OUT AND ABOUT IN
Hungary

OUT AND ABOUT IN
Hungary

Well-PRess Publishing – Miskolc
2004

AUTHORS:
Gyula Bedécs, Piroska Benedek, János Dávid, Lajos E. Nagy, Zoltán Faragó, Gabriella Filip, István Gazda,
László Görömbölyi, György Ifju, Ilona Katona, László Kelemen, Erika Kiss, Márta Klinkovics, Gábor Kurucz,
László Lackner, Ágnes Őrsi, Zsuzsa Nyíri, Katalin Pálfy, István Páll, Ágnes Rácz,
Éva Regős, Imre Söptei, Gábor Tillai, József Varga,
as well as our colleagues at the national parks and photographers listed in the relevant section.

HUNGARIAN PROOFS READ BY:
János Dávid, Tamás Ormos, István. Páll, Enikő Sárközi, Gábor Tillai, Ottó Trogmayer;
2nd Edition: György Ifju and the colleagues at the regional marketing directorate at Magyar Turizmus Rt.

TRANSLATOR: Matthew Palmer
ENGLISH PROOFS READ BY: Michael Webb, János Wodala

DESIGN:
Tamás Futó

GRAPHICS, WATERCOLOURS:
István Nemes, Tamás Futó

MAPS:
Agát Co. TOP-O-GRAF Cartographic Office

CHIEF EDITOR:
Katalin Pálfy

EXECUTIVE EDITOR:
Erzsébet Körtvélyesi

LABORATORY WORK: Well-PRess Studio – HEAD OF STUDIO: Piroska Benedek
PRINTING: Friedrich VDV GmbH, Linz – Executive Director: Heinz J. Friedrich

Well WR PRess Kiadó

PUBLISHER:
Well-PRess Publishing Limited
3527 Miskolc, Bajcsy-Zsilinszky u. 15., Tel.: (+36) 46/501-660, Fax: (+36) 46/501-663, E-mail: wellpress@vendegvaro.hu

EXECUTIVE PUBLISHER: Erzsébet Körtvélyesi, György Esterházy
Publishing Deadline (2nd updated edition): 15th March 2004

ISBN 963 9490 26 1

"Now one sole purpose shines on me:
the sheen the dew has showed,
which lingers like a radiant veil
by everybody's road, —
the road of every man and beast
Who through the dew will pass;
for them the ancient vision shines
athwart the silent grass."

(Pál Gulyás: from "Daybreak Walk
on the Highway"
/translation
by Watson Kirkconnell/)

Forward

In seeking your destination you may instead find yourself on a voyage of discovery. Whilst a journey by definition has an aim, what you finally find may be something quite unexpected. During this particular Hungarian journey we intend to fire your imaginations before accompanying you on your chosen course.

The book you have in front of you has two basic aims: firstly to make your visit all the more enjoyable, and secondly to tempt you into some of Hungary's unknown and less-visited corners.

Before diving straight into the regions it is probably a good idea first to consult the Encyclopaedia, in the first chapter of the book, which we have called the *Hungarian Treasury*. It is here you will find the concepts and keywords which could prove useful during your stay. Some entries may stimulate an interest, which eventually takes you into regions you had not previously intended to visit.

It is in the Treasury you will also find descriptions of typical Hungarian products, some of which you may have heard of before going to Hungary, as well as Hungary's World Heritage Sites and the National Parks. This being a travel guide endeavouring to go beyond the realms of geographical, historical and tourist interest, you will also be introduced to the arts, literature, music and folklore of the region. We haven't neglected science and technology either, devoting some of the introductory section to the great inventors and scientists who have done so much to help promote the image of Hungary abroad.

The second part of the book takes you through both the larger and more intimate landscapes of Hungary. Arranged in nine regions, the chapters cover both the provincial centres and the cultural backwaters. We start not in the provinces, but in and around the cap-

ital, Budapest (an area which also includes the Central Danubian Region, the Danube Bend and Csepel Island) before heading for the four regions making up Transdanubia. Following the landscapes of the southern and the northern parts of the Great Hungarian Plain, we stop off at Lake Tisza before completing our journey in Northern Hungary.

We haven't overlooked the fact that there are also everyday practicalities accompanying journeys of this kind, consequently you will find addresses, telephone numbers, notes, lists of cultural and sporting events, tourist attractions and leisure activities once we have covered all the individual regions.

During the course of the compilation of this book many specially selected people were employed all over the country in an effort to make sure that the information is both accurate and up-to-date. This is an important consideration bearing in mind how rapidly things are changing in Hungary at the moment. We also employed local people to write and edit the individual regional chapters in the belief that readers would get a more authentic and informed picture of each of the nine regions.

It was by deciding only to include sites of genuine interest, and events which were of more than merely local interest, that we hoped to guarantee stylistic continuity throughout. At the same time, however, we didn't want our authors to feel that they were being restricted in any way. Ultimately it was the job of the editor to make the adjustments necessary to make the text read like a seamless whole. Although we live in an age of mass communications the contributors have written much which has been based on their personal knowledge and experience. At the same time, however, you will find that the authors have not denied the intrepid explorer the thrill of making their own personal discoveries.

The authors and photographers were also given the opportunity to give a special gloss to their regions in their choice of visual materials. There are many places where illustrations have been included to complement as well as enhance the text. There are also numbers of specially inserted texts giving information or quotations directly related to the area in question.

The information which is least likely to change appears in the main text, whilst the data which is more liable to vary appears in the information sections.

This distinction, however, does not detract from the importance of the material not included in the main text in any way. It simply means that the data in the information sections has a fresher feel to it, especially when accompanied some of the more lavishly illustrated advertisements.

Those wishing to study an area in greater detail should either refer to the main text or the information sections. To help you find your way around there is a useful contents section as well as some further suggestions as to how you can get the most out of the book.

The scale of the book, its contents, the manageable format, the maps and the visual materials mean that it is unlike any other Hungarian tourist guide currently available. We have deliberately refrained from lists of historical and art historical dates, and aimed instead at producing a readable and visually stimulating travelling companion. Indeed, we very much hope that our book will prove to be a much-loved friend during your travels around Hungary.

The first years of the new Millennium have seen the publication of the last in the series of Well-Press Publishing's county tourist guides, which have appeared on a regular basis since 1995. It was from the experience gained publishing these guides, and the huge amounts of information collected that we were able to produce the second edition of this book. We are very much hoping that this and the Hungarian and German versions of this guide find their way into every school, hotel and tourist office in the land.

We wish you all the very best on your journeys and hope that you manage to find what you were looking for, whether you were alone or with others.

Erzsébet Körtvélyesi
Executive Editor

Katalin Pálfy
Chief Editor

CONTENTS

CONTENTS

CONTENTS

SYMBOLS USED IN THE ADVERTISEMENTS

The book uses the following symbols throughout for telling readers about the services available at the places advertised in the book.

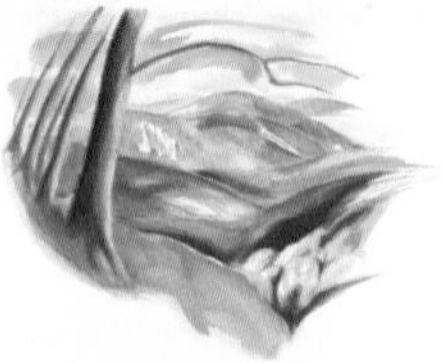

Guarded parking

TVs in the rooms

Air-conditioning

Rooms with bathrooms

Vegetarian food

Restaurant in the building

Special hall, banqueting hall

Dogs welcome

Wheelchair friendly

Medical services

Thermal waters

Open-air swimming pool

Indoor swimming pool

Own swimming complex

Sauna

Solarium

Fitness gym

Bowling

Tennis

Putting green

Riding

Water sports

Fishing

Hunting

Camping

Car rental

Currency exchange

Youth Hostel

Eurocard

Visa

Diners Club

American Express

Number of beds

Breakfast included

Half-board

Recommended Ways of Using the Book

START WITH THE CONTENTS PAGE

As with all books the best way to find your way around the book is to use the contents page. It is there you will find the nine Hungarian tourist regions (with the relevant page numbers), and a colour-coded system to help you find your way around.

The colour used for a particular region on the contents pages lines the edges of the pages devoted to that particular region. Each region begins with an introductory section and ends with tourist information. The watercolours on the contents page are the same as those decorating the opening pages of the individual regions.

ARE YOU INTERESTED IN KNOWING WHAT HUNGARY HAS TO OFFER?

The *Hungarian Treasury* is the first main item on the *contents page*. The entries listed immediately under it tell you there is a short encyclopedia, followed by information about Hungary's specialities, the world heritage sites, the country's famous inventors and scientists, its two main rivers and the national parks. These sections can be found by looking up the relevant page numbers.

LÁNGOS

Before the bread was baked, part of the dough was put to one side, rounded into a lump, and put into the oven amongst the glowing embers. Positioned amongst the flames ("lángok" in Hungarian) it didn't take long for the "lángos" or the "langalló" to get baked and ready to be covered in sour cream. Not having ovens those living in the town first started making their lángos in hot fat, and later went about frying them in oil.

IS IT ONE PARTICULAR REGION YOU ARE INTERESTED IN?

At the beginning of each region there is a map showing you the area covered in the subsequent pages.

The geographical, historical and cultural areas covered in the book don't always correspond with the boundaries of the Hungarian counties. All the towns and villages are marked on the maps, as are the main geographical features. The tourist centres and the best places for setting out on excursions are highlighted.

GYŐR

Tourist centres are considered to be those settlements forming the fulcrum of their local transport systems.

Whether such towns are tourist attractions can only be proved by the extent to which they are visited. Reading through the entries you soon realise there are plenty of places waiting to be discovered.

IN THE KŐSZEG HILLS

From each tourist centre we deliberately take you off in the direction of at least one particular landscape in the region. (Their names are marked on a green background). This involves taking you off to some of the more interesting towns and villages. The suggestions we make should in no way prevent you from stopping off at the other places which are not mentioned in the book to make your own discoveries. The journeys are usually organised so that the last route ends where the next one begins, or as close as is humanly possible. We've also taken the local transport system into consideration.

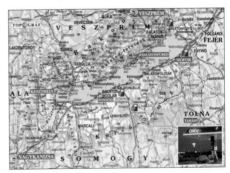

AND IF YOU WANT TO EXPLORE
ONE PARTICULAR TOWN OR VILLAGE …

If you are looking for a particular place you can either look at the contents page of the relevant region, or consult the list of settlements at the back of the book. (The settlements mentioned on the contents page are by no means complete as the places in the main text referred to only in passing do not appear.) The headings on the contents page refer to the place-names which appear in the main text written in SMALLCAPS (in some cases also providing the sub-headings in the main text if written about at any length). The most interesting sites are picked out in bold in the main text. Thus: AGOSTYÁN is inhabited by ethnic Germans, and although strictly speaking part of *Tata*, it still has its own special atmosphere. Just east of the town you will find the 31 hectare **arboretum**.

INFORMATION
ABOUT YOUR DESTINATION

Following the introduction to the regions and the section entitled *All You Need to Know about Hungary* you are given a list of important organisations and companies with their contact addresses. These are organised first thematically and then alphabetically according to the name of the settlement.

TOURIST INFORMATION	
Heritage	672
Folklore	680
Culture	681
Medicinal Tourism	688
Active relaxation	695
Protected Natural Treasures	697
Conference tourism	698

ADDITIONAL INFORMATION
IN THE TEXTS ACCOMPANYING
THE ILLUSTRATIONS

Even though the book is richly illustrated, it still wasn't possible to include pictures of all the sights. What we have done is to make the most of the pictures by including accompanying texts, as well as entries giving you a mixture of quotations and local anecdotes.

The lapidarium includes the mausoleum containing Saint Stephen's stone sarcophagus. The building was designed by Géza Lux and decorated with historical secco wall paintings by Vilmos Aba-Novák.

In sections like this with a pale yellow background you will find additional information about particular places, individuals, events and other matters of special interest.

Advertisements

In the tourist information section you will find lists as well as individual items devoted to tourist-related companies. The latter provide additional information and indeed illustrations. Arranged in alphabetical order they are printed using a different letter type to the main text. The information given in these advertisements is the responsibility of the individual advertisers.

POINTERS AND SOURCES

All places written in SmallCaps are treated in some detail, also appearing in the *List of Settlements*. The names of the photographers whose works are represented are listed at the end of the book in the *Picture Credits*. In the case of the nature photos and the images of works of art we have used pictures which have already appeared in the earlier *VendégVáró* series. We have also made use of the archive materials of the various organisations and institutions.

ALL YOU NEED TO KNOW
ABOUT HUNGARY

This section is just as much for your Hungarian hosts as for you the visitor. For example, what is written will draw their attention to some local peculiarities, which they may not even have thought twice about, and they may even discover a few things they didn't know themselves. As for the traveller the up-to-date information given will hopefully make your visit go as smoothly as possible.

If you want to be brought right up to date we suggest you look up the www.vendegvaro.hu website as well.

There is only one thing left to be done, and that is to wish you a safe journey.

*Well-Press Publishing
and the authors*

Hungarian Treasury

We would like to take the opportunity here in the first chapter of the book to show you that this particular book is no ordinary tourist guide. Whilst attempting to cover the whole of Hungary the book first introduces you, the readers, to all kinds of concepts, objects, customs, events and personalities considered to be representative of Hungary and Hungarianness.

This will mean that when you come to the chapters covering the different regions of the country you should have absolutely no difficulty in understanding what is being talked about.

In the HUNGARIAN ENCYCLOPAEDIA you will find a list of concepts arranged in alphabetical order, giving explanations which we hope will help you make sense of Hungary's various landscapes and the entries describing the towns and villages.

This is why we thought it would be a good idea to have this section right at the beginning of the book. You will find ethnographical and cultural "keywords", as well as historical and geographical entries.

We also include a few festivals and some professions, which people may not necessarily be familiar with at the beginning of the 21st century.

Under the title HUNGARIAN SPECIALITIES we list just some of the typically Hungarian products which are known the world over. In most countries these have kept their original Hungarian names, which have in turn entered the local language.

Those natural treasures and sites of cultural interest in Hungary considered to be of worldwide importance are covered in the seven entries making up the section entitled WORLD HERITAGE SITES.

Many Hungarians appear in the annals of scientific and technological history. Some of their number appear in the section entitled HUNGARIAN INVENTORS AND SCIENTISTS. Whilst you will not necessarily be any the wiser when it comes to the finer details of their research, you will at least learn something about the lives of the world's Hungarian Nobel Prize winners.

The country's two largest rivers, the DANUBE and the TISZA, are covered in the section devoted to Hungary's NATIONAL PARKS.

We hope you enjoy delving into this gold mine of information. Hopefully all this knowledge will whet your appetite for the tours which lie ahead, giving you a taste of the flavours, and a sense of the colours and moods, which give each of Hungary's individual regions their particular character. So without any further ado, welcome to the HUNGARIAN TREASURY!

ATTILA, ETELE

The prince of the Huns (?-453), one of the most powerful rulers during the Age of the Great Migrations. His destructive military campaigns took him into the Byzantine Empire, Gaul and Northern Italy. His empire stretched from the Urals to the Rhine. The Hunnish Empire however was to collapse shortly after his death. During the Middle Ages, known as "the Scourge of God", his name became synonymous with death and destruction. Attila's triple grave is currently being looked for in several countries, one of those of course being Hungary. Priscus Rhetor who, as a member of one of the peace missions, went to Attila's seat beyond the Tisza noted that the king was a small, wide-shouldered man, who never smiled and was at pains to cultivate his frightening reputation. Attila was the most important figure in Hun-Magyar legend, indeed the medieval Hungarian chronicles traced the Árpád kings back to him, thus identifying the Magyars with the Huns.

AUGUST 20TH – AUGUSZTUS 20

August 20th is St Stephen's day, the feast of Saint Stephen, first king of Hungary. He was beatified by Pope Gregory VII. in 1083. The cult of St Stephen is both rich and widespread in Hungary, particularly within the ecclesiastical traditions of the Roman Catholic Church.

The name Stephen (István) is one of the most popular Christian names in Hungary, having been particularly popular over the last two hundred years. The carrying of the relic of St Stephen, the Holy Right Hand, in the streets around Budapest's St Stephen's Basilica is one of the high points in the Roman Catholic Church's celebrations on August 20th. The day is celebrated with both ecclesiastical and official state programmes. The climax comes with the firework display, which draws hundreds and thousands of people onto the banks of the River Danube.

BESENYŐK – PECHENEGS

It was during the period of the Hungarian Conquest that Chief Taksony invited the nomadic Pechenegs to settle in Transdanubia on the west bank of the River Sárvíz. This was when the settlements of Cece, Alap, Szent-Miklós, Tinód and Töbörzsök came into being. The river crossings over the Sárvíz were always important logistically, and it was the job of the settlers to create a defensive outer ring around the royal residence. The clans allied to the prince were positioned along the right bank of the Sárvíz

(Keszi, Kér, Jenő, Ladány, Káloz and Örs). The Pechenegs were also to appear along the right bank, founding the settlements of Hatvan, Fáncs, Egres and Igar. The Pechenegs started to give up their nomadic ways during the 14th century.

BOKSA – CHARCOAL KILN

A charcoal kiln is a dome-shaped pile of wood covered with soil. The soil is there to prevent all but the very smallest amount of air from getting to the wood so that the wood turns to charcoal on burning. During the burning process the wood loses three quarters of its gas and water content, leaving the burners with their charcoal. Charcoal burning became a significant industry in the woods of Hungary at the beginning of the 19th century, at a time when major changes were starting to take place in the larger industries. You still see the smoking charcoal burners' kilns in the Bükk Hills. Charcoal is enjoying a new lease of life. It is easy to light, and burns without a flame making it ideal for grilling and barbecues. Charcoal is also used in blacksmiths' workshops for the refining of copper and in the production of sulphur-free iron and carbon. It also forms a constituent part of filtering and deodorising systems.

BŰVÖS KOCKA – THE RUBIK CUBE

His cube made Ernő Rubik's name known throughout the world. Each side of the cube is divided into nine smaller cubes, each of which can be turned. Of all the infinite combination of turns there is only one leading you to the desired end of having the same colour on each side of the cube.

If someone wanted to try out all the possible combinations on the cube whilst making a turn once a second, finding the 43 252 003 274 489 856 000 combinations would take him or her 14 billion years.

Rubik's cube was patented in 1975, hitting the shops two years later. The toy was named Toy of the Year in the United Kingdom in 1980, and the following year the Museum of Modern Arts in New York bought one for their architecture and design collection.

CIFRASZŰR – TRADITIONAL SHEPHERD'S CLOAK

The formal shepherd's cloak conquered Hungary's rural areas in a matter of a few decades during the 19th century. The cloak-like item of clothing, made from rough, strong, waterproof white felt, protected the wearer from both the wet and the cold. In the Bakony region they are decorated with the wide red felt borders, which provide the coat with its colour. The cut and patterns used told you whether a coat belonged to a peasant or a particular kind of herdsman (a shepherd, a swineherd, or a horseherd).

It wasn't long before the cloak became part of men's formal dress, being worn at weddings and other similar occasions. In some places it was simply impossible to consider marriage, or even courtship, until a young man had a "cifraszűr". Often you had to wait a year or more before you could get your hand on one. It was only when in possession of a cloak that a bachelor could give his loved one the opportunity to express her intentions, for it was by hanging onto a cloak which had been "inadvertently" left at the woman in question's house that she could accept an offer of marriage. A cloak left hanging up in the porch was tantamount to a rejection. It was the authorities who started to ban the wearing of the traditional cloaks, perhaps because they saw in it an expression of some latent peasant consciousness. The golden age of the "cifraszűr" was between 1870 and 1880, when between 800 and 1000 of them would be sold at a major market without any difficulty.

CIGÁNYZENE – GYPSY MUSIC

"Gypsy music" is neither a part of gypsy folklore, nor the same as Hungarian folk music. It is a way of performing, a musical genre, a sound which is immediately recognisable and universally associated with Hungarian culture. Gypsy musicians have played their part in folk music and in the music of the Hungarian royal court since the Middle Ages. The first gypsy orchestra we know of was Panna Czinka's dating from the second half of the 18th century. Now, as then, the smallest type of band consists of two violinists (the leader and the second violinist), the cimbalom player and the double bass.

It is from the second half of the 19th century that one sees the emergence of more musically trained orchestras, whose music, catering for local urban taste, was ideally suited for social events. Today, you are still just as likely to find the best gypsy music in a restaurant as on the stage.

CITERA – ZITHER

The zither is an ancient stringed instrument, which is placed on a table and strummed. It is most likely to be either wedge-shaped with tuning pegs arranged in a stepped fashion down one side, or similarly shaped but curved in a pronounced fashion down one side. The tuning pegs have either-

carved animal or human heads. The player plays the instrument by pressing down between 3 and 6 tuning strings with one hand, changing the pitch of the notes, whilst strumming with the 20 to 25 strings, lying immediately next to them with a plectrum made from a goose's feather. It was Ottó Herman at the end of the 19th century, who was the first person to write about the spread of the zither in Hungary. The zither was a poor person's instrument. They were easy to make, and it didn't take long to learn how to play one. It is for the most part a solo instrument, although at wedding receptions several players would join up and play together. During the 20th century, schools, cultural centres and folk groups started up bands made up of 8 to 20 zither players.

CSÁRDA – INN

These are the wayside inns offering both food and liquid refreshment which can be found on the roads crossing the country's plains. The inns also had a coachhouse, where the carts and coaches could be kept protected from the elements, and where the horses could get some rest. The inns appeared at day and half-day intervals along the main roads leading to the local markets, particularly in places where the local authorities had difficulty enforcing the law, like for example on the borders between two counties where it would be easy for a highwayman to escape the attention of the local county constabulary. It is not surprising, therefore, that there are a lot of romantic highwaymen's stories associated with these inns. Apart from serving passing travellers these inns constituted a social centre for the local communities as well. The 19th century was very much the golden age of the "csárda". With the changes that went on in the transport system the inns began to lose their importance. The inns you can see today were established especially to serve the needs of today's travellers, the holidaymakers. Whilst there are inns whose cuisine is known far and wide, you are still likely to find common or garden hostelries with names as obvious as the "Dew Drop Inn".

CSIKÓS – HORSEHERD

The horseherd was the most respected of the herdsmen. On the Great Plain the local farmers were quite happy to acknowledge the fact that it was the horseherd and his charges who had first refusal on the pastures. On the great estates, however, the horseherd was merely the stable boy who looked after the ponies. The horses were ridden bareback or with a so-called horseherd's saddle by the skilled and well-trained horseherds who were kitted out with a decorated saddle, a traditional horseherd's whip and a 15-17 metre-long rope, which could be used as a lasso. On the Hortobágy the horseherd traditionally wore a blue linen shirt and trousers, a wide-brimmed hat, which was tied down onto the head, a cloak and spurred boots. The Bugac horseherds differed in appearance from those on the Hortobágy. They traditionally wore a white linen shirt and trousers, and a narrow-brimmed hat known as a "túr" hat on account of its coming from Túrkeve.

Délibáb – Mirage

A mirage is caused by the air immediately above the ground heating up at a rapid rate, causing the density of the air to increase suddenly. This causes a break in the rays of light coming up from the objects on the ground, creating the reflective effect. It is at this point that the eye can see an inverse reflection of anything the mirage happens to be situated in front of. A person standing at ground level sees what looks like the water's surface, with any objects on the earth's surface rising through the watery effect being reflected in the mirage. What appears to be water is in fact a mirror image of the sky. Mirages appear on large flat surfaces where the air has risen in temperature suddenly and over a large area. In Hungary they tend to be found on the Hortobágy.

The first scientific explanation for this phenomenon was made by Tóbiás Gruber in 1871, and it is for this reason that the word "délibáb", the first name given to describe the phenomenon, became an internationally recognised meteorological term.

Déli harangszó – Midday Chimes

The ringing of the church bells at midday has its origins in the events of the Battle of Nándorfehérvár (Belgrade) in 1456. On 29th June 1456 on hearing of an imminent battle between the Turkish and Hungarian armies, Pope Calixtus III. ordered the bells to be rung at noon in all Christian countries as a call for believers to pray for a Christian victory. By the time the bull decreeing the ringing of the bells had been issued János Hunyadi's armies, who had gathered under Nándorfehérvár (Belgrade), and benefited from the support of János Kapisztrán's crusaders, had scored a magnificent victory over Mohammed II.'s numerically superior forces. The timing of events prompted the subsequent belief that the Pope had decreed the ringing of the bells at noon to celebrate the Hungarians' triumph at Nándorfehérvár. What cannot be disputed, however, is that Pope Calixtus III., who was the driving force behind the fight against the Turks, made the date he heard the news of the victory (August 6th) a red letter day throughout the Christian world.

Fazekas – Potter

A potter is a craftsman who fashions and then fires clay pots. Pottery is an ancient craft, and peasant craftsmen practised it on the estates of their feudal lords. Later potters operated small businesses in the rural towns organised on guild lines. Archaeological finds suggest that the Hungarians, who arrived into the Carpathian Basin at the end of the 9th century, learnt the pot-

ter's craft from the local Slav inhabitants. Their first potters were of Avar and Slav origin. The arrival of the potter's wheel led to an improvement in the quality of the pots. Lead glazes appeared, making it possible to decorate pots in new ways. The potters no longer restricted themselves to domestic pots, they also made decorative items, which could be hung up on the wall. The pottery centres, which tended to be where the best clay beds were, supplied the local and more distant markets with their products, and guilds were founded to defend the potters' interests. There are many settlements in the central Tisza region, the Upper Tisza, Transdanubia and Transylvania which are still famous for their practising potters.

Fehértavak – White Lakes

White lakes, both large or small, add a bit of variety to the sandy landscape of the Great Plain. Where the wind-eroded hollows coincide with a high water table you are likely to find their choppy milky waters sated with salt. When the waters retreat the drying salt deposits leave white alkali plains behind them. The lakes are partly a reedy paradise, partly mineral-rich bathing resort. The lakes' relatively small size and the shallowness of the waters make them ideal for water sports. Of the white lakes on the Great Plain, Lake Szikszós in Kiskundorozsma, Kunfehértó and Lake Szelidi are perhaps the most popular. Other white lakes enjoy all the benefits coming with being a conservation area, although they are still expected to lead a marriage of convenience with the neighbouring fishing ponds.

Forint

One forint is divided up into one hundred fillérs, although the latter are no longer legal tender. Forints first appeared in Hungary when the Angevin, King Charles Robert, first minted them in 1325, following his arrival from Naples. They were modelled on the Florentine fiorino, and made of 3.25 grams of gold. The fact that the forint's weight remained constant, and the gold was of a consistently high quality meant that it soon became a popular unit of currency in the neighbouring countries as well. Hungary's

currency has been the forint on several occasions during its history. At the beginning of the modern period the half a thaler, a silver coin minted by Ferenc Rákóczi II., was known as a forint. Golden forints stopped being issued in 1786. However, forints continued to be used in paper and silver form until 1892. It was then, with the end of the gold standard, that the crown replaced the forint as the new unit of currency. From 1st August 1946, the pengő, which had suffered the highest rate of inflation ever experienced by a currency, was replaced by the forint (HUF).

GÉMESKÚT – SHADOOF

This is the most common type of well existing in the territories inhabited by ethnic Hungarians, although they are widespread throughout both Central and Eastern Europe. They work using a two-armed lifting system, which hauls the water out of a hole previously dug into the ground. The vertical wood element is often made from living wood. The forked or dowelled end is strengthened with a horizontal iron element on which the all-important jib, lifting the water out of the well, rests. The bucket, which is strengthened with rings in a manner similar to that seen on barrels, is attached to a pole, the so-called "well-whip", which helps to stabilise the whole device. The weight of the water-filled bucket is balanced by a rock or something similar at the other end of the jib. In most areas the shadoofs were built in the yard, but there were also others, which were built for common use. The depth of the well depends on the length of the well-whip. Once the water level had dropped below that of the well-whip the only solution was to use lifting equipment based on the wheel principle.

GULYÁS – COWHERD

The cowherd drove unfettered cattle from the village to the outlying pastures from spring right though to autumn. The village or the farm owning the cows would employ their cowherd from St George's Day, 24th April, when they were let out, to Michaelmas, 29th September, when the cows were "jammed in".

The cowherd was only second to the horseherd in the pastoral pecking order. Amongst the cowherds themselves there was a head cowherd, who employed the young herdsmen, who in turn fed, watered, guarded and looked after the animals in return for food and payment.

The cowherd would drive the animals with a stick he had cut himself, or a traditional ringed whip. The cowherd would catch the freely roaming animals with his lasso, or his rope and stick. The word "gulyás" does of course have another meaning,

and there is indeed a link of sorts with cowherds. The soup is made from beef and potatoes, thickened with pasta and given a bit of extra colour with the added red paprika. What many people elsewhere in the world call "gulash" the Hungarians would describe as "pörkölt", stew.

GYÓGYVIZEK – MEDICINAL WATERS

Hungary is extremely fortunate to be situated on land literally drenched in spa waters. Even in the Roman province of Pannonia the inhabitants of Aquincum were able to enjoy the hot thermal waters bubbling out of the springs situated where the Buda Hills meet the Danube. The baths enjoyed something of a golden age during the reigns of Sigismund and Matthias Corvinus, and the Turks of course were extremely fond of the thermal medicinal waters. The Turkish Baths in Buda survive to this very day. Although the larger provincial spas opened during the 18th century, it was during the 19th century that the spas took off with a vengeance. Balf, Gyula, Hajdúszoboszló, Harkány, Hévíz, Sárvár and Zalakaros are all spas whose reputations spread far beyond the borders of Hungary.

JUHÁSZ – SHEPHERD

The shepherds, who came third in the herdsmen's hierarchy, were given different names depending on where they happened to be. On the Great Plain and in Transylvania they were known as "bács" or "bacsó". There they were responsible for the "bojtárok", who looked after the landowner's or the village's flocks, which were in turn separated into separate flocks according to age and gender. East of the Tisza the "nyájjuhász" was the herdsman responsible for looking after one common flock owned by any number of farmers. In the area between the Danube and the Tisza they looked after the non-milking flocks irrespective of whether they belonged to one or to many different owners. There were also shepherds who had little or no land at all, and consequently kept their flocks on rented land. Although the shepherds used the ringed whip to drive the sheep, the crook was the most famous tool of the trade. The top end of the crook, which was fashioned out of metal, was designed especially so that the hook could catch onto a sheep's rear leg should the occasion demand it.

HALÁSZLÉ – FISH SOUP

What is now one of the most traditional of Hungarian dishes was already legendary during the Middle Ages. Apart from catching the main ingredients, it was the man's job to make the soup as well, although according to Szeged tradition it was the women who were responsible for refining the art of making the main fish dishes, like fish soup.

It was on the banks of the Tisza that the flavours of the fish, the onion and the paprika were blended by preparing the basic soup liquid from small fish, which had been crushed through a sieve, into which the slices of fish were then added. Nowadays, after the fish has been filleted, the bones, the head, the tail and any other small pieces which have been discarded are put into a blender and liquidised to make the basic soup mixture. On the River Danube pasta is added to the fish and soup mixture to give it extra body. It goes without saying that in both the Tisza and the Danube versions the paprika and the onions are indispensable, the only difference being that in the former they use Szeged paprika and in the latter paprika from Kalocsa. So which of the two soups is the real thing? Well, the proof of the pudding... More and more cooks are entering the fray, organising their own cookery competitions and fish festivals. The events at Baja and Szeged are attended by many thousands of people. Indeed, the towns in question like to think of themselves as the Oxford and Cambridge of fish cuisine. Perhaps it's not a coincidence that the Tisza recipe is referred to as the Szeged variety, and the Danube recipe the Baja version.

HÍMZÉS – EMBROIDERY

Embroidery involves the decoration of fabric and leather, using a needle and thread, or in some cases metal wire. Out in the country embroidery is frequently referred to as sewing. Embroidery can be found together with the other decorative crafts, and embroidery combined with weaving has a long history. Indeed, we have proof that it existed as far back as Neolithic times. Embroidery plays a very important part in Hungarian folk art, being a craft of great richness and variety. Changes within the Hungarian peasantry in the middle of the 19th century saw a rise in demand for showy embroidery and weaving. It was a change in taste which was to keep female family members very busy. However, such changes in fashion did not affect the whole country. Whilst there were indeed places where entire interiors, and the local costume, were covered with various kinds of embroidery there were also regions where embroidery remained relatively insignificant. The regions most famous for their embroidery, irrespective of whether the locals did it to excess, were Buzsák, Drávaszög, Kalocsa, Mezőkövesd, Mezőség, Rábaköz, Sárköz and Siógárd.

HUSZÁR – HUSSAR

The Hungarian name comes from the Latin word cursarius (brigand) via the southern Slav languages. These plunderers on horseback appeared along the southern borders of Hungary during the 14th and the 15th centuries. The light infantry belonging to Matthias Corvinus's cavalry were known as hussars, although it was only after the Battle of Mohács that they really came into their own. Even then it was only when the hussars rejected their western-style tactics that their light cavalry was able to fight the Ottoman forces with any degree of success. It was then that they adopted the eastern sabre and spear. At the end of the 17th century the hussars were organised into regular regiments at a time when they also began to use the cannon instead of the spear. During the 17th and 18th centuries most countries in Europe had their own hussar regiments, whose uniforms, weapons and military tactics had a certain Hungarian air about them. The most famous hussar regiment was that founded by László Bercsényi in France in 1720. It was during the Austrian Wars of Succession in particular that the hussars were used on reconnaissance missions and for cutting through the second line of defence. Their most important military action took place in 1757 when, under the leadership of András Hadik, they managed to hold Berlin to ransom having penetrated deep behind Prussian lines. The hussar regiments played an important role during the 1848-1849 Wars for Freedom. After the Compromise of 1867 the Hungarian army numbered some 20 thousand troops. The hussars were to put up their last fight during the First World War. With the emergence of machine guns the hussars lost their importance. Today it is left to the battle re-enactment societies to keep the hussar traditions alive.

HÚSVÉT – EASTER

One of the biggest feasts in the Christian year, marking the Resurrection of Christ, Easter marks the end of the forty days of Lent when it was forbidden to eat meat, hence the appearance of the word meat ("hús") in the word "húsvét". Easter forms the pivotal point of the Church's movable feasts. There are a lot of customs and superstitions connected with the spring festival (traditional songs, the blessing of food, beating the devil from the bounds of the village, frightening away the frost and the hail).

On Easter Monday Easter sprinkling still takes place as does Easter beating in some places, both of whose significance as fertility rituals is widely acknowledged. Events run as follows the male members of the family visit the girls and women they know, and greet them with a special sprinkling poem, and then sprinkle them with water (although nowadays this tends to be eau de Cologne). In return the men and the boys get a painted egg (another fertility symbol) or some money. The most comprehensive collection of painted eggs can found in Zengővárkony. The giving of Easter presents (the Easter bunny bringing children sweets and eggs) is an urban habit with a more recent history. On Easter Monday and "White Sunday" (the Sunday following Easter) young people of the same sex once gave each other presents. Such bonds served as a basis for more important relationships later in life.

KÁLVÁRIA – STATIONS OF THE CROSS

Calvary was the place in Jerusalem where Christ was crucified. The word also has other associated meanings: suffering, humiliation. In its more concrete sense the word refers to the fourteen depictions, either made on a flat surface or carved in the round, of the Stations of the Cross, and the three crosses which are raised slightly higher up on a mound, symbolising the Biblical events surrounding the Crucifixion. The site often includes a chapel or a church, and they are frequently found either at the edge of the village or in the cemetery. You will also see depictions of the Stations of the Cross on the walls inside most Roman Catholic churches.

These stations form the backdrop for part of the Easter celebrations when members of the congregation remind themselves of the sufferings Christ endured. Indeed, it provides a piece of liturgy having elements of the pilgrimage about it. It was from the accounts and descriptions of the pilgrims who had been to the Holy Land that the first Stations of the Cross were put up. During the Counter Reformation it was the influence of the monastic orders which added a new impetus to the building of such sites. The earliest surviving Stations of the Cross in Hungary are those in Sopronbánfalva (1667). Most were built during the 18th century. The word Calvary also refers to the depiction of Christ on the cross.

KARÁCSONY – CHRISTMAS

According to the Hungarian etymological dictionary the Hungarian word for Christmas, "karácsony", means winter solstice, something coming from both the Greek and Slav traditions. The word, however, also has a folk etymology connected with the Transdanubian village of Nagykarácsony. From 1537, the village was referred to as Karácsonyszállás, and locals believe this was because, some time in the middle of December, the storks cross the Danube from the Great Plain. The birds congregate elsewhere before spending the Christmas period in and around Nagykarácsony. The village apparently got its name from a species of falcon, the lanneret ("kerecsensólyom" in Hungarian). During the early history of the Hungarian people, at a time when they were still living in their homeland on the bor-

ders of Iran, they celebrated the end of the year with a "falcon initiation feast". It was an event, which saw the giving and receiving of presents. Subsequently this "pagan" tradition became mixed up with the celebration of the birth of Christ. Hence "kerecsensólyom" became "karácsony". A typical Hungarian Christmas delicacy is the "szaloncukor" a sweet people hang on their Christmas trees.

KARIKÁS OSTOR – HERDSMAN'S WHIP

This is a whip used for driving animals, with a lash made out of tough leather or bound hemp, attached to a wooden handle. Herdsmen used the short-handled whip often known as the "karikás". Frequently, although by no means in all cases, the join between the handle and the lash was strengthened by the insertion of a ring. The whip also appeared on the horseherd's coat-of-arms. The whips are decorated with carvings, interwoven leather, decorative tassels and sequins. On the Great Plain the handle was usually bound in leather, whilst in Transdanubia the horseherds inserted sequins into their wooden handles. The whip is made up of many different elements, the terminology varying depending on which region you happen to be in. The lash itself is made of 6, 8 or 12 thin pieces of leather or hemp woven together by the herdsman. At the tip of the lash is the whipcord, which is what gives the sound when the whip is cracked.

KASTÉLYOK – PALACES

It was after the Turkish withdrawal that the "missio neoaquistica", the New Acquisitions Commission went about coming to terms with the baronial conspiracies and the Rákóczi War for Freedom. This resulted in the bestowing of properties to a group of individuals, who were to become Hungary's new landowning class. The calmer political atmosphere prevailing after 1690 saw the beginning of a period of prosperity in which art and culture were to flourish.

The Batthyánys, Erdődys and the Esterházys, followed by the Pálffys, Károlys, Festetichs and the Grassalkovichs put their vast wealth into the building of new properties. Leaving their old and outdated residences, more often than not hilltop castles, they built elegant new palaces on the most attractive slopes of their estates, initially in the baroque, and later in the classical style. The houses were usually built by foreign architects on the Viennese model, although there were aristocrats who were enlightened, educated and travelled enough to trust their own architectural instincts. The fate of most of Hungary's palaces was sealed towards the end of the Second World

War and in the decades which followed. Apart from the war damage and the subsequent neglect, it was often the loss of their original function which led to the buildings' demise. Today, great efforts are being made to return these buildings to their former glory.

KEMENCE – OVEN

Built of either glazed tiles, mud, sun-dried bricks, brick or stone and situated in either the living room, the kitchen or the baking house, they were, and are still, used for cooking and baking. There are several designs, meaning that they function in different ways.

The most common versions are the heating and baking ovens, which can be fed either from the inside or the outside of the house, but there are also kitchen ovens and ovens standing completely separate from the house, as well as drying ovens. The word "kemence" itself probably pre-dates the Hungarian Conquest, being Slav in origin. The earliest example we have of the word being used in Hungarian is in a document dating from the 14th century.

The Great Plain ovens standing inside the room and heated from the porch are a commonly-found solution, although there are regional variations taking different forms. The stack oven, so called because it is shaped like a haystack, is always surrounded by a bench where you can sit down and keep warm. There was also a flat section between the oven and the wall where the older members of the family and the children could sleep. The oven where they baked the bread and cooked their meals also heated the house.

KOCSI – COACH

"Kocsi" is one of the few Hungarian words, which has been adopted by nearly all other European languages (coach, Kutsche, coccio, coche, etc.).

The name of the vehicle goes back to the village of Kocs in Komárom-Esztergom County not very far from Győr. The first official reference to the coach comes from Sigmund von Heberstein, the Viennese ambassador, who travelled around Hungary in a "Kotschi Wagen".

The large-wheeled three-four passenger mass-produced vehicle, with its raised sides and leather suspension, evolved from the cart, as did the landau, another horse-drawn vehicle, which was to acquire an international reputation.

KUNOK – THE CUMANS

Invited to live on the Great Plain during the reign of Béla IV. the Cumans lived in settlements lying outside the system of Hungarian counties. Their settlements instead came under the jurisdiction of the Cuman Captaincy. Those who lived on the Cuman lands managed to keep their nomadic lifestyle right up until the Turkish period. They mainly bred and kept animals, primarily sheep and wild cows, and were also hunters and fishers. Excellent archers and bellicose in temperament, and with a much-respected light cavalry, the Cumans could be depended upon when it came down to the matter of quelling unrest amongst the nobility.

KUTYÁK – DOGS

The ancestors of today's Hungarian dog breeds all arrived into the Carpathian Basin at the time of the Hungarian Conquest. Whilst some breeds have remained as they were then, like the komondor and the puli, others it is believed were crossed with Italian sheepdogs, as in the case of the kuvasz, for example. The Hungarian breeds are of Asian and Turkish origin, although the Hungarian greyhound, which also arrived into Central Europe at the time of the Hungarian Conquest, has over the last two hundred years often been crossed with the English greyhound. The puli, the pumi and the mudi are all popular and intelligent sheepdogs. The komondor would hide itself amongst a flock of sheep only to appear suddenly and decisively to launch into any potential attackers. The kuvasz is a brave guard dog. The Transylvanian foxhound and the Hungarian retriever, the vizsla, are excellent hunting dogs. It is interesting to note that although the ancient Hungarian breeds have been bred for many different purposes over the past one thousand years, it has never been considered necessary to breed aggressive dogs.

LAKODALOM – WEDDING CELEBRATIONS

Known variously as the "menyegző", the "nász" or the "lagzi", the "lakodalom" is the festive, social part of the wedding ceremony. It is always the bride and bridegroom's parents who organise the wedding ceremony with the help of the master of ceremonies and the other important representatives. A wedding reception was frequently the most important event in a village's year, and perhaps the host family's only opportunity to make an impression. The wedding reception, following the church and / or the civil wedding (compulsory since 1894), involves a series of deeply symbolic rituals: the handing over of the bride to the groom, her reception into the groom's family, the wedding-night,  followed by the bridal dance and the tying of the bride's hair symbolising the bride's arrival into womanhood.

The wedding reception provided a great opportunity for dancing and generally having a good time in addition to abiding by the time-honoured traditional customs and respecting the old superstitions.

Lángos

Before the bread was baked part of the dough was put to one side, rounded into a lump, and put into the oven amongst the glowing embers. Positioned amongst the flames ("lángok" in Hungarian) it  didn't take long for the "lángos" or the "langalló" to get baked and ready to be covered in sour cream. Not having ovens those living in the town first started making their lángos in hot fat, and later went about frying them in oil, which is how they are made in the buffets up and down the country.

Likpince – Underground Cellars

By the Middle Ages the vineyards, which had first been planted in the region by the Romans, had started to work themselves further and further up the local hillsides, and it wasn't long before the landscape was beginning to show serious signs of erosion. The streams, which formed during the summer downpours, cut great chunks out of the soil. The horizontal walls  left on the hollowed out loess tracks provided ideal places for digging out the underground cellars we call "likpincék". In some places they are indeed little more than a hole, which has then been covered with a door, elsewhere you will find a whole row of them. The interiors of some of them suggest the cellars may in fact have been used as dwellings. Indeed, some cellars were still occupied as late as the 1960s, when the walls would be lime-washed and the soil changed once every 4 or 5 years. When used as wine cellars seeing mould growing on the walls was a cause for rejoicing as it enhanced the environment necessary for the wine to mature in.

Lovaskultúra – Equestrian Culture

The lives of those who arrived in the Carpathian Basin during the Hungarian Conquest were closely bound to their horses. Right up until the middle of the 19th century the horse was considered to be a Hungarian's best friend. Horses carried their riders great distances, pulled enormous weights, and helped their owners complete any number of tasks. There was a time when the strength of an army could be gauged by the state of its stud farms. Horses of course played an important role in many of the hussar traditions, as well as in the traditions of the horseherds. Nowadays equestrian culture takes other forms and is used for other ends: amusement, relaxation and exercise for example, and it's something that can be enjoyed by children and adults alike. Apart from breathing new life into the old traditions the equestrian centres currently involved in breeding horses also encourage horse riding of a more competitive nature.

Majális, májusfa – May Day, Maypole

The May Day and Whitsun celebrations usually took place around 1st May. They mark both the changing of the seasons and a major event in the religious calendar. The May Day traditions are somehow inextricably tied up with those going on at Whitsun. The maypole formed part of one of the old European traditions connected to both festivals, although during the 20th century it became associated primarily with May Day. The maypole, all of whose branches have been cleaned off with the exception of the leafy bit on top, symbolises rebirth, and is the focal point for many of the traditional May Day activities enjoyed by young people both in Hungary and elsewhere in Europe. Here in Hungary it was usual for the young men of the village to go into the wood the night before May Day to cut down the trees they would then place in front of all the girls' houses in the village. They then decorated the May trees with ribbons, handkerchiefs, flowers, whole bottles of wine etc. before either putting the tree into a hole specially dug for the purpose, or simply leaning it up against the gate or the well. This usually took place in total secrecy.

Malom – Mill

A mill is a piece of machinery used for grinding grain and minerals, or a building containing such a device. There are different mills using different power sources, like for example, hand-held peppermills, treadmills driven by humans or draught animals, watermills dependent on the energy potential in rivers, streams or reservoirs, and windmills using the local wind currents. Mills can crush and grind any number of materials. In the paper mills, for example, they pulverise the raw materials before the chemicals necessary for the processing the paper are added.

In Hungary there were also fulling-mills where felt was made. Mills were of particular economic and legal importance during the Middle Ages. The millers, when seen en masse as a professional body, were an important and influential social group.

MÁRCIUS 15. – MARCH 15TH

Hungary's national day, March 15th, marks the beginning of the 1848 Hungarian War for Freedom. The Hungarian War for Freedom called for an end to Habsburg rule, independence and a constitutional settlement. One of the leading figures in the revolution was the popular Hungarian poet Sándor Petőfi, whose  poetry became barely distinguishable from his political sentiments. It was with his National Song and the publication of his 12 points outlining the wishes of the Hungarian people that the free press was born. The revolution in Pest, unlike those in Paris, Vienna and Berlin, was bloodless. The revolution however preceded a war for freedom. Although it was ultimately to prove a failure, its spirit lived on.

March 15th was first celebrated as a holiday in 1989, and since 1990 it has been an official national holiday. It is on this day that the state's highest artistic and scientific awards, the Kossuth and the Szécheny Prizes, are presented.

MÁTYÁS KIRÁLY – MATTHIAS CORVINUS

Mátyás Hunyadi (1443–1490) was the first Hungarian monarch (1458-1490) not to have any dynastic ties with the House of Árpád. The son of the general and slayer of the Turks János Hunyadi, and Erzsébet Szilágyi, he oversaw what was the Golden Age of the Hungarian State. He established a strong centralised system of government, brought in financial and tax reforms, and he founded a standing army ("the black army"). Standing up against the great landowners he managed to keep order with the help of the landed gentry, whilst pursuing an active foreign policy. He was crowned King of Bohemia in Brno in 1469, and then occupied Lower Austria. His humanist education meant he spoke several languages, and he was cultured to a degree rarely seen amongst the aristocracy of his day. As the greatest Renaissance ruler in Central Europe his court was a major humanist cultural centre. His library (the Bibliotheca Corviniana) numbered 2500 volumes, There are many sayings attributed to him, and in Hungarian popular poetry he is often referred to as Matthias the Just.

MÉZESKALÁCS – GINGERBREAD

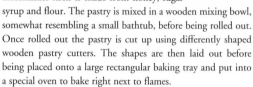

The baker responsible for making "mézeskalács", a Hungarian speciality resembling gingerbread, uses three types of pastry. The mézeskalács itself is made from honey, sugar syrup and flour. The pastry is mixed in a wooden mixing bowl, somewhat resembling a small bathtub, before being rolled out. Once rolled out the pastry is cut up using differently shaped wooden pastry cutters. The shapes are then laid out before being placed onto a large rectangular baking tray and put into a special oven to bake right next to flames.

The second (and in fact the most popular) type of mézeskalács is made with a pastry made using sugar syrup which has been cut up into shapes using metal pastry cutters. They are painted red after baking and given a glaze made out of icing sugar. They are often sold in the form of mirrors or hearts. The third type, which comes in several forms (particularly round macaroons and fingers), is made using spicy pastry. The wooden pastry cutters, which are used to make mézeskalács, are carved either by the head baker or his assistants. Popular forms include circular plates, hussars riding their steeds, babies and hearts. The large coloured hearts with mirrors in the middle would often be kept as love momentoes. They would be bought at the stalls you can still find at patronal festivals, carnivals and markets. The stallholders would travel as much as 80-100 km to such events to sell their wares.

MONOSTOR – MONASTERY

It wasn't just castles and villages that were built during the Middle Ages, there were also the monasteries, those great centres of culture and learning. Of the many monasteries which were built during the 12th and 13th centuries there are but a few which give any impression of their former grandeur.

NAPSUGARAS HÁZAK – SUNBEAM-DECORATED HOUSES

The function of the house's gable was simple; it was simply the wall, which closed one end of the attic of a so-called "gable roof" house. In the southern part of the Great Plain people used this section of wall space as an excuse for doing something  decorative. The simplest versions of this wooden gable can be found in Csongrád, whilst it is on the borders of Szeged that the sunbeam decorations start to appear.

The ethnographer Sándor Bálint believes that the airing holes in the gables, the "God's eyes", have some symbolic meaning. The houses with the most beautiful wooden gables enjoy protected status.

Nepomuki Szent János – St John of Nepomuk

Following his graduation from the University of Prague, Jan Wolfflin or Wölflein (b. 1350 Pomuk, Bohemia, now Nepomuk 1393 Prague) became the archbishop's vicar. According to tradition, as confessor to Wenceslas King of Bohemia's wife he was unwilling to divulge any confessional secrets to her jealous husband. For this he was tortured, tied up and thrown into the River Vltava. His body was buried at the Hradcany. The account which probably lies closer to the truth states that an argument broke out between the Wenceslas and the archbishop about the foundation of a new bishopric, for which the archbishop's vicar was forced to pay the consequences.

The martyr was beatified in 1729, becoming Bohemia's most important Catholic saint. On opening his grave it was found that his tongue was still intact. He is the patron saint of confessional secrets, of confessors, and those working on the water and bridges crossing water.

As Bohemia was then part of the Habsburg Empire the cult of St John of Nepomuk spread to Hungary as well, thanks particularly to the efforts of the Jesuits. It was a cult especially popular amongst the ethnic German populations. It was then that many churches and chapels were dedicated to him (e.g. Székesfehérvár, 1751). The saint often appears on statues standing either in front of bridges or on roads leading to water crossings.

Népdal, néptánc – Folk Songs, Folk Dances

The folk song, together with popular verse, is the great popular lyrical genre. Linked to very specific events within rural culture, it reflects people's thoughts and feelings, the words and the melody forming what is an indivisible whole. The songs form part of an oral tradition, each song having been passed down from generation to generation with variations being created along the way. The origins, and therefore the names of the composers of these songs have for the most part been lost in the mists of time. A folk song can always be freely interpreted, each period bringing with it a new twist to the songs. Folk music has also influenced the work of classical composers. The two most famous collectors of the region's folk songs were Béla Bartók (1881–1945) and his contemporary Zoltán Kodály (1882–1967).

Folk dancing, accompanied by singing, instrumental music or both, formed a very important part of a community's social life. Dancing could either take place spontaneously, or within the context of a more organised event. Some areas developed their own so-called "dance dialects", the survival of which is very important to those who are fond of authentic dance culture.

Október 23. – October 23rd

October 23rd, Hungarian Republic Day, Hungary's third national day in the year, marks the 1956 Uprising. The growing unpopularity the Stalinist régime experienced as the 1950s progressed led eventually to two hundred thousand people pouring onto the streets on 23rd October 1956 in a peaceful demonstration for freedom, democracy and national independence. The ruling party, the Hungarian Workers Party, rejected the demonstrators' demands, and went about forcefully trying restore order. The leading figure in the revolution was Imre Nagy who, as the Prime Minister of the time, brought together a coalition government made up of the democratic parties and the leaders of the uprising. He announced Hungary's withdrawal from the Warsaw Pact, and declared Hungary's neutrality. Following the arrival of the Soviet units on November 4th the formation of a rival government was announced. The suppression of the uprising had some bloody consequences.

Operett – Operettas

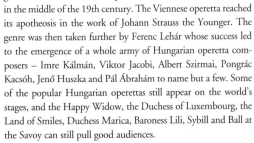

The operetta is a comical musical genre, which includes prose dialogues, songs and dance routines. In the romantic operettas you will always find a prima donna, a bon vivant, a soubrette, a dancing comedian, as well as the other smaller parts. An amusing libretto, which is easy to follow, some rousing melodies, a striking backdrop and dazzling costumes all contribute to the success of an operetta. The genre grew out of French comic opera in Paris in the middle of the 19th century. The Viennese operetta reached its apotheosis in the work of Johann Strauss the Younger. The genre was then taken further by Ferenc Lehár whose success led to the emergence of a whole army of Hungarian operetta composers – Imre Kálmán, Viktor Jacobi, Albert Szirmai, Pongrác Kacsóh, Jenő Huszka and Pál Ábrahám to name but a few. Some of the popular Hungarian operettas still appear on the world's stages, and the Happy Widow, the Duchess of Luxembourg, the Land of Smiles, Duchess Marica, Baroness Lili, Sybill and Ball at the Savoy can still pull good audiences.

ORBÁN – URBAN, THE PATRON SAINT OF VINE GROWERS

It was the grape growers, the barrel makers and the publicans who made Pope Urban, martyred in 230, their patron saint. Many centuries of experience had taught grape growers in Europe that St Urban's Day (May 25th) frequently brought with it a snap frost, which did their vines no good at all. The saying goes that if Urban doesn't bring any frost, there's going to be a good crop. It is for this reason that round about the feast of St Urban festivities are held at which those working in the Hungarian wine regions make their special supplications to their patron saint.

PALACSINTA – PANCAKES

The runny mixture of flour, eggs, milk, salt and sugar can be made into pancakes of various thicknesses. The Hungarian word for pancake is a word of Italian origin first used in Hungary during the 16th century. The first detailed pancake recipes are found in the cookery books belonging to the Princes of Transylvania. Pancakes in the eastern parts of Hungary had long been a popular cake made from a thick mixture often including barley flour and corn before the thinner types of pancake preferred in the towns became popular in the villages at the turn of the 19th and 20th centuries. Whilst we now use frying pans there was a time when pancakes were made on a flat piece of heated stone. The more recent thin, floppy pancakes can be filled with cottage cheese, plum jam or cocoa before being rolled up to make stuffed pancakes.

PÁLPUSZTAI SAJT – PÁLPUSZTA CHEESE

This soft Hungarian cheese is legendary, even to those who get no closer than smelling a particularly ripe example. For those who get as far as actually eating it, it is the cheese's strong flavour and its smell which provide its very charms. Pálpuszta cheese is a mild soft ewe's milk cheese. The difference between the soft and the harder cheeses is that having congealed the soft cheeses are placed in a bath of salt before being injected with a bacterial or a fungal culture during the maturation process. The fungal cultures manage to develop within a matter of weeks, and it is after a further few weeks of maturation that the cheeses find their way to market.

The yellowy-red Pálpuszta comes in a 5decagram aluminium foil package. The rind is edible, and the inside is yellowy white in colour. When mature the cheese is easy to spread, it can even be runny, and the taste is pleasantly salty. It is a great addition to your cheese platter.

PÁSZTORÉTELEK – PASTORAL DISHES

Separated from their families for long periods of time the herdsmen ate very simple hot meals. The basic foodstuffs they could take with them were few indeed: various types of pasta, onions, pig fat and potatoes. Bread they usually got from the village closest to where they happened to be. The meat, which of course was readily available, was always cooked in one vessel, usually a small cauldron. These were of course men doing the cooking, and it is the custom even today for the men to cook all the lamb and beef stews and the game dishes. This applies whether you are eating in a restaurant or with friends at home.

PÁSZTORMŰVÉSZET – HERDSMEN'S ART

The artifacts one finds under the term pastoral art not only show how good the herdsmen were with their hands but they also tell us much about their way of life. Whilst keeping an eye on their flocks there was plenty of time to devote to carving detailed figurative or stylised designs on their staffs, their crooks, their whip handles and their horns. Herdsmen also made objects for their loved ones and friends (washing boards, bobbins, saltcellars, mirrors) as well as things for themselves.

In the pastoral arts it is perhaps the carved horns and the leatherwork which stand out. The weaving, which you can see on the whips and on the tassels, and the sequin designs show that the herdsmen were not entirely lacking in creative ability, something you can see for yourself in the ethnographical collections of the larger museums and at the exhibitions devoted exclusively to the pastoral arts. There are craftsmen who still make such objects today, and they are only too happy to sell you examples of their pastoral folk art at their workshops.

PINCÉK ÉS PRÉSHÁZAK – CELLARS AND WINEPRESSES

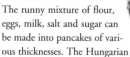

You can find them either amongst the vineyards on the sunny slopes of the hills, or hidden away in the valleys.

The cellars are either simple cellars, or part of a larger complex situated immediately behind the wine-press building. They are covered by barrel vaults over which 1.5–2 metres of soil was spread. The bricks used for building the vaults were often baked on site. The alcoves in the walls of the cellars were used for storing tools and other small items. It was here they also kept their wine-making equipment. The winepress buildings were usually covered with a pitched roof. On the façade you can find an opening and wooden guttering leading down to the barrels situated in the winepress building. The windows were usually shuttered. The winepress buildings often share the Baroque, classical or romantic style features of peasant architecture.

Puszta – Plain

From both a geographical and an ethnographical point of view a plain denotes a wide-open space used for breeding animals. In the historical documentation the word "puszta" also referred to depopulated settlements. The largest plain in Hungary is the Hortobágy, but there are others, like for example the Ecsegpuszta near Túrkeve, and Bugac on the edge of Kecskemét. The changes which took place on the plains in Hungary – as elsewhere in Europe – started during the 13th–15th centuries, and continued, at varying levels of intensity, up until the 18th century. The degree to which the plains could be used depended partly on such things as unreasonably high levels of taxation, plagues and wars, as well as changes in the economic climate. Today we find plains where animal husbandry took place on a huge scale. The animals were left to graze on the pastures, in what were nomadic circumstances, from the spring right through to the first signs of spring, The animals were all separated off according to type and then watched over by their horseherds, cowherds, shepherds, swineherds and their helpers. What one now sees on the plains in the name of animal husbandry is strictly for the tourists.

Pörkölt – Stew

One of the most important ingredients in the Hungarian kitchen is ground paprika, hence the appearance of the word paprika in so many famous Hungarian dishes.
The very word "pörkölt" refers to the way all of the dishes above are prepared. They all start with onions fried in fat to which the paprika and the necessary amount of meat is then added.

Pünkösd – Whitsun

Whitsun is of the most important festivals in the Christian year. Starting on the fiftieth day after Easter it is a moveable feast, which could be as early as May 10th or as late as June 13th. Being at the time of year when spring turns to summer (see the "Whitsun rose" illustrated) there are many ancient customs and superstitions surrounding the feast.
One of the oldest of the many folk traditions is the election of the Whitsun King, something preceded by some kind of show of skill and strength. The Whitsun King reigns for a longer or shorter period of time, although certainly no longer than a year, during which time he enjoys certain powers and privi-

leges. The ceremony is accompanied by singing and dancing, traditional children's games, some of them betraying the remnants of ancient fertility rites, like for example the procession of the Whitsun Queen, when the smallest and most beautiful girl was crowned and carried through the village accompanied by songs and fertility inducing chants.
Common peony (illustrated)

Rácok – Serbs

On the banks of the Danube, particularly on the stretch between Érd and Paks, a substantial proportion of the population used to be ethnic Serbs, They were called "Rác" in Hungarian on account of the fact that the Latin name for Serbia is Rascia.
Some of their ancestors were included amongst those Serbs who accompanied the Turkish armies as freebooters. This explains why they settled along the Turks' warpath. Other groups arrived in 1690, under the leadership of Patriarch Arzén Csernojevics.
Their numbers were for ever changing, partly because of population movement and partly through assimilation. The Serbian population dropped drastically following the repatriations which took place following the First World War.

Rétes – Strudel

"Rétes" is made out of best quality wheat flour, kneaded together with fat, eggs, salt and water.
Once ready it forms a pastry, which can be spread wafer-thin across a table. It is usually filled with cottage cheese or poppy seeds, in some places they use cabbage, walnut or fresh fruit.
The word "rétes" can also refer to a different kind of cake, like for example the poppy seed and walnut bun made by the ethnic Hungarian population in Burgenland in Austria.
At the turn of the 19th and 20th centuries long strudels were curled up in a round tin and baked in the oven. The peasant strudel was usually liberally doused with soured cream before baking so as to stop the soft leafy pastry from drying out.
Strudels were made specially for the New Year, wedding receptions and to give to mothers who had just given birth. Festive eating habits suggest that strudels originated from the kitchens of Transdanubia and the Great Plain.

RIDEGTARTÁS – NOMADIC ANIMAL HUSBANDRY

The Hungarians, who arrived in the Carpathian Basin at the end of the 9th century, bred animals. Once they settled, animal breeding became an even greater enterprise than it had been before. Apart from breeding horses, for which they were traditionally known, the Hungarians concentrated on those animals which were resilient to things like the weather and which didn't demand much time and effort. In particular they liked animals which could be left to graze out on the open plains without causing any undue difficulty. Recently some of the traditional Hungarian breeds of cows, sheep and pigs have been returned to the plains not only for their meat, their skins and their wool, but for their genes, which could ultimately prove important in future breeding programmes. Of the cattle the Hungarian grey is the breed in most demand, while curly-haired mangalica pigs produce excellent ham.

RÓMAIAK – THE ROMANS

The Romans ruled the part of the Carpathian Basin lying west of the Danube from the middle of the first century AD until the end of the 5th century. While a fortification system was

built along the banks of the river, they founded many towns in the province of Pannonia, some of which provide the foundations for some of the towns still in existence today. The settlements were linked by a substantial network of roads, which form the basis of the road network we have today. There are still numerous Roman remains in evidence in Transdanubia. The basic forms of our institutions, our judicial system, our military organisation, and our transport and trade networks alll go back to the Roman Empire, as do the institutions of marriage and the family.

SZÁLLÁSOK

These are settlement types on the Great Hungarian Plain, which have also left their mark on the region's placenames (Jakabszállás, Petőfiszállás, Jánosszállás). Such references have proved the most stubborn reminders of how settlements evolved on the Kiskunság. The "szállás" once played an important role in the plains radiating 20-40km out from the nearest town. Local farmers would allow their animals to stop and graze until they felt their animals had eaten all there was to be had. The "szállások" established themselves in the very best grazing areas, where animals were most likely to stop and eat.

Over time they developed into farmsteads once horticulture had also established itself at these sites. It was in the places where farmsteads tended to congregate that villages, and in some cases towns eventually established themselves.

SZENT ISTVÁN (?975–1038) – SAINT STEPHEN

Originally known as Vajk he was later given the Christian name István (Stephen). He was Prince of Hungary (997-1000) before becoming King of Hungary (1000-1038). Defying the pagan traditions of the time stipulating that the oldest male member succeed his father, Prince Géza made Stephen his successor in preference to Koppány.

Stephen, having put down a Koppány-inspired rebellion, asked Pope Sylvester II. for the crown with which he was subsequently crowned. As a sovereign Christian country Hungary joined the community of European states. Stephen founded the Hungarian dioceses as well as the counties, and he opened up a pilgrimage route from Western Europe to Jerusalem, which passed through Hungary. Following his death on August 15th 1038, Stephen was buried in Székesfehérvár, and beatified on August 20th 1083. His surviving right hand is deemed to be a national relic. The beatification of Saint Stephen, the founder of the Hungarian state is celebrated throughout the country on August 20th, when the relic of the Holy Right Hand is carried around the streets of Budapest.

SZERZETESRENDEK – MONASTIC ORDERS

The western monastic orders played a central role in European cultural and religious history. The foundation of the Benedictine Order (6th century), the Cluniac reforms (11th century), the appearance of the mendicant orders (13th century) and the Jesuit Order (16th century) can be considered the four great milestones in the history of western Christianity. In addition, there were of course the activities of the chivalric orders (12th century) and the teaching orders (17th century). "The monastic orders released the individual from the fetters of society and its inherent constraints, they maintained their independence, taking mankind to new levels, by virtue of being bound by the responsibilities and restrictions of the order." (Adolf von Harnack).

TANYÁK – FARMSTEADS

In the literature the "tanyák" make up what are called "scattered settlements". Indeed, a Dutch expert has suggested that such farmsteads were the models for the American farm. Farmsteads are usually thought to be places where people spend sixteen hours of the day engaged in hard, physical work. Initially, however, they were used by herdsmen and fishermen as temporary accommodation, and it was only in the area between the Danube and the Tisza, where people were engaged in cultivating grapes, fruit trees and other forms of horticulture that such places acquired their present function.

The farmer on his farmstead produces for the town, which is where he sells his produce. He is also responsible for improving the quality of his plants, for using and main-

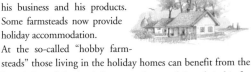

taining his machinery, for packing and delivering his crop, and marketing his business and his products. Some farmsteads now provide holiday accommodation.

At the so-called "hobby farmsteads" those living in the holiday homes can benefit from the knowledge of the local farmers, who are doing their bit for agrotourism. It is not unknown for those providing holiday accommodation to put on special farm programmes.

Töltött káposzta – Stuffed Cabbage

Originally an Ottoman-Turk dish made of boiled cabbage leaves filled with finely cut pieces of meat and gruel, it spread the length and breadth of Europe. It was a well-known dish in the Balkans and Hungary as far back as the 18th century. There are a number of versions of the dish, like for example stuffed cabbage made only of the stuffing, or cabbage, finely cut or otherwise, served with meat balls in tomato sauce. Sometimes vine leaves or horseradish leaves are used instead of cabbage. In Transylvania the stuffed cabbage ethnic Hungarians serve on both ordinary and festive occasions is often stuffed only with

gruel and does not contain any meat. Cabbage stuffed with meat is considered a delicacy everywhere you go, to be served on only high days and holidays. When served at wedding receptions it may in fact be a warm sauerkraut dish. The gruel used

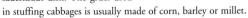

in stuffing cabbages is usually made of corn, barley or millet.

Újév – New Year

The customs of the first day in the year are closely tied to the festivities of the previous day's New Year celebrations. It is then you hear the fireworks going off and see the masks going back to the days when people went about chasing off the old demons and warding off the evil spirits. After bidding farewell to the old year and seeing in the new, 1st January sees the men of the house greeting their relatives and friends. The tradition goes back to the belief that men bring luck and women lose it. On the first day of the year it isn't usual to eat chicken because

chickens peck away at your wealth. Pork is preferred because pigs are good at foraging things out. The way you behave on New Year's Day is supposed to tell you what you will be doing during the rest of the year. It is for this reason that nothing is taken out of the house, especially money.

In the past on the day before the New Year people who kept animals would make sure the animals had enough food to keep them nourished over the festive period because people believed those who worked over the New Year would not get any rest for the rest of the year.

Út menti keresztek – Roadside Crosses

The votive crosses which you will find on crossroads were usually put there either in gratefulness for having being spared from a plague, or in memory of an accident which happened there. There were roadside crosses in Sopron as far back as the 15th century. István Tömörkényi writes: "everyone who passed that way would raise their hat, the women, the girls would take their crosses with them and say a prayer of supplication to the Saviour in the shadow of the column. From then on the landscape lost an old name, they didn't call it Szillapos anymore, but the place where Mihály Mihály's cross is."

The roadside crosses come in many shapes and sizes. The "tin Christs" were the work of local sign painters. Some of the stone crosses put up in the Palóc and the Kiskunság regions during the 19th century amount to minor folk masterpieces.

Vadászat – Hunting

The wild animals of the rich local forests provided mankind with sustenance in both classical and medieval times. The medieval kings were particularly keen hunters, and hunts were often used as a means for conducting important diplomacy. This noble pursuit continues to have a passionate following. Whether at a fresh summer morning or a foggy October morning, winter or spring you are sure to have a hunting experience of one kind or another in the game reserves, which have been developed in some of the country's most beautiful landscapes,

whether in the hillier regions or down on the watery flats. Where there is game there are also plenty of opportunities to take photographs, film or go for a ride on a horse-drawn coach. The

hunting lodges deep in the forests also provide comfortable accommodation complete with traditional Hungarian cooking.

CASTLES – VÁRAK

On finding that Hungary's wooden fortifications were no match for the Tatar armies which attacked in 1241, Béla IV went about ensuring that he and his barons built the stone castles which would enable the country to fend off any future attacks. Initially the castles were built to defend regions and highways and to consolidate the power of their owners. Although a number of the castles were not in fact castles as such, they did perform a defensive function of sorts. In such cases the woods, the hills, the marshes and the surrounding countryside probably provided defences, which were just as effective as the walls of the castles themselves. With a Turkish invasion imminent Hungary' castles were strengthened to such a degree that they would have at least some chance of frustrating the enemy.

Although most of the castles were built on hilltops, it was possible to find castles down on the plains. Castles built in the hillier areas presented a more formidable barrier. Enemies wishing to take one stood the risk of being pelted with stone missiles, and then there were the ramparts and the ditches to contend with. Camping under the castle walls, which were nothing more than continuations of the sheer rock faces, was also out of the question. Castles did of course have gateways, but by the time aggressors got to them it was possible for the defenders to pick out the attackers one by one. Even if the attackers managed to get in by climbing up a bastion on one of their ladders or by some clever manoeuvre it was still possible for a fortress to put up some resistance.

It was firepower which finally defeated the castles. Once an impression had been made in a castle wall with a cannonball it was possible to work away at the walls bringing them tumbling down. Eventually the castles were swept away by the tides of history.

VERBUNKOS

1. From the middle of the 18th century the solo or group male dance was known as the "verbuválás", from which the present word "verbunkos" derives. (The German word "Werbung", means persuasion, winning over, recruitment.)

2. The word also refers to a period of Hungarian musical history (the Verbunkos period), between 1770 and 1830, associated with the Hungarian dance form. It was from the verbunkos that the more recent representative national style of Hungarian music derived, thus forming the basis for the more formal 19th century compositional styles. Such music has a particular instrumental richness, sudden changes of tempo, a distinctive rhythm, a clearly stated major and minor melody and characteristic melodic motifs. The verbunkos form was taken further by János Bihari, Antal Csermák, János Lavotta, Márk Rózsavölgyi and their generation. The verbunkus tradition continued in both piano and chamber music, in the music of the stage, in songs and orchestral works and in the work of Franz Liszt, Ferenc Erkel and Béni Egressy.

VŐFÉLY – THE MASTER OF CEREMONIES

He was the man who was prepared to take on the responsibility of chairing proceedings at the wedding reception. In the past there were always a few men whose organisational skills could be called upon. It was traditional at wedding receptions that each stage of the proceedings, whether it be the arrival of the guests, the toast, the different courses of the meal or dancing with the bride, be introduced with a short verse. These "vőfély verses" are so popular that they have been written down and published. The vőfély looks different from the other male guests, as he directs proceedings clutching a decorated stick whilst wearing an embroidered vőfély scarf over his shoulders. These traditional masters of ceremonies are still very much in evidence today.

ZSINAGÓGA – SYNAGOGUE

The word, which derives from both Greek and Hebrew, means "gathering place", and it is here that Jewish religious ceremonies have taken place since the Babylonian captivity. Synagogues are more varied in appearance than Christian churches and chapels as they were more likely to follow the style of the day. Inside, the most sacred place is the cupboard where the torah is kept symbolising the Ark of the Covenant where the Scrolls of the Law were kept.

The first five books of the Old Testament (the Torah), which are used for readings in the synagogue, are written on a decorated parchment scroll.

Whole Jewish communities disappeared during the Holocaust. Where there were survivors the aging congregations either saw their synagogues fall into a state of disrepair, or suffer the indignity of being used for other purposes.

The two synagogues in Sopron and the two on Buda Castle, however, prove that these buildings, which form such an important part of Hungary's history, can be saved without necessarily serving their original purpose.

There are still about 200 synagogues in Hungary. Most of them have either been totally remodelled, their interiors being scarcely recognisable as old synagogues. There are still some in a ruinous state still awaiting a new role. The largest of the synagogues still in use is the Dohány utca synagogue in Budapest. One of the most beautiful of the Secessionist style synagogues is that in Szeged, whose architect, Lipót Baumhorn was responsible for designing so many of the synagogues which went up over Hungary at the turn of the 19th and 20th centuries.

BIKAVÉR – BULL'S BLOOD

When you hear the words "Bull's Blood" you are more likely to think about the red wine produced in the Eger (and more recently the Szekszárd) wine regions than the hot, red liquid running through the veins of the horned farm animals. There are several legends explaining the wine's rather unusual name, the most famous being connected with the siege of Eger Castle in 1552 immortalised in *Géza Gárdonyi*'s classic novel.

According to the story the Turks were preparing one final assault on the fortress they had laid siege to for more than a month when the castellan of the castle, *István Dobó,* brought up some red wine for his soldiers from the cellars of the castle. The Islamic warriors, not being familiar with the courage which can be stoked up by a fiery Hungarian red wine, concluded that the red liquid dripping down their enemies' beards, which had

seemingly increased the soldiers' strength one hundredfold, was bull's blood. Try as they might the pashas were unable to persuade their soldiers to go back into battle, forcing the Turks to beat an ignominious retreat.

Of all the wines made in the Eger region Bull's Blood still remains the most famous, despite the fact that there are also some fine white wines, like Leányka, Tramini and Italian Riesling, which are produced in much larger quantities. The grapes are grown in the vineyards covering the gentle southern slopes of the Bükk Hills. Bull's Blood is a cuvée, a blend of wines made from several types of grape. The wine's basic character and its colour comes from the Kadarka or the Kékfrankos grape. To this is added Oportó, Medoc Noir, Medoc or Cabernet, depending on the taste of the wine producers in question. Apart from storage there are also many other factors which determine the quality of the wine. Bull's Blood's spicy bouquet, and its full-bodied, harmonious, yet sharp taste is known to wine drinkers both in Hungary and abroad. Indeed, it has managed to bring much well-earned attention to Hungary's other wines.

BÉRES CSEPP – BÉRES DROPS

Here in Hungary this world-famous product has been synonymous with the word health for many decades. Every year millions of people use the medicinal preparation, dreamt up by Kisvárda-born scientist *Dr. József Béres* in the 1970s, as a way of preventing and curing illnesses. The drops are now known all over the world. After two decades of professional and political struggle, of testing and fine-tuning, Béres's special preparation containing trace elements and minerals finally appeared in the top category of the medicinal register in January 2000.

Although the recipe has hardly changed over the last few decades, and the quality remains impeccable, research continues to go on at Béres Pharmaceuticals Ltd, the country's largest Hungarian-owned pharmaceutical factory. The drops are produced in Szolnok.

Béres drops are used successfully in both Hungary and abroad in the prevention of illnesses, and the treatment of health problems facing people of all ages.

Béres drops are among the most popular and best-known medicines in Hungary. Made with scientifically-proved contents the drops have become a symbol of health.

Béres drops can be bought without prescription.
For risks and possible side-effects read the instructions
enclosed or ask your local doctor or chemist.

GYULAI KOLBÁSZ – GYULA SAUSAGES

The sausages, whose name has become synonymous with the town in which they are made, started out life at the end of the 19th century in what were pretty inauspicious circumstances. One of the most important figures in what ultimately became a great success story was the Gyula butcher *József Balogh*, whose sausages became popular at the country's trade fairs round about 1910. It was the efforts of meat producer *András Stéberl*, which eventually brought them international recognition. Stéberl, who learnt his craft in Pozsony (Bratislava, Slovakia), moved to Gyula after the First World War where he was able to benefit from the knowledge and experience gleaned from József Balogh's family butcher's, something which was to prove important later on. Having managed to learn the trade in a year Stéberl took out a manufacturing licence.

Initially he opened a humble little shop, but when things started to happen he built a larger one. By 1940, he had his own meat plant.

Keeping his characteristically seasoned, blended, smoked sausages a close secret Stéberl's sausages were already winning plaudits. In 1935 his sausages won a gold medal at the Brussels World Exhibition.

A memorial plaque to András Stéberl was placed on the wall of his villa on Gyula's Béke sugárút, and it is now the Gyula Meat Plant which continues the sausage making tradition. According to the historian *András D. Nagy* the original Stéberl recipe was the following: *"The meat required for making the sausages (shoulder, leg) should be selected on the basis of how much fat there is on it. We like to add 10-12% of hard fat from the pig's chaps. The selected meat should stand for 24 hours before mincing. For each 10 kg of sausage filling add: 30 dkg salt, 12 dkg paprika, 2.5 dkg pepper, 1.5 dkg caraway seed, 0.5 dkg saltpetre, and 3.5 dkg onion. The mixture is then mixed thoroughly, and then left to stand for a day. With the pig's small intestine used as the skin the sausages are stuffed, pairs of sausages being tied up at about 30 cm intervals. After a half a day of drying the sausages are smoked in cool smoke for 4–5 days."*

HERENDI PORCELÁN – HEREND PORCELAIN

The dense, non-porous, fine, shell-like china has been called porcelain since *Marco Polo*'s journeys in 1298. It was in China that the explorer first saw the studios where the porcelain was made. It was an appraisal of the qualities of the porcelain that led to the material being named after the Italian for shell.

In Europe it was the chemist and alchemist *Johann Friedrich Böttger* who discovered hard porcelain, which in 1709 was still red in colour. In 1710, he achieved a white porcelain similar to that produced in China, opening Europe's first porcelain factory in Meissen's Albrechtsburg.

Vince Stingl (see picture on the previous page) started production at his potteries in Herend in 1826, and it wasn't long before he was making his own experiments into the production of porcelain. By the 1840s even *Louis Kossuth* himself was contributing to the running of the factory, believing it would be a boon to the domestic handicraft industries. By that time *Mór Fischer,* a man who devoted a great deal of time and energy into producing objects of artistic merit, owned the business. In the following year, 1842, Herend porcelain was shown at the national exhibition of applied arts; in 1845 it went to an industrial show in Vienna.

Herend "white gold" is classical hard porcelain made from a mixture of kaolin, feldspar and quartz, which is then sluiced, strained and pressed. The artefacts made from these raw materials are all made by hand.

After the porcelain has been cleaned, decorated and dried it gets its first firing at a temperature of 830 °C. The fired objects are then dipped in a glaze made from ingredients similar to those in the basic mixture, the difference being that it has more glazing liquid in it. The second firing takes place at a temperature of 1410 °C, and it is after this that the snow white, translucent, sparkling "white goods" appear. These are then painted by hand, and fired once or twice depending on whether they have been painted with colours or gold.

It was at the Great Exhibition held in London in 1851 that Herend's perhaps most famous pattern, a design incorporating Chinese-influenced butterflies and flower patterns painted in fresh, lively colours came to the world's attention. Queen Victoria ordered a dinner service in the gold medal-winning pattern for Windsor Castle. Not surprisingly the pattern was subsequently given the name *Victoria*. The Herend Porcelain Factory was the *Habsburg family's* supplier, and it provided porcelain for the aristocracy both at home, producing almost 3000 patterns and 16,000 designs.

KECSKEMÉTI BARACKPÁLINKA – KECSKEMÉT APRICOT BRANDY

The process used for making spirits from fruit is more or less the same wherever you go. The ripe fruits with their high sugar content are put in barrels and crushed. (It is at this point that aroma, made from crushed or undamaged apricot stones, is added in varying amounts.) Once the necessary mould is added the fruits' sugar changes into alcohol. It is the distillation process which preserves the taste of the basic ingredients, and it is the distiller's task to make sure that only the best fruits stay in the mixture. The taste you get in Kecskemét apricot brandy comes from the soil, the sun and the carefully tended trees. Standing where the sand meets the sandy loess the town often feels the effects of the winds.

Although the sand can be light and sodic and sometimes bound, here the sands are loose, sparkling and golden. The sands can easily be moved for cultivation purposes, something which reaps its own rewards. The sand is not very good at retaining to its heat, and a lot of the heat is radiated onto the fruits during the day, the sand cooling quickly during the night.

It is from the light and warmth the fruits get from the sand, the large number of sunny days and the cool nights that the apricots acquire their unique flavour. Many believe that it's the apricot's characteristic flavour which makes apricot brandy such a great drink, others point to the technological improvements which have been made by Zwack Unicum Ltd. The fact remains that the apricots would not have their unique flavour without the region's golden soils, which play such an important part in the ripening process and in prsereving the fruits' flavour. *Edward VIII.* once said of apricot brandy: *"With soda it's better than whisky and soda, and added to tea it's better than tea and rum."*

Makói hagyma – Makó Onions

As well as being one of mankind's most important sources of nourishment, the onion has also been a medicinal plant for many thousands of years. *"There isn't another plant associated with as many legends, myths and superstitions as garlic and the red onion. In the hieroglyphics of the Ancient Egyptian tomb chambers the red onion symbolises growth and fertility. Garlic was cultivated in China more than five thousand years ago, and they are mentioned in the Sumerian cuneiform writings. Herodotus was aware that the slaves building the pyramids were regularly given large quantities of garlic to increase their capacity to work."* (Judit Pákozdi) Throughout history the world's best doctors have written about the beneficial effects of onions. In 1858 *Louis Pasteur* wrote about their antibacterial properties, *Albert Schweitzer* showed onions could be used in the treatment of dysentery. Today, medical journals describe onions as being one of alternative medicine's most important remedies.

Hungary lays a claim for naming onions amongst its list of local specialities because its red onions are grown from seed all over the word. With the right amount of water, nutrients and sunshine a seed planted in the spring will have onions by the autumn. The low rainfall in and around Makó (580mm a year) would normally mean that the onions are small, but this has been avoided by an introduction of a two-year growth cycle. Because the small onions grown in the first year would normally go to seed in the second year without having produced storable onions of any substance, they are given a special form of heat treatment promoting further growth into the second year. This explains the presence of the special onion dryers in Makó, and the onions you find neatly stacked on the stoves in people's living rooms. It may sound strange to find onions in the best room in the house, but you have to remember that the onion, apart from being a means of earning a living, is more than a mere vegetable. Makó has a monument, a house, even a festival dedicated to the onion. The two-year production cycle used in Makó means that the onions contain more bio-active materials in them than in other onions. The bright red skins (used in many places to make herbal tea) and the ivory-coloured insides, with their vitamins, flavour, and 52 types of bio-active materials, all go to make a good Makó onion. What is more, during the first 90 days of storage the flavour of the onions continues to improve.

Paprika

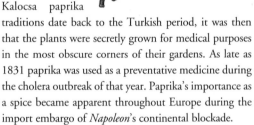

First found in South America it was probably the Turks who brought paprika to Hungary. Indeed, it used to be known as "Turkish pepper". The Szeged and Kalocsa paprika traditions date back to the Turkish period, it was then that the plants were secretly grown for medical purposes in the most obscure corners of their gardens. As late as 1831 paprika was used as a preventative medicine during the cholera outbreak of that year. Paprika's importance as a spice became apparent throughout Europe during the import embargo of *Napoleon*'s continental blockade.

It was in the middle of the 19th century that Szeged became the centre of Hungarian paprika production. The piquancy of the paprika is determined by the amount of seed and paprika fibre used during the grinding process. During the 1920s Kalocsa emerged as a competitor in the production of mild paprika powder. One of the peculiarities in the history of the paprika industry is that Szeged's main paprika growing area is in Röszke, and Kalocsa's in Bátya and Fajsz. (This is also true for the region's mills and packing plants.) Nevertheless, the museums dedicated to the industry can only be found in Szeged and Kecskemét respectively.

Paprika can also be an aesthetic experience. You can see the paprika hanging out to dry under the sunny eaves of many a house as stipulated by ancient tradition. The colour, the flavour and the strength of the paprika is determined not only by the type of paprika used, but by

the way it's dried and ground. This is why paprika is used in a variety of ways. You can make the most out the paprika's colour and aroma if you put it into hot oil; it is then that the colour and the aromatic materials are released to best effect. At the same time you have to be careful not to overheat it because this can lead to the paprika turning brown and becoming bitter in taste.

Onions browned in hot oil to which red paprika is then added forms the basis of many typically Hungarian meat dishes. It is how one starts cooking goulash soup for example.

Consumption of green peppers really started during the second half of the 19th century with the arrival of market gardening. The biggest cultivation area was in the sunny southern part of the Great Plain, centred on Szentes.

It was *Albert Szent-Györgyi*'s research into this vegetable, which was available for analysis in vast quantities all year round, which led him to the discovery of Vitamin C, and his research into how it effected the workings of the muscles. He is the only Hungarian Nobel Prize winner who actually did his research in Hungary.

Szalámi – Salami

The technology required to make salami was invented in Italy at the beginning of the 19th century reaching Hungary a few decades later. When making traditional sausages you simply mince up the meat and the fatty pieces of pork, add spices before stuffing the mixture into the pig's intestines and smoking them. When making salami the mincer is replaced by a device which cuts up the basic materials into grain-sized pieces.

Cutting up the meat manages to reduce the meat's high water content whilst bringing out the flavour of the spices. The skins were made of large intestine (nowadays sterilised plastic), and once ready the salami was smoked, allowed to mature and then packaged.

So how and when did Pick salami became the most immediately recognisable Hungarian brand name in the world? The answer lies in the unique basic ingredients, the unique mixture of spices, and the technology used. It was no coincidence that when *Márk Pick* set up his plant in 1869 it happened to be in Szeged, as southern Hungary had a great pig-breeding tradition.

It is the feed the pigs are given, which gives the meat its unique flavour. The mixture and the quantity of spices used are a closely guarded secret. One thing is certain, however, and that is that there is no paprika in a classic salami. There are of course versions containing paprika, ginger and other flavourings, which are just as likely to contain beef as well. The salami's fully-rounded flavour is there before the stuffing takes place, indeed the spiced mixture takes days to mature. After stuffing, the sausages are smoked in the cool smoke produced from burning hard wood, and it is only a hundred days after that that the salami is finally ready. The maturing process takes place in a special tower built for the purpose in Szeged on

TOKAJI BOR – TOKAJ WINE

This world-famous wine is produced in the wine region known simply as Tokaj, covering the triangle between Sátoraljaújhely, the Sátor Hills in Abaújszántó and Tokaj's Kopasz Hill. The soil, which is of volcanic origin, and its special microclimate, which helps the grapes to ripen, has helped to produce its internationally renowned wines (Szamorodni, Furmint, Hárslevelű and Muscat), all of which are the fruits of many centuries of endeavour.

The wine region's most famous speciality is Tokaj aszú, the vinum regum, rex vinorum, the king of wines, the wine of kings. The first aszú was made in the 1630s, in the court of *Zsuzsanna Lorántffy* by the court vicar *Máté Sepsi Laczkó*. With the right weather the skin of the over-ripened grape splits, leaving a crack for the all-important botrytis cinerea mould to grow in. At the time of the grape harvest, which traditionally starts during the second half of October, the Furmint and Hárslevelű grapes affected by the mould are picked from their bunches, and put in a tub where they are worked into a mixture the consistency of a paste. Wine is then

poured onto the mixture, which is then pressed and put into small oak barrels. The number of "puttony" (3,4,5 or 6) designates how many portions of "aszú" mixture has been added to a Gönc barrel of wine (136 litres). The time required for a bottle of the wine to mature is two years more than the puttony number. Hence a 6 puttony bottle – produced

the banks of the Tisza. Here the meat's water content falls gradually to the absolute minimum, whilst the much-desired mould grows on the skin, enhancing the salami's flavour. In the days before the tower had air-conditioning it was the job of the salami master to ensure that the salami dried out evenly, and to see that it was only the desired moulds giving the salami its flavour. This constant vigilance, which involves the salami being brushed when necessary, is something which is still done today.

In the olden days the temperature in the tower would be regulated by opening and closing the windows, and it was the humidity of the air down on the banks of the River Tisza, which prevented the surfaces of the salami from drying out completely. Despite the fact that today the conditions are carefully regulated by computer there is still much which is traditional in the product.

Part of Pick's success was caused by rapidly changing eating habits. 10dkg of salami has enough protein and fat in it to satisfy an adult's daily intake, and the nutitional content of one kilo of salami is the same as that of 5kg of lean beef. The fact that salami can keep for a long time means it's ideal fare for weekend walks.

Hungarian salami culture has spawned two world-famous companies, one being Pick founded in 1869, the other Herz founded in 1888. Although their recipes differ, the technology they use is the same. Despite their long traditions both companies still have the vitality to take them well into the 21st century.

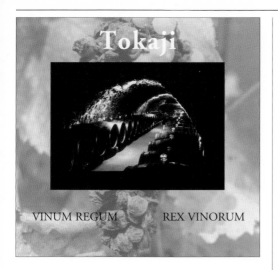

Tokaji

VINUM REGUM   REX VINORUM

the spirit itself is also in harmony with the rhythms of nature. Once the distilled fruits have been put into their storage vessel the spirits at the bottom of the vessel begin to acquire a silkier taste and a darker appearance. The bio-active ingredients in the various added spices are absorbed by the spirits, giving the drink itself a medicinal quality.

using mouldy grapes from the year 2000 – will first appear in the shops in the year 2008.

Many a poem has been written in celebration of Tokaj's wines none more famous than the third verse of the Hungarian National Anthem written by *Ferenc Kölcsey*:

"You on Cuman fields have waved
Gold sheaves for our pleasure,
In the vineyards of Tokay
Pour'd out nectar's treasure.
Often have you rear'd out flags
On wild Turkish towers;
Proud Vienna's fortress groan'd
Under Mátyás' powers"

UNICUM

All over the world spirits producers are reaching for fuller flavours and aromas. One already on the market, Unicum, comes from an old Hungarian recipe. Each fruit is distilled when it is at its ripest before being mixed in the quantities required. In this way

Apart from Unicum only one or two drinks containing medicinal herbs and spices, like Becherovka and Jägermeister for example, have managed to make really satisfying drinks. When using medicinal plants you are dependent on those plants which happen to grow locally, on those plants best able to produce the aromas you want, and whose medicinal qualities can best be exploited. Also for the purpose of the recipe the plants need to be available in just the right quantities at just the right time. The mix is also important, as are the methods used to blend the ingredients together. Then there is the question of how long the spirits should be left to stand and mature. Such details are of course closely guarded trade secrets and based on practices going back hundreds of years.

To sum up, Unicum has managed to capture the tastes and the aromas of Hungary's medicinal plants for more than two hundred years.

ZSOLNAY-KERÁMIA – ZSOLNAY CERAMICS

Following the foundation of the factory in the mid-19th century it wasn't long before the Pécs stoneware factory had acquired a European reputation. Much of this was due to *Vilmos Zsolnay* and his family. It was their desire to experiment which brought them success, and it wasn't long before their historicist, oriental, folk style ware, and Secession-style products could all be found at the industrial fairs of the time.

Interestingly the owner himself also took part in the designing process also bringing in new techniques, new materials and new glazes. In 1893, having won the Grand Prix at the Paris World Exhibition (1878) and the French Government's Légion d'Honeur, Zsolnay made their greatest discovery their famous eozin glaze.

The architectural ceramics they made (stove tiles, insulation blocks, wall tiles, decoration), when used in conjunction with the work of their partner *Ödön Lechner*, was one of the contributing factors to the so-called Hungarian Secession. Zsolnay also invented pyrogranite, which, apart from being frost-resistant, could also be covered in coloured glazes. The most beautiful examples can be seen at the Műcsarnok and the Parliament Building in Budapest, Kecskemét Town Hall, the Aranybika Hotel in Debrecen, and of course at the Zsolnay memorial fountain in Pécs.

As for the decorative ceramics, the most comprehensive collection can be seen at the exhibition hall on Káptalan utca in Pécs. With the necessary permission you can also visit the factory. Apart from Pécs, the Zsolnay factory also has shops in both Budapest and Vienna.

Although not worldbeaters there are products, dishes, plants, wild and domestic animals, which are of local importance. These can be found in the local specialities sections.

World Heritage Sites

Two thousand years of history would have been lost under the waters of Lake Nasser, if nothing had been done during the construction of the Aswan Dam. Instead fifty countries joined forces to save the Abu-Simbel Rock Temple in Egypt. It is thanks to the efforts of the United Nations Educational, Scientific and Cultural Organisation (UNESCO) that this joint initiative has continued. It was in the spirit of this initiative that the international agreement signed under the aegis of UNESCO for the protection of the World Cultural and Natural Treasures was published in 1972. Since the USA became the first country to sign up to the accord 157 countries have also signed the agreement protecting the World Heritage Sites.

These places of importance should relate significantly to their natural and cultural setting so belonging to a particular cultural landscape. At the present time there are more than 750 sites in 134 different countries on the World Heritage Site list, most of which found their way onto the list for their cultural importance.

Every year the member countries have to make a report on the state of the listed places describing what has been done to protect the site, and what has been done to make people aware of its existence. A site runs the risk of being struck off the list if the member country doesn't meet the criteria described in the 1972 agreement. If a site is endangered for one reason or another it is put on the list of Endangered World Heritage Sites. It is this list which draws the world's attention to the causes, whether human or natural, endangering a particular site. Such sites are consequently given particular attention and emergency plans are drawn up to help save them.

The declaration on World Heritage Sites came into force in Hungary in 1985. Since then Hungary has become the proud owner of eight World Heritage Sites.

THE VIEW OF BOTH BANKS OF THE RIVER DANUBE IN THE IMMEDIATE VICINITY OF BUDA CASTLE – has been a World Heritage Site since 1987; ANDRÁSSY ÚT AND ITS IMMEDIATE HISTORICAL SURROUNDINGS were added in 2002.

It was also in 1987 that the 55 houses of the Old Village in HOLLÓKŐ, a village proud of its traditions huddled amongst the Cserhát Hills, were added to the World Heritage list. The thing that makes the village so unique is that unlike most open-air museums showing local folk customs in a museum context this "museum" is a living community, where the traditions are part of everyday life.

The UNESCO World Heritage Committee added AGGTELEK AND THE SLOVAK KARST CAVES to their list in 1995.

THE BENEDICTINE ABBEY AT PANNONHALMA joined the list in 1996. Apart from the Benedictine Abbey itself, the Millennium Monument, the Stations of the Cross and the Chapel of St Mary are also included on the site.

HORTOBÁGY, one of Europe's largest protected grassy plains, first appeared on the list in 1999. The site includes the Hortobágy National Park, covering the Hortobágy, substantial areas of the Nagykunság, the nine-arched bridge at Hortobágy, the Hortobágy Inn and the Pastor Museum, containing an exhibition focussing on old local pastoral traditions. At the end of the year 2000 the EARLY CHRISTIAN BURIAL CHAMBERS in the centre of PÉCS also became a World Heritage Site, and even more recently lands on both the Hungarian and Austrian sides of FERTŐ were added to the list. In 2002, the TOKAJ WINE REGION was added to the list of sites on account of its being a cultural landscape.

Budapest, including the Banks of the Danube, the Buda Castle Quarter and Andrássy Avenue

On the left bank of the River Danube in Budapest, that's the Pest side, you have before you one of the most beautiful panoramas in the world. Directly in front of you stands Gellért Hill, named after the martyr bishop; Tabán, at the foot of the castle; and Castle Hill itself, bordered on the Danube side by the Water Town. Looking back across the river from the Buda side, between the Margaret and Petőfi Bridges, one sees the vibrant city spread out before you. The two cities grew in tandem from north to south along the banks of the river. Historically, the plains of Pest, with their fertile soils, supplied the local inhabitants with food, whilst Buda, a hilly region surrounded by woodland, was the seat of the Hungarian monarchy. However, most of what you can see today is relatively recent, having been built over the last 150 years. Budapest only became one single city in 1873, when Buda, Óbuda and Pest were united. It is on the marl hill on the western side of the Danube that you will find the proud profile of the castle. At the very heart of the rock upon which it stands you will find a cave system, which has over the centuries served as a

hide-out, a storage place and an escape route. Legends suggest that only a fool would enter the labyrinth of caves without any local knowledge.

Although Celts lived in the area in prehistoric times only a few Celtic artifacts have found their way into the city's museums. The Romans left behind a patrol tower on the banks of the Danube on the Pest side, a structure the Hungarians used on their arrival into the area in the 10th century. The Roman remains uncovered at the Pest end of the Elizabeth Bridge formed part of the Contra Aquincum.

It was Béla IV. who decided that a castle should be built on Buda Hill. The outline of the 13th century castle has been picked out in coloured stone in the palace courtyard.

You can get some idea of the appearance of medieval Buda by walking through the winding streets of old Buda. Looking through the gateways of the old town houses towards the courtyards you will frequently find a row of Gothic niches in the walls. The people who lived in these

houses were fortunate indeed to live in such close proximity to the king, as the castle's massive fortifications provided ample protection. A town grew within the castle walls, and it became a place full of churches, houses, as well as new palatial wings. During the 15th century, Matthias Corvinus, whose statue

forms the centrepiece of a large sculptural composition in the castle, kept a Renaissance court whose reputation for artistic and scientific excellence spread across Europe.

The Turks were ultimately to prove too strong for the castle walls, and for 150 years the muezzins' call to prayer could be heard from the towers of the town's churches. Few monuments survive from the 16th and 17th centuries, although we do have the grave of a Turkish military commander from the period, and the hot-water Turkish baths are still popular. The Rác, the Rudas, the Király and the Gellért baths all manage to preserve some of the oriental atmosphere which once prevailed during the Turkish period.

It was with Austrian help that the Ottomans were finally driven out of the region, and the new order was able to establish itself despite the fact that the foreign monarch was only a rare visitor. During the 18th century, Maria Theresa had a larger and more elegant palace built on the site of the old castle. It was at this time that the Castle Theatre, the first Hungarian language theatre, was built in the Palace Quarter. Following the successful suppression of the 1848 Hungarian War for Freedom, the Imperial Court thought it necessary to improve their defences. It was then that the fortress, a blatant show of Habsburg military strength, was built on the top of Gellért Hill.

The final centuries of the second millennium left Budapest with a splendid stock of buildings, some of them the work of the British, Hungarian and

French engineers who contributed so conspicuously to the construction of the new city. The Chain Bridge, proudly guarded by its twin sets of lions, was the first bridge to be built across the river. This was followed by Margaret and then Szabadság Bridge, the final rivet of which was made of silver and hammered in by no less a personage than Emperor Franz Joseph himself.

The next bridge to span the Danube was named after Franz Joseph's wife, although the pristine white Elizabeth Bridge you can see today replaced the original destroyed by the Germans at the end of the Second World War.

The last century also witnessed further unnecessary destruction. Whilst the final months of the Second World War left many historical buildings in ruins, many new buildings appeared which did little to enhance the appearance of the capital. However, the royal residence did become a library, housing Hungary's most valuable collection of books (The National Széchenyi Library), and an art gallery exhibiting Hungarian and contemporary art (the Hungarian National Gallery, the Museum of Contemporary Arts). There is also an exhibition on the history of Budapest and its castle (the History of Budapest Museum, the Castle Museum), which includes some fine International Gothic statues from the medieval palace.

In 2002, Budapest's most elegant boulevard, Andrássy út, which was built during the second half of the 19th century, very much on on the Parisian model, was added to the World Heritage List together with its immediate historical surroundings.

The avenue, which is divided into three clearly differentiated sections, runs from the Millennium Memorial in Heroes' Square, where the Museum of Fine Arts and the Műcsarnok also form part of the heritage area, as does the Millennium Underground Railway Line running the 3,65 km of the boulevard. It was built in just six years in order to ensure, something also stressed in the legislation of the time, that the pleasant atmosphere of the avenue not be dis-

turbed by the noisy horse-drawn tram.

The two sides of the street are lined with town houses, villas and palaces; the work of Hungarian architects who had benefitted from training in places such as Vienna, Zurich and Berlin.

The wide western part of the boulevard which was once laid with wooden blocks, stretching as far as the eight-sided Oktogon, is framed by the three and four storeyed houses with their interior courtyards, so typical of the inner parts of the city. Continuing on to the circus known as Kodály körönd the houses tend to be only one or two storeys high. This changes beyond the circus when one moves into the Villa Quarter, where the houses, no two of which share the same façade, stand surrounded by their

own gardens. It is at this point that pedestrians are likely to bump into any number of places with associations with the greats, the monarchs and the other leading figures in Hungarian history.

The Avenue (Sugárút), as it was first known, is now named after the project's most fervant supporter, Count Gyula Andrássy, the Hungarian prime minister during the period of the Ausgleich, and the Habsburg monarchy's foreign minister. The count used his political nous to ensure that the right legal framework for development was in place, and that sufficient funds from the banks were available for purchasing the plots of land. The building work itself was directed by the infamous Count Frigyes Podmaniczky, whom Gyula Krúdy, one of the great writers of the time once referred to as "the bridegroom of Budapest".

It was cultured entrepreneurial citizens, and the aristocracy who had been fortunate enough to see the world for themselves, who made the Sugárút the finest thoroughfare in Budapest. A century later the avenue continues to be the city's shop window. It is here also that the largest banks and most elegant shops are represented. The Pest intelligensia still tends to gravitate towards the area's recently rejuvenated coffee houses, and the restaurants continue to await those attending the local theatres. Indeed, the juiciest articles in Budapest's tabloids, the latest jokes and the best cabaret sketches are often dreamt up at the tables of these smoky, mirrored, romantic and exotic old coffee houses.

Two marble sphinxes guard the entrance to one of the most important buildings in Hungarian architectural history; Miklós Ybl's masterpiece, the Dalszínház of 1884, now better known as the Opera House. Immediately next to Andrássy út, in the quarter now referred to as Pest's Broadway the divas and the prima donnas of the time were taught to leave no holds barred when entertaining the elegantly dressed gentlemen at the Orfeum.

Before leaving the Octagon take note of the two figures who are casting sly glances at one another. Both statues, one of 19th century romantic novelist Mór Jókai and the other of Endre Ady, a poet with a distain for the society and the politics of his time, stand on the greensward beside the pavements, which during the summer fill with people eating out on the

terraces neatly laid out in front of the restaurants and coffee houses. It is a scene somewhat jarred by the presence of the notorious Terror House (no. 60).

The rows of villas, which once expressed the wealth of their owners, are now occupied by offices and embassies. In front of the gate leading into the Városliget you will find a 36-metre column crowned with a figure of the archangel Gabriel who is said to have appeared to Saint Stephen in a dream holding out a crown to him. To the two sides of the sculptural group, made in 1929, you can see the Museum of Fine Arts and the Picture Gallery (Műcsarnok).

Walking along the Sugárút from end to end you can enjoy the hustle and bustle of the place whilst wondering what secrets these buildings hide. If you decide to take the underground, the displays at the numerous stations tell you something about the history, some of it pretty tempestuous that lies above you.

INFORMATION

The Budapest Tourist Office • BUDAPEST 1364, Pf 215
Tel./fax: 1/317-5964, 1/266-0482, www.budapestinfo.hu
Tourinform • BUDAPEST 1052, V. Sütő u. 2. Tel.: 1/317-9800, Fax: 1/317-9656, www. hungarytourism.hu
Tourinform BUDAPEST 1061, Liszt Ferenc tér 11.
Tel.: 1/322-4098, Fax: 1/342-9393, liszt@budapestinfo.hu
Budavár Info • BUDAPEST 1014, Szentháromság tér 9–11. Tel.: 1/488-0453 Fax: 1/488-0474
The Hungarian National Gallery • Budavár Palace " B–C–D"buildings Open: Tue.–Sun. 10am–6pm
The Budapest Historical Museum • Castle Museum Budavár Palace "E" Building Open.: Mon.–Sat. 10am–6pm
The Matthias Church, The Museum of Ecclesiastical History • Szentháromság tér 2.
Open: Mon.–Sun. 9.30am–5.30pm
The Museum of Military History • Tóth Árpád sétány 40. Open: Tue.–Sun. 10am–5pm
The Ernst Museum • BUDAPEST 1065 Nagymező u. 8., Tel.: 1/341-4355, ernst@ernstmuzeum.hu
The Ferenc Hopp Museum of Eastern Asian Art • Andrássy út 103., Tel.: 1/322-8476, Open: Tue.–Sun. 10am–6pm
The Terror House Andrássy • út 60., Open: Tue.–Fri. 10am–6pm, Sat.–Sun. 10am–7.30pm;
free on 24th February each year; group bookings: 1/374-2600, www.terrorhaza.hu
The Zoltán Kodály Memorial Museum and Archive • Kodály körönd 1., Tel.: 1/352-7106
Open: 1st Jan.–19th Aug., 1st Sept.–23rd Dec. Wed. 10am–4pm, Thur.– Sat. 10am–6pm, Sun. 10am–2pm,
kodaly.budapest@museum.hu
The Picture Gallery (Műcsarnok) • XIV. Dist. Hősök tere Tel.: 1/460-7000, Fax: 1/363-7205;
info@mucsarnok.hu, Open: Tue.–Wed., Fri.–Sun. 10am–6pm, Thur. Noon–8pm
The Museum of Fine Arts • Dózsa György út 41., Tel.: 1/469-7100, 1/363-7205, Fax: 1/469-7171
Open: Tue.–Sun. 10am–5.30pm; titkarsag@szepmuveszeti.hu, www.szepmuveszeti.hu
ANNUAL EVENTS
The Budapest Spring Festival (mid-March–beginning of April), *The Budapest Patronal Festival* (June),
The Crafts Festival (August), *The Budapest Autumn Festival* (October),
FURTHER INFORMATION
www.vilagorokseg.hu – www.vilagorokseg.lap.hu – www.andrassyut.lap.hu – www.sugarut.hu –
varosjarok.imind.hu – www.museum.hu

The Old Village of Hollókő and its Surroundings

The visitor could quite easily be fooled into thinking that time had stood still in Hollókő. However, whilst appearances may deceive, there are still enough rural smells to remind you that you are in the country. To complement the village's fairytale charm there are local legends, which have been handed down from generation to generation, providing their own fictional explanations for the derivation of the village's name. If one were told that the English for "holló" is raven, then it would not require too much imagination to spin a suitable yarn. The official version goes as follows: the lord of the castle overlooking the village was so taken by the local landowner's daughter that he felt it necessary to put her in shackles and conceal her in the walls of his fortress. Fortunately, the woman's nursemaid was able to come to her rescue summoning the black ravens, whose magical powers gained from fraternising with the devil helped her to carry off the enormous rocks from the steps of the castle thus releasing the captive.

The local lands have changed many times during the seven-hundred-year history of the castle, indeed there was a time when the village in fact belonged to the lords of the castle. The castle proved powerless in the face of the marauding Turks, as there was only one steep hillside which could be defended with any degree of success. The most substantial damage, however, was inflicted on the castle after the Turks had left, when the king ordered it to be demolished. Over the centuries that followed the stones from the demolished walls were carried off by the local populace and re-used as building material. Despite this, enough has survived to be of interest to the archaeological community. Indeed, in recent years attempts have been made to return the building to something approaching its original appearance.

The locals suffered greatly at the hands of the successive landowners. Sometimes they were forced to flee from the village, whilst those who stayed had to contend with outbreaks of fire and barren soils. Each setback, however, was followed by a period of consolidation and reconstruction. Families grew, and buildings appeared. The finest decoration was reserved for the house fronts looking onto the streets, the wooden gables being carved with a selection of symbolic motifs. Different generations would live under the same roof, each occupying a specific place in the house's three rooms: the pantry, the kitchen and the front room.

Those really wanting to get a feel of the place can spend a few nights in one of these peasant cottages. The kitchen is the heart and soul, the bread and the lángos still being baked in the old oven. The spinning wheels still spin, the looms still weave, and there are nimble fingers still sowing.

The wedding gifts a wife-to-be takes with her into her marriage require many hours of painstaking work, and the costumes men and women were expected to wear on formal occasions like weddings were by no means cheap. It isn't surprising therefore to find that such items were handed down from father to son, mother to daughter, so that the following generation could take part in social events without a sense of shame. When the occasion demands the locals will still put on their best attire.

Indeed, an inspection of the clothes worn by the dancers with their swirling dresses and pig-tails was usually enough to tell you whether the participants had graduated to the rank of womanhood. Those men who have moved on from being mere boys wore aprons with their names embroidered on them.

There are many festivals on the village's calendar to which visitors are all cordially invited. The Hollókő Easter celebrations coincide with the arrival of the spring. This is when the men go around sprinkling the women of the village, when a lot of songs are sung, a lot of fine food is eaten, and when a lot of other things are going on in the

village. Both sides of the road are lined with people when a newly wedded bride comes out of the doors of the church. At a Palóc wedding the happy couple process accompanied by musicians all the way to the house where, all being well, the table is laid ready for the reception meal. Guests can then enjoy a wide choice of local specialities. Today the local craftsmen and women are still active, producing the objects characteristic of the region which then make their way into the shops. There are also plenty of young people who are only too happy to help ensure the survival of the old Palóc traditions. The streets of the village are all protected, as are the houses and the surrounding woodland with its game, its alders, oaks and its streams.

INFORMATION

Tourist Information • HOLLÓKŐ 3176, Kossuth u. 68. Tel.: 32/379-255

The Village Museum • Kossuth u. 82. Open: 1st Apr.– 31st Oct. Tue.–Sun. 10am–4pm
Ask for the key at Kossuth u. 11. Advance bookings: 32/379-258

The Postal Museum • Kossuth u. 80. Open: 1st Apr.– 31st Oct. Tue.–Sun. 10am–5pm
Visits all year round if organised in advance. Tel.: 32/379-288

The Weaving House • Kossuth u. 94. Open: 1st Apr.– 31st Oct. Tue.–Sun. 10am–5pm Prior bookings: Tel.: 32/379-273

The Farmyard • Kossuth u. 99. Open: 1st Apr.– 31st Oct. Tue.–Sun. 10am–5pm

The Hollókő Nature Reserve – Exhibition • Open: 1st Apr.–31st Oct. except Mondays and Wednesdays 10am–5pm, winter 10am–4pm

ANNUAL EVENTS

Hollókő Easter (Sunday, Monday), *The Palóc Festival* (1st weekend in August), *Castle Tournament* (August)
Traditional Palóc feasts can be organised in advance throughout the summer season.
Arts and crafts and folklore events take place in the *House of Arts* and the *Weaving House*.

The Caves of Aggtelek Karst and Slovak Karst

It is the lush, green meadows covering the hillsides, the white rocky outcrops and the intricate geological forms in the caves which draw the visitors to Aggtelek. The border slicing across the hills and valleys of the Aggtelek and Slovak Karst also mean that the caves go deep into both Hungary and Slovakia.

Whilst it was the skeletons of the tiny creatures living in the waters once covering the area, which provided the main ingredient for the rock, it was the forces of nature which forced the stone into the multitude of forms you can see today. It took many millions of years for what was originally a mountain, created on the back of the shifting plates of the earth's surface, to get to where it is today. During its odyssey, the wind, the frost and the small cracks created by the repeated action of droplets of water reduced the mountain to something no greater than a mere hill, whilst the streams gradually created the valleys. Some of the waters followed set courses down into the depths of the rock, which then dried up to be filled up later with sediment and rainwater. Today the clear ponds provide the only visible evidence of this minor geological episode.

The plate-like karst formations at ground level are evidence that the water has always been king in these parts. Indeed, it is always only a matter of time before the limestone finally submits to the water's influence. The waters which made their way into the bedrock, together with the acids in the tree roots, have effectively worked away at the rock immediately under the earth's surface. Add to this man's destruction of the tree cover and the subsequent loss of the topsoil, and you are left with the landscape we have today. The materials that were taken away from the earth's surface finally made their way down to the enormous caves where they went to form the stalagmites and stalactites rising up from the floor and dropping down from the ceiling.

Stalagmites and stalactites are delicate things, which have been created painstakingly over many, many years. Nevertheless merely touching one could easily damage it beyond repair. The karst caves provide a home for many hundreds of species of animal, the

Baradla, one of the longest caves in Europe, with its array of stalagmites and stalactites, being no exception. The bones and the tools which have been found show that these particular chambers were inhabited by cavemen. In time, however, the caves became forgotten. For generations those living right next to the caves did not even know of their existence, but that was before the intrepid explorers began to fathom the depths, anxious to find out how far the caves actually went. Some of the great Hungarian writers and poets were captivated by the mysterious subterranean world they encountered. The sick and the suffering also found there way to the caves, benefiting from the tranquillity of Béke Cave and its pure cool air.

Leaving the caves for the countryside, walking amongst the heavily scented meadows you can enjoy the wild flowers below you and the rare birds flying overhead on the lookout for food. Horses graze out on the hillsides, and the waters race down towards the village hidden down in the valley. Jósvafő has not changed much over the years. The carved wooden verandas you see as you walk along the streets, the fine painted wooden ceiling in the church, and the hospitality of the locals show that by protecting and respecting the past there will always be something left for people to enjoy in the future.

Amongst the trees growing down in the valleys, and those hanging on for dear life on the sides of the hills you may detect the scent of glowing embers coming from the charcoal burners' kilns. The cartwheel tracks cut into the road leading upwards provide evidence that people also lived up here many centuries ago. From Szád Castle on its rocky bluff you can see the church towers of the tiny villages dotted amongst the surrounding hills, as well as the meandering valleys with their tracks and streams, and the meadows hidden amongst the trees.

Gone are the times when every household was wary of who appeared from the edge of the forest. At the end of the village stands the graveyard with its wooden grave posts. The carpenter's art is also apparent on the wooden bell towers, which can be seen elsewhere in these parts. Yes, it is a rich landscape, and the woods and the caves can be enjoyed

in equal measure irrespective of whether you happen to be in Hungary or Slovakia. Both countries are doing what they can to protect this unique karst environment, both above and below ground in the hope that there will be just as much for future generations to enjoy as well.

INFORMATION
Tourinform-Aggtelek
AGGTELEK 3759 Tel.: 48/503-000, 503-001, Fax: 48/503-002, e-mail:aggtelek@tourinform.hu
Aggtelek National Park Headquarters 3758 JÓSVAFŐ, Tel.: 48/506-000, Fax: 48/506-001

BORDER CROSSINGS BETWEEN HUNGARY AND SLOVAKIA:
AGGTELEK: For all nationalities, open: May–October 8am–8pm, October–May 8am–4pm
TORNANÁDASKA: For Hungarian and Slovak nationals only, open: May–October 6am–8pm; November–April 8am–5pm
BÁNRÉVE: For all nationalities, open 24 hours a day

BARADLA CAVE VISITING TIMES
1st Apr.–30th Sept. daily 8am–6pm; 1st Oct.–31st Mar. 8am–4pm (the last tour leaves at 3pm);
October Saturdays only 8am–6pm.

ORGANISED TOURS ABOVE GROUND IN THE AGGTELEK NATIONAL PARK
Jósvafő Village Walk: 3 hrs (1st Apr.–30th Sept. daily 10am and 2pm, 1st Oct.–31st Mar. daily 11am)
Hikes at Ground Level: 3 and 6-hour hikes, advance booking required (min.3 days before),
with 5 people min. and 30 people max.
Special hikes at Ground Level: 3 and 6-hour hikes, advance booking required (min. 3 days before),
with 5 people min. and 15 people max.
"Scientific Lectures", 1 hour long, by prior arrangement.

MARKED PATHS IN THE NATIONAL PARK
The Baradla Nature Trail, 7.5 km, takes about 3 hours • *The Tohonya–Kuriszlán Nature Trail*, 9 km, takes 5–6 hours
The Borz Nature Trail, 2.8km, takes an 1hr • *Szádvár Nature Trail* 4.5km, 260m ascent, takes c. 3-hrs
• *Alsó-hegy Nature Trail* 8.5km, 350m ascent, takes c. 5-6 hrs
Both cycling and horse riding are permitted on the Aggtelek National Park's nature trails.
The Aggtelek National Park allows both cycling and horse riding along its footpaths.

ANNUAL EVENTS
Aggtelek and Jósvafő Folklore and Arts Festival: folklore programmes and cave concerts (all year round);
The Gömör-Torna Festival (in July)
Aggtelek is also covered in the section dealing with the National Parks.

The Millenary Benedictine Abbey of Pannonhalma and its Natural Environment

Inside the solid defensive walls lies one of the cradles of Hungary's one-thousand-year Christian tradition, for it was to here, the Holy Hill in Pannonhalma, that Hungary's first royal saint, Stephen, brought the Benedictine monks to live by the rules set down by Saint Benedict, and to study the words of the Holy Scripture.

The monastery, dedicated to Saint Martin of Tours, who is believed to have been born nearby, joined the list of World Heritage Sites one thousand years after its foundation. The rank is deserved, not only for the architectural importance of the buildings, but for the spirituality the institution represents. The Benedictine monastery, the monastic church, the Millennium Monument, the Stations of the Cross and the Chapel of St Mary occupying the three hills making up the Sokoró landscape are also considered part of the World Heritage site.

The literary culture and the monks' familiarity with legal tracts meant the monastery became a centre of early medieval book production. Once Joseph II. had dissolved the order in 1786, the institution entered a new era, and in 1802 Francis I. resolved that teaching should take place here, something which continues to this very day. On the walls of the tower you can read the words "Praedicate, Docate" (Preach, teach).

The buildings and cultural artifacts date from different periods in the site's rich and complex history, something which immediately becomes evident when entering the abbey church, an architectural environment which evolved over a number of building campaigns. When entering the church through the west door underneath the stocky neo-classical tower one passes through a bronze door depicting Christian incidents and those connected with the Benedictine order in particular. Normally, however, you enter the monastic precincts through the western wing of the abbey building as part of the guided tour.

The stocky piers with their crocket capitals and the sturdy rib vaults can

be made out in the dim light of the crypt. It is here that the throne, which tradition claims belonged to Saint Stephen himself, stands. To get to the cloisters from the nave you have to pass though the magnificent Porta speciosa, which was built in red marble and limestone

some time before 1224. The walks of the cloister surround a minute garden which can just about be made out through the glass windows. The monks who lived within the confines of the monastery lived by the watchwords of the Benedictine order "Ora et labora" (Pray and Labour).

The library you can see today is the result of generations of endeavour and scholarship. The carved bookshelves, in what is one of the biggest Benedictine libraries in the world, are the work of a local carpenter. The gently curving ceiling is covered with paintings of some of the great figures in

Hungarian history, literature and science, whilst on the end walls you can see grisaille depictions of some of the great classical poets and scholars.

The monument standing on the hilltop nearby was put up one hundred years ago to mark the one thousandth anniversary of the creation of the Hungarian state. The stones of the chapel next door cover the ashes of the monks who resided at the monastery. The lookout tower nearby is named after Mór Boldog one of the first people to be brought up in this abbey, and a man who devoted his whole life to the service of God.

Those who make it to the top are rewarded with a magnificent view. The air at the base of the castle is thick with the scent of the lavender which covers one side of the hill in a lilac carpet during the summer months. Lavender heals, or so they say.

Visitors frequently take away a small phial filled

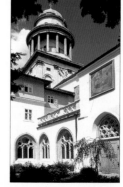

with lavender oil with them. The colourful flowers, the trees and the bushes brought great solace to the members of the order.

It is well worth trying the local wine, made from the sweet grapes growing on the hills nearby in the cool surroundings of the one of the cellars carved into the loess rock faces. The paths in Ravasd Wood weave their way in and out of the ancient trees, whilst in the village of Pannonhalma, situated at the base of the hill, there are still carpenters practising their craft. As the guidebooks say Pannonhalma is where the past meets the present.

INFORMATION
Pax Tourist – The Pannonhalma Abbey Tours Office
PANNONHALMA 9090 Vár u. 1., Tel.: 96/570-191, Fax: 96/570-192, e-mail: pax@osb.hu www.osb.hu
TOURINFORM PANNONHALMA
PANNONHALMA 9090 Petőfi Sándor u. 25., Tel./fax: 96/471-733, e-mail: pannonhalma@tourinform.hu
TOURIST ATTRACTIONS
The basilica and crypt, the cloisters, library, the history of the abbey exhibition and the abbey collections, the chapel of the Blessed Virgin Mary, the Millennium monument
VISITS, GUIDED TOURS
12th November–20th March Tue.–Sun. 10am–3pm – in Hungarian
21st March–31st May and 1st October–11th November Tue.–Sun. 9am–4pm – in Hungarian,
11am and 1pm – in other languages
1st June–30th September 9am–5pm – in Hungarian, 11am and 1pm – in other languages
ANNUAL EVENTS
The Feast of Saint Benedict (21st March), Easter – *organ recital*
Whitsun – *Festal Mass, Corpus Christi, procession* (June)
The Summer Feast of Saint Benedict (11th July), *The Feast of Saint Martin* (11th November)

Hortobágy National Park – the Puszta

Looking at the Great Plain today it is hard to believe that for many thousands of years this was a watery tree-covered landscape where the water meadows teemed with fish and where game was in abundance. But the evidence is there, in the prehistoric remains which have been excavated and in the Bronze Age barrows, which still break the surface of the landscape. Mankind found in this terrain both a place to live and a place to seek refuge, the marshes providing ideal natural defences. The local population was driven away however, once by the Tatars in the 13th century, and once again by the Turks three centuries later, on both occasions forcing families to seek sanctuary elsewhere in the country. The inhabitants of the Plain are indeed made of stern stuff, and fate has often proved a cruel mistress.

The region acquired a new guise 130 years ago when people decided that water provided the area's greatest threat. Once the Tisza had been redirected to flow swiftly down the straightened new course which had been built for it, the mud-flats were deprived of their waters. In addition woods started to thin out, and the landscape once famous for its waters dried out.

It was the cattle owners in nearby Debrecen who let their sheep, pigs and cattle out onto the plains to graze. It was hard work driving such animals to market, especially when the markets were as distant as Vienna, Nuremberg and Venice. But they were hardy animals used to grazing out in the open all year round. Not even in the winter were they allowed to enjoy the warmth and comfort of a stable. The closest the animals would get to comfort were the thatched shelters built out on the plain. It was these leantos and sheep pens which provided the new landscape with a certain amount of variety. During the spring rains regional flooding provides an additional attraction for the birds who otherwise have to be content with the artificial fishing lakes and the boggy areas which survive.

As for the animals, there is the spectacle of the horses either galloping across the Hortobágy, or ambling their way towards a watering place. The bright-eyed puli knows from the movements of his master exactly what he is expected to do with the flock. It was the job of the stronger built komondor and the kuvasz to protect property and the herd, and ensure that neither man nor animal suffered any ill effects.

The road which crossed the waters of the River Hortobágy formed part of an important route, and even today it carries the main road from Budapest to Debrecen.

When built in 1833, the nine-span bridge was the longest stone bridge in Hungary.

There was a time when those wanting to cross the bridge had to pay a toll, and indeed the walled gate posts can still be seen today.

For the weary traveller there was always the wayside inn in Hortobágy to provide you with food, drink and place for the night. But not everyone was guaranteed a soft warm bed, there were those who had to be satisfied with a couch outside on the veranda. Not even the animals were allowed to remain completely without cover, the tired animals being taken away to the "coach house". In such a hostile environment people wore simple clothes. The wind and rain was liable to do their worst during the course of a day's work. As the shepherds and the herdsmen were respected people out in the country, they were not averse to putting on their elegant cloaks for which they were famous. Many people would descend on the annual market to join the droves of animals and the carts piled high with produce, which congregated at one end of the bridge. At the Bridge Markets held today you can buy almost anything, as was the case at the markets of old.

When mankind first went about reshaping the Hortobágy, they could surely not have realised that it would prove to be an environment suitable for so many animals and wild flowers. The Hortobágy National Park has been in existence since 1973, and since then the landscape has been allowed to function as it has done since the 1830s when mankind intervened to the benefit of the herdsmen and their charges. At the same time, however, there is enough flora and fauna, enough marshes and breeding grounds, to remind us of the less tamed landscapes which once dominated the Great Plain.

INFORMATION

Tickets for those parts of the National Park which are open to the general public may be purchased at the information centres and at National Park Central Office.

Hortobágy National Park – 4024 DEBRECEN, Sumen u. 2. Tel.: 52/349-922, Fax: 52/410-645
Pusztainform-Hortobágy – Tel.: 52/369-119, Fax: 52/369-105, E-mail: hortobagy@tourinform.hu

EXHIBITIONS

The Hortobágy Pastoral Museum – Exhibition entitled Shepherding on the Hortobágy
Open: 15th–31st Mar., 1st–30th Nov. 10am–2pm; 1st–30th Apr., 1st–31st Oct. 10am–4pm; 1st May–30th Sept. 9am–6pm.
Info.: Tourinform Hortbágy, Tel./fax: 52/589-321, During the winter: 52/369-350;
E-mail: hortobagy@tourinform.hu

The Western Inn – Permanent exhibition entitled Arts and Crafts on the Hortobágy
Open: 15th Mar.–31st Oct. 9am–6pm, Info.: Tel.: 52/378-054, 30/278-7378

Nagyiván Peasant House – Ethnographic exhibition: Open: 1st May–15th Oct. if arranged in advance
(Tel: 59/415-324, 415-659) and with a National Park entrance ticket

Meggyes Csárda Museum – Ethnographic exhibition
Open: if arranged in advance Tel.: 70/231-4073 and with a National Park entrance ticket.
How to get there: turn off road no.33 at the sign by the 60km marker and go along the mud track.

Puszta Animal Park – Showing ancient Hungarian animals
Open: 15th Mar.–15th Nov. 9am–6pm, Closed during the winter (Opening times may vary depending on the weather)
Info.: Tel.: 52/701-037

Hortobágy Panorama – Exhibitions entitled The Hortbágy National Park in Pictures; Birds of Prey Protection
Open: 15th Apr.–30th June, 1st Sept.–15th Oct. 10am–4pm, 1st July–30th Aug. 9am–5pm (closed Mon.) with a National
Park entrance ticket, or a ticket bought at the door. Info.: Tel.: 52/529-935

Szálkahalom Guard House – Exhibition: The Natural Treasures of the Nyírőlapos-Nyárijárás Plain
(on road no.33 by the 79km marker). Open: 15th Apr.–30th June, 1st Sept.–15th Oct. 10am–4pm;
1st July–30th Aug. 9am–5pm (closed Mon.) Info.: Tel.: 52/529-935

ANNUAL EVENTS

International Art Workshop (February–March), *Crafts Show – Hortobágy/Máta* (April–September)
International Horse Show (July), *Bridge Market* (August)
Hortobágy is also covered in the section dealing with the National Parks.

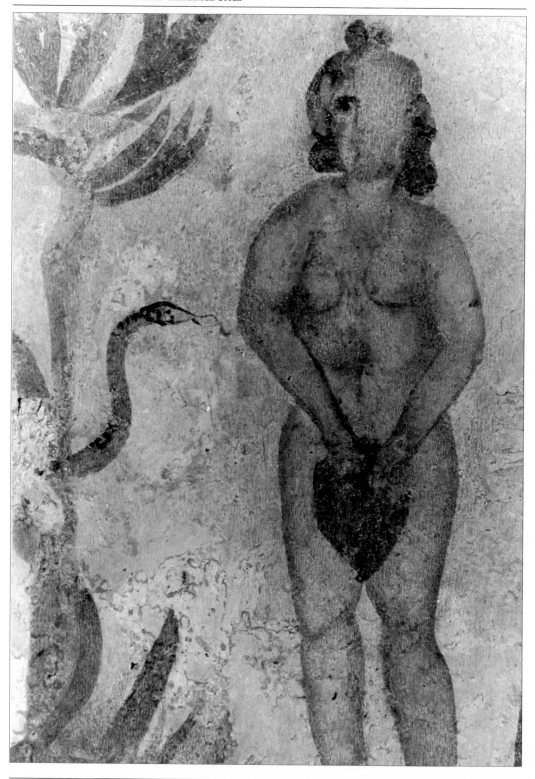

Early Christian Necropolis of Pécs – Sopianae

Pécs, the jewel in the Mecset Hills' crown, has evolved gradually over the last two thousand years. Arguably the most beautifully-situated town in the country, Pécs has played an important role in the arts and the sciences, whilst at the same time being a cultural centre. Although mankind has inhabited the region for six thousand years, it was the Romans who built the first houses here. Sopianae served as an administrative centre for the Valeria province of Pannonia a district named after the Roman Emperor Galerius's wife. The head of the district created a civilised urban environment at the heart of what was a rich agricultural region. During the course of the trading, the battles and the feuds which went on with the neighbouring eastern provinces the local population came into contact with new ideas and doctrines. The loss of respect for the old Roman gods coincided with a decline in the ability of the authorities to exert their power within the empire as a whole. The Romans went about persecuting Christianity, those believing in one god automatically being considered enemies of the empire. The great change came in 313 AD when Emperor Constantine passed the Edict of Milan. The Emperor himself converted to Christianity, and stated in writing that his subjects were free to practise the Christian faith. It was during this period that the monuments at the World Heritage Site were built.

Although the Roman burial chambers in their wooded graveyard were later built over, the Christian faith was to pay an important role in the life of the town in many of the centuries which were to follow. Indeed, it was the Bishop's

Palace and the Cathedral, no less, which were built over the two thousand-year-old burial site. Although it had been known for going on two hundred years that buildings dating from the fourth and sixth centuries lay on the site the consensus was to leave the remains undisturbed until such time as the remains could be restored properly. They also realised that once excavated such finds would have to be looked after with great care. So it is that of the twenty Roman buildings which have been uncovered only three can now be visited by the general public.

Some of the structures are more richly decorated than others, and experts believe that the chambers were those of early Christian martyrs. Above the chambers archeologists have found some buildings which look as though they may have served some liturgical purpose.

The Early Christian Mausoleum in the centre of the square is the largest and most significant funerary building in Hungary. Constructed above a burial chamber it probably amounted to a tall, narrow chapel. In the chamber underneath you can now see the white marble sarcophagus in its original position. The wall paintings in the burial chambers, which contain Early Christian motifs and iconography, are the work of contemporary wandering Italian artists. On the northern wall of the chamber you can see a depiction of Adam and Eve, as well as Daniel in the lion's den. Since then the monogram has been used in churches and on religious objects as a symbol of Christ's protecting and healing powers. The blind passages coming out of the chamber were also used for burial purposes, although they also provided hiding places for the Hun, German and Avar populations in the period following the collapse of the Roman province. Burial chamber number 2 is famous for the jugs and glasses which are represented on the walls. These, together with the vine scrolls and the bunches of grapes, provided the decoration for the burial cham-

ber. In the Early Christian period such depictions symbolised both the Holy Sacraments and the refreshment expressed in the Latin word refrigerium. Because of the restoration work, which is still going on, it is still not possible to visit the chamber discovered back in 1782, with its depictions of Saint Peter and Saint Paul. In 2003, archaeologists once again came across a reasonably well-preserved tomb chamber underneath what is known as tomb chamber no. 5. It will probably be open to the general public from 2004.

One reason for the complex becoming a World Heritage Site was that apart from being an ancient complex, the burial chambers embodied the power and the faith of the Early Christian Church.

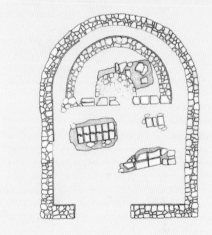

INFORMATION
The Late Roman (Early Christian) Tombs
The information given below may change due to the work currently going at the site.
Eventually seven of the tombs included in the World Heritage Site will be open to the general public.
Information: *The Archaeology Department of the Janus Pannonius Museum*
Pécs 7621 Széchenyi tér 12. Tel.: 72/312-719, 72/324-950
The Early Christian Mausoleum
Szent István tér – Open: 15th Apr.–31st Oct. Tue.–Sat. 10am–6pm, Sun. 10am–4pm;
1st Nov.–14th Apr. Tue.–Sun. 10am–4pm
The Jug Tomb Chamber Pécs, Széchenyi tér
Open: 15th Apr.–31st Oct. Tue.–Sun. 9am–5pm (either separately, or with a combined ticket, which is also valid
for the Episcopal Palace; Info.: Episcopal Palace
The Episcopal Palace: Tel.: 72/513-030

The Fertő/Neusiedlersee Cultural Landscape

The lake is the clear, gleaming surface of water which appears amongst the reeds. The natural unity of the watery environment wasn't disturbed when the Austrian-Hungarian frontier was redrawn in 1921, taking the border right through the middle of the lake. Nature conservationists in both countries now see over what is a National Park extending beyond both sides of the lake. The area first received world recognition in 1989 when the Neusiedler-Seewinkel in Austria became a UNESCO-recognised nature reserve for its strictly protected watery habitats and its rich and varied wildlife.

In 2001, the lake and its immediate surroundings became a World Heritage Site. The site includes the Neusiedler-Seewinkel together with the historical centre of Rust. On the Hungarian side the site includes Lake Fertő and Fertőrákos in the Fertő-Hanság National Park together with the ancestral country houses in Nagycenk and Fertőd.

The saline lake lying in the basin situated between the Leitha Hills in Austria and the plains in Hungary was created nine thousand years ago. Its shallow, malodorous hydrogen sulphide waters provide the largest such expanse of water in Europe. The water plants growing in the area provide a habitat for many thousands of nesting and migrating birds making Lake Fertő one of the biggest water bird paradises in Central Europe.

Next to the bounteous reed beds, where birds settle unhindered, you will also find lidos and other popular bathing places. In Fertőrákos Bay there is also a yacht marina and a quay from where you can take a boat tour of the lake.

Those interested in the reed beds and the local wildlife can visit the Fertő-Hanság National Park exhibition or go on one of the nature trails. You can also visit the places of natural interest on the lake if accompanied by qualified naturalists.

You can read more about the natural treasures in the section devoted to the National Park.

The region's natural resources can be inspected on the shores of the lake. The exhibition at the now disused limestone quarry in Fertőrákos celebrates the geological and cultural history of the area. The stone quarried there can be seen in many of the famous buildings gracing Vienna, Sopron and many of the surrounding settlements. The old quarry, whose appearance has been compared to a Greek temple, now provides a venue for cultural events.

The beauty of the landscape around Lake Fertő and the drained marshes coveted by the local landowners gave the region a certain importance. The local population has traditionally grown grapes on the sun-drenched hillsides, and stored their wines in the wine cellars you can find in the villages.

What is now the Hungarian part of the World Heritage Site was once dominated by the rich local aristocratic families. The income the Esterházys enjoyed from their vast estates went towards building Fertőd, the two-hundred-year-old palace, whose splendour once rivalled that of its French and Austrian counterparts. The magnificence Goethe ascribed to the Esterházys provided the epithet for Miklós Esterházy, the palatine of Hungary and the most important man in the country after the king himself. The Hungarian aristocrat enjoyed pomp,

and was a great patron of the arts. Indeed, he had an opera house and a puppet theatre built in his palace. Joseph Haydn, whose works were often performed for the first time in front of his keen patrons at Fertőd, worked in the family's service for two decades.

Today, concerts dedicated to Haydn's music are held in the palace. The palace in Nagycenk, which formed the centre of an estate, was one of the residences of 19th century politician, István Széchenyi. A great traveller, the Count was always eager to introduce what he had seen on his travels into his home. In one of the wings of the palace you will find an exhibition devoted to the great reformer's contribution to Hungary's national and cultural life. After his death "the greatest Hungarian" was buried in the mausoleum which you can find at the palace.

In Rust, "the town of storks and fine wines", which lies in the hills just across the border in Austria, you will find the Fisherman's Church (Fischerkirche). The Austrian nature conservationists also put on a number of programmes and walks for those visiting the Austrian part of the World Heritage Site. Those who are keen on enjoying the ever-changing countryside around Lake Fertő and the rich local culture can explore the highways and byways on both the Austrian and Hungarian sides by car or by bicycle.

Information

Tourinform Fertőd: Fertőd 9431, Madách sétány 1. Tel./fax: 99/370-544, Tel.: 99/370-182
E-mail: fertod@tourinform.hu

Fertő–Hanság National Park Central Office: Sarród 9435, Rév-Kócsagvár Pf. 4., Tel.: 99/537-622
Fax: 99/537-621, E-mail: fehnpi@ktm.x400gw.itb.hu

Neusiedler See National Park, Information Centre: Tel.: 0043-2175-3442
Fax: 0043-2175-34424
E-mail: neusiedlersee.np@netway.at

Fertőd Palace Museum: Tel.: 99/537-640; *Haydn Room:* 99/537-013
Open (from March 2004) 15th Mar.–15th Oct. Tue.–Sun. 10am–6pm, 16th Oct.–14th Mar. Fri–Sat.-Sun. 10am–4pm.

Nagycenk, István Széchenyi Memorial Museum – Széchenyi Palace: Tel.: 99/360-023, Fax: 99/360-260

Fertőrákos, The Shrine of Mithrász (Border crossing for Austrian and Hungarian cyclists)
Opening times: 1st May–31st Aug. 9am–5pm, Sept. 10am–2pm

The Crystal Museum: Fertőrákos, Fő u. 9.
Open: 1st May–31st Oct. 9am–7pm

The Tokaj Wine Region
Historic Cultural Landscape

When in other places and circumstances mould is a sign of disease and a reason for anger and regret, here it is a source of great pride and joy: when the Botrytis cinerea mould reduces the grapes to shrivelled raisins. The resulting mouldy mixture is then left to mature in wooden casks mixed with the golden yellow honeylike juices from the grapes themselves.

Both the walls of the cellars, which have been carved out of the local riolite tufa, and the bottles of wine, which are carefully stacked inside are covered with a velvety greyish green blanket of another mould, Cladasporium cellare, cherished for its ability to create the ideal climate for the maturation process. Having been left in this state for perhaps as much as a few decades you are left with an fine sweet wine.

In order to ensure the preservation of both the winemaking traditions, some of which go back as much as a thousand years, and the wine region as a distinctive unit, the Tokaj-Hegyalja wine region in the eastern part of the North Hungarian Hills together with its nine settlements (Tokaj, Bodrogkeresztúr, Bodrogkisfalud, Mád, Mezőzombor, Rátka, Szegi, Tarcal, Tállya), and six famous wine cellars was added to the list of UNESCO World Heritage Sites in 2002.

The wine region is bordered to the east by the River Bodrog. The capital of the Hegyalja, Tokaj, grew up around the confluence of the two rivers. The name of the town, which is of Turkish origin, was inspired by the woods which ran along the banks of the river.

The vine is indigenous to the area. Indeed, in the area immediately to the north of the World Heritage area, in Erdőberény, they found ancient vine leaf dating from the Miocene period. It is in fact possible to trace all the grape varieties found in Tokaj today back to that particular Vitis tokaiensis grape type.

130 types of grape are grown in the region, the most commonly found being the unusually fragrant and slightly tart Furmint, the lime honey-

flavoured and fruity Hárslevelű and the slightly more acidic, yellow Muscat.

Of the Tokaj-hegyal-ja's white wines it is the Szamorodni and the Aszú types which are the most well known. The quality of the aszú wines is catagorised accord-ing to the number of "puttony" the wine has, a number which varies from three to six. The number is determined by the number of portions of aszú mixture the wine contains. The more puttonys the more valuable the wine. About 20kg of aszú grapes can find their way into a Gönc barrel containing about 136 litres of wine or must. Wines containing more than six measurements of aszú are called Essence.

The southern slopes of these rich-soiled volcanic hills, which then run down into the river valleys, get as much sunshine as the southern part of the Great

Plain. The long, humid, sunny autumns are good for the moulds which cause the grapes to shrivel which in turn helps produce the aszú.

With this fortunate balance of natural forces at their disposal the local farmers and landowners have made the most of their knowledge and their respect for tradition to make Tokaj wines both unique and unmistakably Hungarian.

Although grapes have always provided the region with a living, written sources from the middle of the

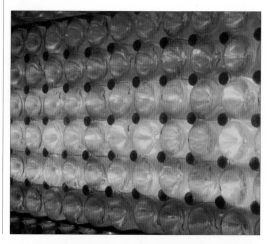

13th century tell us that Walloon and Italian farmers settled in the area following the Tatar Invasion of 1241, bringing with them their own wine-making techniques. Sweet wines made from raisins were not unknown in the southern regions of Europe, although such wines must have been something of a novelty in the cooler Carpathian Basin.

Over the centuries Hungarian monarchs and nobles gave the golden Tokaj wines as gifts to numerous European rulers. The Russian tzar Peter the Great and tzarina Catherine II. guarded the vineyards and wine cellars, which they rented in the Tokaj wine region with their own soldiers. In the middle of the 18th century Maria Theresa sent Tokaj wine to the pope to be used as the wine drunk during the mass. The wine trade brought wealth and prosperity to the region, and it is the old wine-merchants' residences which give the streets in these parts their charm. Clever traders were quick to latch on to the selling power of the Tokaj name, and it was for this reason that during the 16th century thirteen settlements created their own association ensuring that only they were entitled to use the name of the town.

Recognising the importance of the wine region a statue issued by Charles III., King of Hungary, actually stipulated the borders of the area used for wine production, the first instance in the world of a wine region being demarcated in this way.

It was a statute which indicated not only rank and recognition, but led to an insistence that vines be dressed and wines made according to traditional practices. Tokaj was celebrated in music and in

verse, not only in Hungary, but Europe as a whole. Voltaire, Beethoven, Goethe, Schubert and Liszt all praised this golden nectare and its positive effects on the body and the soul.

Apart from the facilities of the large-scale producers. the Tokaj-Hegyalja Wine Road, which makes its way through 28 settlements, takes you in the direction of lots of smaller family concerns. Apart from the famous Tokaj Museum with its exhibitions on the local ethnography, geography and the history of the local wine industry there are plenty of smaller collections dotted around the place focussing on the treasures of the Tokaj-Hegyalja.

INFORMATION

Tourinform Office TOKAJ 3910, Serház u. 1. Tel.: 47/552-070, 47/552-070, 47/352-259; tokaj@tourinform.hu

Tokaj Historical Wine Region World Heritage Association

TOKAJ 3910, Rákóczi út 54., Tel.: 47/553-014, 352-752, Fax: 47/352-006

The Tokaj Museum TOKAJ 3910, Bethlen Gábor utca 7. Open: Tue.–Sun.: 10am–4pm; Tel.: 47/352-636

Tokaj Gallery TOKAJ 3910, Bethlen G. u. 15. Open: 1st Apr.–15th Oct. Tue.–Sun. 10am–4pm; Tel.: 47/552-000

Wine Museum TOLCSVA 3934 Kossuth Lajos u. 55. Tel.: 47/384-240, Sun. and holidays : 47/384-251

Open: Tue., Fri.–Sun. 10am–noon, Thur. 2–4pm, and at other times if arranged in advance

Ethnic German Peasant House RÁTKA 3908 Open: Mon.–Fri. 8am–4pm,

and at the weekend if arranged in advance Tel.: 47/374-019

EVENTS:

The Hegyalja Festival (beginning to mid-July); *The Tokaj Wines' Festival* (May–June)

Harvest Week (last week in September)

Further information:

www.tokaj.hu – www.tokaj.lap.hu – www.tokaji-borut.hu

The Hungarians are a *"nation of scientists"*. Whilst this may be rather bold statement, it can in fact be supported by the facts. Many of Hungary's mathematicians, physicists and doctors have gained reputations abroad, and the number of Hungarian Nobel Prize winners is considerable for a country of Hungary's size.

That *János Bolyai*'s writings on the geometry of real space helped to broaden *Albert Einstein's* field of enquiry is well known, and *Ignác Semmelweis* is often recognised as being the saviour of many mothers for his contribution making to puerperal fever a thing of the past.

Hungary can also be proud of its famous academic families, some producing generations of great doctors (*Lenhossék, Korányi, Bókai, Szent-Györgyi*). The *Eötvös family* was another such family of scientists. *Loránd Eötvös* thought up the torsion balance named after him, which proved so important to those engaged in the examination of natural gas and oil during the 20th century. Albert Einstein followed up Eötvös's ideas on the *Theory of Relativity*.

In the following pages we will be devoting time to some of the lesser-known Hungarian scientists and inventors whose work has nevertheless proved just as important as those mentioned above. They are covered in chronological order.

IGNÁC BORN

Ignác Born was born in Gyulafehérvár (Alba Iulia, Romania) in 1742, and died in Vienna in 1791. He was a miner and mineralogist, chemist and scientific administrator, who, from 1776, was responsible for the Royal and Imperial Natural History Collection, and was the author of its catalogue.

In 1774, his work on the minerals, and indeed the mines and metallurgy of Transylvania, the Banat and northern Hungary (the part which is now Slovakia) was published in German in 1774, the same year that he founded the Scientific Society in Prague. The catalogue of his famous mineral collection was published during the 1770s.

He undertook his experiments into the processes of amalgamation metallurgy in Szklenó (Sklené Teplice, Slovakia) near Selmecbánya (Banská Štiavnica). 27 experts from 8 different countries went to see him present his experiments in September 1786, which turned out to be the world's first international technical and scientific conference. It was also at this time that the first international scientific society of its type (the Mining Society) was founded. In Vienna, Born organised the national masonic lodge, of which *Mozart* was a member, and it is probable that the figure of Sarastro in Mozart's opera the Magic Flute was modelled on Born. Born's name survives for posterity in the mineral bornite. Respected by both Mozart and Goethe he was certainly no ordinary scientist.

JÁNOS NAGYVÁTHY

János Nagyváthy was born in Miskolc in 1755, and died in Csurgó in 1819. The author of the first Hungarian agricultural treatise he studied law in Sárospatak, and later taught theology in Losonc (Lucenec, Slovakia).

His first major study appeared in 1791 under the title "The Diligent Country Farmer", published with the support of Count *Ferenc Széchényi*. The book's great virtue was that it gave an overview in Hungarian of Nagyváthy's area of expertise. The book prompted *György Festetics* to invite him to manage his Keszthely estate. Indeed, it was Nagyváthy who prompted the count to found the grammar school in Csurgó in 1792, to build the church in 1796, and to found an agricultural institute in Keszthely in 1797, which was to become the first independent higher educational agricultural institute in the world.

János Nagyváthy was director of the famous Georgikon for the first six months of its existence. In 1797, he moved to Csurgó, where he devoted much of his time to his own farm. It was a time when he committed a lot of his important work to paper. These pieces, with titles like "The Hungarian Farmer's Wife", "The Practical Hungarian Cultivator", "The Hungarian Farm Manager", however, were only published after his death. It was he who brought the strictest accountancy practices into Hungarian agriculture.

ÁNYOS JEDLIK

Ányos Jedlik was born in the small village of Szimő (Zemné, Slovakia) in 1800, and died in Győr in 1895. More than one hundred improvements, inventions, patents, and new devices are associated with his name, a name indeed which enjoys an elevated position in the history of technology in Hungary.

To begin with he studied at the Benedictine Lyceum in Győr. He taught at the Academy of the Benedictine Order in Pozsony (Bratislava, Slovakia) from 1831, and in 1839 was given the position of Professor of Physics and Mechanics at the University of Sciences in Budapest. He was to teach there until 1878. In addition he was Professor of Physical Science and Mechanics at the Institutum Geometricum, that is the Engineering Institute (one of the forerunners of the University of Technical Science) from 1838 to 1850. During the events of 1848 he joined the national guard, something he was constantly reminded of following the suppression of the rebellion. From 1858, he was an associate member of the Hungarian Academy of Sciences, and from 1873 an honorary member. From 1879 he lived in the Benedictine Lyceum in Győr.

Amongst his famous inventions one should mention the electromagnetic armature invented in 1829, the first electric motor in the world to be made for experimental demonstration purposes, which contained the main parts required to make direct current electric motors: the stator, the rotor, the alternating commutator.

Another famous discovery, which he made in 1861, was his electrical starter motor which differed significantly from the magneto-electronic generators used at the time. Once again, it was only made for experimental-demonstration purposes. The industrial version, which emitted considerably larger amounts of voltage, was made by *Siemens* and *Wheatstone* six years later.

In 1828, Jedlik discovered how you can make soda water, also making the equipment necessary for its production. From 1842 he concerned himself with optics and the principles of photography. He was also to make an important contribution in the development of the Bunsen-electric battery, and his double fluid battery cell won him a bronze medal at the Paris World Exhibition in 1855. He had it patented, and a factory was built in Pest to produce them. In 1863, he expounded the voltage multiplication principle, and at the 1873 World Exhibition in Vienna he used his most recent inventions to produce a charge of about one million volts and sparks 90cm long. It was an event which caught the eye of the Siemens-led jury who awarded Jedlik the "For Progress" medal.

He was the first person in Hungary to write a textbook in Hungarian for undergraduates. Jedlik was also a contributor to the German-Hungarian Scientific Technical Dictionary. It was for this reason that he played an important role in inventing a Hungarian technical vocabulary which coincided rather fortunately with the final phases of the Hungarian language reform. He also took part in the compilation of the Universal Hungarian Encyclopaedia (1859–1876).

In Győr there is a statue of Ányos Jedlik, and there is a permanent exhibition dedicated to his life and work in the village where he was born.

JÁNOS IRINYI

A Hungarian scientist's inventiveness also contributed to the invention of the phosphorus safety match. Matches have been with us for a long time, but housewives were not keen on using the early versions as they tended to ignite in rather an explosive fashion. It was the chemist *János Irinyi* who managed to solve this particular problem.

Irinyi was born in 1817 in Nagyléta, and died in the village of Vértes in 1895. He studied abroad at the universities of Berlin and Vienna. It was in 1817, during an unsuccessful experiment with his teacher in Vienna, *Pál Meissner,* that he came upon the idea of putting phosphorus on the tips of matchsticks instead of potassium chloride and lead peroxide. A Viennese pharmacist bought the idea off him for a sum, it is thought, of 7000 forints.

Irinyi was one of the most active members of the Natural Sciences Society. He was also a member of the Industrial Association, of

which *Louis Kossuth* was the vice-president. He also wrote "The Elements of Chemistry" published in Nagyvárad (Oradea, Romania) in 1847. It was originally planned to be a textbook, but the press of the time thought that it was "terribly opinionated". No further books of his were published after the 1848 War for Freedom.

Although Irinyi returned to his farm in Nagyléta in 1844, he didn't disappear from public life. In 1848, he sent the first draft of the famous Twelve Points to the March Youth from his Vértes home. With the outbreak of the War for Freedom he was one of the first to reach for his gun. Kossuth named him chief inspector of the state factories, and in 1849 he turned his attention to the gunpowder factory and the arsenal in Nagyvárad. Reacting to *Görgei*'s desperate call he produced rockets for the army stationed in the town.

After the suppression of the uprising, Irinyi was forced into hiding, and later he was to spend a few months as a prisoner in the Újépület in Pest. After his release he went first to his parents in Nagyléta, where he undertook some tests on various types of agricultural machinery (he designed a seed-drill and a number of harrows), ultimately being the first person to use a machine which was capable of planting, ploughing and harrowing all in one. He also enjoyed some good results in his experiments into improving soil quality.

OTTÓ HERMAN

Ottó Herman's work is well represented at the museum named after him in Miskolc.

Born of a German-speaking family in Breznóbánya (Brezno, Slovakia) in 1835, he died in Budapest in 1914. He was interested in nearly every aspect of the natural world. It was only when attending school in Miskolc that he acquired the Hungarian language, and became acquainted with Hungarian culture. He failed, however, to take his school leaving exams.

He became a qualified locksmith in Vienna before being called up to serve in the army, which he did for five years. He took part in the organisation of the Carbonari Movement in northern Italy, before joining the ranks of the Polish freedom fighters. Returning to Hungary in 1863 he became a photographer in Kőszeg. He then went to Kolozsvár (Cluj-Napoca, Romania) on the recommendation of *Kálmán Chernel* where he became a laboratory assistant at the Transylvanian Museum Association run by *Sámuel Brassai*. He worked as a guard at the National Museum from 1871, and in 1875 he made it into the zoological department, which was where he founded the "Natural History Journal", a publication he produced for two years. From the middle of the 1870s he played an active role in the scientific life of the country, becoming involved in the work of the Natural Science Society. Under the aegis of the society Herman wrote "Hungary's Spiders", "The Hungarian Fishing Book", "The Ancient Professions: Fishing and the Life of the Herdsman". In 1901 he wrote "The Benefits and Damage Caused by Birds", and in 1914, "The Language of Hungarian Herdsmen".

In 1893, Herman founded the Hungarian Ornithological Centre (the predecessor of the Ornithological Institute). He also started the "Aquila" journal. He was a prolific writer publishing fourteen books and over 1100 writings on many branches of the sciences.

JÁNOS MATHIÁSZ

One of the most important figures in the field of the improvement of grape varieties was *János Mathiász*, who was born in Ádámföld (Mosurov, Slovakia) in 1838, and died in Kecskemét in 1921.

No less than sixty-six grape types are associated with his name, twelve of which have become famous worldwide. The vineyards currently growing Mathiász grapes abroad (mainly grapes for eating) cover an area of over 10 thousand hectares.

In order to escape the phylloxera outbreak in 1890 Mathiász moved his plantation to Kecskemét, where he bought 17 "holds" (one "hold" = 0.57hectares) and later 33 "holds" of so-called immune sand in the Talfája-dűlő. When cultivating on quicksand he used grape types from the nearby Miklós Plantation and some plants of French stock, and with these he was able to supplement the grape types he had already improved himself.

He tried to come up with grape types which ripened at different times, giving him grapes from the middle of the summer right through to late autumn.

On the sand beds he grew 1,300 new grape types, 180 of which were excellent strains, including: Pearl of Kecskemét, Kecskemét Treasure, Lajos Thallóczy, János Mathiász's Glory, József Munkátsy, Mihály Vörösmarty, Ilona Zrínyi, Mihály Tompa, General Bem, Ignác Darányi.

Of his improved grape types six are still under licence, these being Cegléd Beauty, Hungarian Millennium Memorial, Flower of Kecskemét, Mrs János Mathiász's Muscat, Mrs Gusztáv Szaunter, Queen Elizabeth Memorial, and a later grape type he created in 1916, which has subseqmently become well-known, Queen of the Vineyards.

The latter is pretty widespread in Italy, as well as being popular in France and the United States. More than one million grape plants from his farm make their way to Hungarian growers all over the country.

János Feketeházy

One of the most interesting of the bridges joining Pest with Buda is Szabadság Bridge, standing underneath Gellért Hill. This and another bridge in the middle of Szeged, which was also worthy of inspection before it had to be rebuilt following the damage inflicted on it during the Second World War, were both designed by *János Feketeházy*, who was born in Vágsellye (Sal'a, Slovakia) in 1842, which was also where he died in 1927.

One of Hungary's most accomplished engineers he completed his studies at both the Universities of Vienna and Zürich. After the great flood in Szeged (1879) he submitted a design for the building of the bridge across the River Tisza with the co-operation of the Eiffel company. Feketeházy also designed the bridge over the Sebes and the Körös on the road to Nagyvárad (Oradea, Romania), and the bridge over the Rába in Győr. It was his design which won the competition to build the Franz Joseph Bridge (now Szabadság Bridge) for the 1896 Millennium Exhibition in Budapest.

Feketeházy also designed the metal roof for the Budapest Opera House, as well as those for the Economics University and Keleti Railway Station.

Miklós Konkoly-Thege

The pre-eminent figure in the history of Hungarian astronomy was born in Budapest in 1842, which was where he died in 1916. The academy's astronomical observatory in Buda relies very much on the instruments he provided. As a landowner the proceeds of his estates went mainly towards financing his scientific research. There is a small planet named after him, as is the Konkoly Observatory on Sváb Hill (Széchenyi Hill), which was opened in 1921. There is also the Konkoly Medal, which is awarded every year.

He was a pupil of the internationally renowned astronomer *J. F. Encke*, and got his doctorate from the University of Berlin in 1861. He carried out valuable observations on comets, measuring the spectra of 29 different examples. He also observed meteorites and devoted time to examining the sun's spots. He also made some groundbreaking spectroscopic recordings of composition of meteors. In 1876, *Konkoly-Thege* took part in the compilation of the Spectroscopic Catalogue of the Universe. His observatory observations ran to 16 volumes. In 1883, in Brunswick in Germany, he published a work on Astrophysics, and in 1887 he wrote the first ever handbook on astrophysics. His book on astrospectroscopes was published in Halle in 1890, followed by his "Introduction to Photography" in 1891. As the director of the National Meteorological and Geomagnetic Institute he organised the weather forecasting, and together with his colleagues produced the first weather charts. It was his idea to build the astronomical observatories at Kalocsa, Herény and Kiskartal, projects which he himself co-ordinated. It was his research, which provided the basis for the Hungarian Academy of Science's astronomical observatory in Budapest bearing his name. A scientific conference was held in his honour in 1991. He is one of the few scientists to have been elected a member of the London Royal Astronomical Society.

Jenő Gothard

Britain's famous scientific community held him in such high regard that they felt it fitting to name a crater on the moon after him.

Jenő Gothard studied in Vienna, after which, in 1881, he founded the private astrophysical observatory in

Herény. In 1886, he became the first person to prove the existence of the central star of the Lyra annular nebula (NCG 6720) with the aid of a photograph. He discovered the relationship between the novas and the planetary nebulae, using spectroscopic photography, a method he himself had thought up. His photographs of comets and nebulae and his recordings of comets were all recognised internationally, and he also achieved some significant results in the photographing of pale, diffuse extra-terrestrial objects.

The Hungarian Academy published his "Spectrophotographic Studies" in 1891. He was also a major contributor to the development of the telephone and X-rays in Hungary, as well being one of the designers of the Ikervár hydroelectric power station. Many of his most important experimental devices are in the possession of the Budapest University of Sciences' observatory in Herény bearing his name. The observatory in Herény near Szombathely has a small museum dedicated to Gothard's life and work.

LORÁND EÖTVÖS

His works are kept at the memorial exhibition at the Loránd Eötvös Institute on Kolumbusz Kristóf utca in Budapest's 14th District.

Eötvös was born in the year of the Hungarian War for Freedom, 1848, and died shortly after the First World War. Eötvös was a teacher, a university professor, and a lecturer in experimental physics as well as a famous experimenter and nature lover. He not only loved nature, he photographed it as well. It is no coincidence that there is a mountain peak in Italy named after him. Despite the fact that photography was still very much in its infancy Eötvös was able to produce some excellent stereoscopic pictures, which we are fortunate enough still to have. The double-armed torsion balance named after him proved to be a very important experimental tool for geologists, and it was used all over the world. Eötvös was a member of the Hungarian Academy of Sciences, as well as of many scientific societies abroad. His scientific work was highly regarded by no lesser figure than *Albert Einstein* himself.

Loránd *Eötvös* founded a college in memory of his father *József* especially for talented Hungarian students. He led the University of Sciences, which has since 1950 born his name, and he was also president of the Hungarian Academy of Sciences for a good number of years.

DONÁT BÁNKI

The famous Hungarian inventor *Donát Bánki* was born in Bakonybánk in 1859, and he died in Budapest in 1922. His first machines were made at the Ganz Factory, and from 1899 he carried on his designing work as a professor at the Budapest University of Technology. Bánki's name is associated with the development of the gas and petrol motor, projects in which he enjoyed the help of *János Csonka*, the head of the University's workshop.

It was in their world-famous license: "Innovations in Petroleum Motors"(1893) that Bánki and Csonka wrote about the carburettor half a year before *Maybach* took out the patent. The Bánki-Csonka motor, which included these innovations, was used all over the world. In 1898, Bánki was able to perfect the high pressure combustion engine using water injection. In 1894, he took out a patent on the motorbike.

His other research area, the principles of the steam-powered turbines, he brought to the world's attention in Liège in 1905, and in the USA in 1908. On the same topic he wrote his important work "Energy Transformation in Liquids" (1916). In the same year he patented the water turbine, which also bears his name. The invention was important because it opened the way for small-scale hydroelectric power stations. Indeed, the Bánki solution is still recommended in developing countries requiring a quick solution to satisfy urgent energy needs. He was also involved in the planning of the power station then being built on the Iron Gates on the Danube ("The Plan for the Iron Gates Hydroelectric Power Station", 1918). There is a college, a prize and a park named after him, as well as a statue of him.

József Marek

There are many branches of the sciences in which Hungarians have made telling contributions in increasing man's understanding, and veterinary science is no exception. Hungary's great representative was *József Marek*, who was born in Vágszerdahely in 1868, and died in Budapest in 1952.

József Marek gained his veterinary diploma in 1892. He completed his postgraduate studies at several veterinary colleges abroad before starting his teaching work in Budapest.

His book "Clinical Diagnoses" published in 1902 proved an important handbook and a ground-breaking achievement in the field of the veterinary internal pathology.

Together with *Ferenc Hutyra* he wrote the internationally famous "Veterinary Internal Pathology" (1924), which was subsequently translated into nine different languages. József Marek became an associate member of the Hungarian Academy of Sciences in 1918 and a full member in 1938. He won the Kossuth Prize in 1949. He was awarded honorary doctorates by the Universities of Utrecht, Leipzig, Hanover and Sofia as well as by the University of Technology and the University of Agricultural Science in Hungary.

He became an honorary member of the veterinary societies in England, the United States and France as well as the veterinary associations in Greece, Sweden and Finland. A statue by *Ferenc Medgyessy* was put up in his honour in 1954 in the park of the University of Veterinary Science.

Kálmán Kandó
and the Electrification of the Railways

In the field of technology Hungary has had such a fine body of practitioners, and it was some of them who created the alternating current transformer in 1885, applied the principles of parallel transformer systems, and built power stations in Italy and elsewhere in the world.

The first factory in Europe to focus on the production of electrical equipment was that founded by *Ábrahám Ganz* in Budapest manufacturing power current electronic equipment. It was here that *Ottó Bláthy*, *Miksa Déri*, *Károly Zipernowsky* and *Kálmán Kandó*, amongst others worked.

Bláthy's name is associated with the first inductive ammeter, better known as the gas metre. Kandó is known for being the builder of the first three-phase electrical railway.

Kálmán Kandó was born in Budapest in 1869, and it was there he died in 1931. His name appears on 70 patents. One of the Ganz factory's proudest achievements was building the Valtallina railway in Italy, the world's first major alternating current electric railway. It was from this that Kandó went on to design the high voltage three-phase system, which led to Europe's first electrified main line, and the world's first high voltage alternating current electrified railway line. Between 1907-15 more for Ganz-Kandó electrified lines were laid out in Italy, for which they also bought the Kandó patent.

After 1917 he started to work on the electrification of the railway system in Budapest making it possible for the 50 cycle current produced at the power stations to be used on the railways.

In 1923 he built the first 2500 horsepower experimental engine. After some successful tests Hungarian Railways electrified the main line to Hegyeshalom, along which Kandó-type electric trains ran, albeit in 1932, after his death.

In the meantime Kandó built express trains for the French railways (1923), and in 1927 he worked as an advisor for the Westinghouse Company in the United States. Many institutions in Hungary have been named after Kálmán Kandó, one of them being a College of Higher Education.

LIPÓT FEJÉR

Born in 1880 in Pécs and dying in Budapest in 1959, *Lipót Fejér* was one of the world's most famous mathematicians during the 1930s, being responsible for nurturing a whole generation of scientists. He became a member of the Hungarian Academy of Sciences.

He completed his university studies in Budapest and Berlin. It was there that he started to involve himself with the problems surrounding the Fourier Series. In 1900, at the age of 20, he came up with the theorem published in the Paris Comptes Rendus, which was later named after him.

Whilst Féjer's mathematical theorems mean very little to the uninitiated, the fact that more than thirty foreign universities offered him professorial posts says much for Fejér's abilities. Despite such offers he stayed in Hungary, working through what were some of the most difficult of years, particularly during the Second World War. He continued to give his university lectures after the war to the great benefit of his students.

Many of the famous Hungarian American scientists: *János Neumann, Jenő Wigner, Ede Teller, Kornél Lánczos, Leó Szilárd, Péter Lax, György Pólya* and *Gábor Szegő* to name but a few, all looked back to the alma mater where they all started out on their illustrious careers. In the case of some of the mathematicians and physicians the path led eventually to Nobel Prizes in their chosen fields.

LÁSZLÓ JÓZSEF BIRÓ

Born in 1899 in Budapest *László József Biró* was a journalist and technical designer. It was he who invented the "biro", the ballpoint pen. From 1939 he lived in France and then Argentina, but it was during the 1930s, whilst he was still in Budapest that he started his experiments with the ballpoint pen, having become familiar with the Czech *W. Climes*'s patented idea, which he had shown at the Budapest International Fair of 1931.

The Germans bought out a refillable ink ballpoint pen in 1939 under the name "Exakt". On 10th June 1943 Biró finally brought a patent in Argentina on his dye-filled ballpoint pen, which was known locally as the "Eterpen" but which was marketed in France under the name "Biró Crayon". Since then the pen has become internationally recognised as the humble biro. The history of the invention is described in the book "The Peaceful Revolution". László József Biró died in Buenos Aires in 1985.

JÁNOS SZENTÁGOTHAI

János Szentágothai born in Budapest in 1912, where he also died in 1994, was certainly a scientist of our times. For many years he was the President of the Hungarian Academy of Sciences. He was known and respected in many countries, his name being associated with the study of the brain.

It was in 1946 that he wrote his monograph with *Ferenc Kiss* entitled "The Atlas of the Human Anatomy". In 1952 he wrote a book about the vestibular system and the relationships between the eye muscles. His main field of research, however, was in the study of the synapse, and he wrote a monograph on the related topic of the cerebellum in 1967 in which he described the thalamic system and experiments investigating the chemical make up of the neurons and their endings. His 1971 three volume "Functional Anatomy" was well received, and "Neural mechanisms: Structure, Function and Dynamics", with contributions from his colleagues, was published posthumously in 1997. A well-known university teacher and a popular lecturer at international conferences he was also an accomplished watercolourist.

In 1973, Szentágothai won the American Lashley Prize, and in 1984 he won the F. O. Schmitt Prize.

In Hungary he won the Semmelweis Prize, the Jancsó Prize and the Hőgyes Prize. In 1985, he was awarded the Academy's gold medal.

He was indeed a remarkable figure. It is indeed rare to find such a versatile person cutting such a figure on the scientific stage.

He was quite at home in the fields of science, art and literature, he founded a school of scientific thought and managed to enhance the reputation of Hungarian scientists and of science in Hungary in everything he turned his mind to.

1905
FÜLÖP LÉNÁRD
(Bratislava, 1862–
Messelhausen, 1947)
The Nobel Prize
for Physics
for his research
on cathode rays

1925
RICHARD ADOLF ZSIGMONDY
(Vienna, 1865–Göttingen, 1929)
The Nobel Prize
for Chemistry,
for the elucidation
of the heterogeneous nature
of colloidal
solutions

1914
RÓBERT BÁRÁNY
(Vienna, 1876–
Uppsala, 1936)
For studies
on the vestibular
apparatus
of the inner ear

1937
ALBERT
SZENT-GYÖRGYI
(Budapest, 1893–
Wood Hole, 1986)
The Nobel Prize for
Medicine for his
studies on biological
combustion

1943
GYÖRGY HEVESY
(Budapest, 1885–
Freiburg, 1966)
The Nobel Prize
for Chemistry
for the use of
isotopes as tracers
in research

1961
GYÖRGY BÉKÉSY
(Budapest, 1899–
Honolulu, 1972)
For research
on the functions
of the inner ear

1963
JENŐ WIGNER
(Budapest, 1902–1995)
A shared Nobel Prize
for Physics
for his work
on the principles
governing
the interaction
of protons
and neutrons
in the nucleus

1971
DÉNES GÁBOR
(Budapest, 1900–
London, 1979)
The Nobel Prize
for Physics
for the invention
holography

1986
KÁROLY JÁNOS
POLÁNYI
(Berlin, 1929–)
A shared Nobel Prize
for Chemistry
for introducing methods
for analysing basic
chemical reactions.

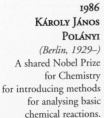

1994
JÁNOS HARSÁNYI
(Budapest, 1920–
California, 2000)
A shared Nobel Prize
for Economics
for his ground-breaking
work in the field
of game theory

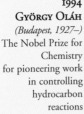

1994
GYÖRGY OLÁH
(Budapest, 1927–)
The Nobel Prize for
Chemistry
for pioneering work
in controlling
hydrocarbon
reactions

1986
ELIE WIESEL
(Sighetu Marmatiei, Romania
1928–)
The Nobel Peace Prize;
"one of the spiritual leaders
in those days when violence,
oppression and racism
left their mark on the world"

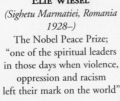

2002
IMRE KERTÉSZ
(Budapest, 1929–)
The Nobel Prize
for Literature for
his work describing
the vulnerability
of the individual in the
face of despotic barbarity.

The Danube

Although people no longer buy their water from the Swabian water carts, which would trundle the roads of the Buda Hills to the tune of *"Tonauwasser! Tonauwasser!"* the river is still an important source of drinking water. The journey to the consumer is, however, by no means direct, going through drilled wells before being filtered through layers of pebbles specially laid down for the purpose. Once used, the water makes its way back into the river, in many cases untreated, in the hope that nature will clean what mankind has polluted. It is left for the Danube, just like all the other rivers, to cope in the best way they can, and somehow, by some miracle of nature the clean waters return...

There was a time, several millions of years ago, after the thick ice cover of the Ice Age had melted, that waters covered the area geologists like to refer to as the Viennese Basin. It was through the so-called *"Porta Hungarica"* cut through the hills that the Danube then made its way into what is now Hungary. A lot of water had to flow before the river eventually found its course. There are sections of the river which were left stranded on the Lesser Plain, and some extensive marshes south of Komárom, and at what was once the mouth of the Zsitva, whose waters originated from the river. The river managed to cut its way though what are now the Börzsöny and the Visegrád Hills, at which point the river was forced to make a spectacular turn to the south, where once relased from the geological constraints of the hills the river spilled onto the Great Plain dividing into a thousand branches.

For hundreds and thousands of years it was the hills forced upwards by the forces of nature, and

the pebble and sandbanks which built up regularly along the course of the river, which interrupted the Danube's progress. This, however, was before man also began to interfere, leaving his indelible mark on the river. The fact that the river flooded, that its banks were in the habit of getting washed away, and the sandbanks in the river tended to make navigation difficult, meant it was only a matter of time before modifications were made. Between 1820 and 1880 the river was shortened by no less than one hundred kilometres, all the "unnecessary" bends being cut off in the process. Nowadays, in our efforts to harness the energies of the river in the name of progress, the *"Bős-Nagymaros"* hydroelectric dam project has led to problems of a more diplomatic nature.

The Danube, however, abides by the ancient Greek saying claiming *"pantha rhei"*, everything flows, everything changes. This goes not only for the waters flowing down the river, but for the life lived along it. There are some stretches of the river, which have managed to avoid mankind's interference, although it is sad to report that the Szigetköz, which had survived more or less untouched up to this juncture, is currently undergo-

ing the significant ecological changes caused by the damming project mentioned above. The Lesser Plain is now covered in a swath of cereal crops, the hillsides in Neszmély are covered in vineyards. The slopes of the Danube Bend are covered in rocks and woodland and down on the Plain, Dunaföldvár sits perched on a layer of loess whilst the Gemenc Flood Plains are covered in thick woods, which not even the midday sun can penetrate.

Of course the banks of the River Danube are not always so quiet and peaceful, and there are some places where the course of the man-made river is so narrow that the Danube occasionally stands at the mercy of the elements. In the past the residents of Érd and Kiskunlacháza would occasionally be forced to move to higher ground to escape the river's rising waters. Those residents of Pest and Buda who were called out of their beds by the bells tolling on the Ides of March also became familiar with the Danube's darker side. By the time the floods had subsided, 5,000 buildings were left either damaged or destroyed.

Elsewhere, in the uninhabited areas, the floods topped up the fertile mudflats, and brought water and nutrients to the woods on the flood plains.

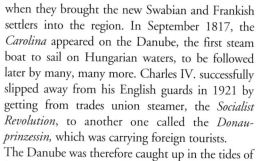

when they brought the new Swabian and Frankish settlers into the region. In September 1817, the *Carolina* appeared on the Danube, the first steam boat to sail on Hungarian waters, to be followed later by many, many more. Charles IV. successfully slipped away from his English guards in 1921 by getting from trades union steamer, the *Socialist Revolution*, to another one called the *Donauprinzessin*, which was carrying foreign tourists.

The Danube was therefore caught up in the tides of history. Apart from the sailors there were a lot of "water people" who lived on and from the River Danube. There were the millers, the gold prospectors and of course the fishermen who provided the fish for the towns' restaurants as well as for their own consumption. Fortunately the fishermen are still with us, as are the fish, although in fewer numbers than in days of old. (One hundred years ago the Pest *"Vizafogó"*, like similar devices on the Black Sea, would pull out fish from the water by the hundredweight.) More recently people have realised that the Danube can also be used for sport and leisure. There is the lido, and there's a certain seaside feel about the quay in Újpest, made all the more convincing by the rowing and other sporting activities. Whilst the Germans worship the Rhine, and the Russians the mother Volga, for the Hungarians the Danube is simply there – or rather *here* and not there. Although it is the Tisza which holds the greater attraction for the people of the Great Plain (it's celebrated in more songs for example than the Danube), the Danube still means a lot to people both in Hungary and the rest of Europe. The Danube has provided, now provides and will always provide a means of communication linking people from different areas, different cultures and different countries.

These floods also made stretches of the river previously unnavigable easy to sail on. As the saying goes *"navigare necesse est"*, on the River Danube just as much as on the high seas although Nato's decision to bomb Serbia's bridges over the Danube has provided some major obstacles. This would be true for the whole year, if it weren't for the droughts bringing down the water levels.

Our prehistoric ancestors were the first to use the waters to suit their own purposes, and the Romans used galleons to help patrol the Danube which formed part of the defensive "limes" defending the northern borders of their Empire. The knights of the *Nibelunglied* arrived along the Danube and sloops rowed along the river to come to the aid of Hunyadi at the Battle of Belgrade. It was also on the waters of the Danube that Matthias Corvinus sailed his flagship the *Bucentaurus*. (It was also on the ice of the River Danube that Matthias was elected by his peers!) The *"Ulmer Schachtel"* (The Ulm Packages) replaced the Turkish galleons on the river,

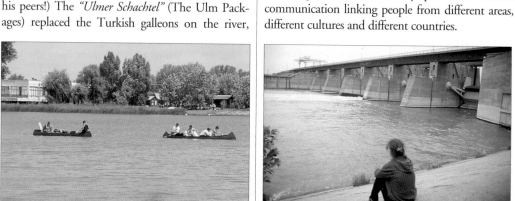

The natural importance of the river and its immediate surroundings has been recognised, and there are two national parks and many protected areas along its course.

The two banks of the river are joined up by road and rail bridges, passenger and car ferries.

The oldest bridge on the Hungarian stretch of the river (and the second oldest permanent bridge along the river as a whole) is the Chain Bridge.

The most recent addition is the St Ladislas Bridge (2003) linking not only Szekszárd and Hajós. North of the capital the only road and rail bridges crossing the Danube are in Komárom, whilst to the south, once past the M0 motorway bridge, there are only two further bridges, those being in Dunaföldvár and Baja. The larger settlements, like Vác and Mohács, have car ferries, whilst the smaller crossings only have passenger ferries.

There are timetabled boat services from Budapest northwards to the Danube Bend along the Vác and Szentendre branches of the river, and hydrofoils connecting Budapest with Vienna and Pozsony (Bratislava). Apart from the MAHART boats there are plenty of travel companies operating sightseeing trips, tours and conference ships in Budapest. There are also marinas for both motorboats and yachts from Esztergom all the way down to Mohács.

Europe's second longest river rises in the Black Forest in Germany and runs into the Black Sea in Romania some 2888 kilometres downstream. Flowing through ten countries it collects water from 800 thousand square kilometres of territory. The Hungarian stretch of the Danube is 417 kilometres long, 240 kilometres of which forms the border with Slovakia.

The river flows into the country near Rajka and leaves it 14 kilometres south of Mohács. Its rate of flow is slowest in Budapest 600m³/sec at high tide (compared with 10 thousand m³/sec at its fastest point). The river is on average 2–3 metres deep, although it can reach a depth of 6–8 metres. The river floods twice a year on average in the early spring and early summer. The almost one hundred years of straightening work on the river has made the river 120 km shorter than it once was and has spared one million hectares of land from flooding. Today, there are 3,000 km of embankment keeping the Danube on its present course.

Apart from the three big islands (*Szentendre, Csepel and Mohács*) there are countless larger or smaller islands along the course of the river. Some of them have in fact become part of the riverbank, or split up into other islands.

The Tisza

Plip...plop... there's a certain atmosphere about the banks of the River Tisza around dusk. On the moonless evenings the willow branches dip to waist height or fall into the waters, and shadows get lost in the dim depths of the river. There are only one or two points of light on the water's surface telling you that there is a river there at all. The plip-plopping sounds come from the direction of the light. The anglers click at the fish, like their great grandfathers and their great great grandfathers before them. Who knows, perhaps prehistoric fishermen did it too. It is the Tisza wels which rule the waters, weighing in at between 100 and 200 kg and measuring between two and four metres. Landing one is a major achievement. But there is more to "the most Hungarian of rivers" than fish and fishing. There has always been a kind of primeval spirit enveloping the everyday lives and the festivities of the people who live along the banks of the River Tisza.

"When in the dusk a summer day had died // I stopp'd by winding Tisza's river-side // Just where the little Túr flow'd in to rest // A weary child that sought its mother's breast."

It is indeed difficult to imagine the Tisza without Petőfi, or indeed Petőfi without the Tisza, despite the fact that the river has changed a great deal in the meantime.

Before looking at the course of the Tisza as it stands today, let's consider how things appeared five, ten thousand years ago, when the Tisza's destiny was still in its own hands. The river created the sandbanks from the solidified gravel rock formations, and the islands and hillocks of sediment

at the foot of the great rock masses of what are now the Carpathians from where the deposits were originally derived. Not utterly humbled by such exertions the river finally made its way into the eastern parts of the Great Plain from whence it meandered onwards down towards the Danube. The Szamos's detrital cone and the more elevated loess beds of the Nyírség took the Tisza westwards and then northwards, where, on encountering the hills created by the River Latorca, the river proceed once again in a westerly direction. The final obstacles the river had to encounter were the deposits left by the River Sajó, at which point the river was sent into a thousand directions. It was in

what is now the Hortobágy that the river tried to find its course, which it did, turning south and eventually proceeding along a series of tortuous bends.

The Tisza's ancient, wild and somewhat maverick existence came to an end 200-250 years ago, when man, who had up until that point given the river a more or less free rein, went about draining the marshes, and then cutting off the more outrageous meanders pushing the river into line with the help of some strategically placed dykes. The Tisza was reduced in length by one third (420 km), whilst the Great Plain gained several thousand acres of additional farmland.

With so many bends having been cut off it is difficult to imagine just how much the river meandered. (The 15 km meander between Vezseny and Martfű could also quite easily have been avoided with the opening of a 2.5 km channel across the bend.)

The Tisza, however, hasn't gone down without a fight. The narrowed and shortened course of the river hasn't always been able to take in the great spring and summer rains, and on occasions *"Roaring and howling through the dyke it swirl'd // Greedy to swallow up the whole wide world"*. Indeed, *Petőfi*'s apocalyptic vision came true in Szeged on 12th March 1879, when the embankments were breached and 6,000 houses reduced to ruins. *"There was no Szeged for the dawn to welcome... Only the ruins, the remnants of which had turned into something resembling an extensive mudflat."* – reported eyewitness *Kálmán Mikszáth*, who was then working as a young journalist in the town. There have of course been more recent occasions when the River Tisza has unleashed its powers, like in 2000 and 2001, when in took vengeance on the surrounding countryside.

Known as the "fair" and "flowering" Tisza its fairness refers to its colour, the yellowy colour provided by the fine sand and clay suspension in the water. The *"flowering"* refers to an insect, the mayfly, and its rare and short-lived flight. The inhabitants of the Great Plain believe that life is all the poorer for not having seen the migrating cranes leaving the Hortobágy or the flowering of the Tisza. The old song goes *"the Tisza is a cemetery when it's in flower"*, referring to those few hours when the surface of the river is covered in a carpet of the silky-to-touch, snow-white winged mayfly. After having hatched, they perform a kind of bridal dance, pair, and after having laid their eggs carefully look after their next of kin, before dying and leaving a white covering over the water's surface and the riverbanks. At dawn the fish in the river wake up to what is an enormous feast of many billions of dead mayfly.

This is however not the only natural wonder you are likely to witness on the river. There are 30 species of fish, from the tiny bleak to the wels, a fish which can weigh many hundreds of kilograms. Where land has been flooded it is possible to see marsh snails and water scavenger beetle in the slightly stagnant waters, and in the dead channels you might see one of the more recent arrivals, the hairy water chestnut. The woods running along the banks of the river, and the willows, poplars and elders growing on the flood plains offer ideal nesting to water birds.

On the branches leaning out over the water you may be fortunate enough to see kingfishers diving into the water with the precision of a crossbow, whilst out on the open river you may see the large black fleshy cormorants, or the long-necked herons making rapid progress. On the more southerly stretches of the river the clay and loess riverbanks are peppered with the holes which provide the nests for the swallows and the bee-eaters. Mankind has been able to eke out a living along the banks of the River Tisza for many thousands of years, firstly by hunting and fishing, and then by building fords and providing ferry crossings and then charging a toll. Villages were founded along the banks of the river, some of which in time have been forced to move further and further away from the river on account of the floods. One thing, however, we can assume has remained pretty constant over the centuries is the locals' partiality for the fish soup which only they know how to cook.

In more recent times man has made a more concerted effort to make use of the river. From the 1850s you start to see the steamers replacing the rafts. First they provided services to Vásárosnamény, and then all the way down to Szolnok. Locks were built at both Tiszalök and Kisköre. Also fords – and a good number of the ferries – all of which were to be replaced by bridges in time. The challenge for the future is to learn how to live in harmony with the Tisza. Steps need to be taken to prevent it being polluted by cyanide, nitrates and goodness knows what else.

Hungary's second most important river was mentioned by both *Pliny* and *Strabo*. Pliny called it the *Pathisous*, Strabo the *Pathissus*. One has to wait until *Anonymous of Ravenna* and the authors of the old Hungarian chronicles, who called it the *Tysia* and *Tisis* respectively, to see the river called anything remotely resembling its present name. The source of the river, of which there are two branches, the Black and the *White Tisza*, lie 1,600-1,700 m above sea level in the Maramures Mountains (Ruthenia, Ukraine).

The two branches join up at Felsőróna (Rona de Sus, Romania), and it is from here that the river is known simply as the River Tisza. 962 km later, 588 km of which are in Hungarian territory, the river flows into the Danube at Szalánkemén (Slankamen, Serbia) near Titel.

Waters covering an area 160 thousand km² flow into the river. When the water level on the river is about average the Tisza is between 100 and 200 metres wide, whilst its depth varies between 1.5 and 8 m. However, there are periods of drought when the Upper Tisza is only 20 cm deep.

Where it is indeed possible some kind of balance with nature needs to be maintained, and where this balance has already been lost steps need to be taken to ensure that a balance is rediscovered. If the problem is left unresolved we will continue to be at the mercy of the elements, and heavy snows and persistant rainfall will continue to cause concern to those living in the nearby towns and villages.

The average rate of flow of 300–500m³/sec can vary enormously depending on the water level. During periods of flooding the quantity of water flowing down the river can be as much as 87 times greater than when the water level is low. There are over 4,000 km of protective dykes and several thousand km² of flood plains between the river and the dykes themselves.

There are 15 road bridges, 6 rail bridges and two carrying both, joining the two banks of the river between Tivadar in the north and Szeged in the south. There are pontoon bridges in Tiszadob and Csongrád, and 16 car ferry services crossing the river, although services do get disrupted during floods, and when the river is icebound.

There are eleven places where passengers can cross the river by boat. Amongst the river's curiosities are the ferries crossing the Tisza, which are pulled across the river using taut cables and gravitational power.

It is also possible to go sightseeing around Szeged by boat. Most river tours concentrate on the picturesque stretches of the Upper Tisza, but you will also find rowers out on Lake Tisza, and some stretches of the Tisza further south. The lidos on the River Tisza are nice and sandy, or gravelly at the very least, all the way through Hungary, and during the summer the water can be as warm as 22–26 °C.

National Parks in Hungary

The fact that Hungary has ten National Parks, all of which are run by the state, is the result of quarter of a century's effort. (It is the Minister of the Environment's job to oversee the countryside, the state's forests, mineral resources and wildlife, which he does with the help of his Secretary of State and the directors of the national parks.) Expressed in the most simple terms the aim of the national parks is to look after a particular area's geological, hydrological, botanical, zoological and cultural historical treasures, to protect totally or almost unspoilt landscapes and to ensure the continuation of basic ecological processes and the conditions demanded of a varied biological environment, as well as to make people more aware of their environment, and to make them feel more responsible towards it. Of particular importance are the protection of the rivers, the subterranean water sources, the forests, the farmland and the renewable energy resources.

Such protection takes place on a number of levels depending on the degree of protection required, as will be seen in the chapters dealing with the different geographical regions. Some areas are strictly protected, whereas as those which are only partly so can be visited by the general public. Some areas are of international, some of national, and others of only local importance. Being familiar with the official terminology is therefore an advantage.

In 1970, UNESCO launched the "Man and the Biosphere" (MAB) research project designed to protect the natural environment. Within the context of the project a number of reserves were established in places where the plants and animal communities and ecosystems were dwindling in number. Five such reserves were marked out in Hungary.

In 1971, the declaration, which was signed in Ramsar in Iran, concentrated on marshes of international importance as well as bird habitats.

The declaration demanded that the member countries compile a list of flood plains considered to be of international importance, and called for the creation of flood plain reserves for the protection of breeding water birds. At the time it was considered an international effort requiring international commitment. Hungary signed the accord in 1979.

Enormous responsibilities go with those natural habitats finding themselves on the list of World Heritage Sites. (Space is also devoted to both Aggtelek, Lake Fertő and Hortobágy in the section dealing with the World Heritage Sites).

Conservation areas are usually small areas containing natural rarities whose protection is necessary for scientific and educational reasons or genetic preservation. Nature reserves are designed to protect that particular area's most characteristic features and maintain a balance between the various elements making up a particular landscape. It is for this reason activities such as the selling off of land for building purposes, building, mining and industrial development which are likely to be alien to that particular environment, are restricted. Other activities which do not fall into this category (like for example farming and forestry) are likely to be tolerated and indeed encouraged. The nature reserves are bound only by local Hungarian legislation. This is not to say that the nature reserves do not contain strictly protected areas. One should also mention the Red Book, in which extinct as well as endangered species are listed.

To some extent environmental protection has an important role to play in the promotion of tourism in Hungary.

The changes which have taken place over the last few years have also affected people's attitudes towards nature and the way Hungary is perceived by the outside world.

Furthermore, the national parks are now much better prepared to meet the needs of all their visitors. Active nature lovers are now deemed to be those who are interested enough in their natural surroundings to go out and explore what's out there around them. In return Nature helps to quench our natural lust for knowledge.

The way one should behave when out in the country is pretty self-explanatory. It's possible to enjoy nature, and of course the national parks, without having to resort to collecting flowers, animals and minerals, leaving litter, making undue noise or upsetting the wild animals. Why would anyone wish to behave any differently?

Marked paths go through the more protected areas, and there is no reason why anyone would want to wander off them. As for motorists arriving at the national parks, it is forbidden to spend the night in your car or camper van in the National Park car parks, and you are not allowed to leave the road and drive along the forest tracks.

In the following pages we would like to introduce Hungary's National Parks following the same geographical order used in the regional chapters, concentrating on the aspects of each park which single them out from the others.

(As the National Parks do not always coincide with our tourist regions, some of the things you are likely to find will also be mentioned in the regional chapters as well.)

The Danube–Ipoly National Park

The Danube-Ipoly National Park is situated to the north of the capital, and covers most of the Pilis and the Börzsöny Hills tucked in between the Danube and the River Ipoly. The National Park covers parts of Pest, Komárom-Esztergom and Nógrád counties, and spreads into three of the regions covered in this book (Budapest, Central Transdanubia and Northern Hungary), where three large tracts of countryside (river valleys, hills and plains) meet. The Danube Bend, where the Danube meeting the hills is most spectacular, is where the river broke through the gap between the Börzsöny and the Visegrád Hills many thousand of years ago. The woods, which come down to the river-

banks, provide one of the park's defining features. The Visegrád Hills are volcanic in origin, the V-shaped valleys and ravines being created by ancient volcanic activity. The "pyramids and the towers" of the andesite agglomerations (the Vadálló Rocks, Thirring Rock), given their present form by the frost, the water and the wind, present a breathtaking spectacle. The Pilis Hills, which are of sedimentary origin, provide the highest point on the Dunazug Hills, rising to a height of over 700 metres. The hills are made of limestone and dolomite which, unlike in the volcanic rock in the region, is where you are likely to find caves. It is not surprising to find, therefore, that the vast majority of the 200 caves in the National Park can be found here. The prehistoric finds in these caves have been rich indeed. The scientific and cultural importance of nine of these caves means they are strictly protected. The Börzsöny, like the Visegrád

Foundation: 1997
Total area: 60,314.3 ha
Biosphere Reserve: Pilis Biosphere Reserve
Management:
    Duna-Ipoly National Park Management
    BUDAPEST II., Hűvösvölgyi út 52.
    Postal address:
    BUDAPEST 1525, Pf. 86.
    Tel.: 1/200-40-33; 1/200-40-66;
    1/200-41-05: 1-200-41-01
    Fax: 1/200-11-68
    dinpig@hotmail.com

The sand dune on the River Danube just below Helemba Island

Hills, is volcanic in origin. The andesite lava trails, which are once again open to elements, are of particular interest. The hills form a series of individual peaks, the highest of which are about 900 m high. The ridges running down from the peaks and the valleys manage to give the impression that the hills are much higher than they in fact are.

It was the river, which was once allowed to meander unrestrained, which made the Ipoly Valley look the way it does today. The straightening of the river, which has been going on for the last twenty years, explains the presence of the dams and the man-made riverbank. Fortunately, 12 km of the riverbank has not been interfered with, and it is there the river is allowed to flood at will, much to the benefit of the flora and fauna living in the immediate surroundings. The Pilis Hills – on account of the rocks they are made of – are

Long-horn beetle

rich in karst water, and hence rich in amply supplied springs. Although there are more springs in the Visegrád Hills and the Börzsöny, they are not as generously endowed with water. There are in fact almost 350 springs in the Börzsöny, more than forty of which can be found at a height of over 600 metres above sea level, something not seen anywhere else in Hungary. Other waters enjoying reputations of sorts are the charming dead channels, the oxbow lakes and the marshes of the Ipoly Valley.

The flora of the Danube Bend acts as a link between the flora of the Transdanubian Highlands and the Northern Hills. On both sides of the Danube you can find those kinds of plants you would expect on flood plains, whilst the banks of the Ipoly are characterised more by the alders growing on the marshes.

The Ipoly Valley

At the present time there are 170 protected species of plant, in the National Park, ten of which are strictly protected.

There are many plants and plant colonies here constituting the final outpost of their particular species. This is the case for example with the *purple hellebore,* which is no longer found in Transdanubia. There are also several so-called endemic species, which survive only in the Carpathian Basin's national parks, as in the case of the *giant fennel* growing in the Pilis Hills which is unique to the National Park.

It is on the steppe slopes that you find the beautiful *pasque flower* and the *black anemone* growing. On the edges of the oak woods you often find *lady orchids,* whilst *anemones* grow and *alpine roses* and *Moldavian monk's-hood* flourish amongst the beeches.

The most beautiful meadows are the Királyrét around the Foltánkereszt, and Ispán Meadow. It is here you can find the protected *cross gentian,* which opens in the autumn. Another interest-

The Hungarian grasshopper

ing feature in the landscape is the *sweet chestnut.* According to the historian Mátyás Bél it was during the 14th century, during the reign of Charles Robert, that the first chestnut trees were planted in the region. You can still find small chestnut woods on the slopes of the Börzsöny and Pilis Hills, some of the trees being of a considerable size and age.

It is in the meadows on the floodplains of Szentendre Island that you occasionally find a whole colony of *meadow saffron.* The wide band of willows and poplars which used to surround the island only survives in a few places. The areas lying a little further inland tended to be either bogs or water meadows, and to the south of the island you will find the *Siberian irises* growing.

There are also considerable areas of meadow on the floodplains of the Ipoly Valley as well. It is here you will find *clematis* growing. The most attractive of the plants growing amongst the alders are the *narrow buckler ferns* and the *blackcurrants.*

The Danube Bend

The varied landscape in the National Park provides habitats for many species of animals, many of which are endangered. Over five hundred of the species enjoy protected or strictly protected status. During the course of the research which went on prior to the establishment of the National Park it became clear that there were a large number of species, which were particularly sensitive and susceptible to change. The biologists also came upon a number of new species which no one had been aware of up to that point. Of particular importance are creatures like the water snails which, apart from requiring large amounts of oxygen, are vulnerable in polluted waters. It is for this reason that they only inhabit a few sections of the Danube.

One of Hungary's longest insects, the *saw-legged grasshopper,* can be found in the Pilis and the Visegrád Hills as well as in the Börzsöny, albeit in small numbers. In the Pilis and on Szentendre Island you can find another protected species, the *Hungarian*

Clematis

grasshopper. They are areas which are also unusually rich in butterflies.

It was when doing the groundwork for the National Park that researchers first discovered the *sooty copper* here. One other curiosity, which you can find on the upper slopes of the Börzsöny, is the *clouded apollo.* The largest populations breed in the clearings on Nagy-Hideg Hill.

On Szentendre Island you can find a local species of *blue,* a survival from the period immediately after the Ice Age. Just looking at the beetles one can mention more than thirty protected species. Of particular interest are the *oak cerambyx* and the *alpine beetles.*

Some species of freshwater fish, endangered throughout Europe, can be found in the rivers, the streams and the marshes of the National Park. One example being the *Petény barbel.*

Particularly rare are the *long-horned beetles* which have, since 2003, provided the symbol for the Danube–Ipoly National Park.

The spotted salamander

With the loss of their natural habitats and the increasing levels of pollution the amphibian populations are under threat. It is therefore significant that the National Park can boast examples of all Hungary's amphibians. The *common frog* can be found in both the Pilis Hills and the Börzsöny. The marshes down in the Ipoly Valley have proved a particularly rich breeding ground for amphibians. Of the lizards one should mention the *Pannonian lizards*, most of which live in this particular region. The *spotted salamander* can only be found in the Börzsöny, the biggest population living in the Drinó Valley.

The enveloping thick covering of trees in the National Park provides a habitat for many songbirds and birds of prey. Of the falcons and the large-bodied eagles, *imperial eagles*, *lannerets* and *peregrine falcons* all nest here, and there are other predatory species, like for example the *bald eagles* that come here to hunt. The hills have a rich selection of woodpeckers as good as anywhere in Europe. It is in the ancient beech woods of the Central Börzsöny that you will find a significant population of strictly protected *white-backed woodpeckers*. The largest species of owl living in the region is the *eagle owl*. The *black stork* breeds in the more distant woodlands.

The water birds find some important breeding and resting places on the islands and sandbanks of the Danube as well as on the meadows of the Ipoly flood plains. One should also mention the herons nesting in the alders along the River Ipoly. The mammals are well represented by the bat population that are considered to be of particular interest in these parts. The Pilis Hills, with all their caves and underground passages provide an ideal habitat for the bats that are free to live and breed in the dark dank depths, totally undisturbed by human interference. There are, however, other places, like in the Börzsöny, for example, where the bats positively flourish in places where humans have left a trail of destruction in their path, as in the case of the entrances to the derelict mine shafts, which are particularly favoured by the local bat population. Of the four bat species enjoying strictly protected status in Hungary three can be found in the region.

The National Park not only provides an opportunity to broaden your knowledge of certain conservation issues, it also gives you the chance to form an opinion on ecology in general. Much can be learned at the Göncöl Foundation's Nature Trail on the flood plains near Vác. (2600 Ilona u. 3. Tel.: 26/304-484), and the Mogyoróhegy Education Centre in the Pilis Hills (Tel./fax: 26/398-227).

Things to See

The Királyrét Educational Centre

It puts on programmes, lasting anything from a few hours to a whole week, for school groups and other interested parties. There is accommodation for 51 people, with rooms for 2, 4, 6 and 8 people.
Szokolya 2624, Királyrét, Tel.: 27/385-432, Fax: 27/375-114

Esztergom Exhibition Centre

This new exhibition centre is situated in Esztergom-Kertváros in the Pilis Hills where there are natural trails and exhibitions to enjoy.
Tel./fax: 33/435-015

Clematis
Clematis integrifolia

The Pál-völgy Cave

Situated under Buda's Rózsadomb, and formed by the local thermal waters, the cave is most famous for its stalagmites and stalactites.
Open:Tue.–Sun.: 10am–4pm
Tours start at 15 mins. past the hour, and last 50 mins.
Budapest 1025, Szépvölgyi út 162., Tel.: 1/325-9505

Szemlő Hill Cave

The renovation work which took place in 2003, has made it possible for visitors to travel the whole length of the caves, by wheelchair if necessary. The main feature of these caves, shaped as they have been by the local hot waters, is the so-called "pea stone" covering the walls. The unusually clean, dust-free air brings relief to countless asthma sufferers and those with other respiratory diseases. Tours start on the hour and last about forty minutes.
Open: Wed.-Mon. 10am–4pm
Budapest 1025, Pusztaszeri út 35., Tel.: 1/325-6001

Pasque flower
Pulsatilla grandis

The Alcsút Arboretum

Once an extensive English landscape garden, the arboretum now contains over 540 types of trees and shrubs from all over the world.
Alcsútdoboz Tel.: 22/353-219

Egreskáta Farm

The farm provides a home for ancient Hungarian species of sheep, pigs and cattle
Info.: Tamás Vidra 70/3303-839

Ócsa Peasant Cottage and Natural History Education and Exhibition Centre

The cottage contains both an ethnographical collection and a workshop. The exhibition building is suitable for lectures, and is used for teaching and exhibitions with an ecological theme.
Info.: Ágnes Papp 30/948-9150

Alpine beetle
Rosalia alpina

Nature Trails

The Nagy-Szénás Nature Trail – Nagykovácsi
The Jág Nature Trail – Pilisszentiván
The Fót-Somlyó Nature Trail – Fót
The Selyem-rét Nature Trail – Ócsa
The Haraszt Hill Nature Trail – Csákvár
The Strázsa Hill Nature Trail – Esztergom
The Gánt Geological Nature Trail – Gánt
Nature Trail in the Turján – Ócsa

Lynx
Felis lynx

The Fertő–Hanság National Park

The Fertő and Hanság region make up an area of rare natural beauty at the western gateway to Hungary. What was once a huge tract of marshland continues to be an area of unique botanical, zoological, ethnographical and cultural interest. In 1991, what was still known as the Lake Fertő National Park with its headquarters at Kócsagvár in Sarród, became the first national park to actually cross over into a neighbouring country. In 1992, the Nationalpark Neusiedlersee-Seewinkel came into being in Austria, being run from the Apetloner Hof in Apetlon.

The Fertő–Hanság National Park

The territories of the Hanság Nature Reserve grew in 1994 – acquiring the name of the Fertő-Hanság National Park in the meantime. It was from this moment that it also became part of a joint Austrian-Hungarian national park.

Due to Europe's high population density there are few areas in the continent which have avoided mankind's intervention altogether. It is therefore extremely important that those areas enjoying environmental protection try to rid the landscape of any evidence of interference. It is for this reason that the IUCN (International Union for the Conservation of Nature) expects the relatively small national parks to be divided up zonally.

The Fertő-Hanság National Park was the first national park in Hungary to implement this idea. It is for this reason that the park, both on the Austrian and the Hungarian sides, have been divided up into three zones.

The Natural Zone: the interior part of the national park totally untouched by human hand, and not being used for any form of agriculture. Interference can only take place in the interest of protecting certain species and habitats (eg. the reconstruction of habitats).

The Protection Zone: to ensure that the effects of various forms of human activity does not impinge

Foundation:	1991
Total area:	33,087 ha
(In Hungary and Austria together)	
Hungarian territory:	23,587 ha
World Heritage:	Fertőzug, Rust (Austria)
	Fertő, Fertőrákos
The region around the palaces at Nagycenk and Fertőd (2001) Biosphere Reserve:	
	Lake Fertő (1979)
Ramsar territory:	Lake Fertő (1989)
Management:	
Sarród 9435 Rév-Kócsagvár Pf.: 4.	
Tel.: 99/537-620, Fax: 99/371-590	
fehnp@krm.x400gw.itb.hu	

Snowflake woods

directly on the Natural Zone. This so-called environmental protection area also has an effect on local farming. The use of chemicals and artificial fertilizer is not allowed; meadows may not be mown before the middle of the summer; and as for grazing it is the vegetation which should take precedence; it is also an area where ecological tourism is encouraged.

The Outer Zone: this includes the sites of cultural and historical interest in the settlements of the area. It is here that the local population live and work, and where the restrictions concerning the way in which the land is utilised are not as strict as in the other zones. This area may be used "intensively" and where mass tourism can take place.

FERTŐ

The Fertő landscape on the Hungarian side includes the Fertőmellék Hills, the 75 km² of lake, 88 per cent of which is covered in reeds, and the meadows and plains southeast of Fertő going down towards the Hanság.

Gopher

The Fertő is the third largest steppe lake in Central Europe. The waters are on average 50–60 cm deep, being no deeper than 180cm. It is fed by the Wulka and the Rákos, and in its natural state there was no natural drainage. The Fertő is the westernmost example of a continental salt lake.

The lake is characterised by the high salt content in the water and the great changes experienced in its water level. The lake is believed to be 20 thousand years old, about the same age as the Hanság Basin, having been created by movements in the earth's crust at the end of the Ice Age. We know the Romans called it "Lacus Peiso" and that Pliny the Elder remarked that the lake used to dry out completely from time to time. This is something, which has also happened many times since, most recently in the 1860s and 1870s. The silting up of the lake has meant that the reeds on the Hungarian side of the lake are covering ever greater areas. On the southern side they cover an area 5–6 km deep. A 240 km-long channel sys-

Wood sandpiper

tem has been cut into the reed beds on the Hungarian side. The canoe tours organised by the National Park take you along the channels deep into the reed-bed habitats of the Fertő.

The *grebes,* the *herons, ducks, graylag geese, reed warblers, moustached warblers,* and *blue-throats* all breed regularly on the Fertő, and in great numbers. During the migrating season flocks of tens of thousands of *bean geese* and *white-fronted geese* make a stopover here. On the south-eastern part of the Fertő, on the saline ponds of the Meksziкópuszta (Fertőújlak) known as Nyéki szálla, Borsodi dűlő, Cikes you will find *redshanks, sandpipers,* and *plovers* all on the lookout for food. Other visitors belonging to the ranks of the rarer bird species include *bald eagles, osprey, peregrine falcons, red-breasted geese,* and *curlews.*

The *loach, pike-perch, pike,* and *common carp* help to make up the fish stock in the lake. The invertebrates are particularly interesting. Amongst the reeds you will also find some rare insects.

Early marsh orchid

Of particular beauty are the Fertőmellék Hills, which run along the western shore of the Fertő. The landscape lies on Miocene Lajta limestone, which can best be seen at Fertőrákos's Püspök quarries, which were worked from the Roman period right up until 1948. The pillared arrangement you can see in the chambers today is the result of the mining methods used. Every summer, musicians make use of the quarry chamber's excellent acoustics at the concerts held there.

Szárhalom Wood, the largest wood in the Fertőmellék Hills provides a habitat for plants and animals preferring a warm climate. Amongst the shrubs and oaks you will find wild flowers which are fond of warmer habitats, like for example the *variegated iris,* the *pasque flower,* the *pheasant's eye* and the various species of orchid. The Gyöngyvirág Nature Trail starting in Tómalom is the only area here which is open to the general public. The wood provides an important hibernation place for the Fertő's amphibians and reptiles. The crested and the

Alder Woodland

spotted newt, the bombinator, the grass snake, and the brown toad's migration route, however, is interrupted by the main Fertőd to Sopron road. In order to prevent any multiple accidents some subtly designed concrete diversion walls have been built along the most critical stretches of the road (between Fertőboz and Hidegség). These are designed to direct the amphibians and the reptiles towards the culverts taking them across the road.

THE HUNGARIAN FERTŐZUG

In the southeastern part of the Fertő, bordering on Hegykő, Fertőszéplak, Sarród and Fertőújlak, on the alkali meadows and pastures, which were once soaked with salt water, you can find the typical salt-resistant species. Like for example, the *Fertő alkali grass, annual sea-blite, glasswort, sea wormwood* and *sea aster.*

In some parts of the conservation zone (Nyéki szállás, Újakó Meadow, Cikes) at-

Bee-eaters

tempts are being made to recreate the habitat of the old marshes and the saline lakes as they were before they were drained, in the hope that the old plants and animals will return. Whilst large areas are covered in water during the wetter seasons, during the summer the waters recede, and the salt concentration increases until the landscape dries out completely. *Avocets, plovers, redshanks, godwits* and *lapwings* all nest here.

Between the spring and autumn floods the summer winds carry the native-soda and deposits it on the dried out bed of the lake. It is during such periods that you see some peculiar invertebrates out on the dried out saline lakes. It is in such lakes also when there is water, that the *predacious dragonflies* breed.

The grasslands around the Fertő provide pastures for the National Park's traditional Hungarian cows, buffaloes and sheep to graze in. These ancient beasts' constant chewing on the local vegetation and the persistent treading action of their hoofs help to maintain the local natural environment.

THE HANSÁG

It was from the Hanság that the Fertő was conceived. In the dim distant past the whole area was covered by the Pannonian Sea whose waters, once they had retreated, made up what geologists refer to as Lake Győr.

The River Danube, the Rába and the other rivers, which then flowed into the area brought with them the deposits, which proceeded to cover the whole area in sand and gravel. The landscape which you see today was

Kingfisher

formed by the breaking up of the earth's surface, subsidence and subsequent wind erosion.

The basin, then covered by a shallow layer of freshwater, was engulfed by thick lush vegetation which, once it had died, led, with the help of the water covering, to the creation of a thick layer of peat. Other areas, which had been covered with a muddy residue, developed into bogs. The lakes as well as the boggy and the marshy areas provided richly varied watery habitats. The Kapuvár-Hany, famous for its willows, its water meadows and its alder woods, was where the locals went for their loach, mud-minnows, their water birds, honey and their firewood. The land provided the peat which was dug here for more than 160 years. Originally it was used for heating, nowadays the peat is used for potted plants and filtering devices at sewage treatment plants. The alder woods are rich in wood-consuming beetles, and in the wetter habitats the *owlet-moth* and the *prominent* add a bit of extra colour. *Viviparous lizards* can also be found in the meadows.

The natural Mosonszentpéter and Bősárkány promontories divide the Kapuvár-Hany from the Lé-

bény-Hany. It is on these drying water meadows that you can find some marvellous *orchids,* as well as *marsh gentians* and *superb pinks.* It is here also that *bustards* nest, and where the *vipers* sun themselves. The *black woodpecker* nests in the birches, whereas the *hobbies,* the *long-eared owls* and the *tawny owls* prefer the oaks, the ashes, and the elms. The rare *greater spearwort* flowers amongst the reeds, whilst the *water violet* grows amongst the weeds in the channels. *Deer* and *wild boar* can also be seen romping amongst the reeds.

A few small lakes, Lake Király and the lakes of the Tóköz (Barbacsi, Kónyi, Fehér), are all that remain of the Han's once famous watery landscape.

THE RÉPCE FLOOD PLAIN

At the southern tip of the Rábaköz, next to the River Répce, you will find Csáford Wood, which is a remarkable survival from the Ice Age.

The wood is known for the millions of protected flowering *spring snowflakes* which cover the ground under the oaks during the spring. By keeping to the marked footpaths going through the area you will be able to see the many other rare wildflowers growing in the area like the *anemones,* for example.

Those who are more interest in the wildlife can keep their eyes trained on the forest floor for the many species of woodland beetles like the *long-horned beetle,* whose presence has earned it pride of place on the National Park's logo. Ornithologists will no doubt be comforted by the presence of such familiar species as the *chaffinch,* the *robin and song thrush,* as well as the more exotic *hoopoe* and the *black woodpecker.*

Tours in and around the Fertő

The saline steppe: will give you the opportunity to become familiar with the wildlife on the saline puszta, go birdspotting on the lake, as well as see some traditional Hungarian farm animals at the Sziki őszirózsa Nature Trail, which can be visited on foot or by bike.

Reeds and water: become familiar with the reedy habitat of the Fertő by canoe on the watery Vízi Rence Nature Trail (over-14s only!)

Tours in the Hanság

There are exhibitions showing the wildlife of the Hanság (Öntésmajor, Madárvárta). You can also get to know the plants and animals of the marshy alder woods, the water meadows and Lake Király, or go bird-spotting at the Nyirkai-hany. The route leads to the Hany Istók Nature Trail, which can be visited either by bike or on foot.

THINGS TO SEE:

Kócsagvár (Sarród) – including the organisation of field trips, special events and conferences
Hanság Wildlife – exhibition (Öntésmajor)
The Esterházy Bird-watching Hide (Between Osli and Földsziget)

NATURE TRAILS

The Sziki Őszirózsa Nature Trail (Around Fertő)
The Kövi Benge Nature Trail (Fertőrákos, at the top of the Püspök Quarry)
The Gyöngyvirág Nature Trail (in Szárhalom Wood)
The Hegykő Nature Trail (Hegykő)
The Hany Istók Nature Trail (in the Southern Hanság)

Pasque flower
Pulsatilla pratensis ssp. nigricans

Superb pink
Dianthus superbus

Iris
Iris pumila

Pannonian sea aster
Aster tripolium ssp. pannonicus

Pheasant's eye
Adonis vernalis

Snowflake
Leucojum vernum

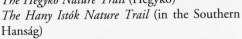

Red deer
Cervus elaphus

Loach
Misgurnus fossilis

Black-winged stilt
Himantopus himantopus

Blue-throat
Luscinia svecica

The Őrség National Park

The *Őrség National Park* covering 43,933 hectares and founded in 2002 is made up of the *Őrség Nature Reserve,* which was itself founded in 1978, the *Inner Őrség,* and the areas of natural interest in the *Rába Valley.* 3,104 hectares of the territory is strictly protected.

The Őrség, and those areas bordering directly on the Vend Region, the Vas Ridge, the Kerka Region and the Rába Valley, make up Hungary's westernmost landscape. It is a countryside of hills and valleys, deciduous and coniferous woods, lush meadows and marshes, crystal clear springs and streams. The peace and tranquillity, the fresh air and the old folk customs, the agricultural traditions and the local produce all contribute to making the region the attraction it is.

The rivers and the streams of the Őrség have helped create a hilly landscape characterised by remote valleys and undulating pebbly ridges. The climate is mild, damp and subalpine in character, failing to reach the extremes. It is one of the wettest areas in Hungary, with an average annual rainfall of 700–950 mm, something which explains why there are so many springs and streams. Some of these streams have been dammed up to form the artificial lakes, which provide some of the region's main tourist attractions *(Lake Vadása, Lake Himfai, Lake Bárkás and Lake Máriaújfalu).*

The most important river in the area is the River Rába, which continues to run along its original course through the northern extent of the region undisturbed by man's attempts to change the landscape. Apart from the Rába, the River Zala (Szala) also passes through the Őrség, as does the Kerka to the south, a stream formed by the waters pouring off the local hillsides. You can also find stagnant pools, which are 1-2m wide and 1-2m deep, used to water the animals and supply water for washing.

Foundation:	1st March, 2002
Territory:	43,933 ha
Management:	
	ŐRISZENTPÉTER 9941
	Siskaszer 26/a
	Tel.: 94/548-034, Fax: 94/428-791
	orseginp@axelero.hu

János Hill, Felsőszölnök

63% of the National Park is covered in woodland. Most of the trees are conifers. The *juniper,* the *common birch, clubmoss,* the various types of *pyrola,* the *sweet mountain fern,* the *hard fern* the *bilberry* and the *red whortleberry* can all be found here. Indeed, this is the only part of Hungary where you will find *creeping lady's tresses,* and other important species include the *green alder* and *wood sage.*

In the hornbeam and oak woods you will find *dog's tooth violet* and *cyclamen.* In the alder woods lying on the banks of the streams you are more likely to see the *rare ostrich feather fern.* The area also has a good number of birch and heather heaths. Along the woodland footpaths you can often find

Yellow lily

wood laurel. The banks of the Rába are bordered by willow and poplars, whilst on the dead channels you will find *water chestnuts,* the *white water lilies* and the *water violets.*

Some of the vegetation which characterised the cool period following the Ice Age still grows in peat bogs and marshes like the Szőce and Farkasfa Marshes and Lake Fekete, the most characteristic insectivore being the sundew. In the spring the marshes are covered in flowering *cotton grasses, Siberian irises, globe flowers, day lilies* and various types of *orchid.* During the autumn it is the *gentians* which take the eye in the meadows. The rainfall and the humidity of the air mean the area is one of the best in the

Wooded pasture on the Lugos

country for fungi. Apart from the well-known mushrooms and toadstools there are some real rarities like the *parrot wax cap* and the *buffcap* which are more usually found in the Alps.

The region's fauna is indeed rich and various. It is here that Hungary's finest butterfly population lives. There are also some rare species of dragonfly, which also enjoy international protection, like for example the *golden ringed dragonfly* and the *yellow dragonfly*. Of the fish the *lamprey* provides what is quite a sight. As for the amphibians the Alpine newt, which can be found in the Vend Region, is also a real rarity. The *black stork*, the *honey buzzard,* the *corncrake*, the *stock dove*, the *crossbill*, the *bullfinch*, the *firecrest* and the *goldcrest* are listed

Marsh gentian

amongst the region's rarer birds. On the banks of the major stretches of water you can find the protected otter.

The Őrség National Park is also rich in buildings and other places of cultural interest. The layout of the villages in the Őrség, known as "szer" settlements, are indeed unique. They are made up of an assortment of scattered hamlets, an arrangement which goes back to the period immediately following the Hungarian Conquest.

A house type including a shortened veranda emerged once bricks were used in construction.

One of the characteristic forms used in the local peasant architecture was the wooden belfry. The finest examples are the thatched belfry in Pankasz (1755), the wooden shingled tower in Gödörház and the log-walled belfry in Kercaszomor. The wooden Calvinist grave posts in Velemér and Gödörháza are also local curiosities.

Although stone castles weren't common in the Őrség, one does see stone churches and church fortifications, some of which are still standing today, like for example those in Őriszentpéter, Velemér, Szőce and Hegyhátszentjakab.

In the Vend Region it is the scattered settlement which is more prevalent, the finest examples being in Kétvölgy, Őrfalu and Apátistvánfalva. Felsőszölnök is the westernmost village in Hungary, situated where three state borders meet. You can get to the Three Frontiers Stone by crossing the Hampó Valley. The thatched houses and the carved crucifixes in the village are rightly famous.

Of the folk arts, pottery and weaving deserve particular mention. Basket-weavers and wood carvers are also active in the region. The curiously-shaped woven objects made of rye stems and hazel bark are used for the storage of agricultural produce. Magyarszombatfa-Gödörháza continues to be a pottery centre to this very day. Older examples of the potter's craft can be seen at the Pottery Museum.

The agricultural traditions of the region are manifested in the ploughed fields, the meadows, the pastures and the woods, which in turn produce the mosaic of a landscape which is so pleasing to the eye.

ACCOMMODATION
The Keserűszer Research Centre
for 15 people; camping possibilities in the research centre courtyard
The Harmatfű (Sundew) Nature Reserve Centre
for 48 people cycle hire available for hotel guests; field trips and summer camps, the organisation of events and conferences.
Information and bookings at NP Headquarters
ŐRISZENTPÉTER 9941, Siskaszer 26/a
Tel.: 94/548-034, Fax: 94/428-791
orseginp@axelero.hu

THINGS TO SEE
The Kőszeg Chernel Bird Hide and Museum
Museum: Exhibition focusing on the lives of the Chernel Family and István Bechtold; The birdlife of the Kőszeg Hills.
Bird-watching Hide: including an exhibition on the treatment and care of sick animals. Bird-watching, teaching
Open: Mon.–Thur. 8am–4pm, Fri. 8am–2pm
At weekends too if arranged in advance.
Info.: *Chernel-kert,*
KŐSZEG 9730, Arborétum u. 2.
Tel.: 94/563-174, 94/563-175
Fax: 94/563-175
E-mail: koszegitk@axelero.hu
The Ság Hill Local History Exhibition
This provides an insight into the local archaeological and geological research, as well as the mining history and varied wildlife of Ság Hill. There is also a display devoted to the life and work of Lóránd Eötvös.
Open: 15th Apr.–15th Oct.
Tue.–Sat. 10am–4pm
Info.: Imre Huszár,
CELLDÖMÖLK 9500, Fazekas M. u. 20.
Tel.: 95/423-096

NATURE TRAILS
The Rezgőnyár Nature Trail – length 300m;
Situated in the strip of woodland next to the Harmatfű Natural History Education Centre you can see the flora and fauna typical of the Őrség National Park, as well as the kind of habitat wolves live in. Professional tour guides are available if necessary, and you are free to visit at any time. It is easily reached from the centre of Őriszentpéter, as well as from Szalafő and Kondorfa.
The Sárgaliliom Nature Trail leads out from Velemér towards Magyarszombatfa, showing the lesser-known natural and cultural wonders of the Inner Őrség. The trail can easily be followed without a guide (but they are available if required), you just have to follow the yellow arrows accompained by their lilies.
The Chernel-kert Botanical Nature Trail
(Kőszeg Nature Reserve) Situated on the western edge of Kőszeg, it was founded in the piece of land known as Címerpajzs-dűlő by the

Őriszentpéter

famous ornithologist István Chernel at the end of the 19th century. The nature trail, which also contains some exotic specimens is primarily concerned with threatened species (of which there are about 100). Apart from the museum dedicated to István Chernel and the exhibition, there is also an ornithological nature trail.

Tour guides are available.

Open: Mon.–Thur. 8am–6pm,

Fri. 8am–2pm

Info.: Chernel-kert (see under Exhibition Places)

The Geological Nature Trail

(Ság Hill Nature Reserve) Here visitors become acquainted with the geological history of the hill by taking the path up to and through the old basalt quarry. The car park next to the Lóránd Eötvös Tourist House is surrounded by information boards showing the rare flowers growing on Ság Hill. You are free to walk along both trails, tourist guides are available if required.

Info.: Imre Huszár, CELLDÖMÖLK 9500

Fazekas M. u. 20. Tel.: 95/423-096

The Őrség Nature Trail – The trail can be found on the edge of the small village of Kercaszomor (272 inhabitants) in the south-eastern corner of the Őrség, not far from the Slovenian border. Apart from introducing the places of historical, cultural, ethnographical and botanical interest, it also contains exhibits relating to the agriculture of the region. The trail, with its 16 stopping-off points, leaves from the main street in the village before taking you into the surrounding woods and pastures. It is 10km long in all. How to get there: either the Őriszentpéter-Bajánsenye or the Magyarszombatfa roads, or if you are walking, by following the National Blue Walk. Tourist guides available.

Info.: The Mayor's Office
Kercaszomor 9945, Fő út 57.
Tel.: 94/444-016, Fax. 94/444-399
E-mail: kercaonkormanyzat@axelero.hu

The Csillaghur Nature Trail (Kőszeg Nature Reserve) – This is a 3.5km trail, showing the characteristic birds and flowers of the Írottkő Nature Reserve. It can be approached from either Kőszeg or Velem by following the signs to the Óház Lookout Tower, and then from the car park above the Kincs-pihenő. Tourist guides available.

Info.: The Írottkő Nature Reserve Associtaion
Kőszeg 9730, Jurisics tér 7.,
Tel./fax: 94/563-121, E-mail: ine@axelero.hu

Királyvölgy Nature Reserve Nature Trail (Kőszeg Nature Reserve) – This 1.5km trail introduces the Írottkő Nature Reserve through 34 separate stopping of points. It can be approached on foot from Kőszeg's Árpád tér. Tourist guides available.

Info.: The Írottkő Nature Reserve Association

The Ciklámen Woodland Nature Trail (Kőszeg Nature Reserve) – This trail is in the arboretum (currently under preparation) next to the Styrian Houses.

How to get there: on foot either from the Hörmann Spring, or from the car park above Kincs-pihenő.

Theme: Forestry in the Kőszeg Hills

Info.: Szombathely Forestry Limited
Szombathely 9700, Zanati u. 26.
Tel.: 94/329-977, Fax: 94/329-973
E-mail: titkarsag@szherdeszet.hu

Green-winged orchid
Orchis morio

Dog's tooth violet
Erythronium dens-canis

Superb pink
Dianthus superbus

Day Lily
Hemerocalis lilio-asphodelus

Honey buzzard
Pernis apivorus

Lamphrey
Endontomizov vladykovi

Goldcrest
Regulus regulus

Stock dove
Columba oenas

The Balaton Highlands National Park

The National Park is made up of both the area immediately to the north of Lake Balaton and the nature reserve founded around Kis-Balaton in 1986. The Balaton Highlands National Park covers a strip of the land varying between one and fifteen

The Balaton Highlands National Park

kilometres in width stretches along the northern shores of Lake Balaton from Balatonszőlős to Kis-Balaton. The park borders on five larger landscapes: the Balaton Highlands, the Southern Bakony, the Tapolca Basin, the Keszthely Hills and the Kis-Balaton Basin, each of which has its own geological character. Some of the features are immediately recognisable to the Hungarian eye, the White Shore on the Tihany Peninsula and Farkó Rock in Aszófő, to name but two. Then there are the familiar shapes of the volcanic basalt rock formations and the caves.

The rich natural environment can be explained by the fact that it is here that the wooded steppe of the Great Plain meets the thick woodland of the Transdanubian Hills creating a natural barrier fixed on a southwest to northeast axis. The meeting of these two landscapes has produced a mosaic of habitats in which the flora and fauna of both are represented. In addition, the influence of the western Balkans can also be felt, explaining the presence of some exotic wild flowers. The landscape includes bogs and water meadows containing species dating back to the Ice Ages, as well as other botanical and zoological rarities. All this has led to the creation of an almost uniquely rich mixture of flora and fauna. The National Park includes some strictly protected plants, like for example the *bear's ear,* the *primrose,* the *fly orchid,* the *early spider orchid,* the *late spider orchid,* the *lizard orchid,* the *gladiolus* and the *woolly foxglove,* as well as almost 200 species of protected plants.

Foundation: 1997
Total area: 57,000 ha
Ramsar territory: The whole water surface of Lake Balaton and its shoreline (Oct.1st-March 31st) and Kis-Balaton: 14,500 ha
Management:
VESZPRÉM 8200 Vár u. 31.
Tel.: 88/577-754, 577-764, Fax: 88/577-731
bfnp@ktm.x400gw.itb.hu
www.bfnp.hui

THE BALATON HIGHLANDS NATIONAL PARK

THE BALATON HIGHLANDS NATIONAL PARK

Balaton scene

The so-called "basalt organpipes" on the edge of the basalt hills are well known beyond Hungary's borders. Of the flowers which can be found on the basalt hills the most famous is a small Mediterranean fern growing on Saint George's Hill, a spot a long way north of its usual habitat.

The section of land immediately next to Lake Balaton between Keszthely and Balatonalmádi is covered in reed beds and marshes, all of which belong to the National Park.

Being the extensive watery environment that it is, the Kis-Balaton is the only environment of its kind in Europe. Rich in flora and fauna its birds have earned it a reputation throughout Europe. 250 species of birds have been spotted here, 27 of which are strictly protected, and 14 of which breed here, like for example the *purple heron,* the *whiskered tern,* the *green-backed heron, the spoonbill,* the *ferruginous duck* and the *little egret.*

The Keszthely Hills, dolomite and basalt hills covered for the most part in woodland, have their own very special mix of plants

The bird's eye primrose

and animals. One of the great botanical treasures is the *leopard's bane.* You can also find many kinds of orchid, like for example the *lizard orchid.* The *Hungarian meadow saxifrage* is one of the area's indigenous species. A characteristic evergreen is the *butcher's broom.* There are also the stalagmites and the stalactites at Csodabogyós Cave to enjoy.

The Tapolca Basin can be divided into two distinct areas. The sometimes pointed (Csobánc, Gulács Tóti Hill), and the sometimes rounded (Saint George's Hill, Badacsony) hills offer quite a spectacle, with their old cellars, churches, castle ruins and vineyards. The extensive marshes which once covered the area have suffered greatly since being drained. Nevertheless, you may be fortunate enough to see the strictly protected gladiolus.

The steppe meadows and bogs on the lower part of the Káli Basin, which form a stark contrast with the surrounding hills with their woods and their vineyards, have some plant colonies rarely found within Hungary, as well as a large number of protected plants.

Water buffalo reservation

Sás Meadow offers the only stable habitat for the *primrose,* a plant surviving from the Ice Age.

The most botanical treasures lie hidden in the Pécsely Basin, and in the meadows up in the nearby hills. It is in those areas rich in streams that you will find the remains of the bogs, the high altitude sedgy habitats and water meadows, which are gradually drying out. For a basin of its size it has an amazingly rich beetle population.

The Tihany Peninsula jutting out into Lake Balaton became Hungary's first-ever nature reserve in 1952. From a geological point of view the most important features are the geyser cones and the basalt tufa rocks. The presence of the botanical and zoological rarities can be explained by its Mediterranean climate. The peninsula is particularly well known for its dry, mossy oak ash, smoke-tree woods and its wild flowers. On the steppe slopes of the Óvár you can see one of Hungary's biggest colonies of sternbergia. The peninsula's rarest nesting bird is the *scops owl.* Lake Balaton and its immediate

Black-headed gull

surroundings amount to one of Hungary's most popular tourist destinations. The tourists who come not only take advantage of the bathing opportunities, they also make for the Balaton Highlands and the ancient monuments in search of the multitude of cultural and natural treasures. Although the shoreline of Lake Balaton and the area immediately behind it hasn't been built up completely, the possibility remains that tourism could have a damaging effect on the environment, if it merely exploited the leisure possibilities without taking proper regard for the environment.

Because the National Park has so much to offer the general public the park's management has tried to encourage a more responsible type of tourism.

THINGS TO SEE:

Lóczi Cave (Balatonfüred)

Situated on the western side of Tamás Hill, this cave, which was excavated in 1894 and opened in 1934, is important both from a natural and touristic point of view.

Saint George's Hill

It was the erosive effects of the warm waters coming up from deep under the earth which created the caves along what was a spectacular Triassic limestone strata.

The Hegyestű Geological Park

On the basalt peak of the Hegyestű you can see all the Balaton Highland's characteristic features. The park is a fine example of man and nature living together in harmony.

The small exhibition at the old basalt quarry shows visitors what they can expect to see in the National Park, and indeed in the geology of Transdanubia as a while.

Salföld Farm

On the edge of Salföld, at the entrance into the Kál Basin just above Lake Balaton, you will find the conservation farm with its stock of traditional Hungarian sheep, cows and buffaloes. Expert guides are available for those wishing to investigate the natural treasures of the Kál Basin.

The Peasant Cottage (Vörs)

The exhibition at the Talpasház shows visitors how life was once lived on Kis-Balaton.

Grasshopper

It includes a fine collection of fishing tackle, and exhibitions devoted to local architecture and everyday life.

The Buffalo Reservation (Kápolnapuszta)

The reservation plays an important role in ensuring the survival of the beasts so closely associated with the Hungarian Conquest, whilst protecting the buffaloes' gene bank. The reservation attracts a lot of visitors keen to see these tranquil amiable creatures in their natural environment.

The Zirc Arboretum

The existence of such an excellent collection of plants has a lot to do with the arrival of the Cistercian order to Zirc in 1182. Even then the site was a distinct entity within the monastic complex. The rainfall the arboretum gets and its microclimate make it possible for even the most exotic trees to grow here.

The Forestry House (Bakonybél)

The house contains an exhibition devoted to forestry and environmental protection, as well as a display devoted to the High Bakony's flora and fauna.

Hegyestű Hill

The types of trees you can see in the woods are described, and visitors are told how foresters go about planning and running the plantation, and what uses the wood is eventually put to. Next to it is an Education Centre, which puts on camps and children's programmes.

Walks and Nature Trails
Guided tours around the nature trails may be organised by making the necessary enquiries at national park headquarters.

The Lajos Lóczy Walk (Tihany)
Although you are free to walk along any of these nature trails, you can ask for a guide if you require one. The first signposted walk in Hungary, the walk was designed originally to make visitors aware of the different rock formations they were likely to encounter in the locality. Following the path you can also learn much about the botanical and the zoological features as well as the surrounding landscape.

The Geological and Botanical Nature Trail (Badacsony)
Signs in two languages accompany visitors along the trail, telling you about the volcanic geological features, the flora and the fauna as well as the local farming practices.

The St George's Hill Basalt Organs Nature Trail (Tapolca Basin)
It can be approached from Tapolca, leaving from the courtyard of the Raposka mine. On this 4km circuit visitors can learn about the geological history of the hill as well as the plants which grow there with the help of the signs, which are written in both Hungarian and German. Having passed the "ice cave" sections of the walk you come to the most interesting part, the basalt organs, which accompany you up to the summit at an altitude of 414 metres. There is a diagram at the top pointing out the main features of the panorama. On a clear day these include the Keszthely Hills, as well as the Balaton Hills, which stretch on as far as Somló. The one-and-a-half hour circuit ends with an introduction to all the protected wildlife you are likely to see in the region. The route is marked by grasshopper symbols.

Kányavár Island, the Búbosvöcsök Nature Trail (Kis-Balaton)
The nearly 2km-long trail is open all the year round. The circuit, which takes between an hour and an hour and a half to complete, is best approached from Zalavár and Balatonmagyaród. Each of the 13 stopping off points is devoted to a species of bird found on Kis-Balaton. The trail, which has a great crested grebe as its symbol, also focuses on the bats of the region and the hydrology of Kis-Balaton.
(Kis-Balaton may only be visited with special permission and in the company of a guide on Mon. 9am; Tue.–Fri. 9am and 1pm; Sat. 9am. These include a visit to the István Fekete Memorial.)

The Boroszlán Nature Trail (Gerence-puszta)
This Boroszlán Nature Trial, which climbs northwards from a height of 240m following Gerence up through picturesque surroundings of the High Bakony, has signs describing the botany, zoology and the geology of the High Bakony Nature Reserve. Laid out in 1994, and situated a few kilometres from Bakonybél, the trail leaves from the Odvaskő Hotel car park on the Gerence Plain. Visitors can choose between embarking on the complete full 7km trail, or the shorter 2km version. The signposts, which are placed along the trail, give information about the natural treasures you can expect to find in the region.

PLACES TO VISIT

The Lóczi Cave (Balatonfüred)
Open: 1st May–30th Sept. Tue–Sun.
10am–5pm

Salföld Farm
Tour guides are available to show you the flora and fauna of the Kál Basin.
Open all year round
Tel.: 88/577-754

The Hegyestű Geological Park
Open: 15th Apr.–31st Oct.

Peasant Cottage (Vörs)
Open: 1st May–30th Sept. Tue.–Sun.

The Jakab Vönöczky Schenk Research Centre (Fenékpuszta)
Groups wishing to visit the strictly protected Kis-Balaton and the *István Fekete Memorial* on Diás Island should assemble at the Research Station on Tuesdays and Thursdays at 10pm, from where they will be taken by a guide.

The Buffalo Reservation (Kápolnapuszta)
Open all year round

Zirc, Arboretum
Open: 15th Mar.–30th Apr. 9am–4pm; 1st May–30th Aug. 9am–6pm; 1st Sept.–30th Sept. 9am–5pm; 1st Oct.–30th Nov. 9am–4pm, 1st Dec.–15th Mar. closed. Closed on Mondays.
Guided tours: Tel.: 88/414-569

Erdők House (Bakonybél)
Open: 1st Apr.–30th Sept. Tue. Wed. Thur. Fri. 10am–2pm, Sat. Noon–4pm, Sun. 9am–Noon; 1st Oct.–30th Mar. Tue. Thur. 10am–2pm; Sat. Noon–4pm Tel.: 88/461-245
And any other day in the year if organised in advance. (Tel.: 88/461-241)
ACCOMMODATION: in Bakonybél phone:
Tel.: 88/461-241
CYCLE HIRE:
In Salföld in the Káli Basin (20 bikes available) and in Bakonybél (5)
SERVICES: A permanent exhibition, publications, videos and postcards are all available at the headquarters of the Balaton Highlands National Park. Staff are available for programmes related to the various field trips and children's camps. They are also happy to help students choose suitable thesis topics as well as offer advice.
Balaton Highlands National Park Headquarters
Veszprém 8200, Vár u. 31.
Tel.: 88/577-754, 577-764; Fax: 88/577-731
bfnp@ktm.x400gw.itb.hu, www.bfnp.hu

Early spider orchid *Ophrys sphecodes*	*Foxglove* *Digitalis lanata*	*Marsh gentian* *Gentiana pneumonanthe*	*Butcher's broom* *Ruscus aculeatus*

Large gold-beetle *Calosoma sycophanta*	*Squacco heron* *Ardeola ralloides*	*Spoonbill* *Platalea leucorodia*	*Heron* *Casmerodius albus*

The Danube–Drava National Park

The Duna-Drava National Park covers a long, narrow tract of land in Southern Transdanubia. The process by which the particularly important habitats were protected along the rivers started in 1962. From the very beginning special emphasis was placed on the two river systems, as well as on the places of particular natural importance in the immediate vicinity. This included habitats below, as well as above, the water's surface, the local woods and farmland. Special attention was also devoted to the use of renewable sources of energy.

THE DANUBE

Whilst the Gemenc covers the landscapes of the Kalocsa-Sárköz and the Tolna-Sárköz, botanically it belongs to the Alföld, the Mezőföld and the Solt Plain. There are indeed similarities with the flora you are likely to find in the Béda-Karapancsa region of the Southern Great Plain.

Most of the sandbanks on the Danube are covered in *purple willows*. The trees' ecological importance lies in the fact that their spontaneous seed dispersal has led to the successful reestablishment of what had been diminishing areas of black poplar woodland.

On the higher-lying areas of the flood plains you can see the white poplars, which form a transitional area between the flood plains and the established woodland with their oaks, ashes and elms. It is here also you will find the protected *black hawthorn*, the *wine grape* and the *adder's tongue*. The oaks, ashes and elms grow on what are the most elevated areas of flood plain, and they are only likely to find themselves underwater during the most serious of floods. The variety of shrubs here is greatest on the floodplains. The *hairy sedge*,

Foundation:	1996
Total area:	49,478.8 ha
Ramsar territory:	Saporca Ó-Dráva River Bed, Gemenc, Béda-Karapancsa, The Pacsmag Fish Ponds
Management:	Pécs 7625 Tettye tér 9. Tel.: 72/517-200, Fax: 72/517-229 ddnp.igazg@ktm.x400gw.itb.hu www.ddnp.hu

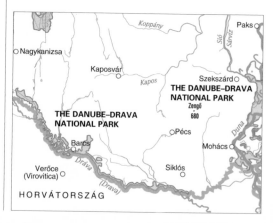

Birds on the Simon–Danube

fritillaries and *lesser butterfly orchids* are all common. The mixture of rare species means that the habitats in the Gemenc region enjoy strictly protected status.

It is on a few of the higher-lying water plains that you will find hornbeams and oaks growing together, as they tend to avoid areas affected by floods. On the Danube and in the dead channels the vertebrates form part of what is a rich fish population. Whilst the sturgeon is becoming ever scarcer the *roach* and *bream* are growing in numbers. In the dead channels and the tributaries you can find *pike* and in some places *crucian carp*.

In the Southern Danube Flood Plains the vertebrates are best represented by the birds, the number of species breeding here coming to well over one hundred.

The *little egret* often breeds here, as does the *night heron,* deep in

Ancient willow

the reeds and in the willows. In the woods growing on the flood plains you can find colonies of nesting *common herons*.

The area's real treasures are the *black storks* and the *bald eagles*, which nest in the ancient oaks and poplars. Both species are easily disturbed, and it is for this reason that the woods are strictly protected.

You may also be lucky enough to see the strictly protected *black kite* and the *lanneret*. The *graylag goose* nests in the reeds of the dead channels, as does the strictly protected *ferruginuous duck* and the *squacco heron*.

As for the mammals, there are bats living in the trunks of the ancient oaks and poplars, the strictly protected *barbastelle-bat* and the *rough-legged water-bat* being of particular interest.

Otters are widespread in the rivers. In the more ancient woodland you can find that rare hunter, the *European wild cat*.

Gemenc wood

THE DRAVA

Once the waters of the Pannonian Sea had retreated, the course of the Ancient Drava began to work its way past the western shore of the lake which covered Slavonia. It was a process, which continued through the Pleistocene period right up to the present day. The really great change came during the 19th century when work started on straightening the river, something which is still going on today.

The straightening has barely affected the Somogy stretch of the river, where the locals still experience the positive and the negative effects of seasonal flooding. Here the river is forever shaping and reshaping the gravel, eroding the river banks and building up sandbanks before sweeping them away.

Hungary's cleanest river, and the one least affected by mankind's desire to control the environment makes its way through 150 km of Southern Transdanubia, sometimes in

Steppe buzzard

Hungarian territory, at other times in Croatia. Going along the Drava you skirt the borders of Somogy and Zala counties starting at the foot of the Zákány-Őrtilos Hills.

The hills' flora has much in common with the flora you find down in the western Balkans. Perhaps the most important vegetation covering the countryside are provided by the Illyrian hornbeams and oaks, the Illyrian beeches, the alders and the ashes growing deep in the valleys.

On the sandbanks along the rivers you can see the little *ringed plover* and the *common sandpiper*, both of which nest in the area. The rate at which the woodland is taking over the terrain has meant that the number of open vegetation-free sand banks, much loved by the local bird population, has fallen. Consequently more time and energy is now being devoted to keeping the banks free of vegetation.

Having gone past Zákány, the Drava spends a considerable time

Gemenc

in Croatian territory. Staying within Hungary you pass through Lankóci Wood. The oaks, ashes and elms growing in the wood have to compete with the shrubs and creepers. The wood's very special atmosphere is explained by the fact that the trees spend a good deal of the year standing in water.

Whilst walking through the woods you can see the *black woodpecker* and the *black stork*. Indeed, you might even see a *field frog*, the males of which turn blue during the mating season.

At Vízvár the Drava returns to Hungary in another guise. The steep riverbanks on the big river bends are constantly being eroded, the heavy silt being deposited on the inner sides of the bend, which build up during the process. Many thousands of *sand martins* use these steep banks to build their nests in. The largest colonies of swallows can be found on the edge of the village of Heresznye. It is on the eroding riverbanks that

Polecat

the colourful *bee-eaters* and the *kingfishers* nest. The dead channels and the ox-bow lakes accompanying the river are full of interesting water plants, *fringed water lilies, white water lilies, water-soldiers,* and *water chestnuts.*

The boggy areas next to the branches of the river, the sedgy meadows and the lakes in the abandoned gravel pits are popular nesting places for the *little grebe,* the *moorhen* and the *water-rail,* and they are regularly visited by *herons* and *storks*. The woods accompanying the rivers are also rich in bird life. It is here you will find the nesting *small woodpecker,* the *song thrush* and the *blackbird,* the *grey-headed woodpecker,* several species of *warbler,* the *bald eagle,* as well as the *goshawk* and the *collared flycatcher*. The best place for meadows and wooded pastures is Drávaszentes, where you will find

The Dead Channel

the trees where the *hobbies* and the *kestrels* breed. Two of the rarest nesting birds there are the *hoopoe* and the *snipe,* both of which prefer the damp depressions.

Downstream from Barcs the territory covered by the National Park widens, and it is here that you can find the Barcs juniper woods, in whose sandy grasslands the *pasque flower* grows. As for the animals, there are *tiger beetles, ant-lions* and *Hungarian grasshoppers.*

Crossing the border between Baranya and Somogy the river shows yet another new face. The Drava has to flow within some pretty tight constraints. There are hardly any sandbanks benefiting from the free flow of the river, and where they

do exist they are heavily wooded showing no signs of any nesting birds.

The most important wooded areas are where the willows grow alone, and where they grow together with poplars. It is here you will find the *yellow iris, hairy sedge,* the *narrow buckler fern* and *black bryony.* You can see *swallows* on the banks of the river, the *common heron* up in the crowns of the alders, and the *little grebe* and the *snipe* nesting in the thickets. The river is particularly important in the water birds' migration patterns. At the end of the winter and in early spring you can see many thousands of them. Apart from the numerous *mallards,* you can see two species of divers, four species of grebe and 12 types of duck.

THINGS TO SEE

The Abaliget Medicinal Cave

Southern Transdanubia's only cave incorporating a stream can be found in the picturesque surroundings of the Mecsek. It is the eroded forms created by the meandering waters, rather than the stalagmites and stalactites, which provide the main attraction.

The "Life on the Flood Plains" Exhibition

In the old hunting lodge on the edge of Szekszárd there is visual presentation of the different habitats on the flood plains, as well as the protected species and the most important animal populations.

The Danube Exhibition Centre (Érsekcsanád)

The audio-visual programmes at the one-time

Ferry Inn introduces you to the delights of the Danube Flood Plain. Particularly interesting are the boat rips down the unspoilt habitats branching off from the river.

The Mohács Historical Memorial Site

A park dedicated to the casualties of that disastrous defeat at the hands of the Turks at the Battle of Mohács on 29th August 1526.

The Pintér Garden Arboretum and Educational Centre, Pécs

The arboretum surrounding National Park headquarters is open to groups all year round.

The Taplós-Góga Exhibition Area

Situated between the Sió and the Bogyiszló Dead Danube the site brings old farming practices and modes of living back to life. Apart from the arts and crafts presentations you can see some ancient Hungarian domestic animals roaming the flood plains.

NATURE TRAILS

The Drava Region:

Babócsa, The Elizabeth Island Nature Trail

The Barcs Juniper Nature Trail (Best reached on road no. 6 between Barcs and Darány)

Csomoros Island Nature Trail (You can get there by boat on the Drava from Barcs)

On the Danube:

The Bárányfok Nature Trail (On the edge of Szekszárd from Gemenc station on the narrow-gauge railway)

The Nyék Dead Danube Nature Trail (Starts at the Dyke Attendent's House in Pörböly)

Lake Malomtelelő (Can be reached from the forestry railway at Gemenc)

The Mecsek and Villány Hills:

The Vár Valley Geological Nature Trail (Eastern Mecsek Nature Reserve leaving Magyaregregy in the direction of Máré Castle)

The Vízfő Nature Trail (in Orfű from the Mill Museum)

The Jakab Hill Geological Nature Trail (From Kővágószőlős leading towards the summit if the hill)

The Abaliget Nature Trail (Above Abaliget Cave)

The Templom Hill Geological Nature Trail (Villány)

Sterlet
Acipenser ruthenus

Little ringed plover
Charadrius dubius

Hoopoe
Upupa epops

Hungarian grasshopper
Acrida hungarica

Water chestnut
Trapa natans

White poplar
Populus alba

Black bryony
Tamus communis

Lesser butterfly orchid
Platanthera bifolia

The Kiskunság National Park

Situated between the Danube and the Tisza the Kiskunság National Park borders on the fields of the Great Plain. The variety, which characterises the park, is due to the way the park is divided up into small landscapes each with its own particular habitat. The plains along the banks of the Danube amount to extensive alkali flats, the Upper Kiskunság Plain, the Upper Kiskunság Lakes and Miklapuszta. The repeated flooding on the Danube, and the fact that the landscape was underwater for long periods of time meant the alkali flats stayed very much as they were up until the mid-19th century. However, once the flood prevention work had been done and the drainage channels built the processes were set in motion which were ultimately to create Hungary's second largest saline landscape.

The surface of the northernmost part of the park, the Upper Kunság Plain, is dominated by wide open meadows and pastures. In the northern part of this particular plain the water-covered bogs and the flood waters break the monotony of the landscape. In many places large patches of white flowers betray the soil's sodic character. The nature of the water supply and the soil mean that only plants capable of living in a salty environment flourish. Indeed, it is *fescue* which dominates the alkali pastures. The *white flowered nasturtium* also grows there, and in the middle of the summer the *lilac lavender* adds some colour to the plain. The *pink carnation,* which has medicinal qualities, can be found on the driest of the alkali plains. In the wetter areas you are more likely to find large numbers of *sea aster* with their tiny flowers.

The Kiskunság National Park

Foundation:	1975
Total area:	48,000 ha
Biosphere reserve:	23,000 ha
Ramsa territory:	Upper Kiskunság Lakes, Lake Kolon

Management:
KECSKEMÉT 6000, Liszt Ferenc u. 19.
Tel.: 76/482-611, Fax: 76/481-074
mail@knp.hu, www.knp.hu
KNP Headquarters Szeged Regional Office
SZEGED 6725, Föltámadás u. 29.
Tel.: 62/498-058
knpi@tiszanet.hu

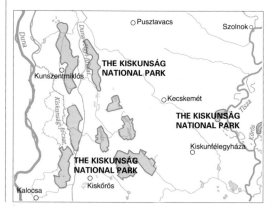

Alkali flat

Of the birds living on the alkali plains the strictly protected *bustard* deserves special mention.

Traditional animal husbandry and the grazing of traditional Hungarian breeds out on the plain once again plays an important part in maintaining the appearance of the landscape. The largest herd of traditional Hungarian cattle in the country can be found around Apaj.

It is here also that you can find a number of settlements originally founded by the Cumans. The Cumans settled on the Great Plain during the 13th century where, continuing their traditional pastoral practices, they enjoyed a certain amount of autonomy. Just as the way the Cumans farmed the land had an effect on the way the flora and fauna on the Plain developed, so the way they lived had a great effect on the way villages were laid out.

The Upper Kiskunság Lakes on the Solt Plain between Szabadszállás and Akasztó constitute Hungary's most extensive saline lake system. The water's chemical and physical qualities mean that the lake provides a habitat for a very interesting cross section of plants and animals. In recent years the number of saline lakes has decreased, consequently the importance of those which remain cannot be underestimated.

You will find significant numbers of *avocet* and *common tern* breeding on the lakes, and several species of sandpiper also breed here in large numbers. The *redshank* is immediately recognisable from its curious appearance and its melodious call. On the lakes and the channels you can frequently see the herons feeding out on the open waters.

Avocet

The areas enjoying the protection of the Ramsar Agreement provide important stopping places on the birds' migration routes.

Miklapuszta – on the southern part of the Solt Plain – is only separated from the Upper Kiskunság Lakes by

Common tern

road 53. It amounts to the largest sodic environment in the area between the Danube and the Tisza. The poor drainage makes the land totally unsuitable for agriculture. The undulation in the landscape is explained by the presence of the old riverbeds and the deposits left by the River Danube. The particularly eroded features have been mixed up with the saline elements. The landscape is characterised by saline marshes, grasslands, which are occasionally submerged in water, and saline beds.

The amphibians and the reptiles you are most likely to see in these parts are the *spade foot*, the *green toad*, the *bombinator*, the *crested newt*, the *pond turtle* and the *grass snake*. As for the birds, the *stone curlews*, the *bustards* and the *Kentish plovers* are all protected. Some of the duck species, like the *shovel-nose* and the *pintail duck*, can also be found here. Large flocks of migrating birds visit Miklapuszta.

Woodcock orchid

The most extensive and most important marshy area from an ecological point of view, known as the "Turján Region", can be found where the Danube Plain meets the sand hills of the Homokhátság. It was the organic matter dating from the period after the Ice Age, filling what remained of the riverbeds, which produced the local peat bogs. It is its geographical position which makes the Turján Region a transitional area, explaining the rich variety of geomorphic forms and the diversity in the natural environment. Despite the fact that man's interference has played havoc with the environment, a large number of species can be found in this drained landscape.

The Peszéradacs Meadows provide a variety of habitats: bogs, water meadows, and marshes, as well as sand beds and sandy woodland. The bogs and sandy birch woods are particularly treasured. In the bogs there are numerous protected and strictly protected species of wild flowers some amounting to substantial

Green-backed herons

colonies as for example in the case of the military orchid.

The flowering marshes and the boggy meadows provide a permanent habitat for some rare butterflies. As for the reptiles the most interesting representatives are the rare and protected *smooth snake*, the *viviparous lizard* and the endangered *Orsini's viper*. The *curlew* is one of the more characteristic local nesting birds. Of the birds of prey it is the *lanneret* and the *red-footed falcon* which feel most at home here.

In the area covered by the region's largest freshwater marsh the surface of Izsák's Lake Kolon varies between 800 and 1200 hectares. The highest point on the Bikatorok sand hills, rising to the west of the lake, is the Revecke Mound, which reaches a height of 126 m.

Lake Kolon grew out of a post-glacial branch of the River Danube, which eventually created what is now a marshy land-

Squacco heron

scape in the advanced stages of development. You will search in vain for a stretch of open water, most of the lake being covered in reed-covered marshes. The average depth of the lake is 60–80cm. The water itself is rich in pondweed, the most characteristic examples being the *rigid hornwort*, the *water-spike*, the *water lily* and *duckweed*.

The southern part of the boggy meadow is rich in orchids, all of which are of course protected. There are also a number of *irises*. As for the amphibians, *spotted* and *crested newts*, and *agile* and *green frogs* are common.

The *great reed-warbler* and the *reed-warbler* both build their small nests in the reeds. The *spoonbill, great heron, common heron, bittern, graylag goose, ferruginous duck, common buzzard,* and the *montagu's harrier* all nest here on a regular basis. The bird-ringing station established on Lake Kolon carries out important

Bustard

research studying the birds and analysing their migration habits.

The largest geographical feature in the area between the Danube and the Tisza is the range of sandy hills, the Homokhátság, which are so characteristic of the Kiskunság and indeed that part of the National Park. Although the sand hills only rise a matter of a few metres above the valleys of the Danube and the Tisza, they form a significant geographical barrier between the two rivers. The sand beds are the remains of the alluvial cones of the Ancient Danube, which piled onto the Pannonian deposits during the Upper Pleistocene and Pleistocene periods. With the silting up of the river basins the Danube left the area leaving the winds to shift the large quantities of loose materials and deposit them elsewhere. It was these deposits (sand, loessy sand, loess) which created the undulations and the hills which run north-west– southeast across the landscape in the direction of the prevailing winds. The depressions in the landscape were once filled with a whole host of saline ponds and marshes. The Fülöpháza Sand Hills, Orgovány and Bugac are the parts of the Homokhatság belonging to the National Park.

The northernmost of these features, the Fülöpháza Sand Hills, are covered for the most part in open beds of sand. It is here that the *fescue* binds together the light soils with its loose nodules. The landscape is at its most beautiful in May. It is then that the *sandy needlegrass* flowers, brighten up the sandy hills, followed by the *immortelle* and the small-flowered *stonecrop*. It is at the height of the summer that the *blue globe-thistle, eryngium* and *tribulus* burst into flower. The *rosemary-leaved willow* grows in the depressions in the damper sandy areas.

Now that the area is no longer used for grazing, the shifting sand dunes have stopped moving. Today there are only two shifting sand dunes in the strictly protected area, the southern part of which can be seen along the marked paths.

There are some substantial juniper groves in the Orgovány and Bugac parts of the National Park, together with a mixture of white and grey poplars. Large numbers of acacias were planted to replace the indigenous tree types. The ancient juniper grove and the juniper groves on the sand hills in Bócsa and Orgovány present quite a spectacle.

Bugac is now probably the best known part of the National Park. It is here you can find the Pastoral Museum. During the high season daily equestrian shows are also held here.

The smallest territory making up part of the Kiskunság National Park can be found in the Lower Tisza region. The best-known part is the Tőserdő, the woods forming part of the Szikra and Alpár Meadows near the stretch of the River Tisza between Lakitelek and Tiszaalpár. It provides an excellent habitat for the flora and the fauna of the Tisza floodplains. The villages are situated on the sand hills and the steeper loess banks, which are such a feature of the landscape. The territory occupied by the National Park includes two dead channels, the Szikra Channel and the Tiszaalpár Channel, both of which contain some important woods. Moving south the countryside opens out into the protected Alpár Meadow.

Both dead channels are 9 km long and they are now connected to the Tisza by a straightened section of river.

The natural oxbow lake, known as the "Dög-Tisza", lost contact with the River Tisza without any human interference. It is here you will find some wonderful *water lilies.* On the banks of the

Shifting sand dune

Szikra Dead Channel it is still possible to study the woodland of the flood plain. The vegetation in the dead channels includes *white* and *yellow water lilies, frogbits,* and *water violets.*

The songbirds living in the Tőserdő are indeed remarkable for the area lying between the Danube and the Tisza. The *grey-headed woodpecker* and the *black woodpecker* are two of the more important species living in the woods on the flood plain. *Owls* and *bats* live up in the trunks of the willows growing on the flood plain.

Two steep-walled loess hills rise out of the landscape in the northeastern part of Tiszaalpár. One of them, Castle Hill, is all that remains of a Bronze Age earthwork; on the other stands a Roman Catholic church.

Both hills are of importance to the landscape and the cultural history of the area. It was this as well as the traditional layout of the village, which led to their being included in the National Park in 1990. Indeed, one of the best views in the whole of the area

Crocus

lying between the Danube and the Tisza is that from the hilltop crowned by the church. The floods which hit the area in the winter of 1998 brought a breath of new life into the 43km² of low-lying flood plains. From early spring the locals are treated to some stunning wildlife with the arrival of some exotic birds.

Pusztaszer, home of one of the two headquarters of the Tisza Nature Reserve, is where you will find some dead channels providing some extremely important habitats. The Lobodár Dead Channel is a watery habitat of international importance. The Sas-ér Woods, which enjoy reservation status, and the alkali plains surrounding Büdös-szék are both strictly protected. The two large fishing lake systems – Lake Fehér and Lake Csaj are both famous for their birds. It is here you can also find the Ópusztaszer National Historical Memorial Park.

In this part of the nature reserve the flora and fauna lying between the Danube and the Tisza mingle with those of the area lying to the east of the Tisza. It is here also that you can find the most important migration routes and the most important resting and feeding places on the Southern Great Plain. *Cranes, wild geese* and *ducks* are regular visitors, and many species of heron nest here. Perhaps the best place to observe all this bird life is at the White Lake in Szeged, where you can watch everything from the observation post on Korom Island.

The banks of the River Tisza in Mártély, which has always been a popular place with artists, has enjoyed protected status since 1971. The straightening work on the River Tisza, which started in 1846, reduced the flood plain to just a fraction of its original size. Two dead channels resulted from

cutting off the bends at Körtvélyes and Ányás. The islands which have been cut off by the oxbow lakes, the low-lying woods down on the flood plains and the meadows are covered in luxuriant vegetation and a rich array of animals.

The Mártély Nature Reserve is a watery habitat of international importance. Tens of thousands of wild ducks and geese live here during the floods, and on the stretches of the river which don't freeze over during the winter. At the end of the summer and during the autumn you can enjoy the sight of the black storks and the herons migrating. The Mártély Dead Channel is also a popular tourist destination with its lido, its camping site, boating opportunities, restaurants and horse riding.

THINGS TO SEE

Nature House
KECSKEMÉT 6000, Liszt Ferenc u. 19.
Tel.: 76/501-596, 76/500-068
mail@knp.hu   www.knp.hu
The National Park's Visitors' Centre has a permanent exhibition showing the history of environmental protection in Hungary, the typical habitats existing in the region between the Danube and the Tisza and a display of ancient arts and crafts. It is here also that you can find the headquarters' "green library" and reading room.
Open: Tue.–Fri. 9am–4pm, Sat. 10am–4pm
Services: Guided tours for groups if organised in advance. Open tours (for individuals and families) based on the events calendar. Lectures and nature-centred activities. Nature documentaries and slide shows. Field trips, camps and special ecological tours

The Open-Air Pastoral Museum – Bugacpuszta
The museum contains exhibitions on pastoral life in Bugac and wildlife in the region. At the site owned by Ménes Ltd. you can see traditional Hungarian animals as well as farm buildings associated with pastoral farming methods. During the tourist season there are also equestrian programmes.
Open: 1st May–31st Oct. 10am–5pm
Tel.: 76/372-688

Medieval Open-Air Museum – Tiszaalpár
The ensemble of buildings built out of traditional materials and using traditional methods is an

example of experimental archaeology.
The museum contains examples of early medieval houses, ovens, granaries, sheep-pens and wells.
TISZAALPÁR 6060, Szent István u. 1.
Open: 1st Apr.–31st Oct. Tue.–Sun. 10am–5pm
Info.: Mayor's Office, Tiszaalpár
Tel.: 76/424-133

Lake Kolon Bird Hide
The KNP together with the Kiskunság Bird Protection Association organise bird-ringing camps and bird-watching programmes, which can be arranged with the camp leader in advance.
Tel.: 20/342-9123, www.kolon-to.com

The Virágh Hall Local History Collection – Kunszentmiklós
Apart from the local history and ethnographical collections there is also an exhibition on the wildlife of the surrounding plains.
Open: 1st May–31st Aug. Tue.–Sun. 10am– 2pm,
1st Sept.–31st Oct. and 1st Mar.–30th Apr.
Only Tue., Thur., Sat. 10am-2pm
KUNSZENTMIKLÓS 6090, Marx tér 1.
Tel.: 76/351-271

Bösztörpuszta – Ancient Animal Paddock
Situated near Kunszentmiklós, you can see some traditional Hungarian species of animals. Groups should report in advance. Tel.: 76/500-068

The Nyakvágó Csárda Museum – Kunszentmiklós
The Csárda Museum manages to maintain the atmosphere of a 19th century wayside inn, together with paraphernalia linked with the local

outlaws. You will find it on the Kunszentmiklós-Szabadszállás road. Open: 1st May–31st Oct., visits to be arranged in advance

Tel.: 76/351-271, 76/482-611

The Szatymaz Education Centre – The White Lake, Szeged

From the second half of 2004 it will show the wildlife of the White Lake as well as the research findings of *Péter Beretzk*. There are guided tours for groups, if organised in advance.

How to get there: on road E75, and 1km south of the Szatymaz roundabout.

Info.: *KNP Szeged Regional Office*

Tel./fax: 62/498-058

The Pusztaszer Seven Chieftains' Memorial

Can be found close to the village of Pusztaszer, and can easily be reached on foot from the Millenium Monument. The obelisk standing on the so-called Árpád Mound in Kecskemét's one-time plain was put up by public subscription in 1902.

HIKING ROUTES

The path marked with a red cross, Bugac

The Karikás Inn in Bugác–The Pastoral Museum/Hittanyák railway station

Length: A 12km circuit

Protected area covered: the KNP Bugac

The path marked with a yellow stripe, Lake Kolon

Izsák station – Soltszentimre station

Length: 12km

Protected area covered: the KNP Lake Kolon, Izsák

The path marked with a blue square, Császártöltés

The Csala Inn, Császártöltés – Hajós Cellars

Length: 20km

Protected area covered: Császártöltés Vörös Marsh, Hajós Meadows

The National Red Stripe Walk

Ladánybene–Petőfiszállás. Length: 100km

Protected area covered: KNP the Fülöpház Dunes, the KNP Orgovány Meadows, KNP Bugac

The Alföld Blue Stripe Walk

The Danube Bridge, Baja–Öttömös

Length: 130km

Protected area covered: The Kéleshalom Sand Dunes, the Hajós Meadows

NATURE TRAILS

The Aqua-Colun Nature Trail – Lake Kolon, Izsák

The Báránypirosító Nature Trail – The Fülöpház Dunes

The Boróka Nature Trail – Bugac

The Cankó Nature Trail – Kelemen-szék, Fülöpszállás

Hankovszky-liget – Kecskemét, Liszt F. u. 19.

The Kontyvirág Nature Trail – Tőserdő

The Poszáta Nature Trail - Lake Kolon, Izsák

The Réce Nature Trail – Felső-Kiskunsági Puszta, Apaj

The Prince Árpád Nature Trail – The Szikra and Alpár Meadows

The Vörös-mocsár Nature Trail – Császártöltés

The Vöcsök Nature Trail – Lake Péter

Information packs and worksheets are available at Nature House.

EDUCATION

The KNP suggests field trips concentrate on the following habitat types:

Sand dunes, sandy plains: Fülöpháza, Bugac

Natron lakes, alkali plains: Kelemen-szék;

Apaj Fishing Lakes; the White Lake, Szeged

Dead Channels: Szikra and Alpár Meadows, the Mártély Nature Reserve

Marshy areas: Lake Kolon, Izsák, the Peszéradacs Meadows

Iris
Iris spuria

Military orchid
Orchis militaris

Mayfly
Palingenia longicanda

Avocet
Recurvirostra avosetta

The Körös–Maros National Park

The Körös-Maros National Park tries to protect what remains of the unique landscape covering the area between the hills in Romania and the River Tisza. A substantial part of this land is closely connected to the local water systems, which include the various branches of the Körös, the River Maros and their dead channels. The landscape includes the woods lying on the flood plains, the marshes which survived the building of the channels and the dykes on the Sárrét and the saline grass lands. There was a time when those areas which were free from flooding were dominated by the wooded heaths and the loess plains. Special attention has been devoted to those which survive. Some rare types of flora and fauna can be found here, for example the *wild sage*, the *pheasant's eye* and the *sternbergia*.

The White Lake in Kardoskút and the fishing lakes in Biharugra provide a watery habitat, whose importance in birds migrating patterns has earned it a place on the list of territories covered by the *Ramsar Agreement*.

The work which went into redirecting the waters in the Maros and in the Körös valleys also provided the region with a lot of additional farmland. The 13 territories making up the National Park stand out like islands amongst the swaths of farmland.

All the territories can be found in an area bordered by the Körös to the north, the Maros to the south and the Tisza to the west.

The rivers are often accompanied by willows, poplars and bushes, whilst on the flood plains the remains of the old riverbeds and meadows bear some resemblance to the old marshes which once dominated the Great Plain.

Foundation:	1977
Total area:	51,125 ha
Ramsar territory:	3,283 ha

(Kardoskút White Lake, Biharugra Fishing Lakes)
Management:

Körös-Maros National Park Management
SZARVAS, Anna-liget 1.
Postal address: SZARVAS 5540, Pf. 72.
www.kmnp.hu   kmnpi@ktm.x400gv.itb.hu

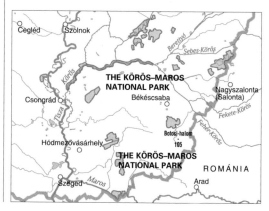

Eagles

The Körös flood plains provide a habitat enjoyed by water birds. During the winter, thousands of wild ducks look for resting places on those stretches of the river which have not been frozen over, followed by eager bald eagles on the lookout for prey. As for the mammals, you are likely to see a considerable number of *otters*.

On the part of the River Maros flowing through Hungary the protected *summer snowflowers* can often be seen out on the flood plains. The strictly protected *black stork*, the *raven*, the *roller* and the *bee-eater* all nest in the woods on the flood plains. The sight of the *Bánát snails,* which are common here, is also deemed to be one of the protected area's great wonders. The Dévaványa-Ecseg Plains making up one part of the Körös–Maros National Park provide many types of habitat. The 20 km of unstraightened river on the Hortobágy–Berettyó provides an important habitat for the birds. The *common heron, night heron* and a few pairs of the strictly protected *little egret* and *squacco heron* all breed on the heron reservation beside the river. Every year a colony of strictly protected *collared pratincole* nest in the areas around the rice plantations. In the watering places alongside the river you can find the protected *ophioglossum,* which is only rarely found on the Great Plain. On the water's surface you can see huge numbers of the *water chestnuts,* which are of "red book" importance in Europe. When times were hard people would make a flour substitute by grinding the fruits. Of particular botanical importance is the *fringed water lily,* which can be found in great numbers, as well as the *water-soldier* and

The Hortobágy–Berettyó

colonies of *yellow water lilies*. It was to help protect Hungary's bustard population that the Bustard Reservation was founded in 1975. The National Park's efforts concentrate on providing the right environment for the birds. This means ensuring that the birds are not disturbed, that they have the wide open spaces they require, food for the winter and safe nesting sites.

The countless streams running from the Sebes Körös and the Bihar Hills within Romania have created an enormous marsh, the most important parts of which make up part of the Kis-Sárrét part of the National Park. The reeds flourish on the Biharugra Fishing Lakes. On the older shallower lakes you can find *fine duckweed* and *common bladderwort*. The leaves of the *bladderwort*, which lie just under the water, contain 10-20 small insect-catching nodules. The plants then feed on the tiny water insects which get caught in them.

The birds living on the lakes are of immeasurable value. One of Hungary's biggest otter populations lives on the lake and in the drainage channels.

Ugra Meadow and Sző Meadow, which stand not far away from the lakes, provide the only reminders of the Sárrét's once watery landscape. With the number of watery habitats continually falling in number returning the two ancient bogs to their original state has become more urgent than ever.

The Ancient Maros once meandered through the landscape south of Békéscsaba. The riverbed it left behind amounts to the most important surface feature on the Kígyós Plain. The waters collecting on the plain cover the landscape in water during the spring and the autumn providing an important strategic resting-place for the migrating water birds. It's a reliable feeding place for the *curlews*, the *sandpipers* and the *godwits*, and a good resting-place for the flocks of geese

Plover

A flock of traditional Hungarian sheep

and ducks. The plain is both a congregation area and a resting-place for the *white storks* and cranes. Wenckheim Palace and its park, which are both popular weekend destinations, belong to the protected area. The park, which was laid out from 1875 onwards, grew out of the wooded heath which existed there at the time.

The *loess plains'* excellent soils meant that almost all the land here fell victim to the plough. On the Great Plain you can only see the original vegetation in very small patches, on the alkali plains, the edges of the fields and the Bronze Age earthworks. These restricted sites are of unique importance. Although few and far between, they nevertheless provide habitats for a number of rare plants and animals. Apart from having some botanical treasures, the Tompapuszta Loess Meadow near Battonya has a population of strictly protected mole-rats.

Pheasant's eye

The Kopáncs, Montág and the Királyhegyes Plains, which together form one all-embracing landscape, also fall under the jurisdiction of the National Park, whose job it is ensure that the flora and fauna of this Csanád landscape has a future.

Hungary's most endangered wild flower, the *Transylvanian pheasant's eye*, which is both an indigenous and a remnant species, grows on the few patches of loess which are left.

Built towards the end of the Bronze Age during the thousand years before Christ, the earthwork once known as the Nagytatár Rampart provides a habitat for the rare and strictly protected *wild sage*. Indeed, the Körös-Maros National Park is the only place you will find it in Hungary.

One of the most important ecological sites in southeastern Hungary is the White Lake in Kardoskút, which developed out of one of the branches of

Fallow deer

the River Maros. The gradual building up of salt not only cut the White Lake off completely from the branch of the river, but managed to increase the salt content in the surrounding plains. The level of the lake rises and falls depending on the state of the weather.

Because the White Lake's flora and fauna, which are closely related to those on the surrounding plains, play an extremely important role in the birds' migrating patterns, the lake has been subject to the Ramsar Agreement since 1979. Of the many nesting birds which can be seen here one should perhaps make special mention of the strictly protected *avocets, plovers* and *Kentish plovers.*

There are years when it is known for 40–50 thousand migrating wild geese, 120 thousand wild ducks and 15–20 thousand cranes to spend the night there during the autumn. The *slender-billed curlew, demoiselle crane, red-breasted goose, lesser white-fronted goose, peregrine falcon* and the *bald eagle,* which delights in pursuing the flock of ducks, are all species of European importance with fluctuating populations.

The tract of land known as Sóstó lying next to the White Lake is where you will find the National Park's ancient Hungarian cattle and sheep populations, which graze the grass lands as they have done for many decades. The White Lake and the area immediately surrounding it are strictly protected and can only be visited with the necessary permission.

The birdlife can be studied at two sites: from the hide, which holds about twenty people at the entrance to the Sóstó animal farm, and a four-man hide situated on the right hand side of the Hódmezővásárhely road as you drive along it from Kardoskút. You can also visit the Kardoskút Museum at the Puszta Centre, if you organise it in advance.

Visitor Centres

Both centres organise their own field trip programmes.

The Körösvölgy Visitors' Centre

The visitors' centre (2003), built next door to National Park Headquarters (Csáky-Bolza Palace), has a permanent exhibition on the natural treasures of the Southern Alföld, a temporary exhibit as well as a 2km nature trail including eight information boards.

The nature trail is accompanied by a herb garden and a fine collection of trees. Information is also available about the programmes and services on offer.

Open: 1st Apr.–31st Oct. Tue.–Sun. 9am–5pm

The Réhely Visitors' Centre

The centre lies half way between Dévaványa and Ecsegfalva. The permanent exhibition introduces the area's unique attraction, the European Bustard, with a video showing the breeding and nurturing going on at the Bustard Range. There is also an exhibition about the natural history of the region. There are guides available if required. At the centre visitors can observe the bustards in their three-hectare site, as well as a wide selection of traditional Hungarian farm animals. There is also a nature trail and a cycle hire service available for those wishing to cycle along the marked tracks through the protected area.

The new Education Centre (2003) offers accommodation, and there are lecture theatres available for in-house training.

Open: 1st Apr.–31st Oct. Tue.–Sun. 9am–5pm

Group visits Tel.: 66/483-083

Dévaványa 5510, Bustard Reservation

Nature Trails

The Réhely Nature Trail (at the Réhely Visitors' Centre): 1.5km; can be completed in less than an hour on foot. There are eight stops focusing on the habitats and the most important flora and fauna of the Devavanya-Ecseg Plains.

The Kígyós Nature Trail (just south of Szabadkígyós, in the northern part of the Great Forest); 5km; with four stops showing the habitats, the flora and fauna of the Kigyós Plain, it takes less than two hours to complete.

The Anna-liget Nature Trail (opening times the same as those at the Körösvölgy Visitors' Centre):

Grey heron
Ardea cinerea

Mantis
Mantis religiosa

Ophioglossum
Phyllitis scolopendrium

Common frog
Rana temporaria

Fringed water lily
Nymphoides peltata

Cornflower
Centaurea cyanus

2km; with eight stops and only visible on foot, one and a half to two hours are necessary to study the habitats of the flood plains.

The Kisvátyon Nature Trail (on the borders of Geszt and Zsadány): 8km; making your way from Zsadány to Biharug turn right 100m past the crossroads – open all year round with a metalled road taking you up to the starting point (which isn't the same as the finishing point).

The Hortobágy National Park

The Great Plain, the treeless pastures – whose beauty has made such an impression on the country's artists and poets – now takes the form of an alkali plain. It was here on the Hortobágy that the Hungary's first national park came into being, an event which was a milestone in the history of environmental protection in these parts.

The National Park is bordered by the Tisza to the west, the Nagykunság to the south and the Hajdúság Loess Ridge to the east. The surface of the Hortobágy has been washed smooth by the floodwaters of the Tisza and its tributaries. The most recent research suggests that previous geological and botanical studies attempting to date the creation of the Hortobágy have been wrong, and that the sodification of the Hortobágy started in prehistoric times, prior to the arrival of the great animal breeding cultures. Whilst of course it would be foolish to discount entirely mankind's effects on the landscape, particularly the grazing of animals and the redirecting of the region's waterways, the fact remains that what is now the continent's largest alkali plain was already a huge open pasture by the middle of the Copper Age.

The climate is continental, moderately hot, although droughts are not unknown during the summer. There is an average rainfall of about 500 mm a year, although there are some years when scarcely 100 mm of rain falls during the spring and summer months. It is not surprising to find that the amount of sunshine enjoyed here is above the national average, and that sometimes the temperatures can be extremely high. The plains are windy, and there are less than ten windless days a year.

The Hortobágy is on average about 92 metres above sea level, the highest point being the Bürök

Foundation:	1973
Total area:	82,000 ha
Biosphere reserve:	53,000 ha
Ramsa territory:	22,000 ha
World Heritage Site:	75,000 ha (1999)
Management:	*Hortobágy National Park*
	DEBRECEN 4024

Sumen u. 2. DEBRECEN 4002, Pf.: 216
Tel.: 52/529-935, 529-920, Fax: 52/529-940
hnp@hnp.datanet.hu
www.hnp.hu

Kunkápolnás Marsh

Mound (105 m). The most striking features on the landscape are the barrows, which may have been the burial sites and lookout posts of the nomadic peoples, who came from the eastern Steppes in the middle of the Copper Age. The presence of these lookout posts provides evidence that these were wide-open plains, for had the mounds been surrounded by thick woodland they wouldn't have been able to serve their function.

Apart from the mounds and the old riverbeds covering the surface of the plain, you can also make out the subtle forms of the saline deposits. These variations in height – which are often only a matter of just a few centimetres – are responsible for the diversity one sees in what appears at first to be a landscape promising little more than monotony. These slight changes in altitude are what makes one area suitable for one cross-section of plants and animals and not for another. The result is a rich tapestry of different habitats.

As has already been mentioned, man has played an important role in the creation of this landscape. It was man who straightened the rivers, drained the marshes, cut down the groves and

Green-backed heron

allowed the animals to graze on the land. The animals are still out there nibbling the grass to the roots out on the alkali pastures.

During the Middle Ages Hortobágy had 12 churches. The prospering villages of the region were destroyed during the Tatar invasion and the Turkish occupation. All that remains of them are the plains bearing the settlements' names (Papegyháza, Zám, Derzs, Máta). The inns, the herdsmen's camps, the pens and the shadoofs which played such an important role in the herdsmen's lives are the only obstacles in views which extend far into the distant horizon.

Inns appear at 10-15km intervals along the roads crossing the plain. It was here that the coach-pulling horses were given food and drink and a place for the night. Nowadays, visitors can sit down to some fine local dishes, take in the atmosphere and perhaps reflect on a romantic past where it was the highwaymen who ruled the highways.

When the borders of the National Park were marked out landscapes representing different stages in the plain's evolution were deliberately

Sunset

included. To find out what the Hortobágy looked like you should head in the direction of the River Tisza to the Tiszcsege Flood Plains, with their trees, dead channels and the marshes all supplied with water from the river.

Looking down on the Hortobágy from a great height it is as if there were a huge colourful carpet covering the earth's surface. The variety is indeed surprising, with each colour being represented in a multitude of different shades. In the middle, shining silver in a line going in a north-south direction is the river after which the area is named. The intermingling of the colours is caused by the close proximity of the landscape's kindred habitats: the alkali plains, the marshes and the woods.

In the summer, amongst the endless alkali pastures, which burn golden yellow, you can pick out the greens of the watery and marshy habitats. The thick vegetation means that you can only occasionally see the twinkling of the water's surface. The variety in this mosaic of a landscape means there is an opportu-

Gopher

nity for all manner of natural processes to run their course.

The rich traditions of outdoor animal husbandry continue to this very day, and you can still see the old traditional Hungarian breeds grazing in the landscape they have played such an important part in shaping.

Some of the ancient crafts have also survived. The potters and the willow and bulrush weavers still make the most of the local materials which are available. Pastoral art took the form of the bone, horn and copper inlay on the herdsmen's whips, and their magnificent cloaks. The motifs they used also appeared on the bells which hung around their sheep's necks and on their crooks. The National Park also attempts to protect these living pastoral traditions.

The long grasses of the loess ridges and the pastures with all their wild flowers on the edge of the plain provide a home for the largest bird found in Hungary, the *bustard*. The barren landscape where the sheep graze provides a habitat for Hungary's only in-

A Hungarian grey bull

digenous sub-species, the *short-toed lark*. At the beginning of May you will see the rare *collared pratincole* amongst the saline ponds covering the landscape. The bleak pastures are separated from the meadows by saline marshes. It is in the thick reeds growing on the marshes that the *green-backed herons*, the *spoonbills* and the rare *wood ibises* live. The surfaces of the marshes, covered with their *fringed water lilies,* and *water lilies* provide an ideal environment in which the grebes can build their floating nests. They are forced to share this enviroment with some noisy colonies of terns.

Out on the meadows you can find the *aquatic warblers,* which are becoming increasingly rare on the continent.

The Hortobágy's five thousand-hectare fishing lakes are also included amongst the National Park's watery habitats. The majority of the lakes were built at the turn of the 19th and the 20th centuries on the site of the saline

Graylag geese

lakes and marshes which dried out during the course of the straightening of the River Tisza. It is for this reason that the names of some of the old marshes live on in the names of the lakes (Csécs, Fényes, Kungyörgy). The fishing lakes have played an important role in saving many of the animals which lived out on the marshes before they were drained, particularly migrating birds, like the rare *lesser white-fronted goose*.

The remains of the alkali oak woods on the edge of the plain – the Ohat Oak Woods and the Újszentmargita Tilalmas Woods – are reminders of what the ancient Hortobágy once looked like.

So far over 340 species of birds have been identified on the plain. The spring winds buffeting the birds gathering on the waters before they fly north is indeed quite a spectacle. During the autumn it is the sight of the migrating cranes and wild geese which delights the local ornithologists.

When making the plain a World Heritage Site in 1999 UNESCO were not only protecting a unique natural environment, they were recognising that the area had been used as an open pasture for 4–5 thousand years.

The Hortobágy National Park has nature trails, exhibitions and programmes all designed to make the area more familiar to visitors. You can find out more about such attractions at the National Park Centre, the plain exhibition sites and at the guesthouses. There are also restored inns, the herdsmen programmes and the Pastor Museum to enjoy: Youngsters can get to know more about the plains at one of the ecological camps. But there is still a lot which needs to be

Red-footed falcon

done: visitors centres and nature trails need to be laid out, and the sights need to be presented in such a way that visitors really feel they have experienced something important.

There are four areas of natural and cultural interest giving you a typical impression of the Hortobágy: the Nyírő-lapos-Nyárijárás Plain, the Hortobágy Fishing Lakes, the Egyek–Pusztakócs Marshes and Lake Tisza. It is here you will find the nature trails. To enter the areas, which are open to the public, you will require tickets, which can be obtained at the information kiosks and at the Hortobágy National Park Centre.

EXHIBITIONS

The Hortobágy Pastoral Museum

Exhibition entitled Shepherding on the Hortobágy
Open: 15th–31st Mar., 1st–30th Nov. 10am–2pm;
1st–30th Apr., 1st–31st Oct. 10am-4pm;
1st May–30th Sept. 9am–6pm.
Info.: Tourinform Hortbágy
Tel./fax: 52/589-321,
During the winter: 52/369-350;
E-mail: hortobagy@tourinform.hu

The Western Inn

Permanent exhibition entitled Arts and Crafts on the Hortobágy
Open: 15th Mar.–31st Oct. 9am–6pm
Info.: Tel.: 52/378-054,
30/278-7378

Nagyiván Peasant House

Ethnographic exhibition:
Open: 1st May–15th Oct. if arranged in advance (Tel: 59/415-324, 415-659) and with a National Park entrance ticket

Meggyes Csárda Museum

Ethnographic exhibition

Open: if arranged in advance Tel.: 70/231-4073 and with a National Park entrance ticket
How to get there: turn off road no.33 at the sign by the 60km marker and go along the mud track.

Puszta Animal Park

Showing ancient Hungarian animals
Open: 15th Mar.–15th Nov. 9am–6pm,
Closed during the winter (Opening times may vary depending on the weather)
Info.: Tel.: 52/701-037

Hortobágy Panorama

Exhibitions entitled The Hortbágy National Park in Pictures; Birds of Prey Protection
Open: 15th Apr.–30th June,
1st Sept.–15th Oct. 10am–4pm,
1st July–30th Aug. 9am–5pm (closed Mon.) with a National Park entrance ticket, or a ticket bought at the door.
Info.: Tel.: 52/529-935

Szálkahalom Guard House

Exhibition: The Natural Treasures of the Nyírőlapos-Nyárijárás Plain (on road no.33 by the 79km marker).

Dwarf almond
Amygdalus nana

Horseradish
Armoracia macrocarpa

Fumitory
Corydalis cava

Spring bluebell
Scilla drunensis

Aquatic warbler
Acrocephalus paludicola

Bustard
Otis tarda

Little egret
Egretta garzetta

Red admiral
Vanessa atalanta

Open: 15th Apr.–30th June, 1st Sept.–15th Oct. 10am–4pm; 1st July–30th Aug. 9am–5pm (closed Mon.)
Info.: Tel.: 52/529-935

TOURS FOR NATURE LOVERS
On foot
Hortobágy Nagyhalastó (1 day)
The Kis-jusztus Hide (1-2 hrs)
The Górés-tanya Bird Repatriation Station and Nature Trail (1 day)
The Nyárijárás–Nyírőlapos Nature Trail (half a day)
The Máta Plain (1 day) – only in the company of a guide
Cycle tours to the Egayek-pusztakócs Marshes
Western Inn–The Fekete-rét Marsh–
The Górés-tanya Bird Repatriation Station–
The Meggyes Csárda Museum–The Kis-jusztus Hide

Travelling by horse and carriage
(Nyírőlapos–Nyárijárás, The Máta Plain)
Riding
Info.: at NP Headquarters
Arts and craft workshop
Making traditional black ceramics, pot-throwing
Hortobágy-Máta ,Open: Apr.-Sept.
TOURIST INFORMATION
Entrance tickets, publications, maps, books and information about the programmes on offer:
Tourinform-Hortobágy Office
HORTOBÁGY 4071 The Pastoral Museum
Tel./fax: 52/369-119, 369-105
The Western Inn
Road no.33, at the Egyek turn-off.
Tel.: 52/378-054
Hortobágy National Park Headquarters
DEBRECEN 4002 Sumen u. 2. P.O. Box 216
Tel.: 52/529-935, 529-920, Fax: 52/529-940
hnp@hnp.datanet.hu

The Hortobágy National Park is also covered in the chapter on World Heritage Sites

The Aggtelek National Park

The National Park is set in the picturesque surroundings of the southern part of the Gömör-Torna karst hills whose rocky peaks rising to a height of 400-500m are accompanied by karst ravines and river valleys.

The valley in which the River Bódva flows, which runs in a northeast – southwesterly direction, marks the border between two distinct areas: the Aggtelek Karst, forming the southern continuation of the Szilice Highlands and the Szalonna Hills, which rise like a monolith out of the landscape. Closely connected to this are the Rudabánya Hills near Telekes.

Foundation:	1985
Total area:	20,170 ha
Biosphere reserve:	20,159 ha 1979
World Heritage Site:	1995

Management:
Aggtelek National Park Headquarters
Jósvafő 3758
Tel.: 48/506-000, Fax: 48/506-001
www.anp.hu, info.anp@axelero.hu
Information:

Tourinform Aggtelek
Aggtelek, 3759
Tel.: 48/503-000, 503-001, Fax: 48/503-002
E-mail: aggtelek@tourinform.hu

To the north of the National Park lies the Slovak Karst Nature Reserve. The whole area forms what is a geographical, geological and cultural entity.

The geography and the geology of the National Park give it its own special climate and its own hydrographic environment. It gets less rainfall than the Central Highlands, amounting to about 600mm in an average year. The average annual temperature is 10 °C, and the hours of sunshine the region gets are below the national average. The unusual local microclimates in the valleys mean that the temperatures are less variable than up in the hills.

In the area in the immediate vicinity of the Sajó-Bódva Reservoir the streams on the surface are fed by underwater streams as well as the permanent and seasonal karst springs. The amount of water flowing in the streams is determined by the amount of precipitation and the thawing of the snows. Indeed, floods lasting a number of days are not unknown.

Baradla Cave

The karst region is characterised by a variety of different rock formations. The extensive karst hills rise dramatically from the valleys, with their small depressions, dolina and karst valleys adding extra variety to the landscape. The once wooded, now bare, hillsides stand out white, their furrowed rock faces known locally as "devil's plough furrows".

The streams running along the blind valleys on the edge of the karst and non-karst regions disappear into the holes, which are either known as "sly" or "devil's holes".

Young barn owls

Once blocked up all there is to show for these holes are the small dolina ponds on the surface. The waters which come out from the depths of the karst supply the dozens of seasonal karst springs. In the places where the waters contain large quantities of lime, tufa deposits are left on the surface.

The caves you can find in the National Park were added to the list of World Heritage Sites for a number of reasons. Firstly, because of the variety of ways in which the caves were created, secondly, for the weird and wonderful forms

Bear Rocks

you can see in them, thirdly, for the peculiar natural environment the caves provide, fourthly, for the archaeological finds and their cultural importance, and finally for their natural beauty.

The most famous forms, which you can see beneath the earth's surface, were created by water dissolving and eroding the rock as it passed down through the holes in the earth's surface. There are some places where the water flows all the year round, in others it only flows after the snow and ice has melted or after substantial rainfall. Most of these holes are now inactive due to the way the karst has been worked. The sheer numbers of odd shapes created by the waters as they make

Telekia

their way along the fault lines greatly increase the importance of the site. The caves, which are made up of vertical shafts and parallel rows of shafts, can be found mainly on Lower Hill.

The hot and luke-warm waters coming up from the depths of the earth played an important role in the formation of the caves in the levels under the karst. The various ways in which the caves were formed determined the passages' size, the way they were divided up and the minerals which could be found down there.

The main branches of the almost horizontal stream-filled caves join up with side passages of various lengths. The steep passages of the seasonally active "devil's holes" descend in step-

Peace Cave

like fashion. The caves can be either simple or complex spaces, some even existing on several levels in a labyrinth-like fashion.

Those going down into the caves will be rewarded with stalagmites and stalactites of various shapes, sizes and colours, and other curious forms. In some places you can also see gypsum and, in the winter, icicles. The Aggtelek karst's geological location, its geological formations and its climatic conditions mean that its flora and fauna is transitional in many respects. Although geographically speaking the wild flowers belong to the Carpathians and Pannonia, the karst conditions mean that the plants belong to what is their own independent botanical region.

Military orchid

78 per cent of the area is covered in trees. The territory provides one enormous habitat for a considerable range of species not otherwise found growing near to each other.

The trees most commonly found living in such a karst environment are the hornbeam and the oak. It is here also that you can find the most substantial population of the only species of grouse living in Hungary, the *hazel grouse*. Amongst the oaks growing on the warmer southern slopes you can find species, which are normally associated with the steppe and the wooded steppe, whilst amongst the oaks and the rocks you can find sub-Mediterranean species and species from Asia Minor.

Imre Vass Cave

The most notable of the indigenous plant rarities is the *golden drop,* which has a place in the international "red book" on account of the fact that this is the only place in the world where it grows. Rare inhabitants of the ancient woods include the *imperial eagle,* the *short-toed eagle* and the *bee-hawk.* It is a habitat also enjoyed by *red deer, roe deer* and *wild boars.* The peace and quiet of the woods also attracts permanent residents like the *lynx* and the *wolf.* Bats are well represented down in the caves – particularly in Peace Cave and the Baradla Cave.

The Aggtelek National Park offers some pretty substantial cave tours. At ground level there are also marked pathways and nature trails. You can also go horse-riding, or visit the hucul stud farm protecting the gene pool of that particular breed. There are also botanical, zoological and ecological walks, and you can also explore the surrounding villages by bike.

Concerts are held in the Baradla Cave Concert Hall, the Great Hall and the Calvinist church in Jósvafő as part of the Aggtelek-Jósvafő Arts Festival.

Aggtelek National Park Central Office
JÓSVAFŐ 3758
Tengerszem oldal 1. Pf.: 6.
Tel.: 48/506-000, Fax: 48/506-001
info.anp@axelero.hu
www.anp.hu

Baradla Cave
Open all year round.
Summer season 1st April–30th September
8am–6pm (Last tour leaves at 5pm.)
Winter season 1st October–31st March
8am–4pm. (Last tour leaves at 3pm)

The Aggtelek National Park is also covered in the chapter on World Heritage Sites

Dogstooth violet
Erythronium dens canis

Iris
Iris sibirica

Toothwort
Dentaria glandulosa

Variegated iris
Iris variegata

Salamander
Salamandra salamandra

Black kite
Milvus migrans

Oak cerambyx
Cerambyx cerdo

Black woodpecker
Dryocopus martius

Lake Tengerszem, Jósvafő

The Bükk National Park

The National Park, which is situated in Northern Hungary, covers the geographical extent of the most extensive tree-covered range of what is hills in Hungary. It was during the Mesozoic era that the volcanic rock broke out through the various deposits left by the sea, which had once covered the area. The areas surrounding the rising range of hills were covered with deposits and rocks of more recent provenance. It is this geological variety which gives the landscape here its diversity. The various forms you can see in the landscape manage to create such a variety of microclimates that, apart from what you would normally expect to find in these parts and those surviving species dating back to the earlier periods in the hills' history, you can also find Carpathian and Mediterranean habitats.

The rich flora and fauna of the Bükk Hills, which rise 300–960 metres between the Carpathians and the Great Plain, make it a kind of biogeographical buffer zone. The hills, which are covered in thick woodland, generally run along a north-south axis with different trees tending to grow at different altitudes.

The steep northern rocky dolomite-limestone slopes and the beech woods made up of a rather stunted stock of trees managing to grow on the scree-covered slopes provide a habitat for numerous rare species and remnant species from the Ice Age. The Bükk's beech and oak woods need special protection because it is here that you can find the *Lady's Slipper,* an orchid whose survival here is of national importance. It is on the steepest of the western slopes that you can find the limes and the mountain ashes under which the remnant sub-alpine species grow. On the slate beds of the lower areas you will find those species of oaks which

Foundation:	1976
Total area:	43,200 ha
Increased protected area:	5,730 ha
Management:	*The Bükk National Park*
	EGER 3304, Sánc u. 6.
Postal adress: EGER 3301, P.O.Box 116	
Tel./fax: 36/411-581, Fax: 36/412-791	
buknpi@ktm.x400gw.itb.hu	
www.bukkinemzetipark.hu	

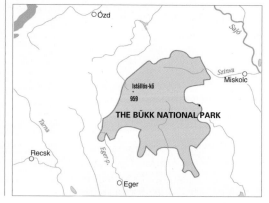

The Bükk, Eger

cannot grow on limestone, whilst in the hot, dry habitats on the acidic soils of the quartz beds and on the dolomite you can find the dolomite oak woods, which provide a habitat for an altogether different group of plants.

Plants of many types find themselves growing almost side by side in the Bükk's scrub forests. They could be sub-Mediterranean species, eastern continental Pontian-type plants, Pannonian plants, flowers benefiting from steppe-like environments or those flourishing on rockier terrain. Bél-kő is the only place in the Bükk, or indeed anywhere in Hungary for that matter, where you will find an indigenous Carpathian-Pannonian species, the *pink carnation.*

There isn't much dolomite in the Bükk, making the meadows growing on it all the more important, particularly the colourful hare's-tail grass, which can only be found in one meadow in the Bükk Hills.

Chalkhill blues

In the northwest-facing meadows you will find the rare *fly orchid*, which is one of the smallest and most northerly of the insect-imitating orchids.

Bug-bane, Hungarian examples of which can only be found in the Bükk National Park, was a product of the cool period immediately following the Ice Age. The local *dragon-grass* with its blue flowers growing on the cooler dolinas on the peaks of the Bükk Hills is the only such grass you are likely to find in Hungary. It gets its name from the characteristic shape of the flowers, which resemble dragon heads.

The plants growing in the warmer seasons manage to find habitats in the woods and meadows on the steep southern slopes, which heat up in no time at all. One such plant is the *smoke-tree,* whose leaves cover the hillside in a sea of red during the autumn.

There are still some species surviving from the Ice Age which, once the temperatures had increased, found

The Szalajka Valley

an ideal habitat on the steep northern rock faces and ravines of the Bükk. This explains the presence of the *yellow violet,* which cannot be found elsewhere in Hungary, the *alpine rock-cress, saxifrage, hare's-tail grass* and the *alpine clematis.*

In the Bükk's most obscure corners you can also find animals going back to the Ice Age, which have managed to adapt themselves excellently to their new surroundings. They can, however, only be found in the most restricted of areas. In some of these small colonies it was only by evolving new species and sub-species that the animals were able to survive. One such example is the *smaller heath moth,* which normally lives in the higher hills in the alpine and sub-alpine zones, but whose curious, endemic, indigenous sub-species here is restricted to a few square metres of cold rocky habitat in the Leányvölgy. There is also a Bükk sub-species of the *Alpine newt,* which lives in the wood ponds, the springs, and often in the deeper

Scops-owl

puddles lying on the higher peaks of the northern Bükk. The *blue slug* is usually associated with the peaks of the Carpathians. These large, stunningly blue creatures require a damp, cool microclimate likely to be hidden away in a valley or ravine.

There are at least 22 thousand species of animals living in the Bükk. In the hot dry southern meadows you will find the *saw-legged grasshoppers,* which give the hills its Mediterranean hum. The *Pannonian lizard* prospers in a very similar kind of terrain. Of the rich and varied insect communities living in the oak woods and the scrubland it is the butterflies which are the most spectacular. There are also many small insignificant-looking species, which are nevertheless treasured either because their habitats in the Bükk are much further north than one would normally expect, or because they are endangered.

The *lanneret,* one of the rarer species of bird living in the Bükk, became widespread about two

The Bükk Hills

decades ago, when a conservation programme was set up to provide the best possible habitat for them. Amongst the rocks and in the derelict quarries you may be fortunate enough to see the *stonecrop*. Quarries are also popular with the local *eagle owl* population. The birds of prey which go hunting in daylight like the imperial eagle, the lesser *spotted eagle* and the *short-toed eagle* are perhaps the most valued zoological treasures in the region. There are also a lot of real rarities centred on the local caves. Some of the species living in the caves only use them on a temporary basis. One such animal is the *long-eared bat,* which only breeds and hibernates in the caves. They are being threatened with extinction in many parts of Europe.

The geological features: the rocks, the ravines and the caves, all the results of geological processes, which have been going on over a period of many millions of years, also enjoy environmental protection.

The pasque flower

The most unified stretch of the hills is the 800 metre plateau, which is divided into higher and lower sections by the Garadna. It is the karst formations which give the hills the appearance they have today.

The main features on the slightly undulating surface of the landscape are the lower peaks and the caves and dolinas which lie between them. These holes take the waters deep into the heart of the hills and caves. Equally characteristic are the peaks of tectonic origin and the ravines. The furrows and the hollows, the perforated limestone surfaces and the "devil's plough furrows" all add detail to the hilly landscape.

853 caves have been found in the Bükk thus far, 45 of which are strictly protected. The deepest cave in Hungary, the 250 metre-deep István-Lápa Cave, belongs to the same cave system as Szepes Cave and István Cave in Lillafüred, whose beautiful stalagmites and stalactites and karst passageways can now be seen by the general public.

Imperial eagle

The features for which the Bükk is perhaps most famous are the limestone tufa rock formations produced from the waters of the karst springs. The limestone tufa builds up across the streams forcing the water to dribble over them. The results are waterfalls like the famous Fátyol Waterfall in the Szalajka Valley, limestone mounds like that at the source of the Szinva, or caves like the Anna Cave in Lillafüred, which was blocked off from the rest of the world by a build-up of tufa. There are also fine lime deposits in the Szentlélek and the Sebesvíz Valleys and at the Harica Springs.

Another stunning geographical feature is Castle Hill in Szarvaskő, where one can make out the lava flows, which form the remains of what was an active underwater volcano. The so-called riolite beehive rocks on the southern edge of the Bükk are also features of great geological and cultural importance.

The Bükk National Park is also blessed with a large number of archaeological sites, the caves once inhabited by our prehistoric ancestors being amongst the most important. The most famous are the *Szeleta* and the *Istállos-kő Caves*. The oldest remains were found at the Kálmán Lambrecht Cave. It was here they found tools belonging to a caveman living about 100 thousand years ago. In Cserépfalu there is an exhibition of finds from the nearby *Suba-lyuk Cave* in the Hór Valley.

NATURE TRAILS
The Bükk National Park
The Szarvaskő Geological Nature Trail
The Rejtek Nature Trail (short circuit)
The Rejtek-Répáshuta Nature Trail
(long circuit)
The Szalajka Valley Ecological Walk
The Szilvásvárad Millennium Nature Trail and Forestry Walk
The Olasz Gate Nature Trail
The Nagy-mező – Kis-kőháti-zsomboly–Jávorkút Nature Trail
The Szinva Walk
The Felsőtárkány Triple Circuit Nature Trail
The Bél-kő Nature Trail
The Mátra Nature Reserve
The Gyöngyös Sár-hegy Nature Trail
The Parádfürdő, Ilona Valley Nature Trail
The Zemplén Nature Reserve
The Regéc Nature Trail
The Karancs-Medves Nature Reserve
Salgó Hill

The Somoskőújfalu Geological Nature Trail and Park
The Eastern Cserhát Nature Reserve
Sámsonháza, The Buda Hill Geological and Botanical Nature Trail
The Ipolytarnóc Prehistoric Nature Reserve
Ipolytarnóc Geological and Geological Nature Trails and Park
The Hollókő Nature Reserve
The Hollókő Castle Tour and Biological Nature Trail

THINGS TO SEE
The Ipolytarnóc Prehistoric Remains
1.5km from Ipolytarnóc the nature trail entitled Our Geological Heritage, which can only be seen in the company of a guide, takes you from the bottom of a Lower Miocene tropical ocean to the drinking places of the ancient jungles via the tufa lava flow of a distant volcanic explosion. The 6km biological nature trail and the 700m geological trail can be seen without assistance.

Martagon lily
Lilium martagon

Monk's hood
Aconitum variegatum ssp. gracile

Lady orchid
Orchis purpurea

Meadow saffron
Colchicum autumnale

Stag beetle
Lucanus cervus

Beehawk
Pernis apivorus

Peacock
Inachis io

Wild boar
Sus scrofa

The Anna Cave, Lillafüred

The interesting thing about this 400m-long cave is that the chambers were formed by the workings of tumbling water. The travertino walls and ceilings mixed as they are with coatings of moss, evergreen and roots presents quite a sight.

The St Stephen Cave, Lillafüred

The shallower sections of the system currently cover a distance of 710 metres, 170m of which is lit and open to the public. A 52-metre man-made tunnel takes you from the road to the great chamber.

EXHIBITIONS

"Mankind and the Landscape" – Hollókő

This exhibition, situated in one of the buildings making up the village museum outlines the history of the World Heritage village and the Nature Reserve while focusing on the Palóc culture and the life of the Hungarian peasant.

History of the Countryside Exhibition – Boldogkőváralja

The exhibition, which is designed to show the natural historical and cultural heritage of the Zemplén Nature Reserve, is spread over five areas. Apart from the botanical and zoological rarities you can see some of the tools used by local craftsmen and the Boldogkőváralja geological collection. There are also displays about the castle and its owners.

Arboretum – Erdőtelek

Situated in the northern Alföld at the foot of the Mátra Hills "this highly significant" arboretum can be found in the 3 hectares of land making up the garden of Buttler House. Its scientific importance is shown in its more than 700 trees, shrubs and perennials that come from many different parts of the world.

Ecological and Cultural Historical Exhibition – Ároktő

Presented by the Borsod Mezőség Nature Reserve as well as Ároktő and its environs.

"A Natural Overview of the Bükk" – Szilvásvárad, Orbán House

A colourful exhibition of the flora and fauna of the Bükk Hills together with the local geological collection.

"Low on the stone-ribbed landing-stage I perched
and watched the swimming rinds of melon-fruit.
I barely heard, while through my fate I searched,
the surface chatter through the depths were mute.
As if from my own heart, the Danube flowed,
muddy and wise and heavy in its load."

(Attila József: By the River Danube
translation by Watson Kirkconnell)

Contents – Budapest and the Danubian Basin

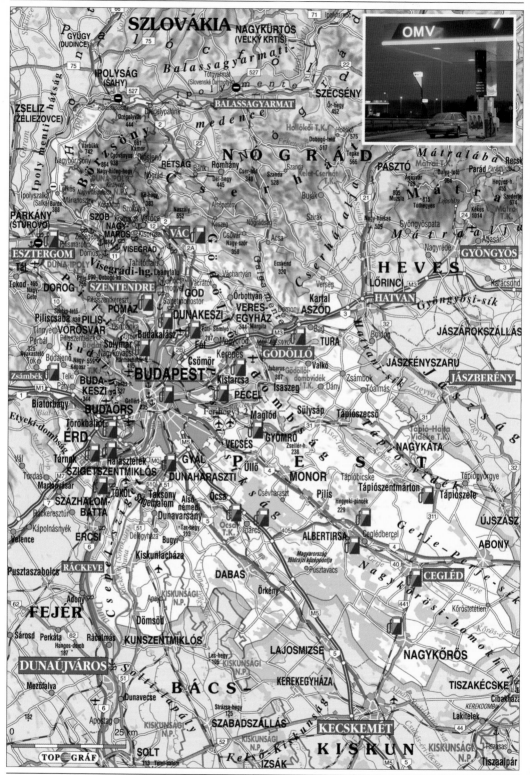

BUDAPEST AND THE DANUBIAN BASIN

What we have decided to call "the heart of the country" includes all of Pest County, that part of Komárom-Esztergom County situated on the Danube Bend, and the western part of Nógrád County lying in and around the Börzsöny Hills. The title is apt from a geographical, historical and a political point of view (something we shall be turning to in due course).

The landscape has been shaped by two things: water and mankind. It is of course the River Danube and the multitude of streams feeding it which account for the first. The rivulets trickle patiently down the hillsides, occasionally having to negotiate rocks and other natural obstacles, carving newer, deeper channels when the need arises. Way back in prehistoric times man made his mark on the landscape, clearing trees, planting crops, building and removing dams, before future generations built, built, built...

There are roads in the foothills and castles on the summits. And there are the villages and the towns with their *Hungarian*, *Serb*, *Slovak* and *Swabian* inhabitants. The landscape became the heartland of the Hungarian church, with its quiet parish churches, its monasteries and a seat worthy of the Primate.

Then there is the landscape. The Börzsöny, the foothills of the Cserhát, the Gödöllő Hills, the Tápió, the plains lying between the Danube and the Tisza, the Pest Plain, Csepel Island, the Zsámbék Basin, the Buda and the Visegrád Hills, the Pilis and the Danube Bend. Indeed, you have all of Hungary's rich and varied landscapes crammed into one small area.

The name Börzsöny or Berzseny, although sounding very Hungarian, is in fact Slavonic in origin. The word in fact means hill dwellers, the people living amongst the hills. Geologists talk about the Börzsöny in terms of its being a young range of hills. The range is only 15 million years old. The 600km² of hills wedged in between the *Ipoly*, the *Danube* and the *Nógrád Basin*, are mainly of volcanic origin. The volcanoes were situated near the hills now known as *Nagy-Inóc* and *Nagy-Hideg*. Because the hills are quite high, having considerable snow cover during the winter months, they are well suited to

The Péter Pázmány Catholic University

winter sports. The hills are also rich in springs and streams. The highest peak in the Börzsöny is the *Csóványos* (939m). The earliest known inhabitants of the Börzsöny were the *Quadi*, a people of Germanic origin. Indeed, it was to fend the Quadi off that the Romans built bridgeheads between Szob and Verőce, the remains of which can still be seen at Verőce. A number of Avar cemeteries have also been uncovered. Even the chroniclers of the Hungarian Conquest mention Nógrád Castle and the Szob ferry. The ramparts on *Templom Hill* in Bernece-barát and the castle built for the bailiffs (ispán) of Hont and Nógrád date from the time of the foundation of the Hungarian State. Bernece, Kemence and Nógrád are all place names of Slavonic origin. During the 12th and 13th centuries castles and earthworks, which amounted to keeps surrounded by ramparts, appeared on the peaks of the region's hills (Bibervár, Pusztatorony, Csehvár, Kámor, Királyrét-Várhegy, Zuvár). Nearly all the villages in the area are of medieval origin, the exceptions being Kismaros, Kóspallag and Zebegény, which were all founded during the 18th century. The region's gold,

silver and copper mines are mentioned in royal documents dating as far back as 1312. It was only after centuries of mining, in the 1700s, that the mining eventually came to an end.

The "huta" (foundry) mentioned as having stood on the Királyrét Plain is the only remaining reference we have to the medieval iron industry in Szokolya.

Following the fall of Vác in 1545, the region fell into the hands of the Turks. The inhabitants of the smaller villages were forced to seek refuge in the woods. Indeed, 15 settlements were completely destroyed during the Turkish period. All that's left of them are their names (Hánta, Orszán, Szomolya, Társa). During the 15 Year War at the end of the 16th century, Tiefenbach, the castellan of Kassa (Košice, Slovakia), managed to drive the Turks out of the region.

During the course of the 18th century Germans settled in the depopulated villages. The Germans in Kismaros came from Württemberg, those in Nagymaros from Mainz. Slovaks from the northern counties of the Kingdom of Hungary settled in Damásd, Szob and Zebegény. It was at this time that Kemence became the seat of the historical county of Hont. In 1742, the county's nobles, along with all those of the other counties, commended their "lives and blood" (*vitam et sanguinem*) to

Ráckeve, painted vaulting

Maria Theresa. She was to visit Vác in 1764. In 1785, Joseph II. carried out some administrative reforms which resulted in the hillier regions of the county coming under the jurisdiction of Pest.

The limestone rock near Vác, known as *Naszály* (652m), looks down onto the Danube from the *Southern Cserhát*. Its valuable stone was dressed in Vác.

The *Gödöllő Hills*, which jut out into the Great Plain, only rise above 300m in a few places. The highest point is *Margita Hill* (345m) lying between Gödöllő and Veresegyház. There are also some rocky outcrops around Fót. Indeed, ever since *Mihály Vörösmarty* wrote his poem *Fót Song*, *Magastető*, *Kőhegy* and *Somlyó* have all held special places in Hungarian literary history.

The *Rákos*, whose source you can find at the base of Margita Hill, runs through Isaszeg and Pécel before reaching the ancient Danube pebble beds of the *Rákos Region*, which form a small arc around the inner parts of Pest. Not many people realise that Rákoskert and Rákosliget do in fact lie higher than *Gellért Hill* on the banks of the Danube. This explains why the capital's villas were built out there. Of all the settlements in the area it is Mogyoród which is mentioned earliest in the chronicles. It was there, in 1074, that Béla I.'s two sons, Geisa and Prince Ladislas defeated King Salamon. Csömör is first mentioned in 1135, and Kerepes (*Werbőczy*'s birthplace) in 1148. The whole region was in fact inhabited by the end of the 12th century. During the Turkish period the area was very much a border region, a protectorate under the authority of the Pasha of Buda. During that time the population fell dramatically.

The "Committee for New Acquisitions", the *Neoaquistica Commissio*, set up following the Turkish occupation to determine who owned what, decided to reward Antal Grassalkovich, the Counsel for the Chamber, with large tracts of land in the Pest region. It was he who went about re-settling the depopulated villages, making Gödöllő the centre of his estate.

The borders of the small, compact *Tápió Region* are easy to make out as they follow the course of the Tápió from the Gödöllő Hills down to the Zagyva Flood Plains. The name is ancient Turkish

The Pilis

in origin. The 13th century chronicler *Anonymous* refers to the small river as the *Tapy*. It was once a bottomless bog broken only by the sand dunes and a range of hills created from the sand blown from the Danube's alluvial soils. The ancient bog became more accessible following the straightening of the River Tápió in 1926.

At the time of the Hungarian Conquest the area was occupied by the Megyer clan. Iazygians, Cumans, members of the Palóc community and Slovaks from the northern counties (1711) were settled in the region by the local landowners to make up for the population lost during the Turkish occupation. The palaces and country residences, so conspicuous in the villages, are reminders of a bygone age. *Sándor Petőfi* once lived at Bognár Palace in Tápiósáp, and it is in the cemetery at Tápiószele that you can find the grave of Etelka Csapó, in whose memory Petőfi wrote his cycle of poems *Boughs of the Cypress*.

SPECIALITIES FROM BUDAPEST AND THE DANUBIAN BASIN

It would be difficult to imagine life without some of Budapest's and indeed Hungary's great cakes, for example the *Dobos*, the "zserbó", otherwise known as a *Gerbeaud Slice*, the *Jancsi Rigó Slice*, named after the famous gypsy band leader, or what the Germans call the *Kugler*, the French the *mignon*. Then there are the sweets, the *chocolate liqueurs*, the *negró*, ideal for a sore throat, *Tibi* chocolate, *Dianás*, liqueur-filled boiled sweets, and *szaloncukor* chocolates. There are also some spirits which the local producers are particular proud of. Indeed, they become extremely reticent when it comes to discussing the recipes for such aperitifs as the *Hubertus liqueur*, or *Budafok Serbian Vermouth*. When it comes to lighter alcoholic drinks the region produces beers, *Dreher*, *Dreher Bak* and *Arany Ászok* to name but a few.

Those going to Nagymaros should be on the look out for sweet chestnuts and raspberries, whilst those walking on Szentendre Island should keep an eye out for *strawberries* and *gooseberries*. The right bank of the Danube is famous for *peaches* and *apricots*, and Tetény for *almonds*. Both Solymár and Pomáz are renowned for their cherries. If you happen to be at the market in Szob, it is the *redcurrents* you should try.

As for vegetables and herbs there are *rosemary* (Soroksár), *mushrooms* (Budafok), Körös *lettuce*, St John's *radish* (Csepel Island) and Vecsés *sauerkraut*. In one of the country's most famous canning and bottling plants in Nagykörös they produce *bottled gherkins* and *canned liver paté*.

The area lying between the Danube and the Tisza is characterised by sandy hillocks, areas of shifting sands and saline lakes. Before mankind left its indelible mark, the landscape was covered in wooded plains, oaks, marshes and bogs. Now, the oaks have for the most part been cut down and the bogs drained. In their place you can see poplars, junipers and needlegrass. Apart from the acacias and the fir trees you will find that vines and fruit trees are benefiting from the chalky sub-soils and the long hours of sunshine the area enjoys. Indeed, the region is famous for its boiling hot summers and freezing cold winters.

The *Pest Plain* stretches from the edge of the capital to the plains lying between the Danube and the Tisza. The hillocks and the terrace effects of the region were created by sediment from the River Danube. The Pest Plain is very much a transitional area between the Central Hills to the west and the Great Plain to the east. There are plenty of nice places to go bathing on the banks of the Danube. 54-kilometre-long *Csepel Island*, which covers an area of 247km², is the biggest island on the Hungarian section of the River Danube. It was created from silt deposits 100-150 thousand years ago. For most of the last one thousand years of its history it was a royal hunting ground. Anonymous tells us that in the Middle Ages people were able to gain access to the island by using the *Megyer ferry*. Both the landowners and the monastic orders were frequently locked in legal disputes over the ownership of Csepel. The island was later to become one of the hotbeds of the Reformation in Hungary. During the 16th and 17th centuries its population exceeded that of Buda. The population was made up of Italian stonemasons, rich Hungarian bankers and Serbian and Greek merchants. The Turkish writings we have from around 1650 refer to the island as *"Sheep Island"*. Following the 1848 War for Freedom the development of the southern part of the island slowed down, whilst that of the northern part speeded up. It was in 1882 that the *Berthold and Manfréd Weiss Canning Works* opened, becoming a munitions factory in 1889. The island's new, industrial profile really came to the fore after the Second World War, and Dunaharaszti, Halásztelek,

Szigethalom, Szigetszentmiklós, Taksony and Tököl were swallowed up by Budapest's suburbs. In 1950, the northern tip of the island became part of Budapest proper.

Over the last half a century the banks of the Danube flowing down the eastern side of the island, the *Ráckeve (Soroksár) Danube*, have become popular weekend destinations with those living in and around Budapest, particularly anglers.

The main branch of the Danube flowing down the western side of the island, known as the Old Danube, belongs to Transdanubia strictly speaking. Crossing the Danube south of Budapest it feels as though you are moving from one plain to the next. North of the capital the picture is totally different, as you are up in the hills in an area where property is much sought after. By the time you reach *Visegrád* the hillsides go right up to the banks of the river, leaving just enough space for a riverside road.

Of the region's sub-regions it is the *Buda Hills* which are the most-visited. In fact these limestone and dolomite hills are technically part of the range stretching diagonally across Transdanubia. Beyond the *Pilisvörösvár Fault* rise the *Pilis Hills*, the highest of the limestone and dolomite Transdanubian Hills. The Visegrád Hills are in fact the same age as the hills in the Börzsöny which lie just to the other side of the Danube. The Buda Hills form a horseshoe stretching from the *Hármashatár Hill* via *Hárs Hill* to *Szabadság Hill* around the outer districts of Buda. The *Gellért* and *Castle Hills* are now totally engulfed by the city. Of particular natural historical interest is *Sas Hill*. The *Csiki Hills*, which continue out from Szabadság Hill, form the dolomite cliffs, which provide the picturesque backdrop to Budaörs.

The further one gets from the Danube the higher the peaks get (*Nagy-Szénás*: 551m). Hot natural spring waters gush out of the fault line running parallel to the river on the Danube side of the hills. The hot springs at the foot of the Rózsadomb supply the Császár, Lukács and the Király Baths, whilst those on Gellért Hill feed the Rác, Rudas and Gellért Baths. The waters from the springs situated a bit further north (the Csillaghegy, Róma and Pünkösdfürdő) are not quite so

One of Budapest's new attractions is the Újpest Embankment which takes on the appearance of a seaside promenade during the summer.

hot, and are better suited for swimming and bathing than medicinal treatment.

By the middle of the 19th century, Buda only stretched as far as the foot of Sváb Hill. Until the phylloxera outbreak of 1880 the southern and western slopes of the hills were covered in vineyards. The first vines were planted by Geisa II.'s (1141–1161) vine-dresser. Buda's red wines received generous praise from the crusaders returning from the Holy Land. Budapest's first cog-railway climbed its way up through the vineyards. Until 1870 there wasn't a single permanent resident up in the Buda Hills.

Picturesque Szentendre

The Grigoletti high altar painting in Esztergom Cathedral

The *Buda Nature Reserve* and the *Buda Sas Hill* nature preservation areas were established to maintain the original appearance of the landscape. Once upon a time the *Zsámbék Basin* was a marshy, reed-covered plain with pastures, meadows and fishing ponds. The waters of the basin now make their way down to the Tök, a stream whose source lies near Tinnye. The dammed up waters on the borders of Bia have created a lake (*Lake Bia*) covering an area of about 83hectares.

To the north of the basin you see *Nagy-Szénás*, which belongs to the Buda Hills, bordered by the hills' highest and most substantial peaks *Nagy-Kopasz* (558m) and the *Black Hills* (*Fekete-hegyek*) (466–493m). The southeastern fringes of the hilly region between Törökbálint and Biatorbágy include *Iharos* (333m) and *Kőhegy* (302m).

Slavs were living in the area when the Hungarians arrived in 896. Zsámbék's golden age came in the centuries immediately following the Conquest. It was then that the town lay on the busy route linking the ecclesiastical centres of Esztergom, the seat

of the archbishop, and Székesfehérvár, the coronation town. The town managed to weather the Turkish period, and was described as being an agricultural town in 1715, a distinction it was later to lose. At the beginning of the 18th century settlers came from Germany to populate the empty villages of Torbágy, Törökbálint and Telki. It was they who rebuilt Perbál, and sent settlers into Zsámbék. More recently the basin around Zsámbék has developed two very distinct characteristics. Whereas Zsámbék and its surrounding villages have assumed a more independent character, the villages closer to Budapest have been drawn more into the capital's sphere of influence. The capital's residential areas are beginning to spread out into places like Páty, Perbál, Budajenő and Telki. The *Danube Bend* is part of this picturesque landscape, which also includes the *Pilis* and the *Visegrád Hills*, the latter rounding off the dolomite and limestone hills.

The highest point in the Visegrád Hills is the famous *Dobogókő* (700m) with its superb views. Of the Pilis's steep rocky peaks *Pilis-tető* is the highest at 757m making it the highest of all the Transdanubian Hills. The hills are wooded, but there are also meadows and clearings rich in wild flowers. The highest peaks are covered in beeches, whilst hornbeams and oaks are more common on the lower slopes. The vegetation at ground level is extremely varied, and sub-Mediterranean in character. Of particular interest to the botanist is the *fennel* growing on the rocky slopes of Pilis-tető. When it comes to wild animals there are stags with their full set of antlers and wild boar, both of which tend to attract hunters into the region.

Between the hills, the *Danube Bend* links up with the towns lying on the stretch of the river immediately to the north of Budapest. This area is the third most-visited area in Hungary after Budapest and Lake Balaton.

Apart from the beauty of the river and the surrounding countryside, the area's popularity can be explained by its history, and the cultural history of the towns and villages in particular. It is here that you can discover 19th and 20th century Hungarian painting, from *Károly Markó* the Elder to *István Szőnyi*.

The landscape tells us much about the development of the Hungarian State. It was here that Hungary's first monarch, King Stephen was born, and it was one of the first castle-administered areas and the centre of the Christian church in Hungary. Even when Székesfehérvár, Buda or Gyulafehérvár (Alba Iulia, Romania) became seats of the monarchy the area didn't lose its royal significance. Indeed, the opulence of the Angevins, Sigismund, and Matthias Corvinus made Visegrád and its environs all the more magnificent. Having left Esztergom, leaving the royal buildings to the church, it was neighbouring Visegrád which became the main royal residence during the reigns of Louis the Great and Matthias Corvinus.

The region suffered during the Turkish period. Following the fall of Budapest, Visegrád was next to fall (1543). It wasn't long before the entire length of the Hungarian Danube was in Turkish hands. Liberation came in 1686. At the turn of the 17th and 18th centuries the northern counties returned to the descendants of their previous owners, and the Germans were invited to settle and make a living on the vineyards. Following the Compromise of 1867 the area became popular walking country and the place one went to for a holiday. Politicians (*Ferenc Deák*), writers (*Zsigmond Móricz*) and artists (*Károly Ferenczy, Géza Gorka*) moved out into the region's towns and villages.

Szentendre Island starts just south of Visegrád. Originally made up of six smaller islands, the island covers an area of 56km². Owned by the Tahi and the Rosd families during the Middle Ages, the island fell into the hands of the sultan (khász) during the Turkish period, a time during which a number of villages disappeared. Of the village of Torda, where the Vác ferry leaves from, only the Pokol Csárda remains.

Nowadays the best ferry crossings are at Kisoroszi, Tótfalu, Pócsmegyer and Szigetmonostor on the western side, and Surány and Horány on the eastern side. The manner in which the settlements have developed over the centuries has been much influenced by the destruction caused by the Old-Danube flooding. Floods are not unknown even today.

The island's great treasure is undoubtedly its drinking water, which is filtered through the thick layer of pebbles covering the island. This drinking water is taken to Budapest by pipe.

At the top of the Danube Bend, in Szob, the *Ipoly* and the *Kemence* flow into the Danube. The *Mogyoród*, the *Csömör*, the *Szilas* (or Palota) and the *Rákos* all join the Danube just north of Újpest. The *Galga* flows into the *Zagyva*, and the *Tápió* into the *Tisza*.

The banks of the Danube offer great opportunities for those interested in fishing, boating and traditional or extreme water sports. The lidos on the banks of the Danube, where the water quality allows, resound to the sound of children all summer long. Those walking or cycling out under the enormous riverside poplars and willows are likely to come across lots of interesting wildlife, particularly in the *Danube-Ipoly National Park*. (There is more information on the local flora and fauna in the chapter dealing with the National Parks.)

Picturesque Szentendre Island

Budapest's Castle Hill, a World Heritage Site since 1987

BUDAPEST

"Unlike Potsdam or Karlsruhe, whose existence was dependent on the benevolence of a prince, Pest is a product of the energies and the natural talents of the people. This town lies in the middle of one of the richest countries in Europe, on the banks of a river spanning half the continent, ... the town's climate is first-class, and the town has the potential to spread in all directions. From all this one can but forecast the brightest of futures for Pest-Buda." (Lord John Paget, 1835.)

Lord Paget proves that he is not only a fine writer but that he had great foresight. Over the following half a century the city was to become one of Europe's great cosmopolitan centres. But before we indulge ourselves any further, let's go back to the very beginning.

It is difficult to say exactly when the town was born. Did the wood, earth and stone Celtic fortifications

The city's most recent birthday marks a quite recent event. The Budapest Carnival, held during the last weekend in June, celebrates the departure of the last Soviet soldier from Hungarian soil in 1990. In fact the city's official birthday is November 17th, the anniversary of the unification of Buda, Pest and Óbuda in 1873.

(*oppidum*) built many thousands of years ago on *Gellért* and *Castle Hill* really mark the beginning? Perhaps it all started with the Celtic settlements built next to the warm waters of what are now the *Roman Baths*? The Romans left their first marks on the Pest side of the river, with the construction of the *Contra Aquincum* (Március 15. tér)

million if one includes the workers coming in from the provinces and the tourists. Much of the country's trade and industry is centred on Budapest, and it is here you will find all the state offices. Furthermore, the rail network and seven of the country's eight main highways converge on Budapest.

The Romans adopted the name Ak-Ink (Plentiful Water) for their ever-growing provincial capital. Aquincum, with its roads, squares, shops and baths, can be found in Budapest's 3rd District.

The waterfalls and the lake on Margaret Island are like an oasis at the heart of the big, bustling city. It's a pleasant place to end a long day beating the streets of the capital.

1259 is another candidate for Budapest's birthday for it was then one hears the first mention of the three settlements which later made up the core of the city one finds today: Buda (*Vetus Buda*), Új-Buda (*Nova Buda*) and Pest (*Castrum Pest*). If by birthday you mean a rebirth, then another possibility would be 1686, the year Budapest was recaptured from the Turks. There are other contenders: the great flood of 1838; the turmoil of 1944–1945; or the phylloxera epidemic of 1880, which destroyed all the vines. The vineyards having been lost the way was opened for the property speculators to push the boundaries of Budapest up the slopes of the hills.

On 1st January 1950, seven towns and 16 villages were engulfed by the capital. With this the number of districts grew from 10 to 22. The city currently covers an area of 525km², one third of which is taken up by hilly *Buda* and two thirds by "flat" *Pest*. 1.77 million people (2001) now live in Budapest's 23 districts, a figure which exceeds two

For many centuries the city has shared its history with that of the country as a whole. Following the Hungarian Conquest, in about the year 900, the prince's clan settled in what is now *Óbuda* and *Csepel Island*. During the Árpád era, however, the monarchy based itself in Esztergom and Székesfehérvár. Following the Tatar invasion of 1241, Béla IV. started building the fortress on what is now *Castle Hill* (1255). This was followed soon after by the construction of the Church of the Blessed Virgin Mary. It wasn't long before Buda became a fully-fledged medieval town.

It was Sigismund, the Holy Roman Emperor and King of Hungary (1387–1437), who turned Buda into a town of European standing. Matthias Corvinus (1458–1490) made further contributions with his initiatives in the arts and sciences. Buda began to decline shortly after his death and prior to the Turkish attack on Buda in 1541, which marked the beginning of one hundred and fifty years of Turkish occupation. Buda was finally liberated in

1686. The turn of the 17th and 18th centuries saw frantic building activity in both Pest and Buda, a period which provided the town with its Baroque palaces, churches and town houses.

The beginning of the 19th century saw an upturn in the economic life of the town. The *Improvements Committee*, founded on the initiative of Palatine Joseph, brought some of the latest ideas in urban planning to the town. The fact that such new principles were actually carried out was due primarily to the River Danube.

The Chain Bridge was completed in 1849 making it the first permanent bridge to cross the Danube between Regensburg and the Black Sea. Although the bridge linked Buda and Pest, the two towns, together with Óbuda, were not to become formally united until 1867.

The flood of March 15th 1838 reduced five thousand buildings to ruins, opening the way for the construction of a new, modern town.

The horse-drawn trams went into service in the city centre in 1866, and 1874 saw the building of the *cog-railway*, the third one of its kind in Europe. By 1888, trams were running from Nyugati (Western) Station to Király utca, and in 1896 the first *underground* on the continent was built in time for the Millennium celebrations marking the thousandth anniversary of the Hungarian Conquest. Budapest's vibrant cultural and artistic life and the growing reputation of its spa waters made the city one of the finest capitals in Europe. "He who is tired of Budapest..." To give yourself at least a chance of becoming acquainted with the city you need time, and quite a lot of it. Indeed, if you were to ask Budapest's 1.8 million inhabitants for the ultimate tour you would be sure to get 1.8 million different answers. Everyone's got their own favourite street corner, their own favourite restaurant, park or promenade.

Perhaps the best advice we can give the visitor would be to get stuck in there and discover Budapest for yourself. There are of course places which come into the "unmissable" category, but in seeing those it would be a pity to miss out on all the other things out there to be discovered.

There are all those secret courtyards, backstreets and markets, those stalls selling pork chops served up with gherkins. And those glorious façades lying right above you...

Some of the best bits of Budapest are there, just above your head.

Budapest is not only happy to have tourists, it is tourist-friendly as well. Just by travelling the lengths of three tram lines, tram number 19 in Buda, and numbers 2 and 6 in Pest, you can see nearly all the major sites in Budapest, and it will only cost you the price of three tram tickets. However it is wise to start at the beginning of the line to make sure you get a seat. But please note, this is but a taste of what is to come.

The Parliament Building (Imre Steindl, 1885-1904) is one of the largest buildings in the country. The statistics are indeed impressive: length 268m, width 118m, height 96m, area covered 17,745m². Parliament first sat here on June 8th, albeit not without 1896, in the year the nation celebrated the one thousandth anniversary of the Hungarian Conquest.

THE CITY CENTRE

"A country has to have a heart", István Széchenyi wrote, when the idea of a united Budapest first came to him. If Budapest is Hungary's heart, then it is **Kossuth Lajos tér** which makes Budapest tick. During the first half of the 19th century the place was a rubbish tip. The square was given its present name in 1927, when the "first" statue of Kossuth was put up (*János Horvay*, the statue can now be seen in Dombóvár). It was dismantled following the Second World War, being deemed too sombre and pessimistic. The main figure in the present composition was sculpted by *Zsigmond Kisfaludi Strobl* (1952). The landscaped parts of the square are dotted with references to bygone ages. You will find the **national flag**, and the **eternal flame** to those who died during the revolution, the statue of **Ferenc Rákóczi II.** put up on the two hundredth anniversary of his death (*János Pásztor*, 1935), and the symbolic grave of those executed in 1956. The square is usually full of people on Hungary's three national holidays.

The **Parliament Building** is essentially a study in the Gothic Revival style Baroque and classical references. The ceremonial staircase leading you up to the hall lying under the 27m vaulted ceiling is covered by paintings by *Károly Lotz*. The royal statues in the hall now guard the *Hungarian crown* and the crown jewels controversially placed there on 1st January 2000. There are guided tours around the building, where you can visit the Parliament Chamber and the *Parliament Library*, which is also open to the general public.

On the eastern side of Kossuth Lajos tér stands the **Ethnographic Museum** (12.), which was previously the *Hungarian Royal Hall (Alajos Hauszmann, 1893–1896)*. Next to it stands the *Ministry of Agriculture and Regional Development* (11.) designed by the architect who came third in the competition to design the Parliament Building (*Gyula Bukovics, 1895–1897*). Underneath the arcade looking onto the square you can see a **pantheon** of the greats in Hungarian agriculture, whilst on the corner with Alkotmány utca there is a **memorial tablet** to those shot dead on 25th October 1956, with a depiction of the Hungarian flag with the centre burned out.

The *Imre Nagy* (1896–1958) *Memorial* (*Tamás Varga*, 1996) in Vértanúk tere was put up on the 100th anniversary of the politician's birth. In Báthory utca there is the **lantern** put up in memory of another Prime Minister, who lost his life in office, *Count Lajos Batthyány* (1806–1849).

Szabadság tér is dominated by Budapest's one surviving Soviet *war memorial*. In Hold utca, which runs parallel to the square, you will find one of Budapest's most beautiful Hungarian Secession-style buildings the **Postal Savings Bank** (*Ödön Lechner*, 1900). On the other side of the road it is worth looking into the **Market Hall,** which has

It is worth going up the basilica's northern tower. You can do it by lift and the view is stunning. In the southern tower hangs the biggest bell in Hungary. It weighs nine tons. Two statues of St Stephen can be found in the church, one above the doorway in the entrance porch, the other over the high altar (Alajos Stróbl). In the Chapel of the Holy Right Hand behind the chancel is kept one of Hungary's most important relics, the mummified remains of St Stephen of Hungary's right hand. (Its reliquary is illustrated below). On August 20th, St Stephen's Day, the relic is carried in a procession in the area immediately surrounding the church.

recently been renovated at great expense. It is one of five opened in February 1897. The huge classical neo-Renaissance **St Stephen's Basilica** (*Hild József, Miklós Ybl, József Kauser,* 1851–1905), once the property of the City of Budapest, has recently been given to the Roman Catholic Church (Szent István tér). Last year (2003) saw the completion of a 20-year renovation project.

In the middle of Deák tér stands one of the town's most beautiful fountains. The central figure in the **Danubius Fountain** is the Danube, surrounded by figures symbolising the Tisza, the Drava and the Sava (*Miklós Ybl, Leó Fessler,* 1880–1883). Budapest's three *underground lines* intersect at Deák tér next to the Kiskörút. These include the *millennium line* with its own **museum**. The old bus station in Erzsébet tér is a protected building.

The niches in the façade of the Opera House contain the figures of Ferenc Erkel and Franz Liszt (Alajos Stróbl), whilst the main parapet contains a series of famous opera composers from Monteverdi to Smetana. Those who go on an afternoon guided tour of the building will be able to see the frescos inside (Bertalan Székely, Károly Lotz).

The facilities lying underneath the park in the middle of Erzsébet tér include a business, exhibition and conference venue and an underground car park. The **Lutheran church** and the **National Lutheran Museum** next door are two of the square's more notable buildings, as indeed is the monumental *Anker House*.

The laying out of the 2.3 km-long Andrássy út (1872–1885) now a World Heritage Site, had a great effect on the atmosphere of the city (*Lajos Lechner*). *Miklós Ybl* designed the **State Opera House** (22), one of the most beautiful neo-Renaissance public buildings in Hungary (1875–1884).

It is of course great to go and see an opera, and it doesn't have to be a pleasure reserved only for the autumn and winter, as the Budapest Opera opens its doors during the first weeks of August.

In Nagymező utca you will find the *Miklós Radnóti Theatre*, the *Thália*, the *Capital's Operetta Theatre*, the *Mikroszkóp Stage* and the *New Theatre*. The theatres offer everything from traditional Hungarian cabaret through operettas to the avant-garde. Those wanting entertainment with a Parisian flavour should go to what is an exact copy of the *Moulin Rouge*. It would be a shame to miss one of Budapest's more specialist museums, the **Hungarian Museum of Photography**, situated in imperial and royal photographer *Manó Mai's* old studio.

Jókai tér contains a statue of the novelist Mór Jókai (*Stróbl Alajos*). Liszt Ferenc tér contains a statue of the poet Endre Ady (*Géza Csorba*, 1960), and a statue of the composer Franz Liszt (*László Marton*), the founding president of the **Academy of Music**. The Secession-style *Music College* is the best daytime concert venue in Budapest. At night the square is full of crowded coffee houses, cellars, pizzerias and music cafés. If Nagymező utca is Budapest's Broadway, Liszt Ferenc tér is its Times Square.

On the Sugárút and in the Liget

The Nagykörút crosses Andrássy út at the *Oktogon*. There was a time when it was the famous *Abbázia Coffee House* which attracted people there, not the fast food restaurants. On Andrássy út, known to the locals as the *Sugárút*, every residence has a story to tell. There is the **Franz Liszt Museum** (67.) in the *Old Academy of Music*, where the founding president and composer used to live. The **Budapest Puppet Theatre** is in the old *Picture Gallery* (69.). 60 Andrássy út, the one-time headquarters of the Fascist Arrow Cross Party and then of the Communist secret police, now houses a controversial exhibition devoted to *terror and violence*.

In Kodály Körönd you can see statues of *Miklós Zrínyi*, *Bálint Balassi*, *Bottyán the Blind* and *György Szondi* all looking towards *Zoltán Kodály's* one-time residence (1.), which is now a **museum**. Those not

The iron bridge crossing the boating lake built for the 1896 millennium celebrations is busy all the year round.

familiar with the area could easily walk past the *Lukács Cake Shop* as its entrance is concealed by a bank. Andrássy út leads into the capital's most elegant and most celebrated public space, Heroes' Square. This in turn leads to the Liget with its zoo, its castle, and the boating lake which is used for skating on during the winter. In fact the **Liget** is the capital's largest park (1km²).

Many generations have been to the *"Lizse"* to relax or to have fun. The benches under the plain trees offer shade and romantic possibilities.

> *The first written reference to the Liget comes in an account of Batu Khan's victory at the Tatar invasion (1241). It was during one of the national assemblies held there during the Middle Ages that the ambitious Tamás Bakócz, the peasant's son turned archbishop, recruited one hundred thousand peasants for a crusade, including the warriors of György Dózsa and Lőrinc Mészáros. Later Leopold I. donated the territory to Pest. The first villas were built out here at the beginning of the 19th century, although it was only at the turn of the 19th and 20th centuries that urbanisation really began to move on apace.*

The **Millennium Monument** standing in front of the Liget was built for the one thousandth anniversary of the Hungarian Conquest (sculptor: *György Zala*, architect: *Albert Schickedanz*).

The allegorical depiction of Peace (György Zala) crowning the Millennium Monument.

In the middle of Heroes' Square stands the **Memorial to the National Heroes** (the Tomb of the *Unknown Warrior*). Behind it you can see the 85x25m colonnade (1896–1926). On the two flanks you have representations of *War* and *Peace*, and at the inner end of the cornice, supported by a pair of columns, *Work* and *Prosperity*, *Knowledge* and *Honour*. Between the columns you will find a row of bronze statues representing Hungarian kings and the military leaders and politicians who participated in the Wars for Freedom against the Habsburgs.

A 36m Corinthian column stands at the centre of the **Millennium Monument** on top of which stands the 5m-high figure of the Archangel Gabriel, holding the Hungarian crown in his right hand and a Patriarchal cross in his left. It won the *Grand Prix* at the 1900 Paris World Exhibition.

After the Prado in Madrid it is at the Museum of Fine Arts that you can find the largest collection of El Grecos.
There is hardly an old master not represented in the collection.
There is also a fine collection of antique sculpture.

At its base you can see the equestrian statues of Prince Árpád and the six chieftains.

The classical façade of the **Museum of Fine Arts** has a tympanum containing a copy of the sculptural group found on the *Temple of Zeus* in Olympia (1900–1906). Opposite stands the eclectic-Neoclassical **Picture Gallery** (1895), which has the largest exhibition space in Hungary. Both buildings were designed by *Albert Schickedanz* and *Fülöp Herczog*.

The Time Wheel is now making its way slowly across the parade ground. This 2.5m wide, 60 metric-ton hour-glass made of red granite, stainless steel and bulletproof glass symbolises Hungary's membership of the EU. It will take the 4.4 cubic metres of sand one year to flow from one container to the other causing the whole contraption to move forwards 15 metres in the process. At this rate it will take 50 years for the wheel to cross the square.

The area immediately behind the Picture Gallery used to be known as "boot" square, because the sole of Stalin's bronze foot was once all that survived of the gargantuan statue of Stalin following the 1956 uprising. Pál Pátzay's statue of Lenin was put up in its place. Lenin, however, didn't suffer the indignity of being blown up. He was gently lifted away by crane and deposited in the sculpture park on the edge of Budafok where he survives with many other displaced comrades (XXII. District, on the corner of Balaton út and Szabadka út).

During the winter months the eastern part of the Liget boating lake turns into an ice rink. Crossing the bridge you can make your way to the Vajdahunyad Castle complex.
The ensemble includes copies of Hungarian buildings dating from the Romanesque period right through to the Baroque.

It was Flóris Rómer's idea (1866) to found the Zoo (Állatkerti körút 6-10). To mark the opening its first manager, the colourful János Xantus, was given a giraffe by Queen Elizabeth. The walls of the Zoo, the entrance and some of the buildings were designed in a Hungarian Secession style made popular by Károly Koós. How many elephants can claim to live in a house decorated with Zsolnay majolica?

The construction of the minaret-like tower next to the elephant house caused a storm when it was built, just as it did when it was recently renovated. Ambassadors from some of the Islamic states protested against the construction of such a holy building for such a profane purpose. Fortunately the minaret has survived. For a small charge you can climb up the tower and enjoy the view. There was a time when you could hire a telescope, but this had to be stopped when it was discovered that the male visitors tended to focus their attentions on the sunbathers lying on the ladies' sun lounge at the Széchenyi Baths next door.

Budapest's **Vajdahunyad Castle** was originally built to provide temporary wooden exhibition space for the 1896 Millennium Exhibition. However, the locals were so enamoured with the castle that they asked *Ignác Alpár* to build them another one out of stone. It now houses an **Agricultural Museum** containing an excellent collection of hunting trophies.
The castle courtyard, which has a Renaissance atmosphere about it, is a venue for outdoor concerts during the summer and a Nativity play, with real animals and a real live Jesus, during Advent.

The buildings of the Széchenyi Baths were built between 1909 and 1913. The drinking hall in the eastern wing has recently been restored (2003), and it is there you can get your chilled version of the 77°C St Stephen's Spring waters to take home with you.

In this part of the Városliget you can see the **Fairground**, the **Capital's Big Top**, and Europe's largest medicinal bath, the **Széchenyi Medicinal Baths and Swimming Pool**. For those who are looking for something a little bit out of the ordinary and a little old-fashioned, we recommend the one-hundred-year-old "ringlispíl" roundabout in the **Little Fairground**, a *Europa Nostra Award* winner, which will be particularly popular with the children. Also in the Liget there is the **Transport Museum**, the *History of Aviation Collection* and the *Petőfi Csarnok*, otherwise known as the **PeCsa**, which is particularly popular amongst Budapest's youth. At the weekend you will find the *Pecsa-bolha* flea market there, the best **outdoor market** in Budapest.

Going on the new roller-coaster at the fairground has its ups and downs.

Following the Underground

"It's been an old mania, to walk down to the end of the Stefánia..." – is a refrain still heard in Pest today. But of course it's no longer the coaches and the horses which go to the edge of the town where the villas stood... Today you can make the trip by underground, but walking out there can also be very pleasant.

The country's biggest sporting complex, the **Népstadion** (*Károly Dávid*, 1948–1953), recently renamed the **Ferenc Puskás Stadium,** covers 192,916m², and has a capacity of 78 thousand (Népstadion út). The **Olympic Hall**, the recently built **Budapest Sports Arena** and the **Millennium Sports Centre,** with Hungary's only velodrome, are all situated nearby.

When **Keleti (Eastern) Station** (*Gyula Rochlitz, János Feketeházy*, 1884) was built in Baross tér it was one of the most up-to-date stations in Europe. Now that it has been renovated it is once again somewhere approaching its former glory. In the niches in its façade you can see statues of *James Watt* and *George Stephenson*.

The statue of Gábor Baross (1848-1892) (Antal Szécsi, 1898) on the Thököly út side of Keleti Railway Station was put up in recognition of his contribution to the construction of the Hungarian railway system. The engine shed at Budapest's other major station on the Pest side, Nyugati (Western Station), was designed by Eiffel's office in Paris. The one hundred-year-old tram stop sign outside the station commemorates Budapest's first ever tram departure in 1888. To get to the Railways Historical Park (XIV. District, Tatai út 95.) you can either catch the nostalgia train from Nyugati Station or catch bus no. 30 from Baross tér.

The helium balloon, known as the Budapest Eye, takes off from the roof of the Westend Shopping Centre just opposite Nyugati Station. Once airborne passengers get a fine view of the city.

It was along today's Rákóczi út that the mourners followed the ashes of Ferenc Rákóczi II. and those of his exiled supporters from Keleti Station to the National Museum. The *National Theatre* stood on the corner of the Nagykörút and Blaha Lujza

tér until its demolition in 1965. Near the *Semmelweis* (once known as the *Rókus*) *Hospital* (Gyulai Pál u. 2.), where the road suddenly narrows, you will find the **Saint Roche and the Rozalia Chapel** (1740), built during a period when plagues were known to claim many victims.

On the façade of the chapel there is a tablet marking the height of the 1838 flood.

On the Múzeum körút, next to the *Loránd Eötvös University*, stands the classical façade of the **Hungarian National Museum** (*Mihály Pollack*) containing both the oldest and the largest public collections in the country.

Like the Chain Bridge, the National Museum is a symbol of the awakening Hungarian spirit and its citizens' demands for freedom, as expressed in the words "Rise Hungarians, your country calls!" Apart from having a permanent display covering the history of the region from prehistoric times up until the present day, the museum also hosts temporary exhibitions.

It was in the streets behind the museum that the buildings were gradually transformed into what was to become the "palatial" 8th District.

Apart from the *Central Antiquarian Bookshop*, the Múzeum körút also has some old courtyards on the odd-numbered side of the street which are worth looking at. It is here you will see sections of the old town wall which are as much as 6–8 metres high.

In Budapest the **Astoria** is more than just a hotel. There is the busy crossroads, the underground station going by the same name and all the subways conneced with it.

Near the Astoria, on the wall of Rákóczi út 2., an elegant street lamp reminds you that the first electric street lighting in Budapest was used here in 1909.

A modern office building now stands on the site of the first *National Theatre*. It's worth going up the lift in the glass corner feature to enjoy the view from the top floor. 3, Károly körút is a typical Pest block with a passageway going through it. The back entrance opens onto Dohány utca where you can see Budapest's main **Synagogue** opposite you.

The Moorish-style Synagogue (Lajos Förster, 1859), which stands on the corner of the old Jewish quarter, is one of biggest and most beautiful synagogues in the world.

In the garden next door to the synagogue there is metal composition depicting a willow, the *Memorial to the Jewish Martyrs* (*Imre Varga*, 1991) each of whose leaves represents one of Hungary's 600,000 holocaust victims. You can also visit the world-famous **Jewish Museum**. Concerts are held in front of the synagogue, which is also home to the *Jewish Summer Festival* at the end of August.

TOWERS AND QUAYS

Ferenciek tere gets its name from the **Franciscan Church** (1717–1743) founded during the 13th century. On the side wall stands a relief (*Barnabás Holló*) in memory of Miklós Wesselényi, hero of the 1838 flood. In front of it you can find the *Nereida Well* (1835), the first carved public well in Pest.

Next to the church you can find the Kárpátia Restaurant which, together with the Apostolok next door, is one of the last surviving traditional Pest restaurants. Not only do the painted walls and the wooden panelling hark back to a bygone age, the menu too preserves traditions going back many hundreds of years. It's probably best to take your coffee at the recently rebuilt Central Coffee House, where the spirits of times past waft around the marble tables and thonet chairs.

Március 15. tér, a square named on the one hundredth anniversary of the 1848 revolution, is where you will find the **Belváros Parish Church,** the oldest building in Pest. The church was originally built in the 11th century from the stones of the adjacent *Contra Aquincum*, and it was here that the martyr bishop Gellért was buried in 1046. The church was rebuilt during the 14th century, and the chancel has a row of cusped Gothic wall niches dating from this period. The two chantry-chapels date from the Renaissance period. During the Turkish period the church was used as a mosque, and the mihrabot (the prayer alcove) can still be seen in the eastern wall.

It was around the present Baroque church (1725-1739) that the old centre of Pest grew. The Kecskemét, Hatvan and Vác roads all joined up here, and the Pest ferry departed from the Pest Pier nearby. The classical-style tomb is the work of István Ferenczy (1792-1856), pupil of Canova. As for the more recent works there is the altar painting by Pál C. Molnár, member of the so-called School of Rome, and a statue of St Anthony of Padua (László Kiss) in the porch.

To the east of the church stands the neo-Baroque building of the one-time **Piarist Monastery and Grammar School** (*Dezső Hültl*, 1915), which has recently been occupied by the *Sapientia Theological College*. The chapel, which once served as the *university theatre*, is once again used for religious worship. If you move one block further down, you come to the 200-year-old *Százéves* restaurant, the only surviving non-religious Baroque building in Pest.

Váci utca runs through the town's most elegant district up towards Elizabeth Bridge. The northern stretch of the road ends at Vörösmarty tér, a square known for its elegant hotel, famous department stores, boutiques and galleries. The streets running parallel to Váci utca are just as interesting. There is for example the Gothic Revival Paris Court in Petőfi Sándor utca, whose concourse manages to join up three separate streets.

On the last Thursday of every month the public gets the opportunity to sit in on an open session of the *Budapest City Council*. This takes place in the richly decorated council chamber in the **New Town Hall** (Váci utca 62–64.) (The council offices are actually in the Baroque Invalidus Palace, the *Old Town Hall* building in Városház utca.)

The real centre of Pest is Vörösmarty tér with the legendary Gerbeaud (Zserbó) Patisserie, its street artists and its lively street culture. During Book Week the square is full of tented books stalls, and the Christmas Market fills the square with candlelight and the distinctive smell of cinnamon. It is from here that the official opening procession for the Budapest Spring Festival sets off in the middle of March. It is in the southern part of Váci utca, beyond the pedestrian zone, that you start coming across the small restaurants (and they are no ordinary restaurants), coffee houses and elegant shops before finally reaching the Great Covered Market.

It isn't worth attempting to drive your car into the area between the Kiskörút and the Danube. Driving is a troublesome business, and there are hardly any parking places on offer anyway. It's easier to visit everything on foot, and you can also see a lot more while you are at it. It's here you will find the **University Church** in Papnövelde utca (*András Mayerhoffer*, 1742), the quiet benches in **Károlyi Garden** (behind the Károlyi Palace, the *Petőfi Museum of Literature*) and the **museum** in *Endre Ady*'s final Pest residence (Veres Pálné u. 4–6.).

On Apáczai Csere János utca on the banks of the Danube stand the elegant hotels, the palaces and the shady walks. In particular one should mention the palace known as the Pesti Vigadó, which will be closed for renovation from 2004, with its gallery, concert hall and ballrooms, as well as its pub and casino. Don't forget to stroke the sculpture of the Little Princess (László Marton, 1990) sitting on the railings next to the tram stop in front of the Vigadó, before sitting down on one of the benches and taking in the world-famous view of the Danube with Buda beyond.

BUDA: PEARL OF THE DANUBE

Elizabeth Bridge, which crosses the river at its narrowest point (290m) in Hungary, links Pest with Buda at the foot of *Gellért Hill*. The original bridge, blown up by the Germans in 1945, was rebuilt in 1965 (*Pál Sávoly*). The hot-water springs at the foot of 130 metre-high Gellért Hill supply the *Rác*, the *Rudas* and the *Gellért Baths*. At the southernmost point of the hills you will find the **Statue of Liberty** depicting a woman holding a palm (*Zsigmond Kisfaludi Strobl*, 1947).

The "Rudas" is one of Buda's few original Turkish remains, built in the mid-16th century by Pasha Musztafa Szokoli. Those locals suffering from rheumatism fall into two camps, Rudas bathers and Lukács bathers Both groups vehemently defend the merits of their own particular bath, and would never dream of fraternising with the "enemy".

According to legend Gellért Hill got its name from Bishop Gellért, who was thrown off the face of the hill by Hungarian heathens in 1046. It is said that the infamous Gellért Hill witches used to take the name of the saint in vain, and held covens on the hill until the 17th century. The Citadel was built on top of the hill following the suppression of the 1848 revolution to pacify the rebellious town. It later lost its military character, and now has a hotel, a restaurant, a casino and a disco.

The **terrace** situated on the side of the hill in front of the **Citadel** offers perhaps the best view of the city both night and day. (If work goes according to plan Budapest's second cog-railway, running between the Citadel and the Rácfürdő, will be ready in 2005.)

Walking up on the hill you come across the **Astronomical Observatory**, the *Saint Gellért Memorial*, the famous *Gellért Hotel*, and the **Rock Church** built into Saint Ivan's Cave. Whilst the drinking fountain in front of the hotel offers medicinal waters, and the wall beside *Gellért Hill reservoir* can also prove a refreshing place to sit on a hot summer's day, and the *Buda Girl* and the *Pest Boy* on the balustrade make an interesting photographic composition.

It is from Gellért Hill and the quay down by the Danube that the fireworks are usually lit for the country's big firework display on August 20th. (For more about this and the rest of the national celebrations see the *Hungarian Treasury*.)

According to medieval travellers *"When it comes to towns, in Europe there are three pearls, Venice for its waters, Florence for its plains and Buda for its hills".* It is indeed seldom that one gets such a sense of openness like that felt on the banks of the Danube in a city. This contrasts with the intimacy of Buda's Castle district. Buda's *Castle Hill* is a wedge-shaped outcrop lying parallel to the Danube. Archaeologists have discovered that the 10km of **caves and cellars** within the hill were inhabited during the Palaeolithic period.

It was here, following the Tatar Invasion (1241) that Béla IV built a **castle**. The royal settlement, which built within its walls grew rapidly, culminating in the building projects which went on during the reign of Matthias Corvinus.

The magnificence of the medieval palace can now only be guessed at from the written sources and the superb International Gothic sculptures which survive. During the Turkish occupation, the castle and the town gradually fell into a state of disrepair. The palatial area and the town were rebuilt during the 18th and 19th centuries.

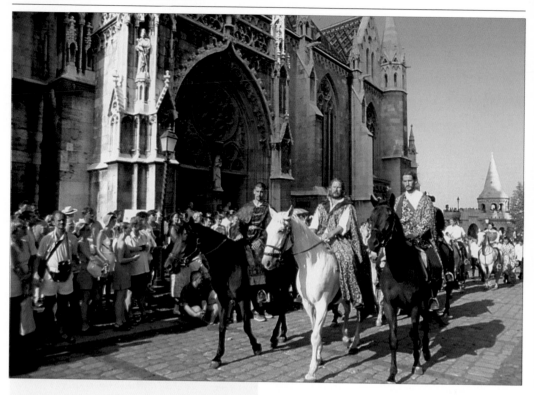

Horsemen in historical costume on parade in the Castle

The castle suffered substantial damage during the Second World War, as it was here that the Germans had their centre of operations, a centre which ended up being their final stronghold. The scars of the street fighting which took place here can still be seen on some of the buildings. (The last war ruin – the one-time Army Headquarters – also belongs to the castle.)

Relaxing at the castle

Dísz tér got its name from the changing of the guards which used to take place here (18th century). During the course of the Middle Ages this square, lying on the border between the castle and town, became the town's main market square. It was here also that public executions took place, and where Ladislas V. had Ladislas Hunyadi, Matthias Corvinus's brother, beheaded in 1457.

The main figure of the *war memorial* is by *György Zala* and the base by *Albert Schickedanz* (1893). The memorial lies on the site of Saint George's Church. In the corner of the square you will find the smallest theatre in Hungary, the *Korona Podium*, and a cake shop of the same name. The theatre's special atmosphere and frequent foreign language productions makes it a popular venue.

During the Middle Ages Szent Miklós utca used to stand where **Szentháromság (Trinity) Square** is today. The houses which stood here were destroyed during the siege of 1686.

The 14.4 metre-high *Trinity Statue* (1713, *Fülöp Ungleich, Antal Hörger*) was put up to commemorate the plague of 1709.

Building on the **Church of the Blessed Virgin Mary** (now more often referred to as the Matthias Church) started between 1255 and 1269, during the reign of Béla IV. Parts of the northern tower date from this period. *St Mary's Portal* on the south side of the nave dates from the reign of Louis the Great (1342–1382). During the Turkish period the church was used as a mosque. Most of what you can see of the church today is the result of an unfortunate restoration conducted by *Frigyes Schulek* between 1874 and 1896. (Visits are possible in the company of a guide.)

The frescos you can see in the Matthias Church are the work of Bertalan Székely and Károly Lotz.
In the Loretó Chapel stands a 16th century marble Madonna. In the Chapel of the Holy Trinity you can see the 1862 sarcophagi which cover the remains of Béla III. and his first wife Anna of Chatillon, both of which were found in Székesfehérvár in 1848. The crypt and the gallery house the Museum of Ecclesiastical Art, which contains an exact copy of the Hungarian crown. The church's excellent acoustics and the fine organ make it a popular concert venue.

You can still find Vilmos Ruszwurm's famous Empire-style patisserie in Szentháromság utca. The small road ends in an atmospheric little square. Here you will find in the Café Miró, site of Buda's first-ever coffee house, the statue of the hussar and equestrian general Count András Hadik. The bronze of this "most hussar of hussars" is for the most part mottled green in colour apart from one particularly shiny spot in the horse's nether regions. The brilliance of the offending part can be explained by the frequent fondling it attracts from students of the Technical University groping for a bit of extra luck during their exams. No figures are available to prove whether this custom brings the desired effect. Interestingly tourists have also resorted to giving the balls a quick rub, for reasons only they can explain.

There is another equestrian statue in Buda, that of St Stephen, standing next to the Matthias Church. The base has reliefs depicting some of the key moments in the king's eventful life (Alajos Stróbl, Frigyes Schulek, 1906).

The **Fisherman's Bastion** (*Frigyes Schulek*, 1902), which is currently being renovated, has never been used for defensive purposes. The bastion did, however, get its name from the Fisherman's Guild, whose responsibility it was to defend that particular stretch of the town wall. The seven towers symbolise the seven chieftains who led the Magyars during the Hungarian Conquest.

Hungary's first printing press went into operation in **András Hess tér** in 1472. It is here also that you can find a statue of Pope Innocent XI who helped to finance the fight against the Turks. The statue was put up to mark the 250th anniversary of the liberation of Budapest from the Turks (*József Damkó*, 1936). A Dominican friary was built on the site during the 13th century. On the wall of the tower you can see a copy of a relief of Matthias Corvinus, which can be found in Bautzen in Germany. The construction of the modern *Hilton Hotel* around the medieval friary has been deemed an architectural success.

One popular subject for an arty photo is the reflection of the Fisherman's Bastion in the windows of the Hilton Hotel. It's also worth going to

There is more to the castle than just Szentháromság tér. It's worth walking along Tárnok, Fortuna or Úri utca all the way to Kapisztrán tér at the northern tip of the castle district.

one of the many performances held in the Hilton's Dominican courtyard.

In the **House of Hungarian Wine** they keep wines from all the Hungarian wine regions, most of which can be tasted for the price of an entrance ticket. In the courtyard of the **Museum of Hungarian Tourism and Trade** (Fortuna u. 4.) you can see a one hundred-year-old vine which, having survived the phylloxera outbreak and a couple of World Wars, still manages to produce a few grapes.

Once you have got as far as Kapisztrán tér you might as well climb up the tower of the medieval *Church of St Mary Magdalen*, otherwise known as the **Garrison Church**. The northwestern end of the castle quarter is dominated by the enormous **Museum of Military History**. During the summer, productions are put on for both children and adults. It was in about 1247, following the Tatar invasion, that Béla IV. built the first castle in what is now the **Palace Quarter**. It served as a royal residence right up until the Turkish Conquest. Charles Robert, Hungary's first Angevin king (1308–1342, however decided to take the monarchy to Visegrád in response to the antagonism he received from Buda's patricians. It was only during the reign of Sigismund (1387–1437) that Buda Castle became a building with any great architectural pretentions.

The first reference to what was called the Friss (Fresh) Palace came in 1439. It was also at this time that the so-called Csonka Tower was built, although it was left unfinished following Sigismund's death. Matthias Corvinus later added decorations and new furniture. The palace was taken by the Turks in 1541, and the building was subsequently to endure fires, earthquakes and plagues. By the time the palace was recaptured in 1686 there wasn't much left to admire. It was Maria Theresa who rebuilt it and enlarged it (Franz Anton Hildebrandt, 1770), although this necessitated the demolition of part of the medieval palace. Further enlargements were made to the plans of Miklós Ybl. Following his death the task of designing the wing facing the Danube was left to Alajos Hauszmann (1895). Hauszmann doubled the length of the facade to 304 metres, and placed a central dome-like feature in the middle.

Now the Palace Quarter is one of the capital's most important cultural centres. It is here that you can find the **Hungarian National Gallery,** which has the most comprehensive collection of Hungarian art; the **Museum of Modern History;** the **Széchényi National Library** and, the most recent addition, the **Ludwig Museum** of Contemporary Art. The **Budapest Historical Museum** exhibits the remains of the old royal palace, including some superb Late Medieval sculptures. The cable railway takes people from Clark Ádám tér up to the Palace Quarter.

Around 20th August every summer the courtyards in and around the palace, and Szent György tér host the Art and Crafts Fair and the International Wine Festival.

The Buda Castle funicular railway, built in 1870 and renovated in 1986, is 95m long, and its rails go up a 48 degree gradient. The carriages are arranged in step-like fashion, and offer unique views of Budapest. At the top there are some great vantage points, for example the square in front of the palace, the stone cornice around the equestrian statue of Eugene of Savoy, whose armies reconquered Buda from the Turks in 1686, and of course the Fisherman's Bastion.

It took six and a half months to dig the 350m **tunnel** through Castle Hill (*Adam Clark*, 1857). Local wags suggested that the tunnel had been built to park the Chain Bridge in. In the square, named after the great Scotsman who built both the tunnel and the bridge, you will find the **"O" milestone** (*Miklós Borsos*) used for all Hungary's main roads, except road number 8, and the funicular railway. The banks of the Danube, like Castle Hill, enjoy *World Heritage Status.* (For further details see the *Hungarian Treasury.*) One of the main attractions of the *Water Town* (*Viziváros*) lying directly under the castle is the upper promenade with its wonderful views onto the Pest river front. The promenade is one of the busiest cycling paths in the country, being part of a cycle path network covering more than one hundred kilometres.

BRIDGES AND ISLANDS

It would be hard to imagine the Danube without its nine **bridges**. The oldest is the *Chain Bridge (Lánchíd)*. The first bridge to cross the Danube in Hungary and the second permanent bridge across the river between the *Black Forest* and the *Black Sea*, it was built around the middle of the 19th century in response to a suggestion by *Count István Széchenyi*.

When the road traffic is banished from the Chain Bridge during the summer weekends, it becomes a an engineering spectacle, an ancient monument and cultural venue all in one.

Budapest's Chain Bridge is a national symbol of progress and the awakening of the national consciousness. It also symbolises the meeting of East and West. The locals are in fact so fond of their bridge that they organise a "birthday party" in its honour. It's a tradition which stretches all the way back to 1999, the bridge's 150th birthday. The bridge was planned by the Englishman Thierney William Clark and built by the Scottish "tunneler" Adam Clark (1839-1849). The bridge's two lion statues (János Marschalkó, 1852) survived the Second World War. At the Pest end of the bridge you will find Roosevelt tér, in which you can find the neo-Renaissance Hungarian Academy of Sciences (Friedrich August Stüler, 1864).

Directly opposite the bridge lies the Secession-style Gresham Palace (Zsigmond Quittner, the Vágó Brothers, 1907), which has been turned into the luxury Four Seasons Gresham Palace Hotel Budapest.

The World Heritage area goes as far as **Margaret Bridge** (*Emile Gouin*, 1876) at the southern tip of the island named after Margaret, daughter of Béla IV., who lived at the Dominican Nunnery situated there.

1.5km² Margaret Island was built up from a number of smaller sandbanks. During the Middle Ages, when it was known as Nyúl (Rabbit) Island, the island was a place of refuge for women who were only too happy to care for the sick and the fallen. Béla IV turned the houses into a nunnery, which was where his daughter Margaret was sent having been brought up by the nuns of Veszprém.

It was here on Margaret Island that Miklós Toldi fought his famous duel with a Bohemian warrior in the Late Middle Ages, an episode immortalized by the poet János Arany. A few generations later the island saw many an aristocratic duel. Today, people are more likely to go to the island for a bit of peace and quiet armed with a picnic hamper full of goodies. Árpád Bridge on the northern tip of the island was built during the 19th century to allow easy access to the Grand Hotel and the Thermal Hotel lying nearby.

The island, once out of bounds, can now be visited for the price of an entrance ticket. There is plenty for the sporty types (the **Youth Sports Centre**, the **Swimming Pool**, the **Jogging Track**, the **Palatinus** swimming pool), as well as the walkers and chess players amongst you.

Under the water tower you will find the **Margaret Island Open-Air Theatre** which puts on operas and musicals. Leaving the bridge you see the **Centenary Monument** (*István Kiss*, 1972) commemorating the 100th anniversary of the unification of Pest, Buda and Óbuda.

Apart from the bus (number 26), you can only get there by taxi, on foot, or by peddle car.

There are several other islands breaking up the flow of the Danube as it makes its way through Budapest. It was on **Hajógyár-sziget** (Shipyard Island) that the Romans built a palace. Some have suggested that it was here that Emperor *Marcus Aurelius* wrote his *Meditations*. Were he to return during the month of September, he would find the island teaming with **waterskiers and waveboarders.** The island now hosts Europe's biggest pop festival, the *Island Festival,* which is held at the beginning of August. During the week-long festival there are over four hundred concerts, covering everything from heavy metal to jazz.

On the Edge of the City

It would be foolish to write off the suburbs. The sights may be fewer and further between, but the intrepid explorer will nevertheless be richly re-

Public sculptures lead visitors up to the National Theatre

warded. Amongst all the concrete and all the high-rise in *Óbuda* you come across **Fő tér** with all its old buildings, houses and museums (*Lajos Kassák, Viktor Vasarely, Imre Varga*), and the atmospheric little restaurants often found in Gyula Krúdy's (1878–1933) novels. Having made your way all the way out to Óbuda it's worthwhile taking a photograph of *Imre Varga's Umbrellaed Girls.*

Travelling three stops further down the HÉV from Fő tér (in the direction of Békásmegyer, Szentendre) you go back two thousand years. It is here that visitors can see the **Aquincum Museum** with its Roman remains and excavated treasures. In one of of Buda's urban centres, not far from Moszkva tér, the old halls of the Ganz Factory have been developed into the exciting **Millennium Exhibition and Cultural Centre.** The southernmost suburb of Buda is *Budafok* (formerly known as Promontor), well known for its wines and champagnes. Its 30 km **cellar system** is so large that it is capable of storing about one million hectolitres of wine. You can visit the *Törley Champagne Works* with its **museum** (Kossuth Lajos u. 82–94.). On the edge of Budafok, on the old Balaton road to be exact, you will find Budapest's most curious museum, the **Statue Park**.

At Budafok's statue park the stars are the statues which popped up all over Hungary between 1950 and 1990. At the entrance to the museum you can buy all kinds of Communist souvenirs, such as model worker medals, socialist and revolutionary songs, and memorabilia of more recent provenance.

At **Rudnyánszky Palace** (Csókási Pál u. 9.) in *Nagytétény* visitors can see a fine antique furniture collection. The *Campona Shopping Centre* has the only **tropical aquarium** in Central Europe. At one end of *Lágymányos Bridge* (1995) you can see the **National Theatre** (*Mária Siklósi*, 2002) next to which it is hoped a new urban district will develop around the **National Concert Hall, House of Traditions** and **Ludwig Museum** complex and the **House of the Arts**.

It's worth going out to *Kőbánya* on the Pest side to see the stands of the **Budapest International**

Fair area which hosts important trade fairs (the spring and autumn *Budapest International Fair*, the *Agricultural Show*, the *Travel Exhibition* etc.) The district's most important architectural monument is the **Church of Saint Ladislas** (Szent László tér 25.) designed by *Ödön Lechner* and covered inside and out by Zsolnay majolica. Kőbánya is to beer what Budafok is to wine. Keen industrial archaeologists will be delighted to learn that there are now guided tours around the *Dreher Brewery*.

The Church of Saint Ladislas in Kőbánya contains windows by Miksa Róth, and pews by Ottó Tandor. Organ recitals are frequently held here.

Underground line number 3, the blue one, takes you out to Kispest, the part of Budapest where *Ferenc Puskás* cut his footballing teeth. Just a few minutes walk from Határ út station you come to one of the city's most beautiful housing estates, the *"Wekerle"*. The estate was laid out in 1908, primarily to the plans of *Károly Kós,* who envisaged five thousand people living there. It was the first such piece of urban planning in Budapest.

After all those palaces, houses, monuments and statues why not escape the hustle and bustle and head for the Buda Hills. You should head for the Normafa and then climb your way up to the Elizabeth Lookout Point on János Hill where you can look down on the very city you have managed to escape from.

Part of the Buda Castle caves

After reaching the heights you can sink down to the depths. With the exception of Monaco there is no other capital in the world which has anything quite like the Buda **caves**. The *Pálvölgy Caves* are famous for their stalactites, whilst the *Szemlő Hill Caves* have some interesting *aragonite* rock formations.

You don't have to traipse around the whole town to find greenery. Instead you can simply catch the underground out to Klinikák, and then walk to the **Botanical Gardens**, where the floating leaves of the *Victoria Regia* contribute to a unique

The Botanical Gardens were laid out on the site of the Festetics Garden in 1847.

Budapest experience. It is here also that you might bump into *ernő nemecsek* (written in small letters) from *Ferenc Molnár*'s world-famous novel *The Paul Street Boys.*

And we haven't even scratched the surface! There are one thousand buildings of architectural interest in all, 223 museums and art galleries, forty theatres, seven concert halls and the two opera houses. There are also the Carnival Parades and the Autumn Festival. If you are unfortunate enough to miss ninety excruciating minutes at a Hungarian football match, you can always play tennis at the Roman Tennis Academy instead. We will leave it to you to decide which of the capital's one thousand restaurants, coffee houses and other attractions you would like to visit.

One of Central Europe's busiest airports: Ferihegy

But before we leave Budapest perhaps it would be a good idea to just to count down the city's eleven forms of transport.

We've already noted the Danube ferries and the pleasure boats, but we haven't mentioned **Ferihegy Airport,** which keeps Budapest and Hungary linked up to the rest of the world. We've got some use out of the underground, the trams, the buses and the trolley buses. But there is still the *cog-railway*, the *ski lift* and the **Széchenyi Hill Children's Railway** to ride on.

So there are all kinds of ways of exploring what we, not surprisingly, think is the most beautiful capital city in the world. Now it's your turn to decide.

Sailing on a pleasure boat along the Danube is one very pleasant way of spending a summer's day.

The high altar and the frescos in and under the dome are the work of Franz Anton Maulbertsch (1771-1772).
A century later the transept walls were decorated by István Takács, and the half-dome in the chancel painted by Béla Kontuly.

VÁC

The first cathedral was built by King Geisa I. He was also buried there in 1077. When capital of the kingdom Visegrád had a positive effect on the development of Vác, although much of what was gained was lost during the Turkish occupation.

During the Baroque period however the *Althan Brothers,* both of whom acquired the title of bishop; *Károly Eszterházy* and *Kristóf Migazzi* rebuilt the town. The steamboats operated between Pest and Bratislava from the 1830s followed by rail service between Pest and Vác (1846). Széchenyi, Louis Kossuth and Petőfi were amongst its first passengers.

It was the houses, which were built for the railway company employees, which led to the growth of Vác up in the direction of the Deákvár Hills. At the same time the Migazzi's Baroque townscape hardly changed at all.

The *pilgrimage place* known as the **Hétkápolna** (Derecske dűlő 2.) got its name from the seven small Baroque chapels representing the seven sorrows of the Blessed Virgin Mary. The spring coming from the riverbed of the old Danube is said to have miraculous eye-healing qualities.

On the right side of the road you can see the prisoners' cemetery where political prisoners were interred. The **War Memorial**, an iron pyramid standing on an artificial mound with a cannonball on top, pays homage to the heroes who fell during the War for Freedom.

The bridge over the Gombás (Diadal tér) in Vác is the only such structure in Hungary (Ignác Oracsek, 1753-1758) to have all its original statues (József Bechert).

The Baroque **Franciscan Church** and its **monastic buildings** (Géza király tér 12.) were built from the remains of the castle and the old cathedral. The picture behind the high altar depicts the stoning of St Stephen the Protomartyr.

The **Episcopal Palace** (Migazzi tér 1.) and the **Cathedral** (*Isidore Canevale*, 1761–1777) were built with funds given by Bishop Migazzi. The cornice over the entrance of the Cathedral is inscribed with the letters DOM, *Deo Optimo Maximo*.

There may be a grain of truth in the saying "to be as rich as the Bishop of Vác" because Kristóf Migazzi, apart from being Bishop of Vác, was also Archbishop of Vienna and a cardinal. Contemporary chronicles tell us the incomes enjoyed by the archdiocese of Vienna were half those of the diocese of Vác. You can see for yourself at the Cathedral Treasury and Diocesan Museum (Március 15. tér 4.).

The Baroque **Piarist Church** (Szentháromság tér, 1725–1745) has a tabernacle made of Venetian glass underneath the high altar painting of Saint Anne donated to the church by Bishop Pál Forgács.

The Piarist Church was built at the same time as the monastic buildings (1727) and the school. It is now known that the artist Károly Lotz (1833-1904) was a novice at the friary and attended the school, and that Imre Madách took an exam there in 1832.

The Vác World Carnival is organised at the end of July, the Gregorian Festival at the end of August, whilst on the days leading up to the national holiday on August 20th, there is the Danube Bend Expo and Trade Fair. The Wine Festival also takes place in August.

Március 15. tér has been the centre of the town since the Middle Ages. Once it had ceased to be a market square a **fountain** (*Frigyes Pogány, Miklós Horler*) was built right in the middle of it.

The **Dominican Church** dates from the 17th and 18th centuries (Március 15. tér). Some intesting painted coffins can be seen at the **Momento Mori Museum** in the crypt (Március15. tér 4.)

The one-time Kúria Hotel (20.) goes back to 1770. It was in what is now the András Cházár Primary School and a Student Hostel (Március 15. tér 16.) that András Jólészi Cházár founded the first deaf and dumb school in Hungary (1802).

The *Vác Diocesan Collection* can be found in the **Grand Provost's Palace** (4.).

One notable building is the **Stone Gate** (Köztársaság u.), the early classical triumphal arch Bishop Migazzi built on the occasion of Maria Theresa's visit to the town (*Isodore Canevale*, 1764). The *State Prison* (Köztársaság u. 64–66.) was originally built to be an academy for young nobles before becoming a barracks in 1784, and then the *Hungarian Military Academy*. The building has been a prison since 1855. The chapel in the courtyard is the only Gothic building remaining in the town.

The road next to the prison leads down to the Danube, the river which has played such an important role in the economic life of the town. In front of the houses leading down towards the Danube you will find the nicest shaded **promenade** on this stretch of the river, where there are statues, playgrounds and a bandstand right next to the water. The **ferry** leaves from here taking cars and buses across to *Szentendre Island*.

THE DANUBE BEND

VERŐCE

During the 14th and 15th centuries this popular tourist resort belonged to the bishops of Vác. With the waning of Visegrád the town declined in importance. Following the Turkish occupation Verőce was repopulated with Slovaks, and Germans from Württemberg. The locals hold their traditional *May Day celebrations* on Magyarkút Meadow, and during the first weekend in October everyone gathers to take part in the *Verőce Grape Harvest. Kossuth Prize-winning* artist *Géza Gorka* (1894–1971) lived here, and his one-time house and workshop has now become the **Pottery Museum** (Szamos u. 22.).

The present two-bayed **Saint Andrew's Church** was built in a Baroque style from the materials of its medieval predecessor by Mihály Károly Althan (1736–1743). The chancel is raised, and crowned with a dome. The altar contains a copy of the *Czestochowa Madonna*, as well as statues of saints.

Lady orchids

From the Youth Camp near KISMAROS *Station in the Morgó Valley you can catch the narrow-gauge railway (see picture) taking you to Szokolya and the Királyrét holiday resort. From there you can make your way up to Kisinóc, Nagy-Hideg Hill and the Csóványos in the Börzsöny.*

If you follow the red path from Verőce Station, you go up the *Les Valley* before eventually arriving at Magyarkút. The blue path takes you to the village of Nógrád, the *Naszály* (626m) near Vác, the *Násznép Cave* and the *Sárkány Well*.

The village of SZOKOLYA, once prime royal hunting territory, it now known for the columned gateways of its **Palóc houses** (Fő u.). It was in the Calvinist vicarage that *Ádám Mányoki* (1673–1757), Ferenc Rákóczi II.'s painter and painter to the Court of Saxony, was born. The painter *János Viski* (1891–1987) was also born here, and their work is on show at the **Mányoki-Viski Exhibition and Memorial Room** (Fő u. 56.).

NAGYMAROS

There is a great view over the Danube Bend from the **Julianus Lookout Tower** on *Hegyestető* (482m). It was here in Visegrád's twin town that the famous hunter and ornithologist and African scholar, *Kálmán Kittenberger* lived and worked. His statue in the main square was unveiled at the opening of the *World Hunting Exhibition* in 1971.

The locals are very proud of the **Roman Catholic church** (Szent Imre tér), with its 14th century nave, and tower dating from 1509. Only the tower remains in its original condition as the rest of the church was re-vaulted and remodelled in the Baroque style following the the Turkish occupation.

Nagymaros prides itself on its water sports and leisure facilities. There is an open-air swimming pool and a boat house, as well as the Sólyom Island camping site and yacht marina.
The latter hosts the San-Team Cup and the Danube Kayak Tour during the second weekend in June.

Zebegény

Looking at the town today it's hard to believe that the first people to live in Zebegény were Slovak

Those who are interested in technical matters should visit retired ship captain Vince Farkas's Shipping History Collection, which has a fine selection of sailing tackle and model ships (Szőnyi u. 9.).

tree fellers. However vine growers from the Mainz region settled here in 1735 and continued to grow grapes until the phylloxera epidemic, at which point they went into fruit growing.

The Secession-style **Roman Catholic Church** (Petőfi tér) was designed by *Károly Kós* and *Béla Jánszky* (1908–1909). The frescos of *Constantine the Great's Vision* and the *Discovery of the True Cross* are by *Aladár Körösfői Kriesch*, whilst the ornamentation was the work of *György Leszkovszky* and his pupils (1910–1914).

Going up to the classical **Calvary Chapel** (1853) you pass the nine Stations of the Cross which are painted onto metal panels. Those climbing up to nearby **Trianon monument and lookout point** will be rewarded with a superb view over the Danube Bend. In the cemetery nearby lies the grave of artist *István Szőnyi* (1894–1960), whose house has been turned into a **museum** (Bartóky u. 7.).

Kóspallag's name comes from the expression *"kos parlag"*, which means sheep pasture. The history of the plain goes back to 1756 when Count Antal Grassalkovich settled Slovak families here. The **stone cross** dating from the beginning of the 19th century at the southern end of the village marks where the Márianosztra military hospital's graveyard stood during the Napoleonic Wars.

> *To get to "Bíber Castle", the Roman watch-tower, you need to travel towards Vác. The view from the lookout tower at nearby White Hill (Fehér-hegy) is also popular. Once in the Börzsöny Nature Reserve you can go to the Kóspallag Fishing Lake and Nagyirtáspuszta where there is a path leading up to Nagy-Hideg Hill and the Csóványos Lookout Tower.*

Törökmező, which got its name from the Turkish military camp which once stood here, is now a popular tourist destination.

It was in Szob, at the mouth of the *River Ipoly*, famous for being the last stop before Slovakia, that *Zoltán Kodály's* father worked as a stationmaster. The composer lived in the town between 1883 and 1885. The **Luczenbacher Palace** in Szob (Árpád u. 8.) fell into the hands of the *Lazarite Order* after the First World War. Now it is the order's Saint *Ladislas Grammar School*.

MÁRIANOSZTRA

Mentioned in 1262 under the name *Nostre*, the village gets its present name from the patron saint of the church (*Maria nostra*). The church is one of the country's most famous **pilgrimage places**.

The parish church formed part of the Pauline Monastery built by King Louis the Great in 1352. Only the Gothic chancel survived the Turkish occupation. The painting of the Madonna (illustrated) is an 18th century copy of the Czestochowa Madonna, painted and presented by Father Cyprián Laszkiri. The Pauline Order, founded in 1274, regained custody of the church in 1989.

The Baroque **monastery** (1773–1774) was home to *Pál Ányos, Ferenc Verseghy* and *Benedek Virág,* the Pauline poet. Following the dissolution of the order (1786) it was used as a store before becoming a *prison* in 1858.

Pilgrimages take place on the feast of *The Five Holy Wounds of Christ,* in the first weekend in July; the *Mother of All Sorrows,* at the beginning of September, and the feast of the *Immaculate Conception* in the first weekend in December. It is then worshippers make their way to the **Stations of the Cross** (1772–1777) at the eastern end of the village.

NAGYBÖRZSÖNY

The Miners' Church in Nagybörzsöny stands to this very day (József Attila u. 1.). It dates back to the 13th century. The Gothic tabernacle dates from the 1417 enlargement.

The village originally nestled around **Saint Stephens's Church** on top of the small hill. It was only during the reign of Sigismund, following the settlement of Saxon miners into the area, that the village moved to its present position further down the valley. The **water mill** is still in operation (Széchenyi tér 10.), and the one-time house, mill and stable complex now has an exhibition about the history of flour-milling.

If you have a permit you can go fishing in the *Farkasvölgy.* When it comes to walking, however, you are free to walk along any number of paths going up into the *Börzsöny.* Since September 2002 it has once again been possible to travel on the **narrow-gauge forest railway** up towards Nagyirtáspuszta.

There was a time when the Nagybörzsöny Mill worked night and day. Now it's an industrial museum.

NÓGRÁD *gets its name from the Slavonic Novi Grad, New Castle. The castle's Renaissance fragments suggest that it enjoyed its heyday during the reign of Matthias Corvinus. Part of the Gunpowder Tower still stands, despite the fact that it was struck by lightning in 1683 whilst the castle was in Turkish hands. Following the destruction of the defences, the Turks were forced to beat a hasty retreat. The castle, up on its rocky outcrop, was never to regain its former role.*

IF STONES COULD TALK

The paths up into the Börzsöny leave from Diósjenő. There's a particularly nice 8.5-kilometre walk, which takes you up to the Börzsöny's highest peak, the Csóványos (939m). Castles once dominated the region's peaks, and it is possible to walk up to Pogány Castle, Cseh Castle and Kámori Castle. One alternative is to relax beside Diósjenő Lake.

Diósjenő

You can get to western Nógrád's tourist centre at the foot of the eastern Börzsöny by road (number 2) or by train on the Vác to Balassagyarmat line.

According to the Roman historians, and the inscription on the monument which you can find there, it was by Lake Diósjenő that the Pannonian legion under the leadership of Marcus Aurelius annihilated the barbarians threatening the right bank of the River Danube in 173AD.

The **Monument to the Hungarian Conquest** in the meadow behind the Börzsöny office of the *Danube-Ipoly National Park* tells us it was the Jenő clan who settled here. At the entrance to the **Calvinist church** (Dózsa György út, 1791) you can see a tablet referring to the fact that the great *Louis Kossuth* was not only a figure of national importance, but Diósjenő's honorary judge.

Whilst staying at the camping site in Diósjenő, or in the village itself, you can make the most of the facilities available at the **open-air swimming complex** and the fishing possibilities at 27-hectare *Lake Jenő*.

At the Bánk Lido on the banks of the lake you can go fishing or boating. The main events on the water stage take place during the Bánk Summer Festival from 15th July to 20th August. It's a great folk event, with concerts, folk music programmes and theatrical performances.

BÁNK is a popular **tourist resort**. The 7-hectare lake is surrounded by several hundred holiday-houses. The 19th century **Slovak Peasant House** (Petőfi út 98.) is full of old costumes and everyday items the local Slovaks wore and used.

DRÉGELYPALÁNK

The name of the village is connected with Drégely **Castle,** which lies four kilometres away on one of the Börzsöny's more outer-lying peaks. Built after the Tatar invasion (1241) it was already considered out of date by the time the Turks invaded. It was only when the Turkish arrival was imminent that the walls were strengthened. The famous siege, celebrated in a poem by *János Arany*, started on 4th July 1552, and lasted for four days.

The castle's 141 defenders, led by György Szondi, refused to give up the fight against Basha Ali of Buda and his 10–12 thousand troops. Archaeological work started on the castle in August 2000.

Basha Ali, however, held his enemies in high regard and honoured the valiant castellan with a hero's funeral; he even took the castellan's pages under his wing. The castle was badly damaged during the siege and was never rebuilt. Only a handful of soldiers were appointed to stand guard. During the Turkish period a huge stock-ade (palánkvár) was built on the site of what is now the Baroque **Roman Catholic church**. In its time the stockade was capable of providing lodgings for two thousand mounted soldiers. It was this fortification which provided the village with the second part of its name.

In the main square of the village you can find the Baroque Holy Trinity Statue (illustrated), the Szondi Memorial and a stone sarcophagus (Pál Kő). In the Szondi Memorial Room (Fő u. 22.) you can see documents referring to the tempestuous Turkish period and the centuries which followed.

Gödöllő

The golden age of the town coincides with the life of Antal Grassalkovich, Maria Theresa's favourite. The model agricultural practices he espoused formed the basis of the agricultural centre Gödöllő has become, with its university and research centre. The old buildings and the beautiful town centre, which made the town a popular holiday destination between the wars, fell victim to the post-war high-rise town planners.

The **Royal Palace** (Szabadság tér 1.) is one of the most important Baroque buildings in Hungary (*András Mayerhoffer*, 1744–1750). Enlargements were made to the designs of *Miklós Ybl* after the Hungarian state had given the palace to Franz Joseph and Queen Elizabeth as a coronation present. In 1920, the palace became Admiral Horthy's summer residence.

During the Grassalkovich period the town did, however, suffer some losses. The Calvinist church was demolished and replaced by the three-bayed

Queen Elizabeth's salon at the Royal Palace

Baroque **Palace Chapel** (1750), which has a high altar painting depicting Saint John Nepomuk, and a Venetian mosaic portrait of Antal Grassalkovich on the back wall. The reliefs on the **Column** in Szabadság tér also date from that period (*Martin Vogel*, 1749).

The Gödöllő Royal Palace Museum has been open to the general public since 1996. The guided tours take you through Queen Elizabeth and Franz Joseph's chambers, "The Age of the Grassalkovichs" and the "Queen Elizabeth" exhibitions as well as the Weapon Cabinet. After a more than two-hundred-year break the palace's Baroque theatre is once again open to the general public. The International Harp Festival held at the beginning of October is just one of the interesting programmes hosted by the palace.

The trees in *Elizabeth Park*, first planted in 1898, are now protected. The mound behind the statue of Queen Elizabeth (*József Róna*, 1901) with the statue of Saint Stephen (*György Zala*), was built up from soil coming from all 63 counties of historical Hungary. The empty interior of the Baroque **Calvary Chapel** (*János Mayerhoffer*, 1771–1775) is now used for storing water.

What was originally the neo-Baroque Premonstratensian Grammar School (*Róbert Kertész* and *Gyula Sváb*, 1922–1928) became Saint Stephen's University before eventually becoming the *Gödöllő Agricultural University* (GATE).

Prince Koloman (1208-1241), Béla IV.'s younger brother, on losing the Kingdom of Halics was given the Count of the Zips in what is now Slovakia. It was there he came into contact with the Premonstratensian order at Jászó (Jasov, Slovakia), who were in the process of constructing their monastery. Koloman gave them gifts and properties, and it is these acts of charity which the sculpture recalls. The Premonstratensian Grammar School in Gödöllő was built from the incomes deriving from those donated lands.

The new wing was built in 1964, the interior of which has Europe's largest bronze relief, *Amerigo Tot's Apotheosis of a Seed* (Péter Károly u.1.).

At the turn of the 19th and 20th centuries the Gödöllő **Art Colony** included some of the most talented Arts and Crafts artists of the time (*Aladár Kőrösfői Kriesch, Sándor Nagy* and *Ede Torockay Wigand*) was a bastion of the Hungarian Secessionist movement. Their works can be seen at the **Gödöllő Municipal Museum**.

The HÉV finally reached Gödöllő in 1911. Up until then the Budapest-Kerepes line had been diverted to serve the travel requirements of a royal family anxious for better links with the capital. The **royal waiting room** of the station, which lies near the palace, was designed by *Miklós Ybl*.

The more than three-hundred-thousand-hectare **arboretum** (Isaszegi út) is open to the public at weekends.

The **Lázár Equestrian Park** in the *Domony Valley* north of the town awaits keen horse riders.

EMBRACED BY HILLS

Máriabesnyő

The Pope gave Máriabesnyő the rank of Basilica minor in 1992.

Máriabesnyő, now belonging to Gödöllő, is mentioned as far back as 1249. After the Fifteen Year War the village went to waste (Besnyő-puszta), and since the 18th century it has been a **pilgrimage place**. The **Pilgrimage Church**, which can be found on road number 30, was built by the landowner Antal Grassalkovich and his wife (*János Mayerhoffer*, 1762–1769). It was while they were digging the foundations for the *Loretto Chapel* that a small 13th century **Madonna and Child** came to light. It wasn't long before news spread of the statue's miraculous powers.

In the Grassalkovich family vault down in the crypt you can see a tumba by *Johann Georg Dorfmeister* (1772).

In nearby *Babat Valley* you will find the Grassalkovich's stable palace, which is decorated by reliefs by *Marco Casagrande*. You can relax in the romantic surroundings of the *Kisbag High-*

wayman's Inn, on old route number 30, or the *Csinto Inn* by the *Petőfi Spring* which doesn't lie far away.

Mogyoród

It was here that King Salomon clashed with Ladislas and Prince Geisa in 1074, and where a church and a monastery were built with the spoils. Both church and monastery were destroyed during the Tatar invasion in 1241.

The village became depopulated during the Fifteen Year War in 16th century. The village was also struck by plague in 1750.

The **Roman Catholic church**, built by Mihály Althan, bishop of Vác between 1747 and 1749, was constructed from the remains of the medieval monastery. The altar painting depicting Saint Michael is a copy of a painting by *Guido Reni*. The altar figures were sculpted by the Óbuda Master *János Szabó*. The statue of Saint Michael on the transept pillar is by *Károly Bebó* (1749).

To the south of the village you will find the Hungaroring (1986), which since the reconstruction of 2003 is now 4,384m in length. On race days up to 220 thousand spectators attend the car and motorbike events, 30 thousand people occupying the grandstand. The most important event on the racing calendar is the Hungarian Grand Prix held in August.

The 36-hectare site offers leisure opportunities even when there aren't races going on: those visiting the *Adventure Park* can test their driving skills on the various rides. There is also the **Aquapark** and a camping site nearby.

Fót

We now move onto the *Pest Plain* on the edge of the *Gödöllő Hills* and into the outer suburbs of the capital. The Károlyi family bought the land here and here abouts and it is their **palace** you can see in Vörösmarty tér. With wings designed by *Miklós Ybl* (1847) the building is considered to be one of the top ten most important ancient monuments in the country. Count László Károlyi and his wife were permanent residents in six of the rooms.

The *István Károlyi Children's Centre* occupies some of the palace as well as the buildings scattered around the enormous park. The Marble Hall on the first floor, the only room still contain-

In Fót's romantic Roman Catholic church (Miklós Ybl, 1845-1855) you can see, amongst other things, Karl Blaas and Karl Müller's frescos depicting the life of Christ, and Karl Blaas's high altar painting. The Károlyi family vault can be found in the crypt. The three white carrara marble sculptures are by Pietro Tenerani (1858). In the chancel the altar, with its multicoloured marble inlay, is the work of Gaetano Bianchini.
There are guided tours around the church (Vörösmarty u.).

ing its original furnishings, is currently used for civil wedding ceremonies. There are guided tours around the house, but this can only be done with prior permission.

It was *András Fáy* (1786–1864), the writer and economist, who built the **winepress building** (1837) on the slopes of Somlyó Hill. The building, decorated by the actor *Gábor Agárdi*'s monumental painting, is now a restaurant.

Most of *Somlyó Hill* is protected. The rocks, the loess wild flowers and the butterflies are of particular interest.

CSÖMÖR

This village, lying just south of the M3 motorway, is first mentioned under the name *Chemer* in a document dating from 1135. Having been laid waste during the Turkish occupation the area was resettled by Slovaks invited by the Wattay family. The village later became the property of the Grassalkovich family before falling into the hands of Baron Sina and a Belgian bank. In 1811, there was an outbreak of cholera in the village. In 1889, the **HÉV** reached Csömör thus linking the village with Pest.

The **Roman Catholic church**, dedicated to the Holy Trinity, is a single-aisled building with a towered west end. On the altar you can see a painting of the *Holy Trinity Crowning the Blessed Virgin Mary*.

The *Corpus Christi Procession,* which takes place on the second Sunday after Whitsun, is perhaps the most colourful event in the church's calendar. The *Spring Village Festival* takes place just before Whitsun, and the *grape harvest* festivities are held in September.

The ancient marshes in Csömör are a protected area. Here you will find the *white Anemone* and the *Marsh Helleborine*.

Sándor Jávorka, the Kossuth Prize-winning botanist, devoted most his time to the study of wild flowers. It was he who discovered the Golden Drop, one of the hundred most strictly protected plants in Europe, on the slopes of Alsó Hill in Tornanádaska in 1906.

DUNAKESZI is the first town you reach on the M3 when travelling northwards out of the capital. It is now joined up to *Alag,* which is where Fülöp Holitscher built the headquarters, the parade ground and the **course** (1871) belonging to the *Hungarian Equestrian Society*. It is the home of Hungarian three-day eventing. In place of the old *Equestrian Society* there is now a riding school, and the sand gallops are used for training all kinds of horses.

The Vácrátót Arboretum's claim to fame is the tallest bald-cypress in Europe. You will also find yew trees, maples, rare pines and ginkgoes. The greenhouses contain coffee bushes, a cocoa tree and some flowering orchids.

The **botanical garden** in VÁCRÁTÓT (Alkotmány u. 2) was planned by the most famous garden planner of his age, *Vilmos Jámbor*. Work on the garden started in 1872 under the leadership of Henrik Band, and went on for 35 years. Despite the death of its founder and all the uncertainties which followed there are still about 15 thousand species of plants to enjoy in the 28-hectare park. The largest botanical collection in Hungary it is run by the *Ecological and Botanical Research Institute of the Hungarian Academy of Sciences*.

From the Danube to the Galga

Those visiting SZADA should head straight for Bertalan Székely's (1835-1910) studio. With the necessary prior arrangements you can see a collection of Székely's sketches, as well as copies of his most famous works. (Illustrated above you can see Bertalan Székely's The Discovery of the Body of Louis II.). The studio is only open during the weekends.

Veresegyház

The local inhabitants are mainly involved in strawberry growing. The village's coat-of-arms and the painted ceiling in the local parish church both depict strawberries. Kristóf Migazzi's coat-of-arms stand over the entrance to St Elizabeth's **Roman Catholic church** 1777–1778. The painting behind the high altar depicting the church's patron saint dates from the 18th century.

The thermal waters were known as far back as the 1900s, although the **swimming complex** and the **medicinal pools** (Találkozók útja) had to be repaired after the Second World War.

The inhabitants of Veresegyháza excel in several traditional pastimes.

Since 1998, the village has had the distinction of having the only **Bear Sanctuary** in the country, if not in Europe. Over thirty bears and wolves live on a 3.5-hectare site specially designed to recreate their natural habitat. The fencing ensures you can walk around the Bear Sanctuary at the end of Park utca in total safety.

Visitors coming to ŐRBOTTYÁN to enjoy the **lake** can also find Hungary's only **bell foundry**. *Miklós Gombos* was responsible for making the bells for Hungary's multi-towered wooden pavilion at the EXPO in Seville.

*GALGAMÁCSA is unusual in that it survived the Turkish conquest at a time when it was one of the largest communities in the Galga Region. The village later fell into the hands of the Grassalkovich family before becoming crown lands. It was here that the naive painter Juli Vankó (1919-1984) was born.
She painted the picture in the entrance porch of the Roman Catholic church built between 1912 and 1913.
Her paintings and ceramics can be seen in the village museum.*

Aszód

It was here that *József Hajnóczy* (1750– 1795), one of the martyrs of the Jacobin Movement, spent his childhood. *Hungarian Lloyd Aeroplane and Automobile Ltd*, Hungary's largest munitions factory, was founded here in 1914.

It was the Podmaniczkys who populated the town with Slovak peasants, German industrialists and Jewish traders. The Podmaniczky's **old residence** (Szabadság tér 8., 1721, wings 1767–1772) and the **Podmaniczky-Széchenyi Palace** (Szabadság tér 7.) are both currently used as schools.

The ethnographic exhibition at Aszód's Petőfi Museum.

Before coming to Aszód aged thirteen, he had studied in Sárszentlőrinc and then with the Pest Lutherans. His parents were forever having to worry about his poor marks and the fact that he was frequently found "hanging around the theatres". It was this which prompted his father to send Petőfi to the Schola Latina in Aszód. The fact that he finally turned to writing poetry can be put down to the three years that he spent under the tutorship of István Koren, a Domony peasant's son turned teacher.

THE TÁPIÓ REGION

Once in ISASZEG you can follow the path marked with a red line from the **war memorial** commemorating the victorious battle of 6th April 1849, with its reliefs of the leading generals, to the mass grave at *Katonapallag*. (During the battle this was where the dressing station was here.) Since 1948 the Calvinist **Peace and Freedom Memorial Church** has kept the memory of the battle alive. The 15th century Goth-

The war memorial in Isaszeg was built with money raised from a national appeal.

The Lutheran G r a m m a r School, built between 1769 and 1771 was still only a single story building when *Sándor Petőfi* was a pupil. The enlarged, classical building now houses the **museum** named after the great poet (Szontágh lépcső 2.). Apart from the Petrovics family mementoes – Petőfi's father was a Petrovics – there are also displays on the history of the *Galga Region* and the local ethnography.

It was in the **Lutheran church** next door that Petőfi's father was baptised and wedded to Mária Hrúz. It was here also, twenty years later, that their son composed his first poem, *Farewell (Búcsúzás)*. There is nothing to rival the 18th century high altar in Hungary's other Lutheran churches. The infamous *borstal* was founded in 1884.

ic **church** perched on the hill in the middle of Isaszeg can be seen for many miles around. It is one of the few such medieval monuments in the *Gödöllő Hills*.

PÉCEL

It is here on the edge of Pest's suburbs that you will find Pécel **Palace** (Kálvin tér 1.). Pál Ráday, Ferenc Rákóczi II's diplomat and leading light within the Hungarian Protestant Church, started to build the palace during the 1720s. The fresco in the banqueting hall on the first floor was painted in 1766 and the fresco on the roof of the library dates from 1763 (*Mátyás Scherwitz*).

GYÖMRŐ became part of Count Teleki's estate at the end of 18th century. The classical **country house** (Bajczy-Zsilinszky u.) was designed by *József Hild* (1837–1840). Next to the road leading out to Üllő you can see the *Ferenc Rákóczi II. Monument* where he gave his famous Gyömrő speech.

The country house in Gyömrő was built on the same spot as its predecessor, which was burnt down in 1835.

When planning a change in his military campaign in Transdanubia Ferenc Rákóczi II. gave a speech to his people outlining his plans (3rd July 1705). "I don't want an empire. I am not asking for treasures; all I ask for is the courage one expects from a true Hungarian. With this firmly in mind I will truly be able to live and die amongst you!"

In Gyömrő's classical-style **Calvinist church** you can find the carved white carrara marble **relief** forming part of the Vay family tomb (*Antonio Canova*).

SÜLYSÁP was created when Tápiósüly and Tápiósáp were joined together in 1970. Following the Hungarian Conquest it was the Kartal clan who settled in Süly. Sáp, then referred to as Saap, appears in a document of 1279 stating the village belonged to the nuns of Nyúl (Margaret) Island. The two **Roman Catholic churches** come from two very different ages. Süly Church (Kápolna u. 7.) is Gothic (15th century) with some later additions, and Sáp Church (Templom u. 7.) is predominantly Baroque.

NAGYKÁTA

On April 4th 1849, the town was one of the sites of the Battle of Tapióbicske, **Keglevich Palace** being used as a military hospital. The **Roman Catholic church** (Szabadság tér) is primarily Baroque in style (1745). The high altar contains statues of Saint George, Saint Peter and Saint Paul. The stained glass windows, dating from the Horthy period, depict Hungarian saints and the coats-of-arms belonging to some of the towns lost by Hungary at the Treaty of Trianon (1920) – Kolozsvár (Cluj-Napoca), Beszterce (Bistriça) and Marosvásárhely (Tîrgu Mures) in Romania, Újvidék (Novi Sad) in Yugoslavia, and Lőcse (Levoča) and Pozsony (Bratislava) in Slovakia.

Visitors to Nagykáta usually head straight for the swimming pool and the thermal baths on Jászberényi út.

The *Sándor Ofella Folk Group* is famous in these parts. The **Farm Museum** on the edge of Nagykáta gives you insight into rural life in the region.

Farmos-puszta on the edge of the town and the marshy countryside around *Lake Nádas* with its many small ponds is a popular stopping off point for migrating birds. The lake isn't suitable for swimming, but it's good for fishing.

5km north of the town at *Egreskáta Farm* you can see the *Danube-Ipoly National Park's* traditional Hungarian cattle and sheep herds.

TÁPIÓBICSKE

The **War Memorial** on the main road out to Nagykáta, built in 1912 from the proceeds of a national appeal, is a copy of the war memorial in Buda.

During the 1848–49 War for Freedom the rebels had to rely on the help of General Damjanich and his troops to push the Imperial Forces back to the Gödöllő-Isaszeg line. It was only then that the Hungarians were in a position to defeat them. István Fejér and his wife Terézia Csikós buried the remains of the fallen heroes in 1882 in a common grave crowned with a white stone cross. The couple left all their worldly belongings to the village in order that the children of Tápióbicske should receive a fresh bread roll on the anniversary of the battle.

The war memorial commemorates the battle which took place on 4th April 1849.

Every May Tápióbicske hosts a major *motocross* event.

TÁPIÓSZENTMÁRTON

It was here in 1923 that the **"Scythian golden stag"**, a piece of shield decoration dating from the time of the Hungarian Conquest, was found. As the original is kept in the *National Museum* there is only a copy at the *Blaskovich Museum* in Tápiószele (see illustration on the right).

It was from the Blaskovich stables that the racehorse *Kincsem* came. The **Kincsem Equestrian Park,** with its numerous traditional Hungarian domestic animals, hosts equestrian shows, and tours in the "Puszta Bus" and has a one-hundred-bed hotel. Another new attraction is the **thermal bath** on Kincsem út.

Ernő Blaskovich, a local landowner, was a great horse breeder, but he was a small man, and was for this reason loath to send Waternymph to stud as the horse's height made up for his lack of inches when he went riding. Eventually, after four years, Waternymph went to stud with a twelve-year-old stallion called Canbuscan, and their first foal was given the name Kincsem (My Treasure). And a treasure he became. Kincsem, who was unbeaten in 54 races, became world-famous and earned his owner a small fortune.

Tápiószentmárton continues to occupy an important place on the equestrian map. Every November there is a showjumping event and a Saint Martin's Day festival at the Kincsem Equestrian Park. More recently many have come to visit the so-called Attila Mound, which is said to have beneficial effects.

TÁPIÓSZELE, which is also famous for its horse breeding, has one of the most beautiful and most interesting museums in the region (Múzeum u. 4.). The **Blaskovich Museum** has a rare interior which survived the Second World War and the ravages of the 1950s.

Apart from having weapons, pipes and paintings from the 16th to 20th centuries the Blaskovich Museum also has some local archaeological finds. There is also a special room devoted to the Blaskovich stud farm and to Kincsem in particular.

CEGLÉD

The development of the town was influenced by the arrival of the Pest-Szolnok line in 1847, Hungary's second railway line. It was in the railway station that the writer *István Tömörkény* (1866–1917) was born. *Kossuth* started his recruitment drive in Cegléd in September of 1848. There are indeed many places in the town referring to this event.

In 1876, whilst Kossuth was in exile in Turin, a deputation was sent from Cegléd to ask Kossuth to be their Member of Parliament. Kossuth, however, recommended his son rather than himself (1876). Following his father's death (1894) Ferenc Kossuth did in fact become MP for Cegléd.

The statue of Kossuth in Cegléd's Szabadság tér (*János Horvay*) later served as the model for the Kossuth Statue in New York.

Visitors to the town can make the most of the **Thermal Baths**. Although further developments are expected three fully-staffed covered pools. A picturesque lake is situated in the three-hectares of grounds.

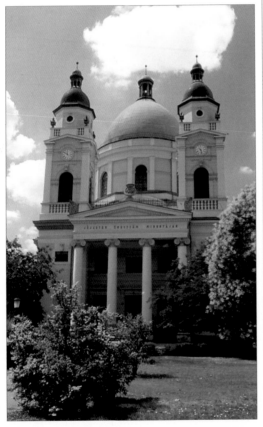

The Kossuth Balcony from the Zöldfa Inn in Bratislava managed to find its way into the garden of the classical Calvinist church (József Hild) in Szabadság tér. From here Kossuth declared the March Decrees, which were later ratified by Franz Joseph and introduced by the country's first Prime Minister Lajos Batthyány.

The classical **Church of the Holy Cross** can be found in Kossuth tér, and the *Trinity Column* (*György Kiss*) stands on the very spot where Louis Kossuth, standing on an oak table taken from the town hall, gave his famous recruitment address.

The Kossuth Museum (Múzeum u. 5.) in Cegléd contains personal items, pieces of furniture and other objects of interest associated with the great politician.

In nearby CEGLÉDBERCEL you will find the **Ruttner Equestrian Farm** offering riding and showjumping to keen amateurs at their covered and open-air arenas.

"YOU CAN ONLY SEE TWO TOWERS"

NAGYKŐRÖS

The Kossuth and Arany cults both flourish in Nagykőrös. It was from the balcony of the **Town Hall**, on 25th September 1848, that Kossuth called upon the people of Nagykörös to mobilize. The *Kossuth Statue* pays homage to this. János Arany lived in the town during the 1850s. This explains the presence of a marble bust of the great poet. In 1925, Kázmér Dezső, the mayor of Nagykőrös, opened a museum mostly made up of items from his own personal collection (1929).

The Great Teachers sculptural group (Imre Varga) includes József Háló Kováts, the translator of Aeneis, and the gunpowder and detonator producers Ferenc Jánosi and Ferenc Mentovich.

The classical-style **János Arany Museum** (Ceglédi út 19.) was once a stud-farm and then a hussars' barracks. The permanent collection opens with the words *"Hey, Nagykőrös, famous town...!"* The exhibition includes a section on the *Calvinist grave posts* you can find in the area lying between the Danube and the Tisza.

The 18th century altar painting of St Ladislas fighting the Cumans in **St Ladislas's church** in Szabadság tér presented by Count Keglevich was painted in Nagyszombat (Trnava, Slovakia). The recent paintings on the walls and ceiling were painted to the designs of *Antal Nemcsics.*

In the garden of the Calvinist church in Szabadság tér, with its eclectic-style west front by Ernő Foerk and Gyula Sándy, stands Alajos Stróbl's statue of János Arany.
The teacher's house, now a school, was where Arany and his family lived between 1856 and 1860, a fact recorded on the marble tablet and the bronze relief.

The Pest County **History of Education Exhibition** can be found in the old school building (Helmeczy u. 1.)

In KŐRÖSTETÉTLEN you can find the **Millennium Monument** (Árpád-halom) put up by the Nagykőrös town council in 1896, on what is believed to have been the very spot from which Prince Árpád departed on his journey of conquest. It was whilst a teacher in Nagykőrös in 1855 that *János Arany* wrote *The Tetétlen Mound* on Gedeon Tanárky's Farm. It was on another Tetétlen farmstead that the poet got to know the herdsman Márton Csonka, a friendship which formed the basis for his poems *Old Herdsman* and *Burial of the Old Herdsman.*

ABONY

Looking around Abony you can see both the ancient and modern. **St Stephen's Church** (1773–1785) in Kossuth tér has a high altar from the same period by the Eger architect *Mihály Sperer*. The depiction of St Stephen the Protomartyr, however, dates from the 20th century (*István Takács*). To mark Abony's formally becoming a town, a chiming clock was added to the late Baroque **Calvinist church** in Kálvin tér. The **Lajos Abony Village Museum** (Vasút u. 16.) has an exhibition on *the history of Abony's farmsteads* as well as a display calling itself *Exploring the Old Historical Monuments*.

The inside of the Abony Village Museum is arranged to look like the interiors of old rural dwellings.

Many of the manor houses belonging to Abony's ancient families (the Vigyázó, Ungár, Sivó, Márton, Györe families) are all protected buildings despite having been remodelled. The **Animal and Leisure Park** also has a historical flavour. You can see traditional Hungarian breeds living in their natural habitat.

Abony is also made famous for a reference to its twin towers in Zoltán Kodály's Háry János.

We now leave the area around Cegléd and head northwestwards for a landscape inhabited by many a distinguished figure. It was in ALBERTIRSA that Samuel Tessedik (1742–1820), the Lutheran priest and founder of the first agricultural college in the country, was born. There is a memorial tablet referring to this on the wall of the vicarage.

The cemetery contains an interesting neo-Romanesque chapel, the **Szapáry Chapel**, designed by the architect *Miklós Ybl* in 1860.

The waters at the **open-air pool** in Dolina utca are recommended for the treatment of many maladies on account of their high mineral content.

PILIS

The village of Pilis may have disappeared completely if landowner János Miklós Beleznay, a favourite and supporter of both Ferenc Rákóczi II. and the Habsburgs hadn't settled its Slovak population here.

> *Memories of the imperial favourite were once preserved at Pilis's Jajgató Hill. Here, Dániel Práczki, a local serf, was tortured and hanged. He had gone to join Péró Szegedinác, the captain of the rebel Serbian forces at Arad (1735). However, Beleznay's Haiduk forces caught up with him just outside Cegléd and drove him all the way back to Pilis. The imperial army and Baron István Orczy's nobles eventually managed to quell what was a two-week rebellion.*

Baroque **Beleznay-Nyáry Hall** (Kossuth u. 31.), built in about 1710, is one of the oldest halls in the region. Many writers are known to have visited, and it was here that *József Kármán* wrote *Fanni's Traditions*. Near the **Millecentenarium Park** in the peaty flatlands you can find the source of the *Gerje* bubbling out of the earth.

Alföld landscape

MONOR's excellent soil makes it ideal for growing seeds. Walking down the *Forrás Valley* and out to *Strázsahegy* you can enjoy a microclimate rich in wild flowers, as well as approximately one thousand **wine cellars**.

ÜLLŐ was owned by Prince Árpád's third son, whose name, in the form of *Illew*, was first mentioned in a document dating from 1289. Many centuries later *Sándor Petőfi* was a guest (1847) and the actress *Lujza Blaha* also lived here for a time. *Katalin Karády* gave her final performance in Üllő before she emigrated.

The most interesting thing at the Roman Catholic church (1707–1752) is the so-called **Cuman Cross** dating from the Turkish period.

Üllő was where the post coaches made their first change of horses having set off from Pest. The rather slow and unwieldy post-chaises were replaced by the smaller, lighter post coaches in the 1820s. The coaches, which carried five passengers and travelled day and night, could do the journey from Vienna to Budapest in 28-30 hours.

THE MIDDLE OF THE COUNTRY

The 11 metre-high hexagonal pyramid (József Kerényi, 1978) on the edge of PUSZTAVACS *marks the geographical centre of Hungary, on the co-ordinates 47° 11' north and 19° 30' east.*
The ball on the top was made by Tamás Molnár and the sun dial by Gábor Gáti.

You can walk for as far as the eye can see...

Dabas is first mentioned in 1264, when it was described as the residence of the royal drummers. The residences you see in the town were built by gentry families who had made their fortunes selling corn during the Napoleonic Wars. The Baroque **Calvinist church** (Bajcsy-Zsilinszky u. 8.) has the porcelain wreath *Louis Kossuth* sent to his father's grave from Turin (1880). In the garden you can see a few classical gravestones rescued from the cemetery in *Alsódabas*. On the late Baroque walls of the **Kossuth House** (Kossuth u. 19.) you can see the inscription: *"In this house lived and died, on 13th June 1839, László Kossuth, Louis Kossuth's father"*. After the arrest of his son his aged father managed to escape to Dabas (1837) aided and abetted by *Miklós Wesselényi*. His grave can be found in the cemetery. What is now the *Kossuth Cultural Centre* (Szent István u. 58.) was once the local casino, one of the first such buildings in Hungary (*Ferenc Löszl*, 1836).

The woods between Ócsa and Dabas can be reached either on foot or by bicycle. The house belonging to the Ócsa Nature Reserve (Bercsényi u. 4.) has an ethnographical museum and an exhibition about the local arts and crafts. You can even rent a bike. Local dishes are also served if the visit is arranged in advance.

ÓCSA

During the course of the 19th century, Ócsa church suffered several natural catastrophes. The 13th and 14th century wall paintings were uncovered in 1900. In the chancel you can see a Madonna surrounded by the twelve apostles, to the north are the legends of Saint Ladislas and Saint Margaret, and opposite them the remains of a Final Judgement.

It was from here that Ferenc Rákóczi II. called the 1705 Szécsény National Assembly (see p.803). The Premonstratensians built what is now the **Calvinist church** (Bercsényi u. 2.) in about 1250. The western towers were given an extra story between 1922 and 1924. The prayer niche (mihrab) dates from the Turkish period.

The Calvinists have been using the church since 1652, although the Roman Catholics have made two unsuccessful attempts to get the church back. The Baroque **Roman Catholic church** (Bajcsy-Zsilinszky u.) was eventually built with help from Maria Theresa and Kristóf Migazzi, Bishop of Vác (*János Mayerhoffer*, 1774).

It's worthwhile looking at the old **wooden grave posts** in the old Calvinist cemetery. The carved motifs refer to the age, economic situation and the married status of the person buried.

Of the almost one hundred thatched cellars you can see carved into the side of *Öreg Hill* only one is original.

It is in DUNAHARASZTI that the *Danube Valley Main Channel* branches off towards Baja from the *Ráckeve (Soroksár) branch of the River Danube*. A channel linking it up with the River Tisza was also planned but it only ever got as far as Dabas. The traditional floating candles ceremony, which takes place on 16th May, commemorates the arrival by boat of the German settlers at the end of the 17th century.

The rare plants on the Dead Channel at Dunaharaszti and in the three hectares around Calvary Hill mean that both areas enjoy protected status. The Ráckeve branch of the Danube is very popular with anglers and lovers of water sports.

RÁCKEVE

Originally one of the areas settled by the Árpád clan, Ráckeve was a popular royal hunting place. In 1440, what was then the flourishing village of Szentábrahám was besieged by Serbian (rác) traders given royal permission to settle there having fled from *Kovin* (Kevi, Keve) lower down the Danube. In the 16th century *Máté Skarica* made the town into one of the bastions of the Hungarian Reformation.

By 1622, like *Csepel Island*, Ráckeve was owned by Pál Esterházy. Later owned by Donát Heister, it was later sold to Prince Eugene of Savoy, the victor at the Battle of Zenta (1697). Following the settlement of the Germans in the 18th century Ráckeve had three distinct ethnic communities.

From 1945 onwards the Savoy Palace was left to fall to rack and ruin. However following renovation work in the 1970s the palace was once again filled with Baroque paintings. The vaulted hall and the drawing room were fitted with chandeliers taken from the demolished National Theatre.

Eugene of Savoy never actually stayed in the **palace** (Kossuth u. 95.) he had built for himself in Ráckeve (*Johann Lucas Hildebrandt*, 1702–1720). It is Hungary's earliest Baroque palace. The Classical dome was built following the fire of 1802. The building, now a conference centre, can be visited if the visit is arranged in advance.

The Church of the Blessed Virgin Mary in Ráckeve (Viola u. 1.) is the only Gothic Serbian Orthodox church in Hungary (1487). The lower part of the free-standing tower is 16th century, whilst the rest of it is Baroque (1758). The walls of the church are completely covered with 18th century Byzantine-style frescos. The iconostasis, the bishop's throne and the throne of the Blessed Virgin Mary, the icon holders and the Easter sepulchre were all made between 1768 and 1771.

The late Baroque **Roman Catholic church** (Szent István tér, 1791–1799) contains the Saint Anthony altar dating from around 1800, and the Saint John Nepomuk altar made in the 19th century. The mythological paintings (1994) are by Ráckeve artist *László Patay* (1932–2002).

On the pillar base of the *Statue of Árpád* (*Gyula Szász*) in Ráckeve (Árpád tér) you can see the prince's coat-of-arms and a depiction of the celebrations on the island following the birth of Árpád's son Zsolt. The **Árpád Museum** can be found in the neo-Baroque *Münich House* (Kossuth L. u. 34.). The collection contains folk art relating particularly

According to local legend, and indeed contemporary literary research, the hero of Sándor Petőfi's famous ballad Brave Soldier János was born in Ráckeve. The heroic deeds of the real János Nepomuki Horváth are recorded at the Árpád Museum.

to life on the river, and items connected to the town's historical guilds and societies.

The *Pereg Woods* lying on the far side of the bridge crossing the *Ráckeve Danube* are popular with anglers and those interested in water sports. The **"boat market"** (Dunasor) is also an interesting sight. Ráckeve's calendar is brightened up by the *Kisduna Folk Music and Dance Festival* held in the second half of August, the Saint Stephen's Day Chinese Lantern Regatta and the Serbian *Festival of the Blessed Virgin Mary*.

THE DANUBE REGION

KISKUNLACHÁZA

Following the floods of 1741 the inhabitants of the riverside village of Laczháza were forced to settle on the site where Kiskunlacháza stands today. It was only at the beginning of the 20th century that the name was given its Kiskun prefix. The most distinctive things about the Baroque **Calvinist church** (*József Peithmüller*, 1771–1772) are the Louis Seize pulpit and the 18th century **pillory post** next door.

The full-length bronze **Kossuth Statue** (*János Horvay*, 1902), a copy of the figure of Kossuth in Cegléd, was put up to mark the one hundredth anniversary of the great politician's birth and paid for by public subscription. According to local legend Kossuth gave a speech on that very spot.

Opposite the late Baroque **Church of St Michael** in Pereg stands **"Angel House"** which contains an interesting ethnographical collection.

Kiskunlacháza's calendar boasts motocross events, the *Pereg Patronal Festival* and the *Kiskun Cultural Festival*. You can go fishing on the *Danube* or on the *fishing lake* lying on the road leading out towards Bugyi.

The old gravel quarries at DÉLEGYHÁZA have been turned into a 200-hectare **lake system.** Lake number 5, Hungary's first naturist outdoor swimming complex, is rented by the *Hungarian Naturist Association*. There are also some very basic camping sites next to the lakes. An ecological village is currently being built. The *Délegyháza Festival* in June marks the beginning of the summer tourist season.

DÖMSÖD

During the Middle Ages, Dömsöd was given to the queen as a wedding present and later belonged to the bailiff of Csepel Island. During the Turkish occupation the Turks diligently defended the Danube Mills for their lucrative wheat tithes. Nowadays the Danube repays those who go fishing on *Dömsöd Island*. It's also good for water sports.

The square in front of the **Calvinist church** (*József Jung*, 1774–1776) was where some of *Ludas Matyi* (*Kálmán Nádasdy*, 1949) was filmed. The days *Petőfi* spent here are recalled in the **Memorial House** (Bajcsy-Zsilinszky u. 6.).

Petőfi's stay in Dömsöd marked the beginning of his career as a poet. As he wrote in his poem "Prophecy":
"The youth's hand siezed a lyre; in exultation He wedded to its strings, his flaming words."

His parents lived in house number 15 on the street which is now named after their famous son. You can also see a sculpture of Sándor Petőfi (László Marton, 1972) in Petőfi tér.

APAJ

Here you can find some traditional Hungarian **plains** which have a lot in common with the famous Hortobágy.

Apajpuszta lies in an area of the *Kiskunság National Park* known as the *Upper Kiskunság Alkaline Plain*. When it rains its calciferous-sodic soil turns into oozy mud, but when it's dry the ground turns rock hard and huge cracks appear upon the surface. Of all the salt resistant flowers which you can find here the best-known is the purple salt aster. The free-range animals, the traditional Hungarian sheep and cattle ensure the survival of the ancient grasslands. About 150 bustards are known to nest here. (For further information see the chapter dealing with the National Parks.)

SZIGETSZENTMIKLÓS

In the Middle Ages this popular fishing village on the *Ráckeve (Soroksár) branch of the Danube* stood on royal lands.

It was here that *Lajos Biró* (1856–1931), the New Guinea expert, lived. The life and work of *Kossuth Prize-winning* musicologist *Jenő Ádám* (1896–1982) is celebrated at the **house** named after him (Árpád u. 29.).

During the last weekend in July Apaj hosts the famous Kiskunság Shepherding and Equestrian Festival at which the old shepherding and horse-herding traditions are celebrated in a colourful programme of events.

The **Baptist church** (1996) is used for organ recitals, and it is here you will find the *International Baptist Theological Academy*.

The 314m *Lakihegy Antenna* is of course instantly recognisable.

"Radio Budapest" first went on air at 5pm on 1st December 1925. By the end of its first month the station already had seventeen thousand subscribers. Today it is calculated that at least four million get their radio signals transmitted from Lakihegy.

SZÁZHALOMBATTA

Despite being known for its power station and its oil refineries Százhalombatta's history goes back a long way. The collections at the **Matrica Museum** (Gesztenyés u. 1–3.) are dominated by archaeological finds. The museum is named after the Roman town which once stood here. It was then during the Roman period that the bridge over the *Benta* was built.

The Archaeological Park (István király u.) is one of the more unusual sights in Százhalombatta. One of the Iron Age 115 mounds (halom) after which the town is named can be found here.

The Baroque **Orthodox church** (Alkotmány u. 2.) was built in 1750 by the Serbs who settled in the area during the 1690s.

Százhalombatta hosts the *Summerfest International Folk Dance Festival* (August), the *Wind Festival* (on the Sunday closest to the 3rd September), the *Batta Festival* (the last weekend in September), and the *Batta Christmas* on the last Sunday before Christmas. An **outdoor swimming complex** can be found in DUNAFÜRED.

BUDA'S SATELLITES

BIATORBÁGY is famous for the *Matuska Szilveszter* railway outrage of 1931. The **viaduct** where it happened stands to this very day. As for the town itself there is the Baroque **Szily-Fáy Palace** (Fő u. 37.). The town's oldest building, the ruins of the 13th century **Church of the Holy Cross,** can be found in the Calvinist cemetery on the road going out towards Sóskút. *József Hild* designed the classical **Sándor-Metternich Palace** (Szentháromság tér 4.) in 1823. When owned by Móric Sándor the palace was renowned for its horses.

Móric Sándor's favourite horse was called Tatár, a run-of-the-mill horse he picked up in Pest. He led the horse by the reins to the grand hall of his Buda residence, from where he proceeded to ride down the staircase to the courtyard. In doing this Tatár had passed his first test.

ÉRD

Archaeologists have proved that a prehistoric settlement existed in and around Érd. Apart from a Bronze Age **earthwork** and a series of Iron Age **barrows** forming part of the Százhalombatta system, Germanic and Avar cooking utensils from the age of the migrations are also in evidence. Following the destruction of the Turkish period the area was repopulated with Greek Orthodox and Catholic Serbs followed later by the *Germans* and the *Slovaks*.

There is a 23m-high 16th century **minaret** (Ó-falu) which stood in the one-time village of *Hamzsabég*. The mosque which once stood next to it is said to have collapsed following the floods of 1838. A concrete niche marks the spot of the *mihrab* (the prayer niche). **St Michael's Church** (Szent Mihály tér) was built in the Baroque style (1702–1723). The walls you can see at *Kutyavár (Érdliget)* are said to be the remains of the building where Matthias Corvinus kept his hounds.

The old salt house has been enlarged and turned into the *Liget Thermal Hotel* (Római út 9.). At *Wimpffen Hall* in the new town you can find the **Hungarian Geographical Museum** (Budai u. 4.).

It was in *Diósd*, which is actually part of Érd that the **Radio and Television Museum** was opened in 1995 on the 70th anniversary of radio broadcasting in Hungary.

BUDAÖRS

This picturesque town is quite rightly known as the western *gateway to Budapest*. It is here that the Vienna and the Balaton motorways converge, and it is not far from a junction with the M0 motorway which by-passes the capital. The town, which was named after the chieftain Örs from the time of the Hungarian Conquest, was depopulated during the Turkish period. It was the Zichy family who repopulated the area with German settlers. The **Ferenc Riedl Local History Collection** (Budapesti út 47.) gives an account of the Germans' existence in the town. Because most of the German population was deported in 1946 and 1947, the museum plays an important role in recording their customs and their culture.

The short walk up to *Calvary Hill* complements a visit to the museum rather nicely. It is there you can find the **Golgotha sculptural group** (18th and 19th centuries). During the spring the town organises the *Budaörs Festival*. If you happen to be in or around Budaörs during the first half of May you might catch the *Airshow* at the **Budaörs Airfield**.

The Csíki Hills and the Twenty-Four Oxen Dolomite Rocks provide Budaörs with its picturesque backdrop. They are also great places for walking. (Illustration: a sandlizard).

The Turkish Jumps, caught between the old main road and the motorway, date from the time when Buda was liberated from the Turks in 1686. Legend has it that the Hungarians drove the fleeing Turks out to the rocks where there was no other alternative but to jump off them to a certain death...

ZSÁMBÉK

Archaeologists have proved that the place was inhabited as far back as the Stone Age. The Celts, the Romans and the Avars also left their marks here. During the Middle Ages the town belonged to a French knight by the name of Aynard.

Leaving Zsámbék the abiding memories are the two Romanesque towers and the remains of the rose window.

In 1490 Zsámbék was John Corvin's, later it was the Zichys' before falling into the hands of the treasury. Zsámbék's **Premonstratensian Church** was built on the site of an 11th century chapel. The church, built in about 1258, was later occupied by the Pauline Order. It was badly damaged during the Turkish period, but having been rebuilt it was then to suffer an earthquake in 1763. It has been a ruin ever since.

The *Zsámbék Saturdays*, a series of concerts and theatrical performances held between June and August either in the *Cultural Centre* or in the ruins of the church, have become extremely popular.

Work on the Zichy Palace (Zichy tér) began in the fourteenth century. During the Turkish period it became one of Pilis County's great border castles. The Zichy family remodelled the castle in 1699, turning it into a country residence.

The so-called **Turkish Road** was built by the Turks during the 16th century. It was restored to its original condition in 1892. Many are attracted to the **Lamp Museum** (Magyar u. 18.), and there is also a **Swabian Peasant Cottage** which is open to the public.

THE ZSÁMBÉK BASIN

PÁTY

The royal saddlers lived here during the Árpád period. The classical **Splényi (Várady) Palace** (Rákóczy u. 35.) has a fence made of gun barrels used during the 1848 Revolution. The old bailiff's house (Rákóczi u. 13.), now the **Community Centre,** has a permanent local history exhibition and also hosts temporary art shows.

In the courtyard of the Páty Community Centre you will find the **Veteran Car and Motorbike Museum,** which is open on Sundays throughout the summer. (It is advisable to book your visit in advance!)

The 300 19th century cellars on **Pince Hill** host the *Cellar Days* held at the end of May.

The atrium at the **Maltese Cross's** house is often used for art exhibitions.

The name TELKI, and that of its Benedictine Abbey, is first mentioned in a document dating from 1198. The writer *János Kodolányi* (1899–1969) was born here, and there is a **room** dedicated to his life and work in the house where he used to live (Fő u.).

BUDAJENő belonged to the Scottish Benedictines who had an abbey in nearby Telki. The Catholic **Cemetery Chapel** (Kálvária Hill) dates from the Árpád period, and there is a 12th century relief embedded in its wall. The Baroque **Roman Catholic church** (Kossuth u.) was built by the Benedictines (*Ignác Oracsek*). The old classical-style **Benedictine Monastery**, now used as a primary school, has the Benedictine coat-of-arms on its façade (c. 1800).

Nowadays, TÖK is most famous for the *Patkó Csárda* (Fő u. 1.). Apart from serving meals the inn offers accommodation and horse-riding facilities. The painted coffered ceiling (*István Szabó*, 1740), which once covered the Baroque **Calvinist church,** can now be seen at the *Museum of Fine Arts* in Budapest.

Apart from being extremely picturesque the cellars in Tök (Szőlő Hill) also have a wine museum.

In PERBÁL, next to the late Baroque parish church, there is a wooden *sculptural composition* amongst the Stations of the Cross dedicated to the local German community deported in the years immediately following the Second World War. At the end of July visiting Germans and the descendants of those who lived here hold a three-day *patronal festival.*

In 1980, Szentendre's efforts in the field of urban preservation were rewarded with the Hild Memorial Medal. What it has is an 18th century townscape unparalleled in Hungary. In the middle of the main square stands the Merchants' Society's monument, the Baroque Merchants' Cross with its painted tin icons, erected in 1763 when the town was spared the plague. Legend has it that plague victims were buried head downwards underneath the monument.

SZENTENDRE

After the Illyrians and the Celts came the Romans. It was they who built the Danube *limes,* the *Ulcisia Castra,* at the beginning of the 2nd century, upon which the town served as an important station. It was later named after Saint Andrew. Following the Tatar invasion the town fell into decline. The town reemerged when the capital moved to Buda in the 14th century.

The different ethnic groups formed separate communities within the town. Szentendre has changed very little since the 18th century.

Szentendre's links with the southern Slavs date back to the loss of the Battle of Kosovo in 1389, when more and more communities sought sanctuary in the Kingdom of Hungary. These new settlers were known as "rácok" after the Latin name for Serbia – Rascia.

Following the recapture of Belgrade by the Turks in 1690 40 thousand Serbs under the leadership of Arzén Csernojevics, the Patriarch of Ipek.

The block of houses on the eastern side of the main square (Fő tér 2–5.) is perhaps the best example of mercantile architecture in the town. The houses were built together under a common roof following a fire at the beginning of the 18th century. Each of the five houses still has its original layout.

The Szentendre Picture Gallery, which took over the ground floor in 1978, now uses the area for its permanent exhibition.

The Baroque Greek Orthodox **Blagovesztenszka Church**, or *Greek Church* (*András Mayerhoffer*, 1752) has a western balcony coming out from the tower and an oak rococo doorway.

Visiting all Szentendre's exhibitions is no mean feat as there are so many of them. The **Károly Ferenczy Museum** (Fő tér 6.) is devoted to the work of the post-Impressionist artist of that name, as well as that of some of his contemporaries. *Margit Kovács*'s pottery can be seen at an **exhibition** laid out in an old Baroque tradesman's house (Vastagh György u.1.). In Fő tér there is a **museum** dedicated to work of one of Hungary's finest modernist painters to have worked in the Cubist manner *János Kmetty*.

Károly Ferenczy: Pebble-throwing Boys

The **MűvészetMalom** (Dunakanyar krt.) is a lively place putting on contemporary art shows, festivals and other cultural events. One should also add the **Roman Lapidarium** (Dunakanyar krt.), the **Puppet Collection** (Sas u. 18.) and the **Transport Museum** (at the end of the HÉV) to our seemingly never-ending list.

The southwestern buttress of the tower at the 13th and 14th century **Roman Catholic church** (Templom tér,) has one of the country's oldest **sun dials**. Inside the church you can see some frescos painted by members of the Szentendre Art Colony (1938). Next door there is a **museum** dedicated to the work of *Béla Czóbel* and his wife *Mária Modok*.

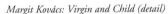

Margit Kovács: Virgin and Child (detail)

Szentendre street scene

In one of the streets leading into it you will find an **exhibition** devoted to the work of constructivist *Jenő Barcsay* (Dumtsa J. u. 10.) The **Marzipan Museum** and the **Museum patisserie** (12., 14.) lie a little further down the road at number 14, and just opposite you can try a real Dobos cake at the **Lajos Dobos Coffee House and Museum**. There are also museums in the town devoted to the works of *Lajos Vajda, Jenő Kerényi, Tibor Boromisza, Imre Ámos* and *Margit Anna*.

The Greek Orthodox Cathedral – the **Beograda-templom** - (Alkotmány u.) forms the centre of the Serbian community. It was built by the ancestors of those who arrived from Belgrade. The paintings on the iconostasis (1777–1781) are by the artist *Vazul Osztoics* from Novi Sad in Vojvodina, and the rococo doorway is the work of local blacksmith *Márton Ginesser* (1772). The Pomáz-born composer *Tihamér Vujisics* lies buried in the church's garden. It is here also that you will find the **Serbian Orthodox Ecclesiastical Museum** (Pátriárka u. 5.).

Rab Ráby House (Ráby tér 1.) in the Dalmatian part of the town probably belonged to a grape grower. It is thought that *Mátyás Ráby*, a local corruption expert, and hero of one of *Mór Jókai*'s novels lived here.

If you take the Pilisszentlászló-Visegrád turning on road number 11 you come to the **Open-Air Ethnographical Museum** (Sztaravodai út).

The Alföld market town town and the collections of buildings from the Bakony Hills and the Balaton Highlands are growing continually. The Ethnographical Exhibition, with its 15 thousand objects, is open all year round, as is the Gallery.

The museum has been exhibiting the buildings, the domestic habits and lifestyle of the *Upper Tisza Region*, the *Lesser Hungarian Plain* and *Western Transdanubia* since 1967.

In the valley above the open-air museum you will find the *Old Spring*, the decorated well cover of which was made during the 18th century. It is here that the local Serbian community hold their traditional summer celebrations.

A WHO'S WHO OF SZENTENDRE
Imre Ámos, painter, 1907–1944
Margit Anna, painter, 1913–1991
Jenő Barcsay, painter, graphic artist, 1900–1988
Tibor Boromisza, painter, 1880–1960
Béla Czóbel, painter, and member of The Eight 1883-1976
Károly Ferenczy, painter, 1862–1917
Béni Ferenczy, sculptor, 1890–1967
Noémi Ferenczy, painter, tapestry artist, 1890–1957
Jenő Kerényi, sculptor, 1908–1975
János Kmetty, painter, 1889–1975
Margit Kovács, potter, sculptor, 1902–1977
Mária Modok, painter, 1896–1971
Lajos Vajda, painter, 1904–1941
Tihamér Vujisics, composer, 1929–1975

ROYAL HUNTING GROUNDS

SOLYMÁR

If you approach the village from main road number 10 you will pass the *British Military Cemetery* containing the graves of the RAF pilots shot down over Hungary during the Second World War. Medieval sources tell us it was here that the king's falconers lived. Sigismund and Vladislas II. in particular were known to have been particularly keen on keeping the birds. **Szarka Castle** (Vár-hegy) was built by István Lackfy in about 1370. After Buda fell to the Turks in 1541, the castle had a military role of sorts. The Turks set fire to it in 1561, and by 1580 the Pilis Valley's last fortification had been reduced to ruins. The castle was excavated between 1929 and 1940.

In Solymár's **Roman Catholic church** (Templom tér, 1782-1799) there is an altar painting by *Ferenc J. Falconer* which includes a depiction of 18th century Solymár.

The footpath marked with a green line leads from the church up *Zsíros Hill* and on to the 550metre-high *Nagy-szénás*. It is possible to go down into the 3km-long *Ördöglyuk Cave*, but only in the company of a guide.

Solymár's *patronal festival* is in September, whilst *the grape harvest parade and ball* both take place in October. The ethnic Germans' traditional *children's dance festival* also takes place here.

> There used to be many famous inns in and around Solymár. Amongst the many hostelries in Solymár there was the Okkeli, in Bia the Holczer Inn and the Gede Tavern. In Pilisszentiván there was the Gábel, in Torbágy the Ómüller and the Hegedűs, and in Nagykovácsi the Kastély.
>
> Whether one drank wine or beer depended very much on the ethnic character of the village, and the background and the social standing of the clientele. In the taverns around Buda it didn't take much in the way of alcohol for the ethnic Hungarians to start mocking the Swabian accents of the ethnic Germans drinking at the table next door.
>
> Mind you they never did it loud enough for anybody to notice.

NAGYKOVÁCSI

During the Middle Ages it was the royal blacksmiths who lived in this upland (342m) village, and in the 18th century it was the Germans who

The old Teleki Palace in Nagykovácsi is now an agricultural vocational secondary school.

settled up here. The present inhabitants come from *Transylvania*, the *Jászság*, and what is now *Slovakia* (1946).

Apart from the Baroque and the classical buildings there is the millecentenary monument, the war memorial (Rákóczi u.) and the **monument** to the deported ethnic Germans. The old Swabian **gravestones** in the cemetery make interesting reading.

The *Linum Arts Festival* in August is named after a rare local *flax* found only in the Pilis Hills. It's an event which includes the *Csillageső International Folk Dance Festival* and the *"crossKovácsi"* fell-running and mountain biking event.

Following paths marked red you can make your way to the **Wildlife Park** in BUDAKESZI.

Whereas Nagykovácsi is the best place from which to reach the *Danube-Ipoly National Park's Nagy-Szénás Nature Trail*, the *Jág Nature Trail* is best approached from Pilisszentistván.

PILISVÖRÖSVÁR

Once upon a time the most important road in Pannonia ran through the town, something proved by the Roman milestones and gravestones uncovered here. Germans settled in Pilisvörösvár following the Turkish occupation.

> The country's largest dolomite mine was opened up on the edge of Pilisvörösvár. As late as the 1920s amply dressed head-scarved Swabian women sold ground dolomite powder on the streets of Buda at a time when it was still used as scouring powder. They also produced "Buda Earth" red dye locally.

The **Roman Catholic church** was consecrated in the 17th century and dedicated to the Blessed Virgin Mary. The Madonna and Child over the high votive altar in the Baroque **St Mary's Chapel** is rococo. There is another Madonna and Child in the **Erdei Chapel** (Kápolna u.), a chapel built from public funds.

You can go riding and fishing at *Örömvölgy Farm* at the end of Bányató utca. The village's famous windband can be heard at the Swabian Ball (end of January-beginning of February), at the *Pilisvörösvár Festival* in August and at the *Grape Picking Parade* (at the end of September).

Walkers are particularly fond of the Nagy-szénás and its immediate surroundings. Rock climbers head for the Csaba Tower. The red paths heading northwards go to Pilisszentkereszt, whilst the blue ones either go to the Legény and Leány Caves via Piliscsév, or to the Klasztrompuszta, where you will find the remains of the mother house (13th century) of the Pauline Order next to the tourist cabin.

PILISCSABA

One of the Romans' great military campaigns ended here. Following the Turkish occupation the village German and Slovak families settled here. The Baroque Roman Catholic church was built by Clarissan nuns from Buda (1778–1781). The **Seated Madonna** dates from the 14th century.

In the old Red Army barracks stands the *Péter Pázmány Catholic University* (*Imre Makovecz*, 1991–1994), a mixture of his house style and older buildings yet to be given the full treatment. The auditorium, the *Stefánium* is also used for concerts, and the student residences offer summer accommodation.

The existence of the holiday centre at *Klotild-liget* is due entirely to the building of the Budapest-Esztergom railway. It is on this stretch of line between Pilisvörösvár and Piliscsaba that you will find the longest **tunnel** in Hungary (779.5m). Hungarian Railways (MÁV) has a timetabled "nostalgia" steam locomotive service between Budapest and Esztergom.

Good fishing can be had at the 4-hectare *Lake Garancsi* situated next to the road going to Tinnye.

Of the 60 thousand hectares of land bounded by Esztergom, Piliscsaba, Pilisvörösvár and the Danube a third belongs to the *Pilis State Forestry Commission*.

POMÁZ

In the *Klissza-dűlő* a **Gothic church and a manor house** built by Louis the Great have been uncovered. The outlines of the walls have been marked out in the ground.

The **Serbian Orthodox church** was built at the beginning of the 18th century. Its iconostasis and carved and painted liturgical furniture should not be missed at any cost.

Pomáz is the best place to set out from on walks up into the Pilis. It doesn't take long to get to Pomáz by HÉV, car or even by bicycle. The yellow path takes you from the village to Oszoly-tető. The green path goes past the János Spring before climbing up to Kőhegy (366m) and then onto the Petőfi Lookout Point (the poet went there in the autumn of 1845). From the János Spring a path marked with a blue cross takes you on a slow ascent to the Lajos Spring and the tourist cabin nearby. The spring was named after Louis the Great who hunted in the area.

CSOBÁNKA

In Csobánka you will find a **pilgrimage church** up on *Hosszú Hill* with a spring, *Szentkút*, next door. This was originally a Serbian **pilgrimage place**. It subsequently became popular amongst the Catholics (1844), a tradition which was German in origin.

The **Saint Hubert Holiday Centre** was built next to what was the *Margitliget Sanatorium*.

Going northwards out of the village, following the red markings past the **Csikóváralja tourist cabin,** you eventually come to the ancient *Holdvilág Ditch*, a site with religious connotations, but mind the vertical iron ladder taking you up towards the *Lajos Spring*!

Going southwards along the red path you come first to the *Kevély Saddle* before the final ascent up to *Nagy-Kevély* (534m). Once there you can enjoy some stunning **views**. If you continue along the red path, you eventually come to the *Csillaghegy HÉV station*.

> *It was in 1898 that Sándor Martin built the sanatorium on the right bank of the Dera at Margitliget (formerly known as Laszlovszky-liget). In 1909, József Wettenstein, the inventor of the serum against tuberculosis, bought the building and turned it into a T.B. sanatorium. During the First World War the building became an orphanage. Since 1950 it has been a Home for the Mentally Handicapped.*

PILISSZENTKERESZT

All that is left of Béla III.'s sumptuous **Cistercian foundation** (1184) next to the *Dera* at the foot of the *Pilis-tető* are a few ruined walls. The monastery was the scene of the events surrounding the murder in 1213 of Gertrude of Andechs-Meran, Andrew II.'s wife, immortalised in *József Katona*'s drama, *Bánk Bán*. The remains of Gertrude's tomb were found here. The tomb can now be seen in the Hungarian National Gallery in Budapest.

> *Who murdered Gertrude of Andechs-Meran? According to József Katona the culprit was Bánk Bán, Palatine of Hungary. The primary source closest in date to the murder itself (September 28th 1213) claims that the murderer was Peter Comes (bailiff). He appears in Katona's play in the guise of Petúr Bán. Bánk's name is first mentioned in documents dating from 1240. In the Hungarian Picture Chronicle, written a good century later, Bánk is described as being the murderer: "Wretchedly Bánk dipped his sword into the queen's blood."*

The Baroque **Roman Catholic church** (1766) was built by the Pauline Order, and the high altar and side altar were probably also their work (1774). The fresco in the chancel was painted by the Franciscan monk *Asztrik P. Kákonyi* (1970s). Patronal festivals are celebrated here, as they are elsewhere in the region (*Szentkút, Máriakálnok*).

Pilis-tető (757m) is great for walking as is the blue path going towards Csobánka down the valley the *Dera* flows along.

The **limeburners' kilns** are still in operation on the edge of the village. Once past them you enter some rugged countryside dotted with paths, bridges and picnic sites.

Dobogókő

This spot, the highest point in the *Visegrád Hills* (700m), is popular all the year round. Up in the hills lies the **Ödön Téry Memorial**, a stone pyramid built in memory of one of the great pioneers of Hungarian tourism (*Sándor Crisztián*, 1926).

The **Tourist Museum** (*Eötvös Loránd-menedékház*) lies nearby. There are further hiking possibilities at the *Prédikálószék*, *Thirring Rock*, the *Vadálló Boulders*, *Árpád-vár*, the *Rám Ravine*, and the *Szőke Springs,* which all lie in the direction of Dömös and Szentendre.

The flax growing in the dolomite soil has a stalk 10-20cm long and yellow flowers, 2 to 6 of which bloom at any one time.

From the Kétbükkfa Saddle it is possible to reach Pilisszentlélek. It was there, in the Pauline monastery, that the nobles shut the lascivious Ladislas IV. (1272–1290) up with his wife in the vain hope that they would manage to produce an heir.

EXPLORING SZENTENDRE ISLAND

Leányfalu

The first residents of the village's villas were artists, poets and writers. *Zsigmond Móricz* often spent his summers here. Indeed, it is his name which graces the new road leading to the holiday centre.

The **Roman Guard Tower** was built in about 370 AD during the reign of Emperor Valentinianus I., only to be destroyed at the turn of the 4th and 5th centuries. Recently the remains have been made more visible.

The red path starts at the camping and swimming complex near the jetty. It leads to the *Pál Gyulai picnic site* and *Csaba Well* before heading towards *Vöröskő* (521m). On a clear day it is possible to see the Börzsöny, the Cserhát Hills and the Great Plain from the top of Vöröskő. There are also other paths heading out towards Paprét, Pilisszentlászló, Visegrád and Tahi.

Those cycling along the cycle path around the Danube Bend will not regret a stop-off at the outdoor swimming complex at Leányfalu to relax in its thermal waters.

Tahitótfalu

The village is built where *Szentendre Island*, the right bank of the Danube, the hills, the plains and the waters all meet. Archaeologists believe that the place has been inhabited for many thousands of years. Roman remains have also been uncovered.

For many hundreds of years the place was famous for its wines. Following the phylloxera outbreak the locals resorted to growing strawberries. The first summer residence and winepress in Tahi (Pataksor 50.) belonged to the famous classical architect *Mihály Pollack*. His grave, in the cemetery in Béke utca, was designed by *Miklós Ybl*.

The altar in the Baroque **Calvinist church** is of particular interest because it was made out of local red Süttő marble (1810s).

KISOROSZI gets its name from the members of the Russian Basilite Order who settled here during Koloman's reign (1095–1114). Having passed *Szentendre Island* rowers often take a rest at the **camping site** on the wooded northern tip of the island, the so-called "szigetspicc".

If you are travelling by road, you have to cross the **bridge** to get to PÓCSMEGYER. During the 19th century the village, which was occupied by the Megyer clan during the Hungarian Conquest, attempts were made at irrigation. After having had to endure frequent flooding, and the floods of 1865 in particular, it was decided to build an embankment.

The popular **resort** of SURÁNY on the Vác branch of the Danube belongs to Pócsmegyer. Those using the Sziget út entrance can sit on the pebbly banks of the river.

During the Middle Ages SZIGETMONOSTOR was owned by the Rosd family. Following the Turkish occupation the village fell into the hands of the Zichy family, before eventually becoming crown land. Today Szigetmonostor, on the main branch of the Danube, is built right up to HORÁNY. From here all the way to Surány you will find plenty of places to **tie up your boat** and **camp**.

The island's only **bridge** crosses the Szentendre branch of the river at Tahitótfalu. Buses wishing to cross the *main branch of the Danube* should proceed to the *Pokol csárda* where the only **ferry** capable of taking buses and larger vehicles leaves from. It takes you into Vác.

View of Esztergom from Párkány (Stúrovo, Slovakia)

ESZTERGOM

Known as the *cradle of Hungary*. The town greets those coming up from the Danube Bend just as the valley opens up before you. Approaching the town you see the "two-horned cathedral", the *"enormous snail"* or what Babits called the *"wise* **basilica"**.

Esztergom Cathedral is the biggest church in Hungary. It is about one hundred metres high and the interior diameter of the dome is 33.5m. The 22m-high columns dwarf the visitor standing in front of the façade. When entering the building you are confronted by the largest altar canvas in the world, *M. Grigoletti*'s depiction of the Ascension of the Virgin Mary. Framed with sculptures by the Italian sculptor *Pietro Bonanni*, the picture is a copy of a painting by Titian. The organ loft is decorated by painted plaster sculptures by *Johann Meixner*.

There are any number of ways of approaching Esztergom: from western Hungary, for example, or from the south along the Danube Bend. Those choosing the latter route should stop just above Basaharc. It is here, at the top of a rock face, that an enormous cross looks onto the Danube. They call it the shiver cross. It was put up more than two centuries ago by a resident of Szentgyörgymeze to "make the shipping community more devout". Local folklore has it that those who walk around the cross will be cured of their shivers.

Apart from the masses, organ recitals and choral concerts are also held in the cathedral throughout the summer.
József Hild was responsible for the final form of this enormous building. The cathedral took almost 50 years to build. Just prior to its completion the building was consecrated, an occasion at which Franz Liszt conducted his Esztergom Mass (1856).

The oldest object in the collection of the Cathedral Treasury is a Crucifixion carved out of rock crystal which was made in Metz in 870. There is also the 13th century Coronation Oath Cross made from precious stones, jewels, pearls and golden filigree. The Matthias Crucifix is an International Gothic masterpiece, and the Suk Chalice one of the most beautiful chalices in the world. There are also drinking horns, seals, embroidered Gothic liturgical vestments and Flemish embroidery.

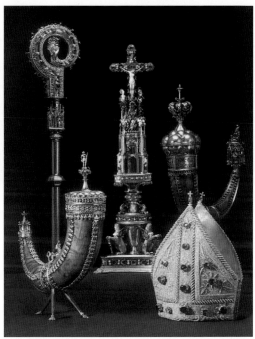

You can find the Cathedral Treasury through a door to the right of Grigoletti's high altar painting. The precious liturgical objects are kept safely behind security glass.

On the southern side of the nave stands the **Bakócz Chapel** (1506–1507), the finest piece of Renaissance architecture surviving in Hungary. It was built for Archbishop Tamás Bakócz by Italian masters using the local red Süttő marble. The altar, made of white Carrara marble, was added later, and is also the work of Italian artists. The chapel originally stood further south, but in 1823 the chapel was dismantled (all 1,600 pieces of it) and rebuilt inside the new basilica.

The **crypt**, which is built in an Ancient Egyptian style, is where the archbishops of Esztergom are buried. József Mindszenty's tomb has been there since 1991.

The 12th century **Royal Chapel** situated in the castle, with its rose window, is a fine early Gothic design. The walls contain fragments of some 14th century frescos which are also of great importance, notably the eight half-length Apostles. At the **Castle Museum,** which was renovated especially for the new Millennium, you can walk through the Árpáds' royal palace seeing where some of the most important episodes of Hungary's medieval past took place.

On leaving the cathedral it's a good idea to take a look down from Castle Hill onto the Danube. For years it has only been possible to cross the Danube to Párkány (Stúrovo, Slovakia) by ferry. The reconstruction of the Mária Valéria Bridge has made crossing the river much more straightforward. The Water Town stands directly under the castle, a scene familiar to those fortunate enough to have a 10,000 forint note.

In one of the rooms in the castle you can see a model of the Porta Speciosa, which stood in the narthex of the medieval cathedral. The room, believed to be János Vitéz's study, contains some 15th century frescos, while on the first floor of the keep there are two fine round-headed 12th century doorways.

The *Water Town* at the bottom of Castle Hill has a predominantly Baroque feel about it. It is here in Pázmány Péter utca that you will find the *Archdiocesan Library*, better known as the **Bibliotéka**. In the same street you will find the *Bálint Balassa Museum*, which holds temporary exhibitions (number 13.). The neo-Renaissance building complex in Zsigmond Berényi utca, the **Primate's Palace** provides a home for both the head of the Roman Catholic Church in Hungary and the **Christian Museum**. What is probably the richest provincial collection in Hungary was founded by Archbishop János Simor in 1875. Perhaps the most famous object on display is *Thomas of Kolozsvár*'s **Crucifixion Altarpiece** from the Benedictine monastery of Garamszent-benedek (Hronsk Beňadik, Slovakia) painted in 1427. It was from there also that the wooden Easter Sepulchre came. There are also a number of Late Gothic altarpieces and Renaissance paintings which deserve attention.

It is worth walking along the Kis-Duna following the bank of the *Primate's Island* into the centre of the town. It is the 18th and 19th century houses lining *Széchenyi tér,* which are most likely to catch the eye. The arcaded Baroque **town hall** (1773) also stands in the square. It was once the residence of *General Bottyán the Blind*, who made his name during the Rákóczi Wars for Freedom.

The royal castle was reconstructed especially for the new Millennium. Miklós Melocco's monument is another recent addition.

Árpád Tóth, Áron Tamási, Lajos Kassák, Dezső Kosztolányi, Frigyes Karinthy and others, making up a veritable pantheon of 20th century Hungarian literature.

Summer is the most interesting season in Esztergom. Events start at the beginning of May with the *Gizella Festival* in honour of King Stephen's wife, and then there's the *Whitsun Fair*. There is a special atmosphere in the town when the theatre is open in the castle and when concerts are going on in the basilica. Many make their way to Esztergom for the Saint Stephen's Day celebrations in August.

From the town you can make your way up to the **Vaskapu tourist cabin** (403m), either by road or by footpath, where there are some great views.

You can always get your bearings by looking up at the two towers of the church in Esztergom's Water Town.

All the buildings in the small streets around Széchenyi tér are of some historic importance.

Maria Theresa added a Grammar School onto the end of the town hall. The Baroque **County Hall**, which stands in Bottyán utca, belonged to General András Török, and the Baroque palace on the far side bears the coat-of-arms of Móric Sándor's family. It's worth going into the **Danube Museum** (Kölcsey u. 2.), which brings the history of the river to life. The collection contains over one thousand maps and more than six hundred letters addressed to István Széchenyi. There are also models, particularly those of boats, as well as objects trawled up from the riverbed (the largest of which can be seen in the courtyard). The building also contains the *"Európai Közép Gallery"*, which puts on exhibitions of contemporary art.

For those of you who are more interested in literature, there is the **museum** housed in the one-time summer residence of *Mihály Babits* in the street named after him. On the wall of Babits's veranda you can see the signatures of *Zsigmond Móricz,*

IN THE REALM OF THE CROWN

PILISMARÓT

You can get to Pilismarot either by catching a ferry from Szob or a small boat from Zebegény. The **outdoor swimming complex** was known as the *Danube Lido* during the 1930s. From Pilismarót getting up into the *Nature Reserve* to do some serious walking is straightforward. Perhaps the most famous destination is the **Hoffman Hut,** which is where the *inn* now stands. The area is good for hunting, and the one hundred hectares of water make it popular with anglers.

> *According to local tradition it was here that his pursuers caught up with Mihály Dobozy, who was in the process of fleeing from Budakeszi where he had stabbed his wife to death rather than let her fall into Turkish hands. It was here that he fought with his Turkish adversaries to the death. (This was a tale depicted in Bertalan Székely's painting "Mihály Dobozy and his Wife"). Historians, however, now believe event took place at Pusztamarót near Nyergesújfalu.*

In Dömös you will find the remains of a provostal church on the hill above the cemetery. The church has a Romanesque crypt containing three aisles and three apses. Today weddings are frequently held here.

The famous publisher *Gusztáv Heckenast* once owned a villa here. The *"wise man of Hungary",* *Ferenc Deák,* was often known to visit. It was here in the peace and quiet of the hills and on the banks of the Danube that Deák worked on the text of the 1867 *Compromise.* The *Basaharc Valley* opens up at the end of the village, which also happens to be where the **Búbánat Valley Holiday Centre** is. It is here also that *Hideglelős cross* rises from a sheer rock face above the Danube.

DÖMÖS

It is not surprising that our early ancestors were taken with the peace and the mysterious beauty of this stretch of the Danube Bend. We know from the miniatures of the Hungarian Picture Chronicle that the Árpád kings held the area in great esteem. Indeed, a royal manor house stood here during the 11th century. Before stopping to look at the sites of historical interest it is worthwhile looking up at St Michael's Hill standing high above the river on the banks opposite.

Dömös's jetty is the only jetty on the Danube to enjoy protected status. It's a light metal structure, which makes leaving Dömös by boat a particularly pleasant experience.

Whilst walking the streets of Dömös it is worthwhile looking for the Baroque **Catholic church** in Hősök tere and **All Saints Chapel**. The **Dömös Gallery and Local History Exhibition** can be found in the local council building (Táncsics M. út 2.).

On the initiative of Dömös-born *József Vertel,* best known for his postal stamp designs, four or five temporary exhibitions are put on here every year. In another room you will find a room dedicated to the painters and sculptors who have worked in the village (*from Károly Kernstock to István Martsa*). There is also a display on the history of the village.

Dömös is also considered to be a *hiking Mecca.* Known as the *Gateway to the Pilis Hills* it offers easy access to all the most beautiful places. You can go to *Dobogókő* (700m), and to the *Prédikáló-*

The Rám Ravine in the Pilis Hills

Looking up at Visegrád Castle you will see Pilis's green forests to the right and the drained stretch of the Danube, with the remains of the half-completed dam system, to the left. On your way to Visegrád you come to the Lepence outdoor swimming pool, which is carved, terraced fashion, into the hillside. Nearby there is the recently-opened spa-hotel (2004).

szék from where you can get some stunning views of the *Danube Bend*. A serious hiker would never say no to the chance of walking the entire length of the *Rám Ravine*.

VISEGRÁD

The Danube Bend can be approached either by path, along main road number 11, or along the road going from the Open-Air Museum in Szentendre via Pilisszentlászló.

Visegrád is first mentioned in texts referring to the construction of the royal palace in Esztergom in 1002, when Stephen I. made the settlement the centre of Visegrád (later Pilis) County.

It was with the building of the 13th century **castle fortifications** and the construction of the royal palace that Visegrád came to prominence. Its golden age came to an abrupt end in 1543 when the town fell into the hands of the Turks.

After the Compromise of 1867, and with the starting of a regular boat service, the town became a popular holiday resort.

From whichever way you approach Visegrád you can't avoid seeing the Salomon Tower. The tower is linked up with the Water Bastion down on the banks of the Danube, the symbolic gateway to the town.

The Salamon tower got its name from a misunderstanding, at a time when it was believed that King Salamon had been imprisoned there in 1082. The reality is, however, that the tower hadn't even been built when the event is supposed to have happened. It in fact dates from about 1258. There is nothing along the whole length of the Danube to compare with its hexagonal ground plan, its height (31m), the area of land it covers (360m²) or its eight floors. The tower is currently occupied by the Matthias Corvinus Museum.

The **Royal Palace** (Fő u. 27.) was started in about 1320. It was here that Felicián Zách made his unsuccessful attempt on the life of Charles Robert (1330). It was here also that the famous Congress of Visegrád took place in 1335.

Building on the palace started during the reign of Louis the Great, and continued during the reign of Matthias Corvinus (1476). This was when the **courtyard** on terrace II. was built, something the archaeologists excavated from under 15 metres of rubble. The so-called *Hercules Well* stood in the middle of the courtyard. The present well is a copy, and bears the coat-of-arms Matthias used as titular King of Bohemia (1469).

On terrace III. stood a chapel covered by a wooden ceiling covered in gold leaf. The so-called *Visegrád Madonna*, carved in red marble and now in the museum, once stood at the entrance to the chapel.

The most interesting part of Visegrád Castle is probably the courtyard renovated with the help of the British government.

On terrace IV., in the **royal couple's private garden,** you can see a copy of the lion's well. It was at this level that the king had his **pool**; the pipes and two pools of which have also been uncovered.

The destruction of the 350-room palace started at the beginning of the 16th century, ending with the fire of 1542. The renovation work, much of which has been based on the writings of 16th century Archbishop of Esztergom Miklós Oláh, was started in 1934 by *János Schulek*. The work is still going on today.

During the *Visegrád Palace Festival* in July medieval tournaments are held down on the recently restored medieval tournament field below the palace.

The **Fortress** was built by Béla IV. mainly for the protection of his family (1245–1255). Construction was continued by Charles Robert, and it was here in the castle that he kept the crown jewels and the archives following their removal from Székesfehérvár. It was from here that Albert of Habsburg's wife stole the *Hungarian Crown* for her as yet unborn son, the future Ladislas V.

The castle's central courtyard was built by Sigismund after 1403. The **western wing of the palace** dates from the reign of Matthias Corvinus. The castle fell into Turkish hands during the course of the 16th century, and the buildings which survived were finally blown up by Leopold I. in 1702.

The **Roman Military Camp** (*Sibrik Hill*), the *Pone Navata*, built in about 330 was capable of housing 200–300 warriors. The hill was named after its one-time owner Miklós Sibrik, Ferenc Rákóczi II's colonel.

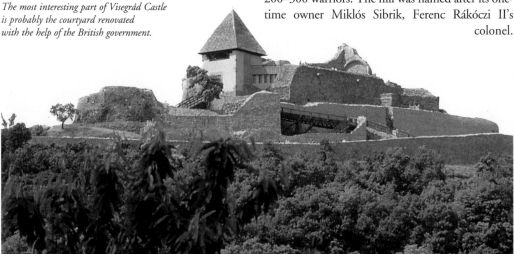

One of the most popular weekend destinations in these parts is *Apátkút Valley*, from where the red marked pathways take you out to the village of Pilisszentlászló.

The Visegrád Visitors Centre on Mogyoró Hill offers all kinds of possibilities: camping, a restaurant, a cultural centre, playgrounds, a wildlife park and many other attractions. Most of the buildings betray the telltale curves of Imre Makovecz's organic architecture (1971).

Hungary's first ever summer bobsleigh track was built on Mogyoró Hill. The 750metre track winds its way down into the valley.

On the way to Pilisszentlászló you pass the *Ördögmalom Waterfalls*, *Telgárthy Meadow* and the *Magda Spring*, which is where you can find parking spaces and plenty of good places for a family barbecue. If you want to visit the **Botanical Gardens** you will have to make the relevant enquiries at the *Visegrád Forestry Commission* (Mátyás király u. 4.).

It is in Visegrád that we say goodbye to the Danube Bend, and indeed to this particular region. We will now be moving on to Transdanubia, starting in the area situated between the northern shore of Lake Balaton and the River Danube.

"Famous Pannonia once
A flowering garden spread;
The Virgin's faithful hand
Watered its garden-bed.

The gardener was our king,
Stephen, his mighty name.
But shadows fell upon
The land of joy and fame."

Roman Catholic Hymnbook
(17th century)

CONTENTS – CENTRAL TRANSDANUBIA

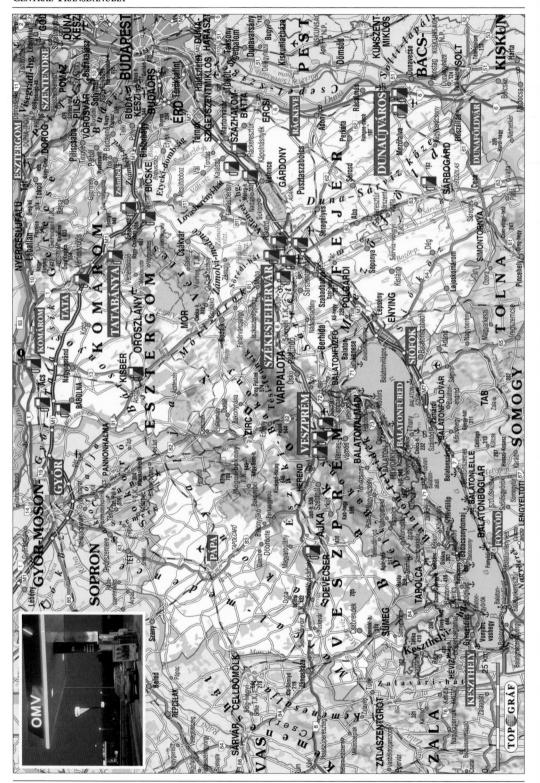

CENTRAL TRANSDANUBIA

The sometimes gentle, sometimes breathtaking, landscape we will be exploring lies west of Budapest and north and northeast of Lake Balaton. It's a region which really defies one particular geographical name, so without trying to complicate the matter any further let's see what there is to enjoy... The region is like a mosaic made up of many brightly coloured pieces. In the cold light of day it is attractive, but then suddenly a slight irregularity in the surface may leave an impression of dazzling beauty. It's a region of great variety. It's a region of individual landscapes where settlements still have their very own individual characters. However in saying this, within such variety there is a common culture, a common tradition, a "Pannonian spirit". But how far does it go back? To the Roman Province of Pannonia? The Pannonians? To the first known inhabitant of the region who lived in Vértesszőlős 350 thousand years ago? Whatever the true answer it cannot be a coincidence that we find the Vértesszőlős man in the Tata Basin amongst the hot water springs.

Let's imagine one summer's afternoon, a *thermal current* suddenly lifted you up and took you high into the sky. Down below you see the contours of the hills and the valleys, and make out the work of human hands. There are the browns of the recently ploughed soil on the shelved hillsides, the clear sparkling blues reflecting off the surface of Lake Velence, and the multitudinous greens on the arable down on the Sárrét disturbed only occasionally by the cooler tones of valley settlement. So why not take off? You may not have the wingspan of a mythical Hungarian eagle, but boarding a light aircraft or a hot air balloon is not entirely beyond the realm of possibility. So jump on board and we'll fly from the banks of the Danube right down to the Balaton Highlands.

On the banks of the great river stand the mighty fortresses of the divided town of Komárom. The two halves are linked, yet divided, by an iron bridge of Danish construction. Under it flows the Danube. Moving from the Danube a little, one still finds plenty of water at the small lakeside town of Tata, where the façades of the Baroque buildings resplendent in Esterhazy yellow contrast with the darker tones of the castle overlooking Lake Öreg.

If one were to sail onwards to the *Gerecse* one would see the wounds, some white, some red, left by those derelict stone quarries which are now gradually returning to the bosom of nature. If you flew low enough you may be able to catch the litany of masses celebrated in Hungarian, Slovak and Swabian German.

Folly in the English Park, Tata

The *Lesser Plain (Kisalföld)* is a landscape of expansive meadows and woods which seem to run one into another. In the *Balaton Highlands* the lime-washed walls of the verandahed houses of the Balaton Heights gradually make way for the royal towns of old. Whether it's Veszprém or Székesfehérvár, nearby Zirc or Pápa, or even Tatabánya, they are all keen to bear the laurels of local supremacy, and each in its own particular way certainly has some compelling arguments.

It's all very well to appreciate the landscape, but one needs a sense of history as well, even if that means dropping a stratum or two.

The *Gerecse* amounts to eight hundred square kilometres of dolomite and limestone hills whose caves are of great interest. The fossily limestone has been mined in the region for as long as mankind can remember. It was mined by Roman slaves for road construction and used by their ancestors for building their stately homes. The abandoned quarries now offer refuge to birds of prey, and their sunny rock faces are covered with rare wild flowers. The *Vértes* is only half the size of the Gerecse, and it is probably this simple observation that accounts for the fact that the hills look considerably higher than

their modest four hundred or so metres. The hills, two parallel ranges which slice diagonally across the landscape from northeast to southwest, rise imposingly between the *Mór* and the *Tata-Vál Valleys* creating a geographical bridge between the Bakony and the Gerecse. The oak woods, the damp ravines and warm slopes create microclimates which vary dramatically from one another, some sub-Mediterranean some subalpine, making hill walking all the more exciting.

The *Sárrét* is of a different character altogether. It lies beyond the eastern reaches of the Bakony where the young oaks, the hawthorn and the sloe bushes grow. It is within such a landscape, not far from Lake Balaton, that Székesfehérvár the medieval coronation, town of *Alba Regia* lies. Its modern counterpart, Székesfehérvár, has managed to combine the traditional with all that is expected of a young dynamic town, and for that reason it is currently arousing the attention it deserves.

Only a few kilometres from Székesfehérvár is *Lake Velence* which was formed about 15–20 thousand years ago. Its water level has always been at the mercy of the elements and there have been occasions when it has dried out altogether, the last occasion being back in the 1860s. Grape-growing is much in evidence along the shores of the lake, not only in the vineyards but also in the cottages, the huts and the cellars.

Lake Velence

The Tés Windmills

Wine is still pressed in some of these cellars today. The 1930s saw the arrival of the tourist industry and by the 1960s planned leisure policies were being put into effect. It was mainly in serving the interests of the tourist industry that so much of the natural habitat was preserved. It was at that time that the *Zámoly-Pátka Reservoir* was built to ensure an adequate supply of water.

The countryside stretching south and east of Székesfehérvár down towards the Danube is known as the *Mezőföld*. The streams running off the Western Hungarian Hills (Dunántúli-középhegység) had been depositing their sediment over the area, when during the ice ages this loess was forced up into the air into a cloud which then settled over the land, leaving the soil with its characteristically yellow colour.

The *stretch of Danube* running southwards from Ercsi is dominated by a succession of settlements which hug the main road from Budapest down to Dunaújváros. In Roman times it was a busy highway taking traffic from *Aquincum* in the north down to Intercisia further south. In later centuries it was the Serbs, once known as the "Rácok", who made their mark on the cultural landscape, as can be seen in place-names like Ráckeve and Rácalmás.

The Danube is not only a river of great natural beauty it is also a natural sports facility. However, you have to be careful. Strong currents and the poor water quality mean that swimming is only possible on certain stretches of the river and in the dead channels.

For sheer variety one should visit the stretch of countryside between the *Balaton Highlands* and the foothills of the *Bakony*, a terrain which complements the hills and valleys of the *Transdanubian Hills*. Beyond, the landscape opens out onto the *Marcal Basin* and the *Lesser Plain* beyond. The *Bakony Hills* pushed their way above the surface of the Pannonian Basin. Its valleys, which were initially filled with the salty water of an ever-intruding and receding sea, later funnelled the rivers and the streams. It is a landscape of rock faces and caves (over one hundred to be exact), the highest peak standing at just over 600 metres.

The wooded *High Bakony* juts out of the main body of hills. Whilst the southern slopes enjoy their full quota of sunshine the level of rainfall, which is slightly higher than elsewhere, means that it provides the natural conditions necessary for the fragrant garlic, the small Mediterranean ferns, and the gladioli. Of the 350 species of bird

CENTRAL TRANSDANUBIAN SPECIALITIES

One of the culinary delights with which nature has endowed this particular region is the delicious *morel mushroom*, although we would suggest that only those with the necessary botanical knowledge go in search of them. It is because the bees here busily feed off the *sunflowers* that the local honey has a characteristic taste and particular traditional medicinal properties.

Now we are on the subject of animals, and with the hunting fraternity very much in mind, it is worth mentioning the *snipe* and the *wild duck*. For those whose heart lies a little closer to their stomachs one has to mention the local poultry soup, which has to be eaten to be believed.

Something which could well turn up in your soup is a slice or two of *Cece white pepper*, something which goes down well at picnics, especially if the sandwiches are made with *Székesfehérvár maize bread*.

For those who are around during the winter months it is worthwhile making the pilgrimage to Alsószentiván to collect a bag or two of *walnuts*, because these too count amongst the region's natural treasures.

which live in Hungary, 190 can be found here. Elsewhere in the *Transdanubian Hills* it is less windy and the climate is a touch warmer. Looking west beyond the Bakony there are the ploughed fields of the *Marcali Basin*, the home of the mighty stork.

Those who live in the Balaton region have traditionally earned their living tending the vines and tilling the land, whereas in the Bakony people have bred livestock and worked in the timber trade. Out towards the Lesser Plain the tendency has been for people to grow crops, produce flour and engage in trade.

During the 12th and 13th centuries the monasteries of the Benedictine and Cistercian orders and the royal and baronial castles sprung up in the Vértes and Bakony. During the Middle Ages monarchs frequently praised the hills for their game, whilst the castles often formed the backdrop for medieval conflicts.

After the destruction of one hundred and fifty years of Turkish occupation, foreign settlers were invited to repopulate the region. Elements of these cultures can still be seen today. It was the settlers who opened up mines and started paper and glass production. It was they who set up the presses, introduced tobacco, organised meat production and built the pottery kilns. These enterprises proved to be the forefathers of such concerns as the Pápa meat guild, the Herend porcelain factory and the Ajka glassworks. The Hungarian aristocracy proved willing artistic patrons, commissioning the building of new churches and country houses, some of which were designed by architects from abroad. It was the aristocrats who founded the schools and made both Veszprém and Pápa into regional centres of learning. The German-speaking population was to stay in the region until the end of Second World War.

People come from all over the world to participate in such events as the Veszprém *Music Festivals,* the Pápa *Baroque Festival,* the Herend *Porcelánium,* the Lake Velence Regatta, the Sümeg Castle *Tournaments,* the Magyarpolány *Passion,* the Székesfehérvár *Royal Festival* and the traditional *Beethoven Concerts* at Martonvásár. Life here is rich indeed, so let's see what there is to see.

KOMÁROM

The strategic importance of Komárom was realised as far back as the Roman period. Then known as *Brigetio*, Komárom enjoyed colonial status, being the second-most important settlement (behind Aquincum) in the Roman province of Pannonia. The confluence of the Danube and the *Little Danube*, was recorded as being where King Stephen built the earthworks which were ultimately to become the seat of the royal county of Komárom.

You can cross the Elizabeth Bridge into the northern part of Komárom (Komarno in Slovakian) if you want. But of course you'll need your passport. The border crossing is open day and night. The new quay on the Danube (2003) has helped to liven up tourism on the river.

The town's layout was determined by the Treaty of Trianon (1920), which dictated that the river would form a border, creating in its wake two separate towns, one Slovakian, one Hungarian. Komárom is known as *the town of fortresses,* there being eight fortresses in all, three on the Hungarian side. In 1809, Francis I., Holy Roman Emperor and King of Hungary, took refuge here when fleeing from Vienna ahead of the arrival of Napoleon. The fortress was designed to house an imperial army numbering some two hundred thousand troops, and it was only in 1877 that building work finally came to a standstill.

On entering the **Fort Monostor** (originally known as *Fort Sandberg*) you are slowly engulfed by the massive earthworks which once protected this huge military installation. First it was the Habsburg Empire and later the Soviet Red Army that occupied the 14-block complex with its 640 rooms... In recent years, however, the buildings have become more visitor-friendly. There are now industrial and military exhibitions, and the *fortress shop* is the only outlet in the world selling *Fort Sandberg wine.*
You can try the local army bread ("bakakenyér") at Hungary's one and only **Bread Museum.**

2,000 masons and 10,000 labourers helped to construct this Austrian-designed fortress. Such a workforce was necessary when you consider that there are 270 thousand square meters of room space inside; 1800 metres of ditches, 9m deep and 9m wide, with inner and outer walls accompanied by corridors lined with gun positions. In its day the "Danubian Gibraltar" was defended by 400 cannons.

Perhaps the most famous episode in the history of Komárom's fortresses happened in September 1848, when the town's soldiers, under the leadership of György Klapka, took control of the castle and in doing so eventually forced Emperor Franz Joseph to come to a settlement with the Hungarian rebels. The *Komárom Festival* pays homage to the event every spring at what is both a cultural and sporting event. It includes the two towns' road race, a tug-of-war on the bridge, and the quay market.

Fort Sandberg: there are 640 rooms down there.

The side entrance to the neo-Baroque town hall on Szabadság tér is marked by an enormous anchor. It also means that you have stumbled upon the Ferenc Juba Hungarian Maritime Museum.

Fort Igmánd with its 106 rooms is open to general public. The *Klapka Museum* houses a fine collection of Roman artefacts (inscribed graves-tones, sarcophagi, and carved mythological reliefs) found on the *limes* which once separated the Romans from the barbarians to the north. (Komárom's third fortress on the Hungarian side, the *Csillagerőd – The Star Fortress* – is still waiting to be opened to the general public.)

There's no better way to end the day than a spot of relaxation down at the local **thermal baths,** the hot spa waters coming up from a depth of 1,260 feet at a temperature of 36–38 °C. The waters are good for the prevention of locomotor disorders (Táncsics u. 34–36). There are hotels, camping possibilities and restaurants situated nearby.

A DAY OUT IN BÁBOLNA

BÁBOLNA

The village is famous for its horses and the large concern which shares its name. It was Joseph II. who put Bábolna on the equestrian map when the **stud-farm** he founded gained a reputation for breeding high-class English and Arab thorough-breds, particularly the cream coloured *Shagya*.

It's certainly worth visiting the **Szapáry Palace** in its new guise as a *horse-breeding centre* (Mészáros u. 1.). In the square in front of the 18th century parish church stands a memorial *(Iván Szabó)* to all the local horses which have fallen in battle. In the **arboretum,** situated on Csikótelepi út, you can walk through the famous horse cemetery free of charge. Also see the recently restored *Officers' Club* (Mészáros u. 16.), now the **local museum**. There is also the fascinating hunting and coach museum run by Bábolna Rt.

KISBÉR, lying just to the south of Komárom, is famous for its 150-year-old stud and all its other equestrian traditions. Recently Bábolna has become the centre of Hungary's *St Martin's Day* (November 11th) celebrations. The venue was chosen for the town's geese, the traditional fare for the day.

Bábolna's famous coach and five horses are a frequent sight.

TATA

As the historical town of Tata is synonymous with the *lake* on which it stands, perhaps it would be wise to begin with the "Water Palace".

Whether one calls it a **castle**, a palace or a hunting lodge, the fact remains that it was first built by Emperor Sigismund at the turn of the 14th century.

By the reign of Matthias Corvinus it had become one of the most beautiful Renaissance palaces in Hungary.

Much of what we can see today, however, tells us more about what the Baroque and the romantic periods thought about the Middle Ages than the Middle Ages themselves.

Tata was once famous for its delftware. It was here that the Farkasházy-Fischer family founded the first **delftware factory** in the country. In the castle you can see Tata's famed lobster motifs, which paid homage to the waters of Lake Öreg. In the **castle chapel,** which stands separate from the building, there is an exhibition of ecclesiastical art featuring altars and sculpture dating from the 18th and 19th centuries.

As far back as the Middle Ages **Lake Öreg** was used to breed fish. Today it's a conservation area, but it doesn't mean you can't cycle around it! Every summer a pleasure boat takes tourists from the castle to the small quay at the *Tóváros* at the far end of the lake. There is also a narrow-gauge railway around the lake which doesn't seem to disturb anybody.

On Tóváros Walk you can see **Pötörke Mill,** once a fulling mill but now a pub, **Czégényi Mill,** which is now an office building, and bit a further on still **Miklós Mill** with its huge wheel.

> *"… that count bloke, who bought the Tata estate from the Krapff family, was my grandfather's grandfather's grandfather's father's elder brother, or would have been"* – is what Péter Esterházy tells us. The later Lord Chief Justice (*országbíró*) *"… was born during a dance, and there was hardly time to get her off to a neighbouring room"*. His mother also just happened to be Imre Thököly's younger sister.…"

Of particular interest is the knights' stove at Tata Castle which looks quite at home in surroundings which hark back to the 14th and 15th centuries.

All date from a time when it was the spring waters which provided the energy to run Tata. Typical of the buildings by the lake is the steep-roofed boat-house, which once used to be the **abattoir**. Near Lake Cseke there is **an English-style garden**. You will find many such gardens in the pages that follow.

Lake Öreg is for the rowers, the windsurfers and the yachtsmen amongst you. Anglers have to be satisfied with the Derítő which lies to the other side of the castle.

The park in Tata boasts Hungary's first folly and its first grotto, both of which were planned by a French-man. The peace and quiet is broken from time to time when a performance starts on the open-air stage in front of the **petit palais**. More recently the park

has been turned into an **Olympic training camp**. It was in its peculiarly English climate that the Hungarian team prepared for the 1948 London

Tata's Lake Öreg is one of the most important aquatic environments in the world. Indeed, it comes under the aegis of the so-called Ramsar Agreement. Its importance lies in its being a resting place for wild geese. During the migrating seasons in spring and autumn, the lake echoes to the sound of between ten and fifteen thousand honking geese.

Olympics.

Today the training camp has become a hotel and sports complex for anybody wishing to make the most of its facilities.

In the town centre the tower built on the far side of the **Capuchin Church and Monastery** is one of the more recent additions to the building, and it is this later date which partly explains why it has got such a slender spire.

You can of course find taller towers in Tata, for example the two on the west front of the **parish church** in Kossuth tér, started by *Franz Anton Pilgram*, continued later by *Jakab Fellner* and

Országgyűlés tér is dominated by the wooden belfry (1763), otherwise known as the clock tower.

The Water, Music and Flower Festival takes over the town during the last weekend in June.
The three days are packed with everything from regattas to fireworks, craft stalls to medieval tournaments, and made all
the more memorable by Europe's most prestigious flower-arranging competition.

completed by *József Grossman.*
Despite not seeing the work to the end Fellner got his final wish and was buried in the crypt of the church.

There is also a sculpture to his memory on the balustrade by *Lajos Ungvári.*

In the **Nepomucenus Mill** designed by *Jakab Fellner* (Alkotmány u.2) you can see the *German Ethnographic Museum.* There are authentic interiors containing the characteristic painted furniture, domestic items textiles and the regional costumes, which were once common in this part of Hungary.

A peculiarly classical experience can be had at the old **Synagogue** (Hősök tere 7.), home of the *Domokos Kuny Museum.* Here one can see copies of Greek and Roman sculptures, including the world-

On the nearby Remeteség Plain, in the grounds of the old Esterházy hunting lodge, 110 hectares of land are currently being turned into a new leisure park. The eighteen-hole golf course has already been built and they have built a conference hall and a swimming pool, all organised by the Old Lake Golf and Country Club.

famous Laocoon Group and the Venus de Milo. Stones of another kind can be found during the summer months at a one-time **quarry** now known as the *Calvary Hill Outdoor Geological Centre* (Fekete u.2.). The displays cover the geology of the last 250 million years. Amongst the highlights of the exhibition are the fossilised shells, octopuses, giant clams and sea lilies originating from the seas which once covered Pannonia. The outdoor geological nature trail up on Calvary Hill in Tata is an interesting place to visit during the summer months.

During the high season there is plenty going on in town for visitors to enjoy. There's a rich theatrical programme, as well as the *Esterházy* and the *Porcinkula Festivals*, the *International Mini-Marathon* and the *Lake Öreg Regatta*.

Agostyán is inhabited by ethnic Germans, and although strictly speaking part of Tata, it still has its own special atmosphere. Just east of the town you will find the 31-hectare **arboretum**.

From the spring through to the autumn, the Bocsájtó Valley is a popular destination for those who fancy a stroll amongst the pines and the rarer types of conifers.

DAYS OUT IN THE GERECSE

These dolomite and limestone hills rise to heights of between 400–600 meters. The peaks, frequently surrounded by eroded valleys, are often made all the more picturesque by the old abandoned quarries. The *Gerecse Nature Reserve* is home to some rare and interesting birds and a unique mixture of wild flowers.

DUNAALMÁS

The *Kőfejtők* wildlife conservation area is not only worth visiting for the fossils but for the exotic wild flowers. It is here, and only here (and there's a **monument** to prove it), that you can see part of the road along which the Roman slaves dragged stone from the quarry to the building site on the *limes*. Apart from a number of sites which are dedicated to the romance between the poet *Mihály Csokonai Vitéz* (1773–1805) and local lass *Júlia Vajda*, whose grave you will find in the Calvinist cemetery, there are also two interesting 17th century **water mills**.

NESZMÉLY

The local wine was praised as far back as Roman times. The wine produced from the grapes grown on *Meleges Hill* compares favourably with wines from the Rhine Valley. There was a time when the monks of the Benedictine Abbey of Klosterneuberg just north of Vienna drank Neszmély wines. After many lean years, Neszmély wines are now enjoying something of a Renaissance. A cycle trip along the Danube, or perhaps a spot of pony trekking, combined with some **wine tasting,** has all the makings of a great day out.

Neszmély also means something to jazz connoisseurs, as it is here that the annual summer International Jazz Festival takes place. There are also the traditional *Bridge-Building Days* which are organised together with the Slovakian villages on the opposite bank of the Danube. Since the year 2000 Neszmély has hosted the *Euro Expo* as well.

Such is the beauty of the countryside here that the Dutch are building the *Panorama Residence Duna* **holiday village** up in the hills around DUNA-SZENTMIKLÓS.

From the Hilltop Wine Hotel you can look down on three hundred hectares of vineyard and enjoy a vista which spreads thirty kilometres over the Danube and beyond.

PÉLIFÖLDSZENTKERESZT

This is a famous *pilgrimage place* which by rights belongs to the village of *Bajót*. It was here some time in the dim distant past that the Knights Templar kept a watchful eye over the waters of a well which were said to have had miraculous powers. The **church** (1735) was built by Imre Esterházy and it was he who declared it an official pilgrimage place.

The church, which belongs to the Salesian Fathers, possesses relics from the True Cross. The Stations of the Cross date back to the 1930s. Of particular interest are the woodcarvings, especially the wooden figures. Although Catholic pilgrims descend on the church all year round, there are three days in the year which are devoted specifically to pilgrimage; 3rd May *(The Finding of the True Cross)*, 14th September *(The Elevation of the True Cross)* and 24th October *(The Feast of Saint Wendel)*.

Of geological interest is the sheer rock face at nearby *Öreg-kő* which is much frequented by climbers. The wild flowers in this area are protected, but if you tread carefully you can make your way up to the **Jankovich Cave**, where human remains dating back to the last ice age have been found. Be warned, however, entrance can only be made with special permission.

The Slovak village of Tardos is the highest village in the Gerecse, standing 300m above sea level. The village, previously known as *Tardosbánya* on account of its mining traditions, is the perfect starting point for hikes and hunting expeditions. Up in the *Malom Valley* there is fishing to be had at the **pond** which lies in the shade of the limestone rock fault not far from the **outdoor centre**.

It was in Tardos that the great expert on Turkey *Lajos Fekete* was born. The house in which he was born (Rákóczi út 168.) may be visited if you arrange your visit in advance.

Although Torda is no longer a mining village it is still very much associated with its **stone quarry**. The stone, although known as "marble" was in fact a very finely grained red limestone.

In neighbouring Süttő they are still quarrying the white limestone. The quarry workers of today have replaced the *Italian marblers* of yesteryear. The marblers were invited to work here during the reign

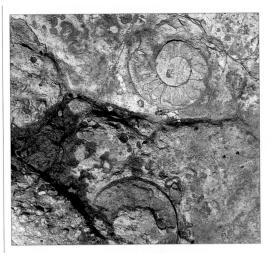

Jurassic ammonite remains in the red limestone.

of Matthias Corvinus. Héreg, a popular assembly point for those wishing to hike or mountain-bike up into the hills, is huddled up against the foot of *Nagy-Gerecse,* which rises up to a height of 634 metres. In recent years Héreg has also hosted a number of equestrian events. One of the peasant cottages on Fő utca has a fine **collection of local artifacts**.

It is a long winding road which takes you to the ethnic German village of Tarján. The old **cottage** in Móricz Zsigmond tér bears witness to bygone days. The village is peppered with wine cellars. The high point in the village's calendar is the three-day festival in August. There is also a well-furnished **youth camp** on the edge of the village.

Tarján is now a flourishing bastion of ethnic German traditions, famous for its folk dancing and brass bands.

TATABÁNYA

In the valley separating the *Vértes* and the *Gerecse*, overlooking the blocks of the modern town, there is a huge bird. This bird, the **mythical Hungarian eagle** (*Gyula Donáth*) to be exact, perches on the edge of *Kő Hill* brooding on the almost as mythical Battle of Bánhida, which may have taken place around 896 when the Hungarian nation found a home in the Carpathian Basin.

This mythological "turul" cast in iron, is the result of the millennium fever which struck Hungary in 1896 on the occasion of the thousandth anniversary of the Hungarians' arrival into the Carpathian Basin. As far as we know its 15-metre wingspan makes it the largest cast-iron bird in Europe.

We hear of the supposed battle in a chronicle written by Simon Kézai. He writes: "Following the rout of the Huns, Szvatopluk son of Marót, began to rule Pannonia." According to legend the Hungarians, who had previously paid him tribute, discovered that he was weaker than them and launched a surprise attack. "Not far from Bánhida they completely annihilated Szvatopluk and the rest of his army".

The *Tatabánya Museum* (Szent Borbálá tér), has a unique **feather collection**, which is the result of *Lajos Boglár's* ethnographic explorations in South America. Next to Bánhida's brick **parish church** (*Adolf Feszty*, 1885) is a classroom as it would have looked in the 1920s (Gellért tér 3.). *Béla Marczis's* collection of over 50 **veteran cars** will be a great attraction for many (Kossuth u. 10). It includes well-

known makes such as BMW, Mercedes and Fiat, and perhaps more interestingly some others which have disappeared completely in the mists of time.

The history of mining in and around Tatabánya is well documented at the Outdoor Mining Museum (Vágóhíd u.). Here, among the original buildings, one can see "old shaft number 15", the remains of one of the most important coalfields in Hungary. You can in fact see everything from the pithead to the miners' house, the mechanical coal-cutters to the hand tools. They are currently building an **education centre** and **leisure park** devoted to the geology of the region. The one-time bath house is now known as the **Sound Bath,** a name acquired because of Lois Viktor's curious instrumental sculptures which fill it.

With the passing of the mining industry the depths are now being plumbed for new treasures. Within a year or two some new natural springs will be coming on line, including the not-so-new thermal waters of the once-famous *Fényes Springs* in Tata.

The motorway passing Tatabánya means the whole region is within a stone's throw of Budapest.

OUT OF TATABÁNYA

One of the most beautiful places to visit is Szelim Cave. At the top of the hill you can climb to the top of the iron pithead tower which also happens to be a memorial to all those who have died in the name of mining.

The castle at **Vitányvár** near Vértessomló, originally built by the Csák clan, is first mentioned in 1324 by which time it had become a royal castle. During the winter months you can make the short journey from Tatabánya to *Koldusszállás* and *Csákányospuszta* by ski lift. In April the hills host the *Gerecse 50* endurance hike.

VÉRTESSZŐLŐS

The scull fragment of the "first Hungarian" was found in 1965.

The village is synonymous with *Samuel*, who was found there on August 21st, 1965. This 350 thousand-year-old bone fragment totally changed our understanding of the early development of mankind. The *Hungarian National Museum* has built an **outdoor exhibition** devoted to the find

in the tufa quarry where the remains were found. The display also includes fossilised plants and bone fragments. Of particular interest is the slab in the glass pavilion in which you can see the footprints left by prehistoric horses, deer and indeed prehistoric men and women.

In the village one of the cottages has been furnished as it would have been when a Slovak family lived there during the 19th century. It contains a very interesting **collection** of domestic artefacts.

To your average Hungarian GYERMELY is associated with pasta. However, to the dedicated angler Gyermely means only one thing *Lake Kablási*. Nearby GYARMATPUSZTA is preferred by the hunting fraternity, who can go about their business in surroundings which were once the sole domain of the local landowner. The **country house** which still stands on the estate can also be visited, as can the 150 hectares of horse-chestnut woodland which lies beyond the Gothic Revival Sándor-Metternich **mausoleum**.

THE VÉRTES

The *Vértes* is but one part of the Transdanubian Hills and it covers an area of 314 km². The hills stand at an average of 3–400 metres above sea level. It is a landscape whose ravines, valleys, caves (nearly 70 in number) and wide open plateaux are accompanied by an assortment of romantic castles and the odd medieval monastic foundation.

Charcoal burners in the Vértes

We have to be grateful to the architects Franz Anton Pilgram and Jakab Fellner amongst others for the views enjoyed from the top of the tower dominating the village of Majk. Unfortunately it is all that remains of the Baroque hermitage. The tower resounds every quarter of an hour to the chimes of Pál Esterházy's Harmonia Caelestis, which was published in 1711.

Some of the fauna and flora is unmistakably Mediterranean. Apart from the forests, there are heaths and scrubland. The *Vértes Nature Reserve* was set up on the southern slopes of the hills in order to protect the local botanical and geological treasures.

MAJK

Here, at the very heart of the *Northern Vértes* we find the refuge of the hermits of the little-known **Camaldulian Order**. You can still imagine them fishing for their livelihood in the clear waters of the surrounding lakes. In accordance with their *regula* the monks' individual cells were arranged in symmetrical fashion around the church. The chapel, where the white friars were under a strict vow of silence, has been remodelled to suit the tastes of residents of a more touristic persuasion. One of the houses contains the **local museum** containing a fascinating exhibition about the history of the order. Every summer outdoor concerts are held in the courtyard.

VÁRGESZTES

The Gothic **castle** in Gesztes which built by the Csák clan, is now a hotel and restaurant. By the reign of Emperor Sigismund, Gesztes had become a royal castle. It survived almost unscathed until the Second World War. Now restored, visitors can climb up onto the roof and enjoy some stunning views. In the park next door you can make the most of the **playground** and the barbecuing facilities.

There is still some of the Vértes's once bountiful game to shoot at...

It is the peace and quiet of the Vértes, its fresh air and romance, that has led to Várgesztes being chosen as the venue for Hungary's first four-star holiday village, the **Villapark**. The park will eventually offer no end of leisure possibilities. At the present time the holiday homes, the swimming pool and the conference facilities are ready. When everything is complete the complex will also have the 4,000 m² *Aquaréna* leisure centre.

The *Zámoly Basin* sits between the steep southern slopes of the Vértes and the granite outcrops of the *Velence Hills*. It funnels the water flowing down from the hillsides into *Lake Velence*.

MÓR

The area around Mór it has been a **wine region** since as far back as the Roman period, or at least that is what the archaeologists tell us. A manuscript dating from 1138 proves that wine was also produced not long after the Hungarian Conquest. However, Mór's speciality, its famous *"ezerjó"* is produced from grapes introduced only in the 18th century.

As you pass through the local vineyards and drive along the country roads you come across many a

You know you are in a wine region as soon as you see the cellars and wine presses. There are some fine examples on Pince utca, Pincesor utca and Hársfa utca, as well as on Vénhegyi út. However, the most famous cellar is the spacious vaulted "Kapucinus" cellar next to the church. The Wine Museum is also open to visitors wishing to enjoy a glass of wine surrounded by the tools of the trade.

The Gothic buttresses betray the Church of the Holy Cross's medieval origins.

cross and **roadside chapel**. If you happen to be in or around Mór at harvest time you could be there in time for the *Mór Wine Festival*.

The centre of the town is dominated by 18th century architecture. There is the Láncos Palace and the **Lamberg Palace** in Szent István tér, which is used as a venue for cultural events. The medieval Church of the Holy Cross, rebuilt between 1889 and 1892, and renamed the **Hungarian Church**, is worth a visit. If you continue a little further, up a slight incline, you eventually get to the Baroque **Capuchin Church,** otherwise known as the **German Church.**

Csókakő Castle, built during the 13th century following the Tatar invasion, had an irregular groundplan and a keep. In its time it was considered unconquerable.

CSÓKAKŐ

Csókakő Castle stands on the southern edge of the Vértes Forest at a height of 208 metres. Its gatehouse and walls glare white above the vineyards.

The **castle** once guarded the main route between Győr and Komárom. During the course of excavation and renovation work the castle's Gothic gateway has been pieced together.

The castle is made all the more popular by the fact that it lies on the *National Blue Walk* (for more information look under the entry for Hollóháza in the chapter on *Northern Hungary*).

CSÁKBERÉNY

This beautifully situated village is made all the more attractive by its 18th century Roman Catholic and Calvinist churches and the **row of cellars** which stand on *Orondi Hill*. For information about the local museum in the *Cultural Centre* (7, Merán park) or anything else concerning the village you should drop in on the *Teleház*, where there is also access to a telephone, a fax machine and a computer.

ZÁMOLY

The *Zámoly Reservoir* is situated next to the road leading up into the Vértes Hills. Whereas the road is of Roman origin the 272-hectare artificial lake dates back only to 1968. It was built, together with *Pátka Reservoir*, to regulate the water level on Lake Velence. It also happens to be ideal for fishing.

The very name Zámoly has a background which goes back to one of the darker episodes in Hungarian history when Peter Orseolo, a pretender to the Hungarian crown during the reign of Andrew I. (1046-60), descended on the settlement with his followers and his foreign allies. It was here that Andrew's knights seized Orseolo and blinded him, muttering the words "You are going to pay for your indiscretions Peter", which sounds a bit like Zámoly when said in Hungarian!

GÁNT

Gánt's the place to come to if you're into bauxite, for it was from deep in this gorge that one of Hungary's bauxite centres developed back in the 1920s.

To really understand the significance of the Gánt mine you need to realise that in 1938 it produced one fifth of the world's bauxite.

Going into the shaft you can follow the whole mining process. The children's particular favourite is "Imre" the Bauxite Engine, which used to pull the bauxite from Gánt to Moharakadó along the narrow gauge line.

The derelict mine, which was in fact the first opencast mine, is now the **Jenő Balás Bauxite Mining Museum**. Visiting the neighbouring **Bauxite Geological Park** offers a unique way of finding out about the geological history of our planet. The tourist house contains *stables* and a *classroom,* which is a great base from which to explore the area.

CSÁKVÁR

Csákvár, which stands on the southeastern edge of the Vértes at the opening of the valley that marks the beginning of the *Zámoly Basin*, was once the home of western Hungary's largest potteries. The **Vértes Local History Museum** (Kossuth u.2) is dedicated to this now lost industry: to its guilds and its characteristic striped and green designs. The exhibition also includes finds from the Roman settlement of *Floriana* which stood where Csákvár stands today.

The huge park standing in the middle of Csákvár surrounds the magnificent **Esterházy Palace** which was designed by *József Hild* in about 1830.

According to the practices of the time the Esterházy Palace also had a functioning chapel, a theatre and a picture gallery, as well as a hunting hall and an equestrian school.

The beautifully articulated façade with its central portico and the grand scale of the courtyard provide the setting for what is now a hospital.

Of particular interest is the 2.5 square kilometre **park**, which was laid out in the best English park tradition. It contains a 40 metre tall *giant redwood*, which is nearly one hundred and fifty years old, as well as *copper beeches, Turkish hazels* and *silver limes*. The garden architecture has been restored, and includes a *Baroque column with a representation of the Holy Trinity*, a *sundial*, a *grotto* and a **Hunters' Chapel**.

Between Csákvár and Gánt you can find the *Haraszt Hill Botanical and Geological Nature Trail* on which you can find characteristic flora of the Vértes region. Nearby, in the *Bárcházi Caves* on

Guba Hill the remains of animals dating back 10–12 million years and people dating back 50 thousand years have been found.

Gessner House, once in the possession of the Esterházys, has been rebuilt and now forms the impressive entrance to the **Vértes Nature Park**, which also provides research facilities and houses a museum and an education centre.

VÉRTESKOZMA

Sixty to seventy 19th century German peasant houses look onto the one road which runs through this obscure hillside village. The place is living evidence of how a well-kept and prospering **holiday village** can preserve an ethnic culture in danger of extinction.

The Bavarians who settled in the Vértes at the beginning of the 18th century lived and worked here undisturbed for a good two hundred years. It was they who brought the potato to the Vértes, half a century before they became widespread in Hungary. The locals carved excellent wooden clogs which they wore to work right up until the 20th century.

VELENCEI-TÓ – LAKE VELENCE

The lake covers an area of 24.9 km². It is 10.8 km long, an average of 2.3km wide and has a circumference of 28.5km. It is, however, on average only 1.45 m deep. It is not surprising that with 2,050 hours of sunshine a year Lake Velence is known as *"lake sunshine"*. The water temperature can be as warm as 26 degrees centigrade and it is shallow enough to be safe for children.

The reeds, which are mainly used for thatching, provide an important source of income for the local economy.

Some serious sailing goes on amongst the reeds. Sailing really took off on an organised basis with the foundation of the Lake Velence Sailing Association in 1957. Fishing, canoeing and rowing competitions take place around the sports facilities in Sukoró and Velence. Windsurfing is also popular.

On the lake every reed bed and every glade has a name (Flamy Glade, Vendel Glade, Owl Nest, Toothless Glade, Disputed Bed, Mr Tés's Baby) each of which no doubt tells its own story.

The boulders on the Velence Hills are the remains of the once glowing lava of the ancient Variszkusz Hills. The once buried volcanic rock has since been pushed up to the surface of the earth.

The **water meadows** have their own special natural environment. More than half of the marshes are covered in reeds. Several kinds of *orchid, iris* and *milk-vetch* can be found there.

There are some great *natural corridors* around Lake Velence like that by *Császár Water* linking up the Vértes and the area around Lake Velence, and the route linking the *Vál and the Saint Ladislaus Valleys*.

If you follow the marked footpaths up through the Velence Hills you will be sure to see the amazing granite outcrops, cliffs and boulders. The highest point, *Meleg Hill*, stands at a height, of 352 metres. Local hikers are all familiar with the hills' other delights: their springs (the *Angelika*, the *Lajos*, the *Pázmánd* and the *Hurkavölgy Springs*), the *Barlang Well* and the 16-metre-long *Pákozd-vár Cave*.

In the forest covering the northern slopes of the Velence Hills you will find oaks, maples

Two hundred species of birds live on or around the lake, one hundred of which actually nest there. The reed beds provide an excellent natural habitat for the fowl and it is for this reason that shooting is absolutely forbidden. (Pictured are a pair of swans)

and hornbeams. On and around Meleg Hill you can also find the very rare Hungarian oak. The cornel and the hazel are much more widespread. On the western side the cerasus is of interest. The base of the granite outcrops are rich in vegetation. The needlegrass prefers the loess beds. The lanneret and the black kite circle above.

LOVASBERÉNY and the *wood* which shares its name must already have been excellent for hunting in the 19th century when Count Cziráky built his **country house** there. By then the Calvinist church (1786) was already standing. The **Roman Catholic church** was subsequently commissioned by the Count and built to the designs of classical architect *József Hild*.

NADAP is the most stable geological point in Hungary, and it is in relation to this point that the altitudes of all the country's hills are measured. An *obelisk* has marked the spot since 1888.

Little egret

Local anglers know of 26 species of fish living in Lake Velence. In his book "Hungarian Angling" Ottó Herman (1835-1914) only mentions thirteen. His book describes the fishing tackle which was once used to fish the lake: the fish-baskets, the harpoons and the nets for example.

In 1928, the Hungarian Ornithological Association built an observation tower on the banks of the lake near Dinnyés. The popular hideout is named after the famous ornithologist István Chernel (1865-1922), the first person to embark on research work here.

Another famous ornithologist was Jenő Radetzky (1909-1992), who carried out his studies in the 420-hectare Velence Bird Reserve and the reed beds of the Dinnyés Fertő Nature Reserve from the 1950s onwards.

VELENCE

In Roman times people made their way here along the road linking Aquincum (Óbuda) to Savaria (Szombathely). In the Middle Ages the lake was referred to as Fertő, a name later shared by a village. It was a gentleman by the name of *Bonfini* who gave the place the much more attractive sounding name of *Venetio*. It was he also who claimed that it was the Venetians who built the village. Velence was once a fishing centre, but by the 1930s it had turned into a tourist resort and later the home of the *Velence Yacht Club*.

The Roman Catholic church was built in 1830 to the designs of *József Hild*. Inside there is a fine altar painting by *Vincenz Fischer*. **Wenckheim Palace**, which currently serves as a public institution, is also worth looking at.

On *Bence Hill* they grow the traditional white grape types (Mézesfehér, Riesling, Hárslevelű). The cellars here form part of the popular "wine trail". It was here that Hungarian poet *Mihály Vörösmarty* (1800–1850) had his **winepress**.

SUKORÓ is the highest (168m), and possibly one of the most beautiful villages, in the Velence area. The **Ethnographical House** (1863) on Szilvás-sor has a collection of local rural artifacts.

On the last Saturday before St Urban's Day (25th May) the St Urban's Day itself festivities are held on the Sárgaföldes-dűlő. There is wine tasting and prize-giving for the best vintages.

During the summer the shallow waters of Lake Velence warm up to 26°C. The water is rich in minerals and does wonders for the faint and weary.

It was at the altar of the **Calvinist church** on the evening prior to the Battle of Pákozd (September 28th, 1848) that prime minister *Lajos Batthyány* gave his famous speech calling for unity between the officers who had joined the revolution and those who had remained loyal to the Habsburgs. Every summer organ recitals are held here.

On the side of the hill stands the Memorial Chapel (Tamás Szabó) to the soldiers of the Hungarian Second Army killed on the Eastern Front during World War II. Since 1999, it has also been possible to pay one's respects to the Unknown Warrior.

Of the granite formations which you can see in the Velence Hills one should mention the individual and grouped rocky outcrops, the rocking boulders, the so-called holey stones and the tors. Some of the best examples can be found at the *Gyapjaszsák* near Sukoró, whilst *Pogány Rock* and *Pandúr Rock* near Pákozd are famous for their *rocking boulders*.

PÁKOZD

In the valley of the *Bella Stream* the remains of a substantial, so-called *group Neolithic settlement* have been found. It has also been proven that there was a Bronze Age earthwork here.

The celebrations marking the anniversary of the Battle of Pákozd help to bring the atmosphere of mid-19th century Hungary back to life.

The famous medieval chronicler *Anonymus* mentions Pákozd by name, and the village also appears in a document dated 1279.

The victorious Battle of Pákozd (29th September, 1848) is marked by a **monument** (1889) next to the main road, an **obelisk** jutting out into Lake Velence, and at the nearby **museum.** In the roof you will find the *Pákozd Mészeg Hill Tourist Centre* with its viewing terrace and exhibition area. Nearby is the recently planted 96-hectare **Pákozd-Sukoró Arboretum** which contains over 250 types of tree and shrub. The **Landscape Museum** is devoted to the natural, meteorological and geographical history of the region.

During the summer, pleasure boats sail over the lake, stopping at *Szúnyog Island* in Pákozd with its thatched, balconied *Fisherman's Inn*.

To the south of Pákozd on the marshes at the foot of *Mészeg Hill* you can find the **Bird Sanctuary**.

AGÁRD is a centre both of tourism and water sports. It was here back in the 1960s that the *Lake Velence School of Water Sports* was founded.

Saint Gellért (after 977-1046) is supposed to have celebrated mass at the medieval church in KÁPOLNÁSNYÉK. It is also the place where the great Hungarian poet Mihály Vörösmarty (1800-1855) was born. The house where he was born has long since disappeared, so the museum dedicated to Vörösmarty's memory is in the house where he was brought up. There is a bust of the great man in the garden (Tamás Vigh).

The thermal baths down in Agárd's Bika Valley is open all year round. The waters in both the indoor and outdoor pools, which come up from a depth of 1000m and at a temperature of 55°C, are recommended for the treatment of both locomotor and gynaecological illnesses. The health facilities and wellness centre which are currently being added will provide a whole list of new services.

GÁRDONY *was once situated on the banks of the lake only for flooding to force the inhabitants to move up onto the hillside. The water's edge was covered in reeds before the swimming complex was built in 1927.*

The **local museum** is devoted mainly to the memory of Hungarian poet Mihály Vörösmárty, but there is also a blacksmith's workshop there and a geological display (Gárdonyi út 13., but visits have to be arranged in advance).

MARTONVÁSÁR

After the Turkish period Martonvásár came into the possession of the family of the Duke of Brunswick. However, the 18th century **country house**, built in finest English Gothick, is more associated with the name of *Ludwig von Beethoven*. It was here that he composed the *Appassionata Sonata*.

The frescos on the vaults of the choir in the **Catholic church** (1773–1775) depicting St Stephen of Hungary and St Emmerich are by *Johann Cymbal*.

The waters of Saint Ladislas Stream have been used to make a small lake. On the island in the lake stands a bust of Beethoven (János Pásztor). Teréz Brunswick's name is associated with the foundation of the first Hungarian nursery school. The Nursery Museum is dedicated to her work and the history of the Hungarian nursery school since 1828.

In recent years Martonvásár has become more renowned for the agricultural and biological research work which has been going on at the *Agricultural Research Institute of the Hungarian Academy of Science*.

The one-time Brunszvik-Dreher Palace in Mártonvásár contains a museum which has in its possession Beethoven's correspondence with the female members of the Brunswick family. The park is currently used for the holding of classical concerts during the summer.

In the park of Martonvásár Palace the island in the middle of the lake is used for hosting outdoor concerts.

THE VÁL VALLEY

TORDAS was a model village founded by the *Hangya Co-operative Society*. It was here also that the Sajnovics family lived, as well as being the home of the astronomer and linguist *János Sajnovics* (1733–1786) who was one of the founding fathers of the Finn-Ugor movement. The family's seat, **Sajnovics Palace**, situated in *Saint Ladislas Valley*, was rebuilt in the romantic style and is now a children's home. It was in the *Vál Valley* that the so-called *Vál Culture* flourished between 950 and 900 BC. Tordas was also the seat of the Ürményi family, whose classical buildings make their mark on the village of VÁL. In such a small village the huge classical **Roman Catholic church** built by Chief Justice József Ürményi comes as quite a surprise.

Three kilometres from the village lies a **woodman's cottage** devoted to the country poet *János Vajda* (1827-1897). The building is in the custody of the next-door neighbour.

ALCSÚTDOBOZ

In the upper reaches of the *Vál Valley*, where the *Mezőföld* meets the *Vértes*, lies one of the most beautiful 19th century **country houses** in Hungary. Designed by *Mihály Pollack,* it was surrounded by a 44-hectare **English landscape garden**.

The renovated chapel now houses Hungary's one and only museum devoted to the history of gardens (Alcsúti út).

The ruined remains of the house's classical facade look picturesque amidst the vegetation. The new owner has recently built some stables and an **equestrian centre** next to the original *Habsburg riding-school.*

The old buildings, which have recently (1996) been turned into the *Pannonia Golf Club,* look down onto an avenue of two-hundred-year-old plane trees which stretch 1.8 kilometres towards the village of Etyek and the charming *Mária Valley*. The golf course is ideal for international competitions and includes a **holiday centre** where you can go riding or cycling, play tennis or swim.

BICSKE

The ruins you can find in the town centre are those of a church built following the Tatar invasion of 1241. Indeed the cemetery contains graves from that period. Of equal archaeological significance are the remains of the Stone Age settlement uncovered on *Galagonyás Hill* in 1931.

The finds (bones, stone implements and cooking utensils) can be found at the museum in Székesfehérvár.

An attraction dating from a later age is the **Batthyány Palace** (1754–1755). When it was remodelled, it was an imposing Baroque building boasting three wings and 64 rooms. The palace had a courtyard and an English-style park with its very own chapel. Its "red room" now houses the *local museum*. Here you can see Franz Joseph and Queen Elizabeth's silver goose feather pen and ink stand. Every summer the park plays host to the *Evening Palace Concerts*, whilst art exhibitions are held in the house.

The astronomical laboratory bears witness to the Batthyány's one-time estate manager Károly Nagy's (1797-1868) interest in mathematics and astronomy. He fought long and hard for the metre and the kilogram to be adopted in Hungary.

ETYEK

On the bank of the *Sajgó* you will find a **local history museum** founded by the Etyek Ethnic German Association in one of the Swabian houses (Magyar utca 7.).

Whilst visiting Etyek you can drop in on BOTPUSZTA to see the five cells of the **Nazarene House**, the church (1750) and its restored *crucifix.*

In 1990, the Etyek Hills, previously famous for having one of the largest single vineyards in Hungary, were finally promoted to the rank of Wine Region. The wines are characterised by their fresh lively flavour, the best known being the Chardonnay, the Pinot Blanc and the Szürkebarát.
Etyek grapes are also used to make Törley champagnes.

The old course of the River Danube and the river as it is today have created Dunaújváros's Youth Island. Those who want to get to the island's fish taverns and camping sites from the eastern bank of the Danube can simply catch the ferry.

DUNAÚJVÁROS

The land next to the village of *Dunapentele* on the Mezőföld was not built on until the 1950s. It was then that construction started on the Duna Ironworks (the predecessor to today's *Dunaferr*) and the new town, then known as *Sztálinváros* (Dunaújváros [Danube New Town] since 1961). The town is a textbook essay in Stalinist classicism and Socialist Realist public art. *József Somogyi's Furnaceman* in Vasmű út actually made it onto the town's coat of arms. Fortunately *Endre Domanovsky's* superb fresco of the *Alliance of the Workers and the Peasants* in the main entrance of Dunaferr Ltd. has been allowed to remain.
The small wooded park nearby is littered with machinery excess to requirement.

> "Work and embrace (sic) have lent the force of steel to the arms of the sturdy workers bridling the iron with asbestine strength; to the limbs of the peasants who took possession of the land; and to those of the fertile women with their sweet smiles." *Pál Morvay's translation of Zsuzsa Fehér's description the Domanovsky fresco.*

Seen together they look like a monument to the steel industry, as well as an exhibition devoted to **industrial archaeology**.

As for the more distant history of the immediate area: a Roman station, *Castellum Intercisa*, which made up part of the *limes* system along the banks of the Danube, stood on the site of the town.

Carved remains from the Roman town of Intercisa can be seen at the open-air lapidarium.

Finds from here and other Bronze age exhibits can be found in the **Intercista Museum** (Városháza tér).
Recently the socialist townscape has been somewhat tarnished by the addition of a number of new churches and sculptures which diverge somewhat from the consistency and uniformity of the old party line, perhaps the most striking example being the glass pyramid of a Lutheran Church designed by prize-winning architect *Tamás Nagy*.
Art-lovers should also pay a visit to the **Institute of Contemporary Arts** (Vasmű út 12.).

GETTING OUT OF DUNAÚJVÁROS

ERCSI

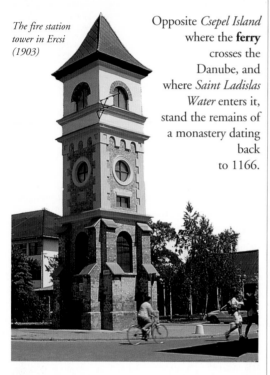

The fire station tower in Ercsi (1903)

Opposite *Csepel Island* where the **ferry** crosses the Danube, and where *Saint Ladislas Water* enters it, stand the remains of a monastery dating back to 1166.

What remained was used to build the **monument** dedicated to the 1,100th anniversary of the *Hungarian Conquest* in the church garden.

Pilgrims come from miles around to see Ercsi's the miraculous picture of the **Blessed Virgin Mary** in the **Church of the Blessed Virgin** (1763–1767). Since 1815, the pilgrimage has traditionally taken place on the Sunday closest to 15th August.

Much of what can be seen in Ercsi is dedicated to the memory of Hungarian writer József Eötvös (1813-71) who spent his childhood here.
There is a museum devoted to him at this old villa in what is now Eötvös utca and a sculpture (Tibor Vilt) of him in front of the Cultural Centre. Those approaching the town from the river will have a good view of the column (Miklós Ybl) which is also dedicated to him.

ADONY

It was here that the Romans set up a **military camp**. Remains have also been found of a 6th–7th century Avar grave and a 7th–8th century horse burial. The **national flag** dating from the 1930s, and the monument to those who fell in the two World Wars reflect the town's more recent history. Nowadays perhaps the most important destination in Adony is the *Freedom Culture Park*. Set around the **Zichy Palace** (c.1820), which now functions as a cultural centre, there is an **outdoor stage** and an **observatory**. The summer programme includes the St Urban's Day Carnival (25th May) and the Wine Festival. The botanists amongst you should explore the Mezőföld loess beds for the rare wild flowers which can be found there, particularly the *milk-vetch* and the *snowdrops*.

The 300-hectare Great Island in the Little Danube (Kis-Duna) at Rácalmás is covered entirely in trees.
Its unique habitat has made it a nature conservation area.
The banks of the Danube, on the other hand,
offer fishing and hunting possibilities.

RÁCALMÁS stands high above the River Danube. It is here that you can find the remains of the medieval **monastery** where King Béla IV. sent his daughter Margaret (later to become St Margaret of Hungary) to be brought up. Later in its long history the monastery was occupied by Greek Orthodox Nuns. Rácalmás's excellent wines are kept in the very same **cellars** which offered refuge to those who were forced to hide from the Turks.

EXPLORING THE MEZŐFÖLD

Because NAGYKARÁCSONY *happens to share its name with the Hungarian for Christmas the local post office has to ensure that all cards posted there from the first Advent until Christmas get a special festive postmark.*

The village also organises a series of special events leading up to the big day. Father Christmas House is open from the middle of November.
Children wishing to do something creative can turn their hands to a little handiwork, and there's always the chance to talk to Santa himself (Petőfi u. 14.).

The lake you can see on the edge of RÉTSZILAS is one of those lakes created by regulating the waters of the Sárvíz. The fishponds are very popular with the *herons, terns, avocets, black storks, pond tortoises* and *otters.*
At *Réti Farm* in SÁREGRES you will find the **Arany-ponty Fishing Museum,** and in the near future a house devoted to the arts and crafts.

A flock of cormorants circle above the Rétszilas Lakes

CECE, which lies on the southern tip of the *Mező-föld,* depends mainly on agriculture for its livelihood: paprika and watermelons in particular. The **country museum,** which can be found in a converted peasant's house, will answer any queries you may have about the farming that goes on here. *István Csók* (1865–1961), one of the great Hungarian Post-Impressionists, was born in nearby Sáregres and it is in his parents' house (Arany János u. 1), that you can visit a small **museum** dedicated to his life and work. It all seems a long way from the Paris Csók lived in between 1903 and 1910.

The interesting thing about the **Zichy Palace** in VAJTA is the fact that it was built in the 1920s to plans which *Mihály Pollack* had drawn up one hundred years earlier. The *Bible College* and *Conference Centre* also operate in the building.

Vajta's most valuable resource is its hot water spring.
Set in beautiful natural surroundings
the thermal waters have medicinal properties.

DÉG

The village is set in the undulating landscape of the Mezőföld next to the stream known as the *Bozót.* In 1769, the village was purchased by the Festetics family. Their **country house,** which was built between 1820 and 1826 to the plans of *Mihály Pollack,* has a splendid pedimented entrance. The oval mirrored banqueting hall with its semicircular alcoves can be found in one of the wings. The house is surrounded by a wooded **park**. There is also a **wild-life park** part of which lies beyond the *Bozót* and the park. When surveying the park you might come across the so-called *"Little Palace"* built in 1772.

The red brick Dutch House, now a venue for art exhibitions, stands on an island in the middle of one Dég Park's man-made islands.

Following the construction of the "Great Palace" it became Pál Festetics's famous stable. Recently Hungary's *largest piece of graphic art* was unveiled in the park. Measuring 17x3m, *Róbert Kőnig*'s work (2000) celebrates the Festetics family's contributions to the life of their country.

There are a fine variety of trees in Dég Park: *ginkgoes, magnolias, black mulberries, catalpas, Judas trees* and *golden rain trees.* The most worthy of mention are perhaps the six oaks whose trunks vary between 3 and 5 metres in diameter. The jewel in the park's crown is, however, the lake which is constantly supplied by three separate water sources. The palace garden is open to the general public.

SÁRSZENTÁGOTA and SÁRKERESZTÚR are surrounded by lakes, ponds and marshes making it an ornithologist's paradise. In the boggy areas one is likely to see *cranes, plovers, tufted ducks, curlews* and *black seagulls.* You will however need binoculars to pick out the *eagles, falcons* and *merlins.*

Botanists will not be disappointed. During the spring you can see *camomile* and *nasturtiums* in the alkaline areas, in the late summer *goosefoot* and *lavender* in the salt marshes, and in the autumn, *asters* cover the ground in vast swathes of blue.

SZÉKESFEHÉRVÁR

It was here in the year 1000, in the lands held by Árpád, that Stephen was crowned King of Hungary. It was the same Stephen, who in 1018, having managed to stabilise the kingdom, opened up a pilgrimage route which went past Fehérvár and on to the Holy Land. This gave rise to the idea of having a *royal town* capable of fulfilling various representative functions. Known as *Alba Regia*, Székesfehérvár hosted **royal coronations** for more than five hundred years, and it was also a royal necropolis and the venue for the royal assizes. It was here that King Stephen was buried in 1038 and canoised in 1083.

It is at the Orb (Béla Ohmann) that the St Stephen's Day (August 20th) celebrations take place. It is also here with the Town Hall, the Bishop's Palace and Franciscan Church as the backdrop that the Fehérvár Carnival takes place on the last Saturday in September.
Géza Lux's lapidarium cum mausoleum is where you can find Saint Stephen's 11th century sarcophagus in a 20th century setting dominated by Vilmos Aba Novák's historical frieze.

The lapidarium includes the mausoleum containing Saint Stephen's stone sarcophagus. The building was designed by Géza Lux and decorated with historical secco wall paintings by Vilmos Aba-Novák.

The outlines of the one-time *Palace Gate* are picked out on the pavement in stone. One part of the old medieval town walls stands behind the park containing *Jenő Bory's Bishop's Well*. From here you can see the cathedral rising above the surrounding rooftops.

The gateway of the **Town Hall** opening onto Városház tér is spectacular indeed. Built at the beginning of the 1700s, the design includes Corinthian columns, mythological figures and a stone balustrade bearing the coat-of-arms of the town. The wing of the one-time Zichy Palace, an architectural exercise in the late-Baroque "Zopf-stil", includes a fine gateway dating from the 1780s. The **Museum of Ecclesiastical Art** in the old Franciscan Friary and the library at the **Bishop's Palace** opposite (1802, *Jakab Rieder*) has some rare manuscripts and some very old printed books. It was the throne *("szék")* that once provided the centrepiece of the now ruined Basilica of St Stephen. The group of buildings, which now form the spiritual centre of what is a **National Site of Remembrance**, were built in 1938 to mark the one thousandth anniversary of the death of St Stephen.

On the pavement in the square just in front of the cathedral you can make out the outline of the quatrefoil-shaped chapel picked out in stone. Just to the north of the cathedral you can see the pointed arches of the oldest surviving building in Székesfehérvár, the recently renovated Chapel of St. Anna (1470). The building also includes some painted fragments dating back to the Turkish occupation.

The statue of Matthias Corvinus (Miklós Melocco) is a useful landmark to use for getting one's bearings. The colourful (and accurate) flower clock is nearby, as is the Vörösmarty Theatre and the Hungarian Royal Hotel.

It was in the wing of the one-time Pelican Tavern (Kossuth u. 15.) overlooking the courtyard that the "Székesfehérvár National Theatrical Society" was founded, and it was here, between 1842 and 1843, that Petőfi Sándor took to the stage. The building is now a theatre, the old theatre hall is now the small Pelican Stage of the Vörösmarty Theatre. The courtyard is used by the Summer Theatre. The columned passageway in the wing on the right-hand side leads to the Pelican Gallery.

The walls of the Serbian Orthodox Rác Church were built in 1733 around an already existing chapel. It was only when the new baroque edifice was completed that the old chapel was finally demolished, meaning that no break in the celebration of the mass was necessary. The church is decorated in superb Byzantine-style paintings and contains a rococo iconostasis.

One of the most popular destinations for a day out is Lake Bánya. This wild, untamed landscape was created by what was a miracle of nature when, one night in 1917, the dark green waters suddenly appeared at the bottom of the quarry. The deep cold waters are not, however, suitable for swimming. The Chapel of Saint Donatus, which stands on the edge of the cliffs, used to be a popular pilgrimage place.

The reliquary of the skull of St Stephen is kept in the Baroque **Diocesan Cathedral** (1758–1778). The cathedral contains frescos by *J.I. Cymbal* and an altar painting by *Vinzenz Fischer.*

The Church of the Mount Carmel Virgin (1745–1748) on Petőfi utca. is also known as the **Seminary Church.** The ceilings, the altars in the first two side chapels and the oratory chapel fresco on the first floor are all *Franz Anton Maulbertsch* (1724–1796).

In the courtyard of Kossuth utca 9. Hungarian historical figures appear every two hours as part of the **Glockenspiel**, to which the music is constantly changes.

The **Cistercian Church** and its monastic buildings (1745–1755) contain frescos, a fine high altarpiece and carpentry *(Károly Bebo)*. The rococo liturgical furniture in the sacristy *(János Hyngeller)* was made by the same workshop as made the furniture in the **Fekete Sas (Black Eagle) Chemist's** (now a museum).

Next to the church, in what was the Jesuit Monastery, now the **Saint Stephen the King Museum**, you can see carved stone fragments from the medieval royal basilica, and finds from the Roman settlement of Gorsium. The *Deák Collection* at the *Municipal Picture Gallery* (Oskola u.) contains Hungarian paintings from the second third of the 20th Century.

At the **István Csók Picture Gallery** (Bartók Béla tér) you can see *Vilmos Aba Novák's* tableau *"Hungarian–French Historical Contacts"*, which won the gold medal at the 1937 *Paris World Exhibition.*

The *Palace District (Palotaváros)* of the town was where a large number of Serbian traders settled in the 18th century. A small group of their houses and the Serbian Church built in 1774 were all renovated during the 1980s. This **museum-like street** recently won a *Europa Nostra Award.*

When leaving for Budapest you can see perched on top of *Csúcsos Hill* the **Monument to the Golden Bull** *(Sándor Rétfalvi)* which is, according to tradition, the place where King Andrew II. signed the Golden Bull in 1222. On the northern edge of the town on *Öreg Hill* stands **Bory Castle**. Dating all the way back to the 1930s, the dreamchild of *Jenő Bory* (1879–1959), the castle is one

The Well and King Matthias Memorial
(Miklós Meloccó) in Liszt Ferenc utca.
Ceremonial Mass at the Cathedral

of Hungary's more unusual attractions. The building now contains a museum dedicated to Bory's sculptures and the paintings of his wife *Ilona Komócsin.*

A good place to switch off and relax is the **outdoor swimming complex**, or perhaps the **swimming pool**. There is also a covered **ice rink,** a *riding school* and the *Csitáry Well. Manchester United* fans may be interested in making a pilgrimage to the *Sóstó Stadium*, home of *Videoton FC.*

The *Sóstó* is all that remains of a salty marsh. Next to it lies the 121-hectare *Sand Pit Nature Reserve* where you can find *orchids, irises, twayblades, early spider orchids* and *milk-vetch.*

THE EASTERN BAKONY

Amidst the beauties of the *Eastern Bakony* between Bodajk and Fehérvárcsurgó lies the **Szurdok Valley** where rocks rise up on either side of the steep road. Equally popular are the rocks on either side of the *Burok Valley* and the wild landscape of the *Kisgyón Nature Reserve*. Even today you can find remnant Ice Age flora in these valleys, for example *alpine garlic* and *reeds*. The area is well known for its rowans and its birds, particularly the *sakerets.*

Another good tourist destination is the *Tűzköves Ditch* which leads up the northeastern face of the 454-metre-high *Hárs Hill*. In the derelict quarry about 120 types of fossils have been found.

FEHÉRVÁRCSURGÓ

Nature has indeed been kind to Fehérvárcsurgó. There is good hunting to be had on the southern stretch of the *Móri Valley*, and the *Gaja* flows through some excellent walking country. History has not made much of an impression on this landscape. There is an Iron Age fort containing nine barrows from the first millennium before Christ.

The **Roman Catholic church** was built on the remains of a 12th century church. If you go inside you can see the *Csurgó Madonna*, the work of one of the village's most famous sons, *Amerigo Tot (Tóth Imre).*

The late-classical **country house** on the Károlyi estate, was remodelled by *Miklós Ybl*. It is planned to turn the house into a venue for international and domestic cultural events, once the renovation work has been completed. Its one hundred rooms, ceremonial drawing room, courtyard chapel and 45-hectare **English-style park** will indeed provide the most pleasant of surroundings.

MOHA is famous for its *mineral waters,* which contain traces of calcium, magnesium, hydrogen carbonate, sodium and potassium. It's especially worth visiting Moha on Shrove Tuesday, when young and old take part in the age-old custom of "hen knocking" with origins which probably go back to some ancient fertility ritual. The waters in Moha go under the name of "Ágnes", a name which dates back to 1869.

The waters from the spring known as *Áldókút* first came onto the market all the way back in 1880.

During "hen knocking" the young men of the village dress up in brightly coloured clothing and go shouting through the village collecting goose eggs, taunting the dogs and playing practical jokes on the residents. In the evening all the eggs collected throughout the day are scrambled and served up.

BODAJK

Bodajk is situated at the southern end of the Móri Valley opposite Csókakő. The village is dominated by **Lamberg Palace** (1839) above, which stands *Calvary Hill* whose Stations of the Cross, crucifix and chapel predate the house by one hundred years. At the base of the **Calvary** stands the church of the Blessed Virgin Mary (1728) and the **Capuchin Monastery**. Together they make Bodajk Hungary's oldest pilgrimage place. The pilgrimage is held on 12th September, the Feast of the Virgin Mary.

At the foot of the hill warm bubbly waters (14–19 °C) surface at the spring. The site, which also includes a pond, has become a popular **bathing pool**. During the winter months guests head for the **ski slopes.** The **youth camp** which lies nearby is open all year. There is also a **sculpture park** at the derelict quarry on *Keselő Hill*.

Running into a deer in the Eastern Bakony is not a particularly rare occurrence.

In ISZKASZENTGYÖRGY the Baroque mansard-roofed Amadé-Bajzáth-Pappenheim Palace lying on the edge of the village is currently being transformed into a hotel. Exhibitions are occasionally held in the banqueting hall. The romantic parkland around the house provides an atmospheric setting.

Summer Wild Geese prepare for migration.

THE SÁRRÉT

During the Ice Age there was one huge lake here collecting up all the waters running off the Bakony. Those waters were subsequently absorbed into the 120 km² of muddy soil known as the *Sárrét*. Because of the 117 species of birds that live here, particularly the *bustards*, and the *sandy needlegrass heathland*, it has become a nature conservation area.

It was in these surroundings that world-famous hunter SÁRPENTELE-born *Count Zsigmond Széchenyi* (1898–1967) learned his craft. All that remains of the park once surrounding his country seat is **Pentele Park** which is now a popular destination for a day out. It is here that you might bump into a **monument** built by the Count's admirers in memory of the man who hunted there in his youth. The Count said of the place: "it means many things, unspoilt plains, mysterious marshes, and the secret and picturesque world of the water bird."

In 1976, some interesting archaeological finds came to light in the park of the classical Zichy-Hadik Palace in SEREGÉLYES. Though not old, the silver and gold plate cutlery and cooking implements from the beginning of the 1900s have been deemed important enough to be displayed at the Saint Stephen the King Museum in Székesfehérvár on an occasional basis. Seregélyes's classical palace (1821) is now the Taurus Palace Hotel.

The reconstructed remains at the outdoor museum give you an idea as to the original appearance of the Roman town.

TÁC-GORSIUM

In the undulating sandy loess soil of the *Sárvíz Valley,* one Roman mile from the village, stand the **ruins** of the Roman town of *Gorsium.* Before becoming the centre of an Imperial cult and a regional centre in the 2nd century, Gorsium had been a military station (46–47 BC).

At the end of April every year the Goddess *Flora* Celebrations are organised in honour of *Floralia* the bringer of spring. The huge **outdoor performance**, involving the massed ranks of 1,200 people, and including a programme of Greek and Roman classical dramas and gladiatorial contests, takes places at the end of August as part of the *Ludi Romani-Gorsium Summer Games.*

SZABADBATTYÁN

Excavations are currently going on at one of ancient Pannonia's most famous villas, on the banks of the

Venus the Goddess of Love

Sárvíz-Malom Channel. It is possible that the so-called *Seuso Treasure,* otherwise known as the *Northampton Treasure* on account of the Duke of Northampton's subsequent ownership of part of the treasure, originally came from this 110x120 m site.

> *The treasures were found by a local amateur archaeologist, György Sümegh, when out walking one day. He hid the treasure in his house, but couldn't resist bragging about it in the village. Following his mysterious death the treasure disappeared without a trace, only to reappear later, first at the Getty Museum in California, and then in 1990 at the Sotheby's auctioning house in New York. The Hungarian state has been pursuing the treasures in the courts ever since.*

The two branches of the *Sárvíz* (the *Nádor* and the *Malom*) meet at the **Cifra Garden.**

Those travelling from Szabadbattyán in the direction of Lake Balaton will only have to take a slight detour via Polgárdi to the get to FÜLE, whose **Sárrét Peasant House** (Széchenyi u. 107.) has a fine collection of woven and embroidered textiles from Fejér County. Visitors can visit the exhibition throughout the holiday.

In the southeastern corner of what is now Szabadbattyán stood the fortress known as Csíkvár, and a granary. The oldest part of the fortress was used as a watchtower during the 15th century, before the Turks added the buttresses and the arrow slits when turning it into a Kula (the Turkish for tower). The tower houses an exhibition about the Turkish occupation.

In 1873 the Nádasdy family decided to turn their 18th century Baroque palace in NÁDASDLADÁNY into a Tudor-style manor house. The furnishings were all modified accordingly, producing some interesting results in the library and the Ancestral Hall. The twenty hectares of the parkland surrounding the house include rarities such as the locust tree and the foxglove tree.

VESZPRÉM

Built on five hills, *"the queens' town"* has a very long history. It was here that Saint Stephen and his wife, the Bavarian Gizella, built St Michael's Cathedral. They also founded the Greek Nunnery lying down in Veszprém Valley. It was there that the Hungarian coronation robe was made, although it was originally intended to be a chasuble. Tradition has it that Queen Gizella herself worked on it.

During the 18th century the town rose from the ashes to become the historic town we can see today.

To get to the **Castle Quarter** you have to go across Óváros tér where some of the finest town houses in Veszprém are situated. One of the most interesting is **Pósa House,** which was built by the Cistercians in 1793. As with all the other houses in the square this too has become a bank, albeit without any apparent adverse effects.

Next to the renovated **Town Hall** stands the locals' favourite statue of a *Girl Carrying a Vase* by *Lenke R. Kiss.*

Up to the 13th century the castle and the town were one and the same, and it was here the town enjoyed its first golden age. It was then the university was founded, and Béla IV. sent his daughter Margaret to be brought up in the monastery nearby. The Chapel of Saint George actually stood during Prince Geisa's lifetime (c. 945–997). According to legend it was here that Saint Stephen's son Emmerich (1007–1031) swore his oath of chastity. The chapel was rebuilt during the 15th century.

The architect of the so-called **Fecskendő House** (1814) on Vár utca was Henrik Tummler, who was also the first person to bring running water to the castle. Here you can visit the *Kisgaléria.* Through **Heroes' Gate** you can find the *Arts House,* which also contains the *Csikász Gallery* and the *Modern Picture Gallery* (Vár u. 3.-7.) containing the *László Vass Collection.*

Going through the courtyard you make your way to the **Fire Tower (Tűztorony):** this and the **Veszprém Pantheon** were built from the remains of a medieval bastion. Dubniczay House (Vár u. 29.) provides some exhibition space for the Castle Gallery, and from the courtyard you can get to the **Brick Museum.**

Veszprém's connection with queens goes back to the Bishop of Veszprém's title of Queen's Chancellor, which brought with it the task of crowning the queen. Bishop Károly Hornig crowned Zita, the last Queen of Hungary, in 1916.

The neighbouring building houses the *Headquarters of the Balaton Highlands National Park.* (For more details see the chapter on National Parks.) Opposite stands the **Bishop's Palace,** built from 1765 onwards to the plans of *Jakab Fellner.* The building includes parts of the medieval palace, but it is dominated by the Baroque of the magnificent entrance hall, the staircase and the banqueting hall. The Archepiscopal Archive and the Archepiscopal Library, which are both open to the public, are made all the more wonderful by *J. Cymbal's* wall paintings. The palace includes the 13th century chapel, often referred to as the **Gizella Chapel.** Its life-size figural compositions are amongst the oldest examples of Hungarian fresco painting in existence.

The 18th century depiction of the *Holy Trinity* in the middle of the courtyard is unmistakably Baroque. The **Cathedral of St Michael** standing behind it was originally built by Saint Stephen and Gizella in

The summer events and cultural programmes which go on in the town - like the Kabóciádé Puppet Festival shown here - are for the most part organised by the Arts Centre (Dózsa út 2.).

the Romanesque style. What one sees today, was mainly built between 1907 and 1910. In the chancel of the cathedral you can see a *reliquary* containing a part of Queen Gizella's arm, a gift

from Passau in Germany where Gizella died and was buried.

Gizella's name is also given to the **Museum of Ecclesiastical Art** which lies near the Franciscan Church. The oldest Hungarian *church* in Veszprém is believed to have been the **Chapel of Saint George,** excavated in 1957.

The **Petőfi Theatre** was the first reinforced concrete building to be built in Hungary. It was designed by *István Medgyaszay* in 1908.

From the balustrade of Veszprém Castle you can see the statues of Saint Stephen and Gizella *(József Ispánky)* and behind them a panorama containing the Bakony, *Benedict Hill,* the *Séd Valley* and the **viaduct.**

Under the arches of the bridge you can find the **Kálmán Kittenberger Zoological and Botanical Garden.** The park has a good record in the breeding, collecting and exchanging of animals. Indeed more than 120 species live there. The complex includes stables, and there are frequent lectures, exhibitions and programmes

The **Dezső Laczkó Museum** *(1912, István Medgyaszay)* in the Erzsébet Woods is devoted to the natural sciences, folk art, history and archaeology. Next to the museum you can find **Bakony House**, an exact copy of a house in the village of Öcs. It was built in 1935 to show how local families from the lower gentry lived.

The Valley Bridge was built in 1938, and its two spans join Jerusalem Hill with the suburb of Dózsaváros.

IN AND AROUND VESZPRÉM

It was in SZENTKIRÁLYSZABADJA on 31st September 1944 that *Miklós Radnóti* wrote the final verse of his *Razglednicas* during the death march that brought him and 6,000 others from the death camp in Bor in Jugoslavia. Rádnóti's Bor notebook was found in his overcoat in the mass grave he shared with 21 other Jewish prisoners just outside Győr. Szentkirályszabadja's tribute to the poet is the **Memorial Museum** (Rákóczi u. 64) which stands in the building Radnoti stayed in that particular night.

The Calvinist church in LITÉR was originally built in the 13th century and was remodelled in the Baroque style. The lion you can see on the portal appears on the village's coat of arms.

BERHIDA boasts the best preserved **14th century church** in Hungary. It is interesting to note that they used cut stone instead of carved timber to hold up the roof, a solution similar to one used in Brittany.

In SÓLY stands one of Hungary's oldest village **churches**. So old is it that it could have stood at the time Stephen (later to become Saint Stephen) and Koppány were battling out the future of Hungary on a field which is believed to have been close by.

ÖSKÜ's **round church** with its wooden shindle roof was probably built from a bastion belonging to *Garay Castle* (12th–16th cent.).

The place where Stephen and Koppány fought is marked by a massive wooden sword on the top of Calvary Hill in Sóly.

VÁRPALOTA

The hectare of nature reserve which occupies the **sandpits** in Várpalota (Gagarin u.) bears testament to the natural history of the Pannonian Basin, and more particularly to the sea which covered the region 25 million years ago. Run by the *Balaton Highlands National Park*, it is open to the general public.

Perhaps Várpalota is most famous for Újlaki (otherwise known as Thury) Castle which stands on Szabadság tér. It had an important function as a border castle in the wars against the Turks. Two of the four corner towers were demolished in 1845, but despite this there is still much to admire today. It is now home to the Hungarian Chemistry Museum, a Mining Exhibition, a picture gallery and a lapidarium.

Várpalota is famous for its churches, those sites which have some connection with the Zichy family, the **frescos** in the Roman Catholic church in the *Inota* district of the town, and the *Gyula Nagy Gallery* in the old Palota **synagogue** (1839) (Szent István u. 3.)

Behind Thury Castle you can follow the path, marked with a red line, which leads up through the woods to **Bátorkő Castle**.

If one looks northwest from Várpalota you can see the Tés **windmills**, both of which are in running order and both of which can be visited by the general public.

THE BAKONY

As you approach Zirc you will see a sign to one of the best-run ski slopes in western Hungary: EPLÉNY. The ski lift is in operation from the beginning of November until the end of the season. That is of course if there is any snow.

ZIRC

The Cistercian **Monastery** has had a stormy history, resulting in its being totally destroyed during the Turkish occupation.

The main altar in the baroque Zirc Abbey (Rákóczi tér) was painted by Maulbertsch in 1754.

It was later rebuilt by the Cistercians in the Baroque style. The monastery is the centre of the Cistercian order in Hungary. The *Antal Reguly Memorial Library* and the *Bakony Natural History Museum* can both be found in the monastic buildings. The latter gives visitors a good introduction to the flora and fauna of the Bakony.

The Zirc Arboretum (Damjanich u.) covers 18 hectares and has about 600 types of trees and shrubs. Some of the specimens are extremely old, like the 400–year-old oak tree.

The horse parade is one of the high points of the Bakony Highwaymen's Festival.

From the edge of BAKONYNÁNA you can follow the signs to the *Gajak* which in turn leads you via the rushing waters tumbling down through the black rocks to the **Roman Bath**.

Along the road which runs parallel with the *Cuha* you eventually get to the **tourist house** at GÉZA-HÁZA, which is open all year round. In FENYŐFŐ you find yourself in the middle of 500 hectares of *ancient pine woodland*, the only natural habitat of its kind in the whole of Hungary.

BAKONYBÉL is well known for its associations with Saint Gellért. It was here that Duke Emmerich's teacher lived between 1023 and 1030. Although the 18th century **monastic buildings** are now used as an old people's home, the Baroque **church,** with its 250-year-old organ, is still a place of devotion.

The ruins beside the Zirc-Győr road mark the site of Csesznek
Castle, now a popular venue for medieval tournaments.

The latest attraction in Bakonybél is the **Bakony Forest House** research centre. Next door you will find the *Forestry Education Centre* and an *Arts and Crafts House* (2002).

In Bánd stand the ruins of the 14th century fortress of **Essegvár**. On *Miklóspál Hill* in Szentgál there is a unique *yew grove*. The yews, numbering about 120 thousand trees, are one of Europe's great natural curiosities.

Herend

The success story started in 1826 when *Vince Stingl* founded his **ceramics business.** Under *Mór Fischer's* leadership the business soon gained a worldwide reputation.

Herend porcelain is one of the world's most immediately recognisable Hungarian products.

In 1851, Herend porcelain had the opportunity to really make its mark. It was then, at the Great Exhibition in London, that the Victoria pattern, based on the Queen's favourite motif, was born. Even today the world's rich and famous buy from the factory in Herend. In 1999, small-scale production was set up in the trade centre for the benefit of visitors. Visitors can also see the world's largest Herend collection. At the **Porcelánium** coffee house you can drink coffee out of real porcelain cups. (Look under "Herend Porcelain" in the *Hungarian Treasury*).

Magyarpolány *is a Europa Nostra award-winning village. Petőfi utca is considered a national treasure, with 43 of the houses having national preservation orders on them, and 40 of them local preservation orders. The village has a famous Calvary (1770-1780). The five carved wooden Stations of the Cross are each covered with their own roof. You have to mount 153 steps to get to the Chapel at the top. The Polány Passion is held on the steps every Whitsuntide.*

AJKA

The first thing that comes to mind when you hear the word Ajka is **glass**, and visitors are fortunate enough to be able to visit the *Kristály Üvegipari Kft. (The Crystal Glass Company)* themselves, to see the engraved lead glass, glasses, jugs and bowls being made. This, however, can only be organised for groups, and with the prior permission of the management.

The **Local Museum** in Szabadság tér includes a permanent exhibition celebrating the life's work of sculptor *Miklós Borsos*.

The **Mining Museum** on Csingeri út has a fine collection of minerals and all the other things you would expect at a museum celebrating the mining industry.

DEVECSER has one of Hungary's most beautiful **libraries**. It is situated in the **Esterházy Palace** (1532–1537, but was subsequently remodelled).

TÜSKEVÁR was once famous for its **potteries,** and the potter's art still survives in the village. The **Somló and District Local Museum** on Kossuth utca is also dedicated primarily to pottery.

SÜMEG

Castle Hill, crowned by its picturesque medieval fortress, can be seen from as far as the *Trans-danubian Hills.* The **castle** was already there by the beginning of the 14th century, but it was only during the second half of the 20th century that it benefited from any kind of restoration.

The ground plan of the castle is pretty irregular. In front of the interior gateway there is a wolf trap. The castle buildings are now partly inhabited and there is a **museum** containing a sabre cabinet, a coach exhibition and an old torture chamber.

Castle **tournaments** are frequently held at the castle. The fun and games take place on a daily basis in August and three times a week in May, June, September and October. In March sports lovers can attend the town's *equestrian event,* while there is an *equestrian camp* to enjoy during the summer months.

In Kisfaludy tér at the base of *Castle Hill* you can see Sümeg's most beautiful building, the **Bishop's Palace**, built between 1748 and 1755. It is in this square that you can see the town's second oldest

Sümeg's castle lies 270 metres above sea level where the Bakony joins up with the Lesser Plain. It covers an area of ten thousand square metres.

building, the **Franciscan Church and Monastery** (1652–1657).

A glorious sight awaits those who decide to visit the **Roman Catholic parish church** on Biró Marton utca, namely some of the most beautiful Baroque and rococo paintings in the whole of Hungary. They were painted to the designs of *Franz Anton Maulbertsch* and his patron, the local bishop. In doing so they both managed to have themselves immortalised in one of the pictures. The scheme is in fact one huge fresco covering the walls and the entire ceiling. There is a certain inevitability about the fact that the church has earned the title of *"Hungary's Rococo Sistine Chapel".*

More and more foreign potters are participating in SÜMEGPRÁGA's *annual Potters' Convention. It is usually held at Whitsuntide or thereabouts, and includes pot throwing, an auction, a fair and a folk programme.*

PÁPA

Pápa was already a town by the end of the 14th century, but the town you see today is essentially Baroque in character. Its history is based on being a trade centre with an educational tradition.

In the town centre there is an old chemist's shop, the *Pomegranate* (Jókai u.), which is more a **museum** than a place you go to buy aspirin.

The Dying Museum (Március 15. tér) is in fact an operational Kluge-type dying workshop dating from the 18th century, and as such is one of the oldest dying workshops in Central Europe. Absolutely everything has survived, from the books to the dying implements. They are all on display at the exhibition.

The Scientific Collections of the Calvinist Church in Western Hungary, its **library, archive** and **museum** have found a home in the *Calvinist Grammar School* (Március 15. tér 9.). The collection contains writings by some of the greats of Hungarian literature. There is also an Egyptian mummy presented by a grateful student.

Some of the greats of Hungarian literature studied at the **Ókollégium** (Petőfi u. 13.).

Next to the **Synagogue,** built in 1846, lies perhaps the oldest Jewish cemetery in the country. There are some gravestones dating back 350 years.

The town hall was built on the site of the Benedictine Monastery (Fő u.). A **Benedictine Church** (1737–1742) still stands next door, on the porch of which you will find a huge crucifix known as

The restoration of the houses in the main square earned the town the Hild Medal.

the *Szerecsen Christ.* The high and the side altars, the pulpit, and the furniture in the sacristy are all very finely carved.

Fő utca, which runs down in front of the **Museum of Calvinist Ecclesiastical History and Art,** leads to the **Catholic Great Church** (1774–1786, *Jakab Fellner* and *József Grossmann*), one of the biggest buildings in western Hungary.

The nave has frescos by *Maulbertsch,* the high altar is by *Grossmann,* the altar painting by *Huber Maurer* and the marble sculpture around the high altar by *Fülöp Prokop.*

At the beginning of August, Hungary's Hussar Associations descend on Papa to participate in the Pápa Historical Festival.

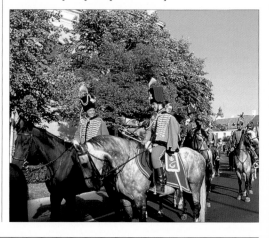

One example of how renovation should be done can be found at the **Eszterházy Palace**. Here the 18th century core of the building has been turned into a music school, a library and the **Károly Eszterházy Museum**. The reading room is in what was the palace chapel, the restoration of which (1988–1989) earned the artists *Éva Král* and *István Felhősi* the *Europa Nostra Prize*.

Its main attraction is the fresco on the ceiling, painted in c. 1750, and the work of Viennese academician Johann Ignaz Mildorfer, to a scheme decided upon by Ferenc Esterházy.

The baths (2003), supplied by 42°C thermal waters, are open all year round. Besides the seasonal outdoor pools, there are plenty of thermal, wellness-fitness and leisure facilities to enjoy, and all in the vicinity of the protected *Inner Castle Garden*. It won't be long before Pápa will also be able to offer health and medicinal facilities, a hotel and a camping site, together with a leisure centre. And all this will be within a stone's throw of the **Thermal Baths.**

IN THE FOOTHILLS OF THE BAKONY

SOMLÓVÁSÁRHELY

At the heart of the Somló **wine region,** you can walk to *Taposó Well,* visit the 15th century **Chapel of St Margaret** or the **Petőfi Lookout Tower** (*1938, István Medgyaszay*). The *Somló Wine House* was kindly built by the people of Pápa as storage for of the local wines. These include wedding-consummation wine and *Somló juhfark,* which were both recommended to the likes of kings to increased the likelihood of being blessed with a male heir.

Somló Castle, which stands on top of the hill, guarded the whole region. All that is left now are

Vinum somlainum omni sanum (Somló wine cures all) was how the chemists of the 18th and 19th centuries put it. This may have been taking it a bit far, but the wine is worth tasting all the same ... Maria Theresa would never go to bed without having a glass, and she ended up having sixteen children!

the ruins. The National Park's *Pál Kitaibel Nature Trail leads* right up there.

GANNA

Is famous for its **round church**, the Esterházy family mausoleum *(Charles Moreau).* The building is claimed to be a smaller version of the *Pantheon* in Rome.

FARKASGYEPŰ

The village can be found in the middle of a 100–120 year-old beech wood. It is a popular destination, and some good fishing is to be had there at the **trout pond**. Its pleasant climate and fresh air meant that a *T.B. sanitorium* was built there between 1928 and 1929.

So, for the time being we must say goodbye, but we look forward to seeing you again in the far-western reaches of Hungary between Győr and Nagykanizsa.

The 14th century ruins of DÖBRÖNTE *Castle are where the Castle Festivities take place every September.*

"And pleasure? It's here, a game.
And the flames burn in the candelabra.
Obligations? They are worlds away!
I can ponder instead on the white stones."

(Ida Solymos: Reflection)

CONTENTS – WESTERN TRANSDANUBIA

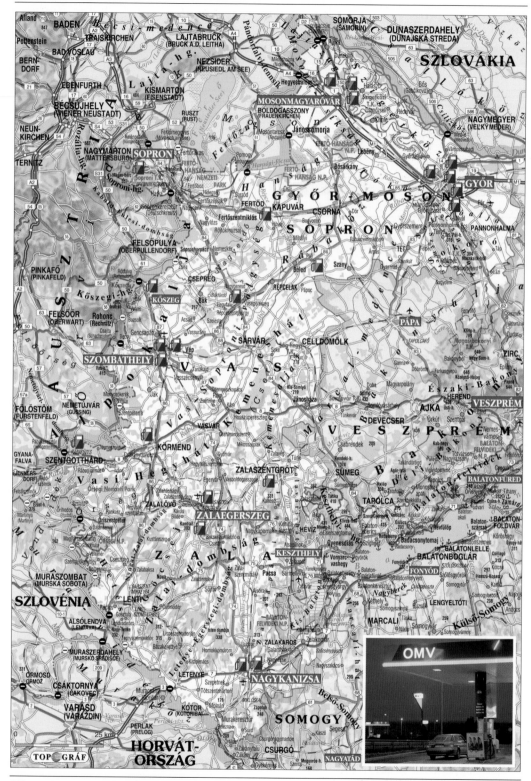

WESTERN TRANSDANUBIA

The following chapter concentrates on the north-western and western parts of Transdanubia, a region which covers the counties of Győr-Moson-Sopron, Vas and Zala.

Seen as a whole, the region was influenced by the same geological processes, which went towards creating the area's smaller landscapes. It is interesting to note that 60–70 million years ago the African and European continental plates shifted, creating a fault line from the *Hernád* through the *Kulcs* to *Zagreb*. During the Pleistocene Age the whole area was covered by the *Pannonian Sea,* a stretch of open water, which gradually silted up over the millenia. At the beginning of the Ice Age the Ancient Danube, the Ancient Rába and the Ancient Drava all flowed through the region down towards the *Drava Valley.* Additional surface movements caused the northern foothills of the Transdanubian Hills to sink bringing a number of streams into the area. The formation of the Keszthely-Gleichenberg Ridge prevented the *Rába* from flowing any further south, forcing the river to make its way westwards thus leaving the way open

for the Zala's predecessor, which at that time flowed into the *Danube.*

During the last third of the Pleistocene Age the subsidence which created the *Balaton Basin* also changed the course of the River Zala. The streams flowing down from the Alps (*Pinka, Gyöngyös, Répce, Ikva*) also experienced similar changes in course, leaving alluvial cones in their trail. The pebbly quartz you can find in the Őrség also resulted from this particular geographical process. The central part of the *Lesser Plain* (*Kisalföld*) began to subside at the same time the Transdanubian Hills began to rise. On entering the *Dévény Gate,* the Danube, not having the energy to spread its deposits all over the Lesser Plain, left sandbanks and islands in its wake. With the passage of time these islands often became eroded, only to appear as islands further down stream.

The islands varied greatly in size. Whilst some islands are so small there is barely room for a single tree, others have whole villages built on them. Dunasziget, Cikolasziget, Sérfenyő Island and the island on the stretch of the Danube between

WESTERN TRANSDANUBIAN SPECIALITIES

When travelling through western Hungary it is important to remember some of your time should be spent sampling the region's patisseries, and that there is much to admire on the local dairy counters. Of the cakes and other baked products on offer there are the *strudels* filled with either pumpkin, poppy seeds, carrot or beans, *bread "lángos"*, *Győr paired rolls*, *Pozsony rolls* (cresent-shaped with walnut or poppy seeds on top), *Rábaköz pretzels*, special pretzels made on a hot volcanic slab *Zala loaf* and babyshaped *"fumu"* are all local specialities.

The region's dairy producers have a lot for which to thank the local climate, the clean air and their excellent dairy cows. As for you the customer you can choose between several kinds of *cottage cheese*, *Őrség goats' cheese*, *Lajta*, *Göcsej cheese*, *Óvár cheese*, *Zala smoked cheese* or *Derby cream cheese*, *Pálpuszta cheese*, and the very special *Moson County cheese* (Csermajor).

If it's fruit you need there are *Cserszeg cherries*, *Kőszeg-hegyalja sweet chestnuts*, *Őrség pears*, *Zala pears*, *Fertőd winter apples* and *bilberries*. And as for vegetables there's *Hegykő celery*, *Moson cabbage*, *Fertőd carrots*, *Kisalföld onions*. *Turnips* are also grown in the region and there are of course the local *roasted pumpkin seeds* and *Őrség pumpkin oil*.

It's also worth trying some of the local meat, the *pork scratchings*, *Sopron cold meats* and *ham*, *meatloaf*, *liver paté* and *spiced ham*.

We should also add the *dark trumpet mushroom*, the *woundwort (solidago) honey*, and the rich taste of the *wood blewit*. Not many people are aware that *buckwheat* and *emmer* are important local crops, or that *honey pálinka* is a local western Hungarian speciality.

Lipót and Ásványráró are probably the most characteristic of the Danube Islands. The former covers an area of 2,000 hectares, the latter over 1,000 hectares.

The dead channels and the oxbow lakes accompanying the rivers are indeed important features of the local landscape. Their still surfaces are caressed by the spreading leaves of the water lilies, whose snow-white flowers occasionally manage to poke their way to the surface. Elsewhere the reeds succeed in choking everything lying in their path. The waters are gradually retreating leaving the vegetation to turn the dead channels into something resembling a marsh.

The countryside generally lies at a level of about 4–6 metres above that of the Danube. It is here that the villages were built, the land was tilled where the deciduous forests (ash, elm, oak) grew alongside woods planted by human hand. Pastures and arable land lie on the irrigated river banks interrupted by the old riverbeds, the 200km of water channels and the occasional oxbow lake. The original natural habitat has managed to survive on the few yards to either side of the water channels where the sedges, the bullrushes, the reeds and the irises grow.

The landscape of Lesser Plain known as the *Rábaköz* stretches along the banks of the *Kis-Rába* as far as the *Sopron-Vas Plain* gravel beds with the Rába flowing to the south and east and the *Répce* to the west.

For many centuries the Rábaköz was very much at the mercy of the elements. When the water level rose the boggy landscape turned into an enormous lake. In the autumn and the spring, the great expanse of water would join up with the waters of the *Fertő*. At that time it was only possible to build on the so-called *"gorondok"*, which rose up like islands from the landscape. This didn't mean that the small villages were totally unaffected by such natural catastrophes. Much of what you can see in the villages today is 19th century, built with the arts and crafts skills of the local population. Indeed, they are skills many people are anxious to preserve even today. Going up towards the Bakony you come across three ranges of hills pointing northwestwards like three fingers in the direction of the Lesser Plain.

As these hills gradually drop in height at their outer reaches they are given other names, like for example the *Sokoró* or the *Pannonhalma Hills*.

As it has always been easier to skirt these hills than cross them, their extensive unspoilt forests have proved a sanctuary for some rare flora and fauna. It is here you can find the pulsatilla, pheasant's eye, the early spider orchid, snowdrops, erythraea, Turk's cap and hemerocallis. On the grassy hillside meadows you will find a fine selection of orchids (early purple, green-winged, military). The long-leaved helleborine tends to grow amongst the oaks. The ancient pines in Écs and the ancient junipers on the shifting sands in Felpéc are indeed sights to behold.

Further west the *Pozsony-Fertő Ridge* separates the *Hanság* from the *Fertő Basin*. For many thousands of years the Ancient Rába and the Ancient Répce, as well as several other small streams, flowed down the alluvial cone of the Danube and Rába into the basin lying two or three metres below. It was with the arrival of today's drier climate that the basin turned into marshland. The natural cycle of growth and decay resulted in the piling up of the decaying remains of reeds, sedges, the bullrushes and many other water plants, which ultimately formed the soil of the *"Hanyföld"*. From the 18th century onwards the local landowners (particularly the Esterházy family) went about turning the area into farmland. In the west they built an embankment between Fertőd and Süttör cutting off the Fertő, and dug a new course for the River Rába, taking the excess water into a network of about 1,000km of channels. This included the *Hanság Main Channel* draining the *Fertő*.

West of the Lesser Plain you come into the western outposts of the Alps and the ancient *Sopron Hills*. The Variscan rocks of the hills can be found deep under a layer of sediment brought up from deep in the Lesser Plain. The rocks themselves only come to the surface on the Austrian border. The Sopron Hills, made up mainly of crystalline gneiss and slate, rise to a height of 558m. The Sopron Hills have all the typical features one would expect to find in hills of their height: gentle slopes, sheltered valleys, extensive beech woods and occasional firs. The grape growers have also

The field frog, one of the marsh's inhabitants

made their mark, their vineyards making their way up the hillsides. The hills are separated from the Sopron Basin by the rocky outcrop at *Balf*. West of the Fertő stand the limestone *Fertőmellék Hills* dating from the period when the area stood at the bottom of an inland sea. This so-called Lajta limestone has been quarried at Fertőrákos since the Roman period.

From a geological point of view the sloping pebbly hills lying between the *Kemenesalja*, the *Marcel* and the *Kemeneshát* are related to the stretch of the River Marcel running down the *Marcel Valley* in Veszprém County. It is here you will find some of the region's indigenous trees. The volcanic formations rising up from the plain give the landscape some variety, the highest hills being *Ság Hill* and *Kissomlyó*.

The pebble-covered hills running almost the entire length of the right bank of the Rába Valley are known as the *Kemeneshát* to the south of which stands the *Őrség*. The Őrség down on the Slovene and Austrian borders is an historical as well as a natural entity broken up by a series of deep, wide valleys. Following the *River Kerka* you eventually come to the *Zala Hills*. The western part of the Őrség is known as the *Vend Region*, an area with Alpine flora, considerable rainfall, and a mild climate. The trees growing up in the hills are for the most part indigenous (pine, beech, oak) and the sunken streams and the wood clearings are full of rare plants. Indeed, the Őrség as a whole provides a safe refuge for the region's wildlife.

The interior of Zalaszentgyörgy church

The Őrség and the Vend Region go to make up the *Őrség Nature Reserve*, which in turn formed the basis of the National Park in 2002.

There are also buildings in the region which enjoy the luxury of protected status. Some of the *"szerek"* (small settlements nestled up on the hilltops) which are so typical of the Őrség have been preserved in their original state. There is no problem relaxing in this Hungarian backwater, and the artificial lakes on the edges of Máriaújfalu, Bajánsenye and Hegyhátszentjakab (*Lake Vadása*) make it ideal for those interested in water sports.

The *Vas Ridge,* which accompanies the Rába to just beyond the Őrség, is covered with both clay dating back to the Ice Age and loess, which has been bound together with the pebble deposits with the passing of time. The valleys have been worked by the changing courses of the rivers and the streams. Apart from the Rába, the most important rivers in the region are the *Csörnöc* and the *Sárvíz*. Mankind's contribution to the landscape has been the network of small villages, the descendants of the settlements carved out of the once all-embracing forests. On the edges of these villages vineyards climb up the slopes of the adjacent hillsides.

In this landscape you will find the indigenous *oaks*, *elms*, *ashes*, *willows* and *poplars*, together with their accompanying undergrowth. In many places these ancient trees have been replaced by *firs* and *acacias*. It is on the warmer southern slopes that you will find the vineyards and the fruit trees. There are still enough old sweet chestnut trees around to suggest that these are what remains of old chestnut plantations. The woods are most likely to echo to the sound of the *coal-tit* and the *golden-crested wren*, whilst it is the *kites*, the *sparrow-hawks*, the *long-eared* and the *tawny owls* which rule the skies. As for the mammals, *badgers* and *beech-martens* are common, and you might be lucky enough to see a *pine-marten.*

On the Rába's few remaining dead channels you can find the *yellow* and *white water lilies* and *sweets-edge*, all reminders of what was once a flourishing natural environment. In the spring the marshes turn yellow with *cowslips*. In the *Szajk Lakes* you can still find the water-chestnut. As for bird life there is the little ringed plover which lives up on the pebbly banks and in the more barren spots. The steep riverbanks are popular nesting places for *swallows* and *kingfishers*. You can even see *otters* swimming in the waters.

The Csernek, forming another part of the *Kemenes Ridge*, gets its name from the Austrian oaks, which once grew here. The further north you go the lower the hills become, and the greater the feeling you are in fact out on a plateau.

References to one of the most extensive woods in the area, the *Farkas Woods*, were made as far back as 1252, when it was the groves and the wooded pastures which were worthy of note. The trees growing today are little more than one hundred years old and the result of some careful and deliberate forest management. It is in the woods around Sitke that you see *asphodels* growing in their natural habitat, a plant very rarely found in Hungary.

Moving from the flood plain you come to the *Vas Valley*, a stretch of agricultural land on the left bank of the Rába going as far as the Vas Hills. The valley touches the Lesser Plain at its northernmost point. The pebbles covering the terrain were brought down by the Ancient Rába.

The closer you get to the border the higher the *Vas Hills* get. The slopes forming the base of the Kőszeg Hills are known as the *Hungarian Alps* whilst those bordered by the Pinka, the Arany and the Perint, are known as the *Pinka Heights.*

The origins of the *Kőszeg Hills* go back about 250 million years to when the African continent collided with Europe. The impact created the hills, the highest of which is *Írott-kő* (882m). It is interesting to note that the streams tumbling down the side of the hills take the most direct possible route. On the southern slopes of the hills, on the so-called *Kőszeg-hegyalja,* you can see what remains of the once extensive sweet chestnut plantations, as well as the vineyards producing the grapes for Kőszeg's famous red wines. *Vas Hill* is also deemed to be part of the Kőszeg-hegyalja.

The potential which lay in the area's cool but constant climate was only really appreciated and exploited during the second half of the 19th century with the arrival of the first tourists. Now the whole area has a network of footpaths providing access not only to the woods and the springs, which have enjoyed protected status since 1980, but to the sites of historical interest lying up in the hills.

The *Zala Hills* are divided up nicely into the *Eastern*, the *Northern*, the *Central* and the *Southern Zala Hills* by the tributaries running up towards the town of Zalaegerszeg and down into the Mura and the Zala. The peaks of the 70km-long *Zalaapát Ridge* in the Northern Zala Hills occasionally reach a height of 300m. The highest point in the Zala Hills taken as a whole is 331-metre-high *Bezeréd Hill.*

Although the *Göcsej*, an area bordered by the *Zala*, the *Kerka* and the *Válicka*, is usually considered to be an ethnographical region, the local flowers and plants provide the Göcsej with another distinctive regional element. There are almost seventy villages here, although the number has varied as villages have not always been particularly keen in seeing themselves considered part of such a backward region. The rolling countryside is covered in dense forest relieved only by the occasional copse or clearing. Up in the hills and down in the valleys tiny streamlets appear only to disappear almost as quickly.

Because the heavy clay soil is so difficult to work, tree plantations have been laid out instead of fields. Today the Göcsej is one of the most densely wooded areas in Hungary. Around Lenti almost 40 percent of the land is covered by forest.

The Göcsej Open-Air Museum

Wood has always played an important role in the architecture of the Göcsej. There are still some examples of the beautiful timber-arcaded houses, together with their original thatched roofs and furniture, but you are sure to see some at the *Göcsej Village Museum* in Zalaegerszeg.

The local dress has always been simple, the basic material used for most of the clothes being locally produced flax and hemp. The local women were never too disheartened by the drudgery of spinning or plucking feathers. It was they who spent the long evenings telling, retelling and composing their folk tales, songs and ballads, ensuring that traditions continued to be passed down from generation to generation.

Göcsej's economic fortunes took a turn for the better with the arrival of the oil industry and other manufacturing industries. With them came the roads and the creation of an industrial working class.

Travelling west from the Göcsej you come to the *Hetés,* a region currently containing eleven villages all lying south of the *River Kerka.* Historically speaking the Hetés continues into neighbouring Slovenia.

It is a flat region, and up until the 18th century it had more than its fair share of bogs and marshes. Even though the lower-lying marshes have been drained completely there are times during and after heavy rainfall when the land reverts to type, becoming covered in water in the process.

Market stalls at the Velem Artists' Retreat

In order to cope with such eventualities special forms of ploughing have been perfected whereby the ploughed furrows actually take the excess waters away.

The folk art in the Hetés is based on rich ornamentation most evident in the woven products. Indeed, weaving has become a veritable cottage industry. The woven artifacts of old Hetés can also be found in both Slovenia and in the museums of Zagreb. The inhabitants of the Hetés made their clothes out of linen to which they added patterns much richer than any seen in neighbouring Göcsej. The local houses, smaller and simpler than those in the Göcsej, were filled with sturdy furniture.

The smallest landscape in Zala is that covering the stretch of the *Mura* between Nagykanizsa and Letenye. The area has a substantial Croatian population, as well as a sprinkling of Swabians. The region's eleven villages have set up their own association aimed at protecting the local architecture and the area's culture and traditions.

It is however the region's rivers and the lakes which provide the area's main tourist attractions. The region is also fortunate enough to be endowed with more than its fair share of thermal waters. Whilst there are many spas (Csorna, Kapuvár, Balf, Bük, Zalakaros, Lenti) the search for new thermal waters has by no means ended. If it is medicinal waters you want you should aim for the Hegykő, Mesteri, Mosonmagyaróvár and Petőháza baths. Sárvár and Győr are the most attractive spa towns in the region, offering more in the

way of leisure and recreation opportunities. The popularity of such places amongst tourists coming from neighbouring Austria and Slovenia means that even the smallest villages are able to operate their own thermal baths.

There are countless opportunities open to lovers of water sports on Lake Fertő, the Moson-Danube, the Danube, the Rába, the Mura and the Zala. The waters are also good news for anglers. Over the last twenty to thirty years the artificial lakes have had an opportunity to blend into the local countryside making them into popular tourist destinations. The countryside along the western border has always been wooded. It is not surprising therefore that a lot of the local buildings were built of wood, and that hunting was traditionally an important means of earning a livelihood. Hunting is indeed still popular today. Apart from a lot of small game, a lot of deer live here, and the wild boar stock is currently growing. The hunting associations' exclusive programmes are becoming increasingly available to foreign hunters as well. At such events successful participants have the chance to take away a few trophies themselves. This is excellent hiking country. There are paths covering all the most beautiful hills, valleys and forests of Western Pannonia. You never know when you might come face to face with a deer. Then there are also the pheasants hiding in the undergrowth, the flowering cyclamen, the snow-flakes and the fritillaries.

In the lines which follow you will be able to become familiar with the region's nature conservation areas, nature reserves and arboretums.

The *Fertő-Hanság National Park,* which also happens to be a *World Heritage Site,* bridges the border with Austria. (For further information consult the chapter on National Parks.) A more recent development has been the creation of a number of nature parks involving two or more neighbouring countries. One of these is the *Írott-kő Nature Park* which covers the *Kőszeg Hills* and the Austrian Geschriebenstein region.

There is also the *Triple Frontier Nature Park* covering the *Őrség*, the *Vendvidék*, the western part of Zala, the *Kerka Region*, the Raab Naturpark in Burgenland, Austria and the Gorickó in the Mura region. Such joint projects, still somewhat of a novelty here in Hungary, will mean that all activities in these areas, even those in the field of trade and industry, will have to take the local environment into consideration.

The region was a province of the Roman Empire, and the so-called *Amber Road* ran from Rédics, up through Zalalövő, Szombathely, Kőszeg and Sopron. There were many Roman river crossings, stations and settlements along the way. Some of the objects uncovered at these sites are on show in Zalalövő, Szombathely and Sopron.

At the time the Hungarian counties were established, the monarchy settled peoples on the peripheries of the kingdom whose job it was to guard the frontiers. The descendants of these border peoples still live in the *Upper* and *Lower Őrség* today. The *Vends* can consider themselves to be the region's oldest inhabitants, and they are indeed a community still eager to protect their customs and traditions. They live peacefully alongside the ethnic Hungarian population as do the local *Croats* and the *Germans*.

It is perhaps not surprising to find that many of Hungary's leading aristocratic families, for example the Széchenyis, the Batthyánys and the Esterházys, had residences in a part of the Kingdom of Hungary not far from Vienna, the one-time centre of the Habsburg Monarchy. It is they we should thank for the beautiful country houses still standing in Fertőd, Nagycenk, Sárvár, Körmend, Egervár and Zalacsány.

When it comes to churches and ecclesiastical treasures there is the Romanesque church at Ják, the Benedictine Abbey at Pannonhalma and the 13th century rotunda at Kallósd.

The people living in these parts have always appreciated their wine, and have always done all in their power to ensure there is enough of it. Perhaps the most famous local grape is the *"Sopron Kékfrankos"* which is grown on the Pannonhalma Hills, around Sopron, in Kőszeg-Vaskeresztes, Sághegy-Kissomlyó, on the western side of Lake Balaton and in and around Zalaszentgrót. The *Keszthely Agricultural University* has been working on some up-and-coming grapes such as the *"Cserszegi Fűszeres"*.

The future of the region lies in the as yet untapped resources of village tourism. Even as we write

Kámon Arboretum

many old peasant cottages are being renovated in the hope that one day they will provide pleasant holiday accommodation. Day-trippers from Austria and Slovenia come in droves, eager to do some shopping or have a day out.

The climate in the area is damp, sub-Alpine, and mild. Scorching summers or the freezing winters are a pretty rare occurrence. About 60–70% of days are overcast, the average temperature is exactly 10.03 °C, and the average rainfall varies between 900–1000mm. On the marshes the air can get pretty humid. After a sudden drop in temperature you are likely to wake up to fog.

Before we embark on our tour of the region it is perhaps just worth noting that this is a region currently buzzing with activity. New thermal baths are opening, new cycle paths are being laid, hotels are being renovated, new guesthouses are appearing and new footpaths and waterways being marked out. At the same time it's good to see that far more care is being taken in looking after the countryside.

Visitors to Győr can see everything from the baroque basilica, built on its Romanesque foundations, to the late 19th century eclectic-style public buildings and the most recent additions to the town's skyline.

GYŐR

The town, built next to the *castrum* protecting the Roman province of Pannonia, became a bishopric and a regional centre at the time of the foundation of the Hungarian state. Its fortress later served to defend Vienna from the Turks. During the 18th century the town's soldiers were replaced by merchants and artisans, the Baroque predecessor to what became a 20th century industrial town.

The romantic and classical elements on the town houses can also be seen at the Győr National Theatre, home of the famous Győr Ballet. It was in 1979 that Győr first gained its first fully-trained dance troupe. In recent years, under the tutelage firstly of Iván Markó and then János Kiss the troupe has created a whole new dance culture.

The historic centre of Győr is dominated by two thoroughfares. The now pedestrianised Baross utca, forming the main north-south axis of the town, crosses the main 19th century Budapest-Vienna road at the town hall (Városház tér 1.). The **town hall** appeared almost overnight (1896–1898, *Jenő Hűbner*), built with the proceeds of the inheritance left to the town by glassmaker József Bisinger.

You have to climb up *Chapter Hill* to get up to the **basilica**. Whilst the eastern apses are all Romanesque, the southern aisle and the **Héderváry Chapel** are Gothic. The west façade is classical in style. *Anton Maulbertsch*'s dynamic frescos hover over *Menyhért Hefele*'s Baroque altars in the central aisle of the building.

The **episcopal palace** opposite the basilica has a sgraffito-covered donjon (1250) to which a 15th century chapel was subsequently attached. Almost opposite the recently uncovered walls of the single-aisled **Church of Saint Lazarus** in Vilmos Apor tér stands a statue of Saint Michael casting Lucifer down into the abyss.

The stained glass windows of the saints of the Árpád dynasty (Lili Árkai) shed their light on the sarcophagus of the murdered bishop Vilmos Apor, who lost his life in the spring of 1945 trying to protect locals from a Russian soldier drunk in charge of a rifle.

In house number 2, a house built on firm medieval foundations, you find a **museum** dedicated to the life and work of the sculptor *Miklós Borsos* (1906–1990). His parents sought sanctuary in the town during the First World War and the sculptor was to maintain his Győr connections throughout his entire life. As a member of the European School following the Second World War Borsos worked in the manner of Brancusi, and met Henry Moore in England during the 1960s.

Kis utca leads up to the massive buildings of the old **Theological College** (Káptalandomb 26.). During the course of its renovation, after which it reverted to its original function, the building regained some of its 18th century character. It also houses the *Ecclesiastical History Collection*.

In Gutenberg tér the origins of the statue of the Ark of the Covenant (Fischer von Erlach, Antonio Corradini) go back to an incident which happened in 1729 when a deserter dressed up as a ministrant was spotted by the castle guards during the course of a procession. In trying to wrestle the deserter away from the procession the guards succeeded in knocking the monstrance out of the priest's hands.
At the request of the citizens of Győr, Charles III. devoted a part of the guards' fines to putting up the statue (1731).

On the well in Duna kapu tér you can see the legend of the Győr weathercock. The Turks put it abroad that Christianity would only return to the town if the weathercock crowed. According to local tradition, when Miklós Pálffy's soldiers broke in through Fehérvár Gate one of the soldiers blew his bugle, which was considered to be near enough to the real thing.

On the banks of the River Danube stand the two heroes responsible for the seizure of the castle from the Turks: *Adolf Schwarzenberg* and *Miklós Pálffy*. It is here that you can really appreciate that Győr is a river town. On the far side of the river you see a row of boathouses, restaurants, hotels, a park, a bandstand and one of Hungary's most beautiful outdoor swimming pools (*Alfréd Hajós*).

The Bástya Walk along the banks of the Rába takes you towards Bécsi kapu tér. On the expectation that the Battle of Mohács (1526) would be followed by a Turkish offensive on Vienna, the court decided to strengthen the defences of Győr Castle. The gun chambers concealed in the corner bastions were therefore filled with enough firepower and ammunition to defend Győr's Viennese Gateway.

The architect of the Baroque **Carmelite Church** (1713–1725), *Márton Wittwer*, was also active in most Austrian towns, creating what was a veritable Danubian school of architecture. The Baroque church is Italian in character, having been based on the ground-breaking church of *Il Gesu* in Rome, the first of all the Baroque churches.

Its crypt, which also serves as a charnel house (*ossuarium*) resorts to an interesting technical solution. The whole roof is supported by a single pillar, and despite standing right next to the Rába, the church's faultless waterproofing has meant that it hasn't let in a single drop of water.

The square immediately in front of Győr's Carmelite Church provides an ideal venue for a whole host of public events.

The Carmelite **monastic buildings**, with their simple façades, often offer accommodation whilst major cultural events are going on in the town. The tranquillity of the courtyard also makes it a popular concert venue. During the *Baroque banquet* guests sit at tables laid in the 18th century manner and eat food prepared with 18th century spices, served up by waiters and waitresses in authentic costume.

The recently renovated stucco exteriors and closed-off balconies of the elegant town houses stand nearby, **Rozália House** (Kazinczy u. 21.) being a typical example.

The enormous **monastery** (9.) in Széchenyi tér originally belonged to the Győr Jesuits before falling into the hands of the Benedictine order. The Jesuits also founded what is now the **Pharmacy Museum** (1654). If you look at the side chapel and the main aisle of the **Saint Ignatius's Church** you can follow the artistic developments of the time from the simpler forms of early 17th century Baroque through to the fully-blown Baroque of the 18th century. The depiction of the Glorification of Saint Ignatius in one of the altars is by *Paul Troger*. The frescos in **Zichy Palace**

On the outdoor stage, on what what was the old parade ground, concerts and dance performances take place as part of the Győr Festival. It is here you can also enjoy a Baroque-style wedding with all the trappings in keeping with the surrounding architecture.

(Liszt Ferenc u. 20.) deserve inspection. The arcaded courtyard is used for chamber concerts. Opposite lies the one-time **Franciscan Friary** (Liszt Ferenc u. 13.)**,** which became the *County Hall* following its reconstruction in 1786.

Next to **Saint Anna's Chapel** (1735) in Rákóczi Ferenc utca lies the **Magyar Ispita** (the town's one-time Foundling Hospital) whose entrance lies in Nefelejcs köz. In the two interior courtyards you can see the Italianate features used by the Baroque builders of Győr Castle. It is here at the *Municipal Museum* that you will find *Péter Váczy's* collection of Roman and Greek terracotta, bronze artefacts, Renaissance and Baroque furniture, paintings and Chinese ceramics.

Leaving the old town hall, in whose cellar prison the heroine of *Mór Jókai's "White Woman of Lőcse"* awaited her execution, you come to **Apátúr House**

The János Xantus Museum covers the history of Győr and its immediate surroundings from the Hungarian Conquest right up to the present-day. It's not often that artefacts relating to the local guilds and the religious life of a community are so well represented.

(Széchenyi tér 5.) home of the *János Xantus Museum.* Benedek Sajghó, the archabbot of the Benedictine Monastery in Pannonhalma built the house in 1741 to offer accommodation to members of the order.

It is believed that the iron tree stump on the corner of the Vastuskós House was the work of wandering apprentices, although it in fact belonged to the local spice company.

On the façade of Apátúr House with its double-windowed balcony and scroll consoles you can see the figures of King Stephen and Saint Benedict.
The old dining room lying inside is used for conferences, and also forms part of the museum.

The beauty of the dining room earned the compliments of Napoleon's officers on the occasion of a ball they held there in his honour. They had the room decorated and the walls covered in painted verses singing the emperor's praises. Because the verses were painted by Italian soldiers the French in the poetry is by no means perfect.

The **house** next door also takes the eye. It is here you will find the *Patkó Collection*, which contains the Far Eastern and African tribal art collected by the local writer and art historian *Imre Patkó*.

Passing the eclectic-style façades you eventually come to the recently renovated **Esterházy Palace** (Király u. 17.) home of the town's *art gallery*. The houses on the northern side of the road follow the inner walls of the castle's 16th century defences, stretches of which have been uncovered, creating an interesting atmosphere in the houses' concealed courtyards. Opposite you find yourself back at the Bécsi kapu tér where the courtyard of the *Sforza Bastion* (5.) houses the **County Museum's Lapidarium**.

On the western edge of the town there is the **Kiskút-liget** with its stadium, ice rink, sports halls. Going southwards a few kilometres to the *Dead Rába Gyirmót* you come to a *nature trail*, the pointing out all the important flora and fauna and recently-opened **thermal and leisure baths** (2003) at the confluence of the *Moson-Danube* and *Rába* complete with its slides and sauna garden.

In the *Szigeti* suburb of Győr just above the *Dead Rábca*, a narrow steel bridge (*Pinnyédi-híd*) takes you to the **Bishop's Wood,** one of Győr's largest green open spaces, which is also not without interest to the botanist.

12km southeast of the town you come to PÉR, whose recently updated (2003) airport can now take international air traffic.

LIVING CRAFTS IN THE RÁBAKÖZ

While the Rábaköz was once never short of the blue dyers who worked in Csorna, Kapuvár and Beled, after a period decline the old **craft** is now enjoying somewhat of a Renaissance. The pottery of the Rábaköz, centred on the village of DÖR, has its own distinctive style. It was the younger members of the Dör potter dynasties who ended up moving out to Csorna, Bodonhely, Rábcakapi, and indeed Győr, where they continued to practise and develop the old Dör traditions.

Each village in the Rábaköz had its own folk costume. It was frequently the embroidery applied to the clothes which gave each costume its own particular character. Woollen embroidery was particularly popular on pillows and tablecloths, as was rich white embroidery.

One of the wonders of Hungarian embroidery is the white embroidery: in its patterns you can see almost all the flowers growing in the local meadows and gardens.

In the Rábaköz you can often see *linear settlements* where the houses are strung out along the roadside, with the church situated in the widest part of the village. The houses arranged on both sides of the thoroughfare extend back from the roadside, their beautiful arcaded brick verandas being a common sight over the garden fences.

Whilst the façade of the **Church of the Ascension of the Virgin Mary** of the Premonstratensian Church in CSORNA is understated, the interior is ornate. Indeed, apart from one 13th century relief everything is Baroque. Above the Altar of the Virgin Mary stands the *Black Madonna*, a local version of the Polish Czestochowa Madonna.

Csorna, the centre of the Rábaköz, is an interesting mix of early and late 19th century buildings. The original Premonstratensian monastery which stood in Fő tér was built during the 13th century. What you can see today is a neoclassical building (1825) with a central balcony bearing the arms of the local deanery. It is here you will find the Csorna Museum with its collection of folk art.

The Premonstratensian Abbey in ÁRPÁS, built at the beginning of the 13th century, was handed over to the Clarissan nuns in the 17th century. Architecture from both periods survives. Although the chancel has a medieval rib vault containing a boss with a hand held up in blessing, everything below it is Baroque. The painting behind the high altar depicting the Blessed Virgin wearing a gown with a map of Hungary in the lining is by an unknown artist.

The early medieval **rotunda** at RÁBASZENTMIKLÓS originally had two horseshoe-shaped apses. The addition of a galleried baptistery brought the number of apses up to three.

The **summer residence** of the Bishops of Győr stands in the middle of SZANY. Its subtly articulated façade is crowned by a tympanum. The balustraded balcony was built during a 19th century remodelling. The village's **local history collection** gives an interesting account of the surrounding landscape and the local economy, taking you back to a time when there were woods on the Rába flood plain and when thousands of cattle would graze on the region's pastures (Kossuth u. 2.). Szany's other important building is its **church**, built at the bishop's volition in 1767. The church was enlarged a century later when the side aisles were added. The Baroque and the classical elements of the two

building periods can clearly be seen on both the façade and inside. BOGYOSZLÓ is worth visiting for its woodcarving, HÖVEJ for its 150-year embroidery traditions and recently-opened museums (2003) and Dör for its pottery.

Woodcarver Jenő Pinter, local craftsman, uses geometric forms and floral patterns in his efforts to carry on the traditions of the Rábaköz woodcarving shepherds (Bogyoszló, Rákóczi F. u. 21.).

THE PANNONIAN INHERITANCE

The *Pannonhalma Hills (Sokoró)* can be divided up into three ranges. The western range running from the *Szőlőhegy* in Szemere down to Nagydém, north of Felpéc, is bordered by sandbeds created when the westerly winds whipped up the sand off the *Sokoró-Bakony Basin* towards the end of the Ice Age. Juniper-covered *Pokolfa Hill* is now a protected area.

The most popular destination on the central range of hills is the *Lila* (314m) crowned by a **land-survey tower,** from where you get a wonderful panorama of the surrounding countryside. To the south, between the pair of hills not far from Écs, stand a collection of rather strange-looking wind-buffeted *ancient fir trees.* The eastern slopes of the hills are covered with broad swathes of vineyards, the grapes growing at a height of 270m in some places.

Grapes were first grown on the land below the woods on the lower slopes a thousand years ago. In 1991, the region was formally recognised as a historical wine region.

Over the last thirty years raspberries have also become a popular crop. Although there are fewer and fewer thatched mud-walled 19th century peasant cottages, some can still nevertheless be found in the villages of the Sokoró.

PANNONHALMA

The **Benedictine Abbey** rising from *St Martin's Hill* enjoys *World Heritage Status* (see also chapter dealing with *World Heritage Sites*).

The first Benedictine monks arrived in Pannonhalma in 996, a small church being consecrated in 1001. The monastery put up resistance against the Tatars in 1241, serving as a fortress for both the Hungarians and the Turks during the Turkish period. The Baroque structures were built between 1722 and 1768. Joseph II. dissolved the Benedictine Order, along with all the other religious orders, only for the order to reform and return to the monastery in 1802. It was then that the enormous library and the church's classical tower were built, giving the monastery its present appearance.

Pannonhalma's 55-metre tower is one of the best-known examples of Hungarian Neoclassicism.

The Chapels of Saint Benedict and the Blessed Virgin Mary, and the star-vaulted chancel are perhaps the most interesting parts of Pannonhalma's triple-aisled, rib-vaulted 13th century basilica. The marble high altar and the pulpit were designed by Ferenc Storno.
From the Gothic southern side aisle you can go down into the crypt, the oldest part of the church.

Moving from the southern aisle into the 15th century cloisters you pass through the late Romanesque *"porta speciosa"*. The most recent of the monastic range dates from 1734–1832. Unfortunately, the most beautiful part of the complex, the Baroque refectory (1734), is not open to the general public. The riches accumulated by the abbey can be found mainly in the archive-library-picture gallery complex. In the courtyard in front of the entrance to the library stands Roman and medieval stonework excavated from the site, while in the entrance hall itself you can see copies of the Tihany and Pannonhalma letters of foundation. In the library itself, amongst the statues of some of the great figures in Hungarian history and science, are 360 thousand volumes of rare books. The abbey can only be visited in the company of a guide. Masses are held in the church on Sunday mornings and feast days.

To the south of the monastery on an artificial mound stands the **Millennium Monument,** with its tympanum and relief by *Gyula Bezerédj* and the four interior historical paintings by *Vilmos Aba Novák* and his pupils. In the position of what is now the **Chapel of the Blessed Virgin Mary** stood a small fortification known as the *"Tarisznyavár"*. A visit to the monastery usually ends either with a visit to the **Stations of the Cross** (1720–1724) or the **arboretum** below the abbey.

In the **peasant houses** in TÉNYŐ, TÁP, GYARMAT, KAJÁRPÉC and GYŐRÚJBARÁT you are able to see the open fires in the kitchens, the cooking and baking utensils lined up on the shelves, and the pots, pans and plates. The earthenware stove supplied the heat during the long winter days, next to which stood a corner bench and a beautifully made up bed. The front room, reserved for special occasions, was where poor cottagers would keep their mirror and their religious pictures.

In ÉCS, under the old fir trees, you will find a church still betraying a few medieval details, whilst near the **Lutheran church** at FELPÉC you will find a juniper grove reminiscent of those often found on the Great Plain.

The pilgrimage **church** at TÉTSZENTKÚT is also worth visiting, perhaps by bicycle, along the Mecsér-Tétszentkút cycle path. TÉT, with its own **cyclists' hostel** and repair shop is at the point where cyclists coming off the Hegyeshalom-Győr cycle path meet those coming up from Lake Balaton.

Just above NYÚL, in the sides of the 20–30-metre vertical rock faces, are the so-called "hole cellars" once used for human habitation.

MOSONMAGYARÓVÁR

You reach the gate of the **castle** by crossing the bridge which replaced the old drawbridge. The boss in the gatehouse vault tells us that it was built during the 15th century. On the side walls you can see seven Gothic wall niches as well as the entrance to the rooms belonging to the castle garrison. The castle is now used by the agricultural community, and it is here you can see exhibitions on the history of the universe, the wildlife of the *Hanság* and the history of the plough.

In the Hanság Wildlife Exhibition, situated in the castle, you can see a large diorama featuring some of the protected animals you can expect to find in these parts, like the cormorants, the lapwings and the herons.

Opposite the castle stands the Baroque **Habsburg House** (Deák Ferenc tér 5.). The building was already a famous inn as far back as the 1600s and on the façade there are tablets referring to some of its most famous visitors. Tradition has it that this was the first place to offer its guests a *menu in Hungarian*.

The imposing **Town Hall** (Fő út 11.), built in 1891 in a Renaissance style, was originally the County Hall.

The 18th century classical **Wallisch House** (14.) is one of the oldest town houses in Mosonmagyaróvár. According to a tablet on the walls of the **old town hall** (6.), built in 1827, it was here that *István Széchenyi* was elected Member of Parliament in 1847.

Outside, it is the stone window frames and balcony fragments of Cselley House in Masonmagyaróvár which grab your attention. Inside there are furniture and paintings to admire (Fő út 103.).

In Városkapu tér the beautiful 1754 Baroque façade and the 17th century **mill** behind it have recently been turned into a hotel.

Saint Gothard's Church stands where Magyar utca widens out into a square. The church, with a dedication rarely found in Hungary, was initially built with support from the town's wealthier citizens, and later with the help of Maria Theresa's son-in-law.

The harbour in the *Moson suburb* of the town is where many hundreds of flat-bottomed horse-drawn cereal barges turned round. It was a place where many inns, coffee houses and town houses were built. The gates of one of the houses lead to a well-kept garden and the **Hanság Museum** (Szent István út 1.).

To mark the unification of the two towns of Moson and Magyaróvár it was decided to build a Transylvanian-style wooden **Calvinist church** (1939) on the border shared by the two settlements. Its particularly tall tower makes the **Church of Saint John of Nepomuk** in Moson (Fő út 110.) immediately recognisable. It's façade bears all the hallmarks of the Baroque style.

In the wooded area near the rivers you will find a **swimming pool** which benefits from the high-quality thermal waters coming up from a depth of 2,000m at a temperature of 74°C. There are guest-houses and other leisure facilities nearby.

THE DANUBE'S TREASURES

The main navigable branch of the Danube is known locally as the Öreg Duna, the Old Danube, and it is on the **Old Danube** that we shall begin.

The Danube, bordered by flood plains sometimes as much as two or three kilometres wide occasionally divides up into several streams, creating lots of small islands in the process. It is on some of these channels that you are likely to find the willow-bushes which herald a wooded hinterland. Where sandbanks appear on some of the wider sections of the river they are covered with picturesque woodland.

Having crossed as many as three or four rows of islands you get to the redirected main river. The Danube moves swiftly through the dams, the ships gliding along what is one of Central Europe's most important stretches of water. The flood plains then continue to the north of the Danube in the *Csallóköz* in Slovakia.

It was in the totally unspoilt surroundings that the *Dunakilit Dam* was built as part of the *Bős-Nagymaros Hydroelectric Power Station*. Following many political and environmental protests, work on the project came to a halt in Hungary in 1989.

However, this didn't stop the Hungarian dam being put into service, forcing the water level to fall drastically by 2.5–3m and causing the water table to drop significantly. In an effort to make up for the loss in water, efforts were made to ensure that the flood plains received at least some supplies of water.

The flood plains, the navvy ponds and the pollarded willows are all the work of human hand. The navvy ponds came into being when the soil was dug out to build the embankments. During floods these fill up with water. It is here algae accumulates, pondweed flourishes and where the frogs come to lay their frogspawn. It goes without saying that everything withers up and dies in times of drought only to reappear again with the arrival of new waters.

The willows which have been pollarded provide the fresh pliable branches needed to make the hurdles used for strengthening the river defences. The willows, with their stubby thick trunks and a crown of radiating new growth, are a frequent sight in the Szigetköz landscape, and one of its endearing features.

On the many branches of the Danube you will find weeping willows and poplars, whilst there are whole plantations of poplars on the flood plains. In the dryer higher-lying areas you are more likely to find hardwood forests filled with oaks, elms and ashes. As for the shrubs, there are cornels, elderflowers and berberis, and the wild flowers include corydalis, violets and anemones.

Flooding explains why so little dating back to the Middle Ages survives in the local villages. Nothing of the medieval churches remain above ground-level. What we have is either Baroque in style (*Halászi, Lipót, Győrzámoly*), or the work of an early 20th century architect using one of the historical styles so popular at the time (*Darnózseli, Dunakiliti*).

It's very pleasant to boat along the Danube. Indeed, boating along the Moson-Danube can amount to quite an adventure.

HÉDERVÁR

Hédervár was named after the Héder knights invited into the area by the King of Hungary during the 12th century. Some of the present **palace** dates from before the 16th century building campaign.

On passing through the entrance, guarded by its sphinxes, you enter the quadrangle. The Renaissance relief you see in the wall dates from the 16th century. Opposite the entrance there are some beautiful 18th century painted trail motifs covering the Baroque staircase and the "sala terrena". The neo-Gothic window and the hunting hall in the southern wing both date from the remodelling which took place one hundred years ago.

It is believed that the red marble font predates **Saint Michael's Church** (1681). The coat-of-arms on the Gothic-style bowl suggests that the donor was a palatine, because he used the symbol of the three hills with a patriarchal cross. The **Chapel of the Blessed Virgin Mary** was built in either the 13th or the 15th century, opinions vary. The chapel was subsequently enlarged, becoming the so-called *Lorettó Chapel*. The rather stern-looking interior can be explained by Károly Khuen-Héderváry's decision to remodel it at the turn of the 19th and 20th centuries. The *oak* near the chapel, which stands 14m tall and has a girth of 710cm, is seven hundred years old. Those parts of the tree which have rotted away have been filled in with cement.

HEGYESHALOM is the busy **border crossing** on the western border with Austria. The **parish church** stands on the small mound (halom) from which the village gets its name. The buttresses and Gothic windows are medieval as is the rib vault, recently uncovered in the chancel. During the restoration work,

the 18th century altar painting of Saint Bartholomew was placed at the west end of the nave.

When leaving Hungary for Slovakia you pass through the rather urban surroundings of RAJKA. The *limes* defending the northern frontier of the empire passed through here one of the Roman watchtowers forming the core of the **parish church**. The traceried windows and the wall paintings on the southern wall date back to the Middle Ages.

The medieval sculpture of Christ over the side door of Rajka parish church was reused as building material during the 18th century enlargement of the church. This explains why one of his hands is missing.

The altars, the interior decoration, the angels and gold-leaf statues are all mature Baroque in style. Although the 13th century **church** in LÉBÉNY managed to survive the Tatar invasion (1241) it was badly damaged during the Turkish wars. Indeed, it was subsequently rebuilt on several occasions.

The large expanses of wall at Lébény are broken only by a few small, round-headed windows. On the southern side of the church, which is where you will also find the entrance, there is a fine portal containing the kind of geometric patterns normally associated with Norman architecture.

ON THE WESTERN BORDER

Our explorations of Western Transdanubia have brought us to the *Hanság* and the *banks of the Fertő*. The draining of the land which took place here has meant that the large areas of surface water have disappeared and that the water table has dropped. As a result the marshes have been replaced by woods and arable land. Of the *Hany's* once mysterious watery landscape only but the faintest of glimpses remain; what there is to appreciate can be seen at *Lake Király*, *Lake Fehér* and *Lake Barbacsi*. In the woods you will find willows and poplars and where the soil becomes moister and boggier the reeds start to appear.

The terrain can be explored on the guided tours around the *nature trails*.

The English traveller and doctor, Richard Bright (1789-1858), wrote on the occasion of his visit to the Fertő in 1815, "After we had left Sopron we looked eastwards towards Lake Fertő, which seemed no distance at all. The shallowness of its waters means that you cannot sail on it. Reeds have grown on its marshy, boggy shores, which are also rich in water birds. Its clear waters are disturbed by the wind, and its water level can easily change with heavy rainfall or drought." The "heart" of the Fertő National Park enjoys special protected status in the form of a reservation-type zone, centred on the southern and south-eastern parts of the lake. It is here you will find sheltered inlets and interior ponds shut off from the rest of the world by the reed beds. There are also the open waters of Silver Lake, 3,000 of whose 7,000 hectares can be found on the Hungarian side. The territory, together with that of the surrounding villages, joined the list of World Heritage Sites in 2001.

The tours are particularly good for school parties. Others can go out to the birdwatchers' hide on the banks of the *Fertő-Hanság Channel*. From there you can walk through the plain lying adjacent to the Austrian-Hungarian border. (For more information see the *Hungarian Treasury*.)

The irises in the Fertő National Park enjoy protected status

You will find JÁNOSSOMORJA on the border of the *Hanság* and the *Moson Plain*. The presence of the ethnic Germans, who brought with them some advanced agricultural practices when they were settled during the course of the 18th century, explains why the villages here differ from the nearby ethnic Hungarian villages. **St Peter's Church** is built in the part of the town which shares its name. The ashlar tower and the columns articulating the west front of the church betray its medieval origins.

The **Church of Saint John,** *Mosonszentjános,* with its low façade and its long nave, situated in the centre of what is now Jánossomorja, has close ties with Maria Kristina of Habsburg and her husband Albert Casimir, the Elector of Saxony. The fine Baroque pulpit, the richly carved Louis Seize pews and the beautiful sculptures and altars suggest the benefactor was not short of funds and artistic intent. Just over the Austrian border you will find the **Andau Sculpture Park**.

KAPUVÁR

Pál Esterházy rebuilt the **castle** from the stones of its medieval predecessor, building the Baroque **fortified palace** you can see today. Before it was blown up, the medieval castle had served as a *"gate"* in the frontier defence system. Now containing by the *Rábaköz Museum* which has a folk art collection and the exhibition *Pál Pátzay* (1896–1978).

Saint Anna's Kapuvár (1884) was originally classical in style before being remodelled into something a little more eclectic. Inside, there is an altar painting depicting Saint Anna with Mary and Joachim.
Of particular interest are the frescos of the Holy Trinity on the left-hand side and the symbols of the cardinal virtues on the right. On the underside of the organ loft you can see some angels wearing local Kapuvár folk costumes.

The growth the town enjoyed at the turn of the 19th and 20th centuries brought with it a number of eclectic-style public buildings which give the town the hints of grandeur it enjoys today. One such building was the **convent and primary school** (now grammar school) built for the Samarian Sisters of Mercy, and Saint Vincent's Primary School (Fő tér 25., 27.).

The classical style **Rába Palace** built for the Esterházy's estate manager is now used as a library. One should also mention the old Law Court on Szent István út.

FERTŐSZENTMIKLÓS's enormous **parish church** stands where the Sopron-Győr road meets the Kőszeg and the Fertő roads. Although built in 1725, the church was given a neo-Romanesque addition two centuries later.

The humble exterior of OSLI's parish church conceals a rich interior. The dainty gold-leafed archangels in their Baroque architectural scenery form the setting for the miraculous figure of the Smiling Madonna.

FERTŐD

The **palace** at Fertőd hosted its first major celebrations in 1770, when Miklós Esterházy (the Magnificent) presented his home and his household to the Viennese aristocracy. Visitors use the main entrance, through the three wrought-iron gates, which lead you into a courtyard surrounded by two curved single-storey wings.

On the walls of the Palace Museum there are several large French mirrors as well as Flemish and French carpets and allegorical sculptures. There is also furniture and frescos all dating back to the Baroque era.

The interest expressed in contemporary French and English travel diaries proves the importance of Hungary's finest Baroque complex.

The palace was originally surrounded by a **French formal** garden based on a system of radiating pathways and neatly kept shrubs. This was subsequently replaced by a more freely composed English-style park during the course of the 19th century which paid more attention to the natural contours of the land.

The complete renovation of Hungary's very own *"Versailles"*, which started in 2003, is one of the most important conservation projects facing the country today. Nevertheless the palace is open to the public on a daily basis (except Mondays) for seven months a year from the middle of March. During the winter the palace and the grounds are open at weekends.

On Madách sétány in the town itself you will find the **Haydn memorial room**, the music school and a local history exhibition.

Joseph Haydn (1732-1807) spent a large part of his active musical life at Eszterháza (the old name for Fertőd).

Leaving the village of SARRÓD, with its renovated peasant cottages, you come to **Kócsagvár** a thatched, wooden building complex put up by the *Fertő-Hanság National Park* in 1993 with support from the European Union's *PHARE* programme.

Kócsagvár isn't only an administrative centre it's a scientific workshop and tourist centre as well. More information about its activities can be found in the chapter dealing with the national parks.

FERTŐSZÉPLAK

The façade of the **All Saints Church,** sitting on its hillock is decorated simply with the letters IHOS (*In Honorem Omnium Sanctorum*). The interior contains everything you would expect to find in a Baroque church. The altars to either side of the high altar create an effect not dissimilar to a triptych.

The **country house** was once owned by the Széchenyi family. It was here that Count Ferenc Széchényi, the founder of the *Hungarian National Museum,* was born in 1754. The residence was originally built from the granary which had belonged to the village's previous owners at the end of 19th century, the Esterházy family. Today the building is waiting to be put to better use. The five buildings at the end of the Széplaki utca show what craftsmen were capable of doing at the end of 19th century. Now housing the **Village Museum,** they give an account of how people lived and worked during the last century (Nagy L. u. 31–39.).

The most striking feature of the parish church at Fertőszéplak is the pulpit, which contains scenes from the life of Saint Peter. The two sculptural compositions in front of the church depicting the Sacred Heart and the Crucifixion were donated by Zsigmond Széchenyi's wife Júlia Barkóczi in 1736.

HEGYKŐ's *thermal bath, a jewel in the region's tourist crown*

The church standing on the hill in the middle of HIDEGSÉG (1748) contains some rare Romanesque wall paintings. Those in the apse of the round chapel depict Christ in Majesty surrounded by Evangelist symbols. The **frescoes** in the nave date from between the 12th and the 16th centuries.

SOPRON

between the *Lesser Plain* and the *Viennese Basin*. It was here that the Romans built the forum at *Scarbantia*. The town wall was built to defend the medieval houses, and the Gothic churches which were situated inside. In the town centre today you are just as likely to find Renaissance and Baroque town houses and 19th and 20th century palaces. In 1975, the town received the gold medal, the *Europa Award*, for its achievements in preserving its ancient monuments.

Going through the vaulted gateway underneath the **Fire Tower** you enter the inner sanctum of the old town.

Fő tér 2. used to be a pharmacy, now it's a museum as well. In a letter written in 1525, Louis II prevented it from being demolished, referring to the need to maintain the unity of the square – an early example of architectural conservation.

The Fire Tower guarding the northern entrance into
medieval Sopron has become a lasting symbol of the town.
The base of the tower dates from the 13th century,
the Baroque balcony being built in 1681.
Tourists can stroll along the atmospheric streets
of the old town almost totally unhindered by traffic.

Tired tourists are often seen regaining their strength
at the foot of the Baroque sculpture in the middle
of Sopron's main square. Sitting there you can see
the Gothic tower of the Franciscan Church,
with its characteristic tympanumed doorway;
the Renaissance town houses and the classical façades
of the public buildings.

During the boundary changes following the First World War there was a plebiscite to decide whether Sopron should become part of Austria or stay in Hungary. A sculptural composition by Zsigmond Kisfaludi Strobl on the façade of the Fire Tower in the main square depicting "Hungaria" summoning together the town's loyal citizens was erected to commemorate the event.

The town is surrounded by the *Sopron Hills* to the south and the west, the *Balf Hills* to the east and the *Ikva Valley* in which the town itself is situated. Geographically the valley serves as a gateway

In the cellar of Sopron's Fabricius House (Fő tér 6.) you will find the Roman lapidarium, whilst on the upper floors there is an exhibition containing some fine 17th and 18th century furniture.

Matthias Corvinus once stayed at Storno House, today it contains a collection belonging to its one-time owner (Fő tér 8.).

The southern side of the main square is dominated by the **Franciscan Church** with its 47-metre tower. The church was originally built by the Franciscans in the 13th century, and was later taken over by the Benedictine Order. On entering the **church** you pass under a donor's coat-of-arms which features a

goat. Although there are a lot of medieval details to enjoy one has to beware of some of *Ferenc Storno*'s 19th century restoration work.

Fortunately the chapter house (1340) at Sopron's Franciscan Church survives. Its carved corbels and its general state of preservation make it one of the wonders of Hungarian Gothic architecture.

The *Mining Museum* and the *Forestry Museum* are in each of the Esterházys' two palaces (Templom u. 2.,4.). **Bezerédj House** (6.) is one of the most beautiful Baroque residences in the town. On the corner of Kolostor utca and Templom utca stands the monumental Lutheran **hall church** built at the end of the 18th century. On the first floor of the vicarage next door (12.) you will find Sopron's contribution to the *National Lutheran Museum*. Orsolya tér has seen many changes in its history. What was once a simple Baroque chapel belonging to the Order of Saint Ursula was replaced by a Gothic Revival monastic church and school (1861–1867). It is here you will find the **Roman Catholic Ecclesiastical Collection**.

Új utca was where the Jewish traders lived during the Middle Ages, and it is here also that the local Jewish community built two synagogues. The **synagogue** at house 22, was probably built in about 1300. The superb restoration revealed the original structure, the Gothic windows, the rib vaults and the rose windows. In the main hall there is a richly ornamented niche where the Scrolls of the Law were kept. Another interesting part of the complex is the **ritual bath** which amounts to a small walled well. Gothic details occasionally jump out of the Baroque house fronts (3., 5.) on Szent György utca. It was during the Reformation that the owner of **Eggenberg House** (12.) was given permission to allow Protestant services to be held in the courtyard, something not permitted elsewhere in the town. One peculiar feature surviving from this period is the stone pulpit built into the middle of the loggia corridor.

The late Renaissance residence (7.) was built by the town clerk. The portal is framed by a frieze of faces, one of which sticks its tongue out at passers-by.

Sopron's Új utca with its synagogue has a distinctively medieval feel.

St George's Church was built in about 1400 in the Gothic style. It was given its current Baroque appearance and liturgical furniture during the course of the 18th century.

The centre of Sopron is arranged around two squares linked together by a number of gently curving streets. Even in the Middle Ages such was the lack of space within the town walls that the width of the plots was severely restricted and a one-way system introduced. On the façades of the town residences you can see some fine Renaissance details in the window frames as well as coats-of-arms over the gateways.

The second medieval gateway into the old town was the Hátsó kapu (Rear Gate). House number 2 was built on the site of a Roman gatehouse and some Roman houses, and the 17th century houses were built of substantial amounts of reused medieval building material. It was within the walls of the Upper House, where the National Assembly elected the palatines, that the decision was made to allow Lutherans to build their own churches (1681). The first floor of the buildings looking onto the courtyard with the Tuscan arcade, has an exhibition devoted to the watercolours of local artist József Horváth.

Leaving the *Hátsó kapu* we enter the *Castle District* running around the oval Old Town. It was here that the great **"rondella"** dating from 1614 was uncovered during the 1950s. Today it is the Secession style **Petőfi Theatre** (*István Medgyaszay,* 1908–1909), which takes all the plaudits. It was in this part of town also that the old **Casino** (Széchenyi tér 15.), perhaps the grandest building in the whole town, stood prior to its demolition during the 1960s. It is here you can now find the **Franz Liszt Conference and Cultural Centre** (2002, Liszt F. u.).

On the eastern side of Széchenyi tér (1–3) you will find the Széchenyi family's imposing early neoclassical palace.

The outer parts of the Castle District acquired their current urban appearance at the end of the 19th century. The **Pannonia Hotel** (1893) is a typical example of the kind of public building you can find here. The **White Horse Inn** (Fehérló fogadó) is considerably older having been visited by *Miklós Zrínyi* in 1644.

St Michael's Church, the parish church serving the *Bécs Suburb* of the town, is one of the finest 14th century churches in Hungary. The curious layout of the eastern part of the church, with its lofty side chapels, is often compared with the cathedral in nearby Wiener Neustadt. Next to the church stands the hexagonal **Chapel of St James** dating from the 13th century.

The growing interest in the local Sopron wines is reflected in the increasing number of local inns. The wines are usually accompanied by traditional *"ponzichter" ("Bohnen Züchter")* bean dishes, made from the beans often grown between the rows of vines out in the vineyards.

The most beautiful of these inns is **Két Mór House**, which is richly decorated and guarded by two moorish figures which feature in the hostelry's name (Szent Mihály u. 9.). At Bécsi út 5., on the recently renovated site of the old bakery, you will find the **Bakery Museum**.

In the *Balf Suburb* of the town, an area also rich in inns, you will find the **Zettl-Langer Collection** (Balfi u. 9–11) of Roman remains, local guild artefacts, pottery and weapons, paintings (including works by *Dorfmaister, Veronese* and *Courtois*) and prints by *Rembrandt* and *Dürer*.

In the southern suburbs of the town stands the Greek-style **Lenck Villa** (Deák tér 1.) built in 1890. The *arts and crafts exhibitions* now held there, give a detailed account of the tools and the tricks of more than twenty different trades. In the suburb once known as *Sopronbánfalva* stands the 12th–15th century **Church of Saint Mary Magdalene**.

The buildings on the *Lővérek* started to appear during the mid-19th century. The streets here are made all the more pleasant by the pretty fences and the thick shrubs growing immediately in front of the houses. The neo-Renaissance building of the one-time **Military Academy**, with its enormous botanical garden, was taken over by the *University of Forestry and Mining* (Bajcsy-Zsilinszky út 3.), which moved to Sopron from Selmecbánya (Banská Stiavnica, Slovakia) following the First World War. The Upper Lővérek is now primarily a residential area, but on the road known as Villasor you can still see some totally unspoilt single and double-storeyed Lővér houses with their verandas (6–30.). On the Lővér körút you will find both an **indoor** and an **outdoor swimming pool.** There are lots of pathways criss-crossing the Sopron Hills, and they all seem to converge on the Lővér Hotel. It is on the 23metre-high **lookout tower** (1935) on Károly Hill that we finally bid farewell to the town.

If you are in Sopron during March you can enjoy the local events contributing to the Budapest Spring Festival.
At the end of May the town hosts the Sopron Wine Festival, and then the end of June and the beginning of July sees the arrival of the Sopron Festival.

The quarry at Fertőrákos feels like somewhere in ancient Egypt. Whatever one happens to think it provides a fine venue for the operas which are put on there every summer.

GETTING OUT OF SOPRON

Hungary's first ever coal mine was opened in BRENNBERGBÁNYA in 1756, and this mining tradition is still apparent in the appearance of the village today. Even the arches in the **church** appear to refer to mining activity of sorts.

FERTŐRÁKOS

The 12 million-year-old Lajta limestone of the hills overlooking Fertőrákos has been quarried for many hundreds of years. The best quality stone has already been quarried; the rubble which remains lies scattered over the galleries.

You can see a collection Hungary's finest minerals at the **Crystal Museum**, the fruit of a Budapest couple's passion for geology (Fő u. 99.)

Fertőrákos's medieval layout survives, as do some of its medieval buildings. The restored house with its fine gabled roof on Fő utca (152.) dating from the early 18th century would have belonged to an German family. It isn't the only peasant cottage that has been renovated for the benefit of the tourists.

The old **water mill** on the Rákos is now used as a hotel. In the courtyard you can see how the moving parts of the old mill worked.

The **Church of the Ascension** was built during the second half of the 18th century, despite appearances suggesting the contrary. It is only when you are inside the church that you really see anything imbued with the Baroque spirit.

Fertőrákos's Roman remains lie carved into the rock, where the altar in the Temple of Mithras survives. On it there is a depiction of a God overcoming the bull of darkness flanked by two figures representing Dawn and Dusk.

Activity at Fertő tends to wind down with the arrival of winter. The sandy shores are deserted, the boats are safely in their boathouses, and the thatched cottages on their stilts are totally empty. The only sounds breaking the stillness are those of the whispering reeds.

The pillory in front of the **Episcopal Palace** (17th and 18th centuries) is the only one in Hungary. A long reed-bordered road takes you from Fertő-rákos to the **Fertő Holiday Village**. Next to the shallow sandy shores of the Fertő stands the grassy, wooded **Outdoor Swimming Complex**. Pleasure boats depart from the small jetty next to the swim-

St Wolfgang's church in Balf with its cemetery and perched on a hill is protected by a stone wall dating back to the 17th century.

ming pool. Beyond the jetty there are some thatched houses on stilts offering accommodation. *Szárhalmi Wood,* running parallel with the western bank of the Fertő, is popular all year round.

BALF

Saint Wolfgang's Church stood on the hill overlooking the village of Balf as far back as the 12th century. The gravestones are the work of stonemasons active in Sopron during the first third of the 18th century. Walking around the graveyard you cannot but notice the tumbledown *wall.* Leaning up against the wall is a small **memorial** upon the base of which you will see the pebbles left by those who have come to remember *"those many thousands who died within sight of victory".* Most of the victims were Jews forced to march out from Budapest to work as slave labourers on an earthwork designed to halt the Red Army along the Austrian-Hungarian border. The words of one of the victims, Antal Szerb, are quoted on the marble tablet. *"Freedom is not the sole possession of one nation, it belongs to mankind as a whole."*

At theWorld Heritage Site's Nagycenk Palace you can see how István Széchenyi dreamt up his plans to improve Hungary's infrastructure, and how such projects were aimed at realising his great rallying call: "Whilst never having been, Hungary will be".

Balf's picturesque **English-style park** contains the slipper chapel (1773), which on first inspection looks like something resembling a jewellery box. Inside you can find frescos, a Baroque altar painting (*István Dorfmaister*) and statues covered in gold leaf (*András Sedlmayer*).

In Balf Park, the hotel, the restaurant and the **swimming pool**, with its wide selection of medicinal facilities, all belong to the sanatorium (Fürdő sor 2). The buttresses and the carved Gothic window frames in the chancel of the **parish church** in HARKA betray its medieval origins. The painting in the chancel is 19th century.

NAGYCENK

The Széchenyi family built the palace which eventually took the Baroque and classical form you can see today. Inside, on the ground floor, the **István Széchenyi Memorial Museum** not only has the furniture you would expect to find in the residence of a 19th century aristocrat, but a collection of documents relating to the life and work of *"the greatest Hungarian"*. The two-storied façade has a central projection crowned by a tympanum incorporating the Széchenyi coat of arms.

The construction of the Széchenyi Palace was started by Antal Széchenyi when the manor house which had stood here was rebuilt in the middle of the 18th century. The house was subsequently much altered by the enlightened figure of Ferenc Széchényi, the founder of the National Museum. The golden age of the estate came when his son István Széchenyi, who inherited the house, asked Mihály Pollack to work on the extensions conducted in 1838. We know that by the time that all alterations had been made in 1840 the house was fitted with all the latest modern conveniences, including gas lamps and flushing toilets. The park surrounding the house has a French feel to it.

In front, two Tuscan pillars hold up the Baroque wrought-iron balcony, which jumps out from the subtly articulated elevation. Above the windows runs a long horizontal relief. The tympanum contains the Széchenyi family's coat-of-arms.

Another real attraction is the **railway museum** founded by some local railway fanatics living in Sopron during the 1970s.

During the summer season visitors can travel right up to the banks of the Fertő in one of several trains dating back to the glorious age of steam.

The railway terminates at Fertőboz, from where you can follow Ferenc Széchényi's and Palatine József's footsteps to the Gloriett. The Gloriett built to commemorate this walk, is an excellent example of neoclassical architecture offering some wonderful views. On a clear day you can see the peaks of the Alps rising up behind the reeds and the shimmering waters.

Even gardening books published in America wax lyrical about the **Lime Avenue** at Nagycenk. Originally (1754) 645 lime trees lined the 2,600m route. The trees still growing today reach a height of 16 metres and their trunks are one metre thick.

Noticing that the local congregation needed more than the crumbling church they were worshipping in, István Széchenyi built them a new one. He financed the project himself and invited Miklós Ybl to draw up the plans. He added, not without a hint of humour, "but don't put a tower above the entrance to the church, it makes the church look like a goose sitting on its eggs. Put the tower to one side, it doesn't matter which, and make sure the church has a gallery inside". Miklós Ybl obliged.

In 1778, Ferenc Széchényi built a Baroque **chapel** in the hope that it would eventually be the family vault. István Széchenyi's tomb and that of his wife Cresscencia Seiler can be found down in the crypt under a pile of wreaths. It is here also that his parents Ferenc Széchényi, the founder of the *National Museum* and Julianna Festetics were buried. From money raised from a national collection organised by István Széchenyi's son the villages were able to put up the *Széchenyi Statue* (*Alajos Stróbl, 1897*).

Opinions are divided about exactly when the **cemetery chapel** in NAGYLÓZS was built. Although some say it dates from the reign of Stephen I. it was probably built in the years immediately following his beatification in 1083. The small church has managed to survive with most of its Romanesque detailing, its round apses and windows intact.

In RÖJTÖKMUZSAJ the **palace**, with its 7 hectares of ancient parkland and a history going back to the mid-18th century, is now a hotel with an attached wellness centre in the old hunter's lodge. The most valuable object in the **parish church** (1879) is the *Vimpác Madonna*.

Tradition says the statue, found on the banks of the Lajta, once decorated the parish church in Vimpác (Wimpassing, Burgenland, Austria) built in 1496. The much-treasured statue was stolen by a Turkish officer, who returned it in gratitude for a miraculous recovery. The Madonna belonged to the Minorite Friary before ending up at the church.

In the centre of PUSZTACSALÁD on the *Répce Plain* far from any town, there is a statue which deserves some attention. But all is not what it appears. The inscription on the base reads: *"Saint Stephen. Made in the 19th century on the occasion of the 900th anniversary of his birth"*. Documents prove, however, that the statue was in fact put up in memory of István Széchenyi rather than the first king of Hungary. In 1860, it was still forbidden to remember one of the great figures of the Age of Reform. So it was that the statue was given a deliberately misleading inscription and put up in what is the smallest and most obscure village on the family's estates.

The Lutheran church in NEMESKÉR *(1732) is
a masterpiece of Hungarian wooden architecture.
The roof's wooden beams rest on a row of wooden pillars.
The limewood pulpit, which was almost definitely a gift,
was added to an altar probably built in situ.
The treatment of the drapery and the apostles' faces
suggest that the artist was not without talent.*

It was in SOPRONHORPÁCS *during the 1800s
that the Széchenyis built their country residence
and laid out their enormous English-style park.
The parish church predates both by a good five hundred years.
Despite much reconstruction work the Romanesque portal
has survived relatively unscathed.
Although inside there is a real hotch-potch of styles
it is not difficult to distinguish the Gothic wall niches,
the stiff-leaf capitals and pointed windows in the choir
from István Dorfmaister the Younger's
and F.A. Maulbertsch's Baroque works.*

KŐSZEG

Those approaching Kőszeg from the north-east get
the best view of what was the only royal free town in
Vas County. From the top of the hills you can see
the Baroque **Calvary Church** rising up above the
entrance to the valley, and the squat **lookout tower**
on *Óház-tető.* The latter stands on the remains of an
800-year-old castle. During the course of the
restoration work (*Kornél Bakay*), which took place
during the 1990s, the portcullis and the extensive
foundations of a 4 to 5 storey keep, covering an area
of 22.5m x 12 metres, were excavated.

There was a time when travellers passing the town
were forced to use the so-called *Cholera Road* during plague outbreaks. Travelling along the road
today you come to the railway station. The Kő-
szeg-Szombathely branch line was built with the
strength and the endeavour of the local population. Going down Rákóczi út in the direction of
the town you come to the **Blackamoor Pharmacy
Museum** (3.). A certain Nicolaus Herpius opened
the shop in 1665. The furniture, which is carved
from cherry wood, dates from the 1850s. Standing
opposite is probably the oldest functioning inn in
the country, the *Golden Ostrich (Arany Strucc)*
(Várkör 124.), frequented as far back as 1597.

*The Trinity Statue
(Servatianus Leithner,
1713) was put up
in memory of Kőszeg's
many hundreds
of plague
victims.*

Of all the buildings in the main square, number 11. is perhaps the most interesting. Originally Baroque it was rebuilt in the neoclassical style. Stucco reliefs representing the four seasons stand to either side of the wrought-iron balcony.

Kőszeg's Town Hall is perhaps the oldest functioning town hall in Hungary. The town has been governed from here continually since the 14th and 15th centuries (Jurisics tér 8.).

In the middle of Jurisics tér, behind the statue of the Blessed Virgin Mary, stands the classical municipal well, which was once surrounded by shuttering to prevent the water from becoming contaminated.

The largest building in the town centre is the Gothic Revival Church of the Sacred Heart (Ludwig Schöne, 1892-1894) in the main square. The interior wall decoration was designed by Viennese artist Otto Kott.

Heading towards the old bridge, along the narrow Városkapu, you eventually come to the old town. The *Alsókapu* was once the most important bastion in the medieval defences. The first floor of the bastion and that of the neighbouring **General's House** (Jurisics tér 6.) now house the *Miklós Jurisics Museum* dedicated to the arts and crafts and the history of the local guilds.

The area around the base of **Heroes' Tower** forms one of Hungary's smallest and most beautiful historical townscapes.

Saint Emmerich's Roman Catholic church, originally built by the Hungarian Protestants between 1615 and 1618, stands at one end of the square. **Saint James the Apostle** was probably the church Kálmán Bishop of Győr built for the Franciscans settling in Kőszeg during the 14th century. It was the Garai family who made the Gothic additions.

The Church of St James is predominantly Gothic in style. The wall paintings depicting Saint Christopher and the Magi are contemporary with the earliest parts of the church. These, as well as a Schutzmantel Madonna, came to light during the dismantling of an 18th century altarpiece. The one-time Jesuit, later Benedictine, monastery (1677-1680, Pietro Orsolini) which joins onto the church is now occupied by the Verbita Order.

Sgraffitos House got its name from the technique used to decorate the house's façade.
The tulip and the geometrical designs used make the town house, which incidentally also has frescoed ceilings dating from the Turkish period, one of the most beautiful houses in Kőszeg (Jurisics tér 7.). The building is now the Írottkő Nature Park's Information Centre.

The valuable oak, walnut and limewood furniture forming the centrepiece of the **Golden Unicorn Pharmacy Museum** were purchased by the *Museum of the Applied Arts* and returned to Kőszeg in 1982.

When **Sigray Palace** (Chernel u. 14.) was renovated it was decided to return it to its early Renaissance form. It's a building now used by the *Europe House Association*.

Next door stands the tallest bastion in the town's defences, the so-called **Old Tower,** otherwise know as *Zwinger Tower*. The archaeological finds uncovered nearby suggest that the bastion was originally built in the 13th century, taking its polygonal form from Angevin precidents. From here you can go down to look at the longest surviving stretch of the town wall. The Kőszeg family also built a **castle** to serve and protect the town. Both the inner and the outer castle were considered totally separate from the town.

Above the gate leading into the inner castle you will find the coat-of-arms of the ducal branch of the Esterházy family, the last owners of the castle, framed by a tent-shaped fresco.

The **inner castle** is in fact the oldest part of Kőszeg. Building on the northern and southern walls, and the four corner towers, was started during the 13th century. During the Turkish siege of 1532 the castle had to withstand 19 attacks within a space of 25 days before the Turks finally retreated.

The siege of Kőszeg Castle was an event of some military interest because, not having siege cannons at their disposal, the Turks made their first attempt to blow up walls using explosives. The defenders, under artillery-sergeant Mátyás Forintos, were able to frustrate the Turks by using countermines.

Every St George's Day since 1740 illustrations of the year's grapevines are drawn in the Grape Book.
The completion of the year's new book is now an event accompanied by great celebrations.

Comedies and musical events are staged in the castle courtyard during July and August.

The castle is now a cultural centre, especially when the **castle theatre** is up and running in the courtyard. It is here also that you can visit the *Miklós Jurisics Castle Museum* with its local history collection and the unique *Grape Book*.

In the **Castle precincts** the original positions of any missing walls and towers are marked out in the ground.

Keeping to the paths, which were for the most part laid out at the end of the 19th century, you can walk to *Óház-tető* and the Seven Springs. For those keen on venturing further you can hike out to the highest peak in Transdanubia, *Írott-kő*, which stands at a height of 883m. The hill once marked the end of the *National Blue Walk* from where you can now continue along the *Southern Transdanubian Blue Walk* towards Szekszárd.

The lookout tower on Írott-kő on the border of Rohonc (Rechnitz, Austria) was built in 1913. Seven years later it was to used as one of the marking points for the new border with Austria following the Treaty of Trianon.
For a long period after the Second World War it was only the Austrians who were allowed to get anywhere near the tower. Hungarian hikers can now approach it from both sides.

The **lookout tower** on *Óház-tető* was first built in 1896 on the site of Óvár Castle.

The present arrangement, with each spring accompanied by a marble tablet naming one of the seven tribes who arrived at the time of the Hungarian Conquest, was laid out to mark the one thousandth anniversary of the event.

IN THE KŐSZEG HILLS

It's worth spending some time in the three small villages of Cák, Velem and Bozsok at the foot of the *Kőszeg Hills* to enjoy the buildings and the surrounding countryside.

Nearly all the Kőszeg Hills lying on the Hungarian side of the border form part of the *Kőszeg Nature Reserve* (1980). On what is a crossroads between two botanical regions you can find eight types of alpine tree not found elsewhere in Hungary, as well as wide-leafed bluebells, white crocuses, mountain arnica and bitter vetch. The landscape is also rich in butterflies and beetles. But if the reserve were to have a symbol it would be the spotted salamander which is common in these parts.

The **row of cellars** standing on the edge of CÁK form one of the most important sites for folk architecture in the area. Large areas of the Kőszeg Hills are covered with sweet chestnuts. There is some argument as to whether they are indigenous or whether they were planted after a phylloxera outbreak destroyed all the vines towards the end of the 19th century.

Winepresses were also kept in Cák's mud-walled and timber-built thatched cellars up until the phylloxera outbreak. Subsequently the cellars were used primarily for storing sweet chestnuts and fruit.

VELEM

Visitors go to Velem mainly for its clean air. The picturesque village of **Schulterhalma,** which can be found on the borders of Kőszegszerdahely despite belonging to Velem, has a mill, built at the beginning of the 20th century, which now functions as a museum.

Most visitors who go to Stirling Villa visit the workshop next door with its exhibition of local arts and crafts. Cultural programmes and markets are held on a regular basis. It was in a bunker on the side of the hill behind the villa that the Hungarian crown was held for safekeeping during the winter of 1944-1945.

The part of Velem having the most history is Szent Vid Hill (582m). Archaeological finds suggest that the area has been inhabited since the 13th–9th century BC. A number of important settlements developed around the hills, whose metal products have been found as far away as Scandinavia. Szent Vid Castle was an important fortress during the Middle Ages. It was here also that a Baroque chapel was built, partly on medieval foundations. Its present appearance dates from 1859. Just in front of the entrance you can see the outlines of the old castle.

In BOZSOK, near the Austrian border, you will find Sibrik Castle, medieval in origin but transformed into a fortified palace in 1614. Its predecessor is thought to have been a hunting lodge belonging to Matthias Corvinus.

According to the carved inscription over the entrance of **Saint Nicholas's Church** in CSEP-REG's main Széchenyi tér, the Gothic building was built by local landowner János Kanizsai, arch-bishop of Esztergom, during the 14th century. All that remains from that time is the massiveness of the tower. Most of the church was remodelled during the 18th century. The classical painting over the main altarpiece is by *Johann Cymbal*. It was mainly due to the efforts of the Nádasdy family during the 16th and 17th centuries that the town became a centre of the Lutheran faith. Ferenc Nádasdy's declared intention to turn to the Catholic faith in Csepreg church in 1643 was therefore an event of some significance.

The region's most popular thermal bath can be found in Bükfürdő. It was in 1957 that the oil prospectors came upon 58 °C waters at a depth of 1,282m underground. It was soon realised that the waters had medicinal properties. The spa was opened in 1962, and three years later the waters were formally recognised as being medicinal. The 34-hectare complex has both indoor and open-air pools, made all the more exciting by the new covered leisure pool (2003).

Bük

The **Szapáry Palace** on Kastély utca was built at the beginning of the 17th century, and remodelled in the Baroque style with the help of some Italian interior decorators at the end of the century. One of its previous owners was Pál Nagy of Felső-bük. It was during a speech in Parliament that the politician suggested that *István Széchenyi* devote one year's income to the founding of the *Hungarian Academy of Sciences*.

Today, the village is very much dominated by the thermal baths. During the 1980s the classical **Nagy Hall in Felsőbük** was turned into holiday accommodation and a restaurant as part of the palace preservation programme. The Baroque **Lutheran church** was built in 1785, although its tower was only added three decades later. There are written records about **Saint Koloman**'s Roman Catholic church in Petőfi Sándor utca going back to 1408, although the church is older than that.

The tower of the Saint Koloman's in Bük was built in 1658. Several medieval details came to light during the restoration of the transept.

SZOMBATHELY

Remains going back to prehistoric times have been found within the boundaries of Szombathely, the county town of Vas. Whilst it is difficult to date such finds with any great accuracy, the fact that Emperor Claudius founded *Colonia Claudia Savariensium*, otherwise known as Savaria, means we can date the town to about 50AD. The centre of the historical town, that is the area around Sörház and Hollán Ernő utca, Berzsenyi Dániel tér and Templom tér, is where you can find the Baroque and classical buildings going back to the 18th and 19th centuries. The so-called **Canon's House** (Hollán E. u. 13.) is a fine example of a Louis Seize-style, late Baroque building of the beginning of the 1780s, whilst the Episcopal **Beer House** (Sörház) (10–12., *Donát Vojta*) is neoclassical in style.

Leaving the Louis Seize-style house belonging to the Canons' musicians (4.) we reach the one-time grammar school (1773) which now provides a permanent home for **Smidt Museum.**

In Berzsenyi tér stands the Episcopal Palace (Menyhért Hefele, 1778-1783). On the parapet are the coat-of-arms of patron, bishop János Szily, and statues of the cardinal virtues.

Its collection of medical, military and cultural artefacts were left to the town by *Lajos Smidt*, head physician at the local hospital.

In the **Episcopal Palace** you will find the *Sala terrena* and the ecclesiastical history collection. It was

in the Sala terrena, covered by paintings by *István Dorfmaister*, that the bishop assembled his collection of Roman sculptural fragments and inscriptions. The **cathedral** (1791–1814) in Templom tér with its statues and the tympanum filled with sculptural depictions of *Faith, Hope and Charity* look down onto a sculpture by *Istvan Tóth* (1909).

In Szombathely's István Járdányi Paulovics Park you will find a restored stretch of the Amber Road.

It was whilst digging foundations in the vicinity of the cathedral that the first Roman remains came to light. In István Járdányi Paulovics Park you will find a number of ruins: part of the road leading to the one-time forum. The finds discovered during the construction of a bank in Fő tér (no. 3-5) can be seen through the glass section inserted into the floor of the bank. They include a junction leading off the Amber Road, a drain, and a 6m Corinthian column. (The rest of the finds were deposited at the Savaria Museum.)

The building was bombed in 1945, and although it was rebuilt some of the liturgical furniture still needs to be replaced.

The **Ecclesiastical Library and Archives** (1777–1780) can be found behind the simple Baroque façade of the old seminary. The library's most valuable books can be found surrounded by the frescos in the *Dorfmaister Room*. It was on the printing press on the ground floor that *Kelemen Mikes's* Turkish letters were first printed.

The road opposite the cathedral and the Episcopal Palace leads to the main square, once the town's main market square. From here a road takes you to the **Iseum**.

Evidence of the cult of Iris, coming originally from Egypt, arrived in Pannonia some time during the 2nd century AD. Evidence of the cult can be found in the temple uncovered in Szombathely between 1955 and 1961.

The reconstructed remains of the temple have been used in recent years as a backdrop for outdoor performances of Mozart's The Magic Flute. Excavations have recontinued at the Iseum, the intention being to rebuild it competely and open it to the general public again in 2005.

Opposite the Iseum you can see one of the most complete **synagogues** *(Ludwig Schöne)* in Hungary. It provides a venue for many concerts and a home for the world-famous *Bartók Seminar and Festival*.

There are two churches which are worthy of attention. Firstly, there is the old Franciscan church in Savaria tér, now known as St Elizabeth's.

The present exterior of this **Roman Catholic church** was built during the 17th and 18th centuries; inside the furniture is for the most part Baroque. In one of the side chapels you can see the oldest depiction of Szombathely (1749).

Many of Szombathely's most famous citizens lie buried in its crypt.

Since the time of Charlemagne, Savaria has been considered the birthplace of St Martin of Tours. According to legend St Martin's Church in Szombathely stands on the site of the house where he was born in about 315 AD. There is, however, no proof that his parents ever lived in the town. What is sure is that a church stood on the site as far back as the ninth century.

If you go down right to the end of Szent Márton utca from Saint Elizabeth's church you come to **Saint Martin's** Roman Catholic church to which are attached the conventual buildings of the Dominican Friary.

The present church was for the most part built in 1638 when the Dominicans settled here, although Romanesque and Gothic details can still be found, such as the Gothic wall paintings uncovered in the chancel.

In 1935, the church was lengthened by 11 metres to the designs of neo-Baroque architect Gyula Wälder. The well in front of the church, which is where you will now find the statue of Saint Martin Baptising his Mother (István Rumi Rajki, 1938) is mentioned as far back as 1360.

The town's cultural calendar includes the *Savaria Historical Carnival*, the *Spring Festival*, *St Martin's Week*, the *Savaria International Dance Festival*, and the *Bartók Seminary and Festival*.

It was in what is now Szombathely's Arboretum, on Szent Imre herceg út, that István Saághy planted 250 coniferous and 300 deciduous trees.

Next to the recently reconstructed pool and the **boating lake** you will find the **Vas Outdoor Museum** (Árpád u. 30.) the second museum of its kind (1973) in Hungary. It contains examples of local peasant architecture, and the collection is still growing.

The stalls at the Vas Outdoor Museum sell locally produced arts and crafts.

On top of the small artificial mound you can see buildings which are typical of the Őrség and the Vend Region, a U-shaped house (from Farkasfa), a fenced house (Szalafő), and some old wine cellars. At the foot of the mound and on the flatter parts of the site you can see houses representing the other local ethnic populations. There's a peasant cottage from the Vas Ridge (Sárfimizdó), a Croatian dwelling (Szentpéterfa), a Kemenesalja peasant cottage (Celldömölk-Alsóság), a blacksmith's (Cák), a Völgység cottage (Nemeskolta), a Lesser Plain house (Lócs), a peasant cottage from the Rába Valley (Sótony), a German dwelling (Pornóapáti), a Kemenesalja poor peasant's cottage (Vönöck) and a Lesser Plain gentry house (Nemesládony). The outdoor museum also keeps traditional Hungarian breeds of chickens, pigs and sheep.

The April and November weekends: corresponding with Saint George's Day and Saint Martin's Day are busy days. It is then that stallholders, comedians and conjurers descend on the museum. On Whit Monday the strong and the brave battle it out for the title of Whitsun King. The children get involved in the *procession of the Whitsun Queen.*

The recently-revived Savaria Historical Carnival which took place in August 2000, included a costumed historical procession showing the most important episodes and periods in the history of Szombathely.

Castles, Palaces and Parks

It was around SZELESTE Palace that Count Andor Festetics laid out a park in the local pastures (1855). Work on the park, which now surrounds the park hotel, was continued in the 1910s by Mihály Baich. The result is an **arboretum** which is a whole landscape in itself.

It was Zsigmond Szentgyörgyi Horváth who built the palace at RÉPCESZENTGYÖRGY during the 1700s. Although the house is in private hands and currently being renovated, the owners are only too happy to show visitors round. The park itself enjoys protected status. Zsigmond Szentgyörgyi Horváth II.'s building activities also went further afield.

Zsigmond Szentgyörgyi Horváth also built the Church of the Elevation of the True Cross in HEGYFALU. The building of the church (1815) influenced the remodelling work then going on at the classical Széchenyi Palace (Kossuth u. 2.). After having been in the possession of a series of owners it was purchased just before 1945 for use as a T.B. sanatorium. Behind it lie 7 hectares of protected parkland.

The recent renovation work on the **Church of Saint Stephen the King** in NAGYGERESD has turned it into one of the most beautiful buildings in the area. During the restoration work on the Baroque church (1755) some 13th century Romanesque and 15th century Gothic details came to light, as did several wall paintings in the chancel and two pastophoria.

SÁRVÁR

During the Roman period the settlement was known as *Bassiana*. In 1534, the fortress became the property of the most gifted politician of his age, Tamás Nádasdy, following a favourable marriage. During the 16th and 17th centuries he and his descendants proceeded not only to strengthen Sárvár but to make it a more attractive place to live in. The outer walls were designed to ward off artillery attacks.

To get to the **fortified palace** today you have to cross the long bridge leading up to the gateway. The corridor through the gatehouse contains some late Gothic wall niches. The ground floor of the arcaded eastern wing, the oldest part of the palace built by Nádasdy, is now used for holding civil wedding ceremonies.

Today the castle contains a museum with exhibitions about the one-time owners of the palace; the Hungarian hussars; cartography; industrial history and the history of the town. In the banqueting hall you can see a battle scene signed by a painter calling himself H.R.M. (Hans Rudolf Miller) painted in 1653. The paintings Miller painted for Ferenc Nádasdy immortalise the great "black bey" battles against the Turks: the Battle of Sziszek, the recapturing of Pápa and Tata, and the incidents at Veszprém, Győr, Kanizsa and Buda.

The banqueting hall also includes Biblical scenes (incl. David and Goliath, and the Annointment of King David) and whilst in the tower room you can see pictures with allegorical themes. All are the work of Baroque artist István Dorfmaister.

Parks have been laid out where the defensive ditches once stood, and it is here you will find a statue of Sebestyén Tinódi Lantos (Iván Szabó).

In the 16th century, the town and castle of Sárvár proved both a cultural and religious centre of the Hungarian Reformation. It was here that the first book in Hungarian was published, János Sylvester's translation of the New Testament (1541).

It is not known exactly when **Saint Ladislas's** church in Kossuth tér was built, but we know the church had a priest in 1385. Today, it is the Baroque pillar incorporating an image of Christ of 1701, which catches the eye. The **Lutheran church** (*Sámuel Geschrey*) on János Sylvester utca is immediately recognisable by its pediment supported by four columns.

On the banks of the Gyöngyös you will find the 16 hectares of garden which include some planes planted by Antal Nábicht (beginning of the 19th century) when he was in the service of the Dukes of Bavaria. Today, there are more than 350 trees and shrubs in the **arboretum** growing around the small lake fed by water from the stream. The park's predecessor is believed to have been the garden laid out by Orsolya Kanizsai, the fruits of which made their way all the way to the Imperial Court in Vienna in the company of Tamás Nádasdy.

Hot 44°C waters bubbling up to the earth's surface from a depth of 1,000m supply the recently renovated (2002) local thermal baths.

It was in the 1360s that the Augustinians founded their monastery in Pápoc. Recent restoration work has brought some of the Gothic details to light. The Romanesque Maria Schnee Chapel, which was later engulfed by the monastery, has survived. Inside it is possible to see the original bases, the rib vaults the shafts and the carved crocket capitals.
The centralised chapel has four apses, and an entrance containing carved medieval stonework.

Celldömölk

Some parts of the town were already inhabited by the early Middle Ages. At the end of Koptik Odó utca stand the remains of **Dömölk Abbey,** founded in the 12th century. The tower and the nave of the **church** are Romanesque, the chancel is Gothic. In the Kiscelli part of the town you can find the old **Benedictine Monastery**, now a pilgrimage church, founded by Odó Koptik, Abbot of Dömölk, during the first half of the 18th century.

In the small chapel situated in the middle of the chancel of **St Mary's Church** stands a copy of the Mariazell Madonna. The patronal festival of the *Feast of the Blessed Virgin Mary* takes place on the Sunday following 12th September. The **Stations of the Cross** (1755) standing behind the church form a spectacle rarely found in Hungary. On the edge of the town stands *Ság Hill* (279m) which forms the smallest nature reserve in the country. The hill is all that remains of a 5 million-year-old volcano. Investigating the interior of the one-time volcano has been made all the more interesting since the *geological nature trail* was laid out.

It was in 1891, on what was still a flat hilltop, that *Baron Loránd Eötvös* (1848–1919) carried out his experiments into the effects of gravity with the help of a torsion balance.

Although the mining on Ság Hill managed to destroy some rare plants, for example the pheasant's eye, pulsatilla and needlegrass, you can still find alyssum, white stonecrop and xeranthemum. In the small clearings you can find groups of erythraea, irises, buttercups and viper's bugloss. The birds of prey all nest in the area. One of the old mining buildings has been turned into a museum containing exhibitions focusing on both local and natural history.

The grapes which once grew around the base of Ság Hill were so good that Ság's high acid-content wines were sold in the pharmacies of Vienna. In recent years much has been done to win back the wines' good reputation.
Together with Somló and Kissomlyó,
Ság Hill is now a recognised wine region.

The **Erdődy-Choron Palace** (in Vár utca) in Jánosháza can be dated back to the end of the 14th century. The spire was added in 1935. After the Second World War the palace fell into state hands, and was consequently turned into a museum. Today the building is privately owned and is currently being renovated.

Heading southwards from HOSSZÚPERESZTEG along road number 8 you come to eleven lakes formed in the 1930s with the damming of the *Csörgető*. Of the **Szajki Lakes** five are suitable for fishing whilst a sixth is popular with bathers. A **wood** has been laid out nearby and there are also leisure facilities.

Although currently Baroque in appearance **All Saints** CSEHIMINDSZENT was in fact mentioned as far back as the Middle Ages. The village is named after the church's patron saint. The church's polygonal chancel contains an altar painting by István Dorfmaister.

József Mindszenty (Pehm), the Archbishop of Esztergom who leapt to world prominence during the course of the Hungarian Uprising in 1956, was born in the village, something commemorated by a **tablet** in the church and a **bust** in the park which can be found next door. By adopting the name of his birthplace in preference to his German-sounding surname he not only emphasised his Hungarian crudentials he also acquired a name with a pleasant religious ring to it.

The parish church at Csempeszkopács, with its single brick-built aisle and semi-circular apse was built on its small artificial mound in the middle of the 13th century.

FROM VAS TO ZALA

In VASSZÉCSÉNY two of the palaces built by the local 18th century landowners, the Ebergényi family, survive.

A 14th century manor house already stood on the site of **Old Ebergény Palace**, which was rebuilt during the 1730s. It was then that the banqueting hall and the chapel acquired their Baroque appearance. The rococo and early classical painted decorations and the stucco-work can now be enjoyed by the guests at what is now a hotel.

The **New Ebergény Palace** (c. 1790) is also now a hotel, whose understated Louis Seize-style buildings resemble the structures *Menyhért Hefele* designed in Szombathely.

The exterior of St Michael Archangel, Csempeszkopács has a fine portal which deserves close inspection.

CSEMPESZKOPÁCS has one of finest Romanesque village churches in Hungary. During excavations at **St Michael Archangel** in Árpád tér archaeologists came across the remains of some Roman tomb fragments.

The church contains some wall paintings dating from various periods. The Apostle heads in the chancel date from the 13th century, the ornamentation on the chancel arch is Renaissance and there are also some Baroque painted figures. The main altar, with its depictions of the Holy Family and the Holy Trinity, date from before 1758. Above the altar stands a statue of Saint Michael.

The rhododendrons planted between the birch trees at the Jeli Arboretum near Kám, flower in May.
In the early spring the bulbs start flowering, and in the autumn you can enjoy the best of the heathers.

Kám

Although the **Jeli arboretum** is worth visiting all year round, it is particularly attractive during the spring. The arboretum, situated on the edge of the *Rába Valley*, was founded by István Ambrózy-Migazzy during the 1920s. His tomb, inscribed with the words *"Semper vireo" (Ever Green)* can be found on the edge of the garden. Since the Second World War its protected status has lapsed somewhat and the woods have been used for forestry projects since 1953; 74 hectares of the woods have been devoted to the naturalisation of various types of conifers.

Vasvár

Vasvár was the historic county of Vas's first administrative centre. Its name betrays the fact that the bailiff had his castle ("vár") here, and that its economy was based on iron (vas). Vasvár's importance as a fortress during the Hungarian Conquest can be seen in the so-called **Roman Ramparts** which are now believed to have dated from the early Árpád period.

One historical monument has survived, the one-time **Dominican church and monastery**. The monks probably settled in Vasvár before the Tatar invasion (1241).

Architectural historians have dated the walls of the monastery to the thirteenth century, and these have survived more or less in their original form. The carved mouldings can be seen in the exhibition about medieval Vas County at the **Vasvár Local History Museum**.

It is said that the *"Peace of Vasvár"* of 1664 between the Turkish Sultan and the Habsburg Emperor was actually signed in the so-called **"Peace House"** on Kossuth Lajos utca (10). There is a tablet on the wall referring to this fact.

The meaning of the letters (S,P,Q,R) found on each of Egervár castle's towers has prompted several possible explanations.
It has been suggested that the letters mark the first letters of four lines of a Latin religious poem, the English translation of which
would be "Who would stand against the might of the Széchenyis?" A more straightforward explanation, and one which probably lies
closer to the truth, was that the letters mark the first letters of the Latin names for the four points of the compass.

GYŐRVÁR

1706 ended with a Kuruc victory, and saw the armies of Count István Andrássy, Ádám Béri Balogh and Imre Bezerédy taking the enemies' commanders-in-chief, including Hannibal Heister. What was left of the defeated army escaped to Egervár Castle. The following day the Labanc imperial forces were allowed to leave in return for the castle. It is said Heister was imprisoned in one of the tower cellars.

EGERVÁR

It was during the 15th century that the local landowner *László Egervári* brought the Franciscans here to occupy the monastery and the **church** he had built for them. The monastery was destroyed and in 1698 the church was described as being in a state of ruin. A later landowner, *Ignác Széchenyi*, rebuilt the church in 1758. During the restoration of 1969 the gothic windows were unblocked and restored to their original glory.

The very first Egervár **Castle** was a wooden fortress built in the middle of a marsh at the time of the Tatar invasion. It is first mentioned in a document dating from 1288. In 1476, *Matthias Corvinus* gave *László Egervári* permission to rebuild the castle, and the wall and fragments from this brick-built Gothic castle can be found in the castle exhibition.

The four-towered, courtyarded Renaissance castle you can see today was built at the end of the 16th century. A century later the castle was purchased by the Széchenyis. Following the Rákóczi Wars for Freedom the imperial court was to have a say in the chronicles of the castle, for it was they who demolished its northern wing in an attempt to rid the building of its military character.

The 13th century **church** in VASBOLDOGASSZONY was rebuilt in about 1700. By that time the limewood altar had already been made. The carved leaf designs suggest that the altar was carved in the part of historical Hungary now lying in Slovakia.

ON THE ROAD TO SZENTGOTTHÁRD

JÁK

Once part of a Benedictine monastery, **St George's** was founded in 1214. However, following two interruptions the church was only finished in 1256 after the death of its founder Márton Nagy of the Ják clan. From the 16th century the Erdődy family became the patrons. The building suffered considerable damage during the siege of the village during the Turkish period. The monastic buildings were demolished following the dissolution of the monastery in 1562. The nave has two aisles divided off by arcades containing octagonal piers.

The historical and artistic importance of Ják church can be seen by the fact that a smaller version of the church was built on the Városliget in Budapest as part of the 1896 Millennium Exhibition celebrating the one thousandth anniversary of the Hungarian Conquest. At about the same time (1896–1904) Frigyes Schulek went about the task of tearing out the Baroque altars in the church itself and putting in neo-Romanesque replacements.

The fresco depicting Saint George behind the main altar was restored in 1991. During the course of the restoration of the St Mary's altar the restorers found the remains of medieval triptych. The lower part of the four apsed double-deckered rotunda, the **Chapel of St James**, standing immediately to the west of the church was an *ossuarium*, whilst the upper part served as a parish church when the monastic church was in use.

The Ják family's manor house and donjon stood on the site of the **abbot's house**. The building now standing there, though built at the end of the 18th century, has been much altered and has recently (2001) become the home of an exhibition devoted to the history of the Ják family and the abbey.

The west end of the Ják church is one of the most beautiful surviving Romanesque sculptural programmes in Hungary. Christ is depicted together with ten disciples immediately above the portal, with the two other apostles placed one on each side in niches in the tower walls.

KÖRMEND

The Batthyány family acquired Körmend in 1604, and then went about the task of rebuilding the palace. Initially they exploited the building's military character before turning it into something more inhabitable. Eventually the house evolved into a Baroque **residence**. The central classical feature on the main façade and the mansard roof were added later.

The palace now houses the **Rába Local History Museum** and has displays on the region's natural history and archaeology, life in Körmend at the turn of the 19th and 20th centuries, local crafts, and an exhibition of exotic birds from around the world. Two of the more curious objects on display are the two bicycles used by two local sportsmen when cycling down to Turin to visit Louis Kossuth.

The Lugos runs into the Rába just southwest of Körmend.

Following the remodelling of the 18th century French-style garden into an English landscape garden (1795), the garden was open to the general public on Sundays. Today, the **garden**, which has shrunk to a size of 36 hectares, contains 70 deciduous trees and 20 conifers, the oldest of which are between 200 and 250 years old. Perhaps the most striking trees are the 150-year-old tulip-trees, the first to have been planted in Hungary. In the old buildings you will find the **Cobblers Museum**.

In front of the main building of the palace stands the statue put up in honour of the optician, *doctor of the poor, László Batthyány-Strattman*, who ran a hospital here between 1902 and 1930.

The exhibition in **Saint Elizabeth's Church** (1731) is devoted to the recently beatified doctor's life of service to his community.

It was during the building activities on the Batthyány Palace around 1800 that the balcony supported by its six columns and the six half columns were added to the main façade.

SZENTGOTTHÁRD

The town gets its name from the **Cistercian Abbey** founded here by Béla III. in 1183. The abbey's subsequent wealth came from the order's forestry activities.

Although the foundations of the **Magtártemplom** (Granary Church) date from the 12th century, the church itself was built in 1677.

It was at the time of the Bocskai Uprising that a Styrian commander blew up the fortified church causing the whole town to go up in flames.
In 1734, Charles III. allowed the one-time abbacy of Szentgotthárd to join up with Heiligenkreuz Abbey, a move which brought a new lease of life to the abbey.

It became a granary only later. From 1664, Szentgotthárd was known throughout Europe, as the place where Montecuccoli's army defeated Köprül Ahmed's Turkish forces.

The foundation stone of the **Church of the Blessed Virgin Mary** was laid in 1748. *István Dorfmaister*'s painting in the first bay depicts the Battle of Szentgotthárd.

EXPLORING THE ŐRSÉG

The layout of the settlements in the Őrség differ from those elsewhere in the region, as does the appearance of the buildings. At the time of the foundation of the Hungarian state the area was populated by people whose job it was to guard the border region. It was something the locals did in return for certain privileges. Although these privileges are no longer valid, the inhabitants of the Őrség have managed to cling onto their identity.

The Őrség in fact crosses into what is now Slovenia. Most of the territory belonging to Hungary forms part of the *Őrség National Park*.

> *There was a time when the whole area was covered in woodland, and the guards had to hack down trees before going about planting crops. Being unable to build on the marshy lowlands and down in the valleys, the locals were forced to build on the hilltops. This explains why the houses are rather spread out and why each hill takes the name of a local family.*

The conifer-covered landscape provides the area with a pleasant *subalpine* climate. It was the rivers which shaped the landscape but now it is the meadows, the streams, the small lakes and the houses perched up on their hills which give it its character.

Lake Vadása, an artificial lake lying between Hegyhátszentjakab and Őrimagyarósd, has become a popular tourist destination in recent decades. There are guesthouses and camping sites nearby.

The architectural character of the area and its arts and crafts were determined firstly by the local materials which were available and secondly by the likelihood of being able to earn a living. The houses were predominantly built of timber, and the furniture and other domestic objects are nearly all made of wood.

For many centuries the inhabitants of Velemér, Gödörháza and Magyarszombatfa have brought in extra income selling pottery.

St James's HEGYHÁTSZENTJAKAB sits on a small hill in the middle of the village. The single-aisled, apsed 13th century **church** was almost totally rebuilt during the 19th century. In 1969, it was decided to take away the Baroque additions to reveal the medieval doorway and the Romanesque windows. At the same time it was discovered that the tower and the chancel were in fact Romanesque, and that it was only the liturgical furniture which was in fact completely Baroque.

The old carnival traditions like "log pulling" are coming back into fashion. During the carnival period the unmarried men and women of the village dress up as brides and grooms and parade down the main street of the villages sitting on a log. Finally, a priest in fancy dress marries them all, and they are free to frit away the proceeds of the auctioned log on the last ball of the carnival.

PANKASZ's most important monument is the oldest and most beautiful bell tower in the Őrség on Kelet Szer Hill. The structure, dating back to 1754, has a shingled belfry surrounded by a steep thatched roof known as a skirt.

A typical feature of the buildings in the Őrség is the thatched roof under which an open or decorated plank gable is concealed.

ŐRISZENTPÉTER, the *capital of the Őrség*, gets its name from St Peter's **church** on *Templom szer.* Although it's essentially a Romanesque church, the exterior wall paintings date from a 14th century renovation which took place after the church had caught fire. The church was also set on fire by the marauding Turks in 1567. The *Agnus Dei* motif was later placed over the entrance to the church.

With the exception of the chancel, the church at Őriszentpéter has managed to preserve its Romanesque character. The style of the stone carvings, resembling those of the so-called Ják school of Romanesque sculpture, suggest that the church was built between 1230 and 1260.

The part of SZALAFŐ known as *Pityerszer* has been turned into an **Outdoor Ethnographic Museum**.

The early 19th century log-walled, thatched, verandahed houses, which you can find in the Szalafő Ethnographical Collection have a living room, a kitchen and a pantry. Most interesting is Hungary's only two-storeyed chamber, which is a combination of living quarters and a barn. The third house, the so-called fenced house, dates from the beginning of the 19th century. The U-shaped building is built around a yard, the fourth side of which has a gate.

VELEMÉR

One of the most-visited sites in the Őrség, the **Church of the Holy Trinity** is set on a small hill outside the village. The church was built during the second half of the 13th century. The outside of the church does not present much of a spectacle, but inside you can see one of the wonders of 14th century wall painting. Painted by *Johannes Aquila* of Radkersburg in 1377, the wall paintings cover a whole host of Biblical themes and personalities. The painted programme includes a portrait of the artist himself on the northern side of the chancel. Although some of the paintings have fallen victim to the ravages of time we have *Flóris Rómer* to thank for the fact that so many of the wall paintings have survived to this very day.

At the parish church in Velemér the painted figures of the four Evangelists, and representations of Veronica and her veil, the Annunciation of the Blessed Virgin Mary, Christ in Judgement and the Schutzmantel Madonna have all survived more or less intact.

ZALAEGERSZEG

The 44metre-high towers of the Baroque **parish church** (Széchenyi tér) have dominated the centre of the town since the middle of the 18th century. The frescos are by the Viennese academician *Johann Cymball*. The paintings over the side altars are representations of Hungarian kings.

The central altar on the northern wall contains the town's oldest work of art, the statue of the Piéta. The 17th century sculpture, which is now painted, once stood in the market square. At that time it was known as the White Picture on account of its colour.

The western wing of the **Göcsej Múzeum** (Batthyány út 2.) contains the sculptures and other artefacts which make up *Kisfaludi Strobl Collection*. The museum also puts on a number of temporary exhibitions.

The bronze flower-like fountain, the Göcsej tulip, standing in the middle of Dísz tér provides refreshment on the hottest of summer days.

In the first floor foyer of the **Sándor Hevesi Theatre** (Kosztolányi Dezső tér 1.) you will find a bust of Hevesi (*János Béres*, 1986): playwrite, critic and director of the National Gallery.

The Arany Bárány Hotel and Restaurant (1894) on the right-hand side of the picture, and the neighbouring archives (Széchenyi tér 3.) were once soldiers' quarters. Maria Theresa had them built in 1765 for soldiers who happened to be passing through. Later a floor was added and extended to provide a neoclassical assembly chamber. The building in the left of the picture is now used as offices.

On hearing that the new neo-Baroque **Franciscan monastery and church** (1925–1926) was being built Zita, widow of the last Habsburg king of Hungary, Charles IV., donated a pulpit to the church.

When surveying the houses and their yards at Zalaegerszeg's Göcsej Village Museum you will come across beehives, mud ovens, barns, shadoofs, dovecotes and stills.

The Museum of the Hungarian Oil Industry, which lies next door, comes as quite a surprise. Founded in 1969, the museum tells you all you've ever wanted to know about the domestic hydrocarbon mining and processing industries.
You can see extraction equipment, drilling towers, steam engines, nodding donkeys and drilling equipment.
The hall of fame dedicated to the heroes of the hydrocarbon industry and geology is growing by the year.

The two towers of the baroque parish church in Zalaegerszeg have become a symbol of the town in the two centuries since they were built.

The Franciscans returned to their monastic buildings in 1990.

Those visiting the **Göcsej Village Museum** enter a Göcsej village as it looked 150 and 200 years ago. Exhibiting local architecture, everyday artefacts and furnished interiors, it was Hungary's first-ever outdoor ethnographic museum (1968). The only building actually standing in its original position is the watermill; all the other buildings were painstakingly dismantled, transported and reconstructed in their original form. When the museum was first opened there were 40 buildings from 22 different villages; today there are considerably more (Falumúzeum u. 18.)

There is a cycle track leading out along Göcsej út out towards Zalaegerszeg's most popular woods, the *Alsóerdő*. It is here you will find a hut, a barbecue area and a 1,820 metre, 20 obstacle **equestrian cross-country course**. Opposite the camp, often used for workshops, the track takes you to the *Azáleás Valley*.

You can walk up to the one hundred-metre-high **TV tower** along Panoráma út instead of driving up by car along the *Bazita* road. On a clear day you can see as far as Lake Balaton to the east and the Alps to the west. North of Zalaegerszeg, on the far bank of the Zala, you eventually come to the **Gébárt Leisure Centre**. *Lake Gébárt* was created in 1975. The northern bank of the lake is good for swimming, whilst on the eastern bank a medicinal thermal bath is being built. The first pool was opened during the summer of 2000. (Both the **outdoor swimming complex** and the **thermal bath** can be found just before you get to Ságod.

It is here you will find **Aquacity**, set in 7.5 hectares of land, with a fine selection of water slides and other attractions.

Those attending courses and art workshops don't have to go far in search of refreshment. The Gébárt Leisure Centre isn't far away (Táncsics u. 2/a.).

EXPLORING THE GÖCSEJ

Seen from an ethnographical perspective the *Göcsej* consists of the 70 villages lying on the banks of the *Zala*, the *Válicka* and the *Kerka*. The names of thirteen of the settlements once situated here ended in the suffix "szeg". The majority of these villages disappeared when they were incorporated into larger communities.

The clay soils here meant that the roads were often impassable, consequently forcing the locals to look to the woods and their vines for a living. The local accent here has a characteristic twang to it, the local dress is simple and buildings tend to be built of wood and clay. Apart from those at the *Göcsej Outdoor Museum,* some fine restored peasant houses can be found in the villages of *Csesztreg, Kávás,* and *Zalalövő.*

The Romanesque **church** in ZALASZENTGYÖRGY was built during the 13th century, although there are also some Gothic additions. The church was so badly damaged during the Turkish period that it underwent a major Baroque reconstruction in 1756. Restoration work has revealed several Gothic frescos in the chancel, and some 17th century wall paintings, traceried windows and a Romanesque window in the nave.

In KÁVÁS there are **two buildings** standing next to each other (Temető út 11., 13.) whose mud-plastered and log walls and thatched roofs manage to recapture the atmosphere of the turn of the 19th and 20th centuries. The thatching technique used creates a stepped effect along the ridges of the roof. These single-roofed buildings are divided up into a living area, followed by the stables and the barn. The stove heating the kitchen was put together using pieces of clay fashioned on a potter's wheel.

ZALALÖVŐ

The *Amber Road* which ran through what is now Ljubljana, Rédics, Zalalövő (Salla) and Szombathely crossed the River Zala at Zalalövő. The Roman bridge lay where the present bridge stands today, and it is the remains of the **Roman buildings** and the exhibition of the Roman finds (Kossuth u. 3.) what draw the visitors.

The L-shaped peasant house (Petőfi u. 35.), so typical of the middling peasant classes, is the only one to survive from the 1920s and 1930s complete with its furnishings and heating system. Its owner built a chimney and remodelled the oven doing away with the open fireplace which had existed there previously.

The peasant cottage on Petőfi utca still has the fittings you would expect to find in a house belonging to a peasant family harbouring certain middle-class aspirations.
Both the stables and the barn survive in the courtyard.
(The curator can be found at the house opposite).

Those wishing to try their luck at some fishing should look for the **fishing pond** west of the village.

Zalabaksa

Leaving road 86 at the bridge over the *Kerka* and continuing for a few more hundred metres, you come to a modern church (Ady u. 16.) in front of which stands *Imre Varga's Queen of the World*.

The tomb of Annus Kósa in the cemetery in Zalabaksa is immediately recognisable by the wrought iron fence and its ruined column.

Travelling from Böde up towards Zalaszentmihály you come upon a Romanesque church perched up on a hill. Apart from being picturesque the church is one of the most important medieval monuments in the region. The church was built in about 1220. During the reconstruction work which took place following the Turkish period the chancel was enlarged (1750), thus giving the church the appearance it has today.

A few years ago a stream bubbled up out of the earth on the edge of Kustánszeg ultimately creating what is a 14-hectare lake.
It has already become a popular tourist resort where people can go boating and fishing.

The **local history** collection in Kustánszeg (Kossuth út 50.) makes a change from a day down at the **lake**. It's there you can see artifacts connected with the local economy and life in the local villages.

Nova

The frescos, and the paintings on the altar next to the pulpit and the high altar in the Baroque **church** (1778) are by *István Dorfmaister*. The church is also famous for the whispering gallery effect around the walls of the chancel. The chancel is supposed to have a whispering gallery effect between two people standing at the chancel arch and the piscina.

In Nova church there is a marble tablet put up in memory of the learned dean Ferenc Plánder, the first person to publish a scientific study of the Göcsej Region. Both the cultural centre and the ethnographical collection are named after him.

The considerable **hunting territory** in these parts lays claim to the world's largest antlered stag. Whilst in the Göcsej it's also worth visiting the **parish church** in Zalatárnok built in the 15th century and remodelled in the Baroque style in 1755.

In Bak there is a wooden **house** by *Imre Makovecz* and a **fishing pond**.

Exploring the Hetés

The Hetés is an ethnographical region, most of which can now be found in Slovenia, covering 11 villages in western Zala. The local population traditionally lived from hunting and fishing, and it was only later that the Hetés became an agricultural region. The local architecture resembles that found in the Göcsej, being a little humbler if anything. The local weaving is more colourful and the designs are generally much richer.

On the last crossroads in Csesztreg on the Lenti road you come to a **peasant house**, which is actually a thatched, shepherd's dwelling built some time during the 19th century (Ady út 29.). It is furnished in a manner one would expect of such a humble dwelling.

The history of the Roman Catholic church in Csesztreg is typical of the region. It was first built in the Romanesque style during the 12th century, reconstructed during the 15th century in the Gothic style, before being remodelled in the Baroque style. The frescos inside are by István Dorfmaister the Younger (Kossuth u.)

Those interested in folk architecture should go west to the southernmost border of the Őrség where you come to Nemesnép with its beautiful **bell tower**, and Szentgyörgyvölgy with a **Calvinist church** famous for its coffered ceiling.

The painted coffered ceiling at the Calvinist church in Szentgyörgyvölgy is indeed a rarity in the region. The closest you will find anything similar is in the Ormánság and Zselic.

The local clay soils provide the raw materials for the Hetés's potters. Rezső Csótár is one of Szentgyörgyvölgy's most famous practitioners.

LENTI

Lenti's **thermal baths** were built in 1978. Once the waters had officially been recognised as having medicinal qualities the **covered pool** was added to the complex. The waters are excellent for treating rheumatic and gynaecological problems, degenerative illnesses and other locomotor disorders (Táncsics u. 2/a).

The thermal baths at Lenti have four outdoor swimming and medicinal pools, and the indoor baths have a further three pools. While 2003 saw the opening of the St. George Energy Park, there is still more to come in the shape of a leisure pool.

The walk from *Lentiszombathely* and *Bárszentmihályfa* takes in some beautiful **bell towers**.

The **Roman Catholic church** in Lenti's main square contains some frescos and an altar painting by the *younger Dorfmaister*. There is also a rather strange 18th century Baroque-style **granary** next to the *Kerka* on the main Zalaegerszeg road (Dózsa György út 7.). The building was constructed from the remains of the castle standing on the very same site, something which becomes obvious when you inspect the part of the building closest to the river with all its gun positions. Although a use has yet to be found for the building, the old defensive ditches have been turned into a horse-shoe-shaped **fishpond**.

The village of GOSZTOLA down on the Slovenian border grows threefold during the tourist season, not a particularly remarkable fact when you realise there are only sixteen permanent residents living in the village all together. It is they who form the congregation of the beautiful **parish church** (Fő u. 22.). As was said during a recently overheard conversation somewhere in the vicinity: "I hear everybody made it to the Sunday service again in Gosztola last week".

LENDVADEDES is somewhat bigger, although with a population of 47 it still has a long way to go before acquiring civic status. Tourists who come to Lendvadedes either have a look at the **bell tower** or head for the **fishing lake** at the edge of the village.

TOUR INTO THE ZALA HILLS

The **church** in NAGYKAPORNAK (Zrínyi utca 2.) has had a colourful history. Originally an aisled church dating from about 1170, both the church and the monastic buildings were remodelled into something resembling a fortress prior to the Turkish occupation. The church was burnt down in 1664, and reconstructed on and off between 1734 and 1779, ultimately becoming the single-aisled Baroque structure you can see today. The church is rich in frescos and has a Louis Seize pulpit containing a relief. During the course of the restoration a number of medieval details came to light.

Ferenc Deák Hall (Kúria út 6.) in KEHIDA-KUSTÁNY was built by the Hertelendy family on the site of Kehida Castle in about 1770. It later fell into the hands of the Deák family. Ferenc Deák lived here for a considerable time, and it is his *bust* (*György Zala*) that you can see in the entrance hall. The **thermal baths** have become much more popular now that the **leisure baths** have been added (Kossuth út 56.).

The one-time guest list included the likes of *Mihály Vörösmarty, Miklós Wesselényi, István Széchenyi* and *Lajos Battyhány*. Nowadays the numbers of visitors are increasing thanks to the **Deák exhibition** opened in spring 2004, following the building's restoration.

The medieval **rotunda** in KALLÓSD is one of the finest of its type in Hungary. Built in about 1260 in a Romanesque style, the rotunda has an internal diameter of 5.8 metres. The exterior is articulated with half-columns, the interior with six pointed niches. Access to the wooden gallery is via a staircase built into the wall.

The rotunda at Kallósd, with its cemetery, sits comfortably amongst the woods of the surrounding countryside.

ZALASZENTGRÓT

While the **thermal baths** – with its four open-air pools – have been open for some time, the covered pools were opened in 2003. The new bridge was built right next to its predecessor, the original, built in 1846, being used right up until 1975. Work has just started on its restoration. This will be the second major rescue operation following that which took place during the Second World War when sergeant-major Hatamov prevented the bridge from being blown up by a German mine. Unfortunately the explosive device went off in his hands. Zalaszentgrót's **Batthyány Palace** (1787, Zala út 1.) lies on the *banks of the Zala* on the site of the old castle. Now a school for special needs children the house stands in 4.3 hectares of parkland. The **medieval ruins** of the monastery can be found on the Balaton road in the *Kisszentgrót* district of the town.

The pride and joy of TÜRJE is one of Hungary's earliest **Premonstratensian foundation**s, built by a French workshop in about 1230. On the southern wall you will find a scene from the legend of Saint Ladislas. After a complicated building history the church was decorated with frescos by the ubiquitous *Dorfmaister*. The **monastic buildings** (Szabadság tér 20.) had already been standing for half a century by the time Dorfmaister was active in the village.

The west façade of the Türje church. The stone-framed, wrought-iron tabernacle on the southern wall of the nave dates from 1478.

The **Roman Catholic church** in ZALAVÉG (Dózsa György út 2.) was built between 1748 and 1751 reusing material from its 14th century predecessor. The painting over the altar is Baroque. In the chancel you can also see a medieval font and a tabernacle from the original church.

The imposing Franciscan Church in Bucsuszentlászló is the region's most famous pilgrimage place.

BUCSUSZENTLÁSZLÓ rises up out of what is a marshy, boggy landscape. The 13th century **church** fell into a state of disrepair during the Turkish period. When the Franciscans arrived in Bucsuszentlászló in the 17th century, they repaired the old church before building their Baroque church and conventual buildings up against it.

The Gothic **church** in ZALASZENTMIHÁLY was built during the 15th century, as can be seen in the fish-bladder tracery of the chancel and southern aisle windows.

In ZALAAPÁTI the Baroque church forms part of the old **Benedictine monastery** (Deák tér 3.) built in 1781.

The **parish church** in CSATÁR rises up from the hills overlooking the *Válicka* valley. Its chancel, nave and tower are for the most part Romanesque, whilst the sacristy, the side chapel and the liturgical furniture are all Baroque.

The founder of the monastery (1149) donated the famous Csatár Bible to the Benedictine foundation. The manuscript, now known as the Admont Bible after the Benedictine monastery which once owned it, is now kept in the Austrian National Library in Vienna (Wien, ÖNB, Cod.s.n.2701-2).

It was in the simple building known as **Deák Hall** (c. 1760) in SÖJTÖR that Ferenc Deák, *"the wise man of Hungary"*, was born on 17th October 1803. His mother died soon after giving birth and baby Ferenc was soon on his way to his relatives in Zalatárnok. He lived in Kehida from 1824.

Deák Hall hosts temporary exhibitions, but the portrait of Ferenc Deák, the contemporary furniture and the documents relating to the great man are on permanent display.

The cyclamen is perhaps Zala's most precious woodland flower. It can also be found in other woods in western Transdanubia.

NAGYKANIZSA

The most important monument in the town is **Vasember (Iron Man) House** (on the corner of Erzsébet tér and Ady u.) a Baroque building later remodelled into something a little more classical. The building got its name from both the armoured soldier in the corner next to the first floor window and because the building was once an ironmonger's. The hall on the first floor is now used for receptions, meetings and civil wedding ceremonies.

Deák tér in Nagykanizsa is a veritable arboretum. You will find symphoricarpos, forsythias, magnolias, silver firs and various types of maple.

The **Turkish Well** in Erzsébet tér is an exact copy of the original you can find in the museum. If you go east along Fő út you come to the **György Thury Museum** (3.), venue for temporary exhibitions, and the **synagogue,** which is just about to be renovated (6.). In the triangular Deák tér you can find *János Istók*'s sculpture of the turul, the mythical Hungarian bird. Behind it you can find the imposing sights of the **National Flag** and the **Felsőváros Church**.

The Baroque **Franciscan monastery** (1702–1714) is in the Alsóváros (the Lower Town) (Ady u. 14.) the monastic buildings are now a library.

The **17th degree of longitude monument** includes a list of all the most important towns lying on this particular meridian (Eötvös tér). Just as you move into the industrial estate when leaving Nagykanizsa for the main road you come across the **castle monument** (1996) marking the site of the now-lost castle.

You can find a bust of Sándor Hevesi (Erzsébet Schaár) in the Sándor Hevesi Cultural Centre in Nagykanizsa, as well as a series of reliefs of the four seasons by János Németh. The centre also holds temporary exhibitions.

The 40-hectare leisure centre situated just 5 kilometres from the centre of the town on road 61 to Kaposvár is becoming ever more popular. The artificial lake offers plenty of opportunities to swim, fish or to go boating.

In front of the 8 metre-high brick gateway stands the bronze bust of the famous castellan György Thury. Another sculpture of the great castellan (Miklós Borsos, 1972) can be found in one of the town's housing estates.

ON NAGYKANIZSA'S DOORSTEP

Going north of Nagykanizsa the first place you get to is HOMOKKOMÁROM with its Baroque Franciscan monastery standing separate from the village on top of its own small hill. The church is now the **Roman Catholic church** (Ady u. 1.).

Inside, the high altar contains a painting of the Blessed Virgin Mary, a fine rococo pulpit, and a small glass coffin containing the skeleton of Saint Felix the Martyr.

The succession of 2–5metre mounds, which can be found on the *sand hills* down towards the border, are forever being shifted and reformed by the region's north-easterly winds.

On the edge of ÚJUDVAR near the **TV tower** the *Csibiti Ravine* creates an ideal environment for ferns. There are stretches where walkers will be able to enjoy some impressive sandstone rock faces.

In ALSÓRAJK, the birthplace of *Zsigmond Kisfaludi Strobl*, there is a **memorial room** devoted to the sculptor (in the council offices). In PACSA there is an artificial lake, which is popular amongst **bathers** and **anglers**.

Between Alsórajk and Pacsa you will find FELSŐRAJK whose recently built five-turreted castle (1999), paying homage to the fortress which once stood on the site, forms the backdrop for outdoor programmes and tournaments.

THE LAND OF THE OIL INDUSTRY

The first thing you see when making the final approaches into CSÖMÖDÉR is the popular **fishing lake**.

Between Csömödér and Kistolmács there is a narrow-gauge railway, which also stops at Páka, Dömefölde, Kányavár, Lasztonya and BÁZAKERETTYE. Trains leave on a regular basis and special arrangements can be made for tourist groups. The train, which leaves from next to the main Hungarian Railways (MÁV) station in Csömödér takes you through some picturesque woodland.

A new part of BÁZAKERETTYE was laid out just before the Second World War to accommodate American oil experts. Nearby you will find the recently renovated **outdoor swimming complex** (Sportút 1.). The **thermal baths** were opened in 2002 and the *hotel* is now open to guests (Olajmunkás köz 13.).

The 46-hectare Budafapuszta Arboretum contains azaleas, rhododenrons, various types of fir trees, cedars and a good cross-section of trees and shrubs. The artificial lakes with their reed beds paint a picturesque picture. The hunter's lodge at the entrance to the park offers seasonal accommodation.

Oil was found on the border of nearby LISPE-SZENTADORJÁN at the end of the 1930s. The **monument** marks the first ever oil bore-hole in Hungary.

Fishing lake, Kistolmács

The cycle route from Budafapuszta to Nagy-kanizsa passes through KISTOLMÁCS. It is here you will find the terminus of the Csömör narrow gauge railway. The 11-hectare **artificial lake** made in 1989 is now rich in carp, pike and bream.

The town's location on the **border crossing** to Croatia has contributed to the development of LETENYE over the past few years. The town hosts a number of cultural events, for example the *Mura Festival*, the annual *National Folk Arts and Crafts Camp* and the *International Wind Band Festival*.

The old **Szapáry Palace** in Letenye now houses a local history exhibition. The once enormous park now covers an area of 5.6 hectares. The most notable specimen is a plane tree with a girth of 550cm and a crown spreading 30m.

Snowflakes can be found flowering in many of the woods in southern Zala.

ON THE BANKS OF THE MURA

The eleven settlements between Nagykanizsa and Letenye making up the *Mura Ethnic Region* are unit-ed in their desire to promote and protect the region's traditions. This is the area's great attraction. TÓTSZENTMÁRTON is known for its Baroque church (1788) and the public statues made during the course of the annual summer **wood-carving work-shops**. An attractive new **church** has just been built in MOLNÁRI. Both SZEPETNEK and MURAKE-RESZTÚR are well known amongst the fishing com-munity, the former for its **reservoir,** the latter for the river. Murakeresztúr lies in good hiking coun-try and there is a **ferry** there crossing into Croatia. You have to go along a wooded back road to get to BELEZNA, which has some **fishing lakes,** a remarkably beautiful church (1899), and a four-hundred-year-old oak tree to enjoy.

A traditional folk dance group from the Mura region.

In SURD, the artificial **fishing lake** and the avenue of protected plane trees prompted the locals to become involved in village tourism. In MIKLÓSFA the cen-tralised, four-apsed **church** with its Baroque fittings is the main attraction.

It is with the small villages on the banks of the *River Mura* that we take our leave of the land-scapes, the villages and the inhabitants of *Western Transdanubia*. Our tour will now continue around *Lake Balaton*.

"*Behind the hill, Our Lady's summer-day*
Resounds already upon golden chords,
As, in the wind of dawn, breathes tremulous
The destined fire of the summer noon;
Yet dew still quivers on the lilac leaf,
And scythe-blades gleam with yet unsullied steel."

(Sándor Sík: Summer and Dawn [extract]
translated by Watson Kirkconnell)

CONTENTS – BALATON

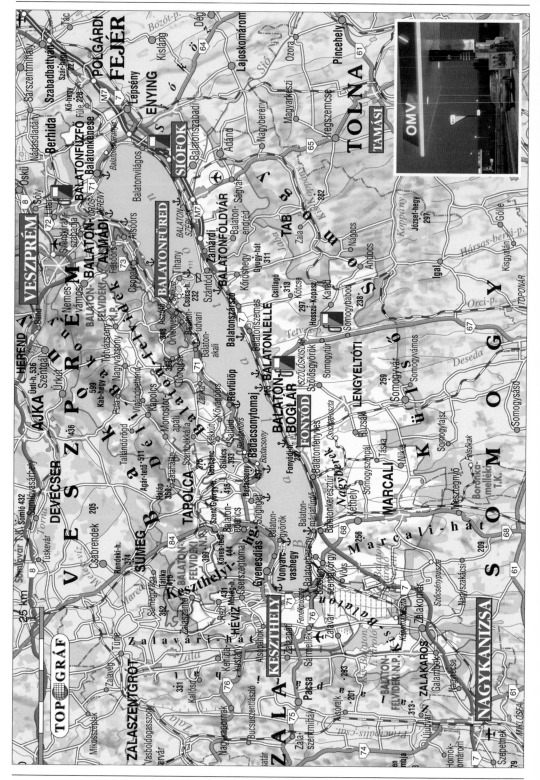

BALATON

In this chapter we will be travelling around the largest freshwater lake in Central Europe, one of the most important natural treasures in Hungary. Setting off from Keszthely Bay we shall be working our way eastwards along the northern shore of the lake before heading westwards along the southern shore. Apart from visiting the towns and villages immediately around the lake, we will be venturing out into the settlements in the surrounding countryside. Lake Balaton presently covers an area of 590km², although there were times during its history when the lake covered a much larger area, stretching from the Danube in the northeast right down to almost the Drava in the southwest. Because the lake has never had a permanent source of fresh water the water level has always been liable to vary considerably.

Today the water level of the lake is controlled by the *Sió Sluice*. However incredible the idea may sound today there was a time during the 19th century when there were plans to drain the lake completely! Fortunately it all came to nothing, but it didn't stop the level of the lake falling by 3 metres when the sluice was built in 1863. This drop in water level had major repercussions on the southernmost tip of the lake (Kis-Balaton, Nagy-berek).

Kis-Balaton (Little Balaton), once part of Lake Balaton, is now completely separate from the lake. However, there was a period during the 19th century when the water was so high that boats of considerable size were able to moor just off Vörs.

The water disappeared from that part of the lake when the railway was built in the second half of the 19th century. Sedge and reeds then grew where the water once stood. These changes meant that the deposits from the *River Zala* ended up being taken all the way to *Keszthely Bay* where they started silting up that particular part of the lake. Once people realised what was happening efforts were made to reconstruct Kis-Balaton. However, a lack of funds meant that it was only possible to build the II. (upper) reservoir. Ornithologists may be lucky enough to see the herons which provide the symbol for the Hungarian nature conservation movement. Work on the rehabilitation of Kis-Balaton, as well as other environmental projects have put an end to the deterioration once seen in the quality of Lake Balaton's water.

Moving east of Keszthely into the hills of that name you come to the so-called *Keszthely Riviera* down on the shores of the lake. The white dolomite of the *Keszthely Hills* can be seen poking its way to the surface. Indeed, it is this easily warmed rock which contributes to the pleasant climate on the shores of the lake below.

The *Tapolca Basin* could also once be counted amongst Balaton's bays. Even today the water level of the lake is scarcely below that of the surface of the basin. This particular landscape is made all the more interesting by the remnant volcanoes once active during the Pleistocene Age. Their lava covered the area with soft, mainly clay, deposits. Where the harder rocks have managed to protect the older formations lying below you can get some idea how high the volcanoes originally were.

Although each small hill is interesting in its own way, we would like to draw your attention to two in particular. You can climb up the great rock mass known as *Várhegy,* which you can see as you make your way to Szigliget, to visit the castle ruins or simply to enjoy the view. Getting to the top of *Saint George's Hill* is not as straightforward, and consequently that bit more exciting. Climbing up from Kisapáti you have to negotiate the 10–20 metre pillars of basalt before reaching the top. The view is stunning.

The basalt pillars on Saint George's Hill

On the far side of the lake you can see the poorer relations, the Fonyód and the Boglár Hills. Approaching Tapolca from the north the first thing you notice are the pyramid-like profiles of the town's high-rise housing estate. Further on the *Bakony* looms in the distance.

The basalt *Badacsony-Gulács Hills* stretch all the way to the lake. The Badacsony is the largest and most interesting volcanic geological formation on the banks of Lake Balaton. If you look at it from the air or from one of the neighbouring peaks you will notice that the Badacsony has a flat table-like summit. Know as "Coffin Hill", it is a popular destination with visitors. There are winepreses, holiday resorts, the *Bujdosók Steps,* basalt rock formations and of course the views down onto Lake Balaton. One of its curiosities is neo-Romanesque Saint Emmerich's chapel in Badacsonytomaj built entirely out of basalt.

Moving eastwards we reach the *Kál Basin* surrounded by its volcanic hilltops. It is here you will find some interesting wild flowers, particularly in *Sásd Meadow,* just one of the water meadows surrounding *Lake Korny.* This is the only place in Hungary where you can find *bird's eye primroses,* the *Siberian iris, hepatica, bogbean* and *gladioli.*

On the borders of Mindszentkálla and Szentbékkálla the rock formation changes to that of a stony conglomerate capable of being moulded by the frost and the wind into some curious shapes. The rocks you are likely to find on the borders of Kővágóörs and Salföld, however, are of a size and hardness which made them ideal for millstones. The region's great treasure is Kékkút mineral water, from a source known as far back as the Roman period.

The red sandstone around Révfülöp and Balatonalmádi was mined and then used to line the southern shores of Lake Balaton. However, the dolomite lying closer to the surface is found in much greater quantities. As in the Bakony, limestone doesn't feature much in the geology of the Balaton Highlands. The *Tihany Peninsula* has some interesting volcanic rock formations. It is here you can find monastic cells carved into the tufa. Elsewhere, for example on *Kiserdő-tető,* it is the wind which has been working the stone.

Quartz can also be found in the region, although the *Aranyház*, the biggest geological geyser formation in the area, gets its name from the colour of the golden lichen covering the rock.

Parallel to the northern shores of Lake Balaton, between Balatonszőlős and Kis-Balaton, lies a band of flat land varying between 1 and 15 km in width now forming part of the *Balaton Highlands National Park*. (For more information see the section on National Parks.)

The currents here have meant that the waters are deeper on this side of the lake. This also explains why the bottom of the lake is stony here. The *"Balaton Riviera"*, covers the stretch of the lake from Ábrahámhegy to Balatonfűzfő. The steep southern slopes of the hills help to warm up the air, whilst the Balaton Highlands and the Bakony shelter the lake from the cooler northerly winds.

The countryside along the eastern shores of the lake is somewhat different, with the steep slopes of the outer reaches of the *Mezőföld* suddenly hitting the lake.

On the southern shore of Lake Balaton, between Balatonkenese and the Nagy-berek, the *Somogy Shore Plain* opens up to a width of 2 to 4 km. Whilst the north-facing valleys of Outer Somogy widen somewhat, the valleys of the Fonyód and the Boglár, and those on the edge of the *Mezőföld*, become narrower. The loess plateaux down on the banks of the lake, which are the same age as the volcanic hills on the northern shore of the lake, are particularly impressive.

It was the winds blowing in from the north which brought the fine deposits which now cover the southern shores of the lake. Once the embankments built for the Danube-Sava-Adriatic Railway (Southern Railway) had been added to what was already a *natural barrier,* the watery environment of the *Nagy-berek* was finally cut off from the lake. Most of the countryside here is covered with reeds, sedge and weeds. It is an environment enjoyed by the local deer, pheasants, partridges and waterfowl. Water can still often be found on the lower-lying areas, and the *Fehér Marshes* provide an excellent breeding-ground and feeding area for the birds. It is here you can find herons, bitterns and a number of types of duck.

Kis-Balaton

In the southwestern part of the Balaton region there is a small landscape, the *Marcali Ridge,* rising up above the lower basins of Kis-Balaton and the Nagy-berek, which differs from the landscapes immediately around it. Here you will not only find hills and hollows but vineyards producing the grapes for the local wines. Those looking for a spectacular view of Lake Balaton should make their way up road 76 to the observation tower above Balatonszentgyörgy. Here, the surrounding hilltops and the Keszthely Hills seem very close indeed.

The fine particles of lime which make the water here so hard form the suspension that makes Lake Balaton perpetually cloudy. Today, Lake Balaton is for the most part between 3 to 4 metres deep. The deepest point in the lake is the *Tihany Well* on the straits between the *Siófok* and the *Szemes Basin.*

Because Lake Balaton usually enjoys more than two thousand hours of sunshine a year it doesn't take long for the shallow waters to warm up. During the long, hot summers the waters rise to a temperature of between 25 and 27 °C, making Lake Balaton one of the most popular lakes in

BALATON SPECIALITIES

Because the local economy relies very much on the tourist industry, the region isn't really known for its agricultural products. Nevertheless, it is worth mentioning *Badacsony cherries* and the region's *peaches*, and *Kál almonds* from the basin of that name.

The pike-perch is the most sought-after fish in Lake Balaton. The local drink is *Badacsony vermouth,* and there are of course the local wines... (For more information on these wines consult the relevant section on the following page.)

Central Europe. The shallowness of the lake, means that the winds coming in from the Bakony can whip up the surface of the water. During the sudden storms which occasionally sweep the lake, waves can be as much as several metres high. So you cannot be too careful. During the winter Lake Balaton sometimes freezes up for long periods at a time, the ice being 20–30cm or sometimes as much as 60cm thick. Once upon a time sledging was popular on the lake, now you are more likely to see ice-surfers and skaters.

The shores of Lake Balaton have been built up in many places and the areas turned into lidos. There are consequently far fewer reed beds than there used to be, but those which do survive continue to play an important role in maintaining the quality of the water. Algae settles on the reed stems lying under the water (which is also where the sponges live), and it is they which manage to rid the water of its impurities.

In 2003, Sunshine Beach in Balatonlelle, the Platán Lido in Balatonboglár, the outdoor swimming complex in Zamárdi and the Föveny Baths in Balatonszárszó all received the EU's Blue Flag for their excellent water quality.

The pike-perch is the most prized of the Balaton fish. The carp are ideal for fish soup and delicious served in batter. The razor-fish, a fish which has brown meat, can be found in Lake Balaton in large quantities. The local bream are extremely tasty if a little boney. There are also large numbers of eels.

Some of the fish living in the lake come from Asia. The grass carp and the white carp you find in Lake Balaton have probably all been introduced as there is nothing to suggest they actually breed here.

You will find vineyards all the way along the shores of Lake Balaton. The grapes were brought to the region by both the Romans and the French monks who founded Somogyvár Abbey.

The county of Somogy was the first county in present-day Hungary to adopt a coat-of-arms, a hand holding a bunch of grapes (1487). According to a letter written by its creator, grapes and wine could be found in such abundance that Somogy could justifiably be named as one of the country's wealthiest counties. One and a half cen-

Festetics Palace, Keszthely

turies of Turkish occupation brought an end to the flourishing wine trade. The local population was forced to flee their homes leaving their vineyards to rack and ruin. The grape-growing culture which re-emerged once the Turks had left was later to fall victim to an outbreak of phylloxera.

The vineyards planted during the first half of the 20th century were positioned on the western slopes of the hills. These new vineyards have been such a success that today the Balaton region is considered to be one of the finest in Hungary. On the volcanic soils of the northern shores of the lake the grapes tend to be white, although you will find some grapes are grown to make the more popular red wines.

The most popular grapes in the Csopak-Füred wine region are *Füred Riesling* and *Cabernet Sauvignon*. *Merlot* is the great success story in the Tihany region, whilst the most famous wine in Badacsony is the Szürkebarát. The wine area on the southern banks of Balaton centering on Boglár and Kőröshegy concentrates on the grape types required to make light fruity wines and champagnes (*Irsai Olivér, Yellow Muscat, Rizlingszilváni, Chardonnay, Király Leányka, Rhenish* and *Italian Riesling*). For the fruity Burgundy-type wines the best grapes are the *Kékfrankos, Pinot Noir, Merlot* and *Cabernet Sauvignon.*

The pleasant climate of the Balaton Basin was also attractive in prehistoric times, something proved by the existence of a prehistoric pigment mine in Lovas. The earthworks in Tihany date back to the Iron Age. Of all the early inhabitants of the region it was the Romans who were the most successful in leaving their mark.

Archaeologists have uncovered some fine Roman mosaics in Balácapuszta, and Roman finds have also been uncovered near Fenékpuszta near the military road joining Sopianae (Pécs) with Savaria (Szombathely).

Following the fall of the Roman Empire it was the Frankish Empire, which spread as far as Lake Balaton. The Franks were then superseded by the Avars, the Alans and the Slavs. Pribina, the Slavic prince, built the centre of his kingdom in Zalavár amongst the marshes of Kis-Balaton. It was here he received *"Europe's apostles"*, the missionaries Cyril and Methodius.

The earthworks (like the ones at Tihany) date from the Hungarian Conquest, as do several place names in the Kál Basin. The name Kál in fact refers to the name of one of the Árpád chiefs, Horka Kál.

The northern shore of Lake Balaton has the appearance of a veritable open-air museum. In the villages there are the medieval church ruins, and out in the vineyards the chapels, dedicated to Saint Donatus more often than not. Then there are of course the medieval castles. Szigliget Castle still has some walls and a tower, there are the pillars at Csobánc, and Hegyesd Castle survives perched on top of its pointed peak. Then there are the crumbling walls of the castles at Rezi, Tátika and Zádorvár.

Like the rest of Pannonia it was only in the 18th century that the region was able to return to something approaching normality following 150 years of Turkish occupation. It was a process helped by the arrival of the considerable numbers of German settlers, who settled in the Balaton Highlands and built or rebuilt the local watermills on those streams what were still bulging with water. The crosses the Germans put up by the roadsides, in the vineyards, and in the villages still offer succour to those seeking it. The crucifixes, which frequently incorporate folk motifs, are usually carved out of sandstone. The local houses often have arcaded verandas of some pretension, and there are indeed examples of the oldest type of house we have, the open-hearthed house (Kékkút, Kővágóörs).

Grape-growing and wine-making provided those living along the shores of Lake Balaton with a living until a phylloxera outbreak temporarily put an end to it all in the 1880s. This disaster fortunately coincided with the beginnings of tourism on Lake Balaton, and it wasn't long before tourism became the most important sector of the economy.

Balatonfüred's history as a spa goes back to the 1730s. Whilst fishing still provided locals with a means of earning a living, it wasn't long before the fishing boats were having to share the waters with ferries and yachts, as well as the rafts and hollowed log boats of old.

The *Balaton Steamship Company* was founded in December 1845 at the suggestion of Count István Széchenyi, and it was on 21st September 1846 that a steamship by the name of the *Kisfaludy* first set sail from Balatonfüred. The *Balaton Shipping Company* now operates 21 landing stages and 16 marinas.

There's a car ferry running between Tihany and Szántód, and there are marinas in Siófok, Balatonföldvár, Balatonszemes, Balatonlelle, Balatonboglár, Badacsony and Balatonfüred. Thirty boats operate regular services, and there are also popular steamers and floating discos.

It was during the 18th century that Lake Balaton became an important part of the Hungarian social scene, whilst swimming as a mass pastime only really took off during the second half of the 19th century. However, it was only when Hungary lost its coast and its mountain resorts following the First World War that Lake Balaton really came into its own. The local landowners divided up their land into plots, selling them off to the builders of the villas you still see dotted around the lake today.

From the 1950s to the 1970s Balaton became one of Hungary's most popular holiday resorts. It was here that the *Zánka Pioneer Town,* the Communist youth organisation's second-biggest complex, was built. The lake's popularity was also helped by the fact that it was here that East German tourists could meet up with their friends and relatives living in West Germany.

The lake hosts yachting regattas, the annual cross Balaton swim, dances and the other social events. In Siófok and Balatonfüred water-skiing courses are marked out on the lake, where beginners are taught in the morning and the experts left to their own devices in the afternoon. Although Lake Balaton may quieten down in the low season, there are programmes in the Balaton Highlands, Zala and Somogy all the year round.

KESZTHELY

The reputation of the town is founded on the activities of the Festetics family and the existence of the *Georgikon* in particular. The centre of the town (Fő tér) is dominated by the **Town Hall,** rebuilt in a late baroque style by *Kristóf Hofstädter* in 1769. It was here that the predecessor of the *Agricultural University,* the *Agricultural College,* operated between 1865 and 1896. In the square, on the walls of the old Franciscan monastery, there is a tablet informing you that the poet *János Batsányi* (1763--1845) went to school there.

The Franciscan **church,** founded in about 1390, contains some splendid medieval wall paintings, the tomb of founder István (II.) Laczkffy (†1397) and that of Kristóf Festetics (†1768). In the neo-Gothic tower, added in 1896, you can see a 14th century rose window, which originally stood on the western façade. To the south of the church in the *Várkert* you can make out the outline of a 12th century rotunda once known as the **Chapel of St Laurence.**

One of the most interesting buildings in the town centre is Pethő, or Goldmark House (Kossuth út 22.) which gained its current appearance during the 18th century. It was here that Károly Goldmark, the famous composer, was born in 1830. The Cultural Centre named after him was in fact the old eclectic-style town hall, built in about 1870.

The most-visited place in Keszthely is **Festetics Palace** (1745–1887). Containing one hundred and one rooms, the most interesting features are the prominent onion-domed tower, the chapel, and the

A French-style garden, later replaced by an English-style garden, stood in the area to the west of the Keszthely's Festetics Palace. The garden eventually covered an area of 42hectares of which only 7.2hectares remain.

pristine two-storey library wing with its 86 thousand volumes, and the oak-panelled staircase in the southern wing. The ground floor rooms are used for temporary exhibitions, and the music room, the old dining room, hosts weekly concert.

When visiting Festetics Palace you are allowed to enter sixteen rooms fully furnished in a manner befitting an 18th and 19th century aristocrat. There is an exhibition of weapons belonging to the Hungarian National Museum in the corridor, and under the tower you can see the pick of Franz Joseph Windischgrätz's hunting trophies. Endre Nagy, a hunter from Zala who worked in the service of the great African hunter for many years, successfully persuaded the duke to leave his collection to the Keszthely Museum.

It was György Festetics who founded the first agricultural college in Hungary, the **Georgikon**. The college (Georgikon u. 20.), whose name is derived from the Christian name of its founder, was founded in 1797. Today the college is a hotel. It is from here that you can walk down the horse-chestnut avenue (Bercsényi út).

The cellar of the multistoreyed granary houses an exhibition devoted to the history of the Balaton wine region. On the ground and first floors you can find permanent exhibitions covering the histories of the Georgikon (1797–1848), the Agricultural College, and the Academy (1865–1945). At the exhibition entitled "The People of the Farmsteads" visitors get a taste of what it was really like being a farm labourer. The attic space houses an exhibition about cereals, a topic closely associated with the building.

The buildings of the **Georgikon Farm Museum** (1971) are arranged around two large courtyards. In the neo-Baroque **Balaton Museum** (1928, Múzeum u. 2.) there is an exhibition devoted entirely to the evolution of the flora and fauna around Lake Balaton. The domed **Helikon Monument** (1921), on the main walk though *Helikon Park,* is where the local schools hold their *Helikon Celebrations* every other year in the years ending in even numbers.

In 1998, three wine taverns were opened in the town. The *Pannonia Wine Tavern* with its collection of wine labels and exhibition devoted to the region's wines, is set in the 19th century surroundings of the Georgikon. It is here, during the *Balaton Festival* held in May, that the national *Cser-*

You can get to the shores of Lake Balaton (Sétáló utca) by going along Erzsébet királyné útja and then crossing the level crossing. The jetty used by the ferry goes a long way into the waters of the lake.

szegi *Fűszeres Wine Festival* takes place. The *Hungaricum Wine Tavern* in Fő tér has a wine-making exhibition in its cellars and a traditional **cooper's workshop** in its courtyard. In the cellar of the *Bacchus Hotel* you will find the huge glass and tile wine tanks dating from 1911, containing wines from all of the Hungarian wine regions.

The **Marzipan Museum** (Katona József u. 19.), with its display of marzipan figures, cakes covered in traditional folk art motifs and marzipan Festetics Palace, is situated on one of the roads next to the palace itself. One of the most recent additions to the **Doll Museum** is the 8x2.5-metre model of the *Parliament Building* in Budapest, made out of fossilised shells originating from quarries from all over Hungary. It took *Ilona Miskei* over fourteen years to make it.

A day in Keszthely would not be complete without a visit to the Island Baths, a curious construction which has always been popular with sun worshippers. Indeed, the row of stalls on the nearby promenade provides one of the town's most attractive sights.

KIS-BALATON

At the present time 28million cubic metres of water, supplied by the *River Zala,* fill this 1,870-hectare artificial lake. The wildlife on Kis-Balaton is best seen from *Kányavár Island* which can be found two kilometres north of Balatonmagyaród.

Kis-Balaton provides an ideal habitat for herons, cormorants, spoonbills, great reed-warblers, coots, great crested grebes and nightingales. Near the 115km marker on road 71 on the Fenékpuszta side of the lake there is an **ornithological station** which can be visited on weekdays all the year round. Visitors will require special permission if they want to go on the guided tours around Kis-Balaton's protected areas. For further information on visiting conditions see section on National Parks.

In FENÉKPUSZTA, south of Keszthely, stands a gateway to a fourth century **fortress**, a three-aisled basilica and what remains of the state warehouse.

250 species of birds can be found in and around Kis-Balaton, 150 of which actually nest there.

The one-time Soviet military runway at SÁRMELLÉK is now run by Zalavár-Sármellék Ltd in co-operation with MALÉV, Hungarian Airlines. Although the runway is currently not used for timetabled commercial flights, it has been used for charter flights since 1993.

ZALAVÁR

It was during the 9th century that the Slav, Pribina, fleeing from Nyitra (Nitra, Slovakia) was given feudal tenure of the lands along on the banks of the River Zala, prior to being given the title of count by the Franks. Pribina built his seat on the Zala floodplains on a site that although served by a single crossing for many centuries, amounted to a fortified island settlement.

It was in Zalavár that Kis-Balaton House was built. The exhibition focuses on the nature reserves and the Balaton water-filtering system. (The photograph below shows the consecration of the excavated ground plan of Saint Adrian's church.)

Saints Cyril and Methodius also came here during the conversion of the local Slavs in the year 867. The **statues** of the saints were put up in 1985. Saint Stephen founded a Benedictine abbey in Zalavár in 1019, and the site was to become a regional centre. Today, both the **Saint Stephen Monument** (1938) and the **Memorial Chapel**, built on the foundations of St Stephen's Chapel (1996), pay homage to the events of this period. Going slightly eastwards you can make out the outlines of **Saint Adrian's Basilica,** which was reduced to ruins during the course of the Hungarian Conquest. The walls have recently been excavated, restored and consecrated. Not far from the castle a sign on the far side of the road marks the site of the old *Récéskút Basilica*.

ZALAKAROS

It was in 1965, during exploratory drilling in the Zala oilfields that the thermal waters feeding the **medicinal baths** were discovered. The two covered baths were added to the complex in 1975.

The so-called "bathing experience" in Zalakaros was opened in 1999, where the underwater currents manage to recreate a whirlpool effect, further thrills can be expected following the 2003 additions.

More recently a herb garden has been laid out, and a medicinal centre is currently being built. From the beginning of June to the end of August the *Cultural Centre* (Fő út 8.) hosts the *Zala Living Folk Arts Exhibition*. There is a completely new display every year. The Behiák **Riding School** is situated on the Zalakaros to Galambok road.

GALAMBOK is recommended to those wishing to visit a renovated peasant cottage (Somogyi út 8.) or try their luck at a spot of fishing.

You will find the KÁPOLNAPUSZTA Buffalo Reservation on Kis-Balaton, to Keszthely roads. It is here that the Balaton Highlands National Park provide, a natural habitat for the two hundred or so water buffalos you can see all the year round.

The **fishing lake** can be found at the edge of the village. You can take a flight in a four-seater plane or a three-seater helicopter from the **airfield** on the Zalakomár road (Hegyalja u. 61.) just two kilometres from Zalakaros.

HÉVÍZ

> *György Festetics played a major role in the founding of the famous Bathing Lake. It was he who started building the bathing cabins. 1865 saw the building of the separate ladies' and gentlemen's mirror baths. A shortage of accommodation meant that guests had to be transported in from Keszthely.*

The **Thermal Bath,** built between 1964 and 1968, was in its day the largest and most up-to-date covered swimming pool in the country. From that moment onwards Hévíz was no longer at the mercy of the elements. In the entrance hall of the winter gardens there is a Roman **altar** (dedicated to Jupiter) which was in fact found in Hévíz, positioned beside a small pool.

> *The second largest thermal lake in the world, the lake at Hévíz with its 35–36 °C waters, covers an area of 4.4 hectares. The water flowing through the lake at a rate of 410 l/sec, means that the 80 million-litre lake is replenished every two days.*

Hévíz is extremely fortunate to have its Thermal Bath (Dr. Schulhof Vilmos sétány 1.), which has been attracting visitors for more than two centuries (ill. below). The State Medicinal Bath Building was built next door in 1952. It was the biologist Sándor Lovassy who introduced the red Indian water lilies into the lake. The water lilies now figure in Hévíz's coat-of-arms.

The church (János Bocskai), complete with its seven towers symbolising the seven gifts of the Holy Spirit, was consecrated in Hévíz in September 1999.

The small village **church** in *Egregy*, now officially part of Hévíz, probably dates back to the first half of the 13th century.

Thanks to its new visitor-friendly image ALSÓ-PÁHOK has become a popular destination in recent years. While *Kolping Family Hotel* is particularly proud of its bio-houses and **wellness centre** (Fő u. 120.), a **holiday village** offering holiday houses, a guesthouse, a swimming pool and sports facilities is currently being built. Not only this, you are also in easy reach of numerous thermal baths and Lake Balaton, which is only 6km away.

CSERSZEGTOMAJ

Equidistant from both Hévíz and Keszthely and situated in some beautiful countryside, the town has its fair share of hotels, guesthouses and tourist attractions. On the road out towards Hévíz you will find the *Club Dobogómajor* (1997), a bio-house built entirely out of wood and other environmentally-friendly materials. Those visiting Cserszegtomaj can also climb the 32-metre-high **Margaret Lookout Tower** or visit the nearby *West Balaton Castle Theatre*.

It was in 1983 that the 3km-long 52-metre-deep **Kút Cave** was opened up. Its appearance has been shaped by the *Ős-Hévíz*, a hot-water spring whose lime deposits have left a host of maze-like formations. Unfortunately, visitors can only see the entrance to the cave. The **arboretum** at the Hévíz

end of the village is nevertheless open to the general public.

Travelling between Cserszegtomaj and REZI you come upon the *Gyöngyös Highwayman's Inn* (1728), which was originally built as a hunters' lodge. Two highwaymen lie buried under the weeping willow growing next to it. The inn itself contains a few relics: arrest warrants and other similar reminders of a bygone age.

The famous wine known as *Cserszegi Fűszeres* takes its name from the village.

The first document mentioning Rezi by name, dating from 1387, refers to the one-time castle, its ruins still stand on the 418-metre-high dolomite rock.
It's a 4km walk up to the castle from the village, but once you are there you are rewarded with some picturesque ruins and some excellent views.

ZALASZÁNTÓ

Of the Romanesque and Gothic details uncovered during the 1957 restoration work at the **Roman Catholic church** (Fő út 20.) most worthy of note are the 13th century features on the south door and the late-Gothic ogee-arched tabernacle in the chancel. The door to the sacristy is the work of a Renaissance master.

In Zalaszántó there is also a **peasant cottage** (Vadász út 20.) complete with domestic animals kept in the traditional manner.

The medieval remains of **Tátika Castle,** situated on the 412-metre-high volcanic hill overlooking Zalaszántó, are hidden amongst the ancient beech trees. You can get there on foot.

For the time being the ten-hectare Human Rights Park on Kovácsi Hill overlooking Zalaszántó only has one building, the Buddhist Stupa (1992–1993) complete with its gold-leaf statue of Buddha.

THE NORTHWESTERN SHORE

GYENESDIÁS

Once a hilltop village, it now forms part of a famous wine and fruit-growing region. Quite a few of the peasant cottages which survived the arrival of the tourist industry now provide holiday accommodation. The landscape is enhanced by the wine cellars lined up on the hillside.

The **Nagymező Leisure Centre** situated above the village has a fine adventure playground not far from the **Festetics Lookout Point** (230.5metres). The paths covering the *Keszthely Hills* take you deep into the *Balaton Highlands National Park*. Within a few hours walkers can get to *Pető Hill*, *Büdöskút Valley* and *Szobakő Cave*. (For more information see the relevant section in the *Hungarian Treasury*.)

In the village itself there is a restored thatched **shepherd's cottage**, which includes an exhibition, a **motocross track**, and horse-riding facilities. Gyenesdiás also has two outdoor swimming complexes, one on the banks of the lake with sandy beaches and lawns, the other with a **giant water chute**.

Those making a point of visiting VONYARCVAS-HEGY usually head for the **chapel** on *Saint*

Michael's Mount, the *Vashegy* **Chapel** (1884), as well as the classical-style *Helikon Tavern* situated out in the vineyards which used to house the Festetics family's winepress.

The lido at Vonyarcvashegy is one of the most popular on Lake Balaton. Its sandy shores are recommended particularly to families with small children.

St Michael's Mount, at the eastern end of Vonyarcvashegy, is visible for many miles around. According to legend in 1739, 46 fishermen were left stranded on a sheet of ice heading out into the middle of the lake. In their moment of distress the fishermen swore that if they were to survive the incident they would build a chapel on top of the hill. At that moment the wind turned and blew the sheet of ice towards the shore. The chapel which you can see today, however, has only been standing for a century or so.

It was only in the 1920s that Balatongyörök became a recognised tourist resort. Today the village's quay is busy with tourists enjoying a good day out. People come to visit the cellars, hike along the marked footpaths and ride along the 10km cycle path to Keszthely (2003). It is also one of the most popular lidos on the Zala side of Lake Balaton.

Szépkilátó Hill rises from the eastern end of BALATONGYÖRÖK where road number 71 starts its descent into the *Tapolca Basin*. It's not surprising that the hill's name translates as the "hill with a beautiful view", for despite its lack of metres it has one of the most outstanding views in Hungary. Standing at the summit you have the waters of the lake below you, Szigliget to the east with *Badacsony* beyond, and the hills of Boglár and Fonyód rising above the southern shores with the lowlands of the *Nagy-berek* next door. To the west you can see the steep outer slopes of the *Marcali Ridge*, with Kis-Balaton down at about the same level as the lake. It was the famous hunter *Endre Nagy* who founded the **African Museum** in BALATONEDERICS. It is here you can see his African hunting trophies, animal hides, his Tanzanian ethnographical collection of bone and wood carvings and African tribal objects.

In the safari park next door you can see camels, buffaloes and zebras.

BASALT HILLS, CAVES, WINES

SZIGLIGET

It was here that many a Hungarian literary masterpiece was conceived. The classical **Esterházy Palace** in the main square, built at the beginning of the 19th century, is now a *Writers' Retreat*. The park contains some mature trees, some of which are over a hundred years old.

The pathway skirting to the chapel takes you past some 19th century peasant houses and some cellars. Underneath the castle you will find the *Old Village*, built during the 18th century. Szigliget **Castle,** built by Pannonhalma Abbey in 1262, was blown up in 1702. Excavations have been going on at the castle since 1990.

Above the old ferry in the eastern part of the village stands the **Csonka Tower**, which is all that remains of medieval Avas Church. The thatched **Szigliget Gallery** exhibits paintings with a Balaton theme. Arts and crafts workshops are also held there.

The *Szigliget Summer Festival,* taking place during the first weeks of August has its fair share of equestrian folk dance and brass bands programmes. The Szigliget-Balatongyörök Bay **swimming competition** also takes place at this time.

TAPOLCA

Tapolca, ten kilometres north of Lake Balaton, is well known for its wines and its *medicinal waters.* Indeed, there are plans to make the town a major health spa. Its most famous attraction is its unique **Cave Lake** discovered in 1903.

The waters in the cave are almost a metre deep and it was possible to row on the crystal clear waters until as late as 1983, when the local bauxite mine inadvertently caused the waters to seep away. Once the bauxite miners were told to hold back on their activities and the mine stopped pumping the subterranean waters from the area in the vicinity of the caves, the waters returned. Since 1998 it has once again been possible to boat on the small underground lakes. The most beautiful rock formations are those formed by the action of the hot waters.

It was a combination of hot volcanic water, limestone, sand and clay deposits which created Tapolca's 4-kilometre-long subterranean water system. The biggest chamber is the Lóczy Chamber, which is 20m long, 3–5m wide and 8m high.

The things to see in this small country town are **Lake Malom** and the **Municipal Museum** (Batsányi tér 11.), with its exhibition devoted to local writer *János Batsányi.* His bust stands by the lake, a tablet commemorates him on the wall of his birthplace (Batsányi u. 12.) and he is buried in the cemetery. In the **School Museum** you can find one of the oldest elementary schools in Central Europe.

It was in the old mill in DISZEL, not far from Tapolca, that antique collector Ákos Vörösváry opened Hungary's first Modern Art Gallery (Templom tér).

BADACSONY

This table-topped basalt hill rising majestically above Lake Balaton is about four or five million years old. BADACSONYTOMAJ is the most popular village on this stretch of the lake. You can get there by boat, by train or by car, but it's also worth while trying the excellent cycle path.

It is on the slopes of the 440m-high Badacsony (part of the *Balaton Highlands National Park* since 1956) that they grow the grapes for the Badacsony region's excellent wines. On the steeper slopes there are some interesting geological formations, the most spectacular probably being the basalt pillars.

They used basalt to build **Saint Emmerich's Church** in Badacsonytomaj. The **Ranolder Cross** has been standing 400metres up the southwestern side of the hill since 1857. It was named after the famous bishop responsible for putting it up.

The body of the great Balaton painter *József Egry* (1883–1951) lies in Badacsonytomaj cemetery. A statue *(László Márton)* of him stands in the park next to Badacsony railway station. The house where József Egry lived, which stands nearby (Egry sétány 12.), is now a **museum** dedicated to the artist's life and work. An artist prone to melancholy, Egry found in the lake the perfect subject matter through which to express his interest in "space and infinite". The exhibition includes documents and pictures covering his whole career, from his first pictures to his famous painting *Balaton Fishermen* of 1923.

There is also a museum in the baroque **Róza Szegedy House,** once inhabited by *Sándor Kisfaludy* (1772–1844) and his wife, complete with its original furniture, personal belongings and grape-picking equipment.

The courtyard is used for holding events having some connection with the Age of Reform. **Kisfaludy House**, which lies a little further up the Badacsony, was once a small winepress building belonging to the poet. Today it is a restaurant. *Kisfaludy Spring* lies in front of the house, whilst the car park nearby marks the beginning of the footpath leading up to the **Kisfaludy Lookout Tower** (437m). From here you can go down the *Bujdosók Steps* right to the water's edge.

The Badacsony Patronal Festival and the Folk Art Bazaar are held during the first weekend in August, whilst the grape harvest in Badacsony in the middle of September is marked by an impressive parade.

It's not difficult to walk to BADACSONYÖRS and to the **Folly Arboretum** with its fine collection of evergreens. The ruins of *Csobánc Castle* are only a 10–15-minute drive away. In addition there is the jewel in the Tapolca Basin's crown, *Saint George's Hill,* with its fine collection of basalt pillars.

The Badacsony Wine Region is set in some enchanting landscape. White grapes dominate the slopes of Badacsony, St George's Hill, Csobánc, Gulács and Szigliget. The most typical wine types are Italian Riesling, Szilváni, Kéknyelű, Szürkebarát, Muscat and Tramini. It is not only the high quality of the wines for which the region is famous, there are also curiosities like the "ice wine" produced when the grapes are harvested after frost. It was in Badacsonytomaj that the maximum size of cultivated plots was established, something which was done to protect the traditional size of the vineyards.

FROM LAKESIDE TO SUMMIT

RÉVFÜLÖP

The village standing at the foot of *Fülöp Hill* (274m) was built at what is the southern entrance to the Kál Basin. Because of the proximity of Balatonboglár on the far side of the lake, Révfülöp has traditionally been used as a **crossing point**. While the red sandstone **ruins** of 13th century *Fülöp* church stand opposite the railway station the ruins of Ecsér church stand at the Kővágóörs end of the village. The **Community House** (Halász utca 6.) shares its premises with the *Tópart Gallery*.

It is from the lido that the famous **Cross-Balaton Swim** starts. The event, which forms part of the *Villa Filip Festival*, attracts thousands of swimmers eager to swim the 5.4km to Balatonboglár. The two communities also link up for the *Golden Bridge Friendship Festival* held at Whitsun each year. The conferences held at the **Lutheran Study Education Centre** also bring people to the village. Every summer some of the country's finest dance groups take to the outdoor stage at the **Sziget Lido**.

There are plenty of marked pathways leading out of the village. The paths marked with a red line take you from the quay through the vineyards to *Fülöp Hill*. From the **Millennium Lookout Tower** you get a fine view of the volcanic rock formations of the *Tapolca Basin* and the Somogy Hills.

The Balaton Highlands National Park Nature Conservation Farm in SALFÖLD *provides an ideal environment in which to see some of Hungary's typical breeds of cows, sheep, oxen and sheepdogs. The Kál Basin is rich in interesting geological features and sites of cultural interest. You can ask for a guide at National Park Headquarters.*

There are marked paths taking you deep into the Kál Basin, an area which is part of the Balaton Highlands National Park. The local stone, a Miocene sandstone containing a compressed mixture of sand, clay and pebbles, can be found in bizarre rock formations, like those near KŐVÁGÓÖRS, *Salföld and* SZENTBÉKKÁLLA. *Locals like to refer to these slabs of rock as "petrified waves".*

Anyone can try the refreshing mineral waters, once enjoyed by the Byzantine Empress Theodora, which now flow into the bottling plant in the small village of KÉKKÚT. *What can be drunk here free of charge can be bought at the usual outlets in either its still or fizzy form under the Theodora brand name.*

Heading for the eastern end of the Káli Basin we continue northeastwards towards Zánka and on through the *Valley of the Arts* to the pride of the *Southern Bakony,* Nagyvázsony.

The name ZÁNKA appears on two railway stations, the old fishing village of that name and the pioneer town (1969-1975). With Communism gone, the camp is now called the **Centre for Children and Youth**. The village and the camp join forces to organise the *Zánka Fisherman's Festival* in July.

Legend tells us it was here or hereabouts that Pál Kinizsi, Matthias Corvinus's most valiant knight, started life as a miller's boy. Before taking the tourist route named after him, it is worth visiting Zánka's famous Calvinist Church, already in existence in 1516, and rebuilt in 1786.

Although DÖRGICSE is situated 10km from Zánka and only five kilometres from Balatonakali it is not deemed to be a Balaton settlement. The three sets of Romanesque church ruins on the road leading out towards Vászoly are worth visiting: the **ruined church** in *Alsó-Dörgicse,* already standing in 1268; the ruins of *Szentpéter-Dörgicse*'s single-aisled parish church in the middle of the village and *Kisfalud-Dörgicse* church.

The six villages in the Valley of the Arts, KAPOLCS, TALIÁN-DÖRÖGD, VIGÁNTPETEND, MONOSTORAPÁTI, ÖCS and PULA came to the public's attention in 1989, when the arts festival organised by the composer István Márta, was first held there. Every summer since tens of thousands of people have attended the festival, including many big names from the world of music. Since that first festival the villages have been smartened up a bit, and many craftsmen and artists have settled in the valley. Those making the necessary arrangements in advance can visit the space observatory in Taliándörögd.

NAGYVÁZSONY

Situated on the main Veszprém-Tapolca road, just 15km from Lake Balaton, this town, with its woods, fishing lake and equestrian traditions draws back visitors year after year.

The **border fortress** is in a better state than it was a few years ago, indeed, the castle chapel is now used for wedding ceremonies. On each floor of the four-storey donjon you can see an **exhibition** dedicated

to its one-time castellan, and Matthias Corvinus's heroic knight, Pál Kinizsi. His red marble sarcophagus stands in the **castle chapel**. It was he and his wife Benigna Magyar who built the *Pauline Monastery,* the **ruins** of which can be found on the edge of Nagyvázsony just beyond the cemetery.

15th century **Saint Stephen's Church** (Rákóczi u.) was built reusing masonry from its predecessor dating from the Árpád era.

Those spending their holidays on Lake Balaton at the beginning of August won't regret turning their backs on the lake for a day or two and heading for the Kinizsi Festival in Nagyvázsony.

Zichy Palace (Kossuth u. 10–14.) was already standing by the end of the 18th century. Its park is now a nature reserve and a venue for summer **equestrian events**. Since the renovations the palace has provided a roof for a 4-star and a 5-star hotel.

ALONG THE SHORELINE TO TIHANY

In BALATONUDVARI's old cemetery next to the main road you will find almost fifty carved white heart-shaped **gravestones**, all dating from the first half of the 19th century. The few gravestones of a similar type existing in Balatonfüred were probably carved by the same person.

The two-arched **bridge** over the *Pécsely* in ÖRVÉNYES stands just in front of the **watermill** situated next to the ruins of the medieval church. The first mention of the mill, which is still in working order, dates back to 1211, although it was rebuilt during the 18th century.

The old **row of cellars** in ASZÓFŐ still echo to the sound of the owners and their clientele. The village also contains the classical **St Ladislas's Church** (1832–1834) and the 13th century **ruins of Kövesd parish church**.

TIHANY

It is the **peninsula's** architecture, history and its natural environment which brings visitors to Tihany. The *Inner Lake,* which is all that remains of a volcanic crater, is popular with anglers.

In the spring the almond and the ash trees cover the Tihany Peninsula in blossom. During the summer it's the luxuriant vegetation which takes centre stage, particularly the surviving lavender beds, whose fragrance is an experience in itself. In the autumn the inner area of the peninsula bursts into an array of autumnal colours. By September the smoke bushes have turned bright red, the dogwood bushes a shade of purple. You can also pick out the flowering ash trees and the yellowy browns of the oaks. Walking through the woods on an Indian summer day is an experience rarely forgotten.

The *Outer Lake* formed part of Lake Balaton when the water level was higher. When the water-level dropped the water remained only in the lower-lying areas. With the lake only rarely getting a top up of water it is gradually turning into a marsh. The Outer Lake is a great place for birds, particularly ducks and herons, a fact which pays testament to

József Csáki-Maronyák: Tihany in the Spring

the success of an ecological approach which has sought to protect the geological, biological and geographical diversity of the Tihany Peninsular. Success also came with the Europa Diploma awarded by the Council of Europe in 2003.

The Tihany Peninsula projects five kilometres into the water, making the Tihany Straits the narrowest stretch of Lake Balaton. There is a **ferry service** linking the peninsula with the marinas, quays and lidos of Szántód on the southern shore. The first document we have relating to the **Benedictine Abbey** is the *Letter of Foundation* of 1055 which, although written in Latin, contains the first recorded piece of written Hungarian. Andrew I., who issued the document, is buried in the **crypt**. His tomb is the only one belonging to a Hungarian king to remain in its original position. Having died in 1055, Andrew I., the founder of Tihany Abbey, was buried 700 years before the present Baroque church was built. The crypt's narrow windows illuminate the tomb, which is decorated with spiral motifs and a cross.

The **abbey church** (1719–1754) was built by Abbot Ágoston Lécs. The liturgical furniture is by the Tyrol-born *Sebestyén Stulhof,* who spent a quarter of a century working on the church. He was also buried here. Since 1994, the monastic buildings have once again been used for religious purposes, although one part of the complex contains a **museum**, a lapidarium and a temporary exhibition

The frescoes inside the church are by Lajos Deák-Ébner (the Doctors of the Church), Bertalan Székely (the four Evangelists), Károly Lotz (Faith, Hope and Charity) and János Novák (Saint Ányos). The church's organ was built in 1764, although it was damaged by a grenade in 1945. In 1993, a new organ was fitted into the 230-year-old organ case.

venue. It was in Tihany that the last king of Hungary, Charles IV., and his wife, Queen Zita, spent their final days in Hungary before going into exile. You can get some good views of the lake from around the abbey, and there are plenty of beautiful old houses to enjoy.

The Pisky Promenade starting from the church leads to the **Doll Museum** (Visszhang u. 4.), which

On 11th August 1999, the day of the total eclipse of the sun, many people were there to witness the walling in of 5,000 bottles of wine into a cellar which will not be opened until the next total eclipse. Interestingly, the bottles contained the local curiosity Somlói Juhfark rather than the more established Tihany Merlot or Cabernet.

was opened to the general public in 1997. It contains dolls and games from the last 200 years. The **open-air stage** in Tihany is the venue for many a summer event. Organised weekend nature walks around the peninsula take place from the beginning of July. The tours leave from the Sajkod entrance to Tihany on the Aszófő road (number 71). Further enquiries can be made at the *Balaton Highlands National Park.* It is here, next to the ruins of **Apát church,** that you can find a sign showing the route of the *Lajos Lóczy Walk.*

Local volcanic activity formed the hillocks overlooking the *geyser meadow* three million years ago. The most beautiful of the geyser-formed rock formations is known as *Aranyház*, a name deriving from the golden yellow lichen covering it.

The houses in the Open-Air Ethnographic Museum (Batthyány utca 36.) are built from a grey basalt tufa which used to be mined in the area. The houses, once belonging to the fisherman's guild, the potter's workshop and the farmhouse all contain their original fittings. The guild chest, the guild tankard, a hollow log boat and other more recent types of wooden rowing boats are of particular interest.

On the ridge of Nyereg Hill stands the most important geological feature on the peninsula. The contorted limestone slabs were formed by the combined effects of water and movements in the earth's surface. Siberian irises and marsh orchids both grow in Bozsa Bay, one of the most strictly protected areas in the National Park. In the reeds you can find grayling geese and marsh harriers, and perhaps otters too. On Csúcs Hill you can still make out the walls of a medieval keep. It is here, on the highest point of the peninsula, that the sternbergia, star hyacinths, and variegated irises flower in great numbers.

It is at the **picnic site** on **Óvár-tető** that you can find *Echo Hill* with its *Echo Rock*. Today any claims to an echo ring hollow.

The Monk's Dwellings make up the only surviving hermitage colony site in Central Europe. The Basilite monks, brought to Tihany by Andrew I., carved their cells into the 20metre-high basalt tufa cliff. Following the landslide of 1952, only a few of the cell groups remain open to the public.

Any resonance has long since been swallowed up by buildings and vegetation, and gone are the days when 16 syllables long echoed clearly off the wall of the abbey church.

Of Tihany's five lidos, one (the *Gödrös*, which lies just above Balatonfüred) is free of charge. Also on that stretch of Lake Balaton you can find the *Club Tihany* holiday centre and the *Balaton Limnological Research Centre,* founded by the *Hungarian Academy of Science* between 1926 and 1927.

BALATONFÜRED

What was Hungary's first **spa town and tourist resort** has since 1987 become an *International Grape and Wine Town.* Here the title "international" is totally appropriate, with the local population of 13 thousand doubling during the high season.

By the beginning of the 18th century, Füred was already known for the beneficial effects the **mineral waters** had on those suffering from heart and arterial problems, locomotor disorders, skin and gynaecological complaints. The spa halls and the well, the latter of which is in Gyógy tér, were built in 1800. Even today many visit the **Louis Kossuth Drinking Hall**. The **Coronary Hospital** behind the hall was built in 1912–1913; the older Louis Seizestyle sanatorium, on the northern side of the square, between 1781 and 1803.

It was on the site of the sanatorium theatre that Hungary's first stone-built theatre was situated (1831). Following two demolitions and two re-constructions only six pillars survive from the original building. The sanatorium theatre and its dining room now form part of the Hotel Árkád. It is here, every July, that the Anna Ball takes place. The first such ball was held on July 26th, 1825 in honour of Anna-Krisztina, a daughter of the Szentgyörgyi-Horváth family. The ball was held in their house, built in 1798, on the western side of Gyógy tér.

The *Anna Ball,* held on the last Saturday in July, is an important social gathering which culminates in the coronation of the ball queen.

The **promenade** and the **jetty** are both popular places. The arrival of the first boat from Siófok at the beginning of April marks the opening of the season in Balatonfüred. It is in the **rose garden**, lying immediately in front of the jetty that the *Opening of the Sails Celebrations* take place in the middle of May, at the same time as the *Whitsun Song* international children's choir festival. The *Wine Festival,* starting in the middle of August, takes place both on the promenade and on the **jetty's open-air stage**, making it a cultural event, as well as a wine festival.

During the Age of Reform, Balatonfüred wasn't simply a spa town, it was a lively social and cultural centre alive with political intrigue. Kazinczy, Csokonai, Ádám Pálóczi Horváth, Széchenyi, Kossuth, Deák and Vörösmarty were all known to visit. Jókai even built a summer residence here, a building which is now used as a museum (Honvéd u. 1.).

In one part of what is in effect a two-centred town, next to the lake, stands the classical **Round Church** (1841–1846). The high altar painting is by *Henrietta Kärgling* and the painting above the side altar by *János Vaszary*. The tablet on the wall of the classical hotel nearby tells you that this was the singer *Lujza Blaha*'s favourite haunt. The street is named after her. In Szent István tér, the centre of the old town, you will find the town hall and the red stone Catholic church. The Calvinist Church stands in Óvoda utca. At the end of Öreghegyi út you come to the 120m-long **Lóczy Cave**. Discovered in 1882 and developed in 1934, the cave has some beautiful rippled limestone walls which you can visit in the company of a guide.

It wasn't only during his lifetime that writers congregated at *"Balaton writer" Gábor Lipták*'s house. Today the building is the **House of Hungarian Translators**.

The shores of Lake Balaton are just a minute's walk from Gyógy tér. A walk taking you through the park where some of the spa's most famous guests planted trees in thanks for the beneficial effects of the waters. One such guest was Rabindranath Tagore, after whom one of the promenades is named. The most famous statues are the fisherman and the ferryman (1941) by János Pásztor standing next to the jetty.

Balatonfüred is one of the venues for Lake Balaton's many sailing regattas.

Count Ferenc Széchenyi's **summer residence** (1792) in *Arács* is now used as a school (Hősök tere 1.). The building was used by *Mór Jókai* as the model for Mihály Tímár's palace in his novel *The Golden Man.*

Going towards Csopak you come to the most famous place in Balatonfüred, the picturesque *Koloska Valley*. There are numerous footpaths taking you through the 761 hectares of protected woodland to the *Koloska Spring*, the inn, and on to the **Jókai Lookout Point**.

Of all the sites on the northern shores of Lake Balaton it is the *Füred Camping Site* which has

the most visitors. Surprising as it may sound it is also open during the winter. Those staying in the heated houses tend to spend their time going skating on the ice marked out at the **Esterházy Lido**.

Going from Balatonfüred towards Veszprém along road 73, you come to the Roman remains at BALÁCAPUSZTA, *situated between Veszprémfajsz and* NEMESVÁMOS. *Although the Roman villa, unparalleled in Central Europe, was uncovered in 1906, excavations are still going on. More and more of the 30-40 main buildings and one hundred outbuildings are coming to light, but it will still be a few more decades before the whole of the 16-hectare site is excavated.*

Balatonfüred is the home of Hungarian yachting. For the yachtsmen who come here it's not just the sailing, it's the tradition which counts. The return to Lake Balaton of Nemere II., the yacht which set the record for sailing around the lake back in 1955, was a cause for great rejoicing. Nemere II managed to complete the circuit in under ten hours. Its new owner renovated the boat in the year 2000 after which it proceeded to win the Nemere II. class competition.

There are several clubs and societies dedicated to preserving the old hussar traditions. Whilst at the Hussar Gallery in Nemesvámos you may be fortunate enough to meet the founder of the gallery himself.

THE LAKE'S EASTERN BASIN

Only the **tower** remains of Csopak's 13th century parish church. Nevertheless, despite an 18th century reconstruction the church manages to retain some of its medieval character. Csopak's oldest

The Balatonfüred-Csopak wine region has finally come back to life after many years in the doldrums.
Now wine experts are devoting ever more time and energy to their vines and their old cellars.

aristocratic summer residence, **Ranolder Villa** (Kishegyi út 13.), dates back to the 1860s. The romantic-style building is surrounded by a *botanical garden* containing a valuable collection of conifers. The **cellar,** (Arany J. u. 3.) once belonging to the residence and the vineyard, laid out during Bishop János Ranolder's lifetime, were considered state-of-the-art in their day. The current owner has renovated the 18th century classical cellar building, which is capable of storing 1,800-2,000 hectolitres of wine, and has brought the processing equipment for his gold medal-winning wines right up to date. For more and more visitors Csopak means *the international dance festival.* Every weekend during the holiday season, the Csopak Dance Group takes to the stage situated in the car park on Fürdő utca. The so-called Gothic **Török House** (15th century) (Petőfi köz 7.) in ALSÓÖRS is the oldest gentry manor house in Hungary. It is also described as the *"Turkish tax collector's house"*, because the top of the chimney bears a passing resemblance to a turban. During the summer the house provides a venue for cultural events, and more recently weddings have been held there.

Motorboats are banned from all parts of the lake. However, visitors are quite free to sail, windsurf, row or use water bicycles.
There is also the Alsóörs flying man competition which takes place at the end of July, when a special stage is built for contestants to jump, cycle, ski or snowboard off. It's an event which manages to attract thousands of visitors.
The Harley Davidson Festival held in June at the Alsóörs's Európa Campsite is a red-letter day in the calendar of the motorcycling fraternity, and an event not to be missed at any cost.
The renovated lookout tower on Alsóörs Cser Hill provides excellent views across the lake, especially when the regatta is on.
The Balaton Regatta held in October in Balatonalmádi is modelled on the Oxford v Cambridge University Boat Race. The competitive edge is taken off somewhat by the fact that both crews, Veszprém and Keszthely, come from the University of Veszprém.

FELSŐÖRS

Just three kilometres north of Alsóörs, you come to the most beautiful Romanesque parish church in the *Balaton Highlands*. The **Catholic Deanery Church,** built in red sandstone at the beginning of the 13th century, has managed to preserve its medieval character despite its 18th century liturgical furniture. The western façade contains three windows separated by knotted shafts, standing above a fine Romanesque portal. Concert recitals are held in the church during the summer months.

Since the year 2000, the general public has been able to enjoy the **Geological Nature Trail**. Over the half-a-kilometre trail visitors can study the Triassic rock formations uncovered during excavations on *Forrás Hill*. Special places have been marked on the trail showing where visitors can take rock samples home as souvenirs.

BALATONALMÁDI

It is still possible to make out the four settlements (*Vörösberény, Almádi, Káptalanfüred* and *Budatava*) which make up the town we can see today.

The paths in Öreg Park are lined with the works of some of Hungary's sculptors. There is Miklós Izsó's Sándor Petőfi, Barnabás Holló's Ferenc Rákóczi II. and Louis Kossuth, and Gábor Mihály's János Váth. Walkers often stop at the "bridge of sighs" linking the Auróra Hotel with the shore, and the eternal flame commemorating the 1848 Revolution.

In the centre of Balatonalmádi stands the town hall, which also contains the "Attic Gallery". You can get to the town by both bus and train. The tunnel takes you from Baross Gábor utca to the biggest and most beautiful bathing area on the northern shore of the lake.

Balatonalmádi is famous for the **Chapel of the Holy Right Hand** (Óvári Ferenc u.) standing next to Saint Emmerich's Church. The fabric of the chapel was transported block by block from Buda Castle some time after 1956. The mosaics are those made by *Miksa Róth* for the original chapel.

The *Red Sandstone Nature Trail* starting in Városháza tér takes you six kilometres, past sites of geological and botanical interest, up to the *Óvár Lookout Point*. The information boards were supplied by the *Balaton Highlands National Park*. *Malom Valley* and *Vödör Valley* are also popular destinations for a day out.

In *Vörösberény*, now considered part of Balatonalmádi, stands the **Calvinist Church**, a medieval structure (1297) with later side aisles and chapels. The surbased spherical vault was added during the 18th century. The defensive wall, with its buttresses and arrow slits, make it the only surviving fortified church in the Balaton Highlands.

The old **Jesuit monastery** (Veszprémi u. 83.), now a hotel, dates from the 18th century. *Xavér Bucher*'s frescos inside the **church**, painted at the end of the 18th century, depict the saints of the Jesuit Order and the church's patrons.

The 60 metre-long 18th century granary belonging to the monastery complex now houses a **wine museum,** offering wine-tasting and purchasing opportunities.

It is the sandy beach which makes BALATONFŰZFŐ popular. When the weather conditions make swimming in Lake Balaton impossible you can always go to the **Balaton Swimming Pool** with its full-size swimming pool, its hot pools and sports grounds. The 13th century **ruins** of *Máma* church (Jókai u. 37.) are used for events like the classical concerts making up part of the *Fűzfő Festival* held around 20th August. The **Partfő** in BALATONKENESE is a loess wall with nine openings once used as cave dwellings. The **village's museum** (Kossuth utca) will be of particular interest to those interested in folk art.

In BALATONAKARATTYA's Rákóczi Park, which is in fact part of Balatonkenese, stands what remains of the **Rákóczi Tree**, an enormous elm which has in fact been dead since 1969. In saying this, it's not entirely sure that Ferenc Rákóczi actually tied his horse to that particular tree...

There are some glorious views over the eastern part of the basin from the **upper shore** at BALATONVILÁGOS. Indeed, it is from here that those arriving from Budapest get their first glimpse of the lake, which is precisely 14km wide at this point. The *Club Aliga* has a cable-ride taking you from a height of 19 metres down to the water's edge at a speed of between 35 and 40 kilometres an hour. Of course only lovers of extreme sports kitted out in suitable equipment should consider having a go on it.

BALATONSZABADI is famous for its peasant architecture and its churches. In the Siómaros part of the village stands the world's first **statue of Louis Kossuth** (1894, *Antal Gerenday*), made just a few months after the great politician's death.

Today we can only guess at the route of the Roman road linking *Tricciana* with *Gorsium (Tác)* and *Aquincum.* However, there are some Roman **ruins** in SÁGVÁR on road 65, just south of Siófok.

SIÓFOK

Imre Varga's statue of Imre Kálmán blends in nicely with the tourists enjoying the shady walks.

It is easy to get to Siófok. The lidos are excellent and there are numerous cultural events going on in the town. During the summer months the population of the town increases five-fold. The beaches, which stretch 17km along the shore, are amongst the longest on Lake Balaton, and the quay is the busiest on the lake. During the long summer months the shady promenades of the **Golden** and **Silver Shores** bustle with activity.

The well-kept parks and walks are dotted with statues and sculptures. The town also has its fair share of buildings designed by *Imre Makovecz,* while it was Siófok-born *Imre Varga* who was responsible for the sculptures you can see in the public spaces. The songs of Siófok-born operetta-composer *Imre Kálmán* often feature in the summer concert programmes.

In the park in front of the quay near the **Balaton Steam Boat Monument** stands the *Meteorological Observatory* where the meteorologists issue their local gale warnings.

It's not just those in boats who should sit up and take notice of the yellow flashing light, because it only takes a few minutes for an incoming storm to make swimming dangerous. If the revolving flashing lights flash at a rate of 30 a minute, that's known as a first-degree warning. A second-degree warning flashes at a rate of 60 a minute, and it is at this point that swimmers should think about leaving the water, and sailors go about taking the necessary measures.

The **Sió Sluice,** which forms part of the marina, was designed to regulate the water-level of the lake. Nowadays low water-levels have rendered the sluice useless, causing it to be shut on a permanent basis. The *Golden Shore* lies immediately to the east.

The Golden Shore, with its leafy walks and villas, really draws the crowds during the course of the Cola-Cola Beach House. The Petőfi and the Beszédes Walks are good places to stroll along all the year round. This is not to say there are no other popular places in the eastern basin of Lake Balaton. There are the upper shores in and around Kenese, and the Balaton Highlands between Balatonfüred and Aszófő.

On the strip of land lying parallel to the shore, you can look at the villas which once belonged to writers such as *Frigyes Karinthy, Mór Jókai* and *Gyula Krúdy. Imre Kálmán* was born in what is now the municipal **museum** (Kálmán Imre sétány 5.). On the same walk you will also find the **Mineral Museum** (no. 10), whose collection of minerals from the Carpathian Basin can be seen in the biggest such exhibition in Hungary. The 45m-high **water tower** (1912) in Szabadság tér is one of the more immediately recognisable buildings on the Siófok skyline.

Most of the wood used for the new Lutheran Church (Imre Makovecz) in the Oulu Park came from Finland. The modern synagogue (Sándor Kovács, 1984–85) was built on the site of its predecessor.

Around the **South Balaton Cultural Centre** (Fő tér 2.) you can enjoy the work of some of Hungary's most respected sculptors. The **parish church** (Fő u. 57.) is also worth visiting on account of its fine paintings and stained glass.

The summer officially starts with the *Whitsun Season-Opening Festival*, with its parade and the *Balaton Girl Competition*.

The Golden Shell International Folklore Festival at the beginning of July gives you the opportunity to become familiar with the cultures of different ethnic groups.

Organ recitals and masterclasses are held at the Roman Catholic church. For sports enthusiasts there is the *International Showjumping Competition* and the *Hungarian Jump Derby.*

FROM RÉV TO LELLE

BALATONSZÉPLAK joins onto Siófok, and once in Zamárdi road signs are telling you that the *Tihany Straits,* the narrowest stretch of the lake, are not far away.

From ZAMÁRDI station there is a marked path up to *Szamárkő.* On *Kő Hill* you can see where ancient sacrifices took place up amongst the isolated rock formations.

The village has quite a few **peasant cottages** (Fő u. 120., 129.), one of the oldest (82.) (1847) has all the features you would expect to find in the Balaton region. Visitors can also visit the lidos, the *Kocsi Csárda* and the **holiday village.** On the *Tóközpuszta,* once the economic centre of Tihany Abbey, there are regular equestrian and folklore programmes.

The most famous attraction in BALATONENDRÉD is the **Kájel Lace House** (Kossuth u. 30.), devoted to the history of lace making.

SZÁNTÓD

It is in this small village that you can catch the only car **ferry** crossing Lake Balaton. Szántód is mentioned as being an important crossing point

in Tihany Abbey's Letter of Foundation of 1055. Andrew I. gave Szántód and its immediate surroundings to Tihany Abbey in whose hands the lands were to remain for many centuries.

Once upon a time small wooden ferries, at the mercy of the elements, linked the two shores of Lake Balaton. At the beginning of the 20th century they were replaced by much larger wooden craft capable of carrying 100 people. The ferrymen used to send smoke signals telling each other how many passengers were on board.

The ferry's first jetty was built in 1803. The ferry inn (1839, Rév u.), next to the row of stalls, has recently been restored. It was here people awaited the arrival of the ferry before crossing to the other side of the lake. A tablet on the wall records that Mihály Csokonai Vitéz, too, waited here.

The site of what is the **Szántódpuszta Tourist and Cultural Centre** belonged to the church lands from the 11th century, with one or two breaks, right up until 1945. The renovation and rebuilding of the centre was deemed so successful that it won a *Europa Nostra Award* in 1995. The building makes all the right references to the history of Hungarian agriculture.

In the one-time **hall** (1716) visitors can see paintings and sculptures, as well as the coach house and the stud. In the **wine cellar,** now returned to its original glory, you can find out how the grapes from nearby *Kő Hill* are processed into wine.

Out on the Szántódpuszta visitors can either go to the two-hundred-year-old inn or the aquarium showing what lurks in Lake Balaton's shallow waters. Alternatively, you can see the traditional Hungarian breeds of sheep and cattle, or visit the memorial room dedicated to the plain's one-time owner Ádám Pálóczi Horváth.

In the imposing **granary** you can find an arts and crafts exhibition. The local history collection is in the **farmhand's house**. On *Chapel Hill* you will find the 350-year-old **St Christopher's Chapel**. From here you get a good view of the northern shores of the lake, stretching from Badacsony to Balatonfüred. You can also go pony-trekking, picnicking or wine-tasting.

BALATONFÖLDVÁR

The town gets its name from the Celtic **earthworks** built there during the Iron Age. The fortress was defended by ramparts to the south and by the raised shores and the lake to the north. You can see the earthworks on top of the high loess banks.

The old plain at Balatonföldvár underwent some substantial changes at the end of the 19th century, when Dénes Széchenyi decided to build baths on his estate. Some of the major figures of the day went on to build summer residences there (Gizi Bajor, Jenő Kwassay, Kálmán Kandó, Jenő Rákosi) and the Széchenyi family themselves owned seven villas.

The town's cultural events take place at the **Gizi Bajor Community Centre** (Kőröshegyi u. 1.). The *Földvár Festival* in the middle of June marks the anniversary of the foundation of the baths. The *Földvár Days* amount to a series of classical concerts. At the *Balaton Folklore Meeting* at the end of July, dance groups from both home and abroad perform their competition programmes. The *Hungarian-Bavarian Festival* in August celebrates a relationship going back one thousand years to when Saint Stephen of Hungary married his Bavarian wife, Gizella.

KŐRÖSHEGY

It is for its Gothic **Roman Catholic church** (József A. u. 1.) (14th–15th century) that Kőröshegy is famous. The church once formed part of a Franciscan monastery, the rest of which gradually fell into a state of total disrepair. Only a few ruins remain.

In keeping with the demands of the Franciscan Order the tower of the church was built next to the chancel rather than over the west end as was more usually the case at the time. Today organ recitals are held in the church.

There are two places in Kőröshegy where you can go riding, either at the Borkút Riding Club above the famous vineyards or the Pannon Equestrian Academy on Marócpuszta, where the Gidrán has been bred for 200 years. The breed can be traced back to Baron Fechtig, the Gypsy Baron made famous by novelist Mór Jókai. The hussars riding these gutsy and hardy buckskin horses earned a reputation which spread the length and breadth of Europe.

When Hungarians hear the name BALATONSZÁRSZÓ they think of the tragic death on 3rd December, 1937, of one of their finest poets, *Attila József.* There is a **museum** dedicated to him at the house where he lived (József A. u. 7.), tracing the most important events in the writer's short life. The gravestone (*Gyula Csóka,* 1981) is simply that, as Attila József's ashes were taken to Budapest for burial.

Opposite Balatonszárszó Station in Tópart Park stands a monument put up in memory of Attila József (Tamás Ortutay, 1998).

BALATONSZEMES

Bagolyvár was built on the site of the old Turkish fortress in 1900, in a style meant to take you back to the age of chivalry (Bagolyvár u. 16.). The tower and spiral staircase contribute to an architectural ensemble which amounts to what is a pretty brave attempt at medieval romance.

The *Post and Telecommunications Museum Foundation*'s **Postal Museum** is situated in the Baroque stables of the old post office (Bajcsy-Zsilinszky u. 46.). On arriving at the entrance to the museum you can see an impressive collection of horse-drawn post coaches and post vans. Once you are inside you can see for yourself how letters get to their destination.

The Baroque **Hunyady Palace** (Gárdonyi utca 1.) was once the economic centre of the local estate. The house, although now a school, has, thanks to its classical verandah lost nothing of its grandeur. The same is true of the nearby granary.

The great Hungarian actor Zoltán Latinovits is buried in Balatonszemes cemetery.
The exhibition entitled "Truth and Opportunity" in the local council buildings is dedicated to his life and work (Bajcsy-Zsilinszky E. u. 23.).

The graphic artist *Károly Reich* was born in the village, and there is a **museum** dedicated to his life and work at his birthplace (Zrínyi utca 17.).

All that remains of *Rádpuszta* parish church (13th century), now part of Balatonszemes, are the 8-10metre-high sandstone walls, the consoles once carrying the vaults and the buttresses.

Those who are in the village in June will be able to make the most of the *Szemes Festival,* which includes art exhibitions at the *Latinovits Cultural Centre,* classical concerts at the Roman Catholic church and a *windsurfing competition* down on the lake.

BALATONLELLE

The giant water slide makes the two-kilometre-long lido at Balatonlelle all the more popular.

Szent István tér and the boulevard leading off it have a certain Mediterranean feel to them. A modern **Roman Catholic church** built from red sandstone was built on the site of an 11th century basilica. Recitals are given on the organ which has three consoles and 29 registers.

Kis Hill is just an hour's walk from the centre of town. Amongst the vineyards stands the Baroque Saint Donatius Chapel (1758) with the vine-dresser's house and cellar opposite.
Despite the 136 hectares of woodland around the chapel, the views are superb. The best times to walk up there are either during Wine Week, between 2nd and 8th August, or on 1st May, for the Kis Hill May Day Celebrations.

It was on the mound opposite the Catholic church that the Jankovich family built their Baroque **residence** (1712). It is now used as a school.

The Szalay family's classical **residence** (1838) in the centre of the town is now used as a cultural centre. Out in the park there is an **open-air theatre** capable of holding 1,200 people. It's used for pop concerts during the summer.

The **Kapoli Museum** (Kossuth u. 35.) is housed in a peasant cottage built towards the end of the 18th century. It puts on temporary art exhibitions and has carvings and reliefs by both *Antal Kapoli* the Elder and Antal Kapoli the Younger.

The new leisure **bathing complex** (2003) offers heated pools from the spring through to the summer, with the steam baths staying open through the winter months as well (Napsugár u.).

To the southeast of Balatonlelle you come to *Irma-puszta's 12 fish ponds*, which are rich in bird life.

There are one or two days in the year when the off-roads call in on Somogybabod *for a spot of fun and games.*

At what was once known as Bosnyák Hall in Somogytúr is a **museum** dedicated to the plein-air paintings of *Lajos Kunffy* (Árpád u. 22.).

THE SOUTH BALATON WINE REGION

BALATONBOGLÁR

Situated half way along the southern shores of
Lake Balaton, the town can easily be reached by
car, train or boat. It is fortunate to have shores
stretching to both the east and the west, indeed
Balatonboglár itself extends as far as both Fonyód
and Lelle.

It is perhaps best to start our tour at the **quayside.**
The boats leaving from here sail to most of
Balaton's other quays on a regular basis. The pier
provides shelter for the yachts at anchor.

*The spherical lookout tower has become
one of Balatonboglár's landmarks.*

*It is the Cross-Balaton Swim which attracts the most tourists
into the town. Participants leave from Révfülöp opposite
and arrive at the Platán Lido in Balatonboglár.*

Vörösmarty tér, in the centre of the town, contains an **ornamental fountain** and *József Müller's*
sculpture of the *Woman Stepping into the Water.*
The local history collection and the arts and crafts
exhibition can be seen in **Fischl House** (Erzsébet
u. 12–14.). The **parish church** was the first
church in Hungary to be built of reinforced concrete (*Iván Kotsis,* 1932).

Boglár's two hills, like the volcanic geological features on the other side of the lake, are made of
basalt tufa and sand. From the **lookout tower**
named after *János Xantus,* on *Castle Hill,* you get
some good views looking north.

On one of the lower hills, known as Cemetery or
Chapel Hill, stand the famous chapels the **Red
Chapel** and the **Blue Chapel**. Their names require
no explanation.

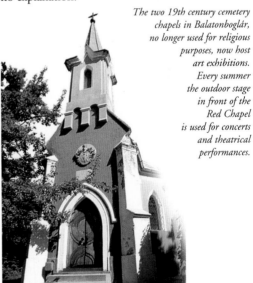

*The two 19th century cemetery
chapels in Balatonboglár,
no longer used for religious
purposes, now host
art exhibitions.
Every summer
the outdoor stage
in front of the
Red Chapel
is used for concerts
and theatrical
performances.*

Balatonboglár, the *International Grape and Wine Town,* is the centre of the *Southern Balaton Wine Region.* The *Wine Road Association* was founded to encourage further interest in the local wines.

The summer season starts at Whitsun with the first in a long series of events. The open-air **stage** in front of the Red Chapel and the **Platán Lido** take turns in hosting the programmes which go on throughout the summer. The *Boglár Grape Harvest Festival* is held on the promenade around 20th August, the holiday season finally winding down during the second weekend in September.

In the neighbouring village of SZŐLŐSKISLAK you will find the **Wine Museum** in Gaál Palace and the famous **Légli Potter's House** (Epres u. 7.), where visitors can not only see the produce but have a go at throwing a pot themselves.

FONYÓD

The two volcanic hills lying next to Lake Balaton, *Castle Hill* (232m) and *Sípos Hill* (107m), take the same form as the hills lying on the opposite side of the lake, the only difference being that here the hills are made of basalt tufa. The southern and western slopes of the hills are surrounded by the low-lying *Nagy-berek.* It was on the lower slopes of Sípos Hill overlooking the lake that the town's churches were built. The walk from the railway station up to the **Berzsenyi Lookout Point** is about four kilometres long and well worth the effort, as the views of the Balaton Highlands from the top are spectacular.

In the days when the water-level of Lake Balaton was higher, that is to say right up until the beginning of the 20th century, Fonyód rose island-like from the watery landscape of the Nagy-berek. It was in 1895 that the villas started to appear on Béla Zichy's estate, a site now known as Bélatelep.

The post office's vocational secondary school (*Imre Makovecz,* Hunyadi J u. 3.) in the middle of the town hosts the Fonyód Helikon readings and other cultural events. During the summer months the main square hosts street theatre, concerts, and arts and crafts fairs.

Down by the lake *István Kiss's Couple,* an aluminium sculpture made in 1960, has become one of Fonyód's most immediately recognisable landmarks. It's a good place to enjoy the distant views and the spectacle of the longest **jetty** (464metres) on Lake Balaton. Every summer an open-air stage is put up by the quay for visitors to enjoy the programmes going on at the *Fonyód Summer Festival.*

Those visiting the so-called Crypt Villa will witness a peculiar and rather disturbing labour of love: a house built during the 1930's by the rather eccentric Ödön Abrudabányai Rédiger for his childhood sweetheart, Magdus. Even today lovers won't fail to be moved by the carved bridal suit, complete with the two reclining life-size marble figures, fashioned by the great romantic himself, covered by a veil of artificial stone (József u. 16.)

Fonyód's most famous historical site is the remains of the Alsóvár Stockade, next to the road leading out towards Kaposvár (Szent István utca 119.). What remains has been excavated and reconstructed. The Százéves Cellar restaurant near the fortress contains a famous 22 metre-long cellar.

The *Mini Gallery* (Szabó Ferenc u. 3.) is open all the year round, whereas the *Summer Gallery* (Fürdő u. 3.) isn't.

The *Castle Tournament* takes place at the castle ruins on the anniversary of the fall of Fonyód Castle (August 3rd). The knights and the archers, dressed up in medieval costumes, put on a quite a spectacle. The *harvest parade* takes place on *Saint Stephen's Day* (August 20th). One of the key moments in the day's proceedings is the blessing and breaking of the new bread.

OUTER-SOMOGY, NAGY-BEREK

LENGYELTÓTI is a friendly little town best known for the **Blue Lake Holiday Village** on the road leading out to Hács. The waters of the small romantic **lake** come from natural springs, and a real tourist centre has developed around the hotel up on the hillside. The late 19th century **Catholic church** on Church Hill was built onto the existing 12th century chapel, the medieval chapel becoming the chancel of the new church. The **Stations of the Cross** line the pathway up to the church.

BUZSÁK

Although most impressive during the summer months, the most popular village at the Balaton end of Somogy County is worth visiting all the year round. During the summer you can see the ladies by the roadside hard at work on their table-cloths, bedspreads and pillows. Even the vestments and the altar frontal in the Baroque church are covered in traditional *Buzsák embroidery*. The locals are also in the habit of dressing up the *statue of the Virgin Mary* on the high altar, something they also do in the village of Andócs.

The village hall in the centre of the village, with its folk art exhibition, was designed by an architect of the *Makovecz School*. Those who are interested in the history of the village and local agriculture should pay a visit to the **peasant's cottage** (Fő u. 8.) which is fitted out with traditional furnishings. In the rooms looking onto the yard there are displays devoted especially to the local embroidery and folk costumes.

Buzsák is indeed a lively village especially when the local ethnic Hungarian and German populations celebrate Whitsun together.

At the Buzsák Patronal Festival in August it is folk art which takes centre stage. In September all eyes turn to the grape harvest.

Whilst there are those staying in Buzsák who find themselves going to the **Csisztapuszta thermal baths** there are others who come in from Balaton-fenyves on the **narrow-gauge railway**. All can testify to the medicinal qualities of the waters at the small two-pool complex.

Although the Benedictine Monastery at Somogyvár was destroyed during the Turkish occupation archaeological excavations have uncovered what was a large monastic complex. A few of the columns from the cloisters still survive as does a full-length figure of Saint Ladislas, the king who founded the abbey. The monastic ruins form the backdrop for the Saint Ladislas Day celebrations.

SOMOGYVÁR

The ruins of the Benedictine Abbey standing on Kupavár Hill overlooking the marshes of the *Nagy-berek* provide one of Hungary's **Historical Memorial Sites**. It was here that chieftain Kopány settled, and where Ladislas I. built his **basilica** dedicated to *Saint Giles* in 1091. Benedictine monks from the monastery's mother convent in St. Gilles in the south of France were the first to inhabit the new **monastic buildings**. Saint Ladislas decided he wanted to be buried at his foundation, and his wish came true in 1095. It was only after the death of King Koloman that his ashes were taken to Nagyvárad (Oradea, Romania). Outer Somogy offers some great alternatives to those staying in the southwestern basin of Lake Balaton.

In 1912, part of Fonyód's shoreline was planted with fir trees. Now known as BALATONFENYVES, bathers will find five lidos within the space of 6km – the Lower Fenyves Lido having benefitted from a recent renovation (2003). It is from here that the **narrow-gauge railway** (Kölcsey u. 9.) heads in the direction of the *Nagy-berek,* the longest and most popular stretch of line going to CSISZTA-PUSZTA. *Railway Day* is held during the first weekend in September, and the week after that sees the *Fenyves Cup* sailing regatta. It was in Balatonfenyves that the only covered **equestrian arena** on the shores of Lake Balaton capable of hosting international equestrian events was built. Pony trekking and riding in a coach and horse out into the Nagy-berek are popular with visitors.

It was in BALATONKERESZTÚR that the Festetics family built the **Church of the Holy Cross**. This Roman Catholic church contains a carved Baroque-rococo pulpit and a magnificent altar. The paintings on the side walls are by followers of either *István Dorfmaister* or *Anton Maulbertsch*.

It was in 1731 that *Mátyás Bél* was guest at the Baroque **palace** built by Kristóf Festetics in about 1720. It was here that he put pen to paper describing his journeys around Somogy County. On the wall there is portrait of Mátyás Bél made at the Zsolnay Ceramic Works in Pécs.

Exploring Inner Somogy

Marcali

Marcali can easily be reached from Lake Balaton by taking the Balatonkeresztúr road.

Széchenyi Palace (Széchenyi u. 17/21), originally Baroque, was rebuilt in an eclectic style in 1912. Although now a hospital, the statues of *Ágoston Tóth*, the founder of Hungarian military cartography, and *István Széchenyi* remain.

The **Roman Catholic church** (Hősök tere) has both Baroque and classical details. The **Local History Museum** (Múzeum köz 5.), situated in the old county prison, contains folk art, arts and crafts and a geological displays. The museum also puts on temporary exhibitions.

The **Bernáth Gallery** (Kossuth u. 25.) was founded in honour of Marcali-born artist *Aurél Bernáth* (1895–1982). Apart from showing works by Bernáth himself there are also temporary exhibitions. Those climbing Nagy Hill will come across *Dániel Berzsenyi* **obelisk,** where the great poet, the so-called Nikla Hermit, had his vineyard.

Those staying in the town can take advantage if the **Thermal and Leisure Centre** (2003), with its 1500m² of water and its sports facilities.

Nikla

You can find the Dániel Berzsenyi Memorial Museum (Berzsenyi u. 96.) in his old residence (1811). The house is filled with personal belongings, selections of his writings and correspondence as well as some of his folk musical instruments.

Dániel Berzsenyi, moved to Nikla in 1804, in order to add his Somogy inheritance to the lands belonging to his wife. The move wasn't an unqualified success and he was forever wanting to return to his native Kemenesalja. His **obelisk** in the graveyard can be seen for miles around.

The *Fehér-víz Marsh,* a reminder of the boggy terrain which used to dominate the landscape, can most easily be approached from Táska. Tourists, however, tend to head for the gentle slopes of *Öreg Hill* and the *Baráczai Vineyards.* Amongst the neat rows of vines you can see the old **winepress buildings**. Their owners are only too happy to thrust a glass of wine into the hands of those who have come up from the railway station by coach and horse.

Even tourists staying at Lake Balaton, are discovering Táska, down on the edge of the Nagy-berek.
Most make their way on the wobbly narrow-gauge railway, which makes its way through the Nagy-berek from Balatonfenyves.

Eastern Kis-Balaton

The even gradient of the shore and the sandy beaches make Balatonberény one of the most popular bathing resorts on Lake Balaton. Its **naturist lido and camping site** (Balaton u. 12.) was the first of its kind on the lake. Further west the reeds and the willows make the shore unsuitable for swimming.

The village, overlooking the lake, has managed to retain its peaceful and friendly atmosphere.

At the **Catholic church** (13th–15th century) (Kossuth u. 102.) it is still possible to see four Gothic windows and the archivolt of the pointed doorway on the southern side of the church. You can find the local history museum at the **Múltház** in the street where the church is situated.

BALATONSZENTGYÖRGY

Although the village is no longer on the shores of Lake Balaton its past, and indeed its present, have close ties with the lake. During the Roman period it was from here that people crossed both the waters of the Kis-Balaton and the River Zala when heading towards Fenékpuszta.

László Festetics not only built the embankment going towards Fenékpuszta and the **bridge** over the River Zala, he also built the hunting lodge, the **Csillagvár** (1820–1823), which resembles some star-shaped fortification. László Festetics was kind enough to build an interesting, safe and indeed comfortable house for his head forester. As you can see today, the walls are thick, the windows are small, just like the kind of fortress people refer to it as. Those living in the house didn't even have to go out for water as there was a well 31 metres deep on site. In 1959, the hunting lodge was furnished in the style of a 17th century farm (Irtási-dűlő).

Nearby there is a **peasant cottage** (Csillagvár u. 68.) bearing all the characteristic features of the local folk architecture.

> *The house was built using massive oak beams. Stakes were driven in between the beams and it was around these that the wattle was woven. The daub was mixed before being rubbed into the walls. Once the walls had been plastered repeatedly and allowed to dry the outer walls were limewashed.*

VÖRS

At Advent each year Hungary's largest **crib scene,** covering an area of 50m^2 is put up in the local Catholic church (1820). At the end of the village known as *Alszeg,* there is a *house on stilts* (Dózsa Gy. u. 17.) once occupied by the poorest of the agricultural labourers. Today it's filled with a collection of traditional Kis-Balaton fishing tackle and other relevant household objects.

The Vörs Fire Brigade Museum (Flórián tér 1.) is full of the equipment once used by the local fire fighters during the 19th and 20th centuries.

The *Kis-Balaton* is a paradise for bird watchers. There are mud tracks out of the village taking you to the **hides** from where you can spot the birds with binoculars. It's possible to get to the water-filled parts of the Kis-Balaton from the west just above Zalavár.

The areas of Kis-Balaton known as "The Land of the Rising Waters" on the western edge of Lake Balaton and the Marcali Ridge is quiet and peaceful, in fact ideal for a spot of relaxation. Those interested in exploring the local flora and fauna should head for the Búbosvöcsök Nature Trail on Kányavári Island.

With this aerial view of the Badacsony we take a final look at Lake Balaton.

"The hills' golden earth curves,
the countless undulations embraced by trees,
the rippled surfaces of plough-furrowed sea,
to the tired eye swells of tranquillity."

(Gyula Takáts: Where I was Born)

Contents – Southern Transdanubia

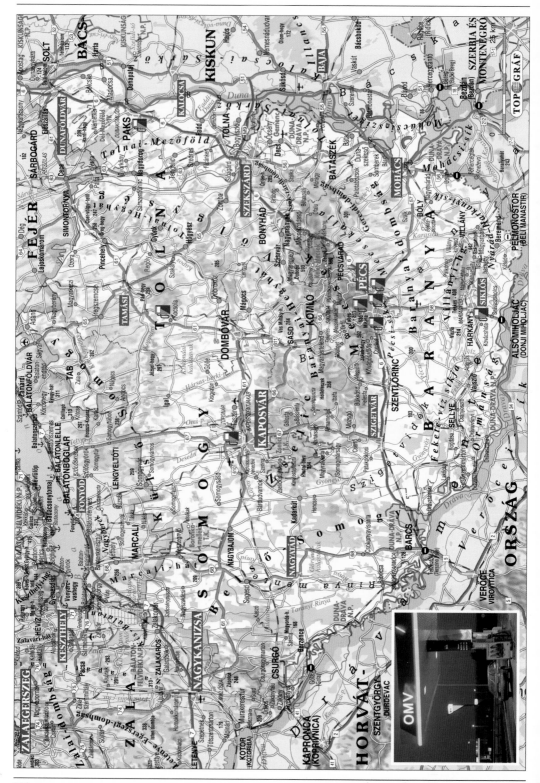

SOUTHERN TRANSDANUBIA

Spreading from *Lake Ba-laton* to the *River Drava*, from the *Danube* to the *Zalaapát Ridge*, Southern Transdanubia can be as flat as the Great Plain, but there are also undulating landscapes with hills quite capable of making walkers short of breath. However, it is the *"hills with a thousand valleys"*, Inner Somogy, stretching north-south from Lake Balaton down to the River Drava, which takes up most of the region. The region's geographical features were formed for the most part by the thick layers of deposit left by the Danube and its tributaries as they carved their way through the landscape. Once the rivers had established themselves the hills of Inner Somogy were left to dry out. The strong Pleistocene winds then whipped up the fine sands into the air and deposited them onto the characteristic sand beds you can see today. The shifting sands stopped moving with the arrival of one of the rainier periods in the earth's history, and in the course of time the sand-hills were gradually worn down and substantially reduced in height.

Today one sees an undulating landscape with wide-open valleys and marshy lowlands created by the rainfall which fell in the region's less distant past. A typical example of these lower-lying areas is *Lake Baláta* near Kaszó. In what is an environment with vastly fluctuating water levels you can find many common marsh and bog plants, some rare like the pitcher plant and the yellow-flowered bladderwort.

Driving across the loess hills of *Outer Somogy* can feel a bit like riding a roller coaster, one moment you're up on the crest of a hill, the next moment you're down in a valley next to a bubbling stream. In most of the valleys dams have been put up, creating reservoirs and fishing lakes much to the delight of the local anglers.

In the western part of the region the hills point northwards to the shores of Lake Balaton. Indeed, geologists have discovered that the ridge of hills continues along the bed of the lake where they are now covered by thick layers of mud. The eastern part of the region is more varied, something best appreciated when driving south from Szántód down towards the *Kapos Valley*. Going towards the eastern part of Outer Somogy you drop down into the *Sió Valley*, where the landscape is more or less flat.

There are a lot of lovely small villages in Outer Somogy, some of them unfortunately becoming depopulated, others slowly coming back to life after a period of slumber, which is especially the case with the villages lying closer to Lake Balaton. Being only a matter of kilometres from the lake and linked by empty country lanes, guesthouses and holiday homes are springing up left, right and centre. Following the recent discovery of spring waters some charming thermal baths have opened in Nagyberény. The combination of the thermal waters and the local countryside has also drawn visitors to the thermal pool at Igal.

The *Kapos Valley* was created from the energies unleashed from deep under the Earth's surface.

The Saint Ladislas Bridge, Szekszárd (2003)

The valley and its river, formed during the course of the Ice Ages, have created a natural border between the countryside lying to the north and that lying to the south. To the south of the Kapos the hilly landscape is made up of steep hillsides and narrow valleys.

The *Zselic* is a romantic landscape, and one fortunate enough still to have a good many of the woods which were once haunted by local highwaymen. The smaller hills are covered with beautiful woods full of beeches, hornbeams and oaks. The villages hidden away deep in the valleys are particularly interesting. The tomb of Pali the Highwayman on the edge of *Vitorág Wood* is always covered in fresh flowers, and there is scarcely a Hungarian who has not heard the story of the priest of Ibafa's pipe or the tales of Miklós Zrínyi's heroic deeds in fighting the Turks at Szigetvár. The Zselic is one of the most popular walking areas in Southern Transdanubia.

Moving east and southeast of Zselic you come to the *Völgység* and the *Tolna Ridge*. There are indeed a lot of valleys in the Völgység, and a lot of the small villages in these valleys have managed to preserve a great deal of their character as well as their ancient monuments. The western and northern edges of the region fall steeply towards the Kapos, the old woodlands having been replaced by vineyards in many places. The thickness of the loess here means that landslides are not unknown during periods of heavy rainfall. The soft yet stable local soil has often been dug into for various purposes. The smaller tunnels are used for cellars or pits of various descriptions, the larger ones for dwellings or as somewhere to keep the animals. In Petőfi's day it was the oxen pulling their carts that plied their way along the tracks in these parts. These lanes remain uncharted backwaters even today.

The steep loess-covered slopes of the *Szekszárd Hills* south of the Sió have proved excellent for the grape-growers and the winemakers. Szekszárd Kadarka is well-known way beyond the borders of Hungary. The footpaths in *Sötét Valley* and around Szálka, not far from the county town of Szekszárd, are popular with walkers.

The highest area in Southern Transdanubia is the *Mecsek*. Its complicated geological history means that there is much for the geologist to enjoy. Granite and other ancient crystalline rock formations come up to earth's the surface near Geresd and Mórágy. Because the rock core here is particularly solid the height of geographical features are measured in relation to it.

Whilst the *Baranya Ridge* rises almost imperceptibly from the north of the main mass of the Mecsek, there is a sudden drop down to the *Pécs Plain* on the other side. The ridge is made of limestone for the most part, although there are traces of rock formations on the surface which are much older.

Above Kővágószőlős in the *Western Mecsek* you will find some curious Permian red sandstone formations. The stone is made up of large pebbles and worn rock fragments embedded in the finer sandstone. On *Jakab Hill* the wind and the ice have carved some particularly interesting forms, know locally as "baby terns". It was here, underneath the ragged sandstone, that Hungary's only uranium mine operated. The local coal-mining industry is also slowly running its course.

Of the limestone caves the largest is the *Abaliget Cave* in the northwestern part of the Mecsek where you are free to study the way the subterranean stream and the waters seeping into the cave have worked the stone. There are also some interesting stalactites down in the caves and karst formations up on the surface.

The highest point of the *Eastern Mecsek*, the area with the most varied landscape, is *Zengő* (682m). The most beautiful parts of the hills, with their beech woods, oaks and hornbeams, make up the *East Mecsek Nature Reserve*, an area where you can find some extremely rare plants (monkey orchids, Italian asperula and leopard's bane). Indeed, there are tracts of land whose vegetation is distinctly Mediterranean.

The thermal baths at Sikonda play an important role in the Mecsek's tourist industry.

Moving south of the Mecsek beyond the less substantial *Baranya Hills* you see the *Villány Hills* rising dramatically before you. The hills are made of Triassic and cretaceous limestone and dolomite. If it's medicinal waters you want you should head for Harkány. At the highest point in the Villány, the

One of the Mecsek's picturesque lookout points: the Zsongorkő on Jakab Hill.

442-metre-high *Szársomlyó,* you can either taste the wines found elsewhere on the *Siklós–Villányi Wine Road* or inspect the most beautiful karrenfeld in Hungary on the southern slopes of the hill.

The steep southern slopes of Szársomlyó also have a Mediterranean flavour. It is the only place in Hungary you are likely to find the Hungarian crocus and the cynanchum. As for insects and reptiles you might find a saw-legged grasshopper, a harvest bug or a grass snake.

The plains immediately next to the *Drava*, on the banks of the *Danube* (*Mohács Island, Sárköz*) and on the *Mezőföld*, which formally belongs to the Great Hungarian Plain, are all susceptible to flooding. Seen from a geological perspective these are relatively recent landscapes, indeed they continue to shift and move around even today.

The *Danube-Drava National Park* was founded to protect the natural flood plain environment lying between the two rivers. Today, efforts are being made to make the area more accessible to visitors. (For more information about their activities see the relevant section in the *Hungarian Treasury*.)

During the Ice Age the streams brought loess deposits down from the Transdanubian Hills onto the *Mezőföld*. You can get a good idea as to

Sweet chestnuts flowering on the hills of Southern Transdanubia

the thickness of the loess at Dunaföldvár, where the bank drops steeply from the Mezőföld down onto the bed of the River Danube.

The climate of the Mezőföld, although not as wet as the *western fringes of Transdanubia*, is considerably wetter than the *Great Plain*. However, it doesn't have to endure the Great Plain's extreme temperatures. It is also in this part of Hungary that you can best feel the Mediterranean's influence on the climate. Moving southwards from Lake Balaton down towards the River Drava the winters become much milder, and the springs arrive much earlier. The southern climate is best felt on the southern slopes of the hills, in the Mecsek and the Villány Hills in particular.

In prehistoric times settlements tended to be built on the small hills overlooking the waters. The peoples of the Iron Age organised in larger social groups managed to organise their economic life from sturdy fortresses built on elevated pieces of land, many of which have been excavated over the last century or so (*Mór Wosinszky* focused his research on the *Lengyel Culture*, and *János Dombay* on the area around Zengővárkony).

Whilst it was the people of the Hallstatt Culture who built the most significant fortress in the region on the top of *Jakab Hill* in the Western Mecsek, it was the Romans who brought urban civilisation. The number of Roman settlements in Southern Transdanubia deriving their names from those of their Celtic predecessors suggests that the Roman Conquest of the area may indeed have been peaceful.

The urban settlements either grew up along the main trade routes or from the main military stations (Dunaszekcső – *Lugio*, Szekszárd – *Alisca*) making up the Roman "limes". By the end of the 3rd century it was Pécs's predecessor, *Sopianae,* which became the administrative centre of the province known as *Valeria.* The cemetery in Pécs dating from one or two centuries later is now a *World Heritage Site.* Thanks to the survival of some of the old Roman milestones and a contemporary "travel guide" *(Itinerarium Antonini)* we know the Roman names of many of the settlements. The artifacts which have been excavated and the local Roman villas (Nagyharsány, Kővágószőlős) suggest it was a period of flourishing business and trade.

Southern Transdanubia played a particularly important role in Hungarian history during the course of the Hungarian Conquest and in the centuries that followed. It was through this countryside that the peripatetic princely households would move from Óbuda in the north to the Mecsek in the south. Saint Stephen created the diocese of Pécs in 1009, partly so that it could enjoy the ideological neutrality which came from being part of a "Somogyország" (Somogyland), and partly as Pécs was a useful centre from which to convert the peoples living beyond the Drava and east of the Danube.

During the Middle Ages the important pilgrimage route linking Byzantium and Regensburg ran through Southern Transdanubia. The region is also linked with the first ever piece of Hungarian literature: the legend Mór, the second bishop of Pécs, wrote about the hermits Saint Benedict and Saint Andrew. During the course of the 11th century two kings were buried in the region, Orseolo in Pécs, and Béla I. in Szekszárd, both places becoming important ecclesiastical centres. Indeed, the region is rich in both Romanesque stone carving and Romanesque parish churches (Szenyér, Mánfa, Mecseknádasd, Cserkút).

It was towards the end of the Árpád period that the smaller feudal centres started to appear, and with the arrival of the Turkish threat in the 15th century Hungary's more dignified families went about building fortified palaces in a Gothic-Renaissance style. Filippo Scolari built the castles in Simontornya and Ozora, and the Garai family Siklós Castle.

In 1367, during the reign of Louis the Great, a decree passed by Pope Urban V. allowed the University of Pécs to open its doors. Founded shortly after the great universities in Prague, Vienna and Kraków, it was the first university in Central Europe not to be established in a royal seat.

Janus Pannonius, Bishop of Pécs, the first Hungarian poet to enjoy an international reputation, worked as a diplomat for Matthias Corvinus during the second half of the 15th century. The burgeoning Renaissance and humanist culture existing in the ecclesiastical and aristocratic centres was utterly destroyed during the course of the Turkish Conquest. However this was not before the Reformation had taken hold in Hungary, thanks to efforts of the likes of *Mihály Sztárai*, *Máté Skaricza* and *György Válaszúti*.

Sebestyén Tinódi Lantos may well have sung his lines *"I now sing a lament to Hungary: // To Mohács its soil drenched in blood;"* in the court of Bálint Török in Szigetvár. Szigetvár, the most important military fortress during the course of the Turkish Conquest, witnessed many heroic deeds in the middle of the 16th century, the most famous being Miklós Zrinyi's stand off with Suleiman the Magnificent in 1566. Indeed, the Ottoman architecture you can see in Baranya County is the finest in Hungary (Pécs, Siklós, Szigetvár).

The most important changes to take place in the 18th century were those affecting the ethnic mix of the population. It was in 1690, that about 40 thousand Serb families from the Balkan Peninsular moved into an area which had become completely depopulated. The Serbs created whole colonies along the banks of the Danube, building their own Greek Orthodox churches (Mohács, Grábóc, Dunaföldvár) in the process.

The Habsburgs encouraged several waves of German settlers to make their way down the Danube, creating what was known as the *Schwäbische Türkei* (Swabian Turkey) in the eastern half of the region in the process. The pure Hungarian population

lations were restricted to small pockets living in the *Sárköz*, the *Ormánság* and the more obscure corners of *Somogy County*.

Elsewhere, a new aristocratic class emerged, also with the blessing of the Habsburgs, when new landowners with no previous local ties were invited into the region. Both the Hungarian aristocratic families who were loyal to the Emperor (Esterházy, Batthyány, Pálffy) and the international aristocrats (Draskovich, Festetics, Caprara) went about building the substantial baroque, and later classical, country houses which can still be seen today (Bóly, Bükkösd, Lengyel, Sellye).

Quite a number of smaller country residences have also survived (Nikla, Zala, Tengelic, Hencse) some of which now play an active role in the local tourist industry.

It is however the Baroque parish churches which dominate the skylines of many of the villages in the region. The local pilgrimage places bear witness to the religious zeal of the Counter-Reformation (Andocs, Máriagyűd).

The old medieval counties continued to be governed from the feudal centres, although it was the more urbanised centres which were to become county seats (Kaposvár, Pécs, Szekszárd). The turn of the 18th and 19th centuries saw the appearance of various educational institutions founded as part of ecclesiastical, aristocratic and other local initiatives. These not only provided education in the fields of law and theology, but in the most up-to-date agricultural practices as well (Csurgó, Pécs, Kaposvár).

Whilst using his stay in Somogy as an opportunity to lambast the locals' lack of education *Mihály Csokonai Vitéz* (1773–1805) was much taken by the cheerful and civilised company *"in this noble county which always revives memories of idyllic rapture."*

It was on his estate in Nikla that the "Diogenes of Somogy County", *Dániel Berzsenyi* (1776–1836), was able to entertain thoughts of European significance.

It was following the Compromise of 1867 that industry was to have its greatest effect on the Mecsek, for it was the Mecsek coal mines which were to provide the miners of Pécs with work. Other reputable companies were also to come into

SOUTH TRANSDANUBIAN SPECIALITIES

The hills and the woods of South Transdanubia have earned a reputation for game, vegetables and processed meats. As for the fruits deserving the title of local speciality there is the *Iharosberény chestnut*, the *Pécs peach* and *Pécs fragrant grapes*. Turning to the meats there is *cabbage sausage*, the local *salami* and *thick Stifolder sausage*. *Wild boar, venison, wild goose* and *snails* all add a bit of variety to the local menus. *Hungarian beef, Bonyhád game* and *yellow Hungarian turkey* are also considered South Transdanubian specialities, as are dairy products such as *Szekszárd cheese*, and *cheese with caraway seeds*.

Mecsek Itóka is the local liqueur, and for those with a sweet tooth there is *lime tree honey, Zengővárkony sweet chestnut honey* and *wild garlic honey*. *Elderflower jam* can hold its own against other jams made from more conventional ingredients. *Mushrooms* are associated particularly with the area around Szekszárd. Bogyiszló is famous for its peppers, Mohács for its *cabbages* and *sweet peas*, and the *early Somogy potatoes* are also particularly sought after.

existence at this time (the *Angster Organ Factory*, the *Littke Champagne Works*, and the *Zsolnay Ceramic Works*).

Many local artists managed to capture the atmosphere of the region: *Mihály Zichy* (1827–1906), one of Hungary's great draughtsmen, *Béla Iványi-Grünwald* (1867–1940), a founding member of the Nagybánya (Baie Mare, Romania) Art Colony, and *Sándor Galimberti* (1883–1915) one of the first Hungarian practitioners of Cubism. It was in Kaposvár that *János Vaszary* (1867–1939) was born, as was *József Rippl-Rónai* (1961–1927), whose villa on Rózsa Hill has become something of a pilgrimage place. *Ferenc Martyn*, the non-figurative artist, also came from Kaposvár.

Apart from the theatre companies in the county seats there are other groups active in the region (the *Pécs Ballet*, the *Bóbita Puppet Theatre*, the *Croatian Theatre*, and the *Deutsche Bühne*).

There are plenty of craftsmen (carpenters, potters, dyers, weavers, etc.) still practising their crafts according to the traditions of their particular ethnic group, and keen folk groups only too happy to perform for visitors (Decs, Nagynyárád, Zengővárkony). The feelings locals have towards their place of birth is well expressed in the lines of Szekszárd-born poet Mihály Babits.

'Italia...your skies are no bluer,
your hills no greener,
than the hills we have here
and the Transdanubian sky,
the playful blue tones of a gentle rolling countryside.
(Mihály Babits: Italia)

We will start by exploring the western extremes of the region, before heading towards Kaposvár. From there we travel southwards to the *Zselic* region, and on to the *Ormánság* where we will go to the *Harkány* area, and then on to the *Villány wine region* before continuing right down to *the banks of the River Danube*. Having looked at the Mecsek we will explore the Tolna and the Szekszárd Hills, which is where we end our tour of Southern Transdanubia before crossing the Danube and embarking on our exploration of the *Great Hungarian Plain*.

Nagyatád

Nagyatád is the economic and cultural centre of the central part of *Inner Somogy,* and one of the few towns in Southern Transdanubia situated down on the plain. The avenue of horse chestnuts in Dózsa György utca leads you to the centre of the town and to the park (Széchenyi tér) where it is the oaks, the birches and the mulberries that catch the eye.

The oldest buildings in the town are the Baroque **Franciscan monastery** (1740) and the **church,** which was subsequently enlarged using distinctively classical elements. The **Municipal Museum** (Széchenyi tér 2.), with its exhibition devoted to the development of the town, stands nearby in a town house built at the beginning of the 20th century.

The **Solar Hotel**, built especially for those using the **Thermal Medicinal Bath** and the **Outdoor Swimming Complex** (Széchenyi tér 11.), has certainly had a positive effect on the appearance of the town. The **Municipal Thermal Swimming Complex,** with its up-to-date pools and beautiful parkland, also awaits guests (Zrínyi M. u. 4.).

The protected area around **Mádl Palace,** next to the boating lake, is covered with oaks and evergreens.

In the International Wood Sculpture Park (Göröndi út) you will find 64 monumental sculptures made by sculptors who have been active in Nagyatád since 1975. 24 other works occupy the public spaces around the town.

The Boronka Region

SEGESD was once the queen's county seat, on account of the fact that Andrew II. (1205–1235) gave the lands immediately to the south of the royal estates centring on Somogyvár to his wife. The place also became an ecclesiastical centre. It was here that Somogy County's first Baroque **Franciscan monastery and church** (Iskola u.) was built. The Széchenyi family's romantic-style palace is currently an old people's home. The park surrounding the palace is the village's great attraction.

Nagybajom

The village is bordered by the *Boronka Nature Reserve* to the north, a watery terrain popular with the local storks. The locals treat these ungainly creatures with great respect. Indeed, the village itself is often referred to as the stork village on account of its 35-40 stork nests.

Dániel Berzsenyi and Mihály Csokonai Vitéz were known to visit the educated, literature-loving landowner István Sárközy (1759–1845). It is in his one-time residence that you can now find the István Sárközy Local History Museum (Fő u. 40.). Particularly impressive are the Biedermeier drawing room and the Empire-style bedroom furniture.

Mesztegnyő

The Hunyadi family built the **Roman Catholic church** and the **Franciscan monastery** in the middle of Mesztegnyő during the 18th century. The altar painting is by *István Dorfmaister.*

The exhibition in the **Village House** (Ladi J. u. 55.), in what was the old boys school, is devoted to the local flora and fauna.

In Inner Somogy you may be lucky enough to see a marsh orchid.

But your exploration of the local flora and fauna shouldn't necessarily end at the exhibition at the local museum. The **narrow-gauge railway**, which was built in 1925 and leaves from the MÁV railway station, takes passengers in the direction of the *Boronka Nature Reserve*. Having travelled a distance of 9km in three quarters of an hour, you eventually find yourself in *Felsőkak*, which marks the end of the line.

The nature reserve, which you can visit either on foot or by bicycle, was founded to protect the natural habitat, particularly the wild flowers and animals living in the marshes and woods accompanying the lake systems in the valleys leading off the Márcali Ridge. On the sand beds a few metres difference in altitude can affect the composition of the flora and fauna considerably, particularly when you move from the marshes to the dry sandy grasslands. On the fishing lakes you are likely to find a lot of waterfowl (cormorants, black stork, shovellers and herons), as well as otters and ospreys on the lookout for food.

In Mesztegnyő it's only a matter of time before everyone discovers who makes the most delicious strudels.

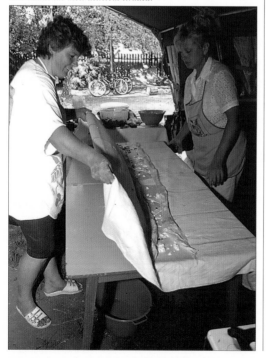

For most of the year NAGYSZAKÁCSI *is extremely quiet, but during the first weekend in August tens of thousands of visitors descend on the village for the Royal Chef Competition. During the Middle Ages, the inhabitants of the village worked as cooks at the royal court in Buda, a historical footnote which prompted the founding of today's culinary event. The organisers make it quite clear that only those ingredients and cookery techniques may be used which were current in the period up to 1490. Entertainment is provided by the dancers, the musicians and the street artists, and there are also plenty of fine Somogy wines in evidence.*

IN AND AROUND CSURGÓ

SZENTA and KASZÓ are famous for **Lake Baláta** and the dense woods which surround it. You can get to the lake on the **narrow-gauge railway** leaving from Szenta station. You are advised to make all the relevant enquiries at the offices of *Kaszó Ltd.*, who also provide guided tours.

The steam locomotive known as *Karácsony* may not be the world's fastest, but it does nevertheless give you plenty of time to take in the passing countryside.

Black storks can be found in quite a few places in Somogy County.

Baláta itself is a depression situated amongst the sand beds. The lake there is dependent on the elements for its water supply, and water levels can vary enormously. Of particular interest from a botanical point of view are the insect-eating plants, like the pitcher plant, the common bladder-wort and the peat-moss, all extremely rare in these parts. Vipers also live here, so you should mind your step. About seventy species of bird breed here and migratory birds use the woodlands around the lake as a resting place. As it is difficult to get to the open water meadows around the lake you are advised to visit the woods and the shores of the lake.

Csurgó

This town, built on the southern part of the *Zalaapát Ridge*, is famous for its contributions to Hungarian culture. It was in 1792 that the enlightened György Festetics founded the **Calvinist Grammar School**, the educational influence of which can still be felt today. Many famous academics, poets and writers studied here, the best know probably being *Mihály Csokonai Vitéz*.

Csurgó's first Grammar School building (1796) is now occupied by the Municipal Museum, which contains a local history collection and exhibitions devoted to the arts and crafts and the paintings of Lajos Raksányi (Csokonai u. 24.).

The most recent school buildings were built in the middle of the town in 1896, which was also when the park was laid out which is now so popular with visitors. Work started on the **Kegyeleti Park** in 1936, and it is here you can find the Csokonai memorial bench and the statues of György Festetics and Péter Méliusz Juhász.

The Csokonai bust is just one of the features in a park filled with columns, statues and tablets dedicated to the students and teachers of Csurgó Grammar School.
One feature of particular interest is the so-called Festetics Gate, a gate which came to symbolise the school from 1940 onwards.

The **Ágneslak Arboretum** in Csurgónagymarton has one of the largest and most important collections of trees in Southern Transdanubia. The landscape created by the estate managers Camil Metzl and Károly Pogány is filled with a wide variety of conifers, maples, magnolias and tulip trees, to name but a few. (Permission to visit the arboretum may be acquired at the *Iharos Forestry Commission*.)

Őrtilos

The steep hillsides near the River Drava mark the end of the *Zalaapát Ridge*. The slopes themselves enjoy the kind of sub-Mediterranean climate only usually seen in the western Balkans. The climate certainly differs from that seen elsewhere in Hungary, and it is here that the woods and streams accompany the participants of the *Three Rivers* cycle race.

On a clear day the views from *Saint Michael's Hill*, rising above the River Drava, stretch over the *Drava* and on towards the *River Mura*. The region's most famous pilgrimage place is **Saint Michael's**, a Baroque church dating from 1740. Patronal festivals are held here four times a year, the most popular being St Anne's Day in July. To the south of the church stands the memorial, the **Festung**, dedicated to the 1848–49 War for Freedom. It is said that during the Turkish period this part of the *Saint Michael's Hill* was used as an important defensive outpost. It was from here in 1848 that Mór Perczel bombarded the Illyrian battalions who had been forced into hiding in Légrád.

At *Lankóc Wood* in GYÉKÉNYES in the *Danube-Drava National Park* you can see what the landscape once looked like here The stony Drava floodplains are rich in both wetland and woodland plants. (For further information see the *Hungarian Treasury*.)

Around the deepest waters you come first to the marshes and further on, where the alders have established themselves, you start seeing oaks and ashes as well. The undergrowth is particularly thick during the early spring, which is when the spring snowflakes flower. In the marshy flats surrounding the woodland you will find Siberian irises. The higher-lying areas, which are covered with oaks and hornbeams, also contain the broad helleborine and wood laurel.

In the middle of Gyékényes what was once the gravel pit is now a clear lake known to the locals as "Kotró".

MEDICINAL WATERS AND LAKES

CSOKONYAVISONTA

It was during exploratory oil drilling in 1942 that the hot spring waters came shooting up to the surface. Not long after the locals realised the water brought relief to those suffering from rheumatic complaints the **baths** were built (Fürdőtelep 1.).

It was in Csokonyavisonta that both the great traveller János Xantus and the politician János Nagyatádi Szabó were born. Legend has it that Karl May modelled his pale-skinned warrior, Old Shatterhand, on Xantus, the founder of both Budapest Zoo and the ethnographical department of the Hungarian National Museum. There is a tablet on the wall of Xantus's birthplace (Xantus János u. 235.).

South of Csokonyavisonta the *Fás Pastures* spread out before you. Following the deforestation which deprived the countryside of all of its indigenous trees, it was the lesser trees which survived. The acid soils on the lime-free clearings are covered with the wild flowers so typical of the Pontian and the Pannonian Steppes.

BABÓCSA

Walking around the village you can still see a few remains dating back to the Turkish era. During the spring the 12-hectare **Basakert**, a name which is itself of Turkish origin, is full of thousands of flowering *daffodills* which are celebrated both at the *Daffodil Festival* and the *Daffodil Run* to Barcs, which take place on the first Sunday in May. Archaeologists who have been engaged in excavation work in the area have found the remains of some earthworks, a Turkish steam bath, a medieval church and a potter's kiln.

Having survived Mohács, András Báthory, the local lord, had to repel the Turks from his castle in Babócsa. Having held out for six days, the 200 defenders were forced to submit to the Turks' superior forces (1555). The by then ruined castle was recaptured by the poet and commander Miklós Zrínyi a century later.

The most interesting feature in the park of Somssich Palace is the limewashed Turkish-style well

Having visited all the historic sites you can enjoy the outdoor **thermal bath**. The village hosts an *International Artists' Camp* in July, its patronal festival in August, and the *Roma Folklore Festival* in October.

BARCS

The town's importance lies in its bridge over the *River Drava* forming the **border crossing** into Croatia. Ecological tourism has really taken off in the region thanks to the proximity of the *Danube-Drava National Park* (for more information see the chapter dealing with the National Parks). The National Park has made it possible to take river tours down the Drava alongside the protected areas. The National Park Educational Centre has also been opened in DRÁVATAMÁSI.

The **Drava Museum** (Széchenyi u. 22.), housed in what was a three-storeyed granary built at the end of the 19th century, has an exhibition devoted to the history of the town, as well as displays on the natural history and the folk art of the *Drava region*. The museum also puts on temporary art exhibitions.

Woods like the *Barcs Juniper Woods* are what result from allowing animals to graze on the dry sandy soils. Between the juniper bushes you can see the kind of vegetation which thrives on acidic sandy soils. During the spring the potentilla grows, and in the summer it's the turn of sheep's bit and various varieties of thyme. Green lizards run around in the undergrowth, frequently escaping the attention of the grass snakes. The most fascinating areas are those damp spots standing on what was once either the bed of the River Drava or the lower-lying areas between the sandhills.

The royal fern is one of the most widespread of Hungary's ferns, reaching a height of 2 metres.
It is on the edges of the Barcs Juniper Wood that you can find the only alder water meadows in Hungary, a site discovered only in 1975.

The most spectacular of the lakes is **Lake Tündérrózsás**, which becomes choked up with water-lilies by the end of the summer. The most impressive are the white and yellow water lilies, whilst the bladderwort, the water violet and the water-chestnut can also be found. It's an ideal habitat for pond tortoises, black storks, herons and osprey.

Local highwaymen Bandi Patkó was fortunate enough to find himself immortalised in a song: "My beautiful landlady – he addressed her – have you seen seven horseshoes on a horse? If you haven't, come over here and see for yourself: the beautiful animal is wearing four. The fifth is me, isn't it? And I've got two hammered into my boots!"

Seemann Palace on the northern side of road 6 has been used as a **hunting lodge** ever since its restoration. In SOMOGYTARNÓCA on road 68 stands the Széchenyis' late-classical, romantic-style palace (1875) and the neo-Romanesque **cemetery chapel** where most of the Széchenyi family lie buried.

SZULOK, a village mostly inhabited by German-speakers, is most famous for the medicinal thermal waters at the **outdoor swimming complex**.

KAPOSVÁR

The name of the town refers to the small castle, which, together with the *Kapos* marshes surrounding it, protected the area. The castle was blown up following the Rákóczi Wars for Freedom and today hardly anything remains to be seen at the end of Vár utca.

One of Kaposvár's main squares is named after Louis Kossuth, and the town has a Kossuth statue (*János Kopits*, 1911). The one-time Member of Parliament for Kaposvár was rarely in a position to devote much time to his constituency as he had already embarked on his period living in exile in Turin.

The Church of the Blessed Virgin (1737–1744, rebuilt in a Neo-Romanesque-Gothic style, 1886) dominates Kaposvár's Kossuth Square. With the reorganisation of the dioceses in 1993 the church became a cathedral.
Above the entrance you can see György Leszkovszky's wall painting "The Pledging of the Church".

The tower of the eclectic-style **town hall** (1903) is Renaissance in style, whilst the wall paintings and the stained glass windows on the staircase depict scenes of old Kaposvár and old local aristocratic heraldry. The old **Erzsébet Hotel** (1901, Noszlopy u.), with its coloured Zsolnay tiles and interesting corner towers, is one of the most beautiful buildings in the town centre.

The now pedestrianised Fő utca takes you from the *Kapos Hotel* down to Széchenyi tér. The Baroque **Csokonai Inn** at the beginning of the street once belonged to the Dukes of Esterházy. It was a building made all the more famous by Csokonai's visits and his amusing epic poem.

On the main façade of Kaposvár's old county hall (classical, 1832) you can make out both the inscription "A Közjónak" (To the Common Good) and Hungary's first county coat-of-arms (1498). Since the construction of the new County Hall (1983) the building has become the Rippl-Rónai Museum.

The statue-lined route from the new County Hall, the so-called **"Wild Flower Road"** (Vadvirágok útja), leads to the village of Szilvásszentmárton in the Zselic. The 21 wooden statues carved by *János Horváth Béres* depict the wild flowers which can be found there.

In the Secession-style **Anker House,** next to the Museum, you will find the *Vaszary Picture Gallery,* which puts on temporary exhibitions and a permanent exhibition of photographs by Kaposvár-born *Juan Gyenes.*

Csokonai went to the Golden Lion pharmacy (1774) for something to relieve his toothache while József Rippl-Rónai was working there as a pharmacist's assistant. It was in the pharmacy that Rippl-Rónai painted a portrait which proved such a success that he was given the job of teaching the Zichy boys. From there he went to the Munich Academy

It is worth stopping at the **Zsolnay Drinking Fountain** (Fő u.), Under the shade of the trees you will find the statue of Kaposvár-born Prime Minister *Imre Nagy* (1896–1958) (*Iván Paulikovics, 1996*).

The pedestrianised street ends in the Secession-style **Dorottya House** in Széchenyi tér. The ground floor is in fact Baroque, and it is in the large banqueting hall that they hold the famous *Dorothy Ball*.

The rooms of the Rippl-Rónai Villa have a very special atmosphere. The furniture complements the paintings beautifully, whilst the pictures themselves depict some of the residents of old Kaposvár.

In the *Toponár* district of the town the *Deseda* feeds the **Deseda Reservoir**, a spot extremely popular with walkers, anglers and lovers of water sports. The ceiling of **Holy Trinity** church in the middle of the suburb is decorated by *paintings by Dorfmaister*.

It was in1061, Kaposszentjakab, now considered part of Kaposvár, that bailiff Otto of Somogy founded a Benedictine monastery on Castle Hill overlooking the Kapos Valley. During the Turkish period the building served as a border fortress, only to lose its strategic importance. The restored ruins can still be seen today.

The theatre company at the Csiky Gergely Theatre (1909–1911, Ede Magyar and József Stahl) in Rákóczi tér was famous for both its plays and operettas.

The most beautiful objects on display at the **Steiner Cast Iron Collection** (Gróf Apponyi Albert u. 29.) are the richly-decorated, pristine, blackened cooking ranges. There are also sinks, picture frames, cups, candlesticks, ashtrays and ornamental plates. The **Municipal Baths** and the **Ferenc Csík Swimming Pool** (Csík Ferenc sétány 3.) were laid out in the Jókai Woods, and their open and covered pools are open all the year round.

On crossing the Kapos you are into the *Zselic*. On top of Róma Hill you will find the **Rippl-Rónai Villa,** where Kaposvár's most famous son lived and worked.

Amongst the hills of Outer Somogy rises Somogyvámos's Puszta Tower (Ihász-dűlő).
The ruins of the 13th century brick Gothic church also manage to dominate its immediate surroundings.

EXPLORING OUTER SOMOGY

The members of the ever-growing Krisna community
who live in the mud brick houses they have built
themselves also run a school and
an extremely popular tourist centre (Fő u. 38.).

SOMOGYVÁMOS

The village is famous nationally for its **Krisna Valley** and the **Indian Cultural Centre**. The Krisna community moved into the village at the beginning of the 1990s. It was the hard work put in by the original fifty members of the community which created the basis for a rich and productive oriental religious environment. Their motto is: *"a simple way of living, a high level of thinking"*. The inhabitants of the farm grow over thirty types of fruit, vegetables and herbs without having to resort to using fertilisers or pesticides.

SOMOGYFAJSZ

The last landowners in the area were the Kund family. When they laid out the 14-hectare park around their eclectic-style **palace** (1872) the owners managed to incorporate the mature oaks, which were already growing on the site. Since then the plane trees have grown considerably, some of the trunks having a girth of 6.5 metres. The trunks of the spruces can be as much as 3.5metres in circumference. The palace now houses the *Somogy*

Somogyfajsz's main attraction is the Ancient Iron Forge Museum, which you can reach by following a 1.5km-long asphalt road out of the village. Archaeologists managed to uncover 21 tenth-century iron furnaces within a 6x8-metre trench. The primitive furnaces are now covered by a beautiful yurt-shaped building.

County Nature Conservation Assotiation, and it is here you should go if you have any enquiries about visiting the *Boronka Nature Reserve.*

The classical **church** in KISGYALÁN (1807) is one of the smallest rotundas in Hungary. Its exterior, pulpit and altar painting have all recently been restored.

István Fekete, the author of many Hungarian children's classics, immortalised the village of GÖLLE in his books. It is here you can find a bust of the author and a museum (Hősök tere 1.) dedicated to his life and work.

IGAL can thank its hot waters for the fact that it is the most-visited village in *Outer Somogy.* The waters at the **Napfény Thermal Baths**, with their recently renovated pools (2003), are beneficial in the treatment of locomotor diseases, as well as circulatory and chronic gynaecological problems. Drinking cures can also be taken.

ANDOCS

Andocs, one of Southern Transdanubia's most famous pilgrimage places, goes back to the 15th century. The present Baroque nave, however, was built between 1743 and 1767. The thousands of pilgrims who visit the **Roman Catholic church** pay their respects to the *Blessed Virgin Mary*, a wooden sculpture which is almost five hundred years old.

In the monastic buildings next to Andocs's Roman Catholic church you can see the many hundreds of items which make up the Virgin's Garment Museum, all of which were given to the miraculous statue of the Virgin Maria in thanks for prayers which had been answered.

According to local superstition, in about 1520, prior to the defeat at the Battle of Mohács, angels carried the chapel complete with the miraculous statue of the Virgin Mary all the way from Kalocsa. Although most of the inhabitants of the villages were forced to flee during the Turkish occupation, the abandoned Jesuit church, the vicarage and the statue of the Virgin Mary managed to survive in one piece.

It was in the small village of ZALA that the artist Mihály Zichy (1827–1906) was born. He was the illustrator of János Arany's ballads, and returned to the village of his birth with his family having spent time in Paris and St. Petersburg.
There is a museum dedicated to Zichy in the house where he was born (Zichy Mihály u. 20.). The exhibition covers the whole of the artist's career including the period when he was fêted at the court of the Russian tsar.
In his studio you can see his drawing table, his paintbrushes and the painting he was working on when he died.

INNEN INDULT DIADALMAS UTJÁRA
ZICHY MIHÁLY

The **Roman Catholic church** (1756–1762), situated up amongst the hills in the village of TAB, contains some frescos by István Dorfmaister. In the **Gallery** (Kossuth Lajos u. 93.), named after the wood carver Ferenc Nagy, you can see the artist's depictions of the great Hungarians and some rural scenes.

It was in the woods around Tab that András Juhász and Pista Patkó and their vagabonds holed up during the second half of the 19th century. Falling in a shoot out with the authorities, a symbolic grave now stands in the nearby Bábony Woods.

THE ZSELIC

Hunters from both home and abroad regularly come to the *Zselic* to hunt the local game (venison, moufflon). The biggest hunting lodges, once belonging to the local landowners, can be found in *Kardosfa* (the one-time centre of the forestry commission) and in *Sasrét*. Next to *Sasrét*'s imposing **hunting lodge** lies the open-air school. A large **stag farm** lies in the fenced off part of the hillside on the edge of Bőszénfa, where they breed the pride of the Zselic forest.

The stags leaving Szénfa Farm are either exported to add fresh blood stocks or sold for their meat and their antlers. Ground antlers are believed to have the special ability to make men more potent. Access to the stag farm is along a stony track from where the animals can easily be seen if you happen to have a pair of binoculars.

The Zselic hillsides are steep and the trails windy. Indeed the beeches, the oaks and the hornbeams give the impression that the hills are of a considerable height. Although the train doesn't go out to these parts you can still get to the Zselic by car or bicycle. Don't be surprised if you come across the occasional hill-walker...

SZENNA

Although the village is situated amongst some beautiful hills it is the **open-air museum** (Rákóczi u. 2.) people come to visit. In Hungary it's rare to find an open-air museum situated right in the middle of a village.

On the small hill and surrounding the Calvinist church on a site covering 3 hectares, the houses and outbuildings which create a village scene from a bygone age, can now boast a Europa Nostra award. The church (1787), which is still used, contains a painted gallery and a coffered ceiling.

The buildings in the open-air museum, which are typical of Inner Somogy, were dismantled on their original site and reconstructed in the museum using as few new materials as possible, together with their pig sties, hen coops and barns. Animals are kept in some of them even today.

BÁRDUDVARNOK

The village, situated in the westernmost part of the *Zselic*, is made up of 16 more-or-less separate settlements. Although there are two ways of getting to the village from Kaposvár we recommend the quieter, more picturesque route taking you through Szenna. Leaving Szenna's vineyards you soon come to the *Petörke Valley* with its captivating hills. The Scandinavian-style wooden **Benedictine Monastery** in *Kaposszentbenedek* cuts an unusual figure in the Pannonian countryside. From here you can continue to the Kaposdada part of the village and J*ános Somogyi*'s **private arboretum** (Kaposdada 5.). Those wanting to try their hand at riding or archery should go to the *Lajos Kassai* Riding and Archery Ranch. The Hungarian Conquest yurt forms the backdrop for the military displays referring back to the Hungarians' arrival into Europe.

Those who are into horse-riding and archery should visit the Lajos Kassai equestrian archery farm.

It's worthwhile stopping at the smaller of the **Goszthonyi Halls** (Bárdibükk 12.) in the middle of Bárdudvarnok. During the middle of August, you may be able to see glassmakers at work in the courtyard and inspect their the finished products.

On the hill overlooking Bárdudvarnok stands the Panorama Society's guesthouse, while down below you can see the small lakes and the stream of the Gólya Valley. You can look for Pali the Highwayman's grave and drink from the Matthias Corvinus Well.

SZIGETVÁR

"To you weapon and warrior I sing, Turkish power,
The anger of Suleiman growing by the hour,
In the Magnificent's arms, yonder,
The dread sabre tearing Europe assunder."

(Miklós Zrínyi: Sziget in Peril)

It was here that *Miklós Zrínyi*, the Ban of Croatia, tried to halt the Turkish army led by Suleiman the Magnificent in 1566. The castle you can see today was built by the victorious Turks.

There are Turkish monuments all over Szigetvár. In the square in the old town named after him you can see the statue of *Márk Horváth* the heroic captain who led the defence of the castle against the Turkish siege of 1556. The **Franciscan Church** was built on the site of one of the Turkish mosques. The only surviving Turkish house in Hungary, the so-called **Turkish House** (Bástya u. 3.), was in all probability a caravan seraglio.

The Turks built the Ali Pasha Mosque
in the centre of the medieval town (Zrínyi tér) in 1589.
During the 18th century the building was turned into a Baroque
church, and since 1789 the inside of the dome has been
decorated with frescos by István Dorfmaister (Zrínyi tér 9.).

In front of the council building stands the statue of an enormous lion, the **monument** dedicated to Zrínyi and the heroes of Szigetvár (1878). On the base of the monument are the words of *Mihály Vörösmarty: "...There around the hero Zrínyi lie the brave warriors..."* On the far side of the bridge over the Almás you can see the **castle**, a fine example of a 16th century border fortress. In front of the entrance stands a statue of *Sebestyén Tinódi Lantos (István Kiss)*.

A handful of Hungarians had to face the might of a Turkish army preparing for an attack on Vienna. Those defending the castle were outnumbered thirty to one. News of a dramatic struggle was to spread throughout Europe. Cardinal Richelieu, said of the situation in Hungary: "It was here the question as to whether great tracts of Europe would spend centuries living under the cross or the crescent was settled."

On the edge of Szigetvár stands the Hungarian-Turkish Friendship Park (1996) built with the help of the Turkish state. Busts of Miklós Zrínyi and Suleiman the Magnificent (Metin Jurdanur) stand in front of a symbolic tomb of the Turkish ruler who in fact died here.

The Zrínyi cult in Szigetvár is kept alive by the Friends of the Castle, who organise an historical conference every September, which runs concurrently with the concerts and exhibitions of the *Zríny Festival* held at the **Vigadó** (*Imre Makovecz*, József Attila u. 9–11.).

The park surrounding the walls of the castle and the pools of the nearby **thermal bath** (Tinódi u.) offer some respite from the summer heat.

The bridge and the equestrian statue of Miklós Zrínyi (József Somogyi) in the castle courtyard mark the position of the 1566 attack. The Miklós Zrínyi Museum, which is joined up to Sulejman the Magnificent' mosque with its archaeological finds and contemporary documents, focuses on the battle (Vár u.).

THE SOUTHERN ZSELIC

Moving north of Szigetvár you come to the 200–250-metre-high hills of the *Southern Zselic* and the 50–100-metre-deep valleys along which the *Gyöngyös* and the *Almás* flow from the Zselic in the north to Szigetvár in the south. The valleys of *Bükkösd Water* on the eastern extremes of the region also run north-south, and where the waters have been dammed up there are reservoirs and lakes, which are excellent for fishing.

The 19th century country houses in CSERTŐ and MOZSGÓ are surrounded by parkland.

Around ALMAMELLÉK there is less arable land and more woodland. It was in 1901 that Baron Rezső Biederman built the railway from Almamellék through Szentmártonpuszta to Sásrét, with its branch line off to Lukafa. The **forestry railway** has a timetabled service, but special departures can also be arranged. The narrow-gauge railway takes you to Baron Biedermann's Baroque **hunting lodge**, which provides overnight accommodation for visiting hunters.

People go to the Ethnographical Workshop in MAGYARLUKAFA to familiarize themselves with traditional craft skills.
The members of the "Bee Hive" Society not only organise exhibitions in the restored stilted house (Fő u. 16.), they also put on summer camps and organize exhibitions.
St Wendelin's Day in the second half of October traditionally sees the end of Baranya County's contribution to the festival known as the Mediterranean Autumn.

In the tiny village of IBAFA you will find the **Pipe Museum**. Apart from the collection of pipes there are all the other accessories associated with smoking, like for example the decorated tobacco pouches, cigarette cases and matchboxes (Kossuth Lajos u. 39.).

The Calvinist church in PATAPOKLOSI is worth visiting if for no other reason than to admire the **painted coffered ceiling**. In the cemetery in SOMOGYHÁRSÁGY you can find the Festetics family **mausoleum**. The Zichy family country residence in KISHÁRSÁGY can only be seen from the outside.

THE ORMÁNSÁG

Although the name *Ormánság* actually describes an ethnographical region, it is a landscape of undulating woodland. On the southern borders of the region, in what is the *Danube–Drava National Park,* you can enjoy the rich wildlife of the watery landscapes and the peaceful dead channels of the Drava. The sandbanks on the river are now the last remaining breeding grounds for some of the river fish. It is here also that the little ringed plover and the small tern lay their eggs.

The overall impression one gets of the landscape is the woodland: the willows, the poplars and the alders, the oaks, the ashes and the elms. Visitors are free to visit large tracts of the Danube–Drava National Park, some parts of which have information boards (see below), special designated areas which are strictly protected and can only be visited with prior consent and in the company of a guide. (For more information see the section on National Parks.)

The winding main streets of the villages closest to the Drava follow what was the course of the old river, whilst the **Calvinist churches** you can see in the villages were built following Joseph II's decree on religious tolerance of 1781. Although the churches tended to be modelled on the Roman Catholic churches which were already standing, the Calvinists' puritanism meant that the interiors were completely lacking in painted and carved images. The walls were whitewashed and it was left to the ceilings and the galleries to provide the little ornamentation which was allowed. The masters who painted the panels on the ceilings were usually carpenters working to pattern book designs.

Visitors to SELLYE are free to enjoy the evergreens dominating the park which surround the 18th century Baroque **Draskovich Palace** (Köztársaság tér). (The palace is now used as student residences, and offers accommodation to visitors during the school holidays.) In the square in front of the palace there is a stilted house, which was brought here from Csányoszró to make up part of the exhibition entitled *Memories of Life in the Ormánság* at the **Géza Kiss Ormánság Museum** (6.). There is also a **bell tower**, which originally came from Gyöngyfa.

Clothes chests are particularly treasured in the Drava region.

Amongst the lawns and firs at Sellye's **outdoor swimming complex** (Fürdő u.) you can go boating on the *lake* as well as swimming in the thermal pools.

Every two years Sellye hosts the *Ormánság Festival.* The anniversary marking the day Sellye officially became a town is marked by the *Watermelon*

Festival. The ceiling of the Calvinist church (1792) in DRÁVAIVÁNYI has **167 painted panels** at the centre of which is the so-called *"royal panel"* set inside a sun giving details of the artist. It is here you can find the only figurative depiction in the whole of the Ormánság, a crowned mermaid holding a sword, together with a dove holding an olive branch in its beak and a fish.

The 15th century Gothic chancel at the **Roman Catholic church** in BOGDÁSA (Kossuth u. 81.) makes it the oldest surviving ecclesiastical building in the Ormánság. The **Village House** is a particularly beautiful old verandahed peasant's cottage.

It was the writer *János Kodolányi* (1899–1969) who introduced the literary world to the region's unique ethnographical character, as well as to its social problems.

The **Memorial Library and Museum** (Kossuth u. 12.) in VAJSZLÓ named after, Kodolányi contains some valuable literary material as well as artefacts from the Ormánság, photos relating to the writer's life and a forestry office dating from the beginning of the 19th century. The *Vajszló Festival* takes place around 15th August, the Feast of the Virgin Mary. Eight painted panels with Baroque motifs decorate the gallery of the Baroque **Calvinist church** in ADORJÁS (Petőfi u. 46.).

The **parish church** (1793) in KÓRÓS acquired a second choir added to the north in 1834. The two choirs are covered with a coffered ceiling decorated in diagonal compositions dominated by the three colours: white, claret and blue; the older panels dating from 1795, the latter from 1835. The designs on the gallery resemble those at Kovácshida.

The centre of the gallery in the Calvinist church (1833) in KOVÁCSHIDA *there is a panel depicting two chalices, which were at the time the symbols of the Reformation movement. The other panels are covered in floral patterns. The vicarage contains an exhibition devoted to Calvinist ecclesiastical art.*

The Drava also supplies the trees on the flood plain with water.

Following the Turkish period, Siklós became Imperial property, and unlike most of Hungary's other border castles was fortunate not to fall victim to Emperor Leopold's demolition teams.

SIKLÓS

This, the southernmost town in Hungary has one of the most complete **castles** in Hungary. During the Ottoman Conquest the Turks used the fortified castle as a fortress.

The Turks built some mosques in the suburbs of the town, and it was the Sanjak of Klissza who built the Malkocs Bey Mosque surrounded by its rose garden between 1543 and 1565.

The Hungarian Society for the Preservation of Ancient Monuments' reconstruction **Malkocs Bey Mosque** won the *Europa Nostra Award* in 1992. The interior of the **chapel** (14th–15th century) at Siklós Castle is one of the most beautiful in Hungary. The saints and nobles depicted in the wall niches date from the time when the Garai family owned the castle.

During the 18th century the Batthyány family remodelled and enlarged the castle in the Baroque style. It is, however, amongst what remains of the Gothic and Renaissance castle that you will find the **dungeon museum** and the **lapidarium**. The castle also contains the Pécs Glove Manufacturing Museum and a permanent exhibition of *István Gádor*'s ceramics.

Every April local artists show their work at the *Siklós Art* exhibition held in the castle. The *Siklós Salon*, an exhibition of contemporary art, is held in May. Every other June sees the *National Wind Band Festival*; the *Siklós Autumn*, which includes the harvest parade and a folk dance programme, is held at the beginning of October.

Some wall paintings, including the donor's coat-of-arms, have recently been uncovered in the chancel of the **parish church** (the Franciscan Church). Art historians date the paintings to between about 1410 and 1420. It was in the Franciscan Church that Palatine *Miklós Garai* was buried.

The one-time **Franciscan monastery** is now the centre of the *Baranya County Art Colony*. The building also hosts the *International Ceramic Symposium*. The work produced by the local and visiting artists is shown at the summer exhibitions put on for their benefit (Vajda J. tér 2.).

LAND OF WATERS AND WINES

You can see the twin towers of MÁRIAGYŰD's *Baroque pilgrimage church on Tenkes Hill for many miles around. Many thousands of pilgrims visit, particularly during the patronal festivals (the Marian festivals, Whitsun and Corpus Christi). The Stations of the Cross on the side of the hill contain Zsolnay ceramic reliefs.*

HARKÁNY

It is along the fault line running along the southern edge of the *Villányi Hills* that the medicinal waters come bubbling up to the surface. The most famous sulphurous and alkaline hydrogen carbonate springs are at Harkány.

Apart from the mud baths and bathing possibilities, the medicinal waters at Harkány are also good for drinking cures because of the number of trace elements in the water (Kossuth L. u. 7.). And visitors haven't stopped coming, especially now the complex has been renovated.

Work started on the spa in the middle of the 1820s, shortly after the sulphurous waters were discovered. After having spent one or two weeks digging the channels the navvies found that their arthritic limbs didn't ache so much. In fact the longer their feet spent in the boggy soil the less their feet ached. It wasn't long before the news spread and people were descending on the place hoping to benefit from the miraculous waters. In 1824, the Batthyány family, seeing that there were other benefits to be had, contributed to the planning of the baths.

Harkány hosts the *Egg Painting Festival*, the *Whitsun Music Festival*, the *Bathing Festival* (in the middle of July), and a *Harvest Festival* (second half of September).

At the peasant house in NAGYTÓTFALU *youngsters can try their hand at some of the traditional crafts.*

NAGYHARSÁNY

It was during the Turkish period that the village first came into contact with the Reformation, and once the Turks had been defeated it was from Nagyharsány that Calvinism spread throughout the whole of the Ormánság. During the restoration of the 13th century **Calvinist church** in 1978, efforts were made to respect the various periods in the building's architectural history. On the southern side of the church there is a Romanesque portal.

Szársomlyó (442m), rising above Nagyharsány, is the highest peak in the *Villány Hills*. For the past three decades it has been possible to enjoy the works of sculptors from both Hungary and abroad at the **sculpture park** on the Villány to Nagyharsány road. Quarrying still goes on the western side of the hill. To the west of Szársomlyó stands a per-

fectly formed hilltop, to the south an unbelievably narrow ridge and to the east stand the steep "Devil's Plough Furrows".

It is in the grassy meadows on the southern face of the hill that you can find the plant for which the hill is famous, the Hungarian crocus. As most of the hill is in fact a nature conservation area (224 hectares) you will have to enquire about the guided tours if you want to visit.

The monumental sculptures on the Szársomlyó were made during the course of a series of international symposia.

The creation of the Szársomlyó is explained in a folk legend, which goes something like this... A beautiful local girl took the devil's fancy. This didn't however worry the girl's mother as the marriage terms set by the devil seemed impossible: namely that the devil had to plough half the hill by the time the cock crowed. The devil tied six pairs of cats to his plough and started. He made such good progress that the old lady got concerned, so much so she started to crow. The devil threw down his plough (in doing so creating Beremend Hill) and shook off all the topsoil from the Bocskora (making Siklós Hill), and when making one almighty kick only succeeded in burying himself completely. It is from the place where he buried himself, known as Harkány, after the name of the girl, that the sulphurous waters now bubble up to the surface. If you look carefully you can still see the cats claw marks on the rock face (the Devil's Plough Furrows).

The Roman finds uncovered at the base of the hills prove that people have been growing grapes and making wine here for a very long time. Today the **Villány–Siklós Wine Region** covers an area of about 2,000 hectares. The Villány and Villánykövesd vineyards are famous for their red wines.

The Villány-Siklós Wine Road which makes its way through the slopes of the Villány Hills is 30 km long and crosses 8 villages.

"*Villány wine is an elegant wine, I always take Villány wines to balls. You can only get the very best out of the wine when freshly bathed, shaved, and wearing tails or a dinner jacket, if you are a gentleman, plunging necklines for the ladies. The wine manages to arouse just the amount of excitement required to engage your dancing partner in conversation. Discreet, cultured, and refined.*"

(Béla Hamvas: The Philosophy of Wine)

The *Kékoportó*, *Kékfrankos*, *Cabernet Sauvignon*, *Cabernet Franc* and the *Merlot* are the most popular grapes. As for the white wines you should go to

Máriagyűd, Siklós, Nagyharsány, Kisharsány and Nagytótfalu for the *Italian Riesling*, *Hárslevelű*, *Chardonnay*, *Tramini*, and the *Rhenish Riesling*.

In VILLÁNY, the village after which the wine region is named, you will find a **Wine Museum** (Bem u. 8.) in the main street situated amongst the historic wine cellars. It was to enhance the reputation of Villány wines that the *Custodes Vinorum de Villány* (the Villány Wine Order) was founded. It is here in the village that you can find its headquarters.

The *Red Wine Festival* is organised every other year during the first weekend in October (in the years ending in odd numbers).

The opening ceremony of the *Pécs International Wine Song Festival* held in VILLÁNYKÖVESD in the second half of October takes place in the almost two-hundred-year-old Batthyány **"wine cathedral"** whose huge wooden barrels store up to 4,000 hectolitres of wine. The sight of all those huge barrels in its Baroque setting takes the breath away.

Driving towards Villánykövesd the two rows of cellars, in some places three, overlooking the village of Villány, can be seen for miles around.
For this is a wine region with a noble tradition.
On the hillside overlooking the village of Villány there are 57 cellars, all crammed one next to the other.

St. Elizabeth's church in PALKONYA at the northeastern foot
of the Villány Hills was built by the local landowners,
the Batthyány family. It is one of the finest rotundas
in Hungary, with a rather archaic wooden structure
holding up the dome-shaped roof.
The higgledy-piggledy streets
with their traditional verandaed,
limewashed houses create quite an effect.
The appearance of the village you can see today was completed
when the German population built the cellar settlement
during the 19th century.

MOHÁCS

*Our ancestors originally settled on the hills overlooking
the Danube, which in those days flowed in two branches south
of Baja. The vast majority of the Mohács Plain was flooded
to both sides of the river. The Danube, with its twists and turns,
its sandbanks and its dangerous currents made sailing
a tricky business. During the floods there were so many fish
that the locals were able to pick them out of the water
with their bare hands.*

*When in 1526 the forces of Louis II. prepared to
face the Turkish army they spent their final night
in Mohács. The tragic events of the battle started to
unfold on 29th August on the plains under the
town, near the villages of Majs, Sátorhely and Udvar, to the south-west of Kölked. Beaten by the
sheer numbers of their enemies, nearly half of the
Hungarian troops fell in the battle, as did nearly
all their commanders.*
*The fleeing king drowned in the waters of the Cse-
le, a stream swollen by the heavy rains which had
fallen previously. By the river you can see the Louis
II. Memorial (György Kiss). The town's History of
the Battle Museum (Szerb u. 2.) takes visitors
through the events of that fateful day.*

You approach the **Mohács Historical Memorial
Site,** along an avenue of chestnut trees, on the
road out to Sátorhely. The gateway *(József Pölös-
kei)* contains 28 thousand bolts symbolising the
number who fell in battle. The walls of the atrium
are covered with tableaux showing how the battle
progressed.

The **Votive Church** *(Aladár and Bertalan Árkay)* in Mohács's Széchenyi tér was built on the 400th anniversary of the Battle of Mohács. The one-time **Episcopal Church** (Szepessy tér, 1742) was built at about the same time as the **Episcopal Palace**.

It was during the 18th century that Mohács became a multi-ethnic town. Alongside the Hungarian and the Croat population lived large numbers of Serb settlers. They were soon followed by an influx of Germans. The local black earthenware jugs started their journeys to long distant markets from the quay on the riverside. Their colour was acquired from being baked in smoky wood-powered kilns.

The **Dorottya Kanizsai Múzeum** (Városház u.1.) hosts an exhibition entitled *Croat, Serb and Slovene Ethnic Groups in Baranya County* covering the history of various costumes and beliefs, including the origins of the "busójárás" and a display of masks and rattles.

The five mass graves uncovered at the Historical Memorial Site are marked with rose bushes and gravestones. The wooden grave posts for the simple foot soldiers and the funeral-bells of the military commanders provide symbols for the battle (József Király, Sándor Kiss, Pál Kő, István Szabó Jnr.).

The carnival-like events of the "busójárás", where some also wearing wooden masks, is a spectacle attracting tens and thousands of visitors. During the parade the terrifying straw-stuffed sheepskined figures are accompanied by sawdust-sprinkling "jankele" children and the loud report of medieval cannon fire. After nightfall a huge bonfire is lit in the main square and the figure of the straw-filled manakin symbolising winter is set alight.

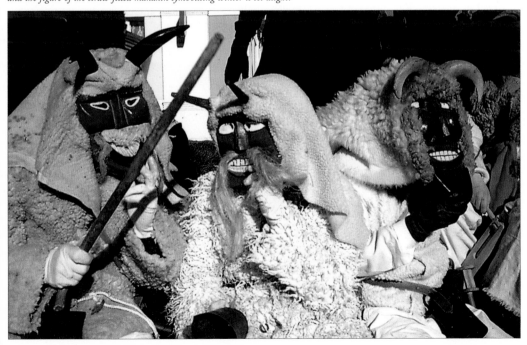

You are well advised to go to the **halászcsárda** in Szent Mihály tér to try the local fish dishes. It is from the quay here that the ferries leave for Mohács Island.

The 48-metre tower of the **Greek Orthodox church** (18th century) rises above the single-storeyed houses of the old Serbian quarter.

It is around the **Busó statue** *(István Laluja)* in Kóló tér that the masked participants meet up before setting off on the Carnival Procession. According to local legend it was the men of the *"busójárás"* in their terrifying masks who finally scared the Turks out of the town. Ethnographers, however, believe that the ritual goes back much further, to a fertility ritual the Hungarians brought with them from their homeland.

ALONG THE BANKS OF THE DANUBE

DUNASZEKCSŐ's Roman predecessor, *Lugio,* was essentially a military station. It was here on the now protected *Várhegy* that a bronze likeness of the Roman Emperor *Marcus Aurelius* came to light *(Pécs, Janus Pannonius Museum).*

The **local holiday cottages** on the slopes of the wooded hills between Bár and Mohács, are ideally placed for fishing, hunting and water sports. During the summer, when the water level of the Danube is particularly low, you can go swimming on the river's two sandbanks, which you can get to on the *Mohács Island* ferry.

NAGYNYÁRÁD is the regional centre of the village tourist industry and local folklore initiatives. *János Sárdi*, a blue-dyer, is more than happy to show you around his workshop and explain how the original printing blocks were used in the **blue-dying** process (Dózsa György u. 5.).

Guests can also take part in cellar parties, grape harvests and pig-killings, as well as learn a few local folk crafts, such as weaving and bead-threading (Zalka Máté u. 29.).

In the area around Mohács a number of Swabian villages have got involved in **village tourism**. The local folk art and the traditional festivals make staying in SZAJK, SOMBEREK and PALOTABOZSOK all the more memorable.

Bóly was shaped by the building activities of the Batthyány-Montenuovo families. The house (1808) is currently used as a children's home, so you will have to ask for permission if you want to inspect the house and its 27-hectare park. (1809). The historicist (neo-Romanesque, Gothic Revival) family mausoleum was built by Júlia Batthyány a century ago.

In BÓLY you can walk around the candle-making and blue-dying **workshops** and the gingerbread-making kitchen. Bóly is also famous for the **row of cellars,** which feature on the *Mohács-Bóly White Wine Road*. While the **local museum** in the old granary building is devoted to local German population and the settlers from Upper Hungary (now Slovakia), *Békás-puszta*, one of the most important economic centres of the local estate, has its own collection of agricultural implements.

There are ever more stables available to those deciding to spend their holidays out in the countryside.

PÉCS

"Once Italy alone in books rode free;
But now fine verse pours forth in Hungary.
My country hails its bard with welcome rare;
They are its glory, and in this I share."
(Janus Pannonius: In Praise on Pannonia
translation by Watson Kirkconnell)

The Romans, built a settlement here known as *Misina*. Saint Stephen founded the bishopric here in 1009. It was here also, in 1367, that Louis the Great founded **Hungary's first university**. From the time of Janus Pannonius up to the Turkish Conquest the town was a centre of Renaissance culture in Hungary.

Following the Turkish period the town was rebuilt, giving the town an unmistakably Baroque character. It was in the middle of the 19th century that heavy industry arrived in the region when coal mining started in the Mecsek. It was a time also when companies, which were later to enjoy international reputations, first went into business, as in the case of the *Littke Champagne Factory* (with Europe's deepest, five-storey, cellarage system), the *Zsolnay Factory*, the *Angster Organ Works* and the *Pécs Brewery*.

The *Elizabeth University of Sciences*, Pozsony (Bratislava, Slovakia) moved to Pécs during the 1920s. Becoming the *Pécs University of Sciences*. *"Museum Street"* came into being during the 1970s, and it was then too that the rest of the town acquired the character it has today.

Széchenyi tér is dominated by the most important piece of Ottoman architecture surviving in Hungary today, the **Pasha Kasim Mosque**. What is now the Roman Catholic parish church is a particularly popular place for weddings, and the square outside often echoes to the sound of folk music.

The Turkish traveller Evlia Cselebi said of the mosque: "Pasha Gázi Kászim's mosque is indeed pleasing and beautiful, it is why so many people visit. Its domes are made of blue stone and it is one hundred paces long and a hundred wide. It has a fine mimber, mihrab and muezzin's mahfil and a kursiye inlaid with precious stones whose beauty is beyond words."

One of the most important buildings dating back to the Turkish period is the Jakováli Hasszán Pasha Mosque which is where the Islamic students studying in Pécs go to worship today.

It is in Széchenyi tér, the old market square, where the town's great celebrations and festivals take place (the Easter celebrations, the Pécs Festival, the Grape and Wine Festival).

The eozin glazed bull's heads on the Vilmos Zsolnay memorial fountain (Andor Pilch, 1912) in Széchenyi tér pay homage to the Nagyszentmiklós Treasure Trove.

The *Janus Pannonius Museum*'s **ethnographical exhibition** (Rákóczi út 15.) has a collection of 18–19th century objects representing the various ethnic groups living in the county of Baranya. The classical **Episcopal Library** (*József Piatsek*, 1830) is currently the Library of the *Pécs University of Sciences* (Szepesy u. 3.).

The Janus Pannonius Museum's **Arts Collection** stands in the old buildings in Káptalan utca. The oldest surviving residence (Káptalan u. 2.) is home to the **Zsolnay Ceramics Exhibition**, which celebrates the work of the factory so famous for its eozin glaze. On the ground floor you can find a number of statues by *Amerigo Tot*.

Works by op-art artist *Victor Vasarely* can be seen in the **museum** dedicated to his work (3.). The museum also contains works by other artists who shared Vasarely's interest in geometric, kinetic and conceptual art. In the underground **Mecsek Mining Museum** you can inspect the machinery used in the coal and uranium mining industries.

All the major Hungarian art movements of the first half of the 20th century (Nagybánya, The Eight, the Bauhaus, Szentendre, the Rome School, the European School) and important individuals (Rippl-Rónai, Gulácsy, Moholy-Nagy, Barcsay, Egry) are represented. The old Deanery Palace Rockery is dotted with works by Péter Székely. In the other historical buildings on Káptalan utca (nos. 5–6.) visitors can enjoy the works of some of Hungary's less-heralded artists (Endre Nemes Museum, Erzsébet Schaár, Ferenc Martyn Museum).

In the enormous vaulted cellar underneath the *Cistercian Louis the Great Grammar School* in sculpture-studded Széchenyi tér stands the *Pécs Gallery*. Opposite the **Town Hall,** whose neo-Baroque appearance dates from 1907, stands the so-called **Elephant House** (7–8.) with its *Arts House* and *Hild Courtyard*. The **Janus Pannonius Museum**'s *Archaeological Exhibition* (12.) has a rich collection of finds covering excavations throughout the region. In the romantic-style **Synagogue** (1865, Gerster and Frey) you can find the first ever organ produced at the *Angster Organ Factory*.

The **Modern Hungarian Picture Gallery** has one of the richest collections of Hungarian art in the country.

You can find the **Csontváry Museum** in the neo-Renaissance Palace on Janus Pannonius utca (11.), dedicated to the paintings of one of Hungary's best-loved painters, *Tivadar Koszta Csontváry* (1853–1919).

Illustrated: a piece of garden sculpture from the Zsolnay Factory.

The copies of the stone carving done for the medieval Pécs basilica (11th and 12th centuries) give you some idea as to the quality of the carvings produced by the local workshop (the people's altar, the steps down to the crypt). You can see the originals in the Cathedral Lapidarium.

Walking on Szent István tér you are in fact walking on across what was the **cemetery** of Roman **Sopianae**. Archaeologists have been excavating the Christian cemetery chapels and tombs dating back to the 4th century that lie five or six metres under the ground. One particular chapel was built on top of the remains of the community's martyrs and other important personages, around which Sopianae's less prominent citizens were buried. Many two-storey buildings have been found in the area around Dom tér and Apács utca.

In the first tomb chamber, found as far back as 1780, you can make out paintings on biblical themes, as well as vegetable and animal motifs. It would appear therefore that part of the chapel was also used by Christians in later centuries. This earlier Christian tradition may have caused Saint Stephen to found a diocese in Pécs in 1009. The triple, and six-apsed chapels, the so-called **Jar Tomb Chamber**, the **Ancient Christian Mausoleum**, with its wall paintings, is such a rarity in Europe outside Italy that the site was added to the list of *World Heritage Sites* (2000). In nearly all the surviving tomb chambers the surviving painted fragments have been given glass protection to prevent any further damage. Although restoration work is still continuing apace some of the ancient Christian building complex is open to the general public at certain times of the year. Viewing restrictions will continue until work on all of the seven buildings has been completed.

The interior of the three-aisled **St Peter and St Paul Basilica** *(Friedrich von Schmidt,* 1891) was decorated by German *(Moritz von Beckerath, Karl Andreä)* and Hungarian *(Károly Lotz, Bertalan Székely)* artists. The most beautiful example of Renaissance art in Pécs is the pastophorium put up by Bishop Szathmári in the **Chapel of the Corpus Christi**. Since its restoration, the **Episcopal Palace** on the western side of the square, which is also built into the old town wall, has been open to the general public on Thursday afternoons. Next to it stand the neoclassical, late-Baroque **archives** and the **diocesan offices**.

The 15th century barbican defended the main entrance to the Episcopal Palace. In the Barbican Garden the almond trees offer some shade to Miklós Borsos's statue of Pécs's most famous bishop, the Italian-trained scholar and the writer of Latin poems, Janus Pannonius (1434–1472). It was made on the occasion of the 500th anniversary of his death. It depicts a young man holding two volumes of poetry inscribed with the initials PJ.

On the eastern side of Sétatér the founder of the one-time *Littke Champagne Factory* was able to put the ancient and medieval underground **cellars** to excellent use. It was here the champagnes were stored, where they matured and where they are now measured out (12.).

The **Pasha Hasan Mosque** (Korház tér) is the only Ottoman religious building in existence in Hungary complete with minaret and original Turkish furnishings.

It is also worth visiting the **Szerecsen Pharmacy** (Apáca u. 1.) for the pieces of furniture incorporating Zsolnay tiles. The **Pécs National Theatre**, built during the 1890s *(Lang and Steinhardt)* provides a home for the theatre, the opera and the ballet.

Book week in the square in front of the theatre.

Of the old houses along Király utca it is worth paying special attention to the **"Vasváry House"** with its *Zsolnay* ceramic decoration, and the *Caflisch Patisserie* founded in 1789. The Baroque buildings of the one-time *Lyceum* (church and monastery) stand at the end of the pedestrianised street. The lizards and tropical fish at the **Aquarium** and the **Terrarium** in the restored underground cellars (Munkácsy u. 31.) come as quite a surprise.

It is in the drying loft of the old tanneries that you will find the **History of Pécs Museum** covering the history of the town from the liberation from the Turks (1686) to 1948 (Felsőmalom u. 9.).

It was on the road leading towards Buda that the *Zsolnay Factory* was built, and where the *Zsolnay Mausoleum* now stands.

The Zoo, on the wooded southern slopes of the Misina, provides a home for animals from both Hungary and abroad. From here you can go for a walk through Almond Wood out towards the Lapis and the Remeterét. There is also a narrow-gauge railway, taking visitors from the Zoo out towards the Dömörkapu.

Victor Vasarely's sculpture entitled Sign stands in front of the Pauline Church (Hunyadi út) built in 1938.

The sub-Mediterranean climate at the foot of Tettye's limestone rock faces has proved beneficial to some exotic trees (cypress, fig, laurel, Judas tree) all of which can be seen at the **Pintér Garden**, which is where you will also find the headquarters of the *Danube–Drava National Park* (Tettye tér 9.). The TV tower (1974) on the top of the *Misina-tető* (534m) offers an excellent **panorama**. Those taking off from the runway at POGÁNY (2003) will also get a good view of the town.

The Tettye Passion Play in Holy Week is a major event on the cultural calendar.

THE WESTERN MECSEK

It is from the **Éger Valley Outdoor Centre** on the western edge of Pécs, near the village once known as Magyarürög, that you can best reach the highest point in the *Western Mecsek, Jakab Hill* (592m). The flat peak and its strategic position made it an ideal site for a late Bronze Age-early Iron Age fort. In the middle of the earthworks stand the **ruins of the medieval Pauline monastery**. The lookout point on *Zsongor Rock* (570m) is the best place from which to survey the surrounding landscape.

Underneath the almost vertical rock face of the Eagle's Nest, on the southern side of Jakab Hill is a footpath that leads you to the bizarre rock formations lying further on. The rocks rise on the southwestern faces in pillar-like features sometimes resembling petrified toadstools.

The story goes that in CSERKÚT there were two rich and proud families who were always feuding. One day both families fell under a beggar's curse promising to turn the families into stone at their moment of greatest happiness. This day turned out to be the day both families' daughters got married. The weddings were held at the Pauline Church on Jakab Hill. With the guests of one of the families going down the hill as the others were going up, neither family was prepared to give way. At this the two stubborn fathers declared they would sooner turn to stone than let the other party through. And so it was.

The medieval church at Cserkút is famous primarily for its wall paintings.

Some medieval details survive at Kővágószőlős **church.** Some of the Baroque furniture, however, comes from the liturgical furniture which stood in Pécs Cathedral prior to its drastic 19th century restoration. In ORFŰ, situated at the northwestern foot of the Mecsek, are a series of artificial lakes, the oldest and smallest of them, *Lake Orfű*, is excellent for boating and fishing. The millers working at the **Mill Museum** are quite happy to show visitors around the mill. You can also buy their flour and home-made bread.

On the eastern side of the largest lake, *Lake Pécs*, stands MECSEKRÁKOS with its old verandaed house (Fő tér 3.). Looking back from the northern banks of the lake you get a wonderful view of the *Western Mecsek*.

At TEKERES old German peasant cottages run along both sides of the village's only street. It is here, around the *Ottó Hermann Lake*, that you will find the **fish** and **water bird reservation**. The fourth of the lakes in this particular system *(Kovácsszénája Lake)* is set aside especially for anglers.

There are plenty of opportunities to relax around the lakes near Orfű.

The cave in ABALIGET in the side of Bodó Hill (219m) was discovered in 1768. Visitors are allowed along about 500 metres of the 1,380 metre-long cave. In addition the humidity, the high radon content, the total lack of dust and the lower air pressure mean that the cave is ideal for those suffering from respiratory problems. Nearby you will find the Bat Museum opened by the Danube-Drava National Park.

Two country residences in BÜKKÖSD were built during the 1780s. Baranya County's most elegant Baroque-façaded building was built to the designs of the famous architect *Johann Bernhard Fischer von Erlach* (1656–1723). The beautiful park (1739) surrounding the **Petrovszky Palace** contains the hillside Louis Seize-style **chapel**.

There is also a **palace** in MEGYEFA on the eastern side of the valley (Petőfi u.). SZENTLŐRINC stands in the *Bükkösd Valley* separating the Mecsek from the Zselic. The local thermal waters supply the local **swimming complex.** Students now occupy the **Esterházy Palace** (1696–1717). The *Saint Laurence Day* festivities starting each year on August 10th include the patronal festival, a street party and the *Farmers' Festival*.

The *Zselic* joins the *Mecsek* in the western side of Bükkösd and Szentlőrinc. The gently rolling hills make the countryside great for walking. The marked footpaths take you to Gyűrűfű, Ibafa, and HELESFA, where a 70-hectare **lake** (2003) has been created surrounded by a **holiday village**.

TOURS IN THE NORTHERN MECSEK

The medieval **church** in MÁNFA, one of the most famous in Hungary, was a single-aisled church with a round-apsed chancel, which must have been enlarged towards the end of the 12th century. It was then that the square-ended chancel and the western tower were built.

In the protected Melegmányi Valley you can make your way on foot to the famous lime tufa dams. The limestone deposits have created lots of tiny waterfalls along the stream.

The interior of Mánfa parish church almost doubled in size during the course of the 14th century.

It was in 1928, during some exploratory drilling in SIKONDA, that the thermal waters were discovered 420m underground. The thermal water with its carbon dioxide content is recommended especially for those suffering from rheumatic pains and locomotor problems. The waters were formally given **medicinal status** in 1995. The microclimate in the *Sikonda Valley* is also ideal for convalescence, refreshment and rest.

Those visiting the **thermal and leisure bathing complex** (from autumn 2004), as well as those fishing on the **lake**, or staying in their weekend cottages or at the **youth camp,** will enjoy what is indeed a unique climate.

The Bánát peony is the most beautiful protected plant in the Eastern Mecsek.

KOMLÓ

It was the mining industry which was primarily responsible for the growth of the town in the valley along which the *Kaszárna flows*. The town's *Cultural Centre* (Templom tér) can be found in what was the **Miners' Working Men's Club**. Behind it, in the Hasmány-dűlő you can see the ruins of the 13th–15th century parish church. On the walls of the entrance hall to the Theatre and Concert Hall on Kossuth Lajos utca you can see the famous relief known as the **Attila József Altar** by *Miklós Melocco*.

The natural history collection at the **Local History Museum** (Városház tér 1.), entitled *The Natural World of the Mecsek*, includes geological exhibits and fossilised material (a dinosaur footprint, mammoth remains, the imprints of microscopic organisms).

MAGYARHERTELEND was once famous for its pottery. There was a time when pottery was made in all the houses in the village. The men saw to getting the raw materials whilst the women threw the pots. An upturn in the village's fortunes coincided with the discovery of the 40 °C thermal waters during exploratory drilling for uranium in 1958. The waters now supply the **baths**. Since then another well has been bored supplying pools with water at a temperature of 62 °C.

The Eastern Mecsek

In MAGYAREGREGY in the *Vár Valley* there is a cold-water **outdoor swimming complex**, above which stands **Máré Castle**, first mentioned in documents referring to an endowment made by Charles Robert in 1316. On the ground floor of the buildings standing around the castle courtyard there is an exhibition dedicated to the natural history of the Mecsek.

The existence of SZÁSZVÁR on the borders of Baranya and Tolna is due entirely to the coal mining industry. Following the closure of the mines it is left to the **Mining Museum** (Kun Béla u. 2.) to keep the memories of the industry alive. The parish church in the main square is built partly on the remains of the one-time **Episcopal Castle**. The building of the church is dated to the episcopate of Bertalan, Bishop of Pécs (1219–1252).

It was in 1799 that Pál László Esterházy, Bishop of Pécs, built both the parish church and his country residence in PÜSPÖKSZENTLÁSZLÓ. Four wings protrude from the oval-shaped **church** creating a Greek cross. The façade of the neoclassical-Baroque **palace** contains the Episcopal coat-of-arms made from Zsolnay ceramics. The park is now a protected **arboretum**.

It was in the 1980s that some youngsters who were looking for something more profound from life discovered Püspökszentlászló, which was where they founded the Life Orientation House in 1995.
Peony House is used as a base for walkers exploring the area (Zengő, Kisújbánya, Pusztabánya, Óbánya).

PÉCSVÁRAD

The **Benedictine Abbey** is situated on the southern foot of the highest peak of the *Mecsek, Zengő* (682m). It was Pécsvárad's first abbot, Asztrik, who brought the crown from Rome to give to Saint Stephen. Stephen then gave his manor house together with all its substantial endowments to the Benedictine missionaries arriving in Hungary.

The Castle Museum is housed in that part of the castle built from what remained of the medieval buildings in the 18th century. During the course of the archaeological investigations the walls of the 11th century monastery and what was once a chapel have been found. There is also a permanent exhibition of sculptures by Sándor Kígyós (1943-1984).

The **Church of the Blessed Virgin Mary** in Pécsvárad, built between 1757 and 1767, is an imposing Baroque structure. The patronal festival on August 15th signals the start of the castle's *Saint Stephen's Festival,* which lasts up until the national holiday on August 20th. The main festival on the calendars of the Calvinists living in Pécsvárad and Zengővárkony is St Luke's Day, October 18th. It is then every other year, in the years ending in even numbers, they hold the *Maidens Fair.*

There are some great paths from Pécsvárad up to *Zengő* from where you can see the villages in the northern part of the Mecsek.

Mecseknádasd

The traditions of the Sárköz in Tolna County are kept alive Zengővárkony the only village in Hungary to have a museum devoted to straw-weaving: the House of Straw (2002).

ZENGŐVÁRKONY

This village, famous for its traditional folk art and its sweet chestnut woods, lies at the foot of *Zengő* in a valley surrounded by gardens and fruit trees. The women of the village still weave and are only too happy to sell their wares. The local art is on display at the **peasant house** (Kossuth L. u. 6.). In the barn you will find the recently opened (2000) *Painted Egg Collection*, which has over 200 decorated eggs from 17 different countries.

The peasant cottage with its veranda and classical details, looks the same as it did in the middle of the 19th century.

It was the Calvinist priest at the local **church** (1787–1802), *Lajos Fülep* (1885–1970), who first brought the treasures of the Zengővárkony to people's attention. There is a **room** dedicated to him in the library at the vicarage (Arany J. u. 97.).

Whilst the largest plantation of Zengővárkony's famous sweet chestnuts, lying at the east end of the woods, has been in a state of decline since the 1970s, elsewhere plantations have been flourishing. The chestnut harvest takes place in September and October.

MECSEKNÁDASD

It was in 1771, that the church was dedicated to Saint George the Martyr. In 1975, the Church of Scotland presented the church with a portrait of Saint Margaret of Scotland by the Scottish painter *Gregor Smith*. It is here also that you will see a staue of St. Margaret (1993) in the **chapel** named after her set on a stone from *Réka Castle*.

When the Germans settled in the area at the beginning of the 18th century they built their first houses around the medieval chapel of Saint Stephen.

According to legend it was in Réka Castle, that Saint Stephen's granddaughter, St Margaret of Scotland, was born. Stephen granted sanctuary to two princes, Edmund Ironside and Edward, who had been forced to flee England. The lands near Mecseknádasd which they were endowed with were referred to as the Terra Britannorum in one particular historical document.

Edmund died, and his brother, who was brought up in the royal court, married Stephen's daughter Agatha. One of their children, Margaret (1046–1093), who later returned to the British Isles, subsequently married Malcolm King of Scotland.

*Of the 40 springs coming to the surface in the eastern Mecsek
the largest are those in the limestone areas. The lime in the water
has produced the interesting staircase effect you see
along the streams in the Hidas Valley and at the Pásztor Spring.
Csepegő Rock is a popular meeting place
for walkers hiking through the area.*

Panorama from the Eastern Mecsek

Mecseknádásd was the favourite part of *György
Klímó*, the Bishop of Pécs's estates. The village
contains an interesting Baroque **architectural
complex** (church, vicarage and school) in Templom tér, and the **Stations of the Cross** (1798–
1811) which end in a chapel dedicated to the
Mother of Sorrows.

Bishop Klímó had the octagonal wooden shingle-
roofed **Maria Schnee Chapel** (Liszt F. u.) built
next to his Baroque summer residence in 1770.
You can learn more about the local German community at the **German Ethnic Peasant Cottage**
(1977) (Munkácsy M. u. 5–7.).

In ÓBÁNYA, situated in one of the narrow valleys
of the *Eastern Mecsek Nature Reserve*. At the local
history exhibition (Fő u. 70.) you can see the
Óbánya pottery collection numbering 140 pots.
Today, *István Keszler* and *József Teimel* are the
only active potters in the village.

One of the most beautiful walks in the Mecsek is
the one taking you from *Stein Mill* at the top of
Óbánya up the *Óbánya Valley* as far as Kisújbánya.

In the courtyard of the Szekszárd's County Hall you can see the outline of the Byzantine-style eleven-apsed church, and the remains of the monastic buildings.

SZEKSZÁRD

The town is set in a landscape full of contrasts. It it is here that the flat landscape of the *Sárköz* meets the southeastern edge of the *Transdanubian Hills* and the *Szekszárd Hills*.

Going north you come to the *Mezőföld*. Apart from the countryside and the pleasant climate it is the grapes and the local wines for which the area is best known.

During the Roman period the town of *Alisca* stood where Szekszárd is today on the *limes* running down the right bank of the Danube. A lot of finds from this period have been uncovered, many relating to the local grape growing and ancient Christianity. During the Árpád period Béla I. founded the **Benedictine Abbey** in Szekszárd (Zegzardu, Zaczard), the remains of which can be found in the courtyard of **County Hall** (Béla tér 1.).

The village was given civic status in 1905.
You can get the best views of the countryside and the town of Szekszárd itself from Calvary Hill, where you can also see the town's coat-of-arms made by István Kis, decorated with an ear of corn, bells and bunches of grapes. Alternatively you can make your way up the hills rising 205 metres to the west by following Munkácsy utca.

Mihály Babits (1883-1940), one of Hungary's most famous poets during the first half of the 20th century, was born at house number 13 on the road that is now named after him.
It was here he lived and wrote for many decades.
In the garden you can see a statue of the poet by Pál Farkas. The house is now a museum dedicated to Babits's life and work.

In Béla tér in the centre of the old town stands the late Baroque Roman Catholic church (1805) dedicated to the patron saint of the town, Saint Ladislas. It is said by some to be the largest single-aisled church in Europe.
The square immediately in front contains a statue of the Holy Trinity commemorating the plague of 1740.

Since 2003, the new Saint Ladislas Bridge across the Danube, lying to the east of the town and on a level with Hajós, provides direct access to the Great Plain. The 920metre-long bridge, with its two lanes, cycle path lane and pavement, and the 20.5km section of road linking roads 6 and 51, has opened up the town to those living between the Tisza and the Danube.

The **Abbot's Residence** in Béla tér, built in 1765, is the oldest building in the town, next to which stands the **town hall** *(Károly Tormay)*, the official opening of which was attended by Franz Liszt in 1846. *Mihály Pollack* planned the classical **County Hall** (1828–1833), one of the architect's finest designs outside Budapest. Inside there is a fine staircase and an elegant council chamber.
One wing of the building houses the *Tolna County Archive*, which also puts on temporary exhibitions. Another part of building houses the **Franz Liszt Memorial Exhibition** and an exhibition of paintings and decorated stones by *Eszter Mattioni* (Béla tér 1.).

In the centre of Garay tér stands a statue of the Szekszárd-born János Garay who sang of János Háry's heroic deeds. The bronze statue designed by Ferenc Szárnovszky was cast in Paris.

The town's first cinema (1913) is now the **Deutsche Bühne**, the only full-time German-language theatre in Hungary. It was in the one-time *Szegzárd Hotel* (*Ödön Lechner* and *Gyula Partos,* 1893) that the first telephone in Hungary was used in 1877.

Ever since it was put up in the **Prometheus Park** *Imre Varga's Prometheus sculptural composition* has prompted no end of debate. It's for you to make up your own mind what you think.

The **Babits Cultural Centre** *(Ernő Tillai)* and the **Biscuits, Candles and Sweets Museum** (Munkácsy u. 8/a) both await visitors looking for something a little out of the ordinary. The **Arts House** awaits art and music lovers.

The **Mór Wosinszky County Museum** (1895) is a fine neo-Renaissance building. Its exhibitions cover the history of the Tolna landscape, showing how people's ways of life have changed over the centuries. Around the town you will find not only vineyards but plenty of woods, which are excellent for walking and relaxing in.

The synagogue (1896–97, J. Petschnik), which served the Jewish community until 1944, is now a concert and exhibition venue.

THE SÁRKÖZ

The Sárköz stands between the *Sió, Sárvíz* and the *Danube*. Following the draining of the marshy areas the locals were able to make a good living from the resulting farmland. This new-found prosperity was expressed in the local Sárköz costume. Őcsény, the northernmost village in the *Sárköz,* has its isolation to thank for the survival of its local Hungarian folk songs and folk costumes.

It is the women's costumes for which Őcsény is best known. The neck is frilly, the sleeves broad and embroidered. Above the tightly flounced starched petticoats the locals wore a silk skirt, decorated at the front and bound together with a tassled silk apron. The tassles on the neckscarf were long enough to enable you to see the beaded collar underneath. The girls wore headdresses, which always included the colour red, shot through with golden thread.

On the **airfield** on the edge of Őcsény you can go hot-air ballooning, and parachuting. You can even have a lesson on how to fly a kite, a glider or a light aircraft. The next stage in the reconstruction project (2003) will involve the laying of a new concrete runway.

The **Calvinist church** in DECS in the middle of the Sárköz, although originally Gothic, has been rebuilt many times. It is worth looking for the **Cserenci Hunting Lodge** where there is an exhibition dedicated wildlife in the *Gemenc.*

The exhibitions at the peasant cottage in Decs and on the first floor of the Village Hall tell you all you need to know about the local costumes. On the ground floor of the Village Hall there are temporary exhibitions about the local arts and crafts.

In BÁTASZÉK you will find some beautiful old **Swabian houses** conveniently situated next to the railway junction. The *Maria-hilf Chapel* and the *Statue of the Holy Trinity* (1794) were built in a Baroque style (Budai u.). The 83-metre tower of the neo-Gothic **Roman Catholic church** (1901–1903) rises above the centre of the town. Next to it they have excavated and restored Hungary's first Cistercian foundation (1142).

The late Baroque **St Urban Chapel** celebrates its patronal festivals in style.

The Stations of the Cross in Bátaszék is one of the most beautiful in Hungary. Another can be found on the road out to Mohács.

A number of 30 million-year-old **granite tors** can be seen near MÓRÁGY. In the main square you will find the **Calvinist church** (1785) and the **Local History Collection** containing some examples of local Swabian costumes (Szabadság u. 83.).

The history of Mórágy is explained in all three floors of the local museum.

It is worth visiting GRÁBÓC for the beauty of its landscape and for its **Serbian Orthodox church and monastery**. The Serbian monks ended up here having fled the Turks in 1580. They finished building the monastery, the only Greek Orthodox monastery in the country, in 1761.

Ever since the waters of the Lajvér rose, SZÁLKA has been a popular weekend destination. The countryside (see picture) opens up before you as you stand in front of the chapel at Görögszó.

GEMENC WOOD

The *Gemenc* not only has the most beautiful **woodland** bordering on the Danube it also happens to be the largest woodland of its type in Europe. Because of the slight inclination in the land, the *Sió* and the *Danube* both splinter into streams creating lots of small islands in the process. Substantial stretches of the river were left stranded once the rivers had been straightened, making the flood plains even more inaccessible.

The most popular destination for visitors to the Gemenc is Bárányfok, five kilometres east of Szekszárd. It is here you will find the hunting trophy museum, a restaurant and a gift shop. The Gemenc Woods can either be seen from the narrow-gauge railway leaving from Bárányfok or from a pleasure boat sailing along the Sió.

The different types of soils here mean there is also a rich and varied selection of wild flowers. In the isolated wooded areas you can find wild tulips, adder's tongue and summer snowflakes. Black cranes, eagles, osprey and goshawks live in the **bird reserve**. The Gemenc Wood is quite rightly famous for its deer and wild boar.

Life in BOGYISZLÓ is very much influenced by the nearby Danube. The village is well-known for its hot, red, thin, pointed paprika and the traditional Sárköz folk costumes. The **Calvinist church** is late Baroque (c.1790, porch 1822). There are 36 hectares of protected woods nearby where you can find various types of grasses, sedge and a fine selection of orchids.

OUT OF SZEKSZÁRD

TOLNA

It is the River Danube which has very much determined the fate of the town, particularly following the straightening of the river. **Silk thread production** in the town started at the turn of the 19th and the 20th centuries. The story of the factory, which is still in production today, and the silk industry in general, is told at the museum (Bezerédj Pál tér 1.).

Amongst the elegant old town houses on Kossuth utca you will find the Baroque **Roman Catholic church** (1773).

It's worth visiting **Festetics Manor**, and the statue of the *Holy Trinity* statue in the centre of the town put up in about 1790.

Many go to the classical chapel on Tolna's Deák Ferenc utca to look at the Stations of the Cross.

Tolna also has a **German Ethnographical Exhibition,** the *István Kiss* model boat and fishing tackle collection (Bajcsy-Zsilinszky u. 106.) and the *János Martinek Bequest* (Bezerédj u. 5.).

FADD is the home of tobacco and paprika. *Dombori*, which administratively speaking is actually part of Fadd, is a tourist resort situated on one of the Danube's dead channels.

Hopefully the termination of the Fajsz ferry service will not affect the popularity of the *Dombori Dead Channel*. There are other alternatives, like the Gerjen–Kalocsa **ferry crossing**, and the new *Saint Ladislas Bridge* in Szekszárd which is excellent for those living beyond the Danube. Those approaching along road number 6 should turn off at either the 120km marker at Dunaszentgyörgy and continue along road130 turning off before Tolna.

The **Benyovszky Palace** in TENGELIC, rebuilt during the second half of the 19th century, belonged to the *Kossuth Prize-winning sculptor István Kiss* whose monumental public sculptures can be seen in many Hungarian towns. It is his works you can see out in the park. Of more interest perhaps to the ornithologists are the birds which nest near *Lake Bogárzó*.

The classical Csapó Palace in Tengelic was built in 1820 to the plans of architect Mihály Pollack.
What was the park is now an arboretum.
Some of the 56 trees originally planted in the park can still be seen today.
(You can only visit the park with the permission of the owner).

SIÓAGÁRD stands at the bottom of the gently rolling hills which stand where the Sió meets the Sárvíz. The folk art, which is still alive and well, can be studied in detail at the **peasant cottage** (Zrínyi u. 31.).

Of all the villages in Transdanubia it was in Sió-
agárd that the local population persisted in wearing
their local costumes for the longest period of time.
Their clothing and embroidery resembled those seen
in Kalocsa and Nógrád County. The brides wore
ribbons and the young girls red scarves with which
they concealed their hair buns. In the second half of
the 19th century they wore rosy silk bodices together
with a blouse and a petticoat. Later their costumes
became much more showy.

Nearby ZOMBA on the *Szekszárd Wine Road* is the perfect place to try the wines for yourselves.

BONYHÁD

This, the centre of the *Völgység*, is situated on the Roman military road linking Sopianae and Aquincum. Following the Turkish occupation the area was repopulated by Hungarian Protestants and then by ethnic Germans. The ethnic mix of the region was made all the more complex by the arrival of the Bukovinan and the Transylvanian Szeklers after the Second World War. A lot of the houses lining the town's narrow winding streets built around 1800 survive to this very day.

Next to the Baroque **Roman Catholic church** (1769–1782) in Bonyhád's main square stands the **Völgység Museum** in what was the *Dőry Palace*. Today, the classical building contains exhibitions devoted to everyday life and customs in the Völgység from the Turkish period right up until the middle of the 19th century (Szabadság tér 2.). Also amongst the permanent displays is the "Lengyel Cultural Collection" and a collection of German and Szekler costumes and textiles.

Turning out of the main square into one of the side streets you come to the Louis Seize-style *synagogue* built in 1715. The **Calvinist church** with its interesting doorway can be found in Petőfi utca. The **Lutheran church** (1795–1800) has an interestingly shaped tower, a three-bayed nave and a polygonal chancel (Dózsa György u. 67.). The successor to the **Lutheran Grammar School**, the first grammar school in Tolna County (Sárszentlőrinc, 1806), has been in existence since 1870 (Kossuth u. 4.). Its most famous student was the writer *Gyula Illyés* (1902–1983).

General Mór Perczel was born in Bonyhád. The illustrious general, who assembled a rebel army in Bonyhád in 1848, first saw the light of day at house number 46 on the street now bearing his name. His greatest military feat was his victory against the imperial forces at Ozora in the autumn of 1848. Forced into exile it was only after the Compromise of 1867 that Perczel was able to return to his homeland. His tomb lies near the picturesque late Baroque Calvary chapel (1817) on Calvary Hill. Poet Mihály Vörösmarty worked as a family tutor at the Perczel Villa (1740–1746) in nearby Alsóbörzöny.

TAMÁSI

The *Kapos-Koppány Hills* get their name from the rivers flowing through the eastern part of *Outer Somogy*. Despite being built on the lowest part of the *Koppány Valley* the town's roads have to encounter the slopes of *Castle Hill* immediately to the south.

To the south of Tamási lies a 36 thousand-hectare forest, which stretches all the way to Gyula far away to the east. However, you need permission from the National Park to enter it. It is here that the world-famous fallow deer live, and where the Hungarian oak gene bank can be found. There are also eight hunting lodges situated in this most picturesque of settings. It is thanks to the efforts of Ádám Würtz that a fallow deer made its way onto the town's coat-of-arms.

A document dating from 1315 mentions the **castle**, which was defended by Brigadier Ádám Béri Balogh during the course of the Rákóczi Wars for Freedom.

Tamási Castle didn't survive Leopold I.'s programme of fortress destruction, and stone from the castle was used to build the **Miklósvár Hunting Lodge**. For many decades the reputation of the place brought a very select band of hunters to the **Tamási Game Park** from all over Europe.

*Most visitors to Tamási head for the thermal baths
and the camping site next door.
Situated at the bottom of Castle Hill
the baths are open all summer.*

The leisure possibilities at Tamási spread beyond
the baths. *Castle Hill* and *Miklósvár Woods* are
both excellent for walking.

It doesn't require much effort to get from the
thermal baths up to the **lookout point** built on
the site of the old castle. There are also tennis
courts and a fishing lake (Hársfa u. 3.).

Miklós Castle was built by Miklós Esterházy in
1775, although it gained its present appearance in
1809. The old hunting lodge would have fallen into
a state of decay if opera singers *Katalin Mészöly* and
Bálint Horváth hadn't bought it and renovated it.
(The building can only be seen from the outside).

The nave of the Gothic **Rozália Chapel** (Kálvária-
domb) dates back to the 14th century. The chancel
was added later in 1542, and there have also been
Baroque and romantic-style additions since then.
There are some fine statues in the wall niches on the
west front of the Baroque **Roman Catholic church**
(1745). The side windows, the rococo high altar and
the pulpit are also worthy of note (Szabadság u. 4.).

THE KAPOS-KOPPÁNY HILLS

REGÖLY's past includes a Celtic mint and a royal
Alan burial site and a medieval deanery. Its imposing **Roman Catholic church** dates from the end of
the 18th century, a period of great prosperity when
the settlement gained the rank of market town.

*The Pacsmag Fishing Lakes in Koppány Valley have aroused the interest of international environmentalists,
and consequently the waters have been granted protected status as part of the Ramsar Agreement.*

The grammar school in Gyönk, where teaching is currently done in two languages, was founded by a Hungarian from Sárvár and a German preacher from the village of Nagyszékely. At the **German peasant house** you can see the Lutheran priest, *Aladár Lackner*'s ethnographic collection (Táncsics u. 48.).

The medicinal waters at the Gunaras Medicinal Baths (Alkotás tér 1.) are particularly good for those suffering from locomotor disorders.

Gyönk's Lutheran church was built in 1896.

Sándor Petőfi was a student at the Lutheran grammar school in Sárszentlőrinc for two years between 1806 and 1807. The house where Petőfi lived now contains an **exhibition** devoted to him (Petőfi u. 12.).

Dombóvár

The town got its name from the castle owned by the landowner Pál Dombó. Today all that survives of the castle is one single stretch of wall on the banks of the River Kapos, known as **Gólya Castle** on account of all the storks nesting there.

It is worth taking a look at the pulpit in Dombóvár's **Roman Catholic church** (1757) (Arany János tér).

In the suburb of *Gölle* you will find a **museum** (Hóvirág u. 25.) dedicated to the children's writer and former resident *István Fekete*. The **Kossuth sculptural composition** (*János Horvay*, 1928) in the *Szigeterdő* is the one that once stood in front of the *Parliament Building* in Budapest, but was deemed too grim and gloomy to stay.

From the Kapos to the Sió

In the middle of Iregszemcse there is a fine **sculpture park**. The locals are extremely proud of the fact that during his folk song collecting tours of 1906 and 1907, *Béla Bartók* transcribed 307 folk songs here. The classical **Viczay-Kornfeld Palace** is now used as a special school. The English-style park surrounding it is now protected and can only be seen with prior permission from the head of the institute. The 15th century late Gothic **Calvary Chapel** is the oldest building in the village.

In the park of the classical Iregszemcse Palace there are some trees which are several centuries old.

OZORA gets its name from its one-time owner, and the builder of the castle, Pipó Ozorai (Fillipo Scolari). The way this one-time Italian trader rose to being one of the most distinguished men in Hungary during the reign of King Sigismund is the stuff of legend.

Perhaps the most heroic episode in the castle's history took place in October 1848, when the Hungarian hussars and the national guard managed to force the retreating Serb and Croat forces into surrendering. The renovated castle now includes a museum dedicated to the poet Gyula Illyés. Sándor Petőfi also frequented the large inn in Ozora and it was here he was taken by the lifestyle of the travelling players.

In the **Baroque Franciscan church** in SIMONTORNYA you can see the most beautiful frescos in Tolna County. The liturgical furniture carries all the hallmarks of the Baroque style favoured during the reign of Maria Theresa. The church is connected to some single-storeyed Baroque monastic buildings. Although PÁLFA has both a palace and a Baroque church, it is particularly famous for *Lower and Upper Rácegrespuszta*. The writer and poet *Ervin Lázár* was born in the former, *Gyula Illyés* in the latter. Although Illyés's birthplace has been demolished, there is a **museum** dedicated to him, which also includes the **school museum**. (For pre-arranged visits contact the following postal address: Rácegres 7042.)

"Wipe our mute father's shining brow, my sweet, / And bring a chair on the veranda here / Behind the thinning vine; sit silently, / While from our souls, as from before this house, / Veils thin away."
(Gyula Illyés: After Summer)

Simontornya Castle's predecessor was built in about 1270. It got its present appearance at the beginning of the 15th century at the height of the Renaissance in Hungary. The Castle Museum (Vár tér 10.) has an exhibition about the history of the castle.

From the *old town* you pass through a carved gate before entering the **castle courtyard**.

*On the hill overlooking Old Dunaföldvár,
in what was a very important logistic position, stood the castle,
which burnt down in 1858. The surviving donjon has been
known as the Stump Tower ever since.*

It was here that the Benedictine Abbey, founded by Béla II. in 1135, stood. The **Stump (Turkish) Tower** (14th–15th century) with its buttresses is now the castle restaurant and an exhibition venue (Rátkai köz 2.).

Outside the Baroque **Roman Catholic church** stands a rococo *Holy Trinity statue* (1755). The **Franciscan Church and Monastery** in Rákóczi utca have all the typical features of the late Baroque style. On the banks of the Danube you will see **cellars**, the **thermal bath** and the fisherman's inn.

The bridge across the Danube (1928–1930) is a very important crossing point linking the *Great Plain* with *Transdanubia*.

From *Látóhegy* on the edge of NÉMETKÉR, you can see the *Ős-Sárvíz* with its sandy hillocks meadows, and its rare flora and fauna. In the most jealously guarded area, the ten hectares of water meadows, you can see up to 15 kinds of orchid.

*On Ökör Hill near Bikács, the sandy, wooded steppe has s
urvived totally untouched. It's at its most beautiful in May
when the needlegrass is in flower. About one kilometre east
of Ökör Hill you come to 47 hectares of protected water meadows.
Apart from the various hybrids of orchid you can also find
two types of plants dating back to the Ice Age,
the white hellebore and the globe-flower (illustrated above).*

*Near Bölcske archaeologists have come across a Bronze Age
earthwork and a building dating from the Roman period.
The Roman finds from the River Danube can be found
in the lapidarium next to the Roman Catholic church
consecrated in 1796.*

During the course of detailed botanical studies on the *Gyűrűs Valley* near BÖLCSKE a lot of protected species flourishing on the flat loess meadows have been successfully identified.

The **Benedictine Abbey** in MADOCSA was built during the reign of Geisa II. (1141–1161). The Romanesque church with its two towers survives whilst the monastic buildings lie in ruins. The most valuable thing in the large Calvinist church is its organ, the tone of which is helped by the excellent acoustics. On the edge of Madocsa, outside the flood barriers along the Danube, you can find a plantation of *Slavonian oaks*.

In DUNAKÖMLŐD they have uncovered the remains of some **Roman fortifications**. The more interesting finds can be seen at the Szekszárd Museum. *Sánchegy* had an important logistical role during the course of the Rákóczi Wars for Freedom. It was from here that the **crossing place** over the Danube used by Bottyán Vak during his illustrious military campaign in Transdanubia was defended.

Those passing near Dunakömlőd should not miss the opportunity of calling in on the **halászcsárda** to sample the local fish dishes.

Fishermen at Paks have caught wels weighing 7kg.

PAKS

It is on the banks of the Danube, on the south-eastern part of the *Mezőföld,* that you can find the thickest layer of *loess* in the whole of Hungary (almost 60m).

The Romans built a fortification by the name of Lussonium on what is now Sánchegy (the Bottyán Ramparts), which formed part of the limes defensive system protecting the eastern border of the empire.

It was from the second half of the 1960s, that the town entered its most dynamic period of growth, which coincided with the opening of the **nuclear power station**. The first block, situated to the south of the town, was plugged into the electricity grid in December 1982. Today the power station produces about half of Hungary's electricity.

The stringent checks in the environment immediately around the power station are done in accordance with international guidelines. If you want to know how nuclear energy can be used and how the nuclear power station works you can visit the Atomerőmű Rt.'s Visitors' Centre (next to road number 6).

The **Municipal Museum** can be found in Mádi Kovács (once known as the Cseh-Vigyázó) Hall (Deák Ferenc u. 2.).

Daróczy Hall (now a school) was restored by no less an architect than *Miklós Ybl* (1820). The **casino** was the third to be built in historical Hungary after Pest and Pozsony (Bratislava, Slovakia). The **Paks Picture Gallery** is housed in what used to be the classical-style *Erzsébet Hotel* (1820) (Szent István tér 4.). From the latter you can walk to the *banks of the River Danube* to look at the Paks fishing boats.

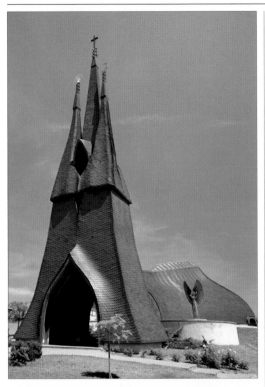

It was between 1750 and 1755 that the arriving Protestants built their first church, the tower of which was built forty years later. In time the German Lutherans also built their own church, the present one acquiring its present appearance in 1884. The Paks Jewry originally came from the Czech, Polish and the German lands, as well as 50 other Hungarian settlements. The synagogue is now used as a library (Villany u. 1.).

NAGYDOROG is a friendly enough place (*drog* in old Slav means friend). The Baroque **Calvinist church** was built during the reign of Maria Theresa.

The old **Széchenyi Palace** is now used as a school. In Kossuth utca you can find local priest *Artúr Stockinger*'s rather unusual **cap and hat collection**. Nagydorog's *Szenes Pastures*, is where we end our tour of Southern Transdanubia.

We hope that you have managed to get at least a flavour of this rich and varied region. Without any further ado it is now time to find the most suitable crossing across the River Danube before planting our feet firmly on the soil of the *Southern Great Plain*.

Imre Makovecz's Roman Catholic Church of the Holy Spirit (Hősök tere) was built in the Kishegy suburb of Paks

"In the Szeged theatre, my love appeared,
That heart-warming name music to my ear.
A reassuring, fair refrain
That, there on the banks of the Tisza river
The applause, the acclaim will be mine to hear,
Because I am yours and you are mine.

Your boxes stretch out open and wide
Embracing the stage from either side,
Taking me gently under your wing;
To artistic concerns a reliable witness,
A stern judge as well as a warm nest,
I thank you all up there for everything."

(Miklós Szabó
on the occasion of the renovation
of the Szeged National Theatre, 1985)

CONTENTS – THE SOUTHERN GREAT PLAIN

OMV

Map showing petrol stations in the region

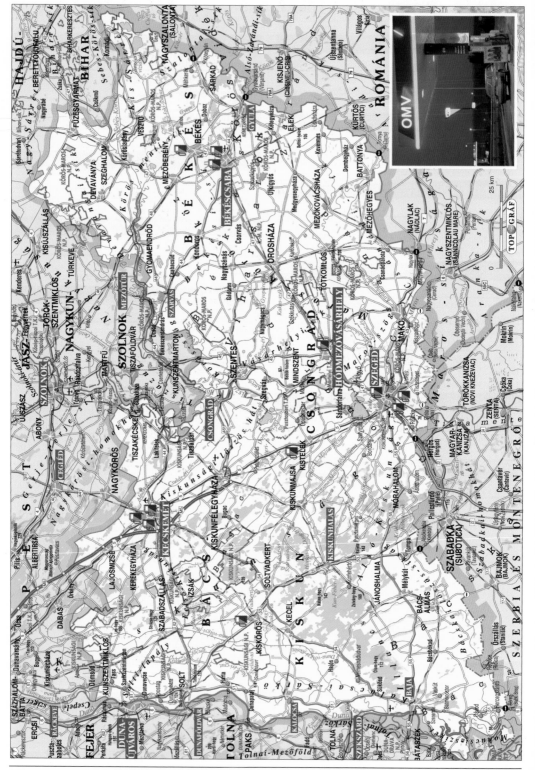

THE SOUTHERN GREAT PLAIN

It was Petőfi who made us fall in love with this landscape. It was he who described the *"Stampeding herds of horses, as they run, / Thunder across the wind with trampling hoof."* You can still see the lonely inns he writes of, although hopefully the old innkeeper is not a sullen man whose *"surly mouth is yawning in his beer."* So, without any further ado, let's look at the region's natural treasures…

The landscape of the southern part of the Great Plain, whilst not actually having been created by the River Tisza, is most definitely dominated by it. The river, rather than helping us to divide the region up, actually binds it together. *"Low flats of yellow shingle spread away, / From where I stood, to meet the meadow hay"* was how Petőfi described it. But a region can also be defined through cold facts and statistics, as well as poetic verse. The Southern Alföld (the Hungarian for "Great Plain") covers three administrative areas, the counties of Bács-Kiskun, Békés and Csongrád, in which there are almost 50 towns and five times that many villages 1,367,000 people live in the region, which covers one-fifth of the territory of Hungary.

It is the winds, the waters, and the hand of mankind, which have created the landscape we see on the Southern Great Plain today. The region lies at the heart of the Carpathian Basin, there is even a monument in Szarvas marking its exact geographical centre. Over the years, and we are talking here in terms of millions of years, the rivers running off the slopes of the Carpathians have left the finest of powdery deposits over the whole region. The sheer quantities of material being carried along in the waters of the Danube, the Tisza, the Körös and the Maros caused the rivers to slow down and meander dramatically. Sometimes the course of the river changed completely leaving a trail of unused riverbeds across the landscape.

The dry sediment, spread over the landscape, would invariably get whipped up by any strong winds and taken off to some distant land. Where thick grasses were able to get a hold of this fine soil there was always a chance that loess would form. Elsewhere sandbanks formed in areas where the deposits were not so fine. It was in these landscapes, differing somewhat from the overall picture, that the loess and sandbanks provided a

Mezőhegyes. The giant plain tree on the Stud Farm.

habitat suitable for plants and animals. Thereafter it was man who was to make his mark on the landscape. Excavations at Gorzsa, Kökénydomb and Kopáncs on the edges of Hódmezővásárhely have shown that villages existed here as far back as seven thousand years ago. The huge mounds (*kunhalom* in Hungarian), which are found mainly east of the Tisza, were probably used for burial purposes. They were constructed at about the same time the pyramids were built...

When people talk about "people shaping the environment" one usually thinks in terms of an active process. But being absent from a particular place also has its consequences. The latter is particularly true of the period following the expulsion of the Turks, and the way in which the southern Alföld reverted to being a wilderness during the 17th century. Whoever happened to be living there had to contend with the marshes, the bogs, the reed beds and the plains, just as the first Hungarian arrivals had to do at the end of the 9th century. They too had to eke out a living from semi-nomadic forms of farming.

The people who lived here, however, were capable of making good that which had been lost. This they achieved, but not before almost totally destroying the woods which lay on the sand beds between the Danube and the Tisza. At the turn of the 18th and 19th centuries the locals were left with what was a barren landscape. Faced with the possibility that the winds would take away all the topsoil, and with it the inhabitants' livelihood, a solution was called for. As *Dezső Horváth* tells us, the people's response was *"to plant acacias, poplars, mulberry bushes, fruit trees and vines. These acted as windbreaks, the guiding principle being that obstacles should be positioned in such a way that the wind would never be able to work up the kind of momentum capable of damaging the following obstacle. And that even if the windbreak didn't actually stop the wind, the wind would at least have been weakened to the extent that it would no longer be able to carry off the topsoil... also the roots not only grow into the sand, the sand also sticks to them."*

It was during the 19th century that the bends in the rivers were dammed up and their courses straightened, allowing the rivers to flow at a much greater speed and opening enormous new tracts of land. Although now flowing on new courses the rivers have managed to hold onto their original wildlife, whilst the dead channels, now totally cut off from their rivers, are used as fishing lakes and reservoirs. The cool, shady channels are popular amongst those seeking relief from the hot summer sun.

The largest area in the region, geographically speaking, is the *Kiskunság*, a region whose name has historical connotations. It was one of the areas the Cumans (*kun* in Hungarian), a people believed originally to have come from eastern Asia, settled in during the 13th century. During the course of the Middle Ages the Cumans were absorbed into Hungarian society. In the Kiskunság the undulating sandbanks alternate with the sandy grassland, the juniper groves, the acacias, the swampy puddles and the ponds which appear after heavy rainfall. Here too you will find stretches of Petőfi's plain. The plains seem to engulf you in Apaj, as they do in Bokros near Csongrád. Even east of the Tisza, around Kardoskút, for example, the plain goes on for what appears to be an eternity.

But to call the Great Plain monotonous is to miss the point. Were you to get down on your knees you would see that the subtle differences in altitude, which here amount to only five centimetres or so, are significant differences indeed to the local vegetation. For such changes in vegetation you would have to climb an additional 50 to 100 metres in more mountainous climes. Ants are capable of changing the earth's surface here on the plain on a scale similar to say a crater or a ravine in a range of mountains. It is no coincidence that out in the Kiskunság the larger fruit plantations are known as hills.

Down towards the border with Serbia the billiard table of a landscape is covered with a loess soil which is ideal for agriculture. It is what *Kosztolányi,* called *"sickly, sotted, sad, sullen Bácska"*. The 30–40 kilometre-wide strip of land running down the banks of the Danube, covering the *Solt Plain* and the *Kalocsa-Sárköz,* was totally depopulated during the Turkish Conquest. With the exception of *Bugac,* subsequent resettlement meant that the area acquired a multi-ethnic character.

The south-eastern corner of Hungary is made up of the two neighbouring regions of the *Körös-Maros Lands* to the north and the *Körös Region,* which both border on the *Lesser* and the *Greater Sárrét.*

The *Viharsarok* (literally Stormy Corner), which is about as far southeast as you can get before crossing into Romania, refers to the radical agrarian movements that once thrived there rather than anything pertaining to the weather.

As for the towns in the southern Alföld, prosperity wasn't guaranteed merely by the ability to produce; proximity to the relevant trade routes was essential. In these parts this meant being close to a river crossing. Some of these commodities traded were salt (a royal monopoly), fish, cereal, cattle and wine. Fortunate enough to enjoy all the necessary prerequisites, Szeged became the region's most important town, a distinction it still holds today.

The ethnic diversity of the southern part of the Great Plain can be dated back to the 18th and 19th centuries. By that time the Cumans had become totally absorbed into the Hungarian population, and it was now time for other ethnic groups to enter the region. In towns that had once been in the pay of the sultan, one now found Germans, living in the eastern parts of Békés County and on the banks of the Danube, Slovaks in Békéscsaba, and Romanians in Méhkerék and Battonya. Around Baja and Szeged the ethnic map was made all the more complicated by the presence of Orthodox Serbs, Catholic Serbs, and Sokác (a small Slavonic ethnic group).

This ethnic diversity can be seen in the way the settlements were laid out. These new villages, unlike the old Hungarian settlements, which had evolved gradually over the centuries, were single entities with streets laid out in accordance with the specifications of the time. Of the "ancient" Hungarian villages only a few survive, hidden amongst the waters and marshes of the Tisza and the Danube.

Some of these new villages managed to grow into towns, like for example the Hungarian settlement of Orosháza, Swabian Bácsalmás, the mixed communities of Mezőberény and Elek, and Slovak Tótkomlós, Szarvas and Kiskörös. It is interesting to note that it was normal to own two homes. Apart from their enterprise, people kept either a town house or a house in a village. Two thirds of the population live in towns, the ancestors of the old agricultural settlements. It is for this reason that the region rather curiously lays claim to being the most urban in Hungary.

The traditional buildings most frequently made use of the building materials which were closest to hand: mud, any wood that happened to be available, reeds and rushes. Quality wood was more likely to be had by those who lived close to a river. The timber gables found on the local houses were decorated according to the taste and the social pretensions of their owners, frequently using the sunbeam motif. The houses in the Swabian vil-

Szeged, sunbeam motifs in the lower town.

SOUTHERN ALFÖLD SPECIALITIES

Have you ever tried *plum jam puff pastry, crunchy caramel cake* or *pork-scratching scones*?

Do you know what makes the *Szőreg rose,* the *Kecskemét apple,* the *Zenta melon,* the *Csengőd sour cherry,* the *Szatymaz peach,* the *Easter rosemary apple,* the *batul apple* and the *Szentes naseberry* different from all the other more established varieties? Everyone knows that *apricots* in apricot brandy come from Kecskemét. The fruits and spices which go to make *"ágyas" schnapps* come from Mórahalom, whilst *Kiffer pear brandy* is only made from the pears of that name.

It is well worth keeping an eye out for *Tisza carp* and *grey wels,* cigánka (a sausage made of blood and liver), *Orosháza goose liver, goose scratchings, goose fat,* brawn ("disznósajt") and *Bácska black pudding* in the local shops and indeed trying them for yourself. If it's a joint of meat you are looking for then why not try *speckled Hungarian hen, guinea fowl, turkey, Hungarian duck* and the local *lamb.*

The local bakeries are likely to have *wholemeal bread, Szeged slices, Orosháza bananas, Mindszent kalács* (a soft sweet white bread), *Békés savoury kalács, Kunság pretzels* and *Dorozsma buns.* It is in these parts that *juniper berries* (Kiskunság), *peppergrass* and *marjoram* are grown. You should find *Szentes* cabbages (both red and white), *paprika, red peppers, asparagus, Szentes radishes* and *Makó and Bátya garlic* down at your local market. You will also probably find *soured peppers stuffed with cabbage, tarhonya* (granulated dried pasta), *Kunság barley, local honey, csalamádé* (a mixture of bottled vegetables), *Kecskemét apricot jam, popcorn corn* and *pritamin red pepper purée* there as well. Why not try them all! You may already have noticed that quite a few of them have already featured in the *"Hungarian Treasury".*

lages tend to have ornamented plastered façades, the distinguishing features being found in the way the verandas were articulated. The Slovaks tended to have richly decorated columned wooden verandas which could be found either at the front or at the back of the house.

So what of the locals themselves? Well, there seem to be two abiding characteristics. Firstly, the desire to express oneself in the most flamboyant way possible, whether that be in the way you articulate your house front, your veranda or your fence. It could also affect what you decide to wear for a special occasion, down to the quality of the needlework. It was the custom during wedding celebrations to parade the bride's furniture (her dowry) in front of all those present. This explains why the local painted furniture is considered the most beautiful in Hungary. Indeed, it is amongst the most highly prized furniture of its type in Europe. *"A potter's soul is full of the flowers and the leafy stalks of garden and meadow…it is only beauty that leads him, it is only beauty he seeks, and on making a pot, he inspects it with a critical eye, turning it briefly in his hands"*– this is how the ethnographer *Lajos Kiss,* described the creative process.

The desire to create, to be always one step ahead of one's neighbour, meant there was nothing which could escape the craftsman's attention, whether that be a harness or a riding whip, indeed, any of the horseman's accoutrements. Indeed, there is still a market and no shortage of work for those craftsmen and women working in Tápé and Makó.

The other trait you are likely to find amongst the locals is their keen interest in the language and culture of their own village and that of their neighbouring communities. It is interesting to note that, in what is a multi-ethnic setting, this curiosity does not extend beyond their immediate surroundings and into the neighbouring countries and beyond. What one has is a vibrant and colourful cultural environment. This pride in one's ethnic roots explains why there are so many organisations involved in the preservation of local customs and traditions, and why so many peasant houses have been restored to their original state and opened to the public.

Sunset on the Tisza

the town hall building in Makó. However, there are also a number of interesting town houses in Baja and Szeged. It is at the turn of the 19th and 20th centuries that the eclectic-style buildings in the region's towns were built. The Secession style made an impression mainly on the townscapes of Kiskunfélegyháza, Csongrád and Szeged, even if it only manifested itself on one particular building.

If the architectural treasures seem to be too few and too far between you can always explore the region's three national parks: the *Duna–Drava*, the *Kiskunság* and the *Körös–Maros National Parks* (for more information about these parks see the opening chapter). It would be foolish to miss the opportunity to explore the wide-open spaces or to experience the intimate atmosphere of a local hostelry.

The southern Alföld also has its fair share of thermal baths. In fact, the locals call the region *Thermal Valley*, though not without a touch of irony. The region enjoys more hours of sunshine than anywhere else in Hungary (more than two thousand hours a year) and there is a thermal bath just a thirty-minute drive from anywhere inside the region.

From the spring through to the autumn you are bound to find something happening. There is the *Szeged Open-Air Festival*, the *Gyula Castle Tournament*, the *Ópusztaszer "Hunniális"*, the *Kalocsa Paprika Festival*, the *Saint Stephen's Day Celebrations* and the so-called *Famous (Hírös) Festival* in Kecskemét. You could also go to a village patronal festival, or see the local village's children's dance group in action. Békéscsaba, Kecskemét and Szeged all have theatres, and there are plenty of musical events going on all year round. In the winter months you could perhaps round off a strenuous day down at the local thermal pool with a spot of culture down at the local museum.

When making your way along the highways and byways of the southern Alföld you will invariably encounter one of the four rivers making its way down through the region. On the left bank of the Danube you will find Kalocsa and Baja. Those using Kiskunhalas as a base are more likely to bump into the Tisza, or perhaps the Maros and down on the border in Békés County there are plenty of rivers going by the name of Körös.

Whilst it is true to say that the villages are beginning to look more and more like each other, and the tendency is indeed towards a greater uniformity, the differences nevertheless remain, in the way people behave, in their culture and in their very being.

There are traces of agricultural, religious and artistic activity in the region going back seven thousand years. Unfortunately, because of the destruction which has taken place in the meantime, very few traces remain. As for the last thousand years, the oldest buildings you are likely to see are only two or three hundred years old. For an explanation one need look no further than the wholesale destruction which took place during the 150 years of Turkish occupation. This, however, does not mean that there isn't anything older.

A few beautiful Romanesque and Gothic churches do survive more or less complete, as for example in Kiszombor, Óföldeák and Szeged, as well as the structures which have either been much rebuilt or left to go to rack and ruin. As far as the churches are concerned it was the baroque period which saw their spiritual and architectural rebirth. Indeed, the baroque style, along with the neo-Renaissance and the eclectic styles, was the style considered most suitable for many secular buildings as well. There are fine palaces in both Kalocsa and Szabadkígyós. As for the classical-style, there is but one building which really scales the heights,

The embroidery in the communities of the northern Kalocsai-Sárköz is an art form which has been handed down from generation to generation. Embroidery was a craft practised in those Catholic villages which miraculously survived the Turkish occupation and by the settlers who came over from Transdanubia, Croatia and Serbia. The motifs and the colours are as rich as the ethnic mix in the region, and the patterns are likely to be found on costumes, bedclothes, walls and furniture in equal measure. Mrs Gál is one of the most famous practitioners of her art. She lives and works in Homokmégy.

Seamstresses were initially pieceworkers taking on jobs at the houses of the upper-middle classes, sewing stencilled bedclothes or tablecloths. Having sewn for the gentry, the seamstresses then went on to use their own new ornamental vocabulary, using new colours and new techniques.
Embroidered patterns began to appear more regularly on clothes, on men's and women's shirts, bodices and waistcoats. The old-fashioned peasant patterns, which had been restricted to strip-like designs, were broken up and applied in an irregular fashion to any surface taking the seamstress's fancy. Indeed, the possibilities open to the embroiderers were further increased with the new coloured cottons coming onto the market.
Arriving in Kalocsa by train you can see the motifs used in the local folk art painted on the walls of the railway station. These can be used as references when wandering around the town looking at the wall paintings and the house fronts.

KALOCSA

Kalocsa is a one thousand-year-old cathedral town. Its first bishop was Asztrik, the Abbot of Pécsvárad, who brought Saint Stephen the Hungarian crown from Rome. In the ecclesiastical hierarchy the diocese is only second to Esztergom, and the archbishops of Kalocsa have often been involved in events (coronations, military campaigns) of considerable historical importance. It was the diocese which initiated the repopulation of Kalocsa following the Turkish occupation, making the town one of the first places in Turkish-held Hungary to experience resettlement. Indeed, it was thanks to the efforts of the archbishop that Kalocsa became a town in its own right, rather than remaining merely an ecclesiastical centre. The fan-shaped layout of the town bears this out. In the middle there is the tightly knit centre, which is where you find the **Cathedral** (1735– 1754, *András Mayerhoffer*) and

When entering the magnificent baroque interior of the cathedral you may be fortunate enough to hear the organ Franz Liszt was known to play on.

the **Episcopal Palace** (1776, *Gáspár Oswald*), and it is from here that the rest of the town opens out.

> *The treasures to be found in the library of the Baroque Episcopal Palace are much older than the building and its wooden rococo wall panelling. The splendours of the Italian interiors are also heightened by the Maulbertsch frescos. The collection contains 140 volumes, and includes written documents, manuscripts, early printed books and maps.*

The *Cathedral Treasury* contains a collection of vestments and devotional objects, including the Saint Stephen herma, which was produced especially for the new millennium, and the head relic of Saint Stephen.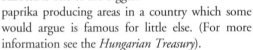
The **Paprika Museum** is dedicated to town's most famous product. Indeed, Kalocsa is one of the biggest paprika producing areas in a country which some would argue is famous for little else. (For more information see the *Hungarian Treasury*).

One particular example of creativity, although in this case in fine rather than folk art, are the computer-generated sculptures of Kalocsa-born artist *Miklós Schöffer*. One of the two **museums** on Szent István király utca is dedicated to his work. Also his illuminated sculpture, *Chronos 8*, a piece of computer-operated Kinetic Art, can be found at the bus station.

Kalocsa folk art (embroidery, painting) and the local folk dancing only really came to the world's attention during the 1930s.

Folk art has not yet been consigned totally to the museum, although there is a fine collection at the **Károly Visky Museum** (Szent István király u.). Indeed, the crafts are alive and kicking and experiencing something of a Renaissance.

The *Kalocsa International Folk Dance Festival* has been going since 1968. It is an event which has helped to keep the folk dance traditions in the region alive, and has ensured that such traditions will continue for a long time to come.

THE DANUBE AND THE KALOCSA-SÁRKÖZ

The old saying about the eastern bank of the Danube goes: *"The Danube will always find its way back to its original course,"* not particularly reassuring when you consider the extent to which the course of the Danube has been manipulated. The average village high street is usually lined with the best houses, some displaying distinctly urban pretensions. The variations in the brick columns and the gateways tell us something about the well-being, and indeed the aspirations, of the inhabitants. Many of the villages have vineyards. If one is to believe the local saying: the vines growing between the paprika fields on the *Kalocsai-Sárköz* may vary in quality, but at least *"drinking the worst Danube wine is still preferable to drinking the best Danube water"*.

DUNAPATAJ
Lake Szelidi's sandy shores, its hotel, camping site, restaurants and open-air stage provide the ideal surroundings for a spot of relaxation.

The sandy beaches, hotel, camping site, private holiday accommodation, restaurants and open-air stage guarantee lots of fun and relaxation.

> *According to a legend connected with the lake, a chief by the name of Bence drove his poor horses so hard that not only did their horseshoes wear away but their hooves did as well. On going to the lake for refreshment, however, the horses felt their strength return.*

Lake Szelidi may have got its name from an event which took place at nearby *Castle Hill*. It happened either when the Turks surrendered on seeing the size of an approaching Hungarian force, or when the Hungarians and the Turks exchanged prisoners at the ending of hostilities. Although now a lake it was once a stretch of the River Danube.

As far back as the Middle Ages the waters were used for healing wounds; today they are more likely to be used for treating hormonal and rheumatic problems, or illnesses affecting the central nervous system. During the summer months the water temperature rises to a pleasant 28 °C.

Lake Szelidi is surrounded by a 360-hectare *nature reserve,* which is a wonder to behold. By the late summer the place is filled with the dazzling purples of the alkaline aster and the reds of the Hungarian goosefoot.

It is certainly worth stopping at HARTA to look at the painted furniture, the local costumes and the farming implements on show at the **German Peasant House** (Templom u. 62.).

In SOLT, which has its own *bridge across the Danube* the carved wooden grave posts are worth looking at. The classical country house in the village, **Vécsei Palace,** belonged to the family of one of the thirteen generals executed in Arad at the end of the War for Freedom on 6th October, 1849. It is currently used as a **library**. On the avenue running through its park (Vécsei tér) you will find the Meleghegy **cellar village** with its five hundred cellars and **Cellar Museum**.

The nearby Danube flood plains are also good for a day out. You can go riding at the **equestrian centre** at *Révbér-puszta,* where you can also become acquainted with the farm animals and what's going on at the **house of arts and crafts.**

ÚJSOLT, which is now a place in its own right quite distinct from Solt, is a **holiday fishing village**. DUNAEGYHÁZA's **outdoor swimming complex,** with its quality waters and beautiful surroundings, make the village a great place for a longer visit. You can also visit the **Slovak Peasant House** (Posta u.). From the Solti-halom **lookout-tower** sitting 124 metres above the Alföld southeast of the village, you get some rare views of the surrounding landscape.

In APOSTAG *you will find the Baroque synagogue (1768), which has recently benefited from a restoration which won it a Europa Nostra award.*

In DUNAVECSE, the **Petőfi Memorial House** (his small dwelling *"on the banks of the great Danube"*) and an exhibition devoted to the ethnographer *Béla Vikár* can be found on Fő út. With this our travels north of Kalocsa have come to a temporary end. We will be returning to the *Kiskunság,* but not before we have gone south to the *Kalocsai-Sárköz.*

In MISKE *there is a special exhibition at the house where the artist Menyhért Tóth was born (Tóth Menyhért sor). It was the sand of the Alföld which inspired these unique visions: the sand, or indeed the water, reflecting the sun. For Menyhért Tóth, who died in 1980, the blinding quality of light was the basis of his surrealism. In the picture above you can see his painting entitled Market Gate.*

HAJÓS was where the Archbishop of Kalocsa settled the German Catholics, who brought the Gothic Madonna you can now see in the parish church from the pilgrimage church of *Bussen*. Thus the church itself became a pilgrimage place.

Hajós, made famous by its Baroque church, its Zsolnay china **Stations of the Cross**, the Baroque **Episcopal Palace** (Köztársaság tér) wine tour and the **cellar village**, is made all the more accessible by the Danube Bridge in Szekszárd.

Hajós's 1,200 cellars are open every day of the year – weekdays and holidays included. Wine-tasting is organised by the Urban Order of Wine Producers, and it is they who swear in those new knights who are prepared to protect and uphold the values to which they aspire.

NEMESNÁDUDVAR is the village where the local Swabians like to keep their **wine**. In a region with a rich ethnic mix, it is well worth visiting some of the local peasant houses which are open to the public, or indeed the odd village museum.

BAJA

All of what you see in Baja has been built over the last three hundred years. By the time the Turks left, Baja had reverted to being a riverbank, with its waters, its fish and wild animals, but little else. Despite having returned to an almost primordial state it wasn't long before Baja had re-established itself as an important port of call on one of Europe's busiest waterways, the *River Danube*. Szentháromság tér lies at the heart of the town. From the raised banks of the *Sugovica*, the tributary running through the town, you can see for miles. Three sides of the square contain the town's most beautiful buildings, the originally Baroque, but now neo-Renaissance **town hall**, and the neighbouring eclectic and classical town houses. Looking as it does onto the river, the bustling clover-shaped square has an atmosphere not found anywhere else

Once the Croatian, Dalmatian, Serbian and German masters and traders had arrived, it was only a matter of a decade before Baja had acquired the rank of town. At the beginning of the 19th century, Baja had the second largest cereal-loading dock in the country (after Pest). The actual layout of the town was determined by the roads leading out to Kalocsa, Halas, Szeged, Szabadka (Subotica, Yugoslavia) and Zombor (Sombor, Yugoslavia) and the river crossing. The town's development was rocked by the catastrophic fire of 1840. The result is today's predominantly classical townscape.

in Hungary. Not surprisingly it's frequently used as a period backdrop in Hungarian films.

The town is a series of narrow winding streets, with town houses standing next to each other very much cheek and jowl. There are small squares and churches, many of the old streets and houses having beautiful cast-iron fences and fittings. There are very few towns in Hungary which have managed to meet the needs of its tourists (restaurants, leisure facilities) and those of its historical buildings so successfully.

In Hungary there are two types of fish soup vying for the hearts and stomachs of the discerning guest: there's the Szeged recipe and the Baja recipe. (At the same time one should perhaps mention the so-called Tokaj "korhely" fish soup which also has pretensions of sorts...)
At the beginning of July the banks of the Danube pay host to the Baja Fish Soup Festival, when passers-by can see and smell the nigh-on two thousand cauldrons of fish soup bubbling away.

Downriver from the town the Sugovica encircles the island. The beauty and the harmony of the "botanical garden" means that its visitors are able to relax both physically and mentally. It is here at the Danube-Rhine-Main dock that you will find the tourist centre.

Baja's **churches** – the Franciscan Church on Bartók Béla út, the Church of St Peter and St Paul in Szent Imre tér, the Serb "Great" Church in Táncsics Mihály utca and the synagogue off Kölcsey Ferenc utca – reflect the town's ethnic, denominational and religious diversity.

The hall containing the portraits of Baja's most famous sons is striking indeed. There you can see *István Türr*, Garibaldi's famous general and one of the builders of the *Corinthian Channel*, and *András Jelky* the wayfaring tailor, whose true-life adventures are still enjoyed by children. However, the greatest figure in **"Baja's Pantheon"** is *Lázár Mészáros*, general during the 1848 War for Freedom. The town also counts Transylvanian-born painter *István Nagy* (1873–1937) as one of its own. *István Türr* gives his name to the **museum** (Deák Ferenc u.), where there also happens to be an exhibition about him. The **art gallery** is named after *István Nagy* (Arany János u.). And *Ferenc Medgyessy*'s sculpture of *András Jelky* stands in the square named after the great traveller. In recent years the **German Cultural Centre** (*István Novák*) has become one of the liveliest places in the town, both as a school and as a cultural venue.

EXPLORING THE BÁCSKA

In SZEREMLE you are likely to experience all the joys of village tourism and living by a river.

BÁTMONOSTOR's **Benedictine Monastery** was one of the region's medieval spiritual centres. Some ruins still remain, and the **local history collection**, which can be found next door, is open to the public.

It is the village's wine which attracts visitors to VASKÚT. This is not to say there are no other attractions. There is good hunting and fishing to be had and the village is famous for its weaving, its embroidery and its friendly hosts.

BÁCSALMÁS

Its Catholic church, and the one-time **Causcher** and **Ulrich residences** are proof that there was indeed wealth in Bácska during the 19th and 20th centuries.

Of particular interest to the visitor are the **Blue Dye Works** (Kossuth u.) founded in 1879 by the very Skorutyák family who run the works today.

Blue dyeing is both an industry and an art. It is industrial insofar as the material is dyed blue in what is an indigo-coloured liquid. The creative part is deciding which printing blocks and which patterns to use.

The appearance of blue-dyed clothing, the shades of blue used and the patterns can tell us a lot about the person wearing the clothes: their age, their ethnicity, and where they live.

South of the town lies a **fishing lake** formed from the *Kígyós Main Channel*. The *Salt Lake, the* southernmost of a chain of alkaline lakes lying between the Danube and the Tisza is recommended to those with locomotor problems. Next to the **outdoor swimming pool** is a picnic site.

KISKUNHALAS

There was a time, at the end of the 19th century when 35 windmills dominated the local skyline. Today there is but one, now a **museum**. The oldest buildings in the town are the Baroque churches, the late-classical **synagogue** (1860) and the **town hall** (1906–1907, *Rezső Hikisch, Henrik Kótai*). The cinema, which lies in the main square has a frieze of figures symbolising the arts along its façade.

Lake Kunfehér to the south and the Salt Lake to the north are all that remain of a landscape once extensively covered with water. Anglers still believe they offer good fishing. Nevertheless, it is the woodland which gives the landscape it special character with its poplars, acacias and pines interspersed with vineyards and fruit trees.

Kiskunhalas has no less than seven museums and houses open to the public. The **János Thorma Museum** (Köztársaság u.) has a local history exhibition, as well as a collection of paintings by the *János Thorma* (1870–1937) himself. Although born in Kiskunhalas, the Thorma family moved to Nagybánya (Baie Mare, Romania) when János was 14. Having trained in both Munich and Paris, he adopted a style similar to that of Bastien-Lepage. The **Collections House** (Bokányi u.) contains some excellent paintings and books, whilst the **Szilády Gallery** (Kossuth u.) has a collection of contemporary Hungarian paintings. The **Hunting Exhibition** (Kossuth u.) contains hunting trophies, whilst at the **Sáfrik Windmill**, which is still in use, you can study what is quite a feat of engineering. **Végh Hall** (Bajcsy-Zsilinszky u.) contains an exhibition dedicated to the work of artist *Balázs Diószegi*.

However, the town's most famous collection is that in the **Lace House**, an exhibition with examples of lace from all over the world (Kossuth u. 37/a.).

Lace is made using one of any number of techniques. In Kiskunhalas they tend to spin it and stitch it. One of the qualities of this delicate, patterned, almost diaphonous material is that it is made from the world's thinnest flax yarn. Ounce for ounce it is more expensive than gold.
The motifs were dreamed up by Árpád Dékáni, art teacher at the local grammar school. Apart from the usual vegetable and animal motifs, you also find depictions of events and personalities from Hungarian history.
Lace-maker Mária Markovits worked to such a high standard that her work was shown alongside the finest Venetian and Flemish lace at the St Louis World Exhibition (1904), where she won a first prize.

At the Lace Museum you can take a close look
not only at the local lace but also the lace of the surrounding regions. In addition you can see how lace is made and indeed buy examples yourself to take home as a souvenir.
The lace illustrated was made in 1938
and required 4300 work hours. It weighs 35g.

THE LAND OF THE SAND WINES

Beside the immaculately kept vineyards, the clumps of needlegrass and the thickets remain untouched as the road disappears over the sparkling sandy hills, past the junipers. It is the vines, however, which dominate the landscape. There are some enormous vineyards, wine presses and cellars capable of storing vast quantities of wine. The tendency now is to go back to picking grapes by hand, rather than continuing with machines, high stringers and screens.

Traditional skills and traditional grape varieties combined with up-to-date practices invariably mean good quality wine. Ezerjó, Kövidinka and Italian Riesling produce pleasant, light, low-alcohol wines. More and more Kékfrankos, Kadarka and Kékoporto is also being produced.

Being responsible for quality control, SOLT-VADKERT plays an important role in the local wine industry. The town is also well placed logistically as a number of important routes converge here. There are five churches in the town, one of them being the 18th century **Calvinist church**, another the 19th century **Roman Catholic church**.

Most visitors go to Soltvadkert to visit Lake Vadkert, known to the locals as Lake Pungent. For over a hundred years now, people with locomotor problems have gone to the lake to make the most of the waters and the mud at the open-air swimming pool, both of which have medicinal properties. Many people also have weekend cottages there.

KISKŐRÖS

It is poetry, rather than grapes and wine, which draws visitors to the town, for it was here that *Sándor Petőfi*, the son of István Petrovics and Mária Hrúz, was born. Kiskőrös is extremely proud of its most famous son, and is extremely grateful to anybody who goes out of their way to promote his work. The Petőfi translators' **sculpture park** (1985) in Petőfi tér is the only one of its kind in world literature.

The literary museum, which now occupies the house where Petőfi was born, is one of Hungary's great secular pilgrimage places (Petőfi tér 5.).

Some of Petőfi's poems have been translated into almost one hundred languages.

Petőfi was indeed known for travelling the highways and byways of Hungary, so it is perhaps apt that Kiskőrös also has the **Public Highways Museum**. It was founded in 1974 by Imre Lévády, a road builder himself by profession; and in what amounts to two covered outdoor exhibition spaces you can see how roads and bridges were built and maintained from the Roman period right up to the present day. Included are the secrets behind the building of the *Amber Road,* which ran from Rome up to the Baltic (a part of which can still be seen in Szombathely). You can also discover how the Scottish engineer *John Loudon McAdam* (1756–1836) went about making *Tarmacadam,* which replaced the old cobbled surfaces at the turn of the 18th and 19th centuries (Dózsa György u. 38.). The local **thermal waters** provide the attratcion at the *Imperial Spa Hotel.*

In Kecel, next to the Pintér Works, is the only park in Hungary dedicated to military technology (Rákóczi F. út). The collection relies entirely on the generosity of individual donors.

In KECEL water is much appreciated in a landscape which has to cope with the summer's baking heat. Those visiting this Kiskunság **Wine Region** town, and Kecel's *Kenderföld* **Fishing and Boating Lake** in particular, will be treated to a *demolition derby* in June, a coach and horses event in July, plus the *harvest festival* later on. Those more interested in natural beauty should head for the marshes along the *Danube Main Channel* and *Berek Wood*.

In the area around JÁNOSHALMA you will find the *Upper Bácska Loess Ridge* and *Ólom Hill*, which rises to a height of 172 metres. The ancient *Kéleshalom Juniper Woods* are a popular weekend destination. The local library has devoted some of its space to the **wine museum** (Bajai út).

The old **synagogue**, despite being little more than a remodelled (1825) peasant house, is of interest because of the harrowing carved inscriptions on the pews. Some of them date from before and some from after the Second World War (some indeed in Cyrillic script), others date from the deportations of 1944 when those who had been rounded up in the synagogue carved farewell messages into the pews. Some of the names you will find duplicated on the marble holocaust memorial on the wall.

Seeing all those fish swimming around in the waters at KUNFEHÉRTÓ is good news not only for the anglers but for all those concerned about decreasing fish stocks. There is plenty for the inhabitants of the area's 800 weekend cottages to enjoy at the *Kunfehértó Summer Festival*.

KISKUNMAJSA is a relatively new town. It is pleasant to walk along the streets looking at the wooden gables and the sunbeam motifs which are so reminiscent of Szeged.

It was whilst looking for oil that the mineral waters came bubbling out from under Kiskunmajsa. The water is particularly good for the treatment of rheumatic and muscular disorders. Next to the covered pool (Kőkút 26.) you can go horse-riding, or travelling in a horse and cart around the peninsula jutting out into the artificially created lake. There is also an inn and a fishing village.

"Despite going through bereavement, destruction and failure, Fire and high water Szeged lives"

(Gyula Juhász)

SZEGED

On the night of 12th March 1879, Szeged was swallowed up by the River Tisza. Of the town's 5,000 houses only 265 survived. Hungarian writer Kálmán Mikszáth, who was a journalist in Szeged at the time, spent that dramatic night in the town hall. "It seemed an eternity before dawn eventually broke. But what were we waiting for? Of Szeged there were but ruins for the sun to shine on" was how he described events. Europe shared in the grief and did all it could to help. Sections of the large boulevard ringing the town were named after the capital cities of the countries donating the most. The chromium steel Flood Monument (1979, György Segesdy) stands at the end of the Tisza Lajos körút.

The town rebuilt after the *Great Flood* of 1879 creates a unified impression. It is made all the more pleasant by its large parks, and the walks along the River Tisza. In addition to the town centre there are also the town's satellite communities – Algyő, *Dorozsma, Szőreg* and *Tápé* – each of which has its own particular atmosphere.

The island, which once stood at the confluence of the Tisza and the Maros, made the site a good crossing place, and consequently a place of great strategic importance. It wasn't a coincidence that boats carrying salt from Transylvania along the River Maros made for Szeged before seeing their cargo continue on its way by river or by road. The salt was transported in rushwork bundles woven by the Tápé weavers. For many centuries Szeged occupied a special place in the hearts of the Hungarian rulers. While monarchs showered the town with privileges, it was the duty of the town to cope with vagaries of the region's rivers. It was the rivers, in the spring of 1879, which were to have their say in the most important event in the town's history.

This misfortune, however, led in turn to Szeged becoming the lucky recipient of a big architectural idea, the brainchild of *Lajos Lechner,* which was to make Szeged the most unified and harmonious provincial town in Hungary. The most important buildings of this period were the Town Hall (Széchenyi tér 10.), and the Secessionist master-piece, the **Reök Palace** (1907, *Ede Magyar,* Tisza Lajos krt. 56.) and the huge **Synagogue** which occupies a whole block, between Hajnóczy utca and Gutenberg utca.

Poet Mihály Babits compared the tower of the town hall to a dainty dancer, without even having the benefit of a petticoat of flowering magnolias.

The town's main thoroughfare is Kárász utca, which leads to the sculptures of Széchenyi tér. There you will find a good selection of the greats of Hungarian history: *Saint Stephen* and his queen, *Gizella; István Széchenyi; Ferenc Deák; Lajos Tisza; Kunó Klebelsberg* and *Pál Vásárhelyi,* who was responsible for straightening out the River Tisza, to name but a few.

The frescos (Vilmos Aba Novák) which covered the huge barrel vault of Heroes' Gate (1936, Móric Pogány) were partly plastered over in 1945, and completely plastered over four years later. The plaster was taken off and the frescos restored in the year 2000.

Lipót Baumhorn, that most prolific of architects, designed the synagogue in 1903. It is indeed one of the biggest synagogues in the world, and many consider it to be the most beautiful. Its size and its excellent acoustics make it the biggest concert venue in the town.

The **Town Hall** (1883), designed by *Ödön Lechner* and *Gyula Pártos,* has, not surprisingly, become one of the town's enduring symbols. The fact that the square in front of the town hall is often used for public events has never succeeded totally in com-promising the elegance of the building.

Operas, musicals, ballets and plays, folk dancing, jazz concerts and many other programmes have made their way onto the rich programmes which form the Szeged Open-Air Festival.

It was in 1935, when standing in Cathedral Square, that Mascagni declared that Szeged's whole future lay in that particular square. This observation could of course have referred to the Festival, but perhaps of greater relevance is the fact that it was here that Nobel Prize-winner Albert Szent-Györgyi worked. One should not forget also that the Hungarian Academy of Science's most active provincial branch is based here. The University of Szeged plans to take over a number of buildings in the square to house some of its more than twenty thousand students.

The legends revolving around Szeged are too numerous to mention. Those taking pride of place, however, are those referring to Attila the Hun's burial place and his triple coffin which are eagerly being sought in the Tisza Basin.
There may indeed be something more to the Agnus Dei found on the town's coat of arms and its official seal. The lamb also appears in the arched doorway to the Dömötör Tower in Cathedral Square.
György Dózsa is said to have been brought up by Szeged's Chief Justice, and it is believed that the judge's daughter was to have been the great peasant leader's prospective wife. This particular story was immortalised in a poem by Gyula Juhász.

There is a real sense of history around the town's other great square, Cathedral Square. Apart from containing architectural evidence of Szeged's one thousand-year-old history, the square marks the ecclesiastical and the academic centre of the town. It is here you can see the **Dömötör Tower**, an early Gothic structure built on Romanesque foundations, the Baroque **Greek Orthodox church** (*Jovan Dobits*), the classical **Hungária House** (*József Hild*), and the neo-Romanesque **Votive Church** (1913– 1930, *Frigyes Schulek, Ernő Foerk*). This group is further enhanced by the one hundred or so sculptures (*Béla Rerrich*) covering the **National Hall of Remembrance**. The new buildings in the square, the *Somogyi Library* and the university educational centre, fit nicely into the surrounding urban fabric.
The square is dominated by the *Cathedral*, which contains Hungary's biggest organ – the hundredth produced by the *Angster Factory* in Pécs (1930). In one of the towers hangs one of the biggest bells in the country. The façade has become the famous backdrop to the *Szeged Open-Air Festival*, which started all the way back in 1931.

The construction of the Votive Church was one of the biggest architectural projects in recent Hungarian ecclesiastical history. It was built (1913-1930) as a result of a pledge made by those who survived the flood of 1879. Like most great churches, the building is still undergoing improvements. The fresco inside the dome was painted by László Patay especially for the new millennium.

The real centre for the town's Roman Catholics is the **Church of the Blessed Virgin and the Franciscan Friary** (Mátyás tér) in the *Lower Town* (Alsóváros). The church was originally built at the end of the 15th century, but was remodelled at the end of the 17th century. The building is the largest surviving medieval complex on the Great Plain. It was here the friars took care of the spiritual and bodily health of those living in the southern part of the county, the latter with the help of herbs.

People travel very great distances to see the Black Madonna, a devotional picture dating from about 1740.
Géza Féja described it as a "clear oriental face, with Mongolian features, yellowy brown, princely". The procession, which forms part of the patronal festival in the Lower Town, combines local folk traditions with traditional Christian liturgy.
The event, which takes place during the first weekend of August, is an opportunity for Szeged folk from both home and abroad to join together as one big happy family. The church itself was built from royal taxes. Indeed, the square in front of the church bears the name of its greatest patron, Matthias Corvinus. Nevertheless, the building remains first and foremost a monument to the commendable self-denial of the Franciscan friars.

The town's schools and music, its bars and churches, are inextricably linked with the town's most fêted poets – *Attila József* (1905–1937), *Gyula Juhász* (1883–1937), and *Miklós Radnóti* (1909–1944). Legends such as those about Sándor Rózsa the rogue king have found their way into novels and films. And there is *Pista Dankó* the great musician, who made Szeged's most beautiful melodies his very own. You can see him carved in white marble (*Ede Margó*) in front of the *Old Hungária*. It is the only public statue of a **leader of a gypsy band** in existence.

The **Black House** (Fekete-ház) on Somogyi utca is for those interested in the art and history of the town. The work of *János Kass*, as well as temporary art shows, can be seen at the **Kass Gallery** (Vár u.).

It is when surveying the steps leading up to the cold and austere interior of the Ferenc Móra Museum during the spring and autumn months, watching the young folk craning their necks for even the slightest hint of sunlight, that you realise that Szeged really is a young persons' town.
The neoclassical building, like the Votive Church, is frequently used as a backdrop for cultural events.

The *Ferenc Móra Museum* can be found in the stately **Palace of Culture**. Apart from having one of the country's finest archaeological collections, the visual arts, natural history and popular culture are also represented. One wing of the classical building (Roosevelt tér 1–3.) almost touches the Tisza, the other looks onto the richly decorated *Stefánia* and the neo-Baroque **theatre** (Deák F. u. 12.).

The **Szeged National Theatre** is most definitely a building befitting a large town, or indeed a city. It is the work of two architects whose buildings grace many a city, Odessa and Budapest to mention but two. The architects in question, *Helmer* and *Fellner*, who were both based in Vienna, designed the theatre in 1883.

On the banks of the Tisza, not far from the so-called Sellő House, you will find a monument (2003) commemorating a certain football match which took place at Wembley Stadium back in 1953. At the top of the 2.5-metre-high bronze, Márton Kalmár has placed a football, from which the twelve studded boots of Puskás and co. come tumbling down.

The Count István Széchenyi lake is one of the best, and perhaps most beautiful, competitive rowing venues in the world.
It has hosted the World Cup, the World Championships and the the National Championships.
The fact that it is excellent for fishing has meant the lake has also hosted the Freshwater Team Angling World Championships.
The lake is situated between the E 75 and road 55.

The Újszeged Botanical Gardens was founded in 1922 to help teach the natural sciences at the university. There are a wide variety of plants, from the palms and cacti in the greenhouses to the exotic plants providing the shade along the pathways. Amongst the Indian lotuses covering the pond you can see Antal Tápai's slender figure of a girl reaching out towards the light.

Visitors to the Wildlife Park can see numerous animals living in something approaching their natural habitats.
And it really is a park, a spacious one too, in which you can actually go up and stroke the creatures.

Újszeged (New Szeged) is a suburb on the left bank of the Tisza. There you can find woods and **baths**, camping sites and hotel accommodation right on the bank of the river (Szent-Györgyi u.), as well as a **sports hall** and a **swimming pool** (Temesvári krt.). It is here you will also be able to find the **university garden** (Lövölde út 42.), known locally as the educational vegetable patch.

Szőreg's contributions to the Szeged experience are its flower garden (particularly its roses), its Hungarian-Serb culture and its medieval monuments. Some remnants of the ethnic settlement patterns survive in the names of the streets: Magyar utca and Szerb utca.

Tápé's rural roots are still very much in evidence. It has a Gothic church and a cross made of sheet-iron. Rush-weaving is still very much alive and kicking, and *József Lele Junior's* **ethnographical collection** (Vártó u. 4.) has successfully preserved artefacts from the village's past. *Pista Dankó* did as much as he possibly could to enhance the dubious reputation of the village by substituting a "because" for a "but" in the lyric: *"Szeged's fame is more than hearsay, (because) it happens to border Tápé…"*

Kiskundorozsma's **alkaline pool** is often used as an alternative to the lido down by the Tisza. It has a boating lake, a **naturist outdoor swimming pool**, a **camping site** and an inn, as well as hotels and gardens. It is also the venue for the *Truck Drivers" Country Rally*. There are those who think that Dorozsma is unjustly famous, and that its fame is only based on one of Pista Dankó's lyrics: *"It's not windy, if the sails of Dorozsma Mill aren't turning."* Detractors are quick to point out that the sails have long since gone and that the mill is now a **museum**.

"Windmills were built on the most exposed hills, to get the most out of the wind… and if the sails didn't turn, the millstones didn't grind… The wind was everything. It gave people their bread, and provided the millers with a living. And if somebody went short, they had to borrow some flour – at least until the next time the wind blew…" (János Herczeg)

In fact wind is the last thing we want as we head towards the *sand beds* accompanying the Hungarian border between the Danube and the Tisza.

On the Sand Beds

The villages out on the sand beds use horticultural practices which alternate between the ancient and the modern. In MÓRAHALOM, amongst the greenhouses, the plastic tents and the fruit trees, you can relax at the new **Leisure and medicinal baths.**

If it's a spot of rural relaxation you are after you could do worse than visiting PUSZTAMÉRGES. There you will find leafy streets, cool cellars, fiery wines and the occasional stuffed cabbage and chicken stew-cooking competition.

Ferenc Polyák's carved peasant sculpture in Mórahalom's main square is dedicated to the rural poor who have had to eke out a living from the sand beds.

Having battled your way through the reeds, groves, vineyards and the farmsteads you finally reach ÁSOTTHALOM. The sand is so deep here that not even Franz Joseph's carriage would have made it to the opening ceremony at the school of forestry had they not spread straw all over the track.

Ásotthalom's tree-planting initiatives extend to the museum at the local technical college (Kiss Ferenc krt.) and the Ferenc Kiss Memorial Wood, which are both devoted to forestry and its traditions.

At BORDÁNY the Kisapáti brothers' vintage car collection offers a unique opportunity to see some very rare working models. Fortunately, they do not show their age and are still very much shipshape and Bristol fashion (Rákóczi u. 60.).

It was amongst the branches of the Sándor Rózsa tree that the rogue leader hid as he neared his end. In 1857, the price on his head was ten thousand forints, quite tempting for any potential informers. The infamous rascal was lost when knocked unconscious by a woman wielding a hatchet, who then tied him up and dragging him off to prison.

WHERE IT ALL BEGAN...

White Lake, which lies between Szeged and Sándor-falva, is held up as a model of how one should go about looking after the environment. You can see for yourselves if you climb up one of the two **lookout towers** at either *Korom-sziget,* a destination best reached from road E75, or the tower on the Sándorfalva road to Ópusztaszer. The **fishing ponds** lie along the Tisza migration path.

There are two exhibitions devoted to the wildlife at White Lake, one is at the Ferenc Móra Museum in Szeged and the other is in the forester's house at the National Historical Memorial Park in Ópusztaszer.

The village of SZATYMAZ *is best known for its part in a legend relating to the arrival of the region's most famous fruit, the peach. "A wanderer who just happened to be passing through spat out the stones of the peaches he was eating. Whether he pressed them into the sand with his heel, or whether it was ploughed in accidentally, we will never know, but what is indisputable is the fact that a tree became of them. ...Even in distant lands they associate its name with the name of the village." (Dezső Horváth). Whether true or not it nevertheless remains a great story.*

Travelling along one of Europe's most important transit routes you come to KISTELEK. The upper storey of the classical and late Baroque **church** (1830) was built to the designs of the tower of Szeged *Town Hall.* According to local legend it was here that *Sándor Rózsa* and his band pulled off the world's first ever train robbery.

Those wishing to take the bus to ÓPUSZTASZER, eleven kilometres away, should wait at Kistelek railway station. The 55-hectare **National Historical Memorial Park** occupies the site of the once thriving medieval market town of *Szer.* The place's importance lies in its relationship to the Hungarian Conquest. In his *Gesta Hungarorum* the 13th century chronicler *Anonymous* says it was here that Árpád and his chieftains settled the country's affairs following their victorious battles. Their "journey" to Szer was immortalised a millennium later by *Árpád Feszty* (1856–1914). The **Feszty Panorama**'s own turbulent history ended in its restoration in 1995.

Those who stand in the middle of the curving surface of Feszty's huge canvas are transported into a bygone age. You are confronted by a huge panoramic view, which seems to move effortlessly towards the horizon. Looking at the painting it is difficult to tell whether the smouldering timbers, the weapons and the plants, which are scattered over the terrain, are painted or for real.

The ruins which you can see are those of a Benedictine Monastery built on the St Gallen model. During the course of their excavations the archaeologists uncovered a bell foundry, which actually included pieces of the casting moulds. Using the moulds the experts have been able to reconstruct a bell which is now on display. It must be one of the few bells of its type in Europe. Natural history exhibitions are held in the yurt huts designed by György Csete and Jenő Dulánszky. 80 cm thick walls, 630 cm wide, and 7.5 tonnes in weight, the slice of giant redwood was a gift from the Hungarian community in California. The most important dates in the history of the Carpathian Basin are marked on the rings of a tree, which started to grow 1,800 years ago.

A special round hall was built to house the panorama. The 1,800 square metres of canvas make the picture the second biggest panorama in the world. The largest scene in the design shows the prince and his chieftains witnessing the victorious charge through the Verecke Pass and into the Carpathian Basin. Elsewhere you can see the nobles following the armies, the arrival of the Hungarian people, and the Hungarians building their settlements and practicing their old heathen customs. The nomad settlement devoted to the Hungarian Conquest is continually growing in size.

The heroic period which started with the founder of the Hungarian nation **Prince Árpád**, and ended with **Prince Geisa** and his son **Stephen,** the founder of the Christian Kingdom of Hungary, is commemorated in the only **sculpture** in which all three historical figures are portrayed together. Further statues of historical figures were added to celebrate the new Millennium (Szoborkert 68.).

From the last Saturday in June onwards you can witness the Hunnialis equestrian programme, which goes on from dawn until dusk. At it you can see how the Hungarian warriors fought, what they fought with and what they wore.

The flora and fauna of the region are shown in the *Kunság Forester's House.* The relationship between man and nature is covered in the exhibition entitled *The Wood: Nature's Temple.* You can get an idea of the state of agriculture in the towns and villages at the turn of the 19th and 20th centuries in the **Outdoor Ethnographical Museum**. While **Hungarians around the World** concentrates on one ethnic group, the diversity of the traditional ethnic costumes once worn in Hungary can be seen in an exhibition of images of town and village life called *Promenade 1896,* which can be found in the rotunda.

MAROS CORNER

21 kilometres of the 50 kilometre stretch of the River Maros running through Hungary does in fact coincide with the state border. Its water level can be unpredictable. In recent years it has ranged from a low of -100cm (in 1983) to a high of 625cm (in 1975). Of the woodlands bordering on the river, the Makó-Landor Woods are the only ones to which the general public can gain unrestricted access.

The villages in the *Bácska* and the *Bánát* were, at one time, just as likely to have been German and Serb as Hungarian. TISZASZIGET is *the lowest point in the country* (75.6 metres below sea level) a fact marked by a column which can be reached by going along the marked footpaths from the village.

Next to road 43, heading towards Romania, in the area around the villages of Klárafalva and Ferenc-szállás, you come to a piece of land known as Kuku-tyin. Here, the locals harvested their oats by boat during floods. According to the idiom, getting sent to Ku-kutyin to harvest oats, is like being sent to Coventry.

KISZOMBOR's 11th century **round church** is one of the most important surviving buildings from the Árpád period. In the village you can also find the Rónay family's **palace,** which many believe to have been modelled on the famous *Miramare Palace* just outside Triest. Unfortunately a proper use has yet to be found for it. The fact that a new **border crossing** was recently opened into Romania, however, proves that solutions can always be found.

According to the art historical literature "the round churches in the Carpathian Basin with their six-foiled interiors are unique in the history of European Romanesque architecture." The Romanesque rotunda was considerably extended in the 18th century, before the extensions were pulled down in 1910 and the rotunda rebuilt, creating a large church. Other examples can be found in Gerény and Karcsa, although the church at Kiszombor is the most complete.

"The lower part of the building looks as though it's growing out of the soil, not without some difficulty. The roof, however, curves and bends sinuously… like the trusses which rise like plant stems… whilst the smaller interior towers grow up inside the main towers." This is what Imre Makovecz has to say about his Onion House (Posta u.) in Makó. Apart from celebrating the onion it also serves as both a community centre and cultural venue. (For more on Makó onions please consult the Hungarian Treasury.)

Makó

It was Makó-born Miklós Szirbik, the Calvinist priest, who began cultivating onions by renting out small plots to smallhold tenant farmers at the end of the 18th century. From these small plots large numbers of onions were produced. When it came to selling their produce, the world was the Makó onion growers' oyster. This was how Makó became *the onion town*. There is even a statue in the town put up in honour of "Mr Onion", and a church with onion connections. There is a statue of the poet *Attila József* who was a frequent visitor to the museum building in the days when it was known as **Espersit House.**

The old county hall, now the **Town Hall** in Széchenyi tér, is perhaps the most beautiful classical palace in the southern Alföld. The rococo **Calvinist church** (Kálvin tér), the Bishop of Csanád's Empire-style **Summer Residence and Chapel** (Kossuth utca) are all buildings bearing witness to the order and tranquillity of a bygone age.

A good way to end the day is to enjoy the medicinal waters of the **baths** (Marcibányi tér 7.) or to head for the lido on the banks of the River Maros.

If you continue your journey in the direction of the border crossing at Nagylak it is worth while stopping a moment to inspect a cross that lies 6 kilometres from Apátfalva. *Resembling a Maltese cross, the cross is carved from Gneiss stone.*

In Magyarcsanád's main street you can see no fewer than four churches, the Catholic and Calvinist churches belonging to the Hungarians, plus the Orthodox Serbian and Romanian Churches. All four ethnic groups are well represented at the **Folk Art Collections** at the *Cultural Centre* (Fő u. 52.).

On the way to our next destination you come across the Great Plain's only medieval **fortified church** (1290). Recently excavated and renovated it can be found in Óföldeák.

Potters' work varies. Even pottery from different parts of the same town may vary in colour, or indeed in the forms used. Potters would also compete against each other: in Tabán they would put red and black motifs onto yellow backgrounds, in Csúcs they put cobalt blue designs onto a white background, whilst in the New Town they made greeny brown-coloured plates, bottles and jugs.

It was in Hódmezővásárhely that they used to decorate the ends of their hemp and linen pillow cases with Hungarian wool which had been dyed black, brown or pink, or with threads coloured a thousand shades of blue. It was the blue of the woad, and the reds and lilacs of the sheep dyes, which were most popular, although there were a whole variety of natural colours which could be made if enough of the necessary plants were available. In many cases they simply used the natural colour of the wool, which meant they had colours covering every shade from black to white.

Practicing craftsmen and women, working from the kind of examples of old traditional patterns which can be found in the museums, are on hand in the Folk Art House (Árpád u.) to give help to those who fancy having a go themselves.

HÓDMEZŐVÁSÁRHELY

Archaeologists have been able to trace the agricultural history of the region back thousands of years. Sometimes the pottery is decorated elaborately, sometimes less so, but all of them are unmistakably the work of human hand. At the present time fifteen potters are active in the town. The history of the local farms and the town would also be unimaginable without the horse. All aspects of animal husbandry, both traditional and modern, are represented at *the St George's Day Agricultural Festival.*

On account of its contribution to the visual and the folk arts, Hódmezővásárhely has won a special place in Hungarian hearts, earning it the nickname *"Peasants' Paris"*. There is nowhere else in the world where the paths of simple folk and trained artists cross so regularly. One example of this was an initiative, which took place at the turn of the 19th and 20th centuries, when artists *János Tornyai, Béla Endre* and others founded the **majolica factory** whose intention was to ensure the future well-being of local potters and their craft.

The local farmers descend on the town of Hódmezővásárhely on Saint George's Day, at the end of April. It is "a spring festival, when according to the mysterious rites dating back centuries, they drive their livestock out in preparation for the summer" (Sándor Bálint). The hotchpotch of traditional and modern elements make the event quite a spectacle. Getting the animals ready for competition gives their owners plenty to do, as they too have to look the part.

Paintings produced in Hódmezővásárhely frequently come across as something resembling a novel. János Tornyai's (1896–1936) paintings of the landscape and the local inhabitants are no exception. The **János Tornyai Museum**, on the road of that name, the **Csúcs Pottery House** (Rákóczi út) and the **Folk Art House** (Árpád u. 21.) are all very much dominated by the region's art history.

The two **art colonies** and the **Kopáncsi Farmstead Museum** are also actively involved in nurturing such traditions. The visual arts are also well represented in the streets, the public sculpture and the imaginatively designed street signs give the townscape a different dimension. There are about forty artists currently living and working in Hódmezővásárhely and they are only too happy to see art lovers and to show them around their studios, even on days when their work isn't being shown at the group exhibitions.

The garden suburb with its sculptures by *Medgyessy* and *Ferenczy* boasts a **thermal bath,** and a new covered pool close to which stands the **town hall** (1879) whose tower rises reassuringly above flood defences surrounding the town.

On the opposite side of Kossuth tér there is the more tranquil spectacle of the **Old Church,** and the **Alföld Gallery** (no.8), which occupies an old Empire-style granary.

The János Tornyai Museum covers the six thousand-year history of the town. The small New Stone Age figure known as the Kőkénydomb Venus is perhaps the most famous exhibit on show, although there is a fine ethnographical collection as well. For the last half a century the museum has shown commendable persistence in continuing to hold the Vásárhelyi Autumn Show displaying the latest works by the artists of the Alföld school.

Kossuth tér is a real cornucopia of the life and culture on the Alföld. Here, near the eclectic bank building and the hotel, is the old promenade where Pista Dankó once used to sing and where Gypsy Béla played.

> *Over the century the citizens of Hódmezővásárhely have had a value system, and a straightforwardness which has held them in good stead. A fine example is the case of András János Nagy's well. He wanted to build a well which would serve the whole community, ignoring the mayor's suggestion that it should only be for the school. His well (1884) became the town's second artesian (252.6m) well, providing clean water for all the residents. Its pipes were made of pinewood not metal (János Kálvin tér).*

With the Baroque and classical architecture of the **Roman Catholic church,** the smoothly profiled bailiff's house, the press-house belonging to the Károlyi family and the Secession-style **synagogue** (remodelled 1906–1908, *Miksa Müller*) Hódmezővásárhely could hardly be considered a typical Alföld town.

AMONGST THE RIVERS

There is a cycle track which takes you northwards along the west bank of the Tisza to Hódmezővásárhely's **leisure complex**. Moving southwards from MÁRTÉLY, in the direction of the *Körtvélyes Dead Channel*, the countryside becomes more tranquil: there are the flowery glades full of birds and wild animals. This is the *Lower Tisza Valley*, the most beautiful part of the flood plain.

At the Mindszent ferry crossing there is sign pointing you to Baks, the village on the opposite bank of the Tisza, and New York, together with the relevant distances. It offers holidaymakers the chance to get their bearings.

Mártély is an atmospheric little fishing village. It is here that the flood plain becomes a tourist paradise. The Dead Channel often receives fresh water from the Tisza, and its banks paint an idyllic picture. It certainly tempts back its fair share of visitors and artists.

At the mouth of the Kurca (situated north of Mindszent) there are lots of fish. The rather unpredictable currents, however, mean that fishing can become a bit of a lottery.

The village of MINDSZENT, its old **ferry crossing** and the River Tisza are usually blessed with blue skies. There are 18 settlements in the Carpathian Basin whose name derives from *Mind(en) Szentek* (All Saints). The village's restaurants can be found next to the **outdoor swimming pool** and on the banks of the Tisza.

Leaving the Tisza and moving eastwards, we come to a region dominated by the *Körös* and its tributaries, and the *Maros*. Eventually you come to Békés County, and the towns of Gyula and Békéscsaba.

SZÉKKUTAS is a must for all lovers of the German TV series as it was here that a young Hugo Hartung fell in love with a certain Piroska Rácz sometime in the 1920s. It was a summer romance that prompted Hartung to write "Ich denke oft an Piroschka" which was also made into both a film and a musical.

KAKASSZÉK Sanatorium, near the Hódmezővásárhely-Kutas Plain, had an excellent reputation in its day. It is currently languishing and seeking a new lease of life. The benefits of the place were discovered when one of the owners' daughters, who was suffering from an incurable illness, went to hide in the rushes. By chance she put her foot in the water, with the result that she was cured. News of her miraculous recovery spread. It was then that Hódmezővásárhely's chief engineer was then sent to Davos on a fact-finding mission. This explains why the sanatorium (now a hospital) happens to be an exact copy of its Swiss model, right down to the fittings.

GYULA

Wherever you happen to go there is something which gives the place its own peculiar charm. In Békés County many such charms can be found in the town of Gyula. The name of the town pays homage to one of the chieftains who arrived during the Hungarian Conquest. It was János György Harruckern who repopulated the town with Hungarians, Romanians and Germans following the Turks' departure. Gyula is now a cultural centre for Hungary's Romanian population.

In the Ferenc Erkel Museum (Apor Vilmos tér) you can find the fourteen carat golden wreath awarded to the great operatic genius himself on the occasion of the fiftieth anniversary of his becoming a conductor. It weighs 525 grams and the decorative lyre at the centre contains 39 diamonds.

In Ladics House (1801, Antal Czigler) you can see the interiors's original furniture, household objects, ornaments, family portraits, library, Chinese porcelain and Venetian mirrors (Jókai u.).

To make a "hundred-year-old" coffee you need 2 cl brandy, half a small teaspoon of cocoa powder and some whipped cream. The drink is made complete with a sprinkling of cinnamon on top.

At the centre of the so-called German Town (Németváros) lies Apor tér. It is here that you will find the late Baroque-classical **Roman Catholic church** (1863–1866) and behind it the one-time choirmaster's house where **Ferenc Erkel** was born. The wing that has been added to the school has an exhibition dedicated to the life and work of the great composer. On one of the walls on Dürer utca is a tablet referring to *Albrecht Dürer's* Hungarian roots.

Czigler also designed the Hundred-Year-Old Cake Shop (Erkel tér 1.), which was founded in 1840 by pastry-cook András Salis. Some of the furniture is original – the thonet chairs, the white carrara marble tables, the counter, the painted walls and the decorative objects.
The old baking oven and the complete set of cooking utensils, crockery and cutlery are now all in the safe keeping of the Confectioner's Museum.

"...Dürer's father went to Germany, settling finally in Nuremberg. It was there he made an agreement with Jeromos Holpert that he would marry his, at that time three-year-old, daughter. This Dürer's father did in 1470 when she was 15 years old. It was through this marriage that Albrecht Dürer was born in 1471. As his father was born in the village of Ajtós, he was known as Albert Ajtósi (in German Türer, Dürer). Dürer's father in fact called himself Albert Ajtósi Dürer, although his son preferred only to use the name Dürer." (Imre Gyula Czeglédi)

The performances of the Gyula Castle Theatre held at the lake stage in the castle courtyard and other venues have been entertaining audiences since 1964. During the course of restoration work at the castle the company was finally given a new permanent home on the northern side of the historic site (2004).

Walking past the impressive 18th and 19th ecclesiastical and public buildings you cross a stone bridge which leads to the **Castle Gardens**. The brick-built medieval castle is indeed quite a spectacle, with its round bastion in one corner. It was John Corvin and his wife Beatrix Frangepán who added the round **Corvin Bastion** to the Gothic palace complex (1403–1445). Following the restoration started in 2003 of the most complete medieval palace in Hungary you will be able to see a dungeon, a blacksmiths, and the *living quarters themselves*.

Opposite, the trees rather hide the Baroque **Harruckern-Wenckheim-Almásy Palace** (1725). Initially it was covered with a wooden shingle roof. What you see today is very much the work of *Antal Czigler,* who rebuilt the palace (1802–1803) following a major fire. There is also a two-aisled agricultural wing with a long vaulted cellar, now a crèche. The northern **Hussar Tower** dates back to the Turkish period, making it considerably older than the palace. The count's one-time riding school (1833, *Antal Czigler*) is now home to the **indoor swimming pool,** which is part of the Castle Baths and the medicinal bathing complex.

The sight of the ancestors of the "English Patient", the Counts of Almásy, riding off from their 19th century riding school, now the covered swimming pool, would indeed have made a scene fit for a film. Then the stables stood in 8.7 hectares of *woodland.* It was under the maple tree, albeit looking a little dried out today, that *Ferenc Erkel* composed his famous opera *Bánk Bán.*

The castle baths (1959) are made special by the 8.5 hectares of woodland surrounding the 25 pools. Some are covered, some open-air, some are good for swimming, others have waves and slides. Wellness fans will also not be disappointed.

Csanád's Landscapes

Kétegyháza is the largest ethnic Romanian village in Hungary. The village's **Romanian peasant house** is full of objects reflecting the life and culture of the village (Kossuth u. 68.). The local landowners, the Almásy family, built a **palace** in the village (*Miklós Ybl*), now used as a school, and a **chapel**.

It was the branch of the Almásy family renowned as great travellers who became famous. Ignác Almásy's son was an orientalist, and his grandson László was an expert on Africa. Al Maza airport in Cairo is named after him, and his life story was celebrated in the Oscar-winning film The English Patient.

It was in 1724, that 50 German families settled in the village of Elek. This was to be followed by 60 more in 1744. It was only a good century later that Romanians and Hungarians settled following the Turkish wars. Even today some of the old Swabian traditions survive, such as the annual *Fasching* Parade and the *Elek World Reunion*.

Baron János György Harruckern Square in the centre of Elek is adorned with an elegant sculptural representation of a woman in traditional German costume, which forms part of the fountain.

70 per cent of the German-speaking population were deported after the Second World War.

Archaeologists working on the edge of Battonya have come across the remains of an 11th century **round church**.

The walls of the chancel, however, were destroyed during the construction of the road ditches. Next to the road to Mezőkovácsháza you will find the *Kistompapuszta loess beds* forming part of the *Körös-Maros National Park*. (For more information see the first chapter of the book.)

The main thoroughfare in Battonya includes the Secession-style town hall (1890) and what was the Hotel and Casino (1885) next door.

The fact that three ethnic groups live here becomes all the more apparent when you begin to count the churches, of which there are six. The Baroque Serbian **Orthodox church,** one of the biggest such buildings in the southern Alföld, has a fine iconostasis. The church – at least until the current restoration has been completed – can only be visited with prior permission (Puskin u. 91.). The **Pravoszláv Church** (1778–1779) currently used by the Serb community also has an iconostasis and is richly decorated (Hunyady u. 56.). The **Roman Catholic church** (1818) contains frescoes by the artist *Pál C. Molnár,* who was born in the town.

At the Mezőhegyes International Mare and Stallion Competition in June the Stud Farm turns into the perfect equestrian venue.

MEZŐHEGYES

"I feel as though some mischievous spirit has taken me off to some far corner of the world. It's quite a sight to behold, as if the elegant residents and their residences, their summer retreats and their palaces, had been transported en masse and deposited in Mezőhegyes." That was how Géza Féja described Mezőhegyes, that strange place amongst the plains with its curious assortment of buildings. The granaries, the silo, and the wooden bell tower say much about the importance of this one-time royal stud farm, "an institution which unquestionably surpassed its equivalents elsewhere in Europe." (Elek Fényes)

The Empire-style gateway leads you towards
the main buildings of the Mezőhegyes Stud Farm.

The pick of the buildings on the complex can be reached through the northern and southern **gates**: both of them were built in the Empire style (1807, *János Hild*). The two sets of barracks are Baroque (1790, *József Jung*). On the northern side of the complex, what is now the *Nonius Hotel* (Kozma F. u. 32.) has Empire and Biedermeier interiors, and Napoleon III. furniture.

At the **Mezőhegyes Stud Farm** it took three generations and 38 stallions thirty years to breed the horse best suited to undertake agricultural work, the nonius.

„Nonius Senior – this originally Norman stallion – Austrian horsemen stole from the Rossieri stud Farm, at the time of the Franco-Austrian War... it was a light bay,... but with cream-coloured markings on the ankle of its hind left leg, and on half its entire right hind leg."

(István Csanádi)

The **Administrative Building** (now belonging to the *Állami Ménesbirtok plc*) with its wooden veranda dates from about 1880.

The covered **riding school** (1809, *János Hild*) still serves its original purpose: in the winter months the horses take their exercise here. The so-called zephyr on the roof tells people which direction the wind is blowing from.

In the Empire-style **Coach Museum** you can see a fine collection of objects related in some way to Hungarian coach driving.

BÉKÉSCSABA

The apparent tranquillity of the towns on the Great Plain is deceptive. Places like Békéscsaba experienced dynamic growth during the course of the last century. The Lutheran **Small Church** (Szeberényi tér) was built in 1745. The centre of the town consists of four interconnected squares. Its most elegant buildings, its parks, woods and the *Elővíz Channel*, which divides the town in two, all manage to give the place a relaxed atmosphere.

The Empire-style Central Granary (1809, János Hild) could almost be a Roman aquaduct.

The giant plane tree has been deemed big enough and old enough to merit protected status. Indeed the statistics relating to the tree are worth noting. It's 35m high, the trunk is 2m thick and in places has a ground area of 4.55m². Its foliage, which is inhabited by long-eared owls, covers an area of 900m².

It is the building materials and the techniques used which make the **Hotel Central** (1885) interesting. It is one of the few wooden-framed buildings in existence in Hungary (Kozma F. u. 22.). The very existence of the stud farm, with its efficient and well-designed buildings, does wonders for what is only a small town. The **Hild Old Barn** (1800, *János Hild*) is the biggest threshing building in Hungary, with two double-level attics and hipped roofs (Kossuth u. 10.).

The architectural and the rarity value of the **stable boys' quarters**, which are sunk into the ground, give them a special importance which goes beyond their intended purpose within the stud farm complex. The vaulted accommodation was built by the imperial architect *Le Favre* in 1785 in an early Baroque style. The rooms were heated from an exterior furnace and originally covered with a layer of grassed-over soil. Unfortunately the building has been re-roofed with tiles. (The granaries and stable boys' quarters, which are still in use, can only be viewed from the outside.)

The settlement, a village, was known as Csaba during the Middle Ages. Having become depopulated following the turmoil of the Turkish period the place was repopulated with Slovak settlers by Baron János György Harruckern. He had been given the whole of Békés County by the Emperor in recognition of his services as court army contractor. The town has managed to preserve its Slovak heritage in its architecture, its cultural traditions, its archaic language and its folk art.

The **Slovak Peasant House** (Garay u. 21.), built in 1865, has a front veranda built of bricks and a wooden one on the side. The ornate wooden verandas, so characteristic of Slovak peasant architecture, are visible elsewhere in the town.

The groundplan of the Slovak Peasant House.is the same as most 19th century peasant cottages, with a drawing room at the front, a kitchen in the middle and a living room at the back. It was from there one could go down into the cellar.

The squares and the houses appear to have bene-fited from the industriousness which was typical of those early settlers: the flowers and the parks are well cared for and the buildings all have a certain character about them.

The façade of the late-romantic, early eclectic **Town Hall** (1871–1873) (Szent István tér) was designed by *Miklós Ybl*. Its cobbled courtyard hosts the summer *Town Hall Evenings*.

The recently renovated neoclassical *Hotel Fiume* has regained its fin-de-siècle grandeur. Next to it lies the **Jókai Theatre**, an eclectic-style building, whose first floor concert hall and 640-capacity theatre plays a key role in the town's cultural and artistic life. In front of it, in the middle of the pedestrian precinct, you will find some trellis-work, making certain references to Slovak peasant architecture. Inside there is a rock garden and a fountain.

Like its famous neighbour Gyula, Békéscsaba can also claim to have a sausage named after it. Indeed the Csaba Festival held in October is dedicated to the sausage and a lot more besides.

Hungary's most famous 19th century realist painter spent some time working as an apprentice in the town. Indeed there is a **house** in Békéscsaba dedicated to him. Evidence of *Munkácsy's* profi-ciency as a carpenter can be seen in one of the doors in **Omaszta Hall** (Gyulai út 5.).

István Mill, which lies on the bank of the *Élővíz Channel*, dates from a time when Békéscsaba was merely an agricultural town. The **Cereals Museum** can be found in the old windmill (Gyulai út). Like neighbouring Gyula, the very name Békés-csaba is synonymous with sausages. The town is also famous for its *festival.*

The Church of the Sacred Heart (1993) in Erzsébethely is a recent example of architecture working together in harmony with its kindred arts and crafts. László Patay's 530 biblical scenes cover five hundred square metres.

The harmony of both the interior and the exterior of the Lutheran church is miraculous considering it was built by three local architects (Ferenc Pumberger, Ferenc Hoffer, Antal Czigler (1807-1824) in three different styles (classical, Baroque and Empire).

The beauty of the great **Lutheran church** can be attributed to its sheer scale. It is in fact the biggest Lutheran church in the country. The hall church is particularly beautiful with its double-deckered galleries and four spiral staircases. The acoustics are fantastic and the church is often used for organ recitals.

"Strolling past the farms on the Nagyrét, Alföld landscapes, smells, colours and sounds bring back fond memories. Such feelings are lost on the townsfolk, as are the peaceful, overgrown tracks, the dog barks and the wind blowing in from distant meadows or the plains which stretch out into eternity..." Zsigmond Réthy's description really catches the mood of Békés County.

SZABADKÍGYÓS

The main building of the Wenckheims' neo-Renaissance **palace** (1875–1879, *Miklós Ybl*) with its towers, loggias and terraces is now a college. It is connected to the outhouses by loggia corridors.

The main block of Szabadkígyós Palace includes a chapel, a dining room/conservatory, a library, a ladies' music room, a gentlemen's drawing room with a smoking room, a day study and an alcoved bedroom. Only the library can be seen by the general public, and only then by prior arrangement (The Food and Agricultural College).

There is also a formal French garden with a fountain and its original ornamental lamp posts. Most of the park, however, provides romantic English park-type surroundings with the oaks, ashes, horse chestnuts and poplars one would normally expect. Here you can also see Hungary's largest hornbeams. Every year the members of the *Wenckheim* family organise their *grand reunion* here. The family **chapel** and the crypt were also designed by *Miklós Ybl*, as was the granary, built in a romantic style. The *Kígyós Plain* is a popular weekend destination. At the beginning of the summer the whole place is covered with plantain and in the autumn with lavender and asters. It is the ancient mounds which bring a certain variety to this landscape *"...one of the most beautiful landscapes for mirages, whose appearance tricks the eye into seeing the sea's rippling surface" (The Wenckheim Album)*. The 4,779 hectares making up the Kígyósi-puszta and the park of Wenckheim Palace are in the care of the *Körös-Maros National Park*. On the protected plain between Gyula and Kétegyháza, you will find the **Farmstead Museum** (Szabadka 12.) Its 14 rooms are full of all manner of agricultural tools and household objects. Next door you will also find a Riding School.

> *According to local historian Lajos Haán, "...within what was the Harruckern sphere of influence, Kígyós was where hunting took place, especially when it involved hunting down wolves. There were occasions when as many as a hundred people set about the task..."*

TÓTKOMLÓS

As you approach Tótkomlós the plain turns into arable land surrounded by open woods and groves. The soil is good for growing cereals, tobacco, paprikas and watermelons. The name of the town may have derived from the word *hop* (komló in Hungarian). The late-Baroque steepled **Lutheran church** (1792–1795) was built by the Slovak families who settled in the village. The classical **house** (1851) on Szép utca is also of interest, with its hipped-roofed, wooden-gabled façade and its double-posted veranda entrance.

At the town's thermal **Rózsafürdő** on the banks of *Száraz Brook* you can have an aromatic bath.

The inhabitants of Tótkomlós have always lived off the land, as you will find out if you visit the Slovak Ethnographical Collection (Széchenyi u.).

In nearby NAGYKOPÁNCS the 12th century ruins of the **Roman Catholic church** survived until they reused the stone to build a new church between 1933 and 1935.

KARDOSKÚT

488-hectare Kardoskút is part of the *Körös-Maros National Park*. White Lake is white because of the sodium carbonate left at the bottom of the lake when it dries up during periods of drought. (See also the chapter on the National Parks.)

The alkaline waters surfaced from the remains of the old riverbed of the River *Maros*. It is now a popular resting and nesting place. Several rare breeds of bird live on the lake, for example, the Kentish plover, the lark and the avocet. During the spring and summer, thousands of mallards, cranes, wild geese and kites descend on the lake.

At the **Plain Centre** next to Lake Kardoskút there is a permanent exhibition dedicated to the region's flora and fauna.

OROSHÁZA

The Zomba bell still hangs from the belfry of the town's **Lutheran church**. With Orosháza depopulated after the Turkish occupation, 70 Lutheran peasant families from Zomba were settled on the plains of Orosháza. It was only in 1830 that their church, in Győri Vilmos tér, gained its current appearance. It was then that the southern transept arm was built onto the watchtower, which had itself been built in 1777. In the southeastern corner of the nave the documents relating to its foundation lie concealed in a piece of stoneware pottery.

The eclectic-style **row of shops** (1890) belonged to the Lutherans. The Lutheran parish hall and the school (1790) are both furnished with Louis Seize style interiors. The most impressive room is an assembly hall covered in a fine wooden panelled ceiling.

You don't have to be an ornithologist to watch the birds from the White Lake Lookout Tower at Kardoskút.

The neoclassical Grammar School (Mikszáth K. u.) is named after Mihály Táncsics who served Orosháza as its Member of Parliament between 1869 and 1872.
In front of the school, a park has recently been laid out, including a sculpture (1994, Tibor Szervátiusz) commemorating the arrival of the first Zomba Lutherans 250 years ago.

The medicinal qualities of Gyopárosfürdő's waters were known to the local doctor as far back as 1869. It wasn't until 1920 that the first wells were drilled and the first pools built. A narrow-gauge railway was also built out from Orosháza. Lake Gyopáros is looking better than ever, with its new medicinal bath and the Great Plain's largest covered Wellness complex to add to the pleasures of the lake. It is here in late autumn that they hold an international falconing event.

The **János Szántó Kovács Museum** (Dózsa György u.1.) has a rich local history collection. József Darvas's one-time **house** (Dózsa György u. 74.) now contains an exhibition dedicated to the politician-writer's life. The old water tower has rather imaginatively been turned into Hungary's one and only **Well Museum** (Könd u. 1.).

Amongst the farmsteads surrounding the town and the peasant houses you will find the **Monor Csárda** (1750) a two-storied thatched building, and one of the favourite haunts of the infamous Alföld outlaws.

THE KÖRÖS REGION

BÉKÉS

It was the willow branches along the banks of the River Körös which supplied the raw materials for the local basket weavers, an old craft which is still practiced here. The town is dominated by the classical town houses (1840–1870) and the Louis Seize-style **Calvinist church** (1748–1775). The galleried nave and the west front were added later *(Antal Czigler)*.

In TARHOS you will find the music school founded by György Gulyás. The school gained a reputation for teaching the playing of music instruments and singing, and it is in Gulyás's school that music courses, concerts, and linguistic and music seminars are held in Békés for Hungarian music teachers living outside the country. Recitals are also held for the benefit of the local music lovers, both in the 18th century surroundings of Wenckheim Hall and in front of the Mátyás Jantyik Museum.

The courses going on at the *Békés-Tarhos Music Festival*, the music workshops and performances all take part in the town during June and July. The opening and closing concerts still, however, take place in the **music pavilion** in the 23-hectare park in Tarhos, with its excellent stock of trees.

Those attending the *Madzagfalva Festival* at the end of September will be able to experience all the fun of a small town event capable of putting on a vast array of programmes.

The monastery was a 10th or 11th century brick structure. The remains suggest that it was a three-aisled basilica with a cloister and a rotunda. The carved fragments point to their being the work of Italian masters.

Where the Kis-Sárrét met the Nagy-Sárrét was once a flat marshy area. "Right up until the end of the 18th century there were most definitely more boats (meaning river craft of whatever size) than coaches... They carved these boats out of a single piece of oak, elm or ash, sometimes they were more than ten metres long. These were longer than anything the horses and the oxen were capable of pulling along the boggy roads of the Sárrét." (Zsigmond Réthy: Land of the Körös)

Vésztő

The roads which go through the middle of the *Kis-Sárrét*, the National Park's *Mágorpuszta* and *Bélmegyer Plains* in the direction of Vésztő are lined by poplars. Their beauty has been noted by many travellers. István Sinka (1897–1969), the poet, was one such person, despite one of his more memorable lines: *"All Beauty is detestable to me / In women, landscape, yea, and everything"*. It is in Vésztő, that you can see the museum dedicated to his work and his legacy.

In the tower of Vésztő's late Baroque **Lutheran church** (1780–1797) you can see the *Ecclesiastical History Collection* (Piac tér). The sculpture-park is filled with the town's most famous historical figures. The Mágor Hills, which stand nearby, have a history going back eight thousand years. On the westernmost hill you can inspect the remains of the Csolt clan's **monastery,** which once stood there.

It was under the ruins of the monastery that Count Ferenc Wenckheim dug a huge wine cellar, whilst his grapes ripened on top of one of the hills next door. The **archaeological trench,** which was dug into the eastern hill, now has a roof over it and is open for inspection. The Stone Age and Bronze Age finds can be found under several metres of soil. Other objects have also been uncovered from the periods and cultures which followed.

GESZT is worthy of mention because of its links with the great poet *János Arany* (1817–1882). The village lay within the Tisza family's estates, and here they built their **palace** surrounded by what was a substantial garden. The Tisza's palace is now an agricultural college. It was in the small thatched cottage lying in the park that János Arany lived in 1851, whilst serving as Domokos Tisza's tutor. It was in Geszt that János Arany described the concept of patriotism to his pupil: *"The greatest objective of all, in this our earthly existence, is always to be Human, and in every eventuality... to love one's Country..."*

SZEGHALOM

The Baroque **Calvinist church** in Kossuth tér (1780–1827) has a complex architectural history. Next to it stands the parochial buildings: the late classical choirmaster's house (Kossuth tér 3.), the Empire-style presbytery and the granary (1820), the romantic-style Calvinist vicarage, the parish office and the church hall (1850). **Kárász Palace** was built in the 1840s, the dancing pavilion being added half a century later. The **Roman Catholic church** (1800) is situated on a 4,000-year-old earth mound (*halom* in Hungarian) which the town is named after. The wooden bell tower has a three-stepped pyramid roof covered in wooden shingles, the only one of its type in the southern Alföld (1892).

One of the town's disadvantages was later to become an advantage, namely its *backwardness*. The peace and tranquillity of the waterside, the abundance of fish, and the rural charm are appreciated by both locals and visitors alike. If you fancy something a little more exotic you should make your way to the **Japanese Museum** (Kossuth u. 10.) in FÜZESGYARMAT to see the collection of exotic artefacts of *István Doma Kikó,* painter to the Tongan court.

Those in need of relaxation should head for the **Füzesfürdő** outdoor bathing complex, which has wellness facilities nearby at the *Gara Hotel.*

MEZŐBERÉNY

Sándor Petőfi was a frequent visitor to the birthplace of his relation and friend, the artist *Soma Orlai Petrich.* According to the inscription on his **monument**, Petőfi crossed the River Körös here on 18th July 1849. In the **German Lutheran church**, in what was a German, Slovak and Hungarian village, you can see a picture next to the pulpit depicting an episode from the Bible (*"Bring unto me the Infant"*) by *Orlai Petrich.*

The park of the Baroque-Empire style **Wenckheim-Fejérváry Palace** is now a municipal park, and a popular place for a day out (Fő út). On the right bank of the Kettős-Körös, in the **Károly Bodoky Waterworks Museum** you can see an exhibition of objects and documents relating to the straightening of the rivers sharing the name Körös.

The main square in Mezőberény, with town hall (1901).

In a region where buildings were traditionally constructed of inflammable building materials, it is not surprising that the Sárrét Museum (Tildy u. 14.) has more than its fair share of old fire engines.

SZARVAS

The town's name first appears in *Anonymous*'s chronicle under the name Szarvas Hill. Later it is referred to as the town of stags (*szarvas* in Hungarian). Szarvas has been an important crossing point of the Hármas-Körös since the Middle Ages. The natural surroundings are enhanced by the presence of the 82-hectare Arboretum and the Erzsébet and Anna Woods which lie on the banks of the Dead Channel.

It was the count who decided to plant an **Arboretum**. Also known as *Pepi's garden*, after the founder's nickname it was created two centuries ago that József Bolza, together with his wife, Anna Batthyány, decided to plant botanical rarities in **Anna Wood** on their Szarvas estate.

In the arboretum you can find the *Körös-Maros National Park*'s **Körösvölgy Visitors' Centre** and Anna Wood Nature Trail. **Csáky-Bolza Palace** now serves as the National Park's headquarters.

The wildlife on the Dead-Körös is protected, although you are allowed to catch 33 types of fish.

In the picturesque surroundings of the bend in the dead channel you will find the **Ligetfürdő** baths, which also has a guesthouse and a camping site sharing the same site, both of which are excellent places from which to explore the area.

The statue you can see of a Roman wolf on the steps leading up to the waterside Bolza Palace (Szabadság u. 2.) refers to the family's Italian ancestry.
The park and the arboretum make one sumptuous whole, which embrace the verdant squares and streets of the town.

It was Pál Bolza who moved the Arboretum to its present position. Today there are 1,600 types of trees and shrubs, and many kinds of fungus providing a habitat for 100 species of bird. It's a great place to go for a day out.

If it hadn't been for Sámuel Tessedik the appearance of the town would have been remarkably different, the Lutheran priest. In Szarvas he founded an agricultural college specialising in plant and soil improvement. The Tessedik Farmhouse (c. 1790) was built surrounded by model agricultural plots (Vajda P. u. 90.).

One of Szarvas's horse-driven mills, which was in operation as late as 1962, is now a museum (Ady Endre u. 1.).

Since 1790, Tessedik's acacia on Szabadság út has grown into an enormous specimen. The **museum** bearing his name has an exhibition devoted to the history of the town. It was also Tessedik who had the **old Lutheran church** built (1786–1788, *Lajos Kimnach*). All the interior fittings, the double deckered gallery, the pulpit altar, the organ and the Louis Seize pews are made of wood (Vajda P. u.).

The **Slovak House** (Hoffmann u. 1.), with its thatched roof and wooden veranda, has a display showing how the local Slovaks lived.

THE HÁRMAS-KÖRÖS REGION

Whereas the region where the various branches of the Körös converged was once a veritable eldorado for birds and fishes, now it's a paradise for the hundreds of holiday-home owners whose abodes hug the river banks and the fishing ponds.

BÉKÉSSZENTANDRÁS is famous for its hand-knotted Persian and Torontal **carpets** (Szent András u.

2.): The country's largest barrow, known as the *Gödény Mound*, lies on the edge of the village. It is a Bronze Age burial site worthy of a visit.

The *Dead Channel system* at GYOMAENDRŐD is very similar to that at Békésszentandrás. It is certainly just as rich in fish and waterfowl. It was *Izidor Kner's* **Printing Works**, founded in 1882, which brought Gyomaendrőd to the attention of the rest of the country. A **Printing Museum** tracing the life of the printing dynasty can be found in Kner's neo-Baroque villa (1925, *Lajos Kozma*) (Kossuth u.16.). The late-classical *Endrőd Farmhouse* (1864) is now open to the public (Sugár u. 20). The Gyomaendrőd **Baths** are a popular destination for those seeking relief for their various complaints.

Gyomaendrőd is keen on preserving its local history and traditions, especially those relating to agriculture and the river. The *Cheese and Cottage Cheese Festival* and the *National Culinary Fish Competition* are popular events.

Visitors to DÉVAVÁNYA are met by a curious Great Plain scene. At the **Réhelyi Visitor Centre** run by the *Körös-Maros National Park* you can not only see a host of traditional Hungarian animals, you can also try spotting the local bustards. In the olden days the bustard had a special significance for the local shepherds, for a young man could not even consider marriage until he had found a bustard feather. Indeed, before he had done this he was not even allowed to go into the local inn.

The National Park's *Dévaványa* and *Ecseg Plains* are rich in medicinal herbs (camomile, mint, meadow sage) all flowering in the meadows. *"This is the landscape of János Arany and István Sinka, and despite the apparent desolation it is rich and exciting. You have to know it to love it!"*
(Imre Dankó)

Birdspotters will have to be patient if they want to see a particular rare specimen. Finding a bustard can frequently take up a whole day.

CSONGRÁD

The name Csongrád is a Hungarianized version of the Slav *black castle*. The castle must have been situated on the dramatic bend on the confluence of the *Tisza* and the *Hármas-Körös*, which according to Anonymous, was one of the centres used by the first Hungarian settlers. Nowadays the town is known for its *grapes* and its *wines*.

The town was founded on what was a good *crossing place* over the Tisza. It was here that armies marching along the main Buda-Belgrade route could branch off towards Arad, and where the Körös and the Tisza supplied the town with goods, people and culture. The area enjoys more than its fair share of sunshine. This, and a thousand years of experience in vine cultivation, means you will find some excellent red wines in the area.

A "mechanised" harvest amongst the endless rows of vines in Csongrád County

The old medieval town centre is almost entirely surrounded by the river. When the town outgrew the island it moved a kilometre further on. What remains is a settlement made up of wattle and daub houses and winding streets.

Researchers believe that the winding streets, the windowless house façades and the closed up fences in the old town were all part of a deliberate defensive system. The almost total lack of yards and agricultural buildings in the centre of the settlement suggests that only the houses were situated there, whilst the outbuildings were all placed together in a ring around the village.

Csongrád's 37 houses in the old town form an **architectural ensemble** without parallel on the Great Plain. They include a **museum** and **guesthouses**, and all in the vicinity of the river.

According to Ferenc Erdei there is no more beautiful stretch of the Tisza. Its beauty is best seen when rowing down the river from north to south, or just floating down with the current. The raised river banks forming a cornucopia of wild flowers accompanied by the willows and the silvery green poplars which complete what is a scene of peace and tranquillity.

During the summer, the town's trees conceal many of the buildings in the new town centre. The art nouveau public buildings and the **medicinal bath** (Dob u. 3.) blend beautifully into the leafy parks. Only the 18th century Baroque **Church of the Blessed Virgin Mary** can be seen from any distance.

The fact that the town is bordered on the one side by the Tisza and on the other by the expanse of water known as the *Serházzug Dead-Tisza*, means that there is not only a calm about the place but a climate of its very own.

At the Mouth of the Kurca

*It all happens at the mouth of the Körös.
On the inside of the Tisza Bend there are
some flat golden sands stretching more than half a kilometre.
After a hard day's sunbathing there is nothing better than
going down to the wine cellars just to the west of the town
to spend a pleasant evening sampling a few local wines.*

It's fun to walk down as far as the old *pontoon bridge* and from there on to the *Nagyrét* and the excavations at **Ellés Monastery,** a building dating back to the 11th and 12th centuries. The whole walk is only 3 km long.

Szentes

During Szentes's most dynamic period of development its streets became lined with buildings of a scale and opulence rarely matched on the Great Plain. Around the spacious Kossuth tér there is the neo-Baroque **Town Hall**, the neo-Renaissance **Old County Hall** building (now the museum and public record office), the classical **St Anne's Church** in Erzsébet tér and the Louis Seize-style Calvinist **Great Church,** all built during the town's golden age.

The town's oldest monument, St Michael's, is a **Hungarian Orthodox church** (1786), which is well worth visiting on account of its iconostasis and its wall paintings (Kossuth u.).

The back streets, however, take you back to the atmosphere of a quiet provincial town. Indeed, the town's museums reflect this duality: the **Pál Péter Town House Museum** (Petőfi u.) has an exhibition showing how well-to-do local citizens would have lived their lives during the 19th and 20th centuries, and the **Friedrich Studio** is dedicated to more recent developments in the art of photography (Kossuth tér).

The sports complex in the Szentes Woods is one of the most beautifully situated in the country. There are 15 tennis courts, bathing and leisure pools, water slides and a camping site. The Kurca, the small river surrounding the complex, is perfect for rowing.

*The shady trees of the Széchenyi Wood is an ideal place
to go out to see József Koszta's (1864-1949) paintings
at the museum named after him.
It is here amongst the luxuriant foliage that his pictures really
come into their own. (Bereghát detail)*

In 1996, Szentes earned the title of *National Sporting Town* thanks to its residents' sporting prowess. The hospital, which was designed by *Károly Dávid,* in fact specialises in the treatment of sporting injuries. The **public baths** (Sima Ferenc u.) with their medicinal waters have a rather oriental feel to them. The town hasn't let the fact that it sits on Europe's largest *geothermal field* pass it by. In what is Hungary's uncontested vegetable capital, 32 thermal water wells supply energy to the greenhouses all year round.

On the edge of the town, to the right of the road leading out to Csongrád you can see a fully functioning pumping station built back in the 1920s. It is there you will find the **Water Works Museum.** Going towards to Hódmezővásárhely the pointed **TV tower** rises 240m into the sky. It is possible to visit it with prior permission.

Not everybody knows that Szentes is in fact a Tisza town. Well it is, and there's a **lido** and a **quay** to prove it.

SZEGVÁR

This is indeed a *"water village".* The Tisza bends around it and the *Kurca* and the *Kórógy* plough right through it. Where the latter widens a bit there is a **lake** which splits the village in two.

The Baroque **palace**, occupied by the Károlyi Counts, and the classical house belonging to the estate manager date from the period after 1776,

when Szegvár was a county town. The estate manager's house is home to the **village museum.** Szegvár hit the headlines when some important archaeological discoveries were made at the edge of the village. The importance of these finds, dating back many thousands of years, means they all have been put into national collections, the most famous being the *sickle-carrying God* from the fourth millennium before Christ. The exhibits in the museum here are copies (Hunyadi J. u. 31–33.).

*In the early years of the 20th century a stable was built
on the New Stone Age settlement where the finds were made.
The most interesting object to come to light was
the sickle-carrying God. It is the earliest known depiction
of God holding an emblem of power.
It could possibly be a representation of Zeus.
His face is flat and covered with a mask.*

It was with great care that the grinding mechanism of the 19th century windmill standing on the upper bank was restored to working order. (Sport tér). Today it provides the setting for the **windmill museum.**

It is the verandaed houses with their solid lime-washed walls, their wooden planked gables, iron ornaments and sunbeam motifs, which give Szegvár its particular character. Indeed it is a village almost without equal in the area east of the Tisza, a region we will have to leave as we head in the direction of Kecskemét.

"In Kecskemét the churches are grouped together in the middle of the town like a clump of trees, and the town's main square is spread out in their shadows... It is here you were likely to meet anyone after church, a case of religious worship enhancing one's standing in the social pecking order." (Ferenc Erdei)

KECSKEMÉT

Originally it was a market town, a stopping place on the main Vienna-Buda-Belgrade trade route. During the Turkish period, Kecskemét was a collecting place for local people fleeing from the invaders. When the time was right the town sprang into action, conquering and then repopulating the surrounding plains, building villages and improving the vineyards. This explains how such vast swathes of land fell into the hands of the town, and why it was better to be a resident of Kecskemét than a local landowner.

Today, the town is well known for its *museums and public collections*. Indeed there are collections that you cannot find elsewhere, like the **Szórakaténusz Toy Museum** where you can relive some of your childhood memories, and the **Museum of Naive Art** where there is innocence of another kind. Both can be found at Gáspár A u. 11.

At the **Hungarian Photographic Museum** (Katona J. tér) there are images covering one and a half centuries of photographic history. In addition there are photographic studios, potters' studios, enamellers' workshops, galleries and even an exhibition showing how **Hungarian spirits** are made (Matkói u. 2.).

With the relevant permission from the directorship of the *Kiskunság National Park* (Liszt F. u.) you can visit some of the peasant buildings in these parts. (For more information see the section on the National Parks in the opening chapter.) The **Bozsó Collection** (Klapka u.) is a good example of how a local artist with an interest in the arts and crafts and a passion for collecting can become part of the fabric of his home town.

A similiar impulse lies behind clockmaker *István Hanga's* **clock collection,** which you can now see in the Calvinist's **Ráday Museum** (2003).

Zoltán Kodály (1882–1967) and writer *József Katona* (1791-1830) were also born in the town. Indeed, the local **theatre** is named after *József Katona,* the inventor of Hungarian drama. The building (*Helmer and Fellner)* itself can be described as being both romantic and neo-Baroque. The **museum**, apart from holding temporary exhibitions, has a permanent collection, which includes an Avar treasure trove (Bethlen krt.).

It was in the buildings of the local railway station that Zoltán Kodály was born. Zoltán Kodály's music for his Psalmus Hungaricus was written for a Hungarian translation of the psalms by another gifted individual, Mihály Végh, the Chief Justice of Kecskemét. One of the many things Kodály left us was the world famous Zoltán Kodály Institute for the Teaching of Music, which offers full-time courses and summer courses to students from all over the world.

One particularly interesting piece of public sculpture in the main square is the "Heraldry Mount" (Gusztáv Pálfy) which shows the distances of towns of interest to those living in Kecskemét.

The **chimes** from the Town Hall which play a version of a melody from *Zoltán Kodály's Háry Suite* also send out the old rallying cry: *"Kecskemét also sends out its finest"*.

The historic surroundings of the main square in Kecskemét, whilst being one of the most beautiful townscapes in Hungary, tells us a lot about how the town grew. The square has something of the intimate atmosphere of a medieval town, despite the vast array of representative public and ecclesiastical buildings.

There is indeed a Gothic building in the town, the **Franciscan church** built in the 15th century. The Calvinist church is Baroque, the Greek Orthodox church is classical, the **Great church** is late Baroque, the Lutheran church is romantic and the **Synagogue** (now the *House of Science and Technology*) is Moorish in style.

The general atmosphere of the town centre is most influenced, however, by three Secession-style buildings, the **Town Hall** (Kossuth tér 1., *Ödön Lechner* and *Gyula Pártos*), the **Cifra Palota** (The Fancy Palace – *Géza Márkus*, Rákóczi út 1.) and the **Calvinist Main Grammar School and Law Academy** (Kálvin tér 1.), designed by *Valér Mende*.

It's worth going inside the Fancy Palace to check out the interior decoration and to search out the fine collection of paintings in the Kecskemét Picture Gallery.

Apart from looking at all the fine monumental buildings it's also a good idea to turn off the beaten track to look at some of the backstreets and alleyways. The fountains and statues bring a certain charm to the town. It is here that you will also come across the occasional late 19th century town house.

IN THE KISKUNSÁG

The town's main square stands 119 metres above sea level. The Outdoor Leisure Centre, however, stands at an altitude of 160 metres thanks to all the soil deposited there when the complex was laid out. The result looks rather like some kind of 20th century Bronze Age earthwork. The Széktó Outdoor Bathing Complex boasts the leisure pool and slide park (2003).

We now come to an area where the flat and sometimes watery landscape of the *Danubian Plain* meets the sandy woods, the sunflowers, corn, grass and vineyards of the *Kiskunság National Park*. On these plains it is only the plants capable of enduring the salty environment which flourish. There are farms and country inns in what is a landscape full of river birds and sheep. There are also stables and country residences to tempt any passing visitors. Those who would really like to become familiar with the local wild flowers should enquire about a guided tour organised by the *Directorate of the Kiskunság National Park*. (For more information see the first chapter of the book).

The roads on the Great Plain are good, and it's easy to find your way through the towns and the new town centres, or to stop and look around the cobbled main squares and the parks. There are plenty of holiday houses, stables, guesthouses, swimming pools and hunting lodges, which have been built for the benefit of the visitors.

Vast swathes of vineyards and fruit trees surround the white-walled farming villages. It is here that the main ingredient for one of Hungary's most famous products, *apricot brandy* (barackpálinka) is grown.

Following a sufficient dosage of culture you can complete the Kecskemét experience by going to one of the town's restaurants or doing something more active. The **Outdoor Leisure Centre** is ideal for a town of its size. It has a swimming pool, an artificial lake, a tobogganing run and a lookout point. The complex is set in 57 hectares of woodland. Kecskemét's cultural calendar has an international feel about it: some of the *Budapest Spring Festival* is held here, there is also the *International Enamellers' Festival*, the *Kodály* concerts, the *József Katona* plays, the two-yearly *Folk Music Festival* and a childrens' get-together known as *Europe's Future*.

During the summer months it is easy to buy fresh fruit cheaply on the streets of the Kiskunság's towns and villages. The fruit sellers have usually grown the produce themselves, and if you find them on a country road they may indeed be trading from the edge of their own plot of land.

The local enlightened landowners turned the many thousands of hectares of land surrounding Kecskemét into model horticultural plots. Ede Wéber, a Swiss entrepreneur, for example, bought a plot of land on which he then employed vine growers from the Balaton region. The plot of land was called Helvécia in homage to the land of Wéber's birth.

At the *Tanya Csárda* (Bene tanya 625) in LAJOSMI-ZSE stands a statue of *Imre Varga* depicted as a *Sower*. It was he who managed to turn part of the plain into a garden. He is celebrated at the **Outdoor Ethnographic Museum**. *Gerébi Hall* and the mature park in which it stands host many an interesting programme. There you can sit by the glowing embers and watch the dancing gypies (Alsólajos u. 224.).

One of the attractions in KUNSZENTMIKLÓS *is the classical Virág Hall, which shares the name of its builder Pál Virágh, and provides a home for the local natural history museum (Kossuth L. u. 4.). One illustrious member of the family was Major Gedeon Virágh, who brought his hussars home from Bohemia in 1848. The building now houses the rich ethnographical, literary and natural history collections of the Kiskunság National Park Museum.*

Whether it's where the *Soroksár branch* rejoins the main branch of the Danube, or where the *Kiskunság Main Channel* starts it's winding course, you will find a landscape scattered with good **fishing waters,** weekend retreats and **holiday homes.** Although TASS almost touches the Danube, locals and holidaymakers not only go to the local **Dunasor lido**, they also make for the popular *Szentgyörgy-puszta* over by the main channel.

There's also a lot happening on the waters around SZALKSZENTMÁRTON where there are also old **gravel pits** to enjoy. It is there that a **ferry** takes you across the Danube to Dunaújváros. The rich variety of building styles in evidence in the **centre** of this rather closed village has earned it a well-deserved *Europa Award* (2003). The village also has its own Petőfi traditions as well. It was here,

between 1844 and 1846, that the Petrovics family rented the inn, which now provides a home for the **Petőfi Museum.**

SZABADSZÁLLÁS is another settlement with strong Petőfi connections. It was here that *Sándor Petőfi* spent his childhood. Indeed, another great poet, *Attila József* (1905–1937), often came here because his mother's family came from the town. Their names can be found on the town's school, arts centre and library. Szabadszállás's imposing two-storied classical **town hall** was built in 1826. What was an important centre for the free Cumans is once again a dynamic town.

You can see a sculpture in IZSÁK that takes the form of a vine press. It is here that they produce some excellent champagnes.

BUGAC

Bugac is deepest plain country. It was here, in the 1930s, that people who felt they understood such matters decided to create a Hungarian version of harmony. The open pastures, the large sandbanks and the junipers which you can be see on the **Bugac Plain** today make it one of the most visited areas in the country. The grasses covering the soil are the very same grasses the animals grazed on at the time of the Hungarian Conquest. Some areas are not open to the public, this is for the good of the rare

The keeping of ancient and naturalised animals using old traditional methods is being done for the good of the gene pool as well as for the sake of the visitors. Seeing the cattle, the sheep, the pigs and the horses together is quite a sight. The Bugac Plain is best reached by turning off the E75 and then following the signs.

plants and animals. However, you can go into the **juniper groves**, either alone or accompanied by a guide. Some of the **sand dunes** are still actually on the move, others are held down firmly by the *junipers* and the *poplars*.

The Buguc Plain would be all the poorer if it didn't have the Bugaci Csárda. It was here, in the 1930s, Ferenc Erdei tells us, that organised tourism first started in Hungary.

> "A plate of hot potato-paprika
> > *beneath a lazy sky,*
> red-slated in warm evening light I saw
> > *the little village lie.*
> Here a slim column'd wisp of smoke – in hope –
> > *its way not understood,*
> wanders and from the chimney-top a-slope waves
> > *to the neighbourhood.*
>
> > *(Attila József: A Village [extract]*
> > *translation by Watson Kirkconnell)*

Things really haven't changed since the lines above were written. Eating and drinking on the plain is a timeless experience complemented nicely by a visit to the pastoral exhibit at the local **museum** or a climb up the **lookout tower** from where you can survey the surrounding landscape. The lookout tower on the Bugac Plain is best reached by taking the necessary turning off road E75 and following the signposts.

The Plain Five, that piece of expert horsemanship, didn't actually exist when the German painter Koch painted it. It wasn't long, however, before the Hungarian horsemen actually brought Koch's artistic vision to life; yet another case of life copying art. If the conditions are right and with a little luck you can do it with sixteen horses.

Whitsun was a time in the year when the horsemen could pit their skills against each other. The best horseman won the title leader of the pack an honour he held for a year. It was a title which brought with it dispensations. He could have wine for free in the local inn, and was invited to all the wedding receptions and social gatherings. Nowadays, the winner of the *Bugac Whitsun Equestrian Festival* is less likely to get as many benefits.

József Kerényi designed the Pastor Museum, and since 1975 he has been seeing to the needs of the visitors on the Bugac Plain.

KISKUNFÉLEGYHÁZA

Our last stop in the Kiskunság is the one-time seat of the *Kiskun Captaincy*, Kiskunfélegyháza. The town currently marks the end of the *M5 motorway*, which will eventually go from Budapest to Szeged, and then on to the Jugoslavian border. Having got this far you might as well stop off in Kiskunfélegyháza to take advantage of its excellent **swimming facilities** (Blaha Lujza tér).

The Town Hall (Kossuth L út 1.), designed by the architects József Vas and Nándor Morbitzer, was built in a local version of the Art Nouveau style between 1909 and 1911.

"Here in this pleasant region was I born,
Where Alföld's broad, fair plains salute the morn
This is the town where first I saw the light;
My cradle-songs still fill its quiet night;
Though they have long been mute, I hear one say:
"O chafer, yellow chafer, fly away!"

(Sándor Petőfi:
In My Native Land [extract] translation by
Watson Kirkconnell)

Ferenc Móra was the author best able to bring the people of the *Kiskunság* to life. The town has honoured him by making his place of birth a museum. Baroque complexes like the **Church of the Blessed Virgin Mary and the vicarage** with its *Statue of Christ* in Béke tér, are rare in this part of the world.

The **Prison Museum** in the *Kun Captain's House* (Holló Lajos út 9.) reminds you of what methods were used to punish and educate criminals.

"This is the town where I first saw the light". This is what Hungary's greatest poet, Sándor Petőfi (1823 Kiskőrös-1849 Segesvár [Sighisoara, Romania]) wrote about Kiskunfélegyháza, despite the fact that he hadn't in fact been born here. Once the family had arrived from Kiskőrös in 1822, the poet's father rented a butcher's shop in the so-called Swan House, a building which had been built in 1820 in a classical style.

THE CENTRAL TISZA REGION

Between Kecskemét and the Tisza the ground level drops 50–60 metres and the soil turns from a sandy colour to something darker. The trees have more foliage, and cabbages, paprika and tomato plants appear amongst the vineyards and the fruit trees.

The narrow-gauge railway, which leaves from the sports grounds in the middle of Tiszakécske, takes its passengers to the best swimming places on the Tisza, as well as the thermal baths. The railway tracks follow the bends in the river.

TISZAKÉCSKE

The **outdoor swimming pool** and the **thermal baths** are most definitely what one would expect in a spa town. The **Community Centre** (Templom tér 6.) puts on cultural programmes and has both a local history collection and an exhibition devoted to pillows. The *Dead Tisza* in Tiszakécske is good for fishing. There are also pleasure boats and a **narrow-gauge railway**. It's a good place to go cycling, riding or have a bite to eat. In fact there's enough to do to make you want to stay longer. In nearby KEREKDOMB **campers** can enjoy the on-site **swimming pools**. The hydrogen carbonate waters in the four pools are good for those suffering from muscular and gynaecological problems (Kerekdomb 1.).

LAKITELEK

Nature also accompanies you right into the middle of the town. The *Tőserdő* lying nearby is one of the most visited places in the *Kiskunság National Park*. This is not surprising when you know there are **thermal baths** and tourist accommodation there. Nearby *Alpár Meadow* was the scene of one of the most important battles during the Hungarian Conquest, which is where you can now find an open-air museum with a medieval theme.

In 1987, Lakitelek was the scene of the lively political debates which went on between opposition politicians prior to the publication of a charter demanding changes to the then one-party system.
The People's College was built with the intention of providing a forum for intellectual discussion and a place where members of the Hungarian diaspora could meet.

Woods full of wild flowers, a dead channel bursting with water lilies, woodland footpaths, clearings, camp fires and a romantic hunting lodge are what you can expect to find in Lakitelek. The original course of the Tisza is more or less in tact, and its original habitat has managed to cope with the ravages of time. (See in the picture a trout-fly).

So it is that with this view of the still waters of the River Tisza that we say farewell to the *Southern Great Plain,* and head for the northern part of this vast geographical expanse. In this particular publication the following region stretches from the Jászság in the west to the borders of Romania and the Ukraine in the east.

"It's as if we were in a magical village
and yet it is so full of people:
… all that one sees betrays the work of hands
and each hand those who lived here
and lived the way only they knew how
I saw the cold wall and the tiny windows
Just about big enough to let in the light"

(Zsuzsa Kapecz: Those Horses)

CONTENTS – THE NORTHERN GREAT PLAIN

THE NORTHERN GREAT PLAIN

The *Northern Great Plain* region is made up of the three large counties of Jász-Nagykun-Szolnok, Hajdú-Bihar and Szabolcs-Szatmár-Bereg which, despite being separate administrative areas, will be taken together to form our next region. Six to ten million years ago the Carpathian Basin was still covered by sea. With the passing of time the area now known as the *Great Hungarian Plain* (known simply as the *Alföld* in Hungarian) became covered with the fresh waters of an inland lake. The rivers which flowed into the area brought with them deposits from the surrounding areas which, over the course of a few million years, resulted in the lake becoming completely silted up. We will be focusing on some of the smaller landscapes like those lying between the *Jászság* and *the Bereg Plain*, and the area between the Mátra and the plains and the *Tisza* water meadows. Of particular importance are the *Hajta Marshes* and the *Zagyva* and *Jásztelek-Pusztamizse Nature Reserves*.

After the Tatar Invasion of 1241, which left the territory in a state of total destruction, Béla IV. repopulated the area with Iazyges ("Jászok" in Hungarian). The Iazyges were Iranian-speaking Orthodox Christians who had split off from the Alan clan. Being both culturally and ethnically different from the Cumans, who also settled on the Great Plain, the Iazyges did not share the political rights enjoyed by the Cumans and were considered to be a subservient people. In 1332, the Iazyges received privileges from Charles Robert which allowed them to have their own captains and judges, as well as their own territory, known as the *Berény-szék* with its own autonomous legal code. The process of economic, religious and linguistic assimilation speeded up during the 15th century, despite the fact that feudal privileges provided a firm basis upon which their ethnic distinctiveness could have survived.

Many crafts prospered in this region: the Iazygian skinners produced the huge sheepskin coats which were once so characteristic of the region, whilst the woven green and white patterns which decorated their tableclothes and other similar items were equally Iazygian.

The ancient Bridge over the River Tarna at Jászdózsa

One of the most beautiful landscapes on the Great Plain can be seen in the *Central Tisza Nature Reserve*, most of which can be found in and around Szolnok. When the River Tisza was straightened in the 19th century the consequences for the local agriculture and the people who lived there were enormous. However, the building of new farmsteads has only really happened in the larger agricultural towns. The villages around Szolnok, which had previously only amounted to a patchwork of communities populated by people of different religious denominations speaking different tongues, became a more or less homogeneous group of settlements inhabited by people sharing the same urban aspirations.

On the banks of the Tisza unaffected by the building of dams and dykes, you can see the so-called Navvy Woods which were planted on the land gained by redirecting the river, and around the holes left by the navvies. The woods were planted to act both as windbreaks and wave breakers. From the point of view of its origins, the *Tiszazug* is the only area in the eastern part of the Great Plain affected by the level of the River Danube. The vegetation one finds in the region, its vineyards and fruit trees, differs somewhat from that the Hungarians found on their arrival in 896. For the tourist perhaps the most important destinations in this particular landscape are *the Tiszakürt Arboretum* and the *Körös-Maros National Park* (further information can be found in the chapter devoted to the *National Parks*.)

Evidence of the Hungarians' presence in the area following 896 can be seen in the local place names and the local archaeological sites. Medieval settlements can be found just above the flood plains. This network of small settlements had already started to thin out during the 14th and 15th centuries, disappearing almost completely during the period of the Turkish occupation when foraging Turkish soldiers, diligent local tax collectors or the armies rode roughshod across the landscape. It was only during the opening decades of the 18th century that the villages started to return to normal.

It was the cultivation of grapes which provided the serfs, and later the agricultural peasants, with a means of earning a living. The local houses were often little more than two-roomed wattle-and-daub structures surrounded by wicker fences. Life was frequently a matter of simply trying to make ends meet, although supplementary incomes could be had from gathering wood, fishing, basket-making, weaving rush mats, and share-cropping. The vines and the fruit trees out on the sand beds are very much a recent development.

The *Nagykunság* joins the Hortobágy and the Nagysárrét almost imperceptibly, bordering the Körös region to the south and the Tiszazug to the southwest. The four to five thousand-year-old barrows form one of the main features of the Great Plain being about 5–10 metres high and 20–25 metres in diameter.

Túrkeve fisherman

Following the Tatar invasion, Béla IV. designated what is now known as the Nagykunság to the Cumans ("Kunok" in Hungarian). Their culture was based on an agricultural economy, mainly pastoral, which contained some very characteristic and indeed archaic traits (shepherd folk art, shamanic religion and sorcery). Mezőtúr is renowned for its pottery. Up until the middle of the 19th century the town was famous for its black ceramics. From the 1860s onwards, it was the yellow domestic pottery decorated with the coloured flowers and leaves for which the town became famous.

One of the area's greatest natural treasures is its thermal and medicinal waters (Túrkeve, Mezőtúr). For many thousands of years the *Hortobágy* acted as a flood plain for the River Tisza. The rather monotonous landscape, so striking today, is the result of many decades of animal husbandry. The huge open spaces and the grazing pastures, together with the occasional boggy depressions, provide an ideal home for the rare species of birds which live there. The *Hortobágy National Park,* enjoys *Unesco World Heritage* status. (For more on both topics please refer to the relevant sections in the *Hungarian Treasury*). Whilst everything is being done to ensure the protection of the flora and the fauna, efforts are being made to encourage the more traditional forms of animal husbandry.

The roadside inns which stand at twenty, thirty or forty kilometre intervals, bear witness to ancient herding practices, the distance between them being about the distance a herd would travel on any particular day. Nowadays a "csárda" is more likely to satisfy the hunger of a passing tourist than that of an exhausted shepherd. The village of *Hortobágy* lies at the foot of the famous *nine-arched bridge.* The annual *Bridge Fair,* which has been held for over a century now, is an event of national importance. Although it is no longer confined to the buying and selling of animals, the market still has much to tempt the tens of thousands of visitors who turn up to inspect the traditional produce and the folk art.

Travelling east from the Hortobágy you move into the *Hajdúság,* an area with its own unique landscape and its own particular history. It was here that the Haiduk ("Hajdúk" in Hungarian),

The Bell House in Hajdúszoboszló

who were originally cattle drivers, took on a military role during the peasant's revolt led by György Dózsa in 1514. It was a role they were subsequently to play on several other occasions. As a result, anyone taking up the sword against authority, particularly if they happened to be a poor peasant living out on the plain, was likely to be labelled a Haiduk. Whilst seeking how best to represent the interests of Transylvania in his role of Prince of that particular principality between 1571 and 1586, István Bocskai managed to gain the support of a substantial number of the so-called Free Haiduk. This was at the very time Bocskai turned against the very same Habsburgs whose help he had sought when trying to drive off the Turks.

The Haiduk were later generously rewarded for their service with lands, special rights and privileges. This was how the seven Hajdú towns (Böszörmény, Dorog, Hadház, Nánás, Polgár, Szoboszló and Vámospércs) came into existence, although in Polgár's case the town was to lose its privileges about one hundred years later in 1715. At the end of the 17th century the remaining six Hajdú towns set up a special Hajdú district enjoying special rights, with Böszörmény at its centre, in an attempt to distinguish their interests from those of the neighbouring county of Szabolcs. This continued to be the state of affairs right up until 1876, when the county of Hajdú became an administrative unit in its own right.

SPECIALITIES ON THE NORTHERN GREAT PLAIN

Debrecen honey dolls and *Hungarian kalács* (a soft sweet bread) and *spicy pretzels* and Hungarian spirits such as *walnut pálinka*, or the pálinkas made from *Szatmár plums* or *Szabolcs apples* all make great presents.

The characteristic fruits of the region are early *apricots* from *Tápiószele, Bereczk quinces, Szabolcs apples, Beszterce* and *Szabolcs plums, Milota* and *Tiszacsécse walnuts* and *Debrecen* and *Pándy sour-cherries.*

The local *Vállaj Swabian Ham* and *Bacon, Csécs Bacon, Choice Debrecen Bacon* and *Smoked Paprika Bacon* are all locally delicacies. They all go down well with the local baked specialities, the so-called *kulcsos kalács,* the sugary *kürtös kalács,* the *vesu,* and the *dübbencs.*

Parenyica ewe's cheese and *mild goat's cheese* are more commonly found in the northern part of the Great Plain than elsewhere in Hungary, as are *Hajdúság cabbages, Hajdúság horseradishes, Kisvarda potatoes* and *Nagydobos pumpkins.*

Then there are *prunes, dried pears* and *apples,* which are good for Hungarian fruit soups, the local pasta, the *roasted sunflower seeds* (compulsory fare at local football matches), and *Nyírség honey,* which is an ideal sweetener for your *camomile tea. Marasmius mushrooms* are the basis for many a fine meal, whereas cakes can be made using *cornel* or *Szatmár plum jam.*

Lebbencstészta, a dish made from pasta and potatoes, and *semolina* are the standard shepherd's fare. It's a good idea to order a Kunság *"kötött galuska"* if you happen to be in a restaurant, and to try quince cheese just to get the full flavour of the Northern Great Plain.

Moving south from Hortobágy and the Hajdúság you come into the *Berettyó Region* which in turn borders on the *Bihar Plain* to its east and southeast. Before it was straightened, the *River Berettyó* too fed the marshes and lowlands of the *Sárrét.*

Moving eastwards from the heart of the Hajdúság you also come to Debrecen, surrounded by the *Erdőspuszta* to the south and southeast and the *Southern Nyírség* to the north. Debrecen, with its population of over two hundred thousand people, is now the second biggest town in Hungary and consequently Eastern Hungary's regional centre. Although Debrecen is mentioned in the *Váradi Regestrum* of 1235, it appeared for a long time afterwards only as one of several villages belonging to the crown. It was only at the turn of 17th century, when it found itself at the intersection of a number of long-distance trade routes, that the town enjoyed any kind of prosperity.

The depopulation of the area during the Turkish occupation led to an extension of the town's borders. This process continued right up to the 1950s by which time even the Hortobágy had been usurped by the municipality. At the time Debrecen was the largest town in Hungary, in terms of square metres at least. Fate has provided Debrecen with its moments of historical importance, particularly on the two occasions when it had to fill the role of state capital. The first occasion being between the months of January and May 1849 when the town became the seat of government during the War for Freedom, the second in December 1944 when Debrecen provided a home for the *Temporary National Assembly.* Debrecen (the *"Calvinist Rome"*) has, since the 16th century, been the centre of the Reformation in Hungary, and the Calvinist *College* an educational centre serving half the country.

Erdőspuszta, lying to the edge of Debrecen, was once filled with a network of farms. Since the 1980s the area has been "repopulated" with tourist facilities.

The *Nyírség* is the country's second largest sand bed. The land between Nyíradony-Nyírlugos and Nyírbogát rises 20–50 metres above the plains east of the Tisza, the highest point lying at *Hoportyó* (183m above sea level) just east of Szalmad, the highest point on the Great Hungarian Plain. The contours of the landscape were shaped during the second half of the Pliocene period, when the waters of the lake covering Pannonia and beyond receded. Subsequently, when the climate was considerably warmer and damper than it is now, the Nyírség became a wooded steppe. These woods disappeared almost completely during the deforestation of the 18th and 19th centuries. During the 1870s efforts were made to try and bind the sands, which were once again open to the elements. This was done by planting trees and laying out vineyards and orchards.

The changes in the water supply in the region during the second half of the 19th century meant the soil lacked adequate drainage, and ploughing became all but impossible in certain areas. It was for this reason that about 3,200 kilometres of water channel were dug, primarily running on a north-south axis. Most of the waters run down the *Belfő* and the *Lónya Channels* into the Tisza. As a result of man's interference the landscape has indeed changed, as has the way the local population lead their lives. The sands have always had a say in the local economy. The shifting sands have been tied down with acacias, whilst vines and fruit trees have been planted on the exposed headland. Indeed, the Nyírség's famous orchards have totally altered the appearance of the landscape. To this very day the Slovaks living in Nyíregyháza (the *"tirpákok"*), who settled in the town during the 18th century, still speak an archaic form of Slovakian. This, and the knowledge and traditions handed down from generation to generation, have aroused much interest amongst Slovak ethnographers.

The *Szatmár* and the *Bereg Plains* skirt the eastern edges of the Nyírség, whilst to the north the River Tisza flows, having come from the Ukraine in the east and Romania to the south. The plains are covered with a 10–12-metre Holocene rock bed, which brings a slight undulation to what is a rather monotonous landscape.

On the western part of the plain stand the Ecsed Flats, formed between the silted up banks of the River Szamos and the shallow basin of the Nyírség Valley during the Upper Holocene period. The

Medieval wallpaintings, Csaroda

flats, which covered an area two-thirds the size of Lake Balaton, were fed by the floodwaters overflowing from the *River Szamos* and the *River Kraszna*. The draining of the marsh started in 1895, and now the whole area is under the plough. This, however, does not mean that the marsh has been lost without trace. During periods of heavy rainfall the land reverts in part to type, the water flooding anything which stands in its way. The waters eventually make their way down to the man-made draining channels. During droughts, however, the subterranean peat sometimes ignites and proceeds to burn for weeks on end.

The *Szatmár-Bereg Plain* has one of the most complex river systems in Hungary. The Tisza, the *Szamos*, the *Túr* and the *Kraszna*, all of which have their sources beyond the borders of Hungary, are capable of frustrating even the most serious attempts at local flood prevention. The countryside once suffering frequent flooding was planted with woods. The old riverbeds, the oxbow lakes, and the badly-drained marshes are now habitats rich in grasses and other typical wetland vegetation.

It is only the plains of the historic counties of Szatmár and Bereg, which survive within the boundaries of present-day Hungary. The fact that this particular area has remained unchanged and untouched means that it is a good place to visit if you want to go in search of a local Hungarian culture which has enjoyed a period of continuity stretching back beyond the Turkish occupation. The inhospitable nature of the landscape meant that not even the Turks were prepared to go to the trouble of occupying it. Consequently many archaic traits have survived here. The local peasant architecture, particularly that in the small villages, has survived, and the countryside has been spared the worst excesses of modern agriculture. However, in recent years the region has had to contend with a number of incidents of river pollution caused by pollutants entering the rivers in the hillier regions further upstream.

The *Szatmár-Bereg Nature Reserve* has managed to preserve what is an ancient landscape. Nevertheless within the reserve you can also find the so-called navvy lakes, dug when the river defences were being built. Today it is difficult to distinguish them from the naturally created lakes. The waters offer a habitat to a number of rare species of animals, for example the *viviparous lizard*, the *bee-hawk*, the *black stork* and the *hazel-grouse*.

Perhaps fortunately for the tourist the *viper*-infested *Lónya* and *Bockerek Woods* are strictly protected and are not open to the general public. An adult would just about be able to cope with a bite from a viper without having to resort to an antiserum, but it still isn't worth finding out for yourself! The nature reserve is run by the *Hortobágy National Park*. Apart from the *Bábtava, Lake Nyíres*, the *Lónya, Bockerek, Ricse* and the *Déda Woods*, the *Túr Dead Channel* and the *Hidéger*, tourists can gain unrestricted access.

About twenty kilometres north of Nyíregyháza the countryside suddenly changes, and you find yourself in a lower-lying landscape cut up into channels occupied by the long, strung-out villages which occupy the higher ground. This is the *Rétköz*, lying between the *Lónya Main Channel* and the River Tisza, which stretches all the way from Vencsellő to Tuzsér. The landscape doesn't stop at the Tisza as it continues into the *Bodrogköz* on the far bank of the river, an area sharing not only its natural features, but its way of life and its economy.

"The life of the Rétség was full of mysteries. Wherever we turned all we could see was reeds and water, and the sky. Wherever the track led, it ended in a silky green carpet. The moss looked reassuring but concealed the uncertainties of the swamp." So wrote *Lajos Kiss,* the ethnographer and local historian.

Once the land had been drained, a whole way of life came to an end. The Lónya Main Channel, which was dug in 1890, ran from Berkesz in the Nyírség as far as the edge of the Rétség, a distance of 44.7 kilometres. The waters collected in the channel join the Tisza just downstream from Gávavencsellő. The one-time flatland villages became agricultural communities. The soil which replaced the waters was rich, and ideal for cabbages, potatoes, carrots, sunflowers and tobacco.

The *Nyíri-Mezőség*, which lies to the west of the Nyírség, amounts to a small tract of land made up of the northern part of the *Hajdúhát* and a short section of the River Tisza. It is here that one can find six villages (Tiszadada, Tiszadob, Tiszaeszlár, Tiszalök, Tiszavasvári and Tiszanagyfalu), all of which differ, particularly from an ethnographical point of view, from those in the surrounding areas. They also share a characteristic layout. The houses were built together in the middle of the village from whence the roads radiated out to the edges of the village, where all the outbuildings, the stables and the food stores were situated. These buildings created a protective ring around the outside of the settlement. It was forbidden to live out there on a permanent basis, and it has only been since the middle of the 19th century that permanent dwellings have been built there. These settlements have much in common with the villages lying on the opposite bank of the Tisza in the *Taktaköz*, although there is in fact a common source in Tokaj and its surrounding villages.

The *capital of the Jászság* is rich in historical monuments. The upper floor of the one-time **Lehel Hotel** (Lehel Vezér tér 33.) (1894, *Szilárd Monaszterly*) now belongs to the grammar school, whilst the *Déryné Arts Centre* can be found on the ground floor. Rococo statues can be found on the banks of the *River Zagyva* in a park which used to enhance the facade of the offices of the *Jász-Kun District Council* (c.1760). The putti symbolise fertility and abundance.

Near the **Town Hall** (Lehel Vezér tér 18.), (1839, *Lőrinc Bedekovich*), is the **Jász Museum** (Táncsics Mihály u. 3.) founded in 1874.

Throughout the 125 years of its existence the Jász Museum has built up a collection of written documents and cultural artifacts relating to the Iazyges. The museum possesses a carved ivory Byzantine horn dating from the 10th and 11th centuries. Known as the Lehel Horn, it gets its name from one of Hungary's heroic sagas, the Lehel Legend. The Lehel Horn has always symbolised the unity of the Iazygian Jász people.

One of the pre-eminent figures of the Hungarian stage, *Róza Széppataki*, was born in the town in 1793. A tablet can be found on house number 2 in the street bearing her name.

The equestrian **hussar statue** in Szentháromság tér (1926, *Viktor Vass*) is a memorial to all those 850 Jászkun Hussars who fell during the First World War. The **Rozália Chapel** was built on the same spot as an earlier plague chapel.

Next to the chapel there are some Baroque statues (*The Man of Sorrows, St John of Nepomuk*). The square is dominated by the Baroque **Roman Catholic church**, originally built in 1332 in the Gothic style, and rebuilt several times subsequently. The tabernacle over the high altar was designed by *Mihály Pollack*, and the painting behind it was painted in Rome by *Ferenc Soldatits* in 1883. The ceiling (1909) is by *Albert Szirmai*. Next to the church you can find *the Stations of the Cross*.

Moving towards the River Zagyva you will find the **Palatine Column** (Nádor u.) built to commemorate the visit of Archduke Joseph in 1798. The **Hamza Foundation Museum** (Gyöngyösi út 7.), dedicated to the art work of the famous film director *Dezső Ákos Hamza* and the fashion designs of his wife *Mária Lehel*, was opened in 1994.

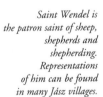

Saint Wendel is the patron saint of sheep, shepherds and shepherding. Representations of him can be found in many Jász villages.

The *Lehel Legend* records the events of 955 when the Magyars were inflicting untold damage on the German lands. On reaching Augsburg they met strong resistance and their two leaders Lehel (Lél) and Bulcsu fell into captivity. Before they knew where they were they were standing before the Emperor Conrad. Being asked to choose their manner of execution Lehel replied "Bring me my horn, and only when I have blown it will I decide." Before he blew he took a step towards the Emperor and dealt him such a blow to his forehead that the Emperor died immediately. It was then that Lehel said, "As you die before me you shall be my slave in the world to come!" The ancient Magyars always believed that the people you killed during your lifetime would become your servants in the afterlife.

The thermal waters at the **Outdoor Swimming Complex and the Thermal Bath** (Hatvani út), which contain sodium hydrogen carbonate, are good for the treatment of bone and locomotor diseases and cartilage problems.

The **Franciscan Church** and Friary in Jászberény were built in the 15th century, and there are indeed some Gothic elements within the Baroque fabric of the church (Ferencesek tere). The high altar was painted by *Endre Holló* and the wall paintings are by *Albin Steffek*. In the park in front of the church you can see the *Stations of the Cross* dating from 1776 and a *statue of the Virgin Mary* (1795).

Jászberény hosts a number of important annual cultural events. At the end of July and the beginning of August there is the Jászberény Summer Carnival, the Csángó Festival (see picture above), the European Minorities Folklore Festival and Conference and an International Folk Dance Camp. The International Honey Fair, which takes place in the first weeks of August, is when the Honey Queen is crowned.

A favourite weekend destination is the Zoological and Botanical Garden where creatures, both exotic and historic, can be found in the more familiar surroundings of the local trees and shrubs (Fémnyomó út 1.).

The **Turkish-Hungarian Monument** was built in *1909 (Jenő Körmendi-Frim)* on top of the bones uncovered within the grounds of the castle.

The **Lehel Sport Leisure Centre and Outdoor Swimming Complex** (Kiserdei út 10.) not only has a swimming pool, a covered thermal pool and medicinal waters, but an ice rink as well.

Travelling about ten kilometres west out of the town you come to *Hajta* which is all that remains of the marshes which once covered the Jászság where the *marsh orchids* grow.

According to local tradition Attila the Hun set up camp at Kerekudvar Plain near Jászberény just to the north of Hajta. According to popular legend he was buried at the bottom of the River Zagyva. A similar legend also exists on the Tisza, not far from Szeged.

JOURNEY INTO THE JÁSZSÁG

JÁSZÁROKSZÁLLÁS

According to legend King Csörsz decided to marry the neighbouring king's daughter. However, tradition stipulated that he had to take his wife-to-be by boat from the Danube to the Tisza. King Csörsz therefore instructed his people to dig a deep channel joining up the two rivers. However, when his reluctant people had dug the channel as far as Jászkisér things turned sour. One of his musicians picked up his violin and struck the king on the head with it. The king died from the injury he sustained, serfdom came to an end and there was universal rejoicing. The king was buried on the very spot where he died, and every single worker on the channel-building project shovelled one spadeful of soil onto his grave. This legend therefore explains the presence of the large ditch and the mound on the edge of Jászárokszállás.

The **Roman Catholic church** (1767, Köztársaság tér 14.), and the Baroque **Külső Inn** (Széchenyi u. 104), are both worthy of mention. At the old coaching inn you can see a Jász horn carved into the keystone of the stone doorframe.

In Jász House (Széchenyi út 31) you can see a house as it would have looked when first occupied by its well-to-do owner. The house, with its six columns, was built in 1892. It was in Jászárokszállás that the characteristic Jászság sheepskin coat was born, and where its famed embroideries still continue to be sown.

The three pools at the town's **Thermal Baths** (Örsi út 18.) contain good quality water which comes up from a depth of 702 metres at a temperature of 52 °C. Its contents and temperature mean that it is very good for locomotor illnesses and rheumatic problems.

JÁSZJÁKÓHALMA

Every 3rd April, a *parade of horses* leaves for Vác in honour of the spring campaign of 1849. Those who are interested in local traditions should also visit the **Péter Horváth Local History Collection** (Fő út 33.). The 15th century **church** standing on *Jákó Hill* is also worth visiting despite the fact that it was remodelled in a late Baroque style. The steeper side of the hill is covered with horse chestnuts, lime trees and acacias. The 19th century

stables (Petőfi út 20.) are open to the public. It is one of the few remaining traditional Jászság agricultural buildings, covered as it is with a thatched roof and built with whitewashed dried earth bricks. There is an active *Local History Society* which organises all kinds of events promoting local traditions. On the last Sunday in July they organise the *St James's Patronal Festival,* and during the first weekend in August in the years ending in odd numbers, the *Folk and Children's Olympics.* The local villages take it in turn to host the annual *Jász World Congress,* when the captain of the Iazygian (Jász) people is elected.

> *If the Mátra looks bigger it's going to rain. (Storm clouds over the Mátra usually empty their contents on the village.) If the Jászdózsa train whistles it will get cold, if you hear the Jászberény train it'll rain. (The Continental Air Stream comes from the east and the Gulf Stream comes from the west, the village is right between Jászdózsa and Jászberény.)*

JÁSZAPÁTI

The square is dominated by the twin-towered Baroque facade of the **Roman Catholic church** (István Király park). The vaulting in front of the chancel is covered with frescos by *Pál Vágó,* and the altar painting is by *Mór Than* (1828–1899).

The cultural centre (Imre Makovecz) has served the town since 1987 (István Király út 8.).

The artist Pál Vágó (1853–1928) was born in Jász-apáti. He often exhibited at the Military Museum and won a French Order of Honour for his painting entitled Hungarian Hussars. He also assisted in painting Árpád Feszty's famous Panorama entitled "The Hungarians Conquest", which can be seen at Ópusztaszer in the southern Alföld.

There is a lot to see of ethnographical interest at the **Farmstead Museum** on Szentandrási út. Those who take the trouble to visit the graveyard will be treated to an excellent late Baroque **stations of the cross.** The thermal waters at the **Outdoor Swimming Pool** (Gyöngyvirág út 22.) are excellent for those suffering from rheumatic complaints.

JÁSZSZENTANDRÁS's neo-Gothic **Roman Catholic church** (Rákóczi út), built in 1903, contains wall paintings by *Vilmos Aba-Novák* and *Ferenc Chiovini* dating from 1933. Many locals can be seen depicted in the paintings.

In JÁSZTELEK archaeologists have found traces of the oldest settlement in the Carpathian Basin, which dates back eight thousand years. One particular 19th century **dwelling** (Úttörő út 15.) now looks the way it would have done when inhabited

Next to the camping site in Jászszentandrás there are three pools on a site covering four hectares.
The water, which is rich in iron, is good for rheumatic and gynaecological illnesses (Mártírok út 14)

by its first occupants. You can inspect the living room, the kitchen and the pantry, as well as the outbuildings. All have their original fittings and they are filled with the household objects and furniture of the time.

JÁNOSHIDA's famous Romanesque **church** (1186) originally dedicated to St John the Baptist can be found on the main street *(Fő út 2.).*

The 70-hectare Pusztamizsei-Zagyva Dead Channel, the lowest lying area in the Jászság, is rich in flora and fauna.
It's a great place to relax or to go for a walk. Every summer ecological camps are organised here.

SZOLNOK

The town stands in the middle of the Great Plain at an important crossing point over the Tisza at the confluence of the Tisza and the River Zagyva. The main building in Kossuth tér at the centre of the town is the **Town Hall** (1884). On the side of the building is a plaque commemorating *Kossuth*'s Szolnok recruitment speech. Opposite lies the late-classical **János Damjanich Museum** built by *Lajos Obermayer* in the 1860s.

The archaeological exhibition entitled "Returning to the Time of our Forefathers" shows how our immediate surroundings and our dwellings have changed over the course of the last one thousand years. The "Craftsman's Art" ethnographical exhibition places its emphasis on the different branches of folk art within the region, particularly pottery and the furrier's art. There is also an ethnographical exhibition entitled "Life around the Central Tisza" and a historical exhibition called "Townspeople at the Beginning of the Century". The Art Gallery focuses on the work of the Szolnok Art Colony. There is also a separate show dedicated to the drawings and caricatures of Tibor Pólya.

The parish church at Jánoshida has managed to come down to us in reasonably good condition. The round-headed doorway into the southern chapel is richly decorated with carved bases, crocket capitals and jamb-shafts. The church was later enlarged in the Baroque style. The roof and the organ date from the second half of 18th century.

The crowning glory of the church are undoubtedly the relief fragments depicting the St Ladislas legend, probably made shortly after his canonisation (1192). JÁSZBOLDOGHÁZA has a very atmospheric **outdoor swimming complex** (Alkotmány út) with some excellent warm waters suitable for the treatment of locomotor diseases. It is also possible to camp here. ÚJSZÁSZ is best known as a railway junction. Of all the landowning families who lived in the town the most famous was the Orczy family. In 1831, *György Orczy* built a **country house** with an attractive garden, greenhouses and a large wood (Akácfa út 90.) The park next to the town's other country house, built in the eclectic style, was laid out in the 1900s. Both houses can be visited if organised in advance.

The **Calvinist church** in Gyula Kellner utca is worth visiting, as are **County Hall** (1878) and **Science and Technology House**, both of which are built in the eclectic style. The *memorial* in Szabadság tér is dedicated to the soldiers who fell at the Battle of Szolnok in 1849.

Crossing the bridge over the Zagyva one can see a sculpture of General János Damjanich standing in front of his troops saluting the colours carved in white carrara marble by *Béla Rudnai.*

Behind it you can see one of the town's real attractions, the **Art Colony**. At the beginning of the 20th century, someone wrote of the colony, *"the Art Colony is to Szolnok what the Eiffel Tower is to Paris. In looking at it you get a feel of the whole place."*

The Art Colony opened in 1902. It was made up of 12 studios and two pavilions set in a park lying on the site of the old castle. It never actually became a school because the artists working there were always eager to plough their own artistic furrows. It was here that Vilmos Aba-Novák painted his painting entitled Szolnok Market (Szent István király u. 6.).

Opposite the Art Colony you can see *Lajos Papi's* **Turkish Well**, as well as the early-classical **Castle Church** (1822–1824) designed by *Ferenc Homályossy* (Szent István király u. 2.).

The suburb of *Tabán,* which used to be a fishing village, has managed to keep its original layout. In one of the winding streets you can find a 1930s **fisherman's cottage,** which is now in the safe hands of the *János Damjanich Museum* (Tabán utca 24.) In the small park in the small housing estate looking onto the banks of the Zagyva you will find a wooden *memorial* to the thirteen generals executed in Arad (now Romania) on 6th

October 1849 at the end of the War for Freedom. In 1562, where the present bridge crosses the Tisza, there used to be a bridge made out of wooden piles. Visitors to the **Sport and Leisure Centre** on the *Tiszaliget* pass a sculpture by *József Lajos* dedicated to the Tisza boatmen. Alongside the hotels and the tourist facilities the Centre has tennis courts, sports halls, a sports field and a fishing lake, while the **thermal baths** five pools, seven slides, water massage and boating lake, which are open during the summer months.

The **Damjanich Swimming Pool** can be found on the banks of the River Tisza (Damjanich út 3.). This too contains thermal waters. The most beautiful part of the town is the **walk** along the riverbank, made all the more attractive by the fountains and the bust of famous local personality, poet and linguist *Ferenc Verseghy*. The walk, bordered as it is by chestnuts, leads up to the **Tisza Hotel** and the **Health Spa** (Verseghy park 2.).

In the neo-Baroque Tisza Hotel you can find a health spa which is very much Turkish in character. The swimming halls are round and domed, and offer hot waters and saunas.

Opposite the Tisza Hotel stands the Szigligeti Theatre (1912, Károly Englert, Tisza park 1.) In 1991, it assumed the appearance it has today, which is something of a mixture combining elements of Art Nouveau and the modern. Outside the theatre stands a statue of Ede Szigligeti (Gábor Benő Pogány) after whom the theatre was named.

On the river walk you can also see the neo-Gothic **Calvinist church** (Tiszaparti sétány 1.) designed by *Ottó Sztehlo* in 1894. The *Molnárfecske Housing Estate*, which lies just a few minutes from the walk, is somewhat of a curiosity. Certainly you would not expect to find Hungary's large nesting site in such an urban setting, but that is what it is. Since 1980, the wooded areas between the residents' balconies have amounted to what is a nature preservation area. The **Gallery**, which you can see at the end of Szapáry út on the banks of the Tisza, was opened in 1972. The building, originally a synagogue designed in the characteristically Moorish style of the architect *Lipót Baumhorn* (1899), is now one of the most beautiful exhibition venues in the country. It is also used for concerts (Templom u. 2.).

One of Szolnok's most important monuments is the Baroque **Franciscan Church and Friary,** to which the classical (once Franciscan) grammar school is attached.

The classical **railway station** is one of the oldest in the country (*Wilhelm Paul Sprenger*, 1847). A few hundred metres away (Temető u. 7.) lies the neo-Renaissance **Church of the Holy Spirit** (1930s) which betrays the influence of the Italian *novocento*.

One spectacular event on the Szolnok calendar is the annual re-enactment of the Battle of Szolnok (1849), which takes place during the Tisza Summer Festival. Spectators can observe at close quarters how the cavalry and the artillery went about their duties.

The **Waterworks Museum** lies on the edge of the town on the road heading out towards Besenyszög. At the so-called *Millér* you can see the machines used in water conservancy and a display devoted to the economic history of the region. At the other end of the town, in *Szandaszőlős*, is the **Hungarian Aviation Museum** (Kilián u.1.), next to road 442.

There are more and more programmes on offer during the summer months, including the Etelköz Festival in August and the Goulash Festival in September.

The popularity of the town is helped by the annual events. In March and April there is the *Szolnok Music Festival,* followed soon after by the *Szolnok EXPO* trade fair.

Szolnok also hosts international kayak-canoe competitions on the **Tisza Dead Channel** and there is a **lido** on the banks of the River Tisza. It is also a good place to go fishing and pony trekking, and to set off on boat trips.

On the Tisza there is no need to worry about your stress levels.

THE RIGHT BANK OF THE TISZA

RÁKÓCZIFALVA is almost a continuation of Szolnok. It is here that a famous prehistoric find came to light. The stylised representation of a woman known as the *Rákóczifalva Venus* can now be seen at the *János Damjanich Museum* in Szolnok. Rákóczifalva really comes to life during the *Rákóczi Spring Festival,* a town whose events calendar is further enriched by the *culinary harvest festival,* with its bread-making competition, auction, market stalls and the food itself, dominated by bread, pig fat, onion and pálinka.

Amongst the more far-flung houses of TÓSZEG lies the *Laposhalom* Bronze Age settlement well known to the European archaeological community.

TISZAVÁRKONY, *lying on the right bank of the Tisza, contains buildings you don't really find elsewhere. They don't have the usual verandas, having an entrance linking up the three rooms instead. At the Folk Artists' Home (1988) woodcarvers, potters, weavers, smiths, and embroiderers exhibit their work. The place also offers possibilities for those wishing to try their hand themselves, as it frequently hosts arts and crafts workshops for both children and adults (Endre király út.).*

The Tiszazug

Tiszazug townscape: Martfü

Crossing the Tisza on the *Vezseny ferry* you soon reach MARTFŰ, one of the ports of call on the international boating tour down the River Tisza. In the middle of the town, in the central square, you will find a modern **town hall**, two **churches** and *Ferenc Gyurcsek*'s statue of Saint Stephen. The town's thermal bath contains water rich in sodium hydrogen bicarbonate, chlorine and iodine.

TISZAFÖLDVÁR also has excellent thermal waters. Its **local baths** (Strand út 27.) have four pools all containing sodium chloride and hydrogen carbonate which are good for relieving rheumatic and muscular pains.

Two or three kilometres from Tiszaföldvár you enter the *Tisza Flood Plains,* which make up part of the *Central Tisza Nature Reserve.* This also joins up with the town's other protected area, the *Körös Flood Plains.*

Apart from the material on local literature, local history and folk art, the **Tiszazug Geographical Museum** (Iskola út 6.) in Tiszaföldvár has the third biggest fossil collection in Hungary.

CIBAKHÁZA is one of the most popular places on the Tisza Flood Plains for those who are interested in nature and those wishing to shoot small game. The regulating of the River Tisza meant 12 kilometres of river was sliced off here. The resulting *Cibakház Tisza Dead Channel* is excellent for fishing or simply for a day out. The **Gödör Outdoor Swimming Complex** is the most popular place for swimming on the Tisza Dead Channel.

In 1995 a **sculpture park** was opened at the *Art-Farm* in TISZAINOKA. There, next to the workshop, is a guesthouse and a camping site. Nearby you can find the recently opened **outdoor swimming pool,** which also offers camping possibilities.

TISZAKÜRT

According to oral tradition the origin of the village's name goes back to the Hungarian Conquest when, at the time of the capture of Alpár, the Hungarians sent messages to each other from the islands lying in the Tisza. It is here you can find the famous **arboretum** (Bolza gróf út 5.) laid out by the children of the founder of the arboretum in Szarvas, *József Bolza.* During the summer there are weekend **cruises** along the Tisza which take the passengers from Szolnok right up to the arboretum. It is just outside the entrance in and around the **outdoor stage** that the *Whitsuntide Village Festival* and the *harvest celebrations* take place.

In what was a wood, a beautiful garden has been created by a process of simply replacing dead and dying trees with trees and shrubs brought from Hungary and abroad. The arboretum is made up mostly of roburs, ash trees and maples. The most famous tree in the arboretum is the so-called "triple plain tree", whose trunk is 6 metres wide at chest height. It is believed that three individual trees grew together to form one single trunk.

At the Tiszakürt Arboretum you can also find some large ancient trees as well as oaks, black walnuts and Turkish hazels.

On Tiszasas's raised main street it is the decorative brickwork on the facades which stands out. The more well-to-do houses have verandas, whilst the plank gates are shared by nearly all the houses.

Even this part of the Tisza Water Plain is protected. The lido, apart from being a good place to swim, has also been discovered by the local anglers. Some families have already seen the possibilities opened up by local tourism.

CSERKESZŐLŐ

In 1943, whilst doing some routine drilling work, biochemists came across some 83 °C **thermal water** rich in minerals. The sodium chloride and hydrogen carbonate thermal waters are considered to be iodine medicinal waters on account of their iodine-ion content. They are recommended primarily for the treatment of locomotor and rheumatic illnesses and gynaecological complaints. Drinking cures can also be taken.

Cserkeszőlő's recently restored outdoor swimming pool with its thermal baths enjoy an international reputation. The place has become a veritable tourists' paradise and will soon include a therapeutic centre.

Southwest of Cserkeszőlő, seven kilometres from the centre of the village to be exact, you reach *Aranyosi Wood*, the highest point in the Tiszazug, and the region's most varied landscape.

The region produces some tangy grapes that mature into light wines in the local cellars.

KUNSZENTMÁRTON

This town is an excellent place from which to explore the *Nagykunság*, the *Tiszazug* and the *Körös Valley*. The nearby Körös Water Brooks are protected as part of the *Körös-Maros National Park*. The woods, meadows, marshes and dead channels provide the environment for what is a unique mixture of flora and fauna.

For culture one need only look as far as the **Local History Museum** on Kerületiház utca, the 18th century **Town Hall** and the Secession-style **Synagogue** (1912, *József Doborszky*) on Deák Ferenc utca. Some of the old crafts survive to this very day. Furriers, potters and sieve-makers are still active in the town. Every June the town hosts the *Tiszazug Music Festival*, and in the middle of November on St Martin's Day there is the *Dalamáris Folk Music Festival*.

In his chronicle György Szerémi relates how the Hungarian crown was kept in Kunszentmárton for a few days during 1541, when János Szapolyai's widow, Queen Isabella, stopped over while fleeing Buda for Transylvania.

At the **Attila József Memorial House** (Rákóczi út 16.) in Öcsöd there is a local history exhibition focusing on the Körös region, and a room dedicated to the poet Attila József (1905–1937).

MEZŐTÚR

This was once a flourishing trading and craft industrial centre. Tanners, potters and furriers all worked here.

At the present time a number of famous potters are active in the town: István Gonda (seen here in the picture), Lajos Búsi, Lajos Kőmüves being but three. They are also there at the stalls, the Mezőtúr fish-cooking and the putting up of the jug and pitcher tree at the International Potters' Convention and Market at the end of June.

The Túr market has been somewhat of a local institution since the 15th century, particularly for traders arriving from the Balkans. According to the medieval chroniclers, foreign travellers stood in wonder at the mountains of wheat, the world-famous wines and the sheer number of herds which had been driven to the market. According to Petofi (1847), "Mező-túr is a fine town…Its horse markets are famous, and it is there you will find Great Plain's shadier characters either stealing horses or trying to sell the ones they have stolen." Even today the market is held every August, and there are cultural evening programmes for the benefit of locals and visitors alike.

The potters were already working in the town as early as the 16th century. *Balázs Badár*, master potter, was the first in a whole dynasty of potters.The **Badár Room and Potters' Workshop** can be found in the *Újváros* (Sugár út 28.) and the **Túr Pottery Museum** in Damjanich út (2.). The earliest examples of Mezőtúr pottery are some fragments of green glazed medieval pottery. Originally the Mezőtúr potters produced black unglazed ware or terracotta utensils. By the middle of the 19th century most of the jugs, along with the black cooking utensils, found themselves being glazed again. The multicoloured floral motifs became popular from the 1860s, but even then the background hadn't become its characteristic yellowy colour. Instead the designs were usually red and green on a white background. The famed biscuit-coloured "dudi" Mezőtúr pottery only appeared in the 1870s. It was at the *Zsindelyes Inn* in Mezőtúr that *Sándor Petőfi* wrote his poem *"Journey on the Great*

The Kunság fur coat was one of the more famous folk costumes.

Plain" in 1847. The one-time inn, now bearing a new façade, is now known as **Petőfi House** (Petőfi tér).

The building of greatest architectural merit is the classical **Calvinist Great Church** in the town centre (Kossuth tér). The **Calvinist Grammar School**, founded in 1530, has provided many a famous Hungarian with a sound education. The school, now known as the *István Szegedi Kis* Grammar School (Kossuth út 1.), was rebuilt in 1889 in an eclectic style.

The tower of the eclectic **Town Hall** (1928, *Frigyes Spiegel, Károly Englert*) (Kossuth tér) offers a fine view over the whole town. One of Hungary's most beautiful fire station towers (1927, *László Fecske*) and the **National Hotel** lie nearby. The **synagogue** in Múzeum tér, which was restored during the 1970s, has been turned into a hall.

The **outdoor swimming complex** can be found in 2.5 hectares of parkland in the *Erzsébet Woods*. The thermal waters are recommended for those suffering from muscular and rheumatic pains. The *Körös Water Brooks* are a part of the National Park, which goes right up to the dikes surrounding the town.

The *Peresi Dead Channel* between Mezőtúr and Gyomaendrőd is 27.6 kilometres long. If you travel along road number 46 leading out of Mezőtúr, you will find a signpost pointing to the **Peresi Peasant Cottage**, which has been cleverly developed out of a pumping station which had been constructed in 1902. Next to the steam-driven-pumps there is an exhibition focusing on the natural history of the *Körös Valley Nature Reserve*.

If you continue along road 46 you will also get to the **Mezőtúr Arts and Crafts Colony** lying in the *Takács Tanya* on the banks of the Peresi Dead Channel.

The *Hortobágy-Berettyó Main Channel* and the *Triple Körös* make the region ideal for anglers and nature lovers. The waters are perhaps best for bullhead pout and bream, although it is not unknown to catch carp as well.

ON COUNT ALMÁSY'S ESTATES

The **Almásy Palace** lying on the edge of KÉTPÓ near the *Tisza II. Channel* now houses the palace hotel, which provides ideal conditions in which to relax.

At KENGYEL near Kétpó you can see one of the landscape's great landmarks, the Bagimajor Windmill.

TÖRÖKSZENTMIKLÓS

The history of the town has been much influenced by the presence of the Almásy family. János Almásy gained control of the ruined town in 1700, and it was he who repopulated it in 1720. The **local history museum** is situated on the road bearing Almásy's name.

The thermal **outdoor swimming complex** can be found on the edge of the town together with a camping site. The arts centre is a *basket-weaving* Mecca. Every year weaving workshops are organised there, after which the work is exhibited at the **Straw Gallery**. The locals founded the *Szentmiklós Association* to bring together all the places throughout the country bearing the name "Szentmiklós" (Saint Nicholas).

Szenttamás also belongs to Törökszentmiklós. Here you will find the one-time Almásy Palace, still set in its 14 hectares of parkland. It is here that you can visit one of Hungary's most famous English thoroughbred stud farms. You can also take the opportunity to go horse-riding. The builder of the country house, Imre Almásy, was the founder of the stud farm and a famous horse breeder in his own right. His racehorses were known throughout Europe. Each year the equestrian days are organised for the benefit of the general public.

The local **Environmental and Ecological Education Centre** in TISZAPÜSPÖKI can be found in an old dam-keeper's house near the Tisza Dam. There is also an **outdoor swimming pool,** a **holiday village** and a fishing village.

Túrkeve

It was here that the three Korda sons, Sándor (Alexander), Vince and Zoltán were born, and where they attended the village school. The cinema on Széchenyi út is in fact named after the film director Alexander Korda.

Miklós Finta was a shepherd in Ecsegpuszta who made the Great Plain hut for the great Millennium exhibition in 1896. The Great Plain also made a great impression on Sándor Finta who was to work as a writer and a sculptor in the United States. His brother Gergely sculpted both in Rodin's Paris studio and here in Hungary.

The Finta brothers donated some of their works to the town, which have, since 1967, formed the centrepiece of the museum bearing their name (Attila út 1.).

The **thermal baths** at Túrkeve have hot waters (68 °C) coming up to the surface from a depth of 2,351metres. The waters contain sodium hydrogen carbonate, iodine and sulphur, which are good for rheumatic complaints and regenerating ageing skin. Apart from the up-to-date health facilities, there is also the wide range of **indoor, outdoor** and **leisure pools.**

You can go horse-riding, or sit in a horse-drawn carriage at the *Győrffy Farmstead*. Indeed, you can have a go at the local crafts or even witness an archery display.

The Túrkeve Festival takes place in October, and the Túrkeve Shepherds' Festival (see picture above) at the end of May. Sheep shearing is particularly popular. Shepherding is celebrated at the festival in many forms: its music, its dancing and its crafts.

Kisújszállás

The **Calvinist church** (Kálvin tér 1.), like so many churches in the towns on the Great Plain, is built in the Baroque style. The most impressive building in the town centre is the **Town Hall** in Szabadság tér, once known as the *"Town Hall Palace"*. The park in front of it contains a number of sculptures.

The **Lajos Papi Arts Studio** is named after the sculptor who lived and worked there up until his death in 1987 (Nyár út 8.). Works from his bequest and from his fine art collection can be seen both in the galleries and outside in the garden. Exhibitions of works by contemporary artists are also put on from time to time.

The **Ethnographical Museum** (Petőfi u. 5.) was once the famous *Morgó Csárda* (1781, *Károly Rabl*). It was in Kisújszállás that they hung out the Kunság's characteristic felt cloaks which were embroidered with vegetable and wreath motifs.

The ancient barrow on the edge of Kisújszállás has witnessed many an historical event.

It is worth visiting the so-called "outer" **peasant house** so characteristic of the region. These houses were the outermost houses in the village and it is for this reason that they incorporate fortified features. These types of houses must be over two hundred years old (Széchenyi út 58.).

The town's **outdoor swimming pool** can be found in the pleasant surroundings of the *Erzsébet Woods,* which lie about 300 metres from the railway station and road number 4. The oaks growing in the park manage to create their own microclimate, which provides ideal conditions in which to enjoy the 48–49 °C thermal waters. The alkali hydrogen carbonate, iodine thermal waters are good for treating locomotor and gynaecological problems and lung, respiratory and circulatory complaints. There is also a camping site, as well as a number of sports facilities.

Life in Kisújszállás is brightened up both at harvest time and when the local archery competitions are held. On the *Dévaványa-Ecseg Plain* on the borders of Kisújszállás and Túrkeve the landscape is covered with the kind of wild flowers likely to flourish in both dry and damp conditions. The plain contains a number of protected wild flowers, for example *wild sage, Star of Bethlehem, asters* and *sulphurwort,* all of which can be found in great numbers.

Admiral Horthy, head of state between 1920 and 1944, was born in KENDERES, *and his body now rests in the family mausoleum following its reburial in 1993. Horthy had previously been buried in Portugal, where he had lived since falling from grace. The one-time Horthy Palace, built in the neo-Baroque style so typical of the era which shares his name, currently functions as residences and a palace (Szent István u. 27.).*

"*Down where the prairies billow like a sea, / Here is my world, my home, my heart's true fane./ My eagle spirit soars, from chains released, /When I behold the unhorizoned plain.*" *(taken from Sándor Petőfi: The Alföld [translation by Watson Kirkconnell])*

HORTOBÁGY

Hortobágy is a totally unique experience. Leaving *Lake Tisza* and Tiszafüred it is not long before you reach the *Patkós Csárda,* and from then on the road leads straight on across the Great Plain to the Hortobágy.

For centuries what is now road number 33 has been an important trade route. It was here that animals were driven to distant markets, and it was here that the "salt route" ran between Buda and Transylvania. The post also went along here. It was next to the *Hortobágy Csárda*, at a place known as the *Máta Ford*, that a wooden bridge was built across the River Hortobágy. Having repeatedly been swept away by floods and burnt down on many occasions, in 1827 the people of Debrecen decided to build a stone bridge. This was done in 1833 to *Ferenc Povolny*'s plans. You cross the famous **nine-arched bridge**, the longest stone bridge in Hungary, when driving along road 33.

The **Hortobágy Csárda** has been putting up guests for nigh on three hundred years. Its guests are still treated to traditional surroundings and a very traditional menu.

Roadside inns lie alongside all of our highways. Approaching the Hortobágy you have the Patkós, the Kaparó and the Hortobágy Csárdas, followed by the Kadarcsi and finally the Látóképi Csárda on the edge of Debrecen. Now all fully restored they offer excellent lunches and evening meals. Try the Hortobágy Meat Pancake, or the guinea-fowl soup, or the "slambuc" (made of pasta and potatoes), which is usually prepared outside over an open fire.

At the Hortobágy Csárda you can see how the original shepherd dishes were prepared, with a little help from the local chef.

For generations the Hortobágy stone bridge has stood firm without any structural iron or concrete.

Opposite the Hortobágy Csárda on the other side of the road you can find the **Pastoral Museum** standing in the one-time coach house (1780). The showcases and displays are full of objects connected in some way with the history, the ethnography and the rural culture of the Hortobágy, and give a great insight into the life people lived out on the Great Plain, and how they eked out a living keeping animals.

In the outdoor pens you can see Hungarian grey oxen, buffalos, Hungarian breeds of sheep, goats, "mangalica" pigs, Transylvanian bald-necked hens, turkeys and Hungarian pigeons.

At the **Great Plain Animal Park** you can see some of the animals which were traditionally kept out on the Hortobágy.

Two kilometres from the nine-arched bridge is Máta with its three hundred-year-old stud farm. The **Equestrian Village** built in Máta during the 1990s known as the *Club Hotel Hortobágy* in-

cludes a four-star hotel and apartments for guests wishing to stay for a number of days. Some of the facilities are also available to non-residents.

For those keen on becoming acquainted with the flora and fauna of the Hortobágy, the local tourist offices can offer a wide choice of programmes. Apart from riding or travelling in a horse-drawn carriage across the Great Plain, you can go rowing on the River Hortobágy or hang-gliding way above it. With the relevant permission it is also possible to go on a guided tour of the part of the **Hortobágy National Park** enjoying *World Heritage* status normally closed to the general public. Several special events take place between May and November, the best known of these being the *Bridge Fair,* which offers a really interesting and varied programme to visitors. (See also the *Hungarian Treasury.*)

The sports events going on during the Hortobágy Equestrian Days held in Máta attract tens of thousands of visitors.

Watching the cranes heading off is one of the great sights during the month of October.

IN AND AROUND BALMAZÚJVÁROS

Having crossed the River Hortobágy and continued a further five miles past the *Kishortobágyi Csárda* you eventually get to the **Darassa Natural History Museum**.

BALMAZÚJVÁROS

Although it is very much a run-of-the-mill agricultural town, Balmazújváros has benefited from being rich in literary connections. It was here that the dramatist *Menyhért Lengyel* came from, and where *Imre Sarkadi* taught briefly in 1953, an experience which led him to write Merry-Go-Round *(Körhinta)*, from which *Zoltán Fábry* made his famous film adaptation. There is also an exhibition dedicated to the writer *Péter Veres* in the **house** where he used to live.

The town's oldest buildings can be found around Kossuth tér. There is the Town Hall, which dates from 1909, and the Calvinist church. The Roman

Catholic church (1781–1786) is famous for the altar painting of the *Assumption of the Virgin* by the Vienesse master *Hubert Maurer*.

Kossuth tér in the centre of the town with its imposing park, its sculptures and statues

In the garden of the *Semsey Palace* (1840) is the recently renovated and family-orientated **Outdoor Swimming Pool** and the **Medicinal Waters.** The waters are 61 °C in temperature are and good for muscular and back problems.

*The enormous 113-metre water slide, the four-lane racing slide, the 101-metre black hole and the white water ride,
as well as the pirate ship with its lighthouse, palm trees, sandy beaches and seaside-like wave bath,
all prove that spa towns are not just for those suffering from rheumatic complaints.*

HAJDÚSZOBOSZLÓ

"Szoboszló is my picture book, I'm forever browsing through it: it's great just to lose yourself in it all, in wonder, in solace, and learning in the process." Ernő Szép wrote these words sometime during the first half of the 20th century. A statue of Szép now stands in the middle of the town (Kenézy u.). One can say without a doubt that many share Szép's sentiments about the town even today, particularly those who come to this *"Rheumatic Mecca"* in search of relief.

Following the destruction inflicted by the Tatars, the settlement remained depopulated until its rebirth during István Bocskai's lifetime. In September 1606 the Prince of Transylvania, whose equestrian statue dominates Hősök tere in the middle of the town, gave the six hundred Haiduk horsemen a homeland in thanks for their support in fighting the Habsburgs during the Wars of Independence.

In 1925, Ferenc Pávai Vajna was the head geologist when his team was looking for gas deposits on the edge of the town. Having drilled the necessary hole it was a strange smelling brown liquid that came shooting out of the earth. This "boiling gold" proved to be medicinal water containing a potent cocktail of minerals. The water's medicinal qualities were only discovered a few weeks later when the women who were then using the waters to do their weekly washing discovered that they no longer suffered from the aches and pains they had been suffering from over the years. The balneologists, chemists and doctors then proceeded to do some scientific tests on the effects of the waters, a process which has continued up to this very day.

The **swimming complex** and the **spa** itself which stand next to road number 4 cover a huge area. Recently the spa has benefited from having been updated. It can now offer the very latest therapies. The swimming complex, one of the biggest in the country, is working hard to ensure that its guests manage to enjoy themselves with a minimum of fuss. In addition, Hajdúszoboszló offers boating and indoor swimming, as well as the **Aquapark**, completed in the summer of 2000 where water freaks will not be disappointed. In the middle of the Great Hungarian Plain the Aquapark makes it possible to enjoy an experience not dissimilar to a day at the seaside.

The hotels are lined up along Mátyás Király út. Most of them have their own medicinal waters as well as their own doctors and nurses. During the summer months the road becomes a busy pedestrian precinct. The crowded streets, the coffee houses and the brasseries all add to the spa's unique atmosphere.

In the park in front of the swimming complex you will find the Bell House (Zoltán Rácz), an interesting architectural construction built around a bell.
The bell was cast in aluminium alloy by Edit Oborzil and Tibor Jenei. The smaller bells were given to the town by Ms Oborzil, who was born and brought up in Hajdúszoboszló.

Next to Szilfákalja út you will find the recently constructed Byzantine-style **Greek Catholic church** which serves a congregation of just a few hundred.

In Kálvin tér stands the Calvinist church, which was built on 15th century foundations. The fragments of fortified wall surrounding it are the oldest surviving remains in the town.

The **Roman Catholic church** on Bocskai utca (1776) is famous for its fresco depicting the development of the town as a spa, and because Pope John Paul II. worshipped here when he was still known as *Karol Wojtyla*, Archbishop of Krakow.

In the **Bocskai Museum,** which lies next door, there is a fine collection of folk artefacts: shepherd coats, women's embroidered sheepskin coats and ornamental carriage ironwork. The work of the town's twenty or so folk artists is also represented. If you are particularly interested in their work, it is possible to commission a piece of embroidery, a carving, an ornamental whip or a piece of ironwork from the individual craftsmen themselves.

Apart from the **hotels** Hajdúszoboszló has guesthouses, private accommodation and two camping sites. While there's plenty going on during the summer months, visitors should not forget that there are the *organic food and wine festivals* to look forward to in the autumn. You can go hot-air ballooning and parachuting at the **airport**, where you can also try your hand at hang-gliding.

DAYS OUT IN THE SÁRRÉT AND BIHAR

NÁDUDVAR

The village, situated where the *Hortobágy* meets the *Hajdúság*, gets its name from the reeds ("nád" in Hungarian) and the houses and the yards ("udvar"), which were once fenced off from each other with reeds. In the 1970s the village became the home of the *Red Star Collective Farm* becoming a modern regional agricultural centre in the process.

When, on 4th January 1849, the entourage led by Louis Kossuth taking the Hungarian government to Debrecen was passing through the village, the cart carrying the crown and the coronation insignia got stuck in the mud. With a little help from the locals the crown jewels were retrieved, but only continued after the retinue and the crown had stayed the night.

Not far from the *Endre Ady Cultural Centre*, the spiritual and cultural centre of the town situated in the main square, you can find the classical **Roman Catholic church**, opposite which stands the **Calvinist church** built in 1774, and remodelled in 1878.

Visitors can wonder at the work of Lajos Fazekas at the Fazekas House (Fő út 159), whose craft is practised by several members of his family.

PÜSPÖKLADÁNY

It is here that the road from Debrecen and Szatmár joins the main route between Kolozsvár (Cluj-Napoca, Romania) and Vienna. These old trade routes were duplicated when the railways were built, and it wouldn't be totally unfair to say that the town is most famous for its railway station. Nevertheless, there is a late-Baroque **Calvinist church** (1792) in Kálvin tér, which just happens to be on the way out towards the **outdoor swimming pool**. Open all the year round, the medicinal waters are good for treating muscular problems. At the treatment centre (2003) you can use the sauna and the salt cave as well as the usual facilities. In the **Ferenc Karacs Museum** (Kossuth utca 28.) there is an exhibition on the history of the *Sárrét* and a folk art display.

The *Farkassziget* **Arboretum,** which lies on the northern limits of the town within the bounds of the *Hortobágy National Park*, has a fine stock of trees. However, it is the 25 hectares of planted woodland which constitutes the main attraction for those interested in the history of forestry and agriculture. At one time these forest systems, standing as they did at right angles to the prevailing wind, played a very important role as wind breaks. Nowadays the tendency has been to cut them all down.

BERETTYÓÚJFALU

Not far from where roads 42 and 47 intersect at *Herpály* you will find some important medieval **church** ruins. Of the magnificent two-towered western facade only a part of the southern tower remains. Archaeological excavations during the 1970s and 1980s uncovered the outline of the ground plan. Both the walls and the tower are open to the public. Of all the beautiful buildings in the middle of the town, most worthy of note is the **Calvinist church** in Kálvin tér, built in 1817 in the late-Baroque style.

Going out towards Biharkeresztes and beyond you come to NAGYKEREKI, which was where the Bocskai and the Báthori families had estates. Of particular interest are the weapons on view at the **Bocskai family's 16th century seat,** and the exhibition on the Haiduk community and the Bocskai family.

DEBRECEN

"What prompted the foundation of Debrecen I will never know", wrote the famous English traveller Robert Townson in 1793. "I am also at a loss to explain why thirty thousand people would choose to live in a place which has neither springs, a river, fire wood nor building materials." Whilst it is indeed true that the town lacks these basic geographical prerequisites, what one sees today is the result of a gradual process during which practical answers have been found to practical problems. The medieval village stood where the Nyírség, the Hajdúság and the Hortobágy meet, where an area of dry land sits slightly above the surrounding flood plains. The gradual growth of the settlement can be explained by the Hajdúság's excellent soils on the one hand, and the grazing to be had out on the Hortobágy on the other. However, it was the fact that the town was positioned on the trade routes connecting Transylvania with Northern Hungary and the Kingdom of Poland, which made Debrecen into a regional centre.

During the Turkish occupation it wasn't just three landscapes which met at Debrecen, but three political entities: the Habsburg and Ottoman Empires and the Principality of Transylvania. The elders of the town were wise enough politicians to be able to maintain the town's independence in the form of something resembling a city state. Centuries of independence did much for the development of the town and to the emergence of the town's much-heralded *civis identity*.

With the arrival of the millennium, efforts were made to return **Piac utca,** the main thoroughfare, to something resembling the boulevard and the great meeting place it was before the street was taken over by the motor car. What was a huge undertaking saw the upper part of Piac utca, between the Great Church and Kossuth utca, turned into a pedestrian precinct.

Piac utca is brought to an abrupt end by the 61 metre facade of the **Calvinist Great Church**. Its construction was prompted by the destruction of the medieval church of St Andrew in the fire of 1802. Although his plan was modified several times, *Mihály Péchy,* a former indent of the College next door, had it built the following year.

The nave was built on the foundations of the old medieval church, the façade running the entire length of the south wall.

The first service at the Great Church took place on November 24th 1819. On April 14th 1849, it was here that Louis Kossuth read out his Declaration of Independence, and where he was proclaimed head of state. His armchair can still be seen in the church today.

Mihály Péchy's other masterpiece in Debrecen is the **Calvinist College,** which was built in tandem with the Great Church between 1803 and 1816.

As a school in what was primarily a mercantile town, the Calvinist College was imbued with an unmistakably Protestant spirit as far back as the 16th century. The school increased in importance during the course of the 18th century, by which time it was considered to be "the school of the nation". Many great figures are listed amongst the college's past students, and the institution itself has had a great effect on Hungarian education.

It was in the spring of 1849, during the War for Freedom, that the *Oratorium* was used to host the National Assembly. It was here also that the *Temporary National Assembly* sat in December of 1944.

What remained of the Calvinist College following the fire was joined up to the rest of the building when the southern wing was added during the 1870s. This explains the College's irregular ground plan.

Close to the college is the **column** dedicated to the memory of those forty-four preachers and teachers, who were condemned to the galleys and deported during the course of the Counter Reformation.

The Great Library is a sight in its own right.

The **Déri Museum** (Déry tér 1.), a fine neo-Baroque edifice in its own right (1923–1930, *Dénes György, Aladár Münnich*), has some fine historical, ethnographical, archaeological, literary and numismatic collections. Most of these come from the collections of the founder *Frigyes Déri* and his younger brother *György*. Many are prepared to believe that the *Munkácsy Gallery*, with its *Jesus Trilogy*, is a cultural experience rarely had outside Budapest.

The composition entitled Christ Before Pilate was painted by Mihály Munkácsy in 1881. By Easter of 1884 he had completed the Golgotha, whilst the Ecce Homo was finished in 1895–1896. The last of the pictures was presented to the museum by Frigyes Déri, whilst the other two arrived in Debrecen on a temporary basis in 1994.

Next to one particular tree in Füvészkert utca the locals are known to tell a famous local anecdote based on an event which took place when the Bishop of Nagyvárad (now Oradea in Romania) sent a canon by the name of Ambrosius to Debrecen to bring the town back into the Catholic fold following the locals' lapse into Protestantism. Having failed to convince a priest by the name of Bálint, the arguments continued as they left the building. In his anger the canon broke a branch off a bush growing by the roadside next to the school, and threw it to the ground saying, "It will be some faith indeed, if it manages to produce a tree from that." Bálint the priest replied, "So, be it".

Walking away from the Great Church, past the elegant **Golden Bull Hotel** (Aranybika) you eventually come to the **Calvinist Small Church**. Capable of holding a congregation of 1,600 the church was built in the 1720s following the destruction of the previous wooden church. The tower was originally capped by a spire. However, it was blown down so often that eventually it was decided to take the spire down for good. The church has been known as the "Stunted Church" (Csonkatemplom) ever since. Walking along Kossuth utca you come to the **Csokonai Theatre,** built in 1865. Parallel to Kossuth utca lies Szent Anna utca with its **Catholic church**. The building of St Anna's Church (1721–1746) marks an important stage in the history of the town, for it was not until the town had a Catholic parish, a Catholic church and Catholic monks that the National Assembly was willing to grant Debrecen the rank of royal free town. Up until then Debrecen had been a purely Calvinist community.

It is well worth walking out to the end of Kossuth utca, where you will find the brick-built *"Verestemplom"*. Once you are there you can visit the **Greek Catholic church** (1907–1910, *János Bobula jr.*) nearby in Szent Anna utca and the **Tannery**, a reminder that leatherworkers were once active in the town (Nagy-Gál István u. 25.) You could also make your way out to the *Tócóskert Housing Estate* in the western part of the town to visit the **Memorial Museum** dedicated to the work of Debrecen artist *László Holló* (Margit tér 20.).

In the **Great Wood** in the northern part of town you can stroll under the ancient trees and out to the **university buildings**.

The wide stairs in front of the university building (1927-1930, Flóris Korb) lead up to a balustrade, which looks onto the atrium forming the centrepiece of the main university building. It's a great gathering place for both lecturers and students.

The atrium is used for official events like the degree awarding ceremonies, freshers' balls and exhibitions. The tables are usually filled with students chatting up their loved ones or copying out their crib sheets. The library faces you as you enter and immediately under it on the wall looking onto the atrium is a list of all the famous people who have contributed to creating the reputation the university now enjoys.

*Waves, bubbles, spray, splashing, sliding, bathing in a cave, enjoying a water massage, sweating in a sauna...
It all adds up to a pretty busy programme whether going to the Aquaticum is supposed to be good for you or simply fun*

Out on the *Boating Lake* nearby you can hire a water bicycle. You could also go to the **Fun Fair** or the **Zoo** lying nearby. In the *Great Woods* you will find the **outdoor swimming complex and thermal baths** with their new indoor Mediterranean leisure centre (2003). Interestingly the waters have the same chemical make-up as those in Hajdúszoboszló.

Moving out six kilometres from the centre of town, opposite the *"Csereerdő"* station on the **narrow-gauge railway**, is the *Devil's Ditch,* a 4th century Sarmatic earthwork otherwise known as the **Csörsz Ditch**. The fortification has been reconstructed complete with its pointed stakes, banking and hurdles.

The Flower Carnival goes on until 20th August, Stephen's Day, attracts hundreds of thousands of people to the town. The event is made all the more colourful by the fifteen to twenty flower floats (from both home and abroad) which parade through the town.
The day ends with a prize-giving ceremony and a parade followed by a firework display in the main square.

Although there is always something going on, the autumn is particularly busy with numerous festivals going on for the best part of a month, including the *Blues and World Music Festival,* the *Alternative Theatre Convention,* the *Jazz Festival,* and a number of gastronomical events.

GETTING OUT OF DEBRECEN

In the main square of MIKEPÉRCS, lying south of Debrecen on road number 47, you will find a Baroque **Calvinist church**, built in about 1800, with a pinnacled tower similar to those found in Transylvania.

The *Erdőspuszta* on the edge of Debrecen is an interesting stretch of countryside characterised by the sandy banks one also finds in the Nyírség, the clumps of oak trees and open meadows. *Lake Vekeri*, apart from being a great place to fish, has a **leisure complex.** There is also a camping site and a park containing an arboretum and stables.

To get an idea of how the Erdőspuszta once looked you should visit the *Fancsika Leisure Centre,* the **Erdőspuszta Show House** and the **Bánk Botanical Garden** lying next door.

In ÁLMOSD's main square there is a **monument** commemorating the victory of Bocskai's Haiduk soldiers over the Austrians on 15th October 1604.

The Calvinist church in NYÍRACSÁD is medieval. Built during the 13th and 14th centuries it also contains some excellent wall paintings (see picture). Guthi Wood is good for hunting, whilst there is also much for the botanist to enjoy. When strolling through the woods you may also come across the ruins of a 13th century church.

The courtyard of 17, Kölcsey utca, Álmosd, contains a bust of the author of the Hungarian National Anthem. It was in this house, built in the local provincial classical style that Ferenc Kölcsey lived from 1812 to 1815. The house is now a museum.

OUT AND ABOUT IN HUNGARY

Going towards Debrecen, after about ten kilometres, the ruined profile of a late Gothic church comes into view. This is all that is left of Zelemér church, which was left to go to rack and ruin at the beginning of the 17th century.

HAJDÚBÖSZÖRMÉNY

The word "böszörmény" in old Hungarian refers to an Islamic Bulgar-Greek ethnic group. Historians believe the site of today's town must have been a collection point for all those people who joined forces to stave off the Hungarian Conquest. One interesting aspect of the town is the way it was laid out. The core of the town was made up of a fortified church surrounded by houses having only very small gardens. This in turn was surrounded by a system of defensive trenches and palisades around which the farm buildings stood. As the population grew, large farmyards, the so-called "zugok", of the kind which are still being uncovered in Hajdúböszörmény, became more prevalent.

The **Calvinist church** was originally built in the Middle Ages. The defensive wall (Bocskai tér) was only added later. The present church is neo-Gothic, dating from 1881. The remains of the

original fortifications have been marked outside the church near the sculptural group depicting a Haiduk dance (*István Kiss*). The seven figures represent the seven Hajdú towns.

In the middle of Bocskai tér stands Barnabás Holló's sculpture (1907) featuring István Bocskai as he stood on December 12th 1605 when handing over the letter of privilege to a Hajdú chief who stands at his feet holding a standard.

Also in Bocskai tér you can find the **Hajdúság Museum** in what was once the central administration building for the Hajdú region. It was built in the middle of the 18th century.

It is worthwhile spending a little time in the sculpture park in the courtyard of the museum. Founded in 1984 the park consists of a series of busts depicting some of the key players in the history of the town and the Hajdúság as a whole.

Behind the Cultural Centre, which takes up the western side of the main square, there is a war **memorial**. The sculpture by *Imre Varga* (1991) is considered by some to be one of his finest. It takes the form of a mourning woman standing on a stylised map of Europe. The map, made up of basalt cobbles, includes a copper plate listing the two thousand residents of Hajdúböszörmény who died.

Bocskai Grammar School was built in 1865. Like the town as a whole, it was a bastion of the Reformation. For many years not a single Catholic lived in the town.

It is interesting to go and visit the outdoor museum in Polgár utca, which incidentally also serves as *the Káplár Camping Site*. Here you can see some fine examples of the local vernacular architecture. A further example is the **Miklós Káplár Memorial House** (Hortobágy utca), devoted to the work of the famous local painter.

The **thermal bath** (Uzsok tér 1.), which is only open during the summer, is recommended especially to those suffering from rheumatic complaints and joint problems. The covered 30-metre pool with its bathing tub is however open all year round.

HAJDÚNÁNÁS

The two immense fields you see on both sides of the road as you enter the town bear testimony to the fertility of the Hajdúság loess beds and the advanced state of agriculture in the region as a whole. As for the development of Hajdúnánás itself the key moment came with the Haiduk settlement in 1605. Two thousand settlers were given land and the Hajdú towns given letters of privilege. The tower of the **Calvinist church** soaring sixty metres into the sky can be seen for miles and miles around. Indeed, it leads any passer-by straight into the main square of the town, Köztársaság tér. The present tower was only built in 1809. The church was surrounded by a defensive wall, the single bastion and the two stretches of wall being all that remain, and even they are re-constructions.

A beautiful late 19th century stuccoed hotel, built on the western side of the main square, now houses the *Cultural Centre*. Directly opposite lies the **Town Hall** dating from the turn of the 19th and 20th centuries. In front of it stands what to many people's minds is one of the finest statues of *Louis Kossuth* (1904, *János Horvay*).

There is a recently restored **house** in Hunyadi utca dating back to the end of the 18th century where you can see how a typical middling peasant family would have lived. It contains examples of the crafts of the region, particularly those artifacts woven from straw and bulrush.

The camping site can be found next to the **outdoor swimming pool** (Fürdő utca 2.). The covered **medicinal bath** (Fürdő utca) is open all the year round.

One of the most unusual sights in Hajdúnánás is the ostrich farm (1993). It is here that you can find out exactly what ostriches can be used for. Luxury items can be made from their skin, and ostrich meat is on the menu at the local Ostrich Restaurant (Kossuth u. 13.).

Unlike the other Hajdú towns the Reformation did not take root in HAJDÚDOROG, and most of the population are Greek Catholics. Indeed, the town is the denomination's diocesan centre. Building on the **Greek Catholic church** was begun in 1610. After much remodelling and several enlargements it acquired its current generally Baroque appearance in 1868. The church was made a cathedral by Pope Pius X. in 1912.

The most notable part of the church is the two-hundred-year-old iconastasis with its 54 panel paintings.

NYÍRBÁTOR

On the road out to Nyírbátor just after Nyír-mihálydi you pass the highest point in the Nyírség, the *Hoportyó,* standing 183metres above sea level.

Continuing your journey it is not long before you are able to make out the town's most famous medieval landmark, the one-time Catholic, and now **Calvinist church** (Báthori u. 24.), built by Stephen Báthory, Duke of Transylvania (1484–1511).

One of Hungary's rare surviving medieval masterpieces, the Calvinist church in Nyírbátor.

In July the church hosts some of the concerts making up the *Nyírbátor Music Festival,* an event going back several decades.

The vast single-aisled church is covered by a fine net vault. The Renaissance doors, the Florence-inspired carved choir stalls and the pews are considered to be amongst the finest examples of Renaissance art in the country. In the chancel you can find Chancellor Stephen Báthory's carved stone sarcophagus and the red marble tomb of Stephen Báthory, Prince of Transylvania.

The **Roman Catholic church** (the one-time Franciscan Monastery and Minorite Church) was built around 1480. It was in the 18th century that it got the Gothic-Baroque appearance you can see today.

Next to the entrance you can find the 30-metre late-Renaissance wooden bell tower (1640), which is the biggest and the oldest in the region.

The Baroque altars and the pulpit are the finest examples of Hungarian Baroque wooden carving we have. It is the *Passion Altar,* also known as the *Krucsay Altar,* by the 18th century Eperjes Master, which is best known. In the carvings you can detect hints of the Late Gothic (Károlyi u. 19.).

The single-storied monastic buildings built onto the **Minorite Church** (1734) are now home to the *Stephen Báthory Museum.* The exhibition covers the history of the town's medieval craft industries and the local folk art.

The Vicars Meadow in front of the museum is where the International Street Theatre Festival, and the Winged Dragon Week takes place every July.

CHURCH HUNTING IN THE NYÍRSÉG

This particular tour is especially for those who like visiting parish churches. Starting at the pilgrimage church in *Máriapócs* we will be going deep into the *Southern Nyírség.* There are natural and art historical treasures hidden in this parts that would be famous in almost any other part of the world.

MÁRIAPÓCS

Ten kilometres west of Nyírbátor lies the Greek Catholics' most famous **pilgrimage place**. The monks of the Basilite Order built the monastery in 1749.

Central to the development of this Greek Catholic pilgrimage place was the Miracle of the Weeping Madonna (1696, 1715 and 1905). Máriapócs's original wooden church was replaced by the twin-towered, single-aisled Baroque church (1731-1756) you can see today. Hundreds of thousands of pilgrims visit the church each year.

The original painting of the Virgin Mary was painted to order by the itinerant artist István Pap. Following the news that the picture had wept (for the first time) the painting was, according to the wishes of Empress Eleanor, taken to Vienna. A master from Kassa (Košice, Slovakia) made a copy which was placed in the northern altar in the church in Máriapócs (which has now wept twice).

The largest numbers of pilgrims descend on the church for the celebrations, which take place on the Sunday closest to September 8th, the Feast of the Blessed Virgin Mary. The **Basilite Ecclesiastical Collection** (Kossuth u. 17.) contains a fine selection of liturgical objects. The importance of the village as a place of pilgrimage is proved by the fact that Pope John Paul II visited Máriapócs in 1991. The **Roman Catholic church,** which lies near the basilica, was originally Gothic, but was rebuilt during the 18th and 19th centuries losing much of its interest in the process.

Nyírbátor is also the home of the *Rabócsi Ring* **rallycross circuit** that was laid out recently.

In NYÍRMIHÁLYDI you can see one of the Southern Nyírség's most beautiful 13th century churches, the **Calvinist church** in Fürdő u. The apsed chancel, which was partly rebuilt in the 18th century, may possibly have originally formed part of a round church. The chancel's small, narrow, splayed windows survive and the remains of a barrel vault have been found over the sacristy. The walls of the nave have the remains of a 15th century Doom.

NYÍRBÉLTEK has a Romanesque **Roman Catholic church** (Széchenyi utca) dating from 1222. The church has changed little since the end of the 19th century. The fragments of wall painting dating from the reign of King Sigismund (1387–1437) (*Golgotha* and the *Twelve Apostles*) are of enormous art historical importance. Decorative motifs can be seen on some of the wall paintings on the nave walls.

In Piricse next to the church stands an eleven-metre-high wooden bell tower (1791) apparently put up in piecemeal fashion by banging together a number of oak beams. The lower roofs and the spire are covered with wooden shingles.

AROUND THE ECSED FLATS

BÁTORLIGET

Travelling down in a southeasterly direction from Nyírbátor you eventually reach Bátorliget.

The *Bátorliget Flats* are surrounded by woodland that manages to beat off any hot air currents travelling in their particular direction. Add this to the effect of the evaporating water, and you are left with a significant drop in temperature. The woods also manage to trap any local mist and fog. Those species preferring a warmer climate are more likely to thrive on the warmer slopes nearby.

In Nyírmihálydi the wooden shingled bell tower dating from 1782 is an important element in the architectural ensemble. The tower itself is covered with wooden boards.

PIRICSE has a 13th century Romanesque **Calvinist church** in Petőfi utca. Interestingly, the main door isn't on the main axis of the church and none of the shared features seem to be of the same size. The points of the narrow windows are formed simply by tilting two bricks up against each other. The nave walls are not parallel; they converge slightly towards the chancel.

The wildlife out on the flats is uniquely rich. It is here that the viviparous lizard lives. The stag beetle (see picture) is perhaps the most interesting of the insects here. For bird watchers there are the black stork and the black woodpecker to look out for.

The Bátorliget Flats are one of the country's oldest and most famous protected natural habitats. This tiny area, covering only 53 hectares, has all the vegetation existing on the Great Plain on one site. Indeed, it is the most varied landscape in the whole of the Nyírség, something made possible by its unique microclimate.

The **exhibition,** in what was the old school, provides a useful introduction to the wildlife on the flats and shows how the flats came into being. Because the flats are strictly protected, the area can only be visited by accompanied parties, and only then with the relevant permit.

The 23 hectares of the *Bátorliget Pastures* are also strictly protected. The sandy grassy terrain affords just the right habitat for the *pulsatilla* and the *meadow anemone,* and it is the only place in Hungary where the *violet pulsatilla* can be found. (Visitors require the necessary permit).

Fényi Wood is also protected. The 298 hectares of woodland is all that remains of the old Nyírség forests. Amongst the oaks the ash trees and the elms it is not rare to find trees which are 200–300 years old. (The area is open to visitors, although visitors are advised not to walk in the areas adjacent to the border.)

On the Nyír Flats you can find the pubescent birch, the Siberian iris (illustrated) and the globe-flower, next to which the orchids grow.

Just a few kilometres from Bátorliget you will find VÁLLAJ, a village resettled with Catholic Swabians some time in the middle of the 18th century. The beautifully ornamented barns are amongst the local curiosities.

The outbuildings which block off the end of the yards are typical of the traditional timber framed building one finds in the historical county of Szatmár. It is interesting to note that the gable facing the yard is built of brick and covered in plaster. This change in building material was an attempt at fire prevention following a fire at the beginning of the 20th century which destroyed nearly all of the old barns. Indeed these "fire-walls" provided protection to all the equipment and the foodstuffs being kept in the building. These expanses of wall provided an excuse to cover the plastered surfaces with decorative patterns.

There is an international **border crossing** in Vállaj. The village on the Romanian side of the border is *Csanálos (Urziceni in Romanian).*

NAGYECSED

The castle the Báthory family built in the 14th century to look over the now drained *Ecsed Flats* was completely destroyed during the Rákóczi War for Freedom. Nevertheless, the excavated **remains** of *Sárvár* and its *monastery* can still be seen. Some of the archaeological finds can be seen at the **József Berey Local History Collection** in Vásártér.

The steam **pumping station** (1915) on the banks of the *River Kraszna* was built at the time the Ecsed Flats were being drained. The pumping station was combined with an electrical power plant to provide 15 settlements, more than thirty thousand people, with electricity.

MÁTÉSZALKA

Mátészalka is another town lying on the edge of the *Ecsed Flats* which would make an excellent base camp for exploring the unspoilt countryside of Szatmár. It's also an ideal place from which to visit the medieval churches lying in the region, whether you are travelling by bicycle, on foot or by car. Every September the town hosts the *Szatmár Expo,* which attracts participants from both home and abroad.

Mátészalka has been a county town on several occasions, firstly, after the Treaty of Trianon in 1920, when it became county town of Szatmár, secondly as county town for Szatmár-Bereg in 1938 and 1939), and finally between 1945 and 1950.

The tower of the **Calvinist church** in Kossuth tér is of medieval origin, as indeed is the western part of the nave. The **Szatmár Museum** (Kossuth u. 5.) can be found in the so-called *Péchy Palace,* which is built in a late Secessionist style. The museum concentrates mainly on folk art. The collection of carts and coaches is unique in Central Europe, not surprisingly perhaps when one considers that the town has one of the largest Roma populations in Hungary. The region's only railway museum, the **Local Railways Collection**, which opened in 1982, can be found next to the railway station (Tompa M. u. 2–4.).

EXPLORING THE SZAMOS REGION

When touring Szatmár it's best to concentrate on one particular area, as each region deserves more than the usual amount of attention.

It was Stephen Báthory, Prince of Transylvania and King of Poland, who presented the inhabitants of the town of FEHÉRGYARMAT with the **bell** which now peels daily from the 15th century Calvinist church. We recommend the **museum** of the *Szatmár-Bereg Nature Reserve* (Vörösmarty tér 3.) to those who are interested in the area's natural history. Moving along the bank of the winding River Szamos you come to a series of delightful and charming villages.

The pride of CÉGÉNYDÁNYÁD is the single-storeyed classical **Kende Hall** (c. 1830, Dózsa út 9.), whose façade is dominated by four lines of verse written by *Ferenc Kölcsey* (1790–1838) taken from his 1833 poem *"To Zsigmond Hende's Manor House".*
"The work of craftsman's hand am I: as from the fair Szamos's
Banks the muse looks up at my raw visage:
House be generous and in joy and peace embrace Your master and his children and welcome his grandchildren."

The plane tree dominating the park at Cégénydányád has a trunk with a circumference of 670cm, and a crown covering 143 square metres. The country house is currently a children's home, but you can visit it with the permission of the principal.

The *grounds* of the country house, which originally covered an area of 50 hectares, contains a fine stock of trees, the 12-metre-high yew tree being perhaps the most impressive.

The most important monument in GYÜGYE is the 13th century Romanesque and Early Gothic **Calvinist church** (Fő út). Often ignored, the church was partly remodelled in the 18th century.

It was then that the painted plank ceiling, with its patterns and foliage designs, was constructed (1767) and the peasant Baroque-style liturgical furniture (the gallery, the pulpit and the pews) fitted. From a stylistic point of view it is one of the more naive of the plank ceilings in the Upper Tisza region.

The Gothic Calvinist church at Szamosújlak *(Petőfi u. 2.) dates back to the 14th century, although it acquired its present form in the 15th century. In 1998, the restoration of the church, carried out under the leadership of György Szekér, won a Europa Nostra Award. The liturgical furniture, which is rather folksy and eclectic in style, was made in 1867.*

It is the **bell tower** which first comes into view when you approach Túrricse. The **Calvinist church** (Zrínyi u.1.) itself was built in a Late Gothic style around 1500, the stone door frames being perhaps the only examples of Jagellonian Gothic existing in Hungary. The wooden ceiling was painted in 1792, and the beautifully carved pulpit canopy completed in 1798.

The 15th century Late Gothic **Roman Catholic church** in Jánkmajtis (Arany J. u. 34.) is of a beauty rarely matched in these parts. There are two fine gothic doorways set between two traceried windows. The interior is relatively large, and the star vault of the chancel has survived complete with a boss bearing a coat of arms. The wooden crucifixion in the chancel arch is Baroque, dating from the 18th century.

In the village of Nagyszekeres you can see perhaps the most beautiful ensemble of buildings in the *Szatmár Erdőhát*. The **Calvinist church** lying in the centre of the village on what is a small artificial island, surrounded by the *Gőgő*, the *Szenke* and a defensive wall, is considered to be one of the finest medieval churches in Szatmár County. It was only built after 1500, although from appearances it looks considerably older due to a use of already outdated architectural forms.

The star vault in the chancel of the Calvinist church at Nagyszekeres and the small Renaissance tabernacle are both worthy of note. The carved pulpit and the organ are both late 17th century. Immediately outside the main door there is a pinnacled bell tower (18th century).

Kisszekeres has a small single-aisled 15th century Gothic church. Built on an irregular ground plan the double-lighted windows of what is the **Calvinist church** are original. The liturgical furniture is all 18th century. The bell (*György Wierdt*, 1646) is one of the oldest in the region still to be rung.

The **Calvinist church** in Gacsály (Petőfi u. 25.) was built during the 14th century in the Gothic style. It is one of the few churches in the region still to have its medieval tower. The church was destroyed during the Tatar incursion of 1717, and it was rebuilt between 1734 and 1759. Of the 172 painted panels, which once covered the ceiling (1759) only 46 survive, and only then in their conspicuously blue frames. Each panel has its own individual design (a vine, a tulip, a rosette, a wreath etc.)

The **Calvinist church** in CSENGERSIMA (13th century, late Romanesque) is one of the oldest churches on the Szamos. The church was in a ruinous state when it was reconstructed during the first third of the 18th century. What is a dead channel of the River Szamos was widened out to form a lake, which surrounds the church on two sides.

Hidden inside the Calvinist church of Csengersima, seen here nestling behind the dead channel of the River Szamos, is a delightful coffered ceiling.

The small wooden porch and the wooden ceiling date from 1761. The 56 decorated panels, painted in what is a provincial Baroque style, are of particular interest. One or two of the panels have patterns which appear to be of Renaissance origin, whilst the panels on the southern part of the ceiling are more Transylvanian in style. The painted gallery and the pulpit both date from the same period, whilst the pulpit canopy was made in 1799.

Recently in Csengersima a new **border crossing** was opened into Romania.

In SZAMOSTATÁRFALVA stands one of the oldest and most interestingly decorated medieval churches in the region. The **Calvinist church** was built in the 13th century in the Romanesque and early Gothic styles. The unplastered walls were built in alternating rows of red and black over-fired brick, a solution not totally unknown to the region. The Romanesque doorway and the coloured window frames create an oriental impression. Attention should be paid to the reconstructed medieval hinge in the southern door. The bell hanging in the rather humble 18th century wooden bell tower was cast by *György Wierdt* in Eperjes (Presov, Slovakia) in 1650.

CSENGER

The 14th century Calvinist church (Hősök tere) is the one remaining example of monumental medieval architecture on the Great Hungarian Plain. It was built of black and red brick.

The octagonal tower of the parish church in Csenger is crowned by a shingled spire and a Renaissance parapet. Inside the church has a painted wooden ceiling (1745, István Felsőbányi Asztalos). The church has played host to some important ecclesiastical events. It was here, at the synod of 1576 chaired by Péter Mélius Juhász, that Calvinist Protestantism was adopted in the form known as the Csenger Confession.

The **Local Museum** in Hősök tere has exhibitions on the history of the town, local archaeology, folk art and the history of the local schools.

Up in the upper reaches of the Tisza you can relax in almost totally unspoilt natural surroundings.

Moving northeast along the road taking you up towards the Ukrainian border you come to Kölcse's **Calvinist church** (Kölcsey u. 93.) It's a single-aisled Gothic church dating from the 15th century. It is likely that only the chancel was in fact vaulted, from where we still have the ribs which ran up to the heraldic boss. The stone carving seen on the two pointed doorframes, the consoled double sedilia and the pinnacled ciborium are of high quality. The wooden ceiling, the rustic Baroque pulpit and the organ all date from the 18th century. The wooden **bell tower** (1794) is squat, the spire sitting on an octagonal base.

Sonkád's Gothic **Calvinist church** (Kossuth u.) was built in the 15th century. Its southern doorway deserves particular attention. Underneath the gallery there is a panel telling us that the liturgical furniture was made in 1715. The rustic Baroque fittings have been recently restored, a project which won it a *Europa Nostra Award*.

The curious thing about the **Calvinist church** and the **bell tower** at Uszka (Fő utca) on the banks of the Batár is the fact that they are joined together, a very unusual solution in this particular region. The late Baroque church was built in 1805, although the furniture is 19th century. The tower, built in the 18th century, is squat and the spire octagonal.

Tiszacsécse

Travelling along the winding roads of the Tisza embankment, through the walnut groves, we reach what *Zsigmond Móricz* called *"fairy island"*. In the middle of a widening stands the beautifully proportioned **Calvinist church** (1820–1825) with a 24metre-high four pinnacled wooden **tower** and a needle-spire piercing the sky.

Zsigmond Móricz (1879–1942), Tiszacsécse's most famous son, was an author of novels, stories and plays particularly popular during the inter-war period. The peasant house on Kossuth u. which is dedicated to his life's work, wasn't in fact his birthplace (as a memorial plate on the wall suggests), but it was where the Móricz family lived for a number of years.

The road then goes along the old course of the Tisza and past the *oxbow lakes* towards neighbouring Szatmárcseke. Before crossing the bridge over the *Túr Channel* it is worth searching out one of the region's most popular bathing places, the *"Bukógát"*. The dam was built to prevent the waters of the Tisza from overflowing into the Túr's waters, whilst allowing the Túr to flow into the Tisza. In the meantime enough water has built up to make it ideal for swimming. On the *Tiszakóród* side there is a camping site set amongst the walnut groves. A speciality in these parts is the walnut. Indeed, Milota dedicates a *whole festival* to the nut at the end of the summer.

The corn bunting is one of the rare birds you can find at the Szatmár-Bereg Nature Reserve.

Szatmárcseke

The likes of the Calvinist boatmen's cemetery, with its wooden headstones, cannot be found anywhere else in Europe.
There are more than 600 robust carved oak grave posts in all. Experts tend to disagree as to the origin and meaning of these graves, however everybody agrees that they aren't of Finno-Ugrian origin as sometimes suggested by the locals.

In the middle of the cemetery stands the classical white marble **tomb** of *Ferenc Kölcsey,* who died in Cseke in 1838. There is also an **exhibition** dedicated to the author of the *Hungarian National Anthem* in the Arts Centre (Kölcsey u. 46.) Every year on 22nd January, *Hungarian Culture Day,* a wreath-laying ceremony is held at the tomb of the great poet.

There is also a **peasant house** with a steep thatched roof furnished as it would have been when occupied by a poor family. The house is open to the general public (Vasvári Pál u. 4.). It contains furniture and local artefacts collected from around the village.

Kölcsey lived in the village for 23 years, during which time his residence become a veritable literary pilgrimage place.

It is not only fresh *plums* which enjoy a good reputation in these parts. This is also jam, with a plum jam competition in Szatmárcseke to prove it. Another local speciality is *"cinke"*, a potato dish made from a mixture of mashed potato and flour which is then rolled into balls, lightly browned in a pan before being served with an accompaniment of sauerkraut, cottage cheese mixed with dill and onion sauce.

The centre of Túristvándi is dominated by the Gothic **Calvinist church** (Móricz Zsigmond u.). As you leave the village on the Kölcse road you move into the *Rókadűlő,* well known for its oaks, wild pear trees and other varieties which seem to have gone wild.

When going along the road, just two kilometres from Szatmárcseke, you come across what is quite a remarkable sight, Túristvándi Water Mill (end of the 18th century).
Its three undershot water wheels are quite a rarity in Central Europe. The mill, which can be found at the end of the village nearest Kömörő, is listed. The traditional fish soup cooking competition takes place in August.

Nagyar

On the edge of the village you can see the remains of an enormous oak tree. According to local tradition it was here under this tree that *Sándor Petőfi* wrote his famous poem *"The Tisza"* in 1847.

When in the dusk a summer day had died,
I stopp'd by winding Tisza's river-side,
Just where the little Túr flow'd in to rest,
A weary child that sought its mother's breast.

(Extract taken from translation
by Watson Kirkconnell)

The two-hundred-year-old *Petőfi tree* suffered a great deal of damage during its lifetime. It was, however, unable to survive the fire of 1995.

Of the three country residences in the village it is the smallest, **Luby Hall** (1780, Petőfi u.1.), which has the most literary connections, for *Sándor Petőfi* stayed here on several occasions when visiting his friend, the lawyer and politician Zsigmond Luby.

The **Calvinist church** (Petőfi u. 6.), built around 1850 in the late Baroque style, reused the walls of a 14th century chapel. During the course of the renovation work, frescos dating from the beginning of the 15th century and the Renaissance period were uncovered.

The bridge at Kisar, on the main road connecting Vásárosnamény and Fehérgyarmat, was a very important **crossing place** over the River Tisza. The **Calvinist church** (Tisza u. 13.) has lost all vestiges of its original medieval character having twice been remodelled in the 18th and 19th centuries. Of its original liturgical furniture only its 18th century walled pulpit remains.

At Kisar you will find Europe's largest flood plain orchard Walnuts, plums and many old varieties of apple are grown on its 50 hectares.

INTO DEEPEST BEREG

Our expedition into Bereg begins on the TIVADAR side of the bridge crossing the Tisza. It is quite possible to lose track of time in the **holiday village** situated on the Tisza Flood Plains.

The recently unveiled monument remembers the massive flood of 1947 resulting from a breach in the embankment. On the night of 31st December torrents of water reduced Tivadar to ruins. It was only a few hundred metres from here that the dyke was breached in the spring of 2001 leaving Bereg submerged in water.

In the main street they have just opened a **Calvinist Youth Conference and Holiday Centre** (2003), where there are several types of accommodation on offer. It's also wheelchair-friendly.

TARPA

A few kilometres away stands the village of Tarpa. The houses, mostly dating from the turn of the 20th century, were built by the village's more prosperous peasants. They are characterised by their plastered classical fronts, tin roofs and wooden-columned verandas.

An old two-floored granary and **house** (Kossuth u. 25/a) are open to the public.

The Tarpa Mill is the only remaining horse-driven mill in northeastern Hungary (Árpád u. on the Tóhát corner). It was built in the middle of the 19th century. The huge floor is covered with a shingle roof next to which there is a small mill house.

Local resident, Tamás Esze, led the Rákóczi's kuruc armies in his capacity as brigadier at the turn of the eighteenth century. Endre Bajcsy-Zsilinszky was Tarpa's Parliamentary Representative during the 1930s and 1940s. The politician's grave faces you as you enter the cemetery.

Above the entrance to the medieval **Calvinist church** (Kossuth u.) you can see the heraldic dragon of the Báthory family in the doorframe (the Gut-Keled branch to be exact). The door itself is a very rare example of a 15th century oak door with its original iron hinges. Recently some Gothic frescos have been uncovered on the northern wall of the church. *Great Wood* and *Téb Wood* are amongst the finest hornbeam-oak woods on the *Bereg Plain*. The so-called Great Hill is in fact the highest point on the Bereg Plain, standing 154 metres above sea level. Since the 1860s, volcanic *dacite* has been quarried there and used for building work and the construction of river defences. The "hill" is covered with a metre of loess, making it excellent for grape-growing.

The most beautiful thing in the 14th century **Calvinist church** in BEREGSURÁNY (Árpád u. 2.) is the rustic Baroque pulpit. There is also *Lake Balácka* and a fine stock of mature trees river in what was the park belonging to Uray Palace. There is a **border crossing** nearby for those with Hungarian or Ukrainian passports.

The most significant building in BEREGDARÓC is its 14th century Gothic **Calvinist church** (Alkotmány u. 2.).

The Calvinists have opened a **Conference and Holiday Centre** offering all kinds of leisure possibilities (2003).

The herd returns from the Bereg pastures.

Just west of Beregdaróc lie *Lake Nyíres and Lake Báb*. *Dédai Wood* gives us some idea of what the *Bereg Plain* once looked like, and which wild flowers and plants thrived beneath its leafy cover. The importance of the natural habitat means that there is only restricted access.

MÁROKPAPI's Early Gothic, single-aisled **Calvinist church** (Kossuth u.) was built during the second half of the 13th century. The bell tower is a rather simple affair compared with some of the bell towers elsewhere in the region.

CSARODA

Csaroda is situated alongside the rather boggy stream known as the *Csaronda*. The **Calvinist church** (2nd half of the 13th century) is one of the most beautiful late Romanesque churches in the country. Above the western facade stands a galleried tower with a fine wooden shingle roof.

Just west of the village stands *Csaroda Wood* and the *Ágakköze*, which you are free to visit.

At Csaroda the wallpaintings vary from the medieval Fathers of the Church (Ambrose, Augustine, Gregory and Hieronymous) sitting at their desks to the blue and red flower motifs, reminiscent of those seen in folk art, dating from 1642.

Tákos's **Calvinist church** is commonly referred to as "Barefoot Notre Dame". This 18th century mud-walled, shingle-roofed church forms the centrepiece of this little village stuck in the middle of the *Bockereki Woods*. The interior has a floor made of beaten clay and a wooden ceiling containing 58 flower-filled panels painted by *Ferenc Lándor* (1766–1779). The liturgical furniture is Baroque in style, and of local provenance. The wooden **bell tower** is a reconstruction based on illustrations of the 18th century original.

The wattle-and-daub Calvinist church at Tákos is also known as the "peasants' cathedral".

The natural wonders that exist in VÁMOSATYA can only be seen by gaining the relevant permission. The place in question, *Bockereki Wood*, stretches out south of the village.

Vámosatya is famous for its **Calvinist church** and its bell tower (Szabadság tér). The single-aisled **Gothic church** (13th-15th centuries) contains a coffered ceiling, pews and a western gallery all made in 1766. The canopy over the pulpit is one of the most beautiful in the region (18th century). The pinnacled wooden bell tower is the tallest in the region, and can be seen for miles around.

LÓNYA

The most famous buildings in the village, which also has a local border crossing for Hungarian and Ukrainian citizens, are the 13th century Romanesque **Calvinist church** and the wooden bell tower (Kossuth u.). Inside the church it is the elaborate pulpit canopy by *Ferenc Lándor* (1776), which

catches the eye. He is the same Ferenc Lándor whose work can also be seen in the churches at Tákos and Csetfalva. The wooden **bell tower** (1781) is crowned with a very fine needle-spire.

During the restoration work which took place after the 2001 floods, some wall paintings came to light resembling those at Csaroda.

Lónya Wood, which stands right next to the border, enjoys strict environmental protection and can only be visited by permission. The 407 hectares of woodland is rich in flora and fauna. It shares with the Bockereki Woods the distinction of being ridden with vipers.

You can cross the Tisza between Lónya and Tiszamogyorós on the **pontoon bridge** or by **ferry** when the river isn't icebound).

VÁSÁROSNAMÉNY

Situated on the confluence of the *Tisza*, the *Szamos* and the *Kraszna*. the town's most important building is the Lónyay family's Renaissance-style palace (17th century), now known as **Tomcsány Palace** (Szabadság tér 26.). It was later enlarged by László Lónyay, and changed into an arcaded, pillared, galleried, four-towered residence.

It was when arriving here in 1703 that Ferenc Rákóczi II. issued the so-called "Namény Warrant" calling Szabolcs's nobility to arms.

In Miklós Eötvös's 18th century hall (Jókai u. 59.), you will find the *Bereg Museum*. The museum's main building, the eclectic **Máthé Hall** (Rákóczi u. 13.), is dedicated to archaeology and folk art in Bereg, and has a fine collection of cast ironwork (ovens, tombstones and other artefacts, both practical and decorative) from the Bereg iron works.

Gergelyiugornya, situated right next to the town, is a popular place to go and swim and relax, the main attraction being the sand dunes and the **Atlantika aqua leisure centre.**

The events of the *Tisza-party* keep visitors entertained for two months over the summer.

KISVÁRDA

This one-time agricultural town, lying on the main road from the Great Plain to the *Carpathians*, still has its original medieval layout. The **Roman Catholic church** (Flórián tér), although Baroque, includes some traceried Gothic windows illuminating the chancel, and patterned and inscribed consoles in the chancel's once-vaulted interior.

The rebuilding of the **castle** started in 1465. The four corner towers, the courtyard and the arcade were added during the 16th century, transforming the building into a Renaissance fortified palace. The complex also included a chapel and a number of outbuildings. Following the Rákóczi Wars for Freedom the castle declined in importance, nearly being destroyed altogether in the first half of the 19th century. The castle garden was subsequently turned into a park containing a restaurant, a dance hall and **baths**.

The Kisvárda Castle Baths have successfully changed with the times. The reconstruction (2003) has brought with it a slide castle, fountains, a white water corridor and a water massage making for a great a water experience.

Every June the Kisvárda castle hosts a festival especially for Hungarian Theatres based outside Hungary.

The old synagogue on Csillag utca, which was built in 1901, now provides a home for the **Rétköz Museum**. Its exhibitions cover the history of the town, the castle and the villages of the *Rétköz*.

THE TISZA BEND

The **Calvinist church** (Kossuth tér) in the village of ZSURK, lying up on the Tisza Bend, was built in 1891. It seems to have kept to the forms and the proportions of the building it replaced. The wooden ceiling, which dates from 1795, comes from the old church, and is one of the few such ceilings to survive in Szabolcs County. It is rococo in style, the longish panels being filled with allegorical figures, vases of flowers and ornamental medallions. The gallery also comes from the old church and is an example of the "landscape gallery".

According to tradition the wooden bell tower that stands in front of the parish church in Zsurk was built around 1560. Its extreme height (41 metres) makes it pretty unique. The base of the six-storey tower is crowned by a galleried, shingled spire. The four corner pinnacles are later additions.

TUZSÉR

The **ferry** across the Tisza connects Tuzsér in the *Rétköz* with Zemplénagárd in the Bodrog köz. The **Lónyay Palace** (18th century), (Ady E. u. 2.), was built by János Lónyay, a member of Mary Theresa's bodyguard. The residence was subsequently enlarged (*Miklós Ybl*, c. 1880) by Menyhért Lónyay, later Finance Minister and Prime Minister during the *Austro-Hungarian Monarchy*. The palace had ten hectares of park.

East of Kisvárda

Anarcs

Situated only a few kilometres southeast of Kisvárda, the village of Anarcs has a Late Gothic **church** (Kossuth u.) dating back to the 1370s. The barrel vault over the chancel is recent, the original Gothic vaulting having been destroyed. The main feature in the church is the enormous 2x1-metre Gothic ciborium, which is inscribed with the date 1475.

Nearby **Czóbel Hall** (Kossuth u. 32.) was built in the classical style. The building's construction in the 1820s is synonymous with the name of László Czóbel. It was subsequently remodelled in the eclectic style. The house has six hectares of gardens which contain sideroxylon and tulip trees, plane trees and oaks, as well the *grave* of the writer *Minka Czóbel* (1853–1947), a previous owner of the house.

Ajak

The locals produce the region's famed high-quality tobacco. It was mainly the local women who were in the habit of wearing their folk costumes right up until the end of the 1960s, although this particular custom did not extend to wearing their costumes beyond the bounds of the village.

The dress codes changed depending on how old you were. Girls between the ages of two and four had to wear a long shirt, a "kantus", a kashmir scarf, a shawl and ribbons; between the ages of 4 and 12 they had to wear a round pinafore, a headscarf, and boots instead of shoes. At their confirmation they had to wear a bridal wreath, whilst those who were more well-to-do would have threaded glass beads. From 12 to 20 girls had to wear a bodice, fine linen underwear, a pleated blouse and a skirt. There were similar variations depending on one's age, right up to the age of 60. There were also seasonal changes with special clothes being worn by those participating in wedding celebrations and at religious festivals such as Good Friday

The **Calvinist church** (Bocskai u.) is a simple building with a beaten clay floor. The entrance was on the southern side as can be seen by the presence of three round windows on that side. Underneath the plaster on the west wall there are some traces of medieval painting.

The Rétköz

Dombrád

Dombrád is the end of the line. Indeed, near the railway station serving the narrow-gauge line to Nyíregyháza there is the **Railway Museum** (Széchenyi u. 63.) and the **Local History Museum**. The **camping site**, a motel, private and company tourist facilities can be found near the **Art Gallery** (Széchenyi u. 63.) on the banks of the River Tisza. It is from here that the boat trips leave. You can reach Sárospatak by crossing the Tiszakanyár Bridge over the Tisza.

It was in a **country house** sitting on top of a hill in Tiszabercel that *György Bessenyei* was born (1747), where he grew up and where he was ultimately to live between 1782 and 1785. Bessenyei was one of the driving forces behind the cultural initiatives which went on during the Enlightenment. A writer, a poet and a thinker, he was at one time Maria Theresa's bodyguard.

Built in the middle of the 17th century, Bessenyei Hall is a typical example of the kind of house the lower nobility inhabited in the Nyírség. The interior is furnished as it would have been during Bessenyei's lifetime, and includes an exhibition dedicated to his life and work (Bessenyei u. 6.).

Tisza dead channel at Ibrány

There is a building of industrial archaeological interest next to the **ferry** between Tiszabercel and Paszab, namely the **pumping station** built at the base of the embankment in 1895–1896. The buildings and huge steam-driven machinery, which have recently been renovated, are still in working order and open to the general public. IBRÁNY, a small village a little further away from the Tisza, has a small Gothic **Calvinist church** (Iskola u.) dating from the 1200s. The local library (Hősök tere) contains an **art gallery**. The **Local History Collection** (Árpád u. 4.) has a good collection of local artefacts from the *Rétköz*. A fine **open-air swimming complex** has recently been opened just five kilometres from the village.

A silver fibula from Ibrány

Ten kilometres southwest of Ibrány stands the 13-metre-high **Black Mound**. 20,000 square metres of soil went into making the burial chamber sometime during the 3rd century AD. The treasures which were found there, albeit somewhat depleted because of the grave robberies, can be found in the Nyíregyháza Museum together with some Hungarian Conquest finds. Although this was considered to be a cemetery of no particular merit, two silver hair ornaments came to light.

The last port of call on this particular journey across the Rétköz is NAGYHALÁSZ. It is here you can see the late Baroque **Calvinist church** (Arany J. u.), which was built in the 18th century, and the recently renovated 18th century **Csuha-Kállay Hall** (Arany J. u. 60.)

Although northeastern Hungary's *"gateway to the east"* now has a population of 120 thousand people you only need to go back as far as the 18th century to trace the origins of the settlement you see today. It was then that some Slovak settlers (known as the *"tirpákok"*) were invited to inhabit the almost completely depopulated lands belonging to the landowner Ferenc Kállay. Although Nyíregyháza can no longer claim to be the easternmost metropolis in the Warsaw Pact, it still has a very important rail junction.

The arcaded **Town Hall** (1841, *Károly Benkő*) adds a Renaissance feel to Kossuth tér despite the fact it was remodelled in 1912. The eclectic wedge-shaped **Savings Palace** (Rákóczi u.1., 1912, *József Hubert*) and its similarly eclectic neighbour the *Crown Hotel* (1895, *Ignác Alpár*), and the red brick neo-Romanesque **Roman Catholic church** (1902–1904, *Virgil Nagy*) give the centre of the town a certain splendour.

A sculpture of Louis Kossuth (Gyula Bethlen, 1912) shares the square bearing his name with a monument commemorating 1824, the year the residents of Nyíregyháza were all relieved of their feudal obligations and allowed to become free peasants. The sculpted column (Sándor Nagy) was put up to commemorate the 150th anniversary of the event.

In Országzászló tér you can see the **Hungarian Hussars Memorial** (1997, *Sándor Győrfi*) and the Secession-style **Nyírvíz Palace** (1913, *Gyula Papp, Ferenc Szabolcs*). Apart from its substantial collection of medals and decorations there is an exhibition dedicated to Miklós Kállay, Hungarian premier from March 1942 until March 1944.

The **András Jósa Museum** (Benczúr tér 21.) is housed in a fine neoclassical building (*Kálmán Maróthy*). Founded in 1868 it is one of the earliest public archaeological and art historical collections in the country.

Benczúr tér quite rightly has a statue of 19th century artist *Gyula Benczúr* (1844–1920) (1941, *Géza Galántai Fekete*). Behind him stands *Zsigmond Kis-*

faludi Strobl's composition *"The Birth of Venus"*. The **Zsigmond Móricz Theatre** (1894, *Ignác Alpár*) looks onto Bessenyei tér, the trees of which encircle the neo-Baroque statue of György Bessenyei himself (1899, *Ede Kallós*).

One of the town's most popular statues is András Kocsis's Peasant Girl in Kálvin tér.

The Greek Catholic Episcopal Palace and the Secession-style Theological College (Miklós Führer, 1908) have been the administrative centre of the diocese since 1914 (Bethlen Gábor u. 5.) A Byzantine-style chapel was built in the courtyard in 1981. The main building now houses the Greek Catholic Ecclesiastical Art Collection. The twin-towered Byzantine-style Greek Catholic Church (Bercsenyi útca) are by Bertalan Vojtovics and Mihály Barzó.

Since 1914, the buildings of the **Greek Catholic Episcopal Palace** and **Theological College** (1908, *Miklós Führer*) have belonged to the Greek Catholic Bishop of Hajdúdorog (Gábor Bethlen u. 5.) A chapel in the Byzantine style was built in the courtyard in 1981. Space has been found in the main building to house the *Greek Catholic Ecclesiastical Collection*. The twin-towered Byzantine-style **Greek Catholic church** (Bercsényi u.) is the work of *Bertalan Vojtovics* and *Mihály Barzó* (1897).

Nyíregyháza's Hősök tere contains an English-style park, the southern part of which is dominated by Zsigmond Kisfaludi Strobl's "Heroes" (1928) a memorial to those who died during the First World War. It is the County Hall (1891-1892, Ignác Alpár) which dominates the western side of the square.

There is a **tablet** on no. 8 Szent István utca recording where the writer *Gyula Krúdy* (1878–1933) lived before moving to Budapest in 1911. The massive eclectic **Louis Kossuth Lutheran Grammar School** nearby was built between 1887 and 1901, and designed by *János Bobula* and *Ignác Alpár*. Just a few paces away is the oldest building in the town, the **Lutheran church** (1784, Giuseppe Aprilis) in Luther tér. The late-Baroque building has a tower soaring 50meters above the main entrance. The tower contains 12 small **bells** (1928), which occasionally delight the passers-by. The **Orthodox synagogue** (1924–32, *Lipót Baumhorn)* lies on Síp utca. In the Kiskörút you come to the **Mihály Váci Arts Centre** (Szabadság tér 9.) opposite which stands the **Municipal Gallery** (Selyem u. 12.).

The event everybody looks forward to in December is the *Santa Claus beauty competition.*

ON NYÍREGYHÁZA'S DOORSTEP

SÓSTÓGYÓGYFÜRDŐ

Sóstó-erdő, the Salt Lake Woods, are Nyíregyháza's lungs. 4km further on you come to the *Salt Lake Spa* (officially recognised as such in 1927) in which there are 46 hectares of **leisure facilities**. The place gets its name from the source of the 9.5 hectares of salt water lying at the lowest point of the complex. The lake is in fact two pools, connected by a single channel, which is opened up from time to time. The pool at the town end is known as the **cold pool** and the other the **boating pool**.

In an effort to bring even more variety to the Salt Water Spa some **tub-baths** were added in the year 2000. These can be found in the *"Bath House"*. The outdoor swimming complex in particular is extremely popular, mainly because of its medicinal waters. The water comes up from a depth of 998metres at a temperature of 50 °C. It is rich in chlorides and carbonates, and consequently recommended for the treatment of the internal organs. (The main entrance is in Berenát utca).

Nyíregyháza Zoo can also be found at the Salt Lake. Its 24-hectare site makes it the second biggest zoo in Hungary behind Budapest Zoo. There are over one thousand animals representing 150 species from 5 continents. The Tropicarium (2002), the nature exhibition known as the Sarvidék Panorama (2003), the Tropical House, the "Shark" Aquarium and the Monkey Forest are just a few of the attractions on offer.

The covered pool and the health facilities are already in place at the **medicinal baths.** The new pools and the spa hotel are expected to be ready by 2005.

The 60m **water-tower** which rises above the Sóstó complex is not only an industrial monument, having been built at the beginning of the last century, it also houses the *Tourinform office* during the summer months.

The centre of the Salt Lake complex is dominated by an early 20th century water tower, the **Svájci-lakk Hotel** (1866) and the **Krúdy Hotel** (1911) which since its renovation (2003) has functioned as cultural events venue and a restaurant.

The Nyíregyháza **narrow-gauge railway** going up to the Salt Lake has been in service for a century. The recently renovated station has been turned into a restaurant. In its heyday the station was also the tram terminus in the days the trams used to share the railway tracks.

The **Salt Lake Museum Village**, which was opened in 1979, covers 7.5 hectares providing a cross section of the kind of rural buildings which can or could once be found in the region. The nearly one hundred buildings contain examples of everything from a Slovak farm to a gypsy encampment.

In the museum some of the buildings are still used. Services are held in the Calvinist church every Sunday morning, and you can shop at the butcher's, go to the pub or see what's going on down at the blacksmiths. During the summer months there is a rich and varied programme. Concerts are held in the church every Wednesday, followed by a reception at which local specialities are served to an accompaniment of folk music or something similar.

THE MID-NYÍRSÉG

NAGYKÁLLÓ

All three churches in the town date from the 18th century, the oldest and the most interesting being the **Calvinist church** with its **bell tower** (Szabadság tér). Although the tower looks medieval it is most definitely 18th century.

The old county hall is one of the town's most notable Baroque buildings (Szabadság tér 13.) having been planned and built by the Italian Aprilis Brothers between 1769 and 1780. Although now used as a psychiatric hospital, part of it can be visited with the permission of the principal.

Szabadság tér 7. was the birthplace of the human biologist Frigyes Korányi (1828-1913), one of the pioneers in the fight to cure TB. One room in the house is devoted to an exhibition about the man and his work. In the Jewish Cemetery that stands nearby you can see the burial place of the great Talmud scholar and rabbi Izsák Ezkiel Taub (Nagybalkányi út). Having gained a reputation for his knowledge, his wisdom, his kindliness and his eloquence, his grave is the most famous of the half a dozen places dedicated to him. People make their way to Nagykálló from all four corners of the globe.

Of all the programmes going on in the town it is the *Nagykálló Festival* at the end of September which arouses the most interest.

Two kilometres from Kiskálló is Harangod, a holiday and leisure centre (see the dance barn above). The village stands on the bank of Lake Harangod where you are free to go boating and water cycling.

The Gothic **Greek Catholic church** in KÁLLÓSEMJÉN (Kossuth u.) is believed to be 15th century. The Greek Catholic population settled in the area at the end of the 18th century. The richly decorated iconostasis was made in the following century.

There are 41 hectares of protected countryside around *Lake Mohos*. This is the only place you can study the wetlands and the floating islands which once covered the *Nyírség*. It's in the last big bog where you are likely to find peat ferns, rare marshland flowers and different types of algae.

Kallósemjén **Palace** (1763, Salvator Aprilis) was the home of the Balog-Semjén branch of the Kallay family, and of *Miklós Kállay* in particular (Kölcsey u. 4.). As premier he was famed for his "see-saw" politics during the Second World War. His body was brought home in 1993 and placed in the family crypt.

The most beautiful sights in ÓFEHÉRTÓ are the Late Gothic wallpaintings dating from the 1400s in the **Roman Catholic church** (Alkotmány u.). During the Reformation the paintings were whitewashed and covered with the kind of red and blue embroidery-inspired designs (1641) you also see at Csaroda and Vámosatya.

The **Roman Catholic church** in Levelek is also a single-aisled, Gothic affair (Hősök tere). It has a gabled, jambed western door.

Those who like their waters warm and shallow should head out to the *Levelek Reservoir* two kilometres north of the village. Filled in 1975 it has become a popular **bathing place,** and is also good for water sports. It is also possible to fish there if you have a permit.

Some of the 341-hectare Bakta Woods (the Great Wood lying north of the road) is a protected area. It is a gene bank for the rare trees which once covered the region. The stag beetle resides amongst the local oak trees.

The 13th century Romanesque **Roman Catholic church** in Baktalórántháza (Köztársaság tér), later remodelled in the Gothic style, is immediately recognisable by its decorative brickwork, which contains a mixture of glazed and unglazed bricks. The chancel contains the fragments of some 15th century wall paintings.

Vaja

The *Vaja Reservoir* stands to the south of the village. The 81-hectare lake is good for fishing.

Peasant cottage, Vaja

The thatched peasant house (Damjanich u. 102.) gives visitors some idea what goes on at the biennial *Shawm Folk Festival,* and how peasants once lived in the Central Nyírség.

In the park outside the **Calvinist church** (Damjanich u.) you will find the **tomb** of *General Ádám Vay*. Vay followed Rákóczi into exile in Poland, and his ashes were returned to Hungary at the same time as Rákóczi's.

The church, which is of medieval origin (14th century) has an interesting two-level 18th century tower complete with a pinnacled spire with a gallery which can be inspected by the general public.

The Vay family's one-time seat was used by Ferenc Rákóczi II. to hold the negotiations of 1703 and 1711 during the course of the Rákóczi War for Independence. Apart from an exhibition dedicated about the period, the courtyard is decorated with a series of busts of the main protagonists (Damjanich u.).

THE NYÍRI MEZŐSÉG

Tiszavasvári

The classical **Dessewffy Palace** (Petőfi u. 1.), built in 1820, is now a school and student residences. The park was laid out in the 19th century. The **historical garden** is protected on account of its stock of ancient and exotic trees. In the suburb of Tiszabüd you will find the **Greek Catholic church** (1764), which is a simple single-aisled Baroque building (Vasvári Pál u.). The tower is a later addition.

The arcaded classical **Calvinist Vicarage** (Garami E. u.) is now home to the *Vasvári Pál Museum*.

The 19th-century Dogály Villa adds a bit of classical splendour to Tiszavasvári.

Although the Calvinist church in Tiszavasvári goes back to the Middle Ages, it has been rebuilt many times. The building we have today has a classical and somewhat fortfied appearance owing to the thickness of the walls (Kálvin u.).

The 65°C waters at the **municipal baths** are recommended to those suffering from locomotor or gynaeological problems. The medicinal complex currently offers a camping site, a **boating lake** and a **youth camp**.

> *János Kabay (1896-1936), the chemist, was born in Büdszentmihály. His initial research related to the methods of extracting morphine from green poppy plants. It was thanks to him that the Alkaloid Chemical Factory (now ICA Alkaloid Ltd), the town's biggest employer, came into being. Pál Vasvári (original name Pál Fejér) (1826-1849), one of the leading figures in the 1848 War for Freedom, was born in Tiszabüd. His pen name was taken from the place where he spent his youth, Nyírvasvári, as Tiszavasvári was then known.*

The *Fehér-szik* offers a habitat for more than forty species of birds. The *warbler*, the *redshank*, the *brown harrier* and the *avocet* can all be seen there except during the migrating season.

TISZADOB

It is probably the most popular village in the *Nyíri-Mezőség* region, situated as it is next to the *Tisza Dead Channel* which manages to surround it almost completely.

Tiszadob has gone to great lengths to preserve its traditional buildings. More than fifty of the **local houses** in the centre of the village are listed. An exhibition devoted to the archaeology of the region and the local folk art can be found in the old library (Andrássy u. 27.).

The **Andrássy Palace**'s fame went well beyond Tiszadob. The palace, situated on the banks of the River Tisza, was modelled on the chateaux of the *Loire Valley*. Gyula Andrássy's formidable-looking residence, bordered on one side by an *English-style garden*, was probably designed by *Ignác Alpár* sometime between 1880 and 1885.

It is out on the 1,030 hectares of land making up *Tiszadob Flood Plain* that you can see the kind of landscape which once characterised the whole region. Work started on the Tisza in the middle of the 19th century, changing the character of the land bordering Tiszadob in the process. In the *Urkomdűlő* lying three kilometres from the village you are confronted by the three obelisks put up in memory of *Count István Széchenyi, Gyula Andrássy the Elder* and *Pál Vásárhelyi*.

Many famous performers from both home and abroad take to the beautifully situated stage for Tiszadob's annual Piano Festival. One of the great attractions in the park is the box maze (below left), and one which is always there to puzzle the children resident at the buildings nearby.

The village has other rarities as well. There is the so-called Tubus Tower (below right), which stands in the middle of the village. The 12-metre-high 19th century granary which tapers very gradually is filled with small triangular openings on its sides (Táncsics u. 2.).

TISZALÖK

Like many villages in the Nyíri-Mezőség, Tiszalök has the characteristic centralised layout. From the narrow network of alleyways you move into the wide-open streets along which herds of animals were once driven. In the old **Szarvas Chemist's** (Kossuth u.– Márton F. tér) you can see an exhibition focusing on life as it was once lived in such agricultural towns.

In 1937, the first of a series of dams across the River Tisza was built just five kilometres from the town.
The second was only built in 1954.
Next door to the hydroelectric dam there is a 24-hectare arboretum boasting 1,200 species of plants.

As you make your way towards Tiszadada on the banks of the *Eastern Main Channel,* you come to a **leisure park** where you can go swimming and fishing. You can then cross the Tisza by **ferry** to Tiszatardos on the far bank.

SZABOLCS

Anonymous the 13th century chronicler mentions an earthwork and describes how, following the Hungarian Conquest, one of the chiefs, Szabolcs, realised that the site was well-suited for a fortification. Once he had discussed his plan with his companions they dug out a huge ditch with the help of the local population building in the process the substantial earthwork known as Szabolcs Castle.

The tenth century **earthwork,** which stands on the edge of the Tisza flood plain, rises to a height of 10–12metres. During the Árpád era assemblies were held in the enclosure.

The Szabolcs ramparts have witnessed one thousand years of history. The warrior statue is but a recent addition.

Near the castle ramparts stands the **Calvinist church** (Petőfi u.), which was in all probability founded by St Stephen. The originally three-aisled church was rebuilt during the 15th century.

The Gothic sacristy door, monstrance and carved font can still be seen inside the church. In front of the church stands a bust of St. Ladislas: it was here that the Synod of Szabolcs was held in 1092 overseen by the king.

On the mound opposite the entrance to the earthwork stands the late 18th century **Mudrány Hall** (Petőfi u. 39.). In the entrance hall there is a large oil painting by the wandering Bohemian artist *Ferenc Wrabetz* depicting the Magyar chieftains on their arrival into the Carpathian Basin. Originally it was intended to grace the walls of the county hall in Nagykálló. The hall now provides a home for the **furniture and costume collection** of the *András Jósa Museum* in Nyíregyháza.

It is with an aerial view of the Tisza Bridge in Záhony that we take leave of the northern and eastern tracts of the Great Plain and move onto our next chapter which deals with the area immediately around *Lake Tisza.*

"I woke one morning on the Tisza shore,
Where in my youth I'd often gone before.
Above the plain the blue sky spread its vault;
I saw the fires of dawn the heights exalt.
The opening smile of morn upon the steep
Began to liven our benumbing sleep.
The mists of night began to smoke, and hide
The valleys and the hills on every side.
Thence I went forward on my misty way
And watched the passing shadows yield to day."

(György Bessenyei: Morning Charm of the Tisza
translation by Watson Kirkconnell)

CONTENTS – LAKE TISZA

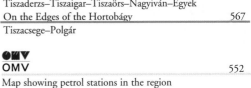

Map showing petrol stations in the region

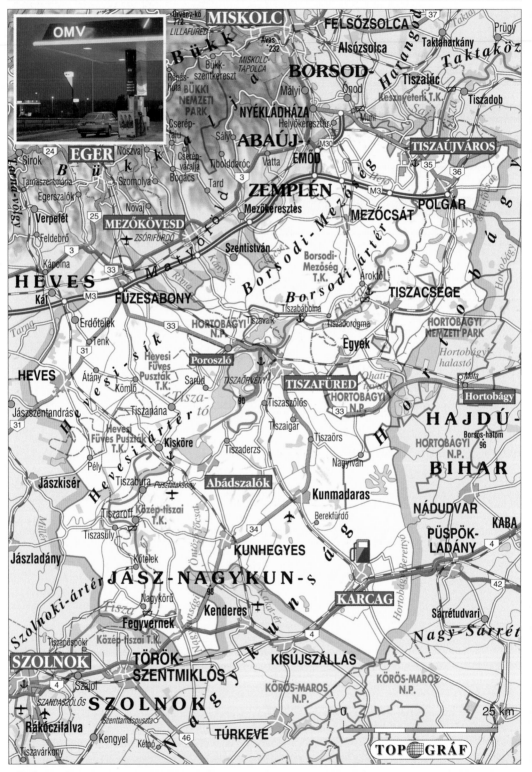

Lake Tisza

Although Hungary's second largest lake was created artificially at the beginning of the 1970s, the landscape around the islands, the dead channels and the oxbow lakes successfully give the impression that they are much older than they actually are. This perhaps explains why the 127km² of water soon became a very popular tourist destination. The variety of landscapes here is explained by the fact that four counties with four very different economic characters, Jász-Nagykun-Szolnok, Heves, Borsod-Abaúj-Zemplén and Hajdú-Bihar all converge on the area around the lake. The *Nagykunság* and the *South Borsod* and *Heves Plains* are all on the doorstep.

The lake is situated on what was a flood plain, and on the flooded territory of the River Tisza in between the water barrages there are sixteen islands and ten water channels. The course of the River Tisza, which can still be made out, reaches a depth of between 10 and 15 metres between mid-March and the beginning of November when the area is deliberately flooded. The huge expanse of water can be divided into three bays (*Abádszalók, Sarud, Tiszavalk*) to which one can add two areas, which are made up of the dead channels and the marshes dating from before the flooding of the area (the *Lake Tisza Bird Reserve*, the *Tiszafüred Dead Tisza*).

Since the lake came into being the composition of the fish population has changed somewhat. The number of sturgeon has fallen, whilst the number of silver crucian carp, carp and pike has increased. You can also find some species of fish from the Far East, which have been introduced into the waters: the silver carp, the grass carp and the white carp. The dead channels, the navvy ponds and the marshes offer ideal environments for amphibians and reptiles. The marsh frog breeds here in great numbers, and you will also find the edible frog, grass snakes and the pond tortoise.

There are nesting places for many species of birds around Lake Tisza. In the *Lake Tisza Bird Reserve* there are nine types of habitat and almost 200 species of birds, amongst them the spoonbill, the common heron, the squacco heron, the greater and the lesser heron, the night heron, the curlew, the white wagtail and the black kite. The Bird Reserve, which forms part of the *Hortobágy National Park* and the *World Heritage Site,* is a protected area.

The sheer power of nature draws many to the lake.

Although much has already been said about the *Hortobágy National Park*, it is worth mentioning here that much of it is situated within the Lake Tisza region, as is the *Nagyiváni Plain* and the area around Karcag. During the spring, the puddles forming on the alkaline soils and the surrounding water meadows attract flocks of wild ducks, wild geese, redshanks and godwits. During the autumn it is the cranes which rest there. The edge of the alkaline beds provides a habitat for the larks, the ever varying numbers of terns and a small group of bustards. Flocks of sheep have been nibbling down the fine grasses of the Hortobágy for many centuries. (The Hortobágy is dealt with in the sections on *World Heritage Sites and National Parks.*)

The *Pusztakócs Marshes*, one of the areas in the Hortobágy richest in wildlife, can only be seen once you have purchased a ticket from the National Park authorities. The *Tiszaigar Arboretum* with its famous Matthias Corvinus tree and its oaks also enjoys environmental protection. The *Borsod Mezőség* and the *Heves Plains* lying in the vicinity of the lake are both nature reserves and well worth visiting.

The Lake Tisza region has been inhabited since the New Stone Age. An important Copper Age treasure came to light in Tiszaszőlős, and finds from the period of the great migrations have been found on the higher-lying areas on the banks of the River Tisza. Excavations at the medieval settlement in Tiszaörvény have shown that the village was an important river crossing at an early date.

Most of the settlements you can see in the area today belonged to the Tomaj clan during the Árpád period. Most of the people living in the region during the Turkish period were forced to leave on more than one occasion only to return each time to rebuild their shattered communities. Most damage was inflicted during the battles immediately prior to the Turks' final retreat. Calvinist settlers came into region during the first half of the 17th century, soon to be followed by Catholics from the northwest invited by the Bishop of Eger as part of his efforts to promote the Counter Reformation.

The potters and the saddlers of Tiszafüred, the Karcag potters and those producing ornamental ceramics in Mezőcsát all enjoy national reputations. In the past the local peasant houses frequently had lime-washed verandas and thatched roofs whilst the residences inhabited by the local gentry betray certain classical pretensions.

Today it is the anglers and the water sports lovers who head for Lake Tisza. The lake is also a great place to go for a family holiday. There are exciting canoeing tours to be had along the Tisza complete with guide if necessary. In the 14km² stretch of water between Abádszalók Bay and the Sarud Basin even speed boats are allowed. It is also possible to cycle all the way around the lake.

In the pages which follow we will first take you to the lake's five biggest towns before exploring the landscape of what is the smallest region in our guide. It is however a region, which is on the threshold of great things especially now the motorway has reached Polgár.

At the lido in Abádszalók the brave can either go jet-skiing or paragliding. Those on a river tour along the Tisza, a life jacket is an essential fashion accessory...

Next to Tiszaújváros's sports centre you can find one of Hungary's most up-to-date thermal baths, complete with a medical centre containing state-of-the-art equipment. There are also open-air swimming pools, a leisure pool and water slides. The 36-38-40 °C iodine waters which come up from a depth of 1200m are medicinal, and there is also balneological treatment and physiotherapy available to everybody who wants it, irrespective of whether it has been prescribed by a doctor. One of the pools remains open through the winter months.

The town has a kayak and canoeing tradition going back decades. Today the Triathlon World Cup held in Tiszaújváros has added to the town's sporting reputation. There is always something going on in Tiszaújváros, whether its the Spring Festival, the Transit Expo Exhibition and Trade Fair, the International Folk Dance Festival or the Hot-Air Ballooning Competition.

TISZAÚJVÁROS

The new town of Tiszaújváros situated near the mouth of the *River Sajó* was built three decades ago. Once called Leninváros the town now prefers to be known as the *National Sports Town*, a title earned by the achievements of the town's kayakers and canoeists.

Both locals and visitors alike get a lot out of the programmes put on by the Tisza Chemical Works at the **Leisure Centre** (Tiszaújváros, külkerület) situated next to the town's sports centre. The **outdoor swimming complex,** situated next to the ice rink, is open from May to September, whilst the ice rink itself is open all the year round.

Tiszaújváros is popular with anglers and those canoeing down the Tisza. It's also a good pied-à-terre for those wishing to explore the surrounding countryside. The **holiday centre** on the southern tip of the **island** is a very popular stopping place with those on their Tisza river tours.

The fish restaurant known as the *"Halászcsárda"* is a great place to relax for both those travelling over land or along the river.

THE BORSOD MEZŐSÉG

Resembling the Hortobágy, the 18-thousand-hectare alkali plain, now known as the *Borsod Mezőség Nature Reserve*, is surrounded by Gelej, Mezőcsát, Tiszadorogma and Mezőnagymihály. It was the loess brought down by the streams flowing off the Bükk and the River Tisza which created the environment for the area's characteristic flora and fauna.

It's no coincidence that this landscape is known as the Little Hortobágy. Looking ahead of you there is absolutely nothing interrupting a view which goes deep into the horizon.

MEZŐCSÁT was once an important local pottery centre. In the **Southern Borsod Peasant Cottage** (Hunyadi u. 8.) there is an exhibition of typical examples of the local pottery including the classic *"miska jug"*.

At the **peasant cottage** (Táncsics út 3.) in ÁROK-TŐ you can become familiar with the local flora and fauna, as well as the history of the region. The inhabitants of the villages of TISZADOROGMA, TISZABÁBOLNA and TISZAVALK are not only keen on their arts and crafts, they also go to great lengths to put on programmes for those interested in hunting, fishing and ecological tourism. At the **lido** in Tiszabábolna you can go boating, fishing, or even catch a pleasure cruiser. Those interested in trying their hand at rush weaving should head out to Tiszadorogma.

POROSZLÓ

It is from this town on the right bank of the River Tisza that we will continue our expedition, starting with the area immediately around Lake Tisza. You can hire water sports equipment from Poroszló's **outdoor swimming complex**, and it is possible to ride around Lake Tisza in a motorboat. You can also make the most of the heated indoor swimming pool, the tennis courts and bowling alleys.

The peasant cottage known as "the gate to Lake Tisza" (Kossuth út 25.) is full of fishing tackle and traditional household objects. Visitors can even visit one of the most beautiful buildings in the town, the Graefl family's palace.

After a long day out visitors can also enjoy some of Poroszló's social and cultural events, such as the Pensioners' Clubs' get-together in July, the *Village Day* on August 20th and the *Patronal Festival* in September.

THE NORTHWESTERN SHORE

The southern end of SARUD touches the Little Tisza, and Lake Tisza is not far away either. The area used to belong to the crown before coming into the possession of the Bishop of Csanád. Those strolling around the village after a hard day at the lido may notice the memorial to the Hungarian Conquest on the wall of the Roman Catholic church. For those who still have some energy to spare this is great cycling country and there are also the new Dream Beach facilities to look up. In 2003, the Eurostrand Camping Site and Youth Camp opened at the Lido.

TISZANÁNA

The stretch of the Tisza just south of the village is good for both swimming and fishing. The *Dinnyés Ridge* is particularly popular, and it is there that some tourist accommodation has recently been built. There are those who already have the date of the *"Hazanéző"* pencilled into their diaries. This is when the residents of both ends of Tiszanána get together for a spot of fun and games. The fact that all the residents participate is indeed significant because the locals still talk in terms of the *Lower End* and the *Upper End* of the village.

Of the **two churches** in the middle of the village it is the Calvinist church which still contains some medieval details. One particularly lively and colourful event on the village's calendar is the summer *Gypsy Day*, followed in October by *Equestrian Derby*. The village also has one of the most beautiful and most romantic lidos on the Tisza.

KISKÖRE

Kisköre has one of the most developed **lidos** in the region. Visitors also have much else to enjoy, from the patronal festival, the art workshops and the *International Triathlon Championship* to the Majorette, the Folklore and the Roma Folklore Festivals.

For many decades the **Village Museum** (Béke út 5.) has been putting together a fine collection of folk art. One of the beams in the house has the date the house was built in 1856 carved into it, and all the fittings and furniture inside date from that period.

At the **Waterworks** (Május 1 u.1.) there is an exhibition of finds excavated from a nearby Avar site.

Kisköre Lock – a weir to be more exact – helps to make the Tisza navigable for ships sailing from Tokaj down to Szeged. It also produces electricity. Those with the necessary permission may use the bridge.

IN HEVES, ON THE RIGHT BANK

FÜZESABONY

The town is an important railway junction. The trains leaving from the station, designed by *Ferenc Pfaff*, take visitors to and from the Bükk, the Mátra and Lake Tisza, three of the most popular holiday destinations in Hungary.

The **parish church** in Füzesabony (1732–35) was designed by the Eger architect *Giovanni Battista Carlone*. The most famous visitor to Füzesabony still remains *Sándor Petőfi*. The tablet on the wall of the *Gelej Tavern* informs you that it was here the poet stayed on more than one occasion.

KÖMLŐ, first mentioned in 1261, has always benefited from its proximity to the River Tisza. Life in the village is brightened up by the *Equestrian Festival* in August and the *Cultural Festival* in November.

The excellent hunting which can be had near TENK is overseen by the *Erdőtelek-Tenk Hunting Association*. The village puts on the *Aranycsengő (Golden Bell) Arts Festival* and the carnival which takes place sixty days after Easter.

In what was the garden of *Buttler Palace* in ERDŐTELEK stands the seven-hectare **arboretum** (Fő út). Situated on the banks of the *Hany* the arboretum became something of a home for rare botanical specimens at the beginning of the 20th century. Of particular interest are the rare species of pine, the rubber trees and the aromatic junipers.

HEVES, first mentioned in 1203, must have been an important place during the Árpád period because the royal county shared its name. The town's **churches** and **palaces,** now used by various administrative offices and social institutions, can all be seen during the course of a short walk around the town centre. It's worthwhile stopping off at the *Domestic Crafts Association* (Kossuth út), which sells arts and crafts products.

Chess is now a sport enjoyed by millions. This partly explains why you can find a Chess Museum in Heves (Hunyadi u. 2.).

On the edge of PÉLY you can find what amounts to an industrial curiosity, the steam-powered **pumping station** built in the 1870s which is still in good working order today. For the ornitholo-gists amongst you there is the **Bird Reserve** on Lake Gánáth. On Pély's 1,200 hectare saline marsh visitors can see red-footed falcons, stone curlews, Kentish plovers and lapwings at close quarters.

ABÁDSZALÓK

The largest lido on Lake Tisza lies on the shores of Attila Bay's 14 square kilometres. The Abádszalók Lido (Feltáró u.) is ideal for swimming and water sports, and the Füzes Camping Site, which forms part of the complex, has a hot-water swimming pool which is good come rain or shine. The place is buzzing with jet-skis and speedboats. The accommodation and facilities on this part of lake make it very popular with anglers.

The construction of the *Tisza II. Lock* and the flooding of the river following the blocking of the river at Kisköre really speeded up the pace of life

The Abádszalók Summer offers two months of rich and varied programmes. The angling competition, the Lake Tisza Cup and the Cooking Competition are held in alternate years both accompanied by the election of Miss Lake Tisza. The equestrian programmes add a bit of extra colour.

The quieter parts of the lake are rich in birdlife. 150 species have been identified. (Illustrated: a kingfisher)

here. The *Village House* (István király u. 41.) is not without interest. The **Doll Museum** has a collection of over 200 dolls dressed up in the traditional costumes worn in the different regions of the Carpathian Basin.

TO THE SOUTHWEST OF THE LAKE

The 15th century Calvinist **church** (Dózsa u. 88.) in TISZABURA, the **Szapáry Chapel** in PUSZTA-TAKSONY and the one-time **Borbély Palace** (Aradi út 28.) in TISZAROFF, a palace hotel with all the services one would expect, all make interesting destinations for the occasional overcast day.
Visits to the medieval church in TISZASÜLY (Szent László u. 4.) and the Sajfok **sluice gate and pumping station** (1878), the country's oldest piece of industrial archaeology, are also recommended. Those wishing to use the local medicinal mud, will for the moment, have to go to the *Gellért Baths* in Budapest.

The schoolchildren of KŐTELEK are called upon to work as tour guides on a daily basis as it was they who founded the village's **Local History Collection** in their school (Kossuth L. u. 6.). The bathers, anglers and hunters all add to the picturesque scene down on the banks of the River Tisza. The village is at its busiest during the course of the *Equestrian Festival.*

Kőtelek's dead channel means that it is rich in wildlife. There is also the rich programme at the Equestrian Festival to enjoy.

NAGYKÖRŰ

One of the houses once belonging to a wealthy farmer is where you will find the **local history collection.** At the summer workshops you can master the arts of rush-binding, lace and candle-making, or try your hand at pottery and leather washing.
During Nagykörű's *Cherry Festival,* horses and traps take visitors out into the cherry orchards. It is worthwhile enquiring after the local fishing, horse-riding, hunting and water sports, as well as the local accommodation and the **Ecological Park.**
On the edge of Nagykörű you can visit that part of the *Central Tisza Nature Reserve* situated on the water meadows of the River Tisza with its sandy beaches and its **lido.**

It was at the end of the 19th century that landowner György Petrovay introduced the Germersdorf cherry to the region. The cherry orchard here also has a unique cherry tree collection (Templom tér 1.) The Nagykörű cherry has its own trademark, and is considered to be one of the region's delicacies and one meriting its own Cherry Festival.

The name of the town is of eastern Turkish origin, probably derived from the Cuman word *qarsaq*, the name of a prairie wolf. The past of what is *the capital of the Nagykunság* has been studied in most detail by ethnographer *István Győrffy*.

The Nagykun Museum, named after István Győrffy (Kálvin út 4.), consists mainly of ethnographical and historical exhibits. Particularly valuable are the artefacts relating to local shepherding as well as the Kunság painted furniture and the Karcag pottery.
One of the exhibitions named the Nagykunság Chronicle after Győrffy's most beautiful book outlines peasant life in the days when animals roamed freely in a landscape still very much at the mercy of the local water system, and as yet untamed by human hand.

The work of Karcag potter Sándor Kántor was very much sought after he had won the main prize at the Brussels World Exhibition. The work of the Kossuth Prize-winning potter can be seen at the thatched Sándor Kántor Potters' House (Erkel Ferenc út 1.). There are still potters active in the town, at Bethlen út 8-10. and 31., and Hunyadi út 42.

For those who are interested in the urban landscape, there is no better place to start than Kossuth tér with its Kossuth statue (*János Horvay*), the enormous single-towered **Calvinist church** and the Secession-style **Town Hall**. **The History of Medicine and Pharmacy Museum** (Széchenyi sugárút) focuses on the work of pharmacist *Gábor Kátai*. The original furniture and the old medical instruments all help to evoke the atmosphere of a bygone age.

The **Greek Orthodox church** (1794, Horváth Ferenc u.) contains a fine iconostasis and an equally fine pulpit. The town's cultural programmes take place at the *Déryné Cultural Centre* (Dózsa György út 5–7.). The pools at the **local baths** (Forrás út 3.) are fed by water from the hot springs coming out of the ground at temperatures of 70 and 41 °C.

The architects who designed the Morgó Csárda in Karcag certainly got their measurements right because they succeeded in aligning the main beam of the inn along the borders of Jász-Nagykun-Szolnok and Hajdú-Bihar counties. This caused great confusion amongst both sets of county constabulary, neither of whom were in a position to pursue a highwayman beyond their area of jurisdiction.

The *Nagykunság Cultural Festival* in August includes the Harvest Parade, the International Choir Festival, a folklore programme, a cookery competition, a motor show and the equestrian event. *Equestrian Day* is held on the first Sunday in October.

The group of classical buildings making up the **Nagykunság Peasant House** (Jókai út 16.) is a minor architectural masterpiece. The building is furnished with local Karcag carpentry known as Cuman Blue. **Morgó Inn** (Baross út 1.), mentioned above, is also a local sight with *Sándor Rózsa* connections.

The 18th century **Cemetery Lodge** (Külterület 3.) at the northern cemetery is one of the last reminders of the medieval subterranean dwelling. Although still inhabited, the people living there are only too happy to show you round if you make all the necessary arrangements in advance.

The area of the Nagykunság around Karcag is the richest in the earthworks known locally as Cuman mounds (kunhalom). They are usually between 5 and 10m high with a diameter of between 20 and 50metres and take the form of either a cone or a dome. A stone monument has been placed in memory of the Cumans on the Kis-Hegyesbor Mound on road number 4 near the 160km marker.

Sixty mills used to operate in Karcag, eleven of them windmills. Today only one remains. The renovated brick-built Barna **windmill** (Vágóhíd út 22.), dating from 1858, was built on a mound so as to allow the sails to get the maximum amount of energy out of the wind.

Despite its name, **Windmill Inn**, the southern gateway to the *Hortobágy National Park*, now contains an exhibition dedicated to the wildlife you can expect to find on the Hortobágy. Bicycle and horse and carriage tours leave from here for Karcag, the more watery habitats and the Great Plain. One popular destination is **Zádor Bridge**, which was once an important crossing point over the *Zádor* before the lands were drained on the Karcag to Debrecen road just east of Karcag. Zádor Bridge's foundation stone was laid in 1806, and the eighty-metre-long nine-arched bridge was built on a stone base, and had nine brick vaulted arches. Its present five-arched appearance resulted from the massive spring floods of 1830 when the torrents of water swept away two arches from both ends of the bridge. In 1833, the remaining arches were reconstructed.

As the straightening work which took place on the River Tisza during the 19th century put an end to the risk of flooding in the area, the traffic on the Karcag to Püspökladány road was taken off Karcag's Zádor Bridge.

A Day in the Nagykunság

Instead of finding oil in BEREKFÜRDŐ *Ferenc Pávai Vajna* found natural gas and hot mineral waters coming out of the earth at a temperature of 56 °C. The popularity of the **spa** (Berek tér 11.) has grown enormously since 1932.

Berekfürdő is for people of all ages.

It is here at the **glassworks** that the immediately recognisable round *Zwack Unicum* bottles are made. At the exhibition next to the factory you can see decorative objects individually blown in blue, violet, smoke coloured and opal white glass.

Louis Kossuth attended the fortress-like 18th century **Calvinist church** in KUNMADARAS (Kálvin út 4.). You can still see the chair he sat in. Nagykunság's characteristic flora and fauna can be seen on the *Kunmadaras Plain* and in the *Kunkápolnás Marshes*, both of which are in the *Hortobágy National Park* once you have bought the necessary ticket.

KUNHEGYES

The twin towers of the classical **Calvinist church** (1827–1848, *Ferenc Homályossy*), the *"Cathedral of the Great Plain"*, can be seen from way out on the plains. Although there are pews for a congregation of 1,200, as many as 5,000 people can squeeze into the church. The Baroque building next door (1739), which is now a library, was originally used as a **salt depot,** one of the architectural relics of the old Szolnok-Debrecen-Transylvania "salt road".

The three-aisled Kunhegyes hall church is the second largest Calvinist Church in Hungary.

The Komlóssy **windmill** (1859) is also considered to be a local folk monument. At the end of the 19th century there were still seven windmills in operation in Kunhegyes. On the edge of the town you can see the most famous of the Cuman mounds, the **Gergely Mound**, which is now protected.

The **thermal bath** in the leisure park is very popular. The *Legénybot* arts workshop takes place in June every year, and August sees the hosting of the *Magyar Kun Cup* youth football tournament. *Kunság Gastronomy* is an initiative bringing old rural culinary traditions back to life by giving visitors the opportunity to try out a few of the local specialities for themselves at the local inns.

Visitors to Kunhegyes can become familiar with basket making and weaving with a little help from the experts.

TISZAFÜRED

Tiszafüred was a centre not only of pottery but of furniture making, carving and painting as well. It was here that the country's most famous saddle-making workshops and basket weavers could be found. Today it is potters *Imre Szűcs* (Belső kertsor u. 2/a.) and *Zsóka Török* (Szőlősi út 27.), who keep their crafts alive. At Ady Endre u. 45. the **Leatherwork Studio** run by the Horváts puts on a permanent exhibition, while putting on masterclasses and courses and having a stall.

One of the town's local peasant classical houses, in fact one which was originally a potter's studio, has been turned into the **Gáspár Nyúzó Potter's Cottage** (Malom u. 12., 1870). Belonging to the Nyúzó family, it was home to two generations of potters and was arranged with a living room-porch-workshop layout. It is now filled with 19th century furniture and fittings.

The sandy beaches and the shallow waters at the lido are particularly popular with the children.

One of Tiszafüred's most famous and popular clay pots is the miska jug which takes the form of an elegant uniformed hussar.

The classical Lipcsey Hall, built in about 1840, now houses the archaeological, ethnographical, historical and natural history collections at the **Pál Kiss Museum** (Tariczky sétány 6.).

Going along the road leading to the camping site you come to the neo-Baroque **Kemény Palace** (1920s, *Ágoston Paulik*) set in the park (Kastély u.) and filled with the furniture of the period.

The Tiszafüred **Thermal and Medicinal Baths** (Poroszló u.) make up part of the holiday centre, as does the **camping site**. One of the big summer events down on Lake Tisza is the *Fish Festival* in July.

The cormorant is one of the water birds you are likely to find on Lake Tisza.

The **Bird Reserve** lying north of the Debrecen-Füzesabony railway line covers 2,500 hectares of the *Hortobágy National Park*. The western half of the reserve is covered in water during the summer. To the east the horseshoe lakes, the navvy ponds, the marshes, the scrubland and the woodland make up a varied landscape. The bird sanctuary in the area enjoying world heritage status can be visited on the guided rowing trips leaving from the quay.

It is, however, possible to watch the birds from the edges of the reserve and the embankments, so it is to these lookout positions that unofficial visitors should go to find a vantage point.

The grandest birds on the reservation are the greater and the lesser herons, the spoon bills, the black storks, and it is here also that the extremely rare and much-loved lanneret lives.

The bays of Lake Tisza near Tiszafüred, like that for example near Tiszaörvény, now present a rich and varied landscape. Its beauty draws anglers, swimmers and lovers of water sport.

ON THE TISZA RIDGE

A riverside panorama, peace and quiet await visitors to *Tiszaörvény*. The territory on the border of TISZADERZS is popular with both hunters and anglers. The riverside near Tiszaderzs is ideal for camping or a day out.

The Romanesque **church** built by the Dominicans in the 13th century has stood in ruins ever since being destroyed by fire (Ady Endre u. 3.).

The 19-hectare **arboretum** at TISZAIGAR has one of the finest collections of trees in the *Central Tisza* region, containing 373 types of trees and shrubs, including firs, cypresses and indigenous oaks. An oak tree standing nearby said to be 400 years old is known as the

A preening heron

Matthias Corvinus tree, despite the fact there is nothing whatsoever linking the tree with the king. A few hundred metres to the west of the tree, in the middle of the pastures, stand two groups of trees believed to be 220 and 240 years old respectively. Many years ago, when a dozen trees still stood there, the trees were named after the twelve Apostles. All that remain are six oaks and two wild pear trees.

The **swimming complex** at the village of TISZAÖRS which is open night and day 365 days a year, has three pools. There is a camping site, a boarding house and further accommodation in the village where you should be able to find somewhere capable of satisfying your requirements.

Over the last 100-150 years nothing much has changed on the borders of Nagyiván.

The **Görbe Inn** on the edge of NAGYIVÁN is the kind of inn you would have expected to find in the 19th century. The **peasant house** in Nagyiván, however, is furnished as it would have been in the 1930s.

Lake Tisza is also popular with birds.

The *Nagyiván Plain* is part of the *Hortobágy National Park.* It is here on the extensive, dry terrain that you will see wild ducks, wild geese, cranes, redshanks, bustards and larks.

The 3,000-hectare *Kunkápolnás Marsh* on the borders of Nagyiván and Kunmadaras is frequently covered with a carpet of white waterlilies and yellow flowers. It is here that black-headed seagulls, grebes and summer geese nest. The red heron and the snow white great herons hide away in the thick reeds. The marshes are strictly protected, and can only be visited with the permission of the National Park (Bem apó u. 1.).

Walking across the plain on a hot dry day you may be lucky enough to see a **"délibáb"**, a Great Plain mirage. In EGYEK, just east of Tiszafüred, the reeds of the *Black Meadow* making up part of the *Pusztakócs Marshes* are similar to the reeds out on the marshes of the Hortobágy.

The marshy, watery habitats *(Nagy-Csattag, Justus-Fekete Meadow)* are restricted areas and can only be visited in the company of a guide.

ON THE EDGES OF THE HORTOBÁGY

Heading out towards Debrecen you come to the **Csárda Museum** built in the *Meggyes Inn* which stood next to what was once the main cattle road. The inn, which survives with all its original furniture, can be reached only along the mud track taking you to the edge of Kócsújfalu. *Hortobágy's* **western lodge** stands where the Debrecen road meets the Egyek road.

Tiszacsege

It was here that there was a ford across the Tisza. The trade route linking Pest with Nagyvárad (Oradea, Romania) crossed the river here.

The Tisza Dead Channel surrounds *Kácsa Island*, now a biospheric reserve. The plants and animals you can see here show you what the natural environment, which dominated the Great Plain looked like before the river was straightened. During the summer, motorboats leave the quay on a daily basis to explore the woods lining the Tisza.

It's worthwhile visiting the **cottar's house** (1833, Óvoda u. 26.), which has preserved its original appearance whilst being furnished in an authentic manner, and the medieval **fortified church**.

Over the last few decades Tiszacsege has become something of a holiday resort. This is mainly because of the thermal waters, which share a composition similar to those in Hajdúszoboszló, were discovered during oil exploration work in 1972. The waters feeding the pools have medicinal properties.

We leave the Lake Tisza Region in Polgár, where they have just started work on their **archaeological leisure park**. The archaeological walk, the Roman ramparts, the Cuman mound and the peasant cottage allow visitors a sight of the region during various stages in its history. There is also a camping site and a sports ground to satisfy visitors' needs. But we won't be leaving the Tisza for long...

In Tiszacsege, the holiday centre offers you many ways to relax. Cyclists can cycle along the embankments of the River Tisza either northwards towards Tiszadob, or southwards down to Kisköre. Horse riding is also a very popular pastime in these parts. Anglers are only too happy to sit down by the flood waters.
There are also horse and carriage tours that explore the more obscure corners of the Hortobágy.

"... It's snowing. The barman coughs.
Steam billows from my mulled wine glass,

the clock slowly strikes six
and I'm tired and totally bewitched."

(Jenő Dsida:
Inn amongst the snowy hills)

Contents – Northern Hungary

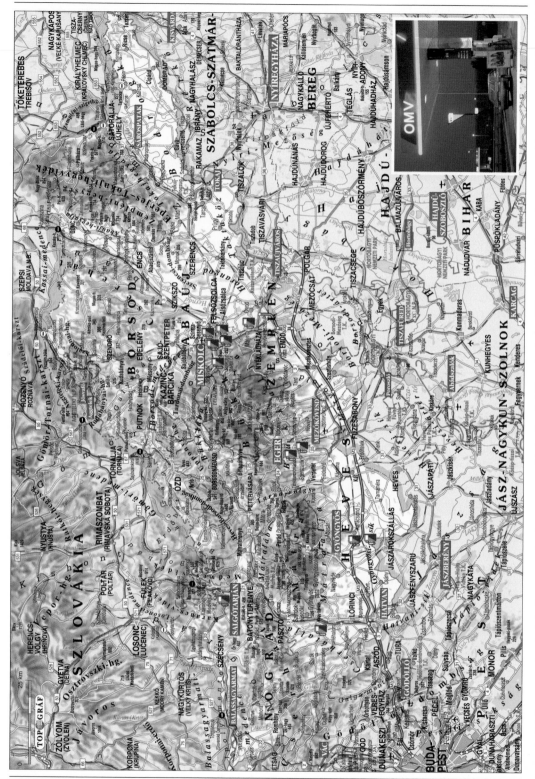

NORTHERN HUNGARY

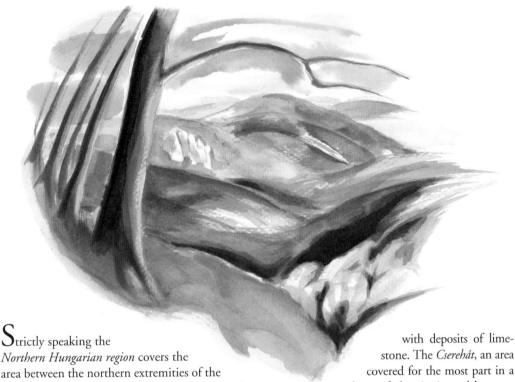

Strictly speaking the *Northern Hungarian region* covers the area between the northern extremities of the Great Plain and the border with Slovakia, stretching from the Danube in the west to the Tisza in the east. The landscape is dominated by the *Northern Hills,* which are in fact made up of a succession of smaller individual ranges, starting with the *Zemplén Hills* in the east, followed by the *Bükk,* the *Mátra,* the *Cserhát* and ending with the *Börzsöny* in the west. In amongst this broad swathe of hills there are other defining geographical features: valleys both large and small, plains and the occasional stretch of undulating countryside. And then there are the cave systems which lurk under the surface.

From a geological point of view it is an extremely rich and varied landscape. The Börzsöny, the Mátra and the Zemplén Hills are all of volcanic origin. To the north of the Mátra the *Karancs* is made of andesite and the *Medves* of basalt, whilst the *Aggtelek Hills* and the Bükk, if only partially so, are limestone. The Mátra's lesser western neighbour, the *Cserhát,* is made up of volcanic rock interspersed with deposits of limestone. The *Cserehát,* an area covered for the most part in a layer of clay, is situated between the Zemplén and the Aggtelek Hills.

The *Cserhát* region, stretching from the Börzsöny down to the Zagyva Valley, contains all the geological formations you are likely to find in the Northern Hills. It is interesting to note that the western Cserhát, stretching from the Börzsöny Hills to the Galga, differs substantially from the eastern Cserhát, which borders on the Mátra. Characteristic of the former are the limestone and dolomite outcrops (Naszály, Romhányi-hegy, and the Csővár-Nézsa), which join up with the *Gödöllő-Monor Hills* to the south. The eastern Cserhát is covered with evidence of lava flows, extinct volcanoes and seams of andesite. The Tepke, the Szanda and the Karancs are also andesite.

The Mátra region is made up of three distinct areas. It is in the *Central Mátra* that you will find the most popular holiday destinations. The streams slicing into the southern slopes have left stone ridges high above them. On the northern side lie the scree slopes, the finest example being the *Tatármező*, the largest such feature in Hungary. *The Mátraalja*, the foothills which lie to the south of the Central Mátra, lead gently down onto the Great Plain. The northern side of the Mátra is known as *the Mátralába*. Lahóca Hill is one of the few volcanic deposits to have survived the ravages of time.

The country's highest and most beautiful karst hills are those bordered by the River Sajó to the east and the north, the Tarna to the west and the Great Plain to the south. The *Bükk Region,* which also include the ancient *Uppony Hills,* constitute the oldest part of the Northern Hills. The Bükk can be divided into three parts. In the *Central Bükk* you will find the Bükk plateau, and all the Bükk's major peaks, or "rocks" ("kő" in Hungarian). So there are *Őr-kő, Bél-kő, Tar-kő* and *Istállós-kő.* The plateau is divided into two by the Garadna Valley, an area rich in karst rock formations. It is here that you will find the caves once inhabited by prehistoric man. Most of the plateau belongs to the *Bükk National Park.* The *Bükkalja* resembles the southern slopes of the Mátra, the undulating landscape being punctuated by the occasional valley. The *Bükklába* is the rolling countryside from which the Uppony Hills rise. It is in this picturesque countryside that you will find the *Csernely Valley* and the *Uppony Pass.*

Stalagmite formation at Baradla

Moving from the Bükk in a north-easterly direction you come to the *Aggtelek-Rudabánya Hills*, a region particularly rich in the karst which continues into the Slovakian part of the Gömör region. Aggtelek abounds in karst rock formations: it is here that you will find the caves and the underground lakes. The amazing underground geological features have earned the caves on both sides of the border the title of *World Heritage Site.* (For a more detailed description look up the relevant entry in the Hungarian Treasury.) The largest cave is the *Baradla* in Aggtelek, whose 24 kilometres go deep into Slovakia. The *Rudabánya Hills* to the south are made of limestone and dolomite. Iron ore was mined here from the 15th century right up until 1985. It was here also that the remains of one of our prehistoric ancestors *(Rudapithecus)* were unearthed. The area immediately around the find is now protected.

The Tokaj-Zemplén Hills belong to the Carpathians' inner volcanic ring, which continues northwards beyond the border into the Szalánci Hills (Slanské Vrchy) in Slovakia.

As the Great Plain was in the process of sinking the volcanic hills began to rise. This movement caused a certain amount of post-volcanic activity. The effects of this can be seen in the Telkibánya area. Geological formations bearing the scars of hot water activity are in evidence near Sárospatak; whilst the scree at Boldogkőújfalu was caused by geological activity during the Ice Age. The volcanic content in the soil, the loess covering and the climate have all made the area ideal for grape growing. To the north of the main axis of the Northern Hills there is a succession of open tracts of countryside each lying parallel to the Hungarian-Slovakian border. Starting from the Börzsöny in the west, this open countryside passes the northern reaches of the Cserhát and the Mátra through what is known as the *Nógrád Basin,* on towards the *Gömör-Heves Hills* and Lake Arló, a geographical feature created by an ancient landslide. Moving on through the Sajó Valley you come to the *Borsod Hills* before finally passing down the Bódva and the Hernád Valleys to the Cserehát. It is here that we have evidence of older rocks breaking through the surface of the subsequent deposits leaving the

Látó-kő in the Bükk

rocky landscape around Szendrő, the granular limestone and the Rakaca marble.

Hungary's highest peak, *Kékestető* (1,014m), crowns the Mátra, followed by its neighbour *Galyatető* (964 m). In the Zemplén Hills lies the 893-metre-high *Nagy-Milic* situated right on the border with Slovakia. It is here that the *National Blue Walk* either starts or finishes, depending on whether you set out on the 1,094 km route from here, or from Írottkő on the Austrian border. The region has three national parks (*Aggtelek*, the *Bükk* and the *Duna-Ipoly*), as well as a number of nature conservation areas and nature reserves. The major rivers, the *Tisza*, the *Bodrog* and the *Hernád* are good for boating on and other water sports. The rivers are popular with anglers as are the region's lakes and reservoirs. (There is a special chapter devoted to the national parks.)

It is not surprising that a landscape so full of forests and streams is also frequently referred to as the country's lungs. The tree cover in the region is well above the national average. In fact, with the exception of the *Gyöngyös-Heves Region* and the *Borsod-Zemplén Levels* the tree cover is at least twice the national average. The wooded areas, which can be found in both rocky and steppe-like terrain, are mainly made up of oaks and beeches. With so many woods around farming doesn't play such an important role in the region, although there are some good soils in the lower-lying areas. In their industrial time the hills provided a livelihood for a large number of miners, as it was here that brown coal, basalt, andesite, limestone and iron ore were mined and quarried. Most of these industries have since fallen on hard times. Forestry and hunting have, however, managed to maintain their importance, and now play a significant role in the now burgeoning tourist industry. However, it is the region's other attractions, the horse-riding, the medicinal baths, the fishing and the local wines which are the real draws.

It is in Northern Hungary that you can find some of Hungary's most important wine-producing regions. A familiarity with Tokaj wines has of course been an important aspect of a fully rounded Oxbridge education for generations.

NORTHERN HUNGARIAN SPECIALITIES

Northern Hungary wouldn't be complete without tasting *Szomolya black cherries, Gyöngyös red gooseberries, Gönc apricots, Eger apples, Heves melons*. And it isn't only the locals who enjoy *Kassa black (gypsy) bacon, Szepes frankfurters*. Then there is *unleavened kalács* (a soft sweet bread), *Miskolc potato bread* and *miller's kalács*. For the adults there are the traditional tipples, *Rákóczi borpárlat (Tokaj brandy), Tokaj essence, cornel schnapps, Gönc apricot brandy, aszú marcbrandy*, and *cherry schnapps*. On special occasions you will find *Matyó kalács* and *Erdőhorvát pretzels* for sale at the markets. *Liptó cottage cheese* and *ewe-cheese* are not only delicious they are healthy as well! The same could be said for *Boldog peppers* and *Hatvan tomatoes*. And there are cooks who will only use *Golden Pheasant tomato purée*, and housewives who are extremely proud of their *rosehip jam*.

Eger Bull's Blood has been de rigueur at student parties since the early seventies at least. Wine producers around Gyöngyös and at the foot of the Bükk hills are currently working hard to win new devotees.

The region around the Northern Hills is the coldest in the country. The annual average temperature on the upper slopes of the hills is only around 6 degrees centigrade. The annual rainfall of between 600–800 mm is considerably higher than down on the Great Plain. On some peaks (for example around Kékestető or on the higher slopes of the Bükk) the climate is similar to the subalpine hills in the western part of the country.

Although Northern Hungary is not known primarily for its medicinal waters, there are nevertheless some spas worthy of note. The pick of the bunch are probably the Zsóry Baths just outside Mezőkövesd where the sulphurous waters are especially good for stomach problems, rheumatic complaints and gynaecological complications. The waters at nearby Bogács are similar in composition and have similar beneficial effects. The spa waters in Eger are good for locomotor problems, and the Salvus waters at Bükkszék are used in the treatment of stomach and rheumatic complaints. Real curiosities are the hot springs at Egerszalók and the carbon dioxide dry bath at Mátraderecske: the *Mofetta*. The waters at Parádfürdő are recommended for gynaecological problems, and the waters, if drunk, are good for stomach disorders.

Doctors recommend the waters of the Miskolctapolca cave bath for the treatment of inflammations and torn muscles. However, you don't have to be ill to enjoy what is a unique experience. Those suffering from respiratory problems are well advised to go up into the rarefied air of the Mátra. It is there you will find the *State Health Sanatorium* in Mátraháza. For decades the *Peace Cave* in Jósvafő has been used for treating asthma sufferers.

You only have to look up at the castle ruins perched high up in the hills, or see the medieval and the Baroque churches and the country houses to realise that this is a region with a rich and colourful history. It was down on the plains just to the south of Miskolc that the Tatar army defeated Béla IV. at the Battle of Muhi in 1241. The Hungarians then retreated up into the hills where they went about building a series of stone fortresses. György Szondi fought heroically, though ultimately unsuccessfully, against the Turks at Drégely Castle (you will be able to read more about Drégely in the chapter on the Budapest region), whilst in Eger, István Dobó managed to stop the Turks in their tracks. It was in Szerencs that István Bocskai was elected prince, and Zemplén County made up part of the Rákóczi family estate.

Whilst on the subject of famous personalities: the village of Monok near Szerencs was the birthplace of *Louis Kossuth*; *Gáspár Károli*, who translated the Bible into Hungarian, was a parish priest in Gönc; and *Imre Madách* and *Kálmán Mikszáth* were both from Nógrád County. The poet *Mihály Tompa* carried out his pastoral duties in the parish of Kelemér in what was then Gömör County, and the biologist *Ottó Herman* spent some of his life in the Miskolc region. These are but a few of the great figures who have local connections.

The *Matyó* and the *Palóc* groups brighten up the ethnographic palette of the Northern Hungarian region. Strictly speaking a Matyó is a member of the Catholic congregation living in a predominantly Protestant community, but nowadays the term is used only to describe those living in Mezőkövesd and in the neighbouring villages of Szentistván and Tard. Traditional Matyó folk art is characterised by the richness of the patterns used and the brightly coloured embroideries. Perhaps Matyó folk art's most famous practitioner was *Bori Kis Jankó* (1876–1954) around whom a cult of sorts has developed. Of the all the Matyó-related sites it is the *Matyó Museum* in Mezőkövesd, which gives the most detailed account of their way of life, their culture and their traditions.

In contrast to the Matyó people it is difficult to tie the Palóc group down to any particular geographical area. However, experts agree that Palóc culture tends to be found in the western part of Borsod County and in northern Heves County, but most frequently in Nógrád County. It is not so much their costumes which define the Palóc identity as the common elements which can be found in their language and their customs. For a more satisfactory account you should visit the *Palóc Museum* in Balassagyarmat.

The red tower with the Lorántffy loggia

Just to round off the introduction to this, the last region in our book, here is the route we will be taking through Northern Hungary in the pages which follow, starting from the east and working our way westwards.

The first stop is *Tokaj*, already featured in the *Hungarian Treasury* section, one of the most important, if not the most important town on the Hungarian wine map. From here we will be making our way through the famous vineyards as far as Szerencs,

The cellar visit is a popular tourist programme in these parts.

before exploring the *Taktaköz* and the *Bodrogzug*. Our next port of call will be the historical town of Sárospatak, from where we will be exploring the *Bodrogköz*, an area rich in sites connected with the Hungarian Conquest. We shall also be travelling through the beautiful landscapes of the *Hegyköz*, as well as visiting the castles and the villages of the western *Zemplén*. We will then move on to *Aggtelek* and its environs, and to the world-famous *Baradla Cave*. We will then go down the *Bódva Valley* as far as Miskolc, Northern Hungary's regional centre. We will of course drop in on Diósgyőr, Miskolc-Tapolca and Lillafüred before making brief tours of the *Bükk* and the *Cserehát*. We will explore the landscapes of the historical county of *Gömör* and the area around Ózd before travelling down to Mezőkövesd in *southern Borsod*, where the matyók live. This lies on the threshold of the *Bükkalja*, the rolling countryside lying between the Bükk and the Great Plain. Our next destination will be *Eger*, a town rich in historical monuments; Baroque art and architecture in particular. We also take in the surrounding villages with their medieval churches and castles (Bélapátfalva, Feldebrő, Kápolna, Tarnaszentmária, Sirok), and the natural beauties in and around Szilvásvárad, Felsőtárkány and Bükkszenterzsébet. Travelling further west we will go to Gyöngyös before ascending the *Mátra* in search of good walking country and sites of historic interest. Then it's down to Hatvan and the *Zagyva Valley*, and then up to the county town of Nógrád, Salgótarján; the *Medves Heights;* the *Cserhátalja* and the *Karancs Valley*. It is here we will visit the *World Heritage* village at Hollókő about which more can be found in the opening chapter.

The final destination is *Balassagyarmat*, from whence we go up into the valleys of the *Inner Cserhát*. To end with we go to Horpács, best known for its connections with the writer Kálmán Mikszáth before ending up finally in Romhány, scene of the last battle in the Rákóczi War for Freedom.

The River Ipoly as it flows past the village of Nógrádszakál.

Tokaj

In Rome it is Tokaj wine which fills the Pope's chalice during Mass. The Kings of Poland always celebrated with a glass of Tokaj, and the Russian tsars toasted their foreign dignitaries with wines from the Tokaj region. So, it would be true to say that Tokaj has a certain reputation. Tokaj aszú – *vinum regum, rex vinorum*, that is to say *the king of wines, the wine of kings* – has made the town one of the best-known in Hungary. Such fame has not surprisingly left its mark on the town.

Tokaj stands to the southeast of the *Great Hill*, where the Tisza meets the Bodrog. The **Tokaj Museum** (Bethlen Gábor u. 7.) tells you all you need to know about the history of the town. The building itself is interesting, having been built by the well-to-do Karácsony family in around 1790. The family was of Greek origin, and their house is richly decorated both inside and out. The interior is covered by some impressive wall paintings.

This is the hill, often mentioned by monarchs, which now enjoys World Heritage status.
At the present time Tokaj is among the 137 towns worldwide referred to as international grape and wine towns.

Looking at the old buildings in the middle of Tokaj you will come across a late-Baroque Calvinist church in Bem József utca, a Baroque Greek Catholic church in Vasvári utca and some fine 18th century town houses on Rákóczi utca, Bethlen utca, Vasvári utca and Hajdú köz.

At the museum apart from being able to see Béla Beres, the dean of Tokaj's collection of ecclesiastical art, you can see a permanent exhibition of texts in praise of Tokaj wine. The writers are as diverse as Anatole France and Sándor Petőfi, and include the words of the Hungarian national anthem which also makes reference to Tokaj's wines. Of the 500 types of grapes existing in the world about 139 can be found in the Tokaj-Hegyalja. 70 per cent of the vines on the plantations are Furmint, 28 Hárslevelű and 1-2 per cent Yellow Muscat. Down in the cellars you can see how wine should be stored and served.

The **Rákóczi-Dessewffy Palace** early 18th century was owned by the Rákóczi family before becoming the treasury's salt store, and then the property of the Dessewffy family. It is now used as a student hostel. Every summer the building hosts art camps, and in August it's the venue for the *Tokaj Writers' Workshop* (Bajcsy-Zsilinszky u. 19.).

The **synagogue** (Serház u.), built on the site of the old brewery, had only just been renovated when it fell victim to a mysterious fire, the effects of which

can still be seen. The Jewish cemetery can be found on the island lying between the Bodrog and the Tisza on the site of the old castle. There you can find 18th and 19th century Louis Seize, classical and romantic-style gravestones with their stone reliefs and their Hebrew inscriptions. The cemetery represents a microcosm of a once thriving community.

The cellars, the restaurants and the guesthouses under the Great Hill offer excellent cuisine as well as fine wines. On *the banks of the Tisza* there are plenty of opportunities to go boating, fishing or camping. Every summer, pleasure boats take passengers on day or half-day trips along the Bodrog and the Tisza.

The harvest parade on the final day of harvest week makes all the right references to the local wine customs and a day-long programme of folk music and dance at which the locals pay homage to Bacchus.

The third verse of the Hungarian National Anthem:
"You on Cuman fields have waved / Gold sheaves of our pleasure, / In the vineyards of Tokaj / Pour'd out nectar's treasure. / Often have you rear'd our flags / On wild Turkish towers; / Proud Vienna's fortress groan'd / Under Mátyás' powers."
(Ferenc Kölcsey – translation by Watson Kirkconnell)

FROM TOKAJ TO SZERENCS

TARCAL

This is one of the older villages lying at the foot of the Great Hill. Dating back to the Hungarian Conquest, Prince Árpád gave the land to a certain Turcol as a reward for winning a horse race. It was in Tarcal in 1100 that King Koloman held the national assembly at which it was decreed that *"because witches do not exist, no laws need apply to them."*

Most of the buildings in the town have a Rákóczi family connection, or are inextricably linked with the period immediately following the confiscation of their lands. It is in the Baroque **Rákóczi House** (Könyves Kálmán u. 52.) – currently the *Tokaj Chamber of Commerce* – that you can make your way into the *Rákóczi Cellars*. With the necessary permission it is possible to go on a guided tour of the cellars tasting some of the wines as you go.

Tarcal has all the atmosphere of small agricultural town. The Baroque **Roman Catholic church** (Templomköz) is built on firm medieval foundations and *Nagy Kopasz Hill* (512 m) is rich in geological and botanical curiosities.

The climatic conditions here are indeed the best in the region for growing grapes and producing wine. The huge wine cellar which lies next to the *Sárga Borház* restaurant on road 37 amounts to quite a spectacle: it belongs to one of the prestigious wine companies operating at the foot of the *Disznókő*.

From Tarcal it is possible to drive up as far as the **TV tower**. The tower affords a marvellous view of the nearby slopes and the Great Hungarian Plain. During the winter you can go up by ski lift.

Aszú grapes.
The dried grapes give tokaji its characteristic aroma, something you can read about in greater detail in the Hungarian Treasury.

Máᴅ's **Roman Catholic church** (Batthyány út) was originally Gothic. The old vicarage houses a **collection of minerals** and an exhibition devoted to grape-growing and the wine trade. *Lake Bor* is also a pleasant place to visit.

In what is one of the outposts of the Hegyalja you will find some fine examples of the kind of peasant architecture which was once widespread in Northern Hungary. Under these houses lie some substantial cellar systems, whose walls are covered with the moulds, which play such an important part in the maturation process.

The Hegyalja's largest Jewish cemetery (Táncsics út) lying on the edge of Mád is of great local importance. "You'll find him with the Mád Jew" is a common Hungarian saying, coming from a time when Jewish wine traders were a common sight on the highways and byways of Hungary. The idiom itself is something you would say when you have no idea where one particular person is.

TÁLLYA

The Rákóczi family had ties with Tállya. It is here you can find their one-time residence (Rákóczi u. 12.), the Baroque **Maillot Palace** (c. 1720), which is now used as a school, and the **Rákóczi Cellar** (Csokonai tér) which, together with its underground passages, covers an enormous area. The cellar was originally used to store all the Rákóczi estates' wines, but could also be used as a convenient hideout if necessary.

In Tállya you are also likely to see some traditional peasant houses.

The Baroque **Calvinist church** (Bocskai út) was enlarged in 1805. The substantial **Roman Catholic church** (Rákóczi út) dominating the immediate landscape is medieval in origin, and was vaulted in 1720. It is one of northeastern Hungary's most beautiful Baroque churches. Hungary's master recruitment musician *János Lavotta* (1764–1820) is buried in the churchyard.

It is interesting to note that during the 1990s geographers discovered that Tállya in fact marks the geographical centre of Europe. And not a lot of people know that.

The grape harvest on the Hegyalja is the most important event in the region's calendar. The different types of grapes are carefully sorted, thus providing the right ingredients for Tokaj's world-famous wines, which are also celebrated at Tállya on the Historical Wine Road.

ABAÚJSZÁNTÓ

Situated on the crossroads of the *Hernád Valley*, the *Zemplén Hills* and the *Hegyköz*, Abaújszántó was for many centuries an important port of call on the international trade route running along the Hernád Valley up towards Poland. It was particularly important for Tokaj's grape growers and wine traders. The village's strategic importance is well documented in the *Local History Collection* (Béke u. 42.) in what is known as the Ulánus or **Kapitány House**. According to tradition it got its name from a visit made by a group of Austrian troops at the beginning of the 19th century. Down in the cellar you will find a deep, dank well. Post-volcanic activity in the Zemplén Hills explains the presence of the hot mineral waters, which are known to come bubbling up to the surface. Abaújszántó is one such place. The waters fill the pools at the outdoor **swimming complex** and the **thermal baths**. (Fürdő-ház 1.). Nearby *Aranyos Valley* is a popular destination for a day out. If you are lucky you may see a few of the 19 or so protected species of birds, 10 of which are known to nest here.

MONOK

The **Kossuth Memorial Museum** (Kossuth u. 18.) is devoted to that part of the great politician's life immediately connected to the Zemplén.

"I was born in Monok, at the foot of Szerencs Hill, where according to legend Árpád first toasted the foundation of his nation. Turin 1890.II.12.."
This is how Louis Kossuth remembered his birthplace. The locals cherish his memory to this very day.

In the garden of **Andrássy Palace** (1750) standing on the side of the hill you will find a 2.5 metre-high bronze statue of the great Kossuth by the sculptor *Zsigmond Kisfaludi Strobl*. It was paid from donations made by the inhabitants of 171 villages.

The **Kossuth Bell** hanging in the belfry of the Calvinist church (1799) is further evidence of the undying respect the village has for its most famous son. In the Roman Catholic church (1814) you will find a relic of St Urban given to the church by Count Andrássy, who had brought it from the *Priscilla Catacombs* in Rome. He believed the relic would be capable of performing miracles, particularly when it came to protecting vines from frost and hailstones.

The oldest building in the village is the Monoky family's **fortified palace** dating from 14th century, with its Renaissance details and classical additions.

Apart from providing a venue for local events the Community House (Imre Makovecz) in Szerencs has proved popular with the tourists.

SZERENCS

According to the 13th century chronicler Anonymous, it was from Isten Hill that Árpád surveyed the landscape and was heard to say: *"Today God brings fortune to this land."* Local legend has it that the origins of the place names Mád, Szerencs and Tállya can be found in the Hungarian translation of Anonymous's Latin original: *"Ma ád Isten szerencsét a tájnak."* This perhaps tells us more about the local population's interest in word games than an interest in local history. The town's one-time role as a mercantile and military centre can still be seen in the curved arches of the town houses on the high street and the fortifications of the castle.

In the **Zemplén Museum,** which lies within the **castle,** you will find an exhibition outlining the *history of the picture postcard*: it is just part of a collection of 825 thousand postcards covering the period from the 1880s right up until the present day, made all the more interesting by 36 thousand *ex libris*. In the castle you can also find the *Castle Hotel* and the *Cultural Centre*. Visitors may catch the *Hegyalja Agricultural Show* during the first half of June and the *Zemplén Arts Festival* at the end of August.

However, to the vast majority of people Szerencs means simply sweets and chocolate. You can find out more at the *Szerencs Sugar Refinery* founded in 1889, and the *Chocolate Factory* of 1923, the latter of which has a **museum** (Gyár u. 1.).

THE TAKTAKÖZ

South of Szerencs, between road 37 and the River *Tisza*, the countryside opens up into a landscape full of lakes. Known as the *Taktaköz,* it is popular amongst anglers, hunters and the ornithologists.

The nature reserves around Lake Hódoslapos and Lake Ökör are rich in wildlife and small game.

The **Zsigmond Móricz Memorial House** (Móricz Zs. u. 8.) in PRÜGY, devoted to the life and work of the great Hungarian prose writer, is on the site of the house where the Móricz family lived between 1887 and 1891.

In TAKTABÁJ the **old Calvinist church** (1784) contains some rococo wall paintings.

NORTHWARDS ALONG THE BODROG

BODROGKERESZTÚR

The landscape is characterised by oxbow lakes, wide open plains, water meadows and riverside woodland.

The *River Bodrog* marks the border of the village as it bends around Tokaj Hill before joining the Tisza three kilometres downstream in Tokaj. The *Bodrogzug* flood plain, lying between the two rivers, also happens to be a nature reserve. Sailing down the Bodrog between Tokaj and Sárospatak is perhaps the best way to see the surrounding countryside.

Participants of the photographic workshop at the quarry in Bodrogkeresztúr.

Harvest at Olaszliszka

As you approach Bodrogkeresztúr you can see, perched high up on the crest of a hill, the late Baroque **Greek Catholic church** (1762), which was built by the local Greek wine traders. The village's **Roman Catholic church** (Felső út) was built at the turn of the 16th century.

> *The pearlite formations lying between Bodrogkeresztúr and Tokaj deserve close inspection: from the base of the almost vertical greyish wall you can find shining pieces of black obsidian (a mineral of volcanic origin). If you are lucky you might be able to find a lump 2-3 cm in diameter.*

OLASZLISZKA's name ("Olasz" is the Hungarian for Italian) probably comes from the 13th century when Italian grape-growers were invited to settle here. The village's 14th century **Roman Catholic church** (Szent István út) is worth seeing despite having been given the full Baroque treatment.

It was in TOLCSVA, on the lower slopes of the Zemplén Hills that the wine producers built their residences. **Szirmay Palace** (Kossuth u. 37.), with its accompanying park, is now used as a primary school. The **Dessewffy Palace** (Szent Imre u. 4.) is now occupied by the *Hegyalja Forestry Commission.* The *Royal Court,* otherwise known as *Rákóczi Palace* (Kossuth u. 63.), now houses the **Wine Museum**. Built for Zsuzsanna Lórántffy, György Rákóczi's widow, the building still manages to conjure up the beauty of 17th century Tolcsva.

The palatial Waldbott Wine House served one of the most important grape-growing and wine producing centres in the region. Built on the highest point of the *Kincsem Vineyard* during the 19th century, the tavern can be seen for miles around. It is now owned by the *Oremus Company.*

Like Olaszliszka, BODROGOLASZI gets its name from the period immediately following the Tatar invasion (1241), when Béla IV. settled the area with Italian *grape-growers.*

The **Roman Catholic church** (Fő út) was already standing on its outcrop overlooking the River Bodrog by the time the Italians arrived.

Situated on the edge of the Bodrogköz, on the banks of the River Bodrog, the fortified palace at Sárospatak was ideally placed. It was between 1534 and 1542, whilst in the hands of Péter Perényi, that the building acquired its predominantly fortified character.

SÁROSPATAK

The golden age of Sárospatak, *Athens of the Bodrog*, coincided with that of the Rákóczi family. The **castle**, which is more a palace than a fortress, is one of the most important Gothic and Renaissance buildings in Hungary.

In 1616, the Rákóczi family acquired the palace as part of Zsuzsanna Lorántffy's will. Subsequently floors were added to the eastern and southern wings of the palace followed by the construction of the **Lorántffy loggia** in 1647, the most attractive architectural feature in the courtyard.

Zsuzsanna Lorántffy's will of 1659 states: *"I leave Sárospatak to the whole of the Hungarian nobility"*. It is therefore apt that one should now find the **Rákóczi Museum** (Szent Erzsébet u. 19.) within its walls. The museum occupies the first floor of the Perényi Wing and the northern wing of the palace, which is dedicated to Rákóczi and the War for Freedom.

The Sub Rosa Balcony Room, which is in the exhibition area, has a ceiling which contains the only remaining Baroque wall paintings in the whole building. It is however for one particular historical event that the room is famous. It was here "under the roses" that the secret negotiations led by Ferenc Rákóczi I. were made prior to the Wesselényi conspiracy.

It was in 1694 that Ferenc Rákóczi gave a **monastery** lying within the outer castle to the Trinitarians. The church now functions as a concert hall, music school and exhibition venue known as the *Muses' Church.*

The tower of the Roman Catholic church looks onto János Andrássy Kurta's equestrian statue.

On the main axis of the street stands one of the largest **hall-churches** in Northern Hungary (14th–16th century). The Baroque altar and the most beautiful pieces of liturgical furniture all came from the Carmelite Church in Buda Castle. In front of the church you can see the outlines of a **round Romanesque church** marked in the pavement. Outside the entrance to the church is a statue of Saint Elizabeth of Thuringia (*Imre Varga*) who, according to legend, was born here.

The **Calvinist College**, established during the 16th century, has played an important role in the cultural history of the town. The College was closed down in 1952 only to re-appear as Sárospatak's Calvinist Grammar School in 1990. The Calvinist Theological Academy resumed its activities in 1991.

The Great Library dates from the foundation of the Calvinist College (Rákóczi u. 1.) in 1531. By the 1980s the library had a collection numbering 300 thousand volumes. The library can be found in the southern wing of the college (Mihály Pollack)built in 1834.

The exhibition at the Calvinist College covers the history of the school, with an exhibition of objects relating to the everyday life at the college. There is also a display devoted to the great Bohemian pedagogue Comenius (Jan A. Komensky) (1592–1670), who spent four years teaching in Sárospatak. It was here he wrote his book on demonstrative education: Orbis sensualium pictus.

The Cultural Centre (Eötvös utca 11.) is perhaps the finest of Imre Makovecz's buildings in Sárospatak. In the square in front of the main entrance there are two sculptures by László Péterffy on ancient Hungarian themes.

Every August, the centre, together with the *Franz Liszt Chamber Orchestra Foundation*, organises the series of cultural events known as the *Zemplén Arts Festival*. Performances are held both at the centre and in many of the villages situated between Sárospatak and Szerencs.

Crossing the bridge over the Bodrog we come to *Kispatak*, whose outdoor swimming complex, camping site, restaurants and quay make it a popular place to relax.

On the dead channels alongside the Bodrog you will find a number of fishing villages. Kispatak has quite a colony of famous potters and gingerbread makers.

The only thermal baths in the vicinity are those at the **Végardó Outdoor Swimming Complex** on the road going out towards Sátoraljaújhely.

The best places for walking are amongst the region's vineyards and by *the lake on Megyer Hill. Longi Wood* is a good place to go in search of rare wild flowers.

Sárospatak is the starting point for the **Rákóczi Tourist Walk,** which heads out towards the southern and western slopes of the Zemplén Hills going as far as *Füzér Castle*.

THE BODROGKÖZ

The *Bodrogköz* still has its medieval network of villages. On the edge of KAROS, a **cemetery,** dating from the Hungarian Conquest and including the grave of Prince Árpád's chieftains, was excavated recently. In nearby KISROZVÁGY is a **copy of a village** dating from the conquest.

At the parish church in KARCSA the brick-built rotunda is 11th–12th century whilst the nave dates from the 12th–13th century.

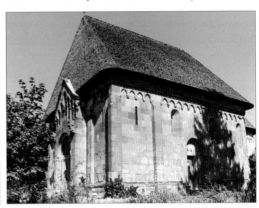

Boating along the Bodrog between Sárospatak and Tokaj is quite an experience.

The church at Karcsa has been the subject of many a tale, the most famous one suggesting that the church was built by fairies. Another tale focuses on the bell. It goes something like this: the fairies were taking the bell across the Karcsa when, on hearing the cock crow, they were forced to drop the bell into the water. Since then the bell has tolled every one hundred years just to remind people of its whereabouts.

PÁCIN, lying right on the Hungarian-Slovakian border, is the jewel in the Bodrogköz's crown. **Mágóchy Palace** is the only place in the whole of Hungary capable of giving a near-authentic picture of a late-Renaissance palace building. It proves also that art continued to be produced during the conflicts against the Turks and the Habsburgs. It is here that you can visit the **Bodrogköz Palace Museum**, which has one exhibition outlining the history of the building, and one concentrating on the region's folk art.

One of the wealthiest aristocrats of his day, Gáspár Mágóchy, built the palace at Pácin. The building was already standing amongst the marshes of the Bodrogköz in 1581.

SÁTORALJAÚJHELY AND BEYOND

SÁTORALJAÚJHELY

It is the **statue of Louis Kossuth** that has become the symbol of Zemplén County's largest town. It is surrounded by the buildings, public statues, squares and cellars which shot up all over the town and the surrounding hillsides during the course of the last few centuries. It was from the balcony of the town hall, then the county hall, that the young Louis Kossuth gave his first public address in 1831.

It is the beautifully maintained parks as well as the buildings of this ex county town which give Sátoraljaújhely its special atmosphere.

The so-called *Barátszer* got its name from the "white friars" of the Pauline Order. The **monastery**, which later became the student residences for the Piarist Order, still has the remains of some early Baroque wall paintings on the southern facade. The refectory ceiling is covered in richly painted stucco and the Baroque furniture is also worthy of note.

The nearby 14th century church with its beautiful wooden tower is now the municipal museum, which contains the first *mechanical clock* in Hungary. The clock-face itself was made in 1501. The **Kazinczy Museum**, which has an exhibition outlining the history of the town and the county of Zemplén, can be found in one of the town's most beautiful buildings (Dózsa György út 11.). During the Age of Reform it was here that the

Zemplén Casino Society met, an institution attended by many of the period's great figures, *István Széchenyi, Louis Kossuth* and *Sándor Petőfi* to name but a few.

Sátoraljaújhely is famous for its wine cellars, and it is the only town which has a church actually built in wine's honour. The wine church, which bears the town's coat of arms, stands next to the railway station on top of one of the town's most substantial cellars.

The old **Jewish cemetery,** standing opposite the railway station, is one of the most important Jewish pilgrimage places in Hungary. It was here that Rabbi *Mózes Teitelbaum,* the worker of miracles, was buried. Legend has it that the wonder-working rabbi also cured the young Louis Kossuth.

The tomb of the miraculous rabbi, Sátoraljaújhely

Leaving the main square along the *Zsólyom* you come to the 14 **Stations of the Cross** ascending *Szár Hill (Kopaszka),* which was laid out in 1936. A road leads out to *Magas Hill* (514 m), a very popular place amongst winter sports enthusiasts. From the lookout point there is an excellent view of the *Hegyköz,* the Slovakian *Bodrogköz* and **Bors Castle,** Ferenc Rákóczi II.'s birthplace.

If calculated in the time it takes to get up, the **chair-lift** (1332m) up Magas Hill is the longest in the country. In the winter it's used by skiers and in the summer by those simply wanting to enjoy the view from the top.

SZÉPHALOM *is a pilgrimage place for those wishing to pay their respects to Ferenc Kazinczy (1759-1831) the reformer of the Hungarian language. The writer lived here for many decades, during which time the place became something of a spiritual centre. Visitors usually head for the Memorial Hall (1862, Miklós Ybl), which stands in the gardens of Széphalom Hall.*

FÜZÉRRADVÁNY is already considered part of the *Hegyköz.* Having driven through the Scotch and Austrian pines you come to **Károlyi Palace** (1857–1859, *Miklós Ybl*). The hundred hectares of parkland, which has some enormous plane trees, and the ground floor of the southern wing of the palace, which contains the *palace museum,* are open to the general public.

It was in FÜZÉR in 1526, following the coronation of *John Szapolyai,* that the Hungarian crown was kept in safekeeping. The castle has been given a new lease of life by the *national castle reconstruction programme.*

The justly renowned Hollóháza porcelain

HOLLÓHÁZA is Hungary's northernmost settlement. Although picturesque, it is more famous for its porcelain, something you can find out more about at the **Porcelain Museum** (Károlyi u. 11.). Those who want a stamp to mark either the completion of the *National Blue Walk*, which ends (or begins!) at the **monument** in the middle of the village, or an ascent of *Nagy-Milic,* should knock at the door of the official rubber stamper at the entrance to the factory.

KÉKED is a popular tourist destination situated on the western slopes of the *Zemplén Hills.* The 500 hundred year-old Gothic **Melczer Palace** (Fő út) lies within a seven-hectare park. Now enjoying a new lease of life as a hotel, it offers a wide variety of services to its guests.

TELKIBÁNYA was once famous for its gold and silver mines. Nowadays it is the countryside which attracts visitors. There is however a **Mining Museum** (Museum u. 34.) dedicated to the village's illustrious mining past. The village was once known as *"gold-buttoned Telkibánya"* and, according to local legend, in its heyday the onion-shaped dome of the tower was covered in gold. During excavations at the 14th century church and the medieval hospital on church hill, enough of the original chancel and the **Chapel of St Catherine** have been uncovered to give us at least an idea of the buildings' original appearance.

Moving southwards along the western side of the hills you come to the village of GÖNC. Here in the *Hussite House* (Kossuth u. 103.), which now serves as a **peasant cottage** open to the general public, you can see, amongst many other things, the measuring units which were once known throughout Europe, as well as the 136.7-litre *Gönc barrel,* which was used both for storing wines and making aszú.

One of the only surviving copies of the original publication of the Hungarian Bible can be found at the Calvinist Church in VIZSOLY*, the village where it was printed.*

The writer of the Hungarian translation of the Bible (1586–1590), *Gáspár Károli,* was the Calvinist minister at what is now the church in Szent István tér. GÖNCRUSZKA has a Romanesque **Calvinist church** (Kazinczy u.) with 14th century and 18th century additions.

HEJCE is an atmospheric little village lying a little off the beaten track. It is from here that you can start your ascent to REGÉC **castle**, which lies on top of a 624-metre-high rocky outcrop. It is here also that you can join up with *National Blue Walk* and the red markings of the *Rákóczi Walk.*

Technically Regéc Castle is considered to be a hill fortress with an irregular groundplan and an inner tower. Regéc's golden age coincided with that of the Rákóczi era. It was here that Ferenc Rákóczi I.'s widow Ilona Zsínyi brought up their son until the age of five. The castle was later to suffer the wrath of the Habsburgs following the Rákóczi Wars for Freedom led by Ferenc Rákóczi II. The furniture which survived from the castle can be seen at the Castle Museum in Sárospatak.

From the ruins of Regéc Castle it is possible to wonder at the beauty of the surrounding Zemplén countryside.

Known as the "reclining lion", Boldogkő Castle also has an historical exhibition which can be found in the residential wing of the fortress.

BOLDOGKŐVÁRALJA, situated at the foot of the picturesque **Boldogkő Castle**, marks the last stop on our tour of the Zemplén. The village has a restored **peasant cottage** containing an **exhibition** devoted to the history of the village and the natural history of the Zemplén. **Péchy-Zichy Palace** (Kossuth u. 2.) is surrounded by a six-hectare garden.

On the edge of BOLDOGKŐÚJFALU lies a rocky geological feature the locals call Doberdó.
On the western slopes of Nagy-Korsós Hill you will find a block of andesite 200-300 m long and one metre in diameter, which was broken up during the Ice Age.

AGGTELEK, JÓSVAFŐ

It is on the Hungarian section of the *Gömör-Tornai karst bed* that you can find the *Aggtelek National Park* (See the relevant sections on the *National Parks* and the *World Heritage Sites*.). What you can see is made from 220 million-year-old Triassic limestone. The rock faces and the lush valleys each have their own individual microclimates. Of the 273 Aggtelek-Karst caves 23 are strictly protected. The most spectacular is the *Baradla*, first mentioned in dated 1594. 25.5 km in length it is the largest cave system in Central Europe. 5.3 km of the caves are in Slovakia. For those interested in outdoor pursuits there are plenty of opportunities to go cycling, riding and fishing. For the ornithologists amongst you there are 130 species of birds to look out for, one of them being the imperial eagle. In the valleys there are several single-street villages which have managed to keep their medieval layouts. For example AGGTELEK, JÓSVAFŐ, which provide the area's touristic centres, and SZINPETRI, and travelling south from Jósvafő, down in the Galyaság, you will find TE-RESZTENYE, ÉGER-SZÖG, SZŐLŐSAR-DÓ and VARBÓC, all of which offer good tourist accommodation.

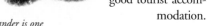

The salamander is one of the area's rarer inhabitants.

On the edge of the village, taking the road towards Slovakia, you come to the enormous cliff face marking the entrance to the *Baradla Cave*. The cliff itself is used for rock climbing competitions. The cave is particularly beautiful when the stream is actually flowing through it. The weird rock formations in the subterranean chambers conjure up a fairytale world. The Canadian geologist, Lloyd Trevor said of the cave system, that of all the places he had visited in Europe during his travels, the Aggtelek Caves left the deepest and most lasting impression. Indeed, he was prepared to rate them alongside the Grand Canyon, the Niagara Falls and Yellowstone Park in geological import-

The St Ladislas column in the Baradla cave. The concerts which are held down there have acquired quite a reputation.

ance. You don't have to be an expert, however, to enjoy the crystaline forms, the colour effects created by the stalagmites, stalactites and the huge subterranean vistas.

The Jósvafő part of the caves has been closed since the beginning of 2004, which means that hikers will have to postpone a certain number of tours (Lake Vörös, Jósvafő, Retek-ág) for the time being. Walkers who have, been out can retire to the town for a decent meal and a glass of wine.

If you travel five kilometres along the winding road in a northeastly direction, you come to Jósvafő, passing the *Red Lake (Vörös-tó)* entrance to the caves on the way.

Part of the so-called *Szakál Manor* (1890) has been preserved in its original condition allowing visitors to see how people once lived in the village. Behind the manor there is a small botanical garden full of local flowers. (Visitors should book in advance: Rákóczi u. 1.).

On the hillside you can see the *Tengerszem Hotel*, under which there is a very pleasant restaurant.

It is also through the Jósvafő entrance that you can reach the **Cave Sanatorium**, which has offered treatment to asthma sufferers since 1967.

Jósvafő church lying in the Jósvafő Valley has a painted coffered ceiling.

With permission it is also possible to visit the **Imre Vass Cave.** From the *Tengerszem Hotel* you can take a pleasant walk up to the *Jósva Spring*, the **Lower Cave** and to the pride of Jósvafő, the hill lake, the **Tengerszem**.

Not far from Jósvafő, on the pastures of the Gergésláp, you can see the Hucul Stud Farm. If organised in advance it is possible to go horse-riding or travelling by coach and horses.
A few kilometres further on you come to SZELCEPUSZTA *a place popular with the hunting community.*

EXPLORING THE ESZTRAMOS

On the edge of SZÖGLIGET high above the *Ménes Valley* on top of a 450m cliff you can see ruins of **Szád Castle**. The castle was probably built by Béla IV. after the Tatar invasion to defend the Bódva Valley. The imperial forces blew the castle up following the crushing of the Rákóczi Rebellion. From the ruins you get a good view of *Aggtelek* and the *Bódva Valley*.

Pheasants' eye, one of the region's protected plants

BÓDVASZILAS is famous for its **Meteor Cave** lying 420 metres up on the side of *Alsó Hill*. The *Titanic Chamber* is the best part of a cave system, which meanders under the earth's surface for several kilometres. The snow-white stalagmites and stalactites gracing the 100-metre-long cavern, one of the largest in Hungary, create an impression of something resembling a jungle. It is only open to researchers and experts.

Hadik Palace (Kossuth u. 1.) makes TORNANÁ-DASKA, situated out on the Slovak border, worth visiting. The medieval palace was continually enlarged and remodelled during the course of the 18th and 19th centuries. The stately home is set in seven hectares of parkland.

> *In such rocky terrain it was only by transporting soil by train from far-away Bácska over a number of years that János Hadik was able to create the necessary environment for his garden. Since 1890 over 200 foreign plants have been planted there.*

In TORNASZENTANDRÁS the **Catholic church** with its two chancels sits particularly well in its surroundings. Inside there are the remains of some medieval wall paintings and an altar, which originally came from the chapel at *Szád Castle*. Some believe that the church was built by one of the architects in the entourage of Gertrude of Andechs-Meran (c. 1184–1213), wife of Andrew II., on account of the church's double chancel arrangement.

> *Esztramos Hill, which originally stood 380m above sea level, suffered the indignity of being reduced 50m in height during the course of a mining history, which came to an end during the 1950s. Originally it was the botanists who took an interest in the hill and its unique flora. This was, however, before the caves were discovered. Although most of the caves were blown up, we are fortunate still to have the Rákóczi, the Földvári and the Surrantós Caves. Those wishing to visit the particularly spectacular Rákóczi Cave, with what is an amazing variety of stalagmites and stalactites, can only do so as part of a pre-organised group visit. You also have to be prepared when it comes to clothing, hiking gear being the required dress.*

On leaving Jósvafő the first place to keep an eye out for is PERKUPA, where the Baroque, Louis Seize and classical-style peasant houses on Petőfi utca are quite a spectacle.

The **Calvinist church** and its accompanying **bell tower** (1765), which is indeed a rare sight in these parts, make SZALONNA a village of outstanding art historical importance. The Romanesque church contains a painted and richly decorated 18th century pulpit, considered to be the finest in the region.

The square nave of Szalonna church was added to the Romanesque rotunda during the 13th century. It was also at this time that the wall painting in the chancel was painted. Master András, a painter born in the Zips region of present-day Slovakia painted the prophets and the Agnus Dei around the chancel arch at the beginning of the 15th century.

It is only one and a half kilometres from Szalonna that the Rakaca appears from out of the ground. The stream runs down to Hungary's largest reservoir before flowing into the River Bódva. Known as Lake Rakaca it has become a popular tourist resort.

It is from *Lake Rakaca* that you can reach MARTONYI to the northwest of which, hidden in a wood, are the ruins of the **Három-hegyi Pauline Monastery**. The surviving 14th century walls and chancel are currently undergoing restoration work. Proceeding along road number 27 you come to SZENDRŐ, whose ruined castle was once a bastion against the Turks. Its walls were used to build the

Calvinist bell tower (Hősök tere 15.) and the **Blue Dyers' House** (Petőfi tér 5.). The latter contains an exhibition dedicated to the art of dying and a display about the medieval castle and the history of the village.

In RUDABÁNYA, one-time centre of the local iron industry, you will find the three-aisled Calvinist church (14th-15th centuries), containing some excellent Late Medieval wall paintings, and the Mining Museum (Petőfi u. 24.). Apart from objects relating to the local mining industry, there is also a display of local prehistoric finds, amongst them a copy of the scull of Rudabánya's very own 10-12 million-year-old man (Rudapithecus hungaricus).

EDELÉNY

According to the 13th century chronicler Anonymous, it was here that a chieftain by the name of Bors built an earthwork, now known as **Borsod Castle**, during the Hungarian Conquest. The fortress was strengthened during the reign of Saint Stephen, when it became the county's administrative centre. The reconstructed ramparts and the outline of the deanery church in the inner bailey can now clearly be seen. Next to the earthworks is the *Bódva Valley* **Outdoor Museum** (Borsodi út 155.) with its farmhouses, outbuildings and working implements. The **peasant cottage** contains the *Kachelmann Textile Collection* and the *Hodossy Bell and Hook Collection*, as well as a permanent exhibition about *Borsod Castle*.

It was during the 19th century when Edelény come under the control of the Coburgs, that the town became a regional economic centre. **L'Hullier-Coburg Palace** (1727–1730), with its 106 rooms and 365 windows, is a splendid marriage of the Baroque and rococo styles. Although conservation work is currently taking place, the building may be visited by the general public..

Edelény Palace is waiting for repairs and a suitable owner.

BOLDVA

Situated on the left bank of the *River Bódva* this ancient Hungarian settlement was a market town before becoming part of the queen's Diósgyőr estate during the 14th century. Although the 12th century **Benedictine Monastery** was destroyed during the Tatar invasion, the church building was subsequently rebuilt and enlarged in the Gothic style. During archaeological investigations the northern part of the monastery was uncovered, whilst on the southern side of the site a rotunda, 12m in diameter, was found.

It was in Boldva in about 1200 that the first surviving piece of Hungarian was written, the *Funeral Oration,* which was found in the pages of the *Pray Codex.*

The Borsod region is rich in shepherding traditions.

View of Diósgyőr Castle with the suburb of Diósgyőr in the background

MISKOLC

Miskolc is situated where the *Szinva* runs off the Bükk into the *River Sajó*. While there are some hills immediately to the west, the eastern and southeastern parts of the town stretch out onto the plain. What is now the most important town in Northern Hungary has always benefited from its proximity to important local trade routes. It was this which initially made Miskolc a lively market town. Miskolc has a rich cultural heritage, something which becomes apparent when you walk down the high street from the Ady Bridge down to the Town Hall.

There is a succession of fine eclectic-style buildings on Széchenyi utca between the "electric police-man" and the theatre which, on a sunny day, make the street one of Hungary's great boulevards.

The crossroads between Széchenyi and Kazinczy utca has been known for decades as the "electric policeman". The explanation is very simple: it was here that Miskolc's first, and for a long time only, traffic light stood.

Opened in 1823, the **Miskolc National Theatre** was the first stone-built theatre built for a theatrical company performing in Hungarian. Since then the building has been renovated and enlarged. Nearby you can find the exhibitions of the **Museum of Theatrical History** (Déryné u. 3.)

At the **Sötétkapu** at the end of Rákóczi utca you will find a tablet on the wall of the Dőry- or Rákóczi House telling you that *Imre Thököly* and *Ferenc Rákóczi II.* stayed there.

Since its renovation the Miskolc Gallery in Rákóczi House has hosted the National Graphics Biennial (since 1961) and the Winter Exhibition (since 1970).

One wing of **Rákóczi House** is devoted to the work of painter and graphic artist *Béla Kondor* (1931–1972). **Petró House** (Hunyadi u. 12.) has an exhibition of drawings by the painter and graphic artist *Lajos Szalay* (1909–1995) and a permanent exhibition of works by *Gyula Feledy* (1928-) also belonging to the Gallery (Deák tér 3.).

In Miskolc's most beautiful square stands the earliest life-sized public statue of Louis Kossuth (József Róna). Here, opposite the Erzsébet Baths, stands the building of the Miskolc Academic Committee (Erzsébet tér 3.) which regularly hosts events of cultural and scientific interest.

Városház tér outside **County Hall** (1836) and the **Town Hall,** buildings containing both classical and Romantic elements, is dominated by *Miklós Melocco*'s curious *statue of István Széchenyi.*

Opposite the Széchenyi statue (illustrated below) the flower clock points you towards Dísz tér where a statue of Saint Stephen (Zsolt Jószay) has recently been put up.

In the town's administrative centre stands the *György Fráter Catholic Grammar School* (Városház tér 6., 1760), which once functioned as the Sisters of Mercy **nunnery and teacher training college**. Continuing along Széchenyi utca as far as **Luther Court** you will find the late-Baroque Lutheran church (1797, Hunyadi u. 8.) containing *Bertalan Székely*'s altarpiece *Jesus on the Mount of Olives.*

Together, the Avas Calvinist Church and its separate bell tower (1557) constitute one of Miskolc's more enduring symbols. It was during the 13th century that building started on the Gothic hall-church. The bell tower chimes every quarter above the oldest graves of the Avas cemetery. The coffin-shaped tombstones date back to the 16th and 17th centuries.

The *Avas* is most famous for its **wine cellars**. The memorial tablet (Középsor 648.) on the *Great Avas* states that it was here that the writer *Ferenc Móra* (1879–1934) enjoyed his last moments of peace and contentment. The stairs passing close by the church lead up to the **Avas lookout point**. The building in *Papszer,* where you will find the **Ottó Herman Museum,** was probably built on 15th century foundations. For many centuries it was the Avas Calvinist Church school. A *statue of Ottó Herman* (*Ferenc Medgyessy*) guards the entrance, whilst inside, apart from a number of exhibitions of local interest, you will find a small, but excellent collection of paintings. Covering Hungarian art over the last two hundred years, there are some fine works by *Pál Szinyei Merse* (1845–1920), *Károly Ferenczy* (1862–1917), *János Kmetty* (1889–1975) and *Gyula Derkovits* (1894–1938) to name but a few.

One of the rare objects you can find at the Hungarian Orthodox Ecclesiastical Museum and the Greek Orthodox Church in Deák tér is the devotional picture of the Black Virgin Mary of Kazán, which Empress Catherine II gave to the Orthodox Church. The 16-metre-high iconostasis contains 88 panel paintings.

The **Minorite Church and Monastery** is an impressive Baroque ensemble (Hősök tere). Up above Petőfi tér you will find the **cemetery** of the wooden church. A wooden church has stood on the site since 1698. The Transylvanian-style timber **Calvinist church** built here in 1938 fell victim to an arson attack in 1997, but was soon rebuilt thanks to the generous contributions of the general public.

In the square of the same name you will find **All Saints**, a single-aisled Baroque church built following the departure of the Turks'. It contains altar paintings by *Mihály Kovács* (1819–1892). In front of the vicarage you can find a statue of **Mary Holding a Vessel,** which is somewhat dwarfed by the neighbouring *International Trade Centre* and the *Rónai Cultural Centre*. Continuing along from the square one comes to the **House of Science and Technology**, the *County Library* and the *Sports Centre*.

The university at the *University Campus* is 250 years old if one includes its previous history elsewhere. The largest provincial university library, the *Central Library* contains the **Selmec Library**, which belonged to the "Berg Akademie" founded in Selmecbánya (Banská Štiavnica in Slovakia) in 1735, one of the forerunners of the present university in Miskolc. The library contains 30 thousand volumes, some of which are real rarities, in the fields of technology and natural history.

The university's ceremonial hall, which contains a rather intrusive porcelain (Hollóháza) frieze by Endre Szász, is used for classical concerts and exhibitions (the International Mineral Exchange and the MicroCad Computer Exhibition), which draw many hundreds of visitors.

The **swimming complex** at MISKOLCTAPOLCA is set in the wooded surroundings of a central park with a pleasant duck pond.

Whilst the outdoor swimming pool is only open during the summer months, Miskolctapolca's unique cave pools are open to visitors all the year round. The pools have also recently benefitted greatly from extensions and renovation work. You can also go boating on the nearby pond.

The ruins of the fortified medieval palace, or castle in DIÓSGYŐR is the most-visited site in Miskolc. You approach the castle up an avenue of mature horse chestnut trees.

A castle was built on the site by the Bors clan during the 13th century. Having being destroyed during the Tatar invasion (1241) Diósgyőr Castle was subsequently rebuilt, coming into the possession of Louis the Great in 1346. His fortified palace is made immediately recognisable by its four corner towers. It was here in 1381 that a peace agreement was signed with the Venetian Republic. Up until 1526 the castle served as the queen's provincial residence. Once the building ceased to be used as a royal residence the castle fell into a state of disrepair until 1678, when it was blown up.

Excavations at the castle started during the 1950s, and with the reconstruction work, which has been going on since 1999, the castle is gradually turning into something like a living museum. The castle history museum has recently been updated, and there is a **waxworks** *(Miklós Köllő)* recreating the spirit of the age of chivalry.

The superb acoustics of the courtyard at Diósgyőr Castle means that it is used for some of the outdoor events making up the Miskolc Summer Festival, like for example, Children's Day, the Diósgyőr Castle Tournament, the Borsod Spinning Festival, the Kaláka International Folk Festival, and the International Dixieland Convention. All in all it's an extremely busy place.

The windy road that goes up into the Bükk Hills takes you to LILLAFÜRED. From Miskolc you can also get to Lillafüred by bus (number 5), which takes you as far as *Lake Hámori*, or on the Lilla-füred **narrow-gauge railway**. By the time you reach the extensive woodland great limestone rock faces are rising to either side of the road. On the top of *Molnár Rock* is a cross dedicated to the tragic love affair between a young miller and the old miller's daughter.

On the other side of the valley it's worth taking a look at the **Metallurgy Museum** (Palota u. 54.) at *Felső-Hámor*. It is from the prehistoric remains found in the *Szeleta Cave* that the *Szeleta Culture* got its name.

The Palace Hotel (1927-1930, Kálmán Lux) is a romantic interpretation of a hunting lodge time from the reign of Matthias Corvinus, with a few extra details thrown in for good measure. In the Matthias Room you can enjoy the hotel's gastronomic specialities whilst looking through some fine stained glass windows.

It was in Lillafüred in 1933 during a writers' conference that Attila József wrote what is considered to be one of the world's finest love poems, his "Ode". – "I look upon the mountain's mane / each leaf reflects / the light of your face."

(Translation by John Bátki)

It is a picturesque landscape which includes a 17,5 metre waterfall and the Saint Anna Cave.

The entrance to the **István Cave** can be found 500 metres further up from the Palace Hotel. The half-hour tour takes you past some fine stalactites and stalagmites. If you want to stay longer you can take advantage of the cave's dustless air and take a cave cure.

THE ROMANTIC BÜKK

The imperial eagle is one the Bükk's protected species.

Man's relationship with the *Bükk Hills* can be traced back over ten thousand years. It is primarily thanks to Ottó Herman's investigations of the local **caves** that we can say this with any certainty. Since 1905, between 40 and 45 sites have been examined, with finds being uncovered primarily at the *Szeleta, Ottó Herman, Balla, Subalyuk, Kőlyuk, Peskő* and *Istállos-kő* Caves. (For further information about the *Bükk National Park* read the first chapter of the book).

BÁNKÚT, *the Bükk Hills' winter tourist and sports centre, offers brand-new accommodation possibilities as well as ski slopes, cross-country skiing loops and taboggan runs all maintained with the most up-to-date equipment.*

the country. In the nearby **Massa Museum** you can trace the history of Diósgyőr's iron industry.

It was in ÓMASSA that *Henrik Fazola's* original **foundry** operated (1772–1814). Moving north of the village you come to the 14th century ruins of the *Szentlélek* **Pauline monastery**. By following the simple red path markings, and then the red triangles you can make your way all the way to *Örvény-kő*, and the **Jókai Lookout Point**.

BÜKKSZENTKERESZT is one of Hungary's highest-lying **holiday village**s (600m). Its clean, healthy air makes it a *subalpine health spa*. The village makes a good starting point for hikes up into the hills, whilst in the winter it's a popular winter sports resort.

There is a **peasant house** there full of glass from the old Bükk glassworks. In HOLLÓSTETŐ you can settle down to a good meal at the *Hollóstető Inn*. At RÉPÁSHUTA there is a **peasant house** showing how life was once lived in this Slovak village lying at the heart of the Bükk. It is near here that you will find *Balla Cave*, one of those already examined by the archaeologists. When exploring the Bükk you invariably come across the lime and the charcoal burners.

Leaving *Lake Hámori* along its northern side it is not long before you reach the ÚJMASSA iron furnace. You can even get there by **narrow-gauge railway**. *Frigyes Fazola's* **iron furnace** (1810) is the only piece of industrial archaeology of its type in

The Csipkéskút Stud Farm can easily be incorporated into a tour of the Bükk Hills.

Down by the Quarries

The waters of the old MÁLYI **gravel pit** are a popular summer destination for the residents of Miskolc. It hosts underwater diving competitions, and it is also good for sailing and windsurfing. A few kilometres further out, in NYÉKLÁDHÁZA, a summer leisure park has developed around *Lake Öreg* and *Lake István*. *Lake Debrecen*, however, is strictly for naturists.

HEJŐKERESZTÚR is where you should head for if you are interested in water sports. The series of old gravel pit **lakes** down by the *River Hejő* are excellent for sailing, rowing or canoeing, windsurfing, water-skiing, fishing and snorkelling.

> *It was in the winter of 1991 that Jacques Cousteau visited the lakes at Hejőkeresztúr with his divers. They were able to testify to the cleanliness of the water and the presence of large shoals of fishes.*

On the edge of the village of MUHI you can see the memorial, put up in 1991 by György Vadász and Sándor Kiss to commemorate the Battle of Muhi at which the Hungarian army suffered a heavy defeat at the hands of the Tatars.

In ÓNOD on the banks of the *River Sajó* it is worth visiting one of the best kept **peasant houses** (Vár utca 17.) in the region. The ruined **castle** was built at the end of the 14th century to protect a crossing place over the River Sajó. Not far from the castle in 1707 the overthrow of the Habsburg monarchy was proclaimed.

On the Slopes of the Cserehát

The medieval structure of the 14th century **Calvinist Church** at SZIKSZÓ also contains architectural elements going back even further. Its defensive wall was built two hundred years later. Leaving Szikszó you come to the gently undulating landscape of the *Cserehát*. In FELSŐVADÁSZ stands the **Rákóczi Palace** (Rákóczi út), now the local primary school, first built during the 16th and 17th centuries but substantially rebuilt during a later period. The Baroque **Roman Catholic church** (Dózsa György u.) also has its own fair share of Rákóczi memorabilia, one in the form of a fine **chasuble** made from buckskin.

SZANTICSKA is the smallest village in Hungary. In the year 2000 it had 19 houses, 2 churches and three permanent residents. The survival of this seemingly moribund village is due almost entirely to the efforts of István Pál. There are, however, no shortage of tourist attractions, and visitors can try their hands at various arts and crafts or visit the photographic exhibition, the exhibition of agricultural machinery, the stable gallery or the beehives. The countryside is perfect for walking and cycling.

In SELYEB you will find the Baroque **Tiszta Hall** (Kossuth út 21), in RÁSONYSÁPBERENCS the Romanesque **Calvinist church**, and in KÁZSMÁRK the painted panelled ceiling of the Gothic **Calvinist church**.

Near ENCS you can go and visit the *Gibárt mini hydroelectric power station*.

In FORRÓ it is worth paying a visit to the **Abaúj Museum** (Szent Imre tér 3.), which has an exhibition devoted to the historic county of Abaúj.

On the edge of Miskolc, driving out in the direction of Sajószentpéter, you come to Király Hill, home of the largest riding school in the region. With its 2700m² arena the complex has hosted both national and international showjumping and horse and carriage competitions. Whilst you are there you can also stroke the traditional Hungarian farm animals.

AROUND GÖMÖR AND ÓZD

There can't have been many people who witnessed the 1752 fire who believed the **Calvinist church** in SAJÓSZENTPÉTER would survive the flames. Nevertheless there are still some Gothic windows left in the nave as well as a Renaissance doorway and a window in the sacristy. The church was restored in the Baroque period following the fire, and the interior contains 173 painted panels.

KAZINCBARCIKA is a fine example of post-war town planning. It is certainly worth driving through the landscaped housing estates to take in a few Stalinist apartment blocks. Continuing up the Sajó you come to PUTNOK, the one-time county town of the historic county of Gömör-Kishont. This explains why the town has more than its fair share of fine public buildings. At the **Gömör Museum** you can find out more about the history of Putnok and the surrounding region (Serényi L. tér 10.).

KELEMÉR

It was here, following the failure of the War for Freedom, that *Mihály Tompa* (1817–1868) spent two years as a priest. For a time Gömör County's finest poet used the pseudonym *Rém Elek*, the name of the village spelt backwards.

The greatest botanical treasures in the area are the small **bogs** created by ancient landslides on the steep hillsides. The *Kis-Mohos* is nearly 16 thousand years old, and the *Nagy-Mohos*, according to the latest studies, even older. There are only two other examples in Hungary, both near Csaroda out on the Ukrainian border.

"The peat bog as a natural environment is a chance survival containing the vegetation which existed in Hungary in the period immediately following the Ice Age." (Botond Czenthe). The fact that the bogs in Kelemér exist at all is as miraculous as some of the plants you can find there such as the sundew, the shield fern, sedge and the bog trefoil.

The small village of GÖMÖRSZŐLŐS has a fine **Outdoor Museum** containing old peasant cottages saved, transported and reconstructed on their present site. The houses are also used for summer **art workshops** and children's camps. There is also an ecological camp to make people aware of the village's four hundred-year-old fruit plantations.

Of the region's older parish churches the most important are those at Ózd-Szentsimon with its excellent 14th century wallpaintings (illustrated above), and the rather drastically restored rotunda at Kissikátor.

Lake Arló, near Arló, *a village also known for its medieval Roman Catholic church, is a rare natural feature created by a landslide. In recent decades it has become a popular weekend destination with swimmers and anglers.*

In Ózd, bastion of the Hungarian *iron industry,* you will find an exhibition devoted to its history at the **Municipal Museum** (Gyár út 10.). On the edge of town there is a **leisure park** with a boating pool, and *Lake Hangonyi* also makes a good day out. Driving from Ózd across the *Lázbérc Nature Reserve* through Borsodbóta you come to Dédestapolcsány. The countryside you pass through is excellent walking country and full of wild flowers. The Uppony Hills, situated on the threshold of the northern Bükk, lie at the very heart of the *Lázbérc Nature Reserve.* The most interesting geographical feature there is the half-a-kilometre-long *Uppony Gorge* leading up to the **reservoir** on the edge of Dédestapolcsány, a village dominated by the hill on which Dédes Castle stands.

The nature reserve is a mixture of oak and beech woodland and rocky landscapes. If it is wild flowers you are interested in, there is meadow-grass stern-bergia, hoary rockrose and toothwort. Apart from the woodland animals you can also see the osprey, the common heron, and the black stork.

MEZŐKÖVESD

The capital of the *Matyóföld* was given civic status by Matthias Corvinus in 1464, and since then the town has been the most important settlement in southern Borsod. The history of the Matyó people can be found in the *permanent exhibition* devoted to them at the **Matyó Museum** (Szent László tér 20.). In the early years of the 20th century the Matyó people were forced to take on part-time jobs in impoverished and distant lands, where the lavishness of their folk costumes was due to their investing the income in their only asset, their costume. The characteristic patterns seen on the Matyó costumes were dreamt up by the Mezőkövesd pattern-makers during the final third of the 19th century.

The term "Matyó" now tends to cover the settlements of Mezőkövesd, Tard and Szentistván in Borsod-Abaúj-Zemplén County. (Elsewhere in the country, however, isolated Roman Catholic communities in predominantly Protestant areas were also described as being Matyó.) This denominational distinctiveness brought with it a particular educational outlook. It was only in the last third of the 19th century that the Matyó settlements caught the public imagination.

The biggest date on the town's busy calendar is the Matyóföld Dance Festival.

One of the main attractions at the Mezőkövesd Museum is the wedding cart piled high with all the objects making up the bride's dowry.

The most famous of the pattern-makers was *Borbála Márton* (1876–1954) better known as *Bori Kisjankó*. It is in the road named after her that you can find the **house** dedicated to her memory (22.). The house looks like many of the other **old peasant houses** on the street (numbers 13, 21, 34.) as well as another house on Mogyoróköz (number 4.). Two of the houses are used as workshops, two of them are open to the public, whilst the others, which have been restored to their original condition, are still occupied. It is here also that you will the characteristic "hadas" *settlement layout* where two related families would live next door to one another, whilst sharing the same yard and the same kitchen. It was an arrangement which survived through many successive generations.

The Architectural Machinery Museum (Eötvös u. 30-32) in Mezőkövesd is the only museum of its kind in Hungary. It boasts the largest collection of agricultural machinery in the country as well as an exhibition on the art of the blacksmith.

The centre of the town contains a pleasing mixture of buildings both old and new. There is the **Roman Catholic church** dating from the 15th century (Szent László tér 22.), which is where you can find *István Takács*'s *Madonna* dressed up in Matyó costume. Outside the church stands a **Baroque column.** The main thoroughfare has a fine Secession-style grammar school, and an arts centre typical of the post-war period.

On the edge of Mezőkövesd you can find the Zsóry Baths, Northern Hungary's largest and most popular outdoor swimming complex and spa. The waters were discovered during routine oil exploration in 1938.

The famous Matyó apron

According to legend the devil once took away a Matyó man on the point of getting married. His bride-to-be begged the devil to return her loved one. The devil said he would, but only on condition that she brought him an apron filled with flowers – a request made more difficult by the fact that it was winter. The girl proceeded to embroider her apron full of roses, winning back her man.

It is in BOGÁCS *that waters come up from 600m underground at a temperature of 70 ºC supplying the outdoor swimming complex. There is also a good fishing lake at the edge of the village. The centre of the village is dominated by the medieval church.*

THE BÜKKALJA

Great Beehive Rock overlooking SZOMOLYA, with its niches carved into the 3-15m rock faces, was used for keeping bees from the 11th to the 15th century.

In TARD *some of the peasant cottages (Béke u. 55, 57) have been restored to their former glory.*

It was from the *castle*, which once stood in the woods surrounding the village, that CSERÉPVÁRALJA got its name. All that remains of the 16th century castle are the ruins. At Gárdonyi u. 5. you can visit a **cave dwelling**, of which there are quite a number in the *Bükkalja*. These houses and **wine cellars** could easily be cut out of the soft tufa and belonged mainly to the owners of the vineyards. As you can see some of the cave dwellings are still occupied today.

CSERÉPFALU stands at the foot of the Bükk Hills at the mouth of great *Hór Valley* in the Bükkalja wine region. On the edge of the village you can find *Subalyuk Cave*, where some of the earliest archaeological finds in Central Europe were found. They included a dwelling belonging to a Neanderthal **caveman** together with the bones of an adult woman and a three-year-old child. The **Subalyuk Museum** can be found in the community centre (Kossuth u. 125.). The **lookout tower** *(György Csere)* offers some marvellous views.

Those who visit nearby KÁCS during the first half of June may well run into the traditional venison-cooking competition. Known as the *Kács Venison Feast* it is accompanied by a hunting trophy, hawking and medicinal plant displays.

Despite being a fine spectacle in its own right there are many historical pageants to entertain visitors to Eger Castle.

EGER

In 1004, it was in the gently undulating countryside between the *Mátra* and the *Bükk* in the valley along which the *Eger* runs that King Stephen decided to found a bishopric. People believe the settlement got its name either from the stream flowing down the valley or the alders (éger) which grow there. Documents relating to the early history of the town have not survived.

The Tatar warriors had no problem taking the town, and it was this which prompted Béla IV. to build a stone fortress in Eger in 1248. It could be argued that Eger's golden era came during the reign of Matthias Corvinus, in the second half of the 15th century, at a time when the humanist Bishops of Eger invested enormous amounts of money in the development of the cathedral town. It was in 1552 that Eger earned its very special place in the annals of Hungary history, at a time when István Dobó was the castellan. On 10th September

1552, the Turks lay siege to Eger Castle, 40–50,000 Turkish soldiers surrounding a castle occupied by a garrison of about 2,000 soldiers. Dobó and his troops, however, swore that they would fight to the very end. On 18th October, after a siege lasting 40 days, the Turks retreated, having failed in their attempt to take the castle. The events surrounding the siege were immortalised in *Géza Gárdonyi's* novel *Eclipse of the Crescent Moon*. The castle eventually fell in 1596, by which time the castle was being defended by mercenaries.

During the Turkish occupation Eger became the centre of its own *Turkish administrative area* (vilajet). Whilst the mosques, which the Turks built out of the town's medieval churches, have all but disappeared (we still have one minaret), some Turkish baths still survive, as does a Turkish variety of grape, the *kadarka*.

It was following the retreat of the Turks that the Jesuits arrived in the town to be followed soon after by the return of the Cistercians, the Franciscans, Servites and the Trinitarians.

In 1828, during the Age of Reform, the first *Hungarian-language Teacher Training College* was opened in Eger. It was at that time also that the new classical-style cathedral was built to the plans of *József Hild*. It was in the courtyard of the Bishop's Palace that Louis Kossuth proclaimed *"here a love for one's country can be taught, not merely proclaimed."*

The Eger wine region came into being in the 1700s, when the vineyards around the town were planted. Most of the resulting wine was exported abroad.

Eger now likes to promote itself as *"the Baroque wine town"*, and indeed, Baroque doorways, elegant statues and the fine pieces of wrought iron-work lurk around every corner.

Even the poet *Sándor Petőfi* had his views on Eger, as seen in his poem *"Near Eger"*

"If I sense good wine, I enter;
Should I not then enter Eger?
If I should avoid this town,
Even God would beat me down."

To get to the entrance of the castle you have to take the steep road up from Dózsa György tér. Once through the main bottom gate you follow the main wall, past **Gergely Bastion** up to the inner gate.

At the Eger Castle Waxworks the siege of 1552 is almost brought back to life.

The walls of the castle are a good place to start a walk around the town. You can get your bearings and enjoy the view.

Between **Dobó Bastion** on your left and the Picture Gallery you will find the medieval *Great Cellar* which during the summer now houses the **exhibition**: *Execution, Torture and Humiliation in Old Hungary*. The **underground passageways**, the lapidarium and the military exhibition can only be visited as part of a guided tour.

It was on the highest point of the southeastern corner of the present castle that *Géza Gárdonyi* lies buried. The great writer's gravestone is inscribed simply with the words *"Csak a teste!"* (Only his body). Next to the *mote* with the crucifixes you can see the ruins of the **medieval cathedral**, dedicated to Saint John. Rising above it you can see a statue of Saint Stephen on top of one of the reconstituted chancel piers. Around the courtyard immediately to the west of the cathedral ruins you can find the **Eger Picture Gallery** and the **Bishop's Palace**. Now much restored the palace was built in around 1470 in the Gothic style. The western end of the arcade is original, whilst the eastern bays are reconstructions. Having made your way all the way up to the castle it is worthwhile continuing on to **Géza Gárdonyi's House** (Gárdonyi u. 20.), whose three rooms and substantial library have been left the way they were when the author lived there. In the shady and well-kept garden you will find a statue of *Géza Gárdonyi* by *Árpád Somogyi*.

Gárdonyi first lived here between 1878 and 1881, and then again from 1897, when he finally settled in the town. When writing "Eclipse of the Crescent Moon" Gárdonyi had to do an enormous amount of research. Right up until his death in 1922 Gárdonyi's working habits were unconventional to say the least. He shut himself away with the shutters closed tight breaking only to do a bit of painting, play some music or bury himself in his secret script.

A weapons cabinet at the **Historical Repository** (Dobó u. 9.) is the private collection of *Sándor Tóth*.

Kossuth Lajos utca, which leads down from the castle to the cathedral, is the street richest in Baroque buildings. It is here also that you will see the locals queuing up for their daily portion of homemade ice cream. One of the oldest buildings in the street is the currently rather depressing spectacle of **Buttler House** (26.), which stands next to a stream. This top end of the street was once the spiritual centre of the thriving Jewish community. You can still make out the Stars of David on the old **Orthodox Synagogue** (1893). Crossing the stream you pass the **Grand Prevost's Residence** (16.) built between 1774 and 1776 to the designs of *Jakab Fellner*. A building outstanding for its ironwork is the *County Library*. The palatial building opposite is the Baroque **County Hall** (1748–1756, *Mátyás Gerl*), whose wrought iron gates by *Henrik Fazola* (1758–1761) deserve close inspection.

If you go into the courtyard inside County Hall, on the right-hand side you will find the clean architectural lines of the county prison, in front of which public executions were carried out.

Back in Kossuth Lajos utca there is the **Franciscan Church** (1736–1755) followed a little further up by the 18th century *Sancta Maria Girls Grammar School* (Kossuth u. 8.). Next to the Canon's House (6) stands the finest residence in the street, the rococo **Lesser Prevost's Residence** (4.) built in 1758. *János Lukács Kracker*'s *Victory of Virtue* (1774) covers the banqueting hall on the first floor. The interior decoration was by *Lukács Huetter*, and the ironwork probably by *Henrik Fazola*.

At the end of the road you will find the **Lyceum**, currently being used by *Károly Eszterházy College*.

The Lyceum Library holds both the Buda Chronicle of 1473 and the Thuróczy Chronicle. The ceiling of the library contains János Lukács Kracker's (1778) representation of the Council of Trent (1545-1563). The frescos in the Lyceum chapel are by Maulbertsch (1793). An astronomical observation tower rises 53m above the west wing of the building. In the Specula astronomical museum there is a camera obscura.

Born in 1725 in Pozsony (Bratislava, Slovakia), Károly Eszterházy studied theology in Rome. Appointed Bishop of Vác in 1759 he eventually became Bishop of Eger in 1762, a position he held until his death. During his nearly four decades as bishop Eger became a fully-fledged county town. It was then that many of Eger's finest Baroque buildings were built. Mary Theresa however refused to grant university status to the Lyceum, built between 1765 and 1785. Teaching did nevertheless start in 1793.

The Lyceum (1765–1785, *József Gerl, Jakab Fellner*) is set around a courtyard. Apart from the chapel and the library there also is a ceremonial hall covered by a huge fresco by *Franz Sigrist* representing the institution's four faculties (law, philosophy, medicine and theology).

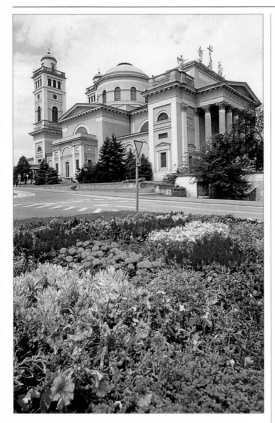

The classical cathedral is 93 metres long, the drum of the dome is
18 metres in diameter and the two towers 54metres high.
The excellent reliefs representing the Life of Christ
by Marco Casagrande deserve attention.
The high altar is by József Dannhauser, and the altar
at the eastern end of the southern aisle by Michelangelo
Grigoletti. In both aisles of the nave there are also
two interesting paintings of Saints Stephen and
Ladislas by János Kracker.

The approach to the **Cathedral** (1831–1836, *József
Hild*) is made all the more impressive by the statues
of Saint Stephen and Saint Ladislas, Saint Peter and
Saint Paul, by *Marco Casagrande* standing to either
the side of basilica's Corinthian portico.

Walking along the main pedestrian thoroughfare
Széchenyi utca, you come first to the **Bishop's
Palace** (18th century). The neo-classical wing
looking onto Eszterházy tér, which is somewhat
later, was built to house Archbishop László Pyr-
ker's excellent art collection, which went on to
help form the basis of the Museum of Fine Arts in
Budapest. The palace is not open to the public,

but you can find a number of exhibitions, for example the Ecclesiastical Museum, in the palace's
old service buildings.

The **Pharmacy Museum** has the oldest surviving
furniture of its type in the town, and opposite
Spetz House (now an arts centre) you can find
the **Cistercian Church** (1731–1733, *Giovanni
Battista Carlone*). At the end of the street, perched
up on a hill, stands the old Serbian community's
Greek Orthodox church (1784–1799, *János
Povolny*) which contains the country's large
iconostasis, which is 18m tall.

The town's famous Turkish **minaret** (Knézich K.
u.) is 40metres high, and has 14 sides. The stone carving has fortunately survived in excellent condition.
Dobó tér is the heart of the town. The sculpture
of *István Dobó* is by *Alajos Stróbl* (1907).

*The Battle Scene in the southwestern corner of the square is
by Zsigmond Kisfaludi Strobl. The square is dominated
by the façade of the Minorite Church (planned 1745,
constructed 1758-1773, Kilian Ignaz Dietzendorfer).*

The medicinal qualities of Eger's famous thermal springs were already known to the Turks.
Cures can be taken at the recently renovated thermal leisure pools and the Turkish Baths (17th century),
otherwise known as the Pasa Arnaut Baths (Fürdő u. 4.), and the Flora Hotel (Fürdő u. 5).

The Valley of the Beautiful Woman is the place
to go to enjoy Eger's wines and to savour
the atmosphere of the local cellars.

The **outdoor thermal complex** stands next to the **Bishop's Garden**, a park laid out in the French manner. Also in the vicinity you can find the new Aladár Bitskey indoor swimming pool (*Imre Makovecz*) with its rather puzzling tower (Frank Tivadar u. 5.). At the well opposite in the **spa park** you can sample Eger *medicinal waters*.

Of all the red wines on the *Eger Wine Road* the most famous is Eger *Bull's Blood*. One thing perhaps that you didn't know was that apart from being enjoyable to drink Bull's Blood has medicinal properties. (See also the *Hungarian Treasury*).

According to legend the name Bull's Blood dates back to the Turkish period when (prior to the siege of 1552.) Dobó's warriors drank Bull's Blood. Thinking that the red liquid dripping from their enemies' beards was bull's blood the Turkish soldiers believed the Hungarian soldiers were endowed with almost superhuman powers.

VENTURING NORTH OF EGER

The old Cistercian Abbey at Bélapátfalva is well known throughout Hungary.

BÉLAPÁTFALVA got its name from the Bél clan, whose **Cistercian Monastery** was founded by Kilit II., Bishop of Eger in 1232. Referred to as Bélháromkút in contemporary documents, it was originally built in the Romanesque style, and remodelled in the Gothic style during the 14th and the 15th centuries. Inside there are some Baroque fittings.

Nearby *Lak Valley* has a **lake** and some **leisure facilities,** making it ideal for fishing and relaxation. The *nature trail* on the *Belkő* side shows some sites of geological interest.

SZILVÁSVÁRAD

Situated 35 kilometres from Eger on the north-western edge of the Bükk on the Eger to Putnok branch line you will find the idyllic *Szalajka Valley,* which is a popular haunt with the locals. The name Szalajka is derived from the Latin – *sal alcalicus* – potash, one of the raw materials needed for glassmaking.

Walking up the 4-kilometre-long valley you come across a number of artificial **ponds** all used for breeding trout.

In the summer you can go up and down the valley on the narrow-gauge railway, which takes you just to beyond the Fátyol Waterfalls. During the winter you can do it by sleigh.

The Fátyol Waterfalls make for both a wonderful and a refreshing spectacle, while the Forestry Museum offers an educational experience.

From the source of the Szalajka stream it takes about a quarter of an hour to reach the cave at the foot of *Istállos-kő* (959m) where, in 1947, one of the Bükk's most important prehistoric archaeological finds was discovered.

The village itself is not without interest. There is the round classical **Calvinist church** (1837–1845) designed by *József Hild*. In **Orbán House** (Miskolci u. 60.) there is a permanent exhibition devoted to the flora of the *Bükk National Park*. (There is more on this topic in the *Hungarian Treasury* as well.)

Next to the one-time stables of the **Pallavicini Palace** (Egri u. 16.) there is a

museum with an exhibition focusing on horses, and the history of *lipica horses* in particular. You can see a cooper's and a blacksmith's workshop, and inspect no end of Hungarian coaches, coach lamps, whips and other horse-riding gear.

BÜKKSZENTERZSÉBET can be found on the edge of the *Heves-Borsod Hills* about 34 kilometres from Eger. It is from here that you can go out to into the *Tarna Nature Reserve* to look at the local wild flowers (loris, woodruff, toothwort, clubmoss) and birds (ravens, bee-eaters or eagle owls).

It is here that the **Ornithology Camp** is organised. Walking along the paths you can find springs which are quite safe to drink from. One of the most popular weekend destinations in the area is *Nagy-kő*, a huge limestone rock which can be approached by track. Wild animals are known to roam the ancient juniper groves and woods surrounding it.

Between Szilvasvárad and the Szalajka Valley you can find one of Europe's most beautiful equestrian arenas, which is capable of holding between 14 and 15 thousand spectators. Opposite the main arena is covered and capable of seating 1,500 people. Locals cannot resist telling visitors that Prince Philip once competed here back in the 1980s.

BETWEEN THE BÜKK AND THE MÁTRA

FELSŐTÁRKÁNY

Travelling from Eger in a northeasterly direction you come to the village which marks the gateway to the *Bükk Hills*. Surrounded by the *Bükk National Park* it is an ideal starting point for an expedition into the hills (for more information see the section on National Parks.) On your travels you are likely to see a number of protected animals (badgers, wild boar) and wild flowers. The *lady's slipper* appears on Felsőtárkány's coat-of-arms.

The waters running off the hills come together to form the stream known as the *Tárkány* just above the village, whilst the *Szikla Spring* supplies a large **pond** at the top end of the village, which is excellent for fishing. There are also several picturesque *nature trails* starting from here. The wooded park around the pond makes an ideal venue for the *May Day* and the *Saint Stephen's Day* celebrations.

Many make the 14 kilometre trip out to Noszvaj, east of Eger, to see the Szepessy-de la Motte-Almásy Palace (1774-1778). The buildings are currently used as a conference centre and a hotel.

If you are lucky, and organised enough to consult the timetable in advance, you may be able to catch the **train** departing twice daily from Felsőtárkány on the *Felsőtárkány Woodland Railway*. The train takes you right up into the Bükk Hills. Special group trips can be arranged in advance.

Noszvaj has a number of early 19th century **cave dwellings**, as well as a **farm house** (Deák F. u. 40.) which has been turned into a museum.

North of the village, and indeed a fair few feet above it, lies *Síkfőkút*, a popular **tourist destination** laid out in the 1930s. From here you can easily reach *Vár-kút* and *Lake Kánya* along the marked pathways. Indeed, armed with a decent map you can explore no end of excellent marked routes though the Bükk's picturesque landscape.

The only place in Europe resembling Egerszalók's hot spring is in Pamukkale in Turkey. Night and day, winter and summer, the 68°C waters pour out geyser-like from a hillside leading down from a coniferous wood, leaving a trail of lime scale as it does so. The hot spring will soon be the centrepiece of a major spa project.

EGERSZALÓK, six kilometres west of Eger, is well known in these parts for its **thermal waters** which come bubbling out from deep under the earth's surface. The water is good for treating bone problems and muscular and rheumatic pains.

It is the *Laskó* which runs down the valley. At the top end of the village the stream has been dammed up to create a 130-hectare **reservoir**. This is popular amongst anglers and lovers of water sports. Egerszalók is part of the Eger wine area.

KÁPOLNA

Many stop here when driving along route three, not the M3 turn-off, to look at the **war memorials,** one old and one much more recent, standing by the roadside. It was on 26th and 27th February 1849 that Kápolna became indelibly associated with the word failure, following the defeat of the Hungarian forces at the hands of the Habsburgs.

According to oral tradition during the Battle of Kápolna in 1849 a cannon ball hit the largest of the three surviving 150-200-year-old lime tree,s and broke it in two. The first memorial was put up in 1869, the new one dates from 1998.

"I kneel a free man in the cemetery recently filled with the shattered bodies of my own flesh and blood. After such a sacrifice your land becomes sacred, even a land which once witnessed great misdeeds. My God! A servile people cannot live on such hallowed soil."

(Kossuth's Prayer)

These were the sentiments expressed by Louis Kossuth when he visited the scene following what was a crushing defeat at the Battle of Kápolna. The three lime trees under which he uttered these words are still standing today and are in the immediate vicinity of the war memorials commemorating the events.

And there is indeed another historical event which is remembered at the edge of road number 3. It was by driving a symbolic stake into the ground in Kápolna on 23rd February 1919, that *Mihály Károlyi* started the symbolic splitting up of the great aristocratic estates.

FELDEBRŐ

The village is known for its full-bodied wine, *debrői hárslevelű* and its medieval church. The wine is celebrated at the *Harvest Festival* during the last weekend in September.

The church is famed for its 11th century **crypt**, on top of which the current 18th century **church** was built. The cemetery lying near the village is proof that the area was of strategic importance as far back as the Hungarian Conquest, when it formed part of the territory settled by the Aba clan.

Once inside Feldebrő church it was possible to look down into the crypt through a series of small windows. Worshippers were therefore able to look down at the altar and participate in the masses celebrated there.

The 20-metre-long nave is divided in two by massive piers. A chancel opens to the east, and to the west there is an opening into a tomb chamber. At the two ends of the tomb archaeologists have found evidence of altars. The walls and vaults include some fine medieval wall paintings.

The southern wall of the **Roman Catholic church** in Verpelét betrays its Romanesque origins as well as some 15th century additions. Next to the church you can see an 18th century *Madonna* surrounded by some interesting reliefs. In the middle of the park there is a **War Memorial** commemorating the Battle of Kápolna (27th February, 1849).

In Verpelét a Blacksmith's Museum has been created out of an old peasant's cottage (Kossuth u. 62.).

The **church** in Tarnaszentmária, one of the smallest settlements in Heves county, is made up of what was a 10th century baptistery. For a time those members of Prince Geisa's family who were buried there were honoured in a manner befitting saints. The fabric of the lower church is original up to the level of the cornice. It was only heightened in the 19th century. (The key can be obtained at Parádi u. 11.)

Sirok

The **cave dwellings** can best be seen on Széchenyi utca. They are carved out of the local tufa; a material which can be easily cut, is relatively resilient and offers good insulation. In these houses the living room is at the front and the kitchen at the back, which is where you can find the oven, whose smoke disappears out through a pipe. The interior walls are lime-washed and the furnishings minimal. There was a time when such dwellings were widespread in the region (*Szomolya, Cserépfalva, Cserépváralja, Noszvaj, Ostoros*). The *Castle Tournament* and the annual motorbike reunion at the nearby *Kút Valley* take place during the summer months.

The 23 hectares of **peat bog** can be found at nearby *Lake Nyírjes*, which is a landscape dating back to the Ice Age. It is particularly rich in snails.

400 metres from castle stand the free-standing rocks known as Monk and Nun. Legend has it that young Bodony fell in love with Tarna, the daughter of the fairy king Darnó. In a fit of anger the evil father killed the lovers, who then turned into stone, Darnó has been crying over it ever since, hence the . village's name Sirok (the Hungarian for "cry" is "sír').

Sirok Castle dominates the village, standing at a height of 294 metres on a tufa outcrop. The original castle was later strengthened by a system of ramparts lying 10 metres below the central tower and its surrounding walls.

GYÖNGYÖS

Gyöngyos, which is situated where the plain meets the hills, is not only the centre of the *Mátraalja wine region,* but the biggest town in the *Mátraalja.* The so-called *Great Church,* **St Bartholomew's,** which you can still see today was built in about 1350. By the end of the 15th century it had become a substantial hall-church.

The Mátra Museum in Gyöngyös can be found in the old Orczy Palace. It has a permanent exhibition about the town and the Mátraalja region.
There is also a natural history and a geological exhibition as well as a display on the history of hunting.
Down in the cellar you can come face to face with a few lizards.

The interior of the Great Church in Gyöngyös, whilst predominantly Baroque in atmosphere, does in fact have a Gothic font.
In the ceiling of the porch there are some frescoes depicting kuruc chiefs.

Gyöngyös's main square acquired its present form after the fire of 1917. A few additional improvements were made in the year 2000. Originally the old town hall stood here, and, although the original houses belonging to the gentry have been much rebuilt, their very presence still enhances the townscape. Behind the Great Church you can find the old Jesuit Grammar School which now houses the Music School.

The memorial bell by the southern entrance refers to the fire which swept the town, leaving the church badly damaged (Kossuth u.). Its reliquaries are considered to be amongst the most valuable existing in the country's Roman Catholic collections. The church's **treasury** can now open to the general public in **Szent Korona House** (Szent Bertalan út 3.).

According to tradition, it was in the so-called **Rákóczi House** (Fő tér 2.) that the Prince himself went into peace negotiations with Pál Széchenyi, Bishop of Kalocsa.

The **Orthodox church,** which is no longer worshipped in, is situated on the other side of the stream running through the town in one of the closed courtyards leading off Vachot Sándor utca. The Orthodox faith came to the region following the Turkish occupation. At that time the Greek, Armenian, Serbian and Macedonian merchants, along with merchants of other nationalities, formed a majority in the town.

The eastern side of Barátok tere is dominated by the **Franciscan Monastery** (1701–1727). The secularisation of church property which went on during the reign of Joseph II. was managed cleverly by Károly Eszterházy, Bishop of Eger, who handed the parochial duties to the Franciscans.

In the chancel stands a tablet telling you that it was here that Bottyán the Blind was buried. At the monastery you can see the only remaining medieval Franciscan library in Hungary to have survived in one piece, as well as an exhibition dedicated to the history of the Order. Apart from texts of religious importance the library also has publications devoted to history, the natural sciences and literature.

IN THE LAND OF SÁMUEL ABA

Nine kilometres northeast of Gyöngyös, not far from the *Sárhegy*, you come to ABASÁR, whose name refers back to the village's 11th century connections with the Aba clan on whose land the village stood. According to legend Samuel Aba founded a Benedictine monastery here. The *Viennese Illuminated Chronicle* states he was in fact buried here.

Some believe the **tomb** found carved into the rock of the *Bolt-tető Cellar* is in fact that of Samuel Aba but this has not been proved. In front of the parish church (Fő tér) you can find a *statue* of Samuel Aba (*Aran Till*). In **Kapás House** you can see an exhibition of artefacts connected with the local wine region (Múzeum u. 15.).

Descendants of the Slovaks who settled in 1710 still live in KISNÁNA. There is a **Slovak peasant house** (Béke út 1.) devoted to life as it was lived during the first quarter of the 20th century. The *Mátragyöngye Folk Choir* devotes a lot of time and energy to the preserving the local folk music and their local costume.

The medieval castle, which looms over the village, is now the home of the Castle Museum. Despite its strategic importance in the wars against the Turks the castle was not given any additional fortifications. The castle gradually fell into a state of disrepair, and by the end of the Second World War people were using what remained to repair their houses.

The vineyards are an important element in the Mátraalja's characteristic landscape.

EXPLORING THE MÁTRA

Travel just a few kilometres north of Gyöngyös,
and you get right into the heart of the Mátra,
one of the most popular tourist areas in Hungary.

You can make your way up to the Mátra Hills either by car or by the **narrow-gauge railway** which goes from Gyöngyös as far as MÁTRAFÜRED. In the hills above the hotels and restaurants of Mátrafüred you can make the short walk up to the ruins of **Bene Castle**. Whilst in Mátrafüred itself the **Palóc Doll Museum** (Pálosvörösmarti u. 2.) also deserves a visit.

Sástó, which lies near Mátrafüred, has been a popular
tourist destination since the 1960s. From the lookout point
you can survey the ever-changing countryside.
The lake boasts the title of the highest-lying boating lake (520m)
in Hungary. It's also good for fishing.

It was in the late 1920s and the 1930s that the first hotels went up in MÁTRAHÁZA. From here you can make your way up to the highest point in Hungary, KÉKESTETŐ (1,014m), where work has been going on at the **ski centre.** The 1800m slope is lit at night, the lifts have been renovated and the children have a lift of their own (2003).
Eventually there will be 5km of slopes complete with snow cannons.

The view from the lookout tower is staggering.
From the viewing deck, which lies 38 metres up the 187-metre
tower, it's possible to see not only the Bükk and the Karancs,
but also the High Tatras in neighbouring Slovakia.

Once up on Kékestető it's worth making the short trip to Hungary's second-highest peak, the 964-metre-high GALYATETŐ. The peak can boast at least one event of great cultural importance, for it was here that *Zoltán Kodály* composed his *Silent Mass.*
Galyatető is in fact part of MÁTRASZENTIMRE, formed during the 1940s when several smaller settlements were joined together under one name. To the west of the village you will find **St Mary's Chapel** at **Fallóskút,** which is a well-known local *pilgrimage place*. The enamel Stations of the Cross are particularly interesting.

If you are to believe all the marked paths existing here, the central part of the Mátra Hills must be one of the most explored areas in Hungary. There are walks of all lengths and all degrees of difficulty. The hills are a great place to explore all year round, and you can go skiiing during the winter months. You are of course advised to book your winter quarters in advance. The youth camp at SZURDOKPÜSPÖKI *near Pásztó helps to broaden the accommodation possibilities available (Gyöngyösi út 35.) at one of the gateways to the Western Mátra.*

THE FRINGE OF THE MÁTRA

PÁSZTÓ

This small town at the foot of the *Western Mátra* is where many walkers depart from on their treks around the region. In the town itself there are the **ruins** of the **Cistercian Monastery,** which lie immediately to the south of the church. There was in fact a Benedictine Monastery on the site (pre-1130) before the Cistercian Monastery was built in about 1172. Much of the stone from the medieval buildings were used when the present building was built in about 1716. One curiosity are the remains of the Benedictine **glassworks**.

In August 2000, Sándor Kiss's composition of St Stephen presenting the crown to the Blessed Virgin Mary was put up right next to the monastery. Following the death of the artist his wife Márta Lesenyei was forced to complete it.

The Baroque monastic buildings in Pásztó are now used as a museum. It contains the Nógrád County Natural History Collection, including exhibitions about both the town and the county, one being entitled "Nógrád County Through the Millennia". There is also a room devoted to the memory of the last Cistercian prior and the European music expert, Benjamin Rajeczky.

In the middle of the monastic ruins lies the Teacher's House, the only 15th century agricultural town house to be reconstructed in present-day Hungary. It is now a museum exhibiting finds from the monastery. In the cellar there is a display devoted to medieval winemaking practices.

The most striking building is **St Laurence's Church** (Múzeum tér 1.). There are still some 13th century details in evidence: some door and window frames, and the sculptures you can see in the niches in the west tower. There is also a fine Gothic chapel on the southern side of the church. There is an interesting 12th century hexagonal chapel on the northern side, which houses temporary exhibitions. To the south of the church stands a sculpture of King Sigismund (1387–1437) by *Sándor Kiss*.

Pásztó has the only **thermal swimming baths** in Nógrad County (Strand út). Every year the town organises the *Pásztó Fair*, which shows the best of the region's produce.

To the northeast of Pásztó proper you come to *Hasznos*, which is now considered part of the town. Here you will find the **Roman Catholic church** with its gothic chancel. From the road above Hasznos you can also make out the two towers of **Cserter Castle** perched up on a small hill. Those who make the effort and climb up to the castle will be rewarded with a fine view.

The stream running underneath the castle has been dammed up to form 27 hectares of **artificial lake**. There are good angling opportunities to be had, and it's also a good place for hang-gliding as *Óvár Hill* and *Ágasvár Hill* both rise up behind it. The *Mátra Nature Reserve* is the most important protected area in the region. It is covered in oaks, hornbeams, beeches and pine plantations, and it is here you can find early purple orchids, bird's nest orchids and helleborines. As for the animals there is the hazel-grouse, the only type of grouse to be found in Hungary.

TAR

In the 15th century it belonged to the estates of *Lőrinc Tari*, King Sigismund's confident. It was through *Sebestyén Tinódi Lantos*'s account of Lőrinc Tari 's pilgrimage to the hellish sulphurous cave known as *Saint Patrick's purgatory* in Ireland, entitled *Inferno*, written one and a half centuries later, that the landowner entered the annals of Hungarian literature. The **ruins** of the Tari family's **manor house** lie on the eastern edge of the village. The fortified castle was burnt down by the Turks in 1552. Right next to the ruins lies the walled **Roman Catholic church**. The chancel is Romanesque, whilst the nave is a 15th century Gothic addition as are the curious apses which were added to the sides of the chancel. The church contains some interesting wall paintings.

Tar church with the ruins of the manor house in the foreground

Next to road number 21, on what was known as Gaál-tanya, there is the **Buddhist stupa** which was consecrated by the Dalai Lama in 1992.

MÁTRAVEREBÉLY

In the pre-Turkish period the village was an agricultural town by the name of *Vereb*. As far back as the 13th century the **Holy Well,** which is now considered part of the village, had already become a significant pilgrimage place. Most pilgrims descend on the shrine on 15th August.

Apart from the patronal festival, another important date on the church's calendar is 8th September, the birthday of the Blessed Virgin Mary. The girls and women from the Palóc villages usually arrive dressed in their colourful folk costumes.

The origins of the Holy Well are said to come from an incident when Saint Ladislas and his troops had been forced to hide in the narrow valley by the Cumans. Completely surrounded and not having access to water the Hungarians asked the Cuman ruler whether they could change religion. In his anger Saint Ladislas thrust his spear into the rocks. When he pulled it out fresh water flowed out from the spot where the spear had been. According to another version Ladislas jumped down from Ágasvár creating the gorge named after him.

The first wooden chapel was built in about 1290 just above the spring. The present two-towered baroque **church** was built in 1757 thanks to the generosity of János Almásy. In 1970, the Pope gave it the rank of *basilica minor.*

The **Roman Catholic church** in the village itself is one of the most beautiful Gothic parish churches in Hungary. The southern doorway is particularly fine. The church also contains an interesting 17th century Renaissance pulpit.

Not far from the top of *Meszes-tető*, which rises above the church, there is a **hermits' cave** carved out of the soft limestone, as well as two **chapels** and facilities such as bedrooms, a kitchen and lavatories for the visitors.

BÁTONYTERENYE

Those entering the town along road number 21 can see the coal-cutting machines standing in front of *Sólyom Hill,* reminding everybody that this was once a coal-mining town.

In place of coal *Nagybátony* has 30,000 picture postcards. *Gyula Barják*'s amazing collection can be seen at the **Postcard Museum** (Alkotmány út 9.). Of particular interest is the selection of postcards depicting the historical county of Nógrád.

In the part of town known as *Maconka* you will find the 13th century **Roman Catholic church** (Rákóczi út), which contains the remains of some medieval frescos. The **Maconka Reservoir**, which stretches for about a kilometre, offers rich pickings for the angler.

In *Kisterenye* you can see the Baroque **Gyürky-Solyomossy Palace** with its rather curious shingled onion-domed tower. Inside there is an exhibition dedicated to the *history of the iron industry.*

The area around Bátonyterenye is also excellent for hunting.

At the **Palóc Cottage** (Petőfi út 6.) in MÁTRA-BALLA there is a collection of traditional garments.

Palóc men haven't worn their traditional costumes for decades. This was caused firstly by their not wearing their traditional white linen trousers during military service, and secondly because they found it embarrassing to wear their traditional peasant dress in front of their colleagues. This took place at a time when people were unable to make a living off the poor soil, being forced instead to earn a living in the factories and the mines. The women's costumes are characterised by the sheer number of skirts they wore at any one time. At major social events they could end up wearing 18-20 petticoats, whereas on a normal day they would be satisfied with only a couple.

MÁTRADERECSKE which lies a few kilometres southeast of Mátraballa is famous for its castle, **Kanázs Castle.** It was probably built by a landowner belonging to the Aba clan.

Life in the village was livened up when the thermal waters were discovered. The **medicinal bath** and the **outdoor swimming pool** are recommended for the treatment of muscular problems. Those suffering from vaso-constrictoral illnesses are advised to go to the dry baths, the *mofetta*, which is currently being developed into a spa health centre. Guest also have access to the sports facilities, the sauna and the gym.

Many make their way to the Palóc Festival in Mátraderecsk on the last Saturday in June.

RECSK

Recsk means just one thing to the majority of Hungarians and that's the labour camp which existed here between 1950 and 1953. Known as the *Hungarian gulag* it lay six kilometres from the centre of the village. Its 1,300 inmates were forced to work in the local quarry. A memorial was put up there in 1991. The **National Memorial Park** to the victims of the Communist dictatorship was opened in 1996. Gold and copper mining started in Recsk in the 1840s. Unfortunately the seams, which lie close to the surface, began to become exhausted during the 1980s. Because of the staggering costs required for further mining exploration, attempts to find new seams have had to stop and the future of the mine is uncertain.

So we head for Parád, the pearl of the Mátra, and one of the most visited places in Northern Hungary. It is also the geographical centre of the Palóc ethnographical region.

It is also worth noting the significance of the elegant avenue of trees on road 24 leading out towards Parád, which were planted by Mihály Károlyi at the beginning of the 20th century. They are just part of an avenue which once stretched all the way to Parádsasvár.

Parád

It was in 1763 that the county health officer *Ferenc Markhot* discovered that the **water** contained traces of alum, and in 1778, that the alum works went into production, the same year the **medicinal baths** were opened.

The five rooms which make up the Coach Museum, which was opened in the Cifra Stables in 1971, trace the history of the horse-drawn carriage. There you will see the Eszterházy carriage, the Károlyi and the Gavallér carriages, the Parliament carriage and the Archbishop of Eger's ceremonial carriage to name but a few.

It was Count György Károlyi who had the stables built in 1880. Their beautifully ornamented exterior and the red marble interiors have earned it the name the **Cifra Stables** (Kossuth u. 214.).

The **Palóc House** in Parád (Sziget u. 10.) shows a local building as it appeared in the 18th century.

Parádsasvár

It is famous primarily for its **glassworks** which were established there in 1767. It was in *Parádóhuta* that Prince Ferenc Rákóczi II. founded the first glassworks in 1708, and it is indeed possible to visit what was the predecessor of today's factory. The Károlyis called their palace *Sasvár*, a name the village has shared since 1950.

There are footpaths to the east and the west (*Sándorrét, Ilona-völgy*) where you can find the **lake** with its 147m-long and 21m-high **dam**. The medicinal waters here have been famous for two centuries or more. The pagoda-like drinking hall was designed by *Miklós Ybl*. The *Csevice Spring* produces a foul-tasting sulphurous sparkling water, which has been taken for curing stomach complaints for two centuries.

The Károlyi Palace, which rises up above the fir trees, was built in 1872 to the designs of Miklós Ybl. Since its renovation it has been known as the Sasvár Palace Hotel.

AT THE FOOT OF THE MÁTRA

GYÖNGYÖSSOLYMOS

This village, now joining onto the edge of Gyöngyös, maintains its own identity through its traditional wedding celebrations. It was here that the local embroiderers and weavers worked out their own simplified versions of traditional patterns, whilst preserving the basic patterns and colours. Their bodices, shawls and golden-thread embroidery add an extra dimension to the *Palóc Festival*.

The most striking building in Gyöngyössolymos is the parish church, with its 14th century tower.

Even by the mid-14th century grapes had proved to be the region's most profitable crop. The village, which is part of the *Mátraalja Wine Region*, still has a number of substantial vineyards of considerable size.

The hills roundabout, which include *Kis-hegy*, provide idyllic surroundings for a spot of relaxation, which in these parts usually means hiking. The **Mátra narrow-gauge railway** passes through the village.

GYÖNGYÖSPATA

The torrents of water known as the *Danka* and the *Zám* flow through the village. **St Peter's Church** was originally built during the 11th century when it also functioned as the centre of the local deanery. The bulk of the present church was built during the 14th century in place of the church destroyed during the Tatar invasion of 1241. There have of course been other additions since.

The parish church in Gyöngyöspata has a high altar, which includes an unusual depiction of Jesse's Tree. The church also contains a copy of the 14th century Nekcse Bible, the original of which can be found at the American Library of Congress.

The famous fourteenth century manuscript known as the Pata Gradual, found in 1886, was written in Gyöngyöspata. The manuscript, which is full of Gregorian chants and chants in Hungarian, was used for teaching purposes.

The local folk songs make more than the usual references to the Blessed Virgin Mary, and those who are familiar with such songs can roll off an almost infinite number of them. At the **peasant cottage** (Dobrányi u.2.) there is collection of local folk costumes.

According to legend Szűcsi, lying just west of Gyöngyös, gets its name from the royal furriers who once lived here. It was here that *József Bajza* (1804–1858), poet and the inventor of Hungarian literary criticism, was born. There is a **museum** dedicated to his memory in the 18th century Bajza Hall (Bajza J. u. 1.). On the southern border of Szűcsi there are some fine **fishing lakes**.

HATVAN

Hatvan may indeed be sixty ("hatvan" in Hungarian) kilometres from Budapest but this doesn't account for the name of the town.

On the corner of Rákóczi út and Bajcsy-Zsilinszky út you will find the neo-Baroque *Újhatvan* **Roman Catholic church**, and opposite it the eclectic-style Cserkész utca **Lutheran church**.

Continuing along the Hort road you eventually end up in Kossuth tér. It is here you will find the **Town Hall** (Kossuth tér 2.). Although originally medieval, most of the town hall is much more recent. In the same square you will also find the late-Baroque **palace** (1754–1763) build by Antal Grassalkovich, the west wing of which is devoted to the town's *Cultural Centre*. The Baroque hall is used for concerts, dances, lectures, exhibitions, conferences and courses. The *Hatvany Room* is used for temporary exhibitions.

The town hall, Hatvan

In Gombospuszta, on the northern fringes of Hatvan, you will find the Baroque Grassalkovich farmhouse, built in 1762. The 18th century buildings are laid out around a courtyard. Of the guardhouses and the cellars which once stood on the corners of the farmhouse two survive. Next to the U-shaped main buildings there are also stables and servants' quarters.

Near the **gravel pit lakes** on the edge of town stands the *Görbeér* leisure park, with its restaurants, summer houses, stables, fishing village and camping site. In the wood there is a hunting lodge, an artists' workshop and a **leisure centre**.

THE ZAGYVA VALLEY

The one-time Grassalkovich-Hatvany Palace was partly built from stone taken from Hatvan Castle.

According to the most recent research the **felt works,** which Antal Grassalkovich built during the 18th century, were situated on the ground floor of the west wing of the palace.

The **Lajos Hatvany Museum** can be found in the old *Beer House* (12.). Apart from hosting temporary exhibitions the museum will, following the planned restoration work, have an important archaeological exhibition.

The villages of HORT and CSÁNY in deepest **Heves watermelon country** are indeed synonymous with this succulent fruit. Csány families were indeed famous for their habit of leaving their homes during the spring and summer months to live in the huts they built in the middle of their watermelon fields in some other corner of the country.

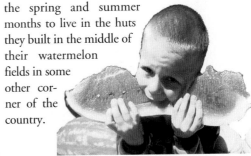

Most of the inhabitants of BOLDOG, south of Hatvan are involved with horticulture, growing cabbages and paprika mainly. During the paprika growing seasons their houses are strung up with paprikas drying out in the sun.

The basic ingredient for the decorated bridal kalács is about 15-20 kg of flour. After baking, the pieces of plaited kalács are set up to form low table-like stand, into which a stick wound up with seven strips of coloured paper is threaded. The whole is then covered with honeyed gingerbread biscuits. For one decorated kalács you need 200-250 biscuits, which could be doll-shaped, hussar-shaped or heart-shaped. These are then decorated with gold-painted walnuts and paper roses to produce what is quite a spectacle.

You can still see that the famous Boldog **folk costume** is still worn on special occasions, the bridal dress being the most impressive. It is only the older women who wear traditional dress during the course of the week.

The first pattern book to be published about Boldog embroidery, published in 1942, concentrated on the Boldog white embroidery. The local arts and crafts can be seen at the peasant cottage (Kossuth u. 32.) including a Boldog bridal kalács (see description above).

SALGÓTARJÁN

The locals joke that the town is famous for not being famous. This of course is not entirely the case. One only has to take one look at the modern town centre, a classic piece of 1960s town planning, to see that it has some quality.

Opinions are sharply divided about the town's aesthetic virtues, or lack of them. But there is no doubting the fact that Salgótarján was the first town to win the Hild Memorial Prize.

The Karancs Hotel and the Attila József Cultural Centre in the main square are venues for a number of cultural events. At the beginning of May there is the International Dixieland Festival, and the summer months see a succession of folk events.

The one old building in the town is the **Roman Catholic church**. A church probably stood on top of the hill as far back as the Middle Ages. The church is now basically Baroque in character.

The old village of Tarján surrounded the cemetery, which was in use from the 12th century right up to the 18th century.

To mark the new Millennium work has started on a **pantheon** (of the town's twelve most important personages) in the square between County Hall and the **Nógrád Historical Museum**. Thusfar, only seven of the intended sculptures have actually been completed.

The sculpture of *István Széchenyi* (*Attila Bobály*) was put up in the square immediately in front of the entrance to the museum in 1995. The museum, the first of its kind in Hungary, is devoted to the history of mining and the history of labour in Nógrád County (Múzeum tér 2.).

The underground **Mine Museum** is only a five-minute walk away. In the shaft you can see how the mining was done and what equipment was used. You can also see a stuffed mining pony which once pulled the underground coal trolleys.

Above ground at Salgótarján's mining museum you can see the so-called open-air museum with its trains, trolleys and the wagons out in the yard (Zemlinszky Rezső út 1.)

From the main square it is easy to find the **Franciscan Church and Monastery** built in the 1930s. It's typical of the period, with walls built of local stone and flat wooden roofs.

Zagyvaróna, five kilometres from Salgótarján, is part of a medieval settlement. The 14th century tower of the **Roman Catholic church** survives. The 19th century tower now standing amongst the trees up on the hill marks the site of *Zagyvafő Castle*, built after the Tatar invasion (1241). Only a few stones remain.

THE MEDVES PLATEAU

What you can see here is Central Europe's largest *basalt plateau*. It covers 13 km², two thirds of which are on the Hungarian side. West of the plateau lies the *Karancs-Medves Nature Reserve* with its woods, springs and ravines, its beeches, oaks, hornbeams and pine plantations. It is here that you can often see ravens, black woodpeckers, white-backed woodpeckers, bee-hawks and hazel-grouses. As for the wild flowers there are pulsatilla, wild hyacinths and lilies

On the edge of the Medves Plateau stands *Somoskő's Castle Hill* cut in two by the Hungarian-Slovakian border, the castle itself falling on the Slovakian side. The **castle** was built by the biggest local landowners, the Kacsics Family, after the Tatar invasion.

The Palóc International High Jump Competition is held every year in the shadow of Somoskő Castle. One of the curious features of the castle and the northern slopes of the hill lying in Slovakia is that Hungarian passport holders can cross the border to inspect the basalt columns.

*The wooden house under the castle has strong con-
nections with the poet Sándor Petőfi. It was here,
according to the poet himself, that an old woman
offered him some goat's milk. The original building he refers to was destroyed by fire, today's being
an exact copy for passing walkers to shelter in.*

From Somoskő it is easy to pick out the soaring
tower of **Salgó Castle,** which was originally built
following the Tatar Invasion (1241).

*Salgó Castle fell into Turkish hands in 1554.
Whilst the Turks were laying siege to the castle they
wheeled the larger pieces of wood up the hill. The
Hungarians who were defending the castle thought
their enemies were rolling up canons not tree
trunks and promptly took flight.*

Getting to the castle is merely a matter of taking a
10–20 minute walk from *Salgóbánya. Sándor
Petőfi* made the effort, and on reaching the castle
ruins wrote his poem entitled *"Salgó".* The castle
ruins, which stand high on the rocks, have an
inner and an outer bailey. The castle has already
got a new slate roof, next the restorers are going to
have a go at rebuilding one of the massive bastions.

*Just south of Salgó around the rock faces at Boszorkány-kő
there is a geological nature trail for visitors to study
the plants growing amongst the rocks.*

THE KARANCS VALLEY

The valley can be reached by travelling westwards
from Salgótarján via *Baglyaskő*. Its interest lies in
the fact that it is all that remains of an *embryonic
volcano*. The feature itself was caused by a crack in
the edge of a crater. A castle was built here after
the Tatar invasion, although by the 15th century
it had already fallen into a ruinous state.

In EGYHÁZASGERGE you will find a Gothic Roman
Catholic church, which includes a **Renaissance
wall cupboard** dating from 1503.

IPOLYTARNÓC

This village, lying 25 kilometres west of Salgótarján, is famous for the prehistoric finds which
have been uncovered here.

*In Ipolytarnóc you can see the fossilised remains
of some giant prehistoric pine trees and some fine foot prints.*

*The finds in Ipolytarnóc survived thanks to a vol-
canic eruption 20 million years ago. The fine volcanic ash buried the animal footprints for posterity.
Eleven species of animals have been identified from
amongst the footprints. They were animals, which
lived in tropical jungles, one of them being an
ancient rhinoceros. There is even evidence of animals
skidding and rain drops splashing. Look out also for
the more than five thousand subtropical leaf prints
and the two thousand animal footprints.*

Going on the Borókás-árok nature trail is like stepping back in time. You can see for example the remains of giant prehistoric pines whose height, according to the most recent estimates, was something in the region of one hundred metres.

It was in the *Csapás Valley* that the world's third most extensive collection of **prehistoric footprints** was found. There is a marked footpath going out to the spot where you can also see the imprints of prehistoric flowers and giant pine trees.

A large structure has been built over the excavated footprints and other fossilised forms. The work put into creating such an educational facility earned its owners, the *Bükk National Park*, a *European Diploma*.

The River Ipoly, forming the border between Hungary and Slovakia, is popular with both walkers and anglers.

Szécsény

Approaching the town from Ludányhalászi you are greeted with the spectacular sight of the Forgách Palace rising above the River Ipoly with the Franciscan Monastery and the Roman Catholic church standing close by.

The Baroque **Forgách Palace** (Ady út) was built in about 1770, from the stones of the old castle. To the right of the ornamental wrought-iron gate you can find the **Sándor Kőrösi Csoma Memorial Exhibition,** which is full of Buddhist religious objects, Tibetan clothes and artefacts collected by Hungary's most famous orientalist. In the **Ferenc Kubinyi Museum** in the palace there is an exhibition about the history of hunting and agriculture including some important trophies.

The Franciscan Monastery west of the palace is built on medieval foundations, although most of it was rebuilt in the Baroque style following the Turkish occupation. One of the most interesting objects is the Rákóczi statue which can be found in the cloisters. According to legend it was here that the great Prince took quarters during the course of the Szécsény National Assembly. In the wall you can find a painted mihrab. During the Turkish occupation the regional governor resided here.

Borjúpást Meadow lying under the one-time castle is a protected area as well as being a famous place. It was at the National Assembly held here in 1705 that Ferenc Rákóczi II. was elected Prince. The garden residence which used to stand here included part of the northwestern bastion of the medieval castle.

The **Roman Catholic parish church** contains an Islamic prayer alcove (Lajos Haynald út 9.)

The main entrance to the medieval town was near the **Prison Bastion**. From here the town wall more or less followed the line of Rákóczi út before heading in the direction of Forgács Palace. Fragments of the medieval walls can still be seen. The walls of the medieval parish church were excavated and an **open-air altar** put up on the site of the chancel.

Every October, the Cultural Centre opens its doors to the Szécsényi Autumn Exhibition. Next to the Cultural Centre stands Castle Square, which is where you can see a section of the castle defences standing as much as a storey high, which protected the so-called Small Gate. The bastion of the gate stood ten metres high as late as 1945 when it was dismantled and the stonework used for road-building purposes.

HOLLÓKŐ

This Palóc village you can see isn't in fact all that old: much of it was built after the fire of 1909. It was then that all the thatched roofs were given tile replacements.

During the course of the rebuilding of the village traditional designs were nevertheless used and the original proportions adhered to. The number of rooms the houses had remained the same (three), and the cellars were reconstructed. The wooden verandas on both the street and courtyard facades with their intricate designs were added later.

Local costumes are still alive and well in Hollókő. The girls and the women are quite happy to wear them at festivals and on Sundays. This was one of the reasons why the village was added to the UNESCO list of World Heritage Sites. (See the section on the World Heritage Sites as well.)

According to legend, the local landowner András kidnapped the beautiful wife of a neighbouring landowner, and kept her in a part of the castle which was still being built. The nursemaid of the lady's witch, however, petitioned Satan, and the sons of Satan proceeded to arrive every night taking the form of ravens. It is from these ravens ("holló" in Hungarian), so it is said, that both the village and the castle got their names. The ravens set about carrying away the walls of the castle, and continued to do so until the woman was released.

Walking down the streets of the old village of Hollókő takes you back centuries despite the fact that the scene is not even 100 years old.

There are plenty of exhibitions on Kossuth utca in the *Old Village*. The **Village Museum** attempts to recreate the atmosphere of the turn of the 20th century. The room facing the street was the Sunday room or "first house" filled with beds, embroidered textiles, painted and carved furniture, glazed pottery and countless religious paintings. The kitchen is fitted out with all the necessary cooking utensils, and the shed contains a collection of gardening tools and farming implements. In the yard there is an oak winepress.

The building, which now houses the **Post Office Museum** (80), used to belong to the *Royal Hungarian Mail*. The exhibition gives you an insight into the changes, which went on in the postal service in Nógrád County, and in the country as a whole. There is a display of old uniforms and the postman's everyday apparel including the weapons they had to carry with them to ward off highwaymen. In the

Hollókő scene

Weaving House they make textiles using old-fashioned looms (94.). At the *Bükk National Park* **exhibition** (99.) there are displays on the geology and the natural history of the Cserhát, a collection of dolls in folk costume and archaeological finds from the castle. The **Community Hall** next to the church is where the folk programmes take place.

The **Roman Catholic church,** which stands at the junction, on the so-called "island" standing between Kossuth and Petőfi utca, provides the image most associated with the village. The shingle-roofed, lime-washed church with its wooden tower was in fact only built in 1889. At the western end of the hill overlooking the village lie the walls of **Hollókő Castle,** restored in 1996. In the building you can now see a small exhibition of weapons, pottery fragments, stone carvings and cannonballs, all of which have been uncovered during excavation work.

There are some excellent views from the highest points of the fortress at Hollókő. You can make out the distinctive outline of the Cserhát in the distance, with the Old Village and the vineyards below.

It is the *Easter Celebrations,* lasting from Good Friday until Easter Monday, which are the high point of the Hollókő calendar. On August 20th there is the *Castle Tournament* and the *Folklore Meeting* and in the autumn the grape harvest. Around Christmas the local Nativity play does a circuit of the village.

The hills surrounding Hollókő are part of the 7,100-hectare *Eastern Cserhát Nature Reserve.* The woods cover rock formations dating back 15 million years, to an age when the landscape was covered in volcanoes. The limestone formations and the sand and clay beds surrounding the hills are rich in fossilised animal and botanical remains.

Horses on the Cserhát

THE CSERHÁTALJA

During the months of March and April it is possible to find the peasants eyes flowering in the local woods. In this landscape a change in altitude brings with it marked differences in natural habitat. There may be hornbeam and oak forests at one height followed by beeches on the wetter and cooler northern faces and scrub on another.

BUJÁK's **castle** has had a rich and colourful past. It was built after the Tatar invasion and destroyed by the Turks. It was in the 1930s that the artist *Oskár Glatz* (1872–1958) lived here. He managed to incorporate the **local folk costumes** into his pictures. The local costume is characterised by the multitude of dresses that might be worn on top of each other at any one time, the pearls and the special blouses and head dresses.

The spinning that was once the task of Buják's women is now the sole preserve of the local folk dance troupe.

The Buják Sunday folklore event is held every year at the beginning of June.

Particularly beautiful are the **Stations of the Cross** in the middle of which you can find **St Anna's Chapel,** all of which were built at the beginning of the 19th century. On the road leading from Buják to Bokor you will come across *Kesely Meadow,* which is full of protected oak trees.

At nearby SZIRÁK stands Teleki-Dégenfeld Palace. Originally built at the end of the 17th century it has subsequently been remodelled countless times. Following recent restoration work the palace became a hotel. The banqueting hall is decorated with scenes taken from the works of Ovid.

Whilst going in the direction of road number 21 it is worth stopping at EGYHÁZASDENGELEG where the **Roman Catholic church** survives in its 1332 form. In neighbouring HÉHALOM the 40-metre classical three-arched bridge is also worth a quick look.

BALASSAGYARMAT

Balassagyarmat proudly bears the name *Civitas Fortissima.* It was on 19th January 1919, that the locals took up weapons and joined forces with the Hungarian troops stationed in nearby Magyar-nándor. Together they managed to drive off the intruding Slovak troops who had begun taking the railway along the Ipoly Valley, as well as the town and the surrounding 18 villages.

Palócföld folk architecture at the open-air part of the Palóc Museum.

The immediate area was inhabited as far back as the Stone Age. One of the original Hungarian tribes settling in the Carpathian Basin was known as the Gyarmat. The area was later owned by the Balassa family, and it was they who built Gyarmat Castle following the Mongolian invasion in 1241. In the period immediately following the Turkish occupation, Slovak, Serb, Greek, Bulgarian and German merchants and manufacturers settled in the town. In 1790, Balassagyarmat became Nóg-rád's county town. The most traumatic event in the town's history came in 1920 when the town was split in two by the Treaty of Trianon, the town's right bank becoming part of Czechoslovakia.

The Baroque **Roman Catholic church** (Rákóczi út), built in 1746, contains the relics of Saint Felician kept in a glass coffin on one of the side altars.

The **Serbian Church,** which lies in the square of the Old Town, is now a gallery. The hexagonal five-storeyed classical **prison** (1842–1845, Madách I. út 2.) is still just that, so you can't go in. The old **County Hall**, which is also classical in style, is where both *Imre Madách* and *Kálmán Mikszáth* enjoyed public office. Their statues can be found in Rákóczi út.

The **Palóc Museum** is situated in the *Palóc-liget*. Apart from a wooden cottage there are some outbuildings, a dovecote, as well as a shadoof, a carved crucifixion and an exact copy of the chapel at Szanda. A number of buildings were brought from the village of Karancslapujtő.

The *Duna-Ipoly National Park* starts where the town finishes. The eastern part of which makes up the *Ipolyszög Alder Plain*. 70 species of birds are known to nest here. (For a more detailed account of the area see the relevant section in the chapter focusing on the National Parks.)

Balassagyarmat's leisure park is known as the Nyírfa. There are six lakes there for the anglers and indeed those who are more interested in doing nothing in particular.

The patronal festival of Saint Anna (26th July) is one of Balassagyarmat's big annual events. There is also the annual summer International Muzsikus Workshop and Music Festival, not to mention the Ipoly Market.

THE INNER CSERHÁT

Travelling on the road to Aszód along the *Galga Valley* you go deep into the heart of *Palóc country*. You can also go up the valley by train, each station making a good place to start a hike into the *Cserhát*, or a cycle tour around the villages.

CSESZTVE was where the writer *Imre Madách* (1832–1864) once lived. This beautifully situated village makes the most of its connections with the writer of *The Tragedy of Man*. There is a **museum** dedicated to his memory in the 18th century classical villa (Kossuth út 7.) where the Madách family once lived. There you can see a collection of early editions, and books published in thirty different foreign languages. There are also theatre posters and personal items and documents belonging to the Madách family.

Madách Hall is surrounded by some beautiful parkland.
Every year at the beginning of October an academic conference is held at Csesztve on some aspect of Madách's life and work.

The Vay-Zichy Palace in Mohora, which although renovated, can only be seen from the outside; the Jánossy Palace in Cserhátsurány and the Bene-Teichmann Palace in Bercel were all built in the final years of the 17th century, and they all have thick walls and corner turrets. The turrets are not merely ornamental devices. At the time they were built the turrets could have been needed as Turkish incursions were still a distinct possibility.

MOHORA was owned by *Kálmán Mikszáth's* father-in-law, Mátyás Mauks. In the courtyard of his country seat, now the local chemist's, there is an old chestnut tree under which the writer was known to sit and work. It was in the small Lutheran church in the village that he got married for a second time, to Ilona Mauks.

One of the greatest actresses of her time, *Klári Tolnay*, was rewarded with a permanent **exhibition** dedicated to her memory in 2000, which you can see in the village at Kossuth út 30.

It is worth visiting CSERHÁTSURÁNY *if but for no other reason than to visit the Roman Catholic church.*
According to local legend the fine 14th century Gothic tower was used as a place of worship during the Turkish occupation.

TERÉNY's great sight is the ark-like ecumenical **bell tower**, in which every part of the mechanism moves when the bells strike. Arts and crafts workshops are held during the summer months, works from which are shown at an exhibition in Balassagyarmat.

Old village customs are alive and well in Terény. One of those, which is particularly popular, is the midsummer's night's custom of fire-jumping on 24th June, which nowadays takes place during the day, involving boys and girls rather than adults.

SZANDA is situated under a group of three hills jutting out from the *Cserhát Hills.* On the easternmost of these you can see the ruins of the **castle**. Six metres of tower stick out defiantly into the sky. Above the *Szandaváralja* end of the village stands the **Little Chapel of the Virgin Mary,** an important Palóc shrine. The arms and legs of the statue of the Blessed Virgin Mary, made in 1891, can be moved, and at festivals she is always dressed up. Embroidered Palóc garments are made as gifts to the statue in thanks for pleas which have been heeded.

The cellars at Szanda go to great lengths to preserve the local wine-making traditions.

BERCEL is Szanda's southern neighbour in the *Gólya Valley.* One of the finest buildings in the village is **Bene-Teichmann Palace** (Kossuth tér 1.) built at the end of the 17th century. It is now used as a chemist's. The Baroque **Kállay Palace** has been turned into a forty-bed hotel (Kenderváros út 11.). Both the Baroque **Roman Catholic church** (1790) and the *Vir Dolorum* statue (1790) can be found on the *Templompart.*

Jákotpuszta, which is also part of Bercel, is where you can find the **Southern Cserhát Ecological Centre** which aims to save ancient and not so ancient local farm animals. The centre is part of an initiative to promote traditional forms of farming and animal husbandry.

However, it can only be visited when the rare breeds of sheep, goats, horses and donkeys are out grazing, between Saint George's Day and Michaelmas.

Szanda Castle, built after the Tatar invasion, fell into Turkish hands in 1546. In was however recaptured by castellan Bertalan Horváth in 1551. He was fortunate to receive a tip-off from a Turk on the run, who told him the whereabouts of a secret tunnel into the castle.

The Nógrád Basin

Horpács

This small village lying in its hollow is famous for being the place where *Kálmán Mikszáth* (1847--1910) lived.

Mikszáth Hall (1910), which stands in the middle of a park, now houses a *museum* dedicated to the life and work of the great author. Apart from the usual personal items and the furniture the exhibition also contains original manuscripts, first editions and toys belonging to his son Jánoska, who died while still young.

Mikszáth was born in the northern part of Nógrád Country in the village of Szklabonya, which now lies in Slovakia. He went to Pest to work as a journalist, but it was only after considerable hardship that he eventually made a name for himself as a journalist in Szeged. It was only towards the end of his life that he bought his property in Horpács.

The most important event in the history of Romhány was the battle which took place on 22nd January 1710, the last major military encounter of the Rákóczi War of Independence.

An eight-metre-high **monument** (1932) crowned by a mythical Hungarian eagle, the turul, marks the site on the road out towards Szátok. According to local legend Ferenc Rákóczi II. directed his troops from underneath an old *hazel tree* on Bereczki út. In a battle of ever-shifting fortunes the "labanc" troops suffered three times as many casualties as their enemies, but still managed to force Rákóczi's "kuruc" army to retreat.

So it is with the historical events at Romhány we take leave of *Northern Hungary*.

Thanks for joining us on our journey. It has been one full of adventures, and we have indeed been well off the beaten track. We hope you managed to get some relaxation along the way. We also hope that our handbook will continue to prove a useful companion on future journeys, whether they be up hill or down dale, or flat out along the plains. If you require any further information, you should at the relevant section at the back of the book.

2heti turizmus

Bi-weekly Tourism is the dominant source of information for the Hungarian tourist trade, it **appears twice a month**, at a circulation of **5000 copies**.

The goal of the review is to provide those involved in an ever-changing tourist market with global information on Hungarian and international trends and changes. The structure of our columns adjusts to the expectations of the trade, we regularly report on the recent problems, market possibilities, and events that interest industry. We deal with business trips in our supplement '**Business Tourism**'.

Target audience: travel agencies, commercial accommodation providers, program managers, event organizers, transport companies, tourist guides, travel insurance companies, tourist information offices, tourist representatives, trade schools, tourism counselling companies, the assigned departments of polity organizations and regional trade associations.

Further information and subscription:
www.turizmusonline.hu

Spa &Wellness

This thematic review presents Hungary's varied health tourism from a **professional point of view**. **10 000 copies** reach the members of this special and complex market, providing the most effective accessibility on both the demand and supply side.

Thermal baths, spa institutions, wellness hotels, fitness and wellness suppliers and vendors, as well as Hungarian doctors and dentists read the magazine. The December issue was also available to the general public, as it was the official review of the **Spa & Wellness Health Tourism exhibition, conference and fair**.

CONTENTS

PRIOR TO THE JOURNEY

Having almost come to the end of the travel guide is there anything we could possibly have forgotten?

Just in case we have we would like to conclude by giving you some practical information which we hope will help to answer any additional queries you may have.

Indeed, what follows may be just as useful to your hosts as it is to you.

By the time you arrive in Hungary all your official documents and bank cards should be in order, but just in case they aren't we have some useful addresses which we hope will get you out of any scrapes.

The addresses may also be useful if you suddenly decide to travel to one of the countries bordering on Hungary.

It's always reassuring to know exactly what to expect, so we have included some useful information about local living conditions and local habits, as well as advice and lots of useful addresses.

We hope this will all prove comforting to visitors, making your stay all the more straightforward.

NATIONAL TOURIST ORGANISATIONS

The Hungarian Tourist Organisation (MATUR)
Budapest 1077
Rózsa u. 4–6.
Tel.: 1/321-5800/ ext. 711
The National Association of Village Tourism
Budapest 1077
Király u. 93.
Tel.: 1/268-0592, Fax: 1/352-9804
The Budapest Tourist Office
Budapest 1056
Március 15. tér 7.
Tel.: 1/266-0479
The Hungarian Youth Hostel Association
Budapest 1077
Almássy tér 6.
Tel.: 1/352-1572/ ext. 204,
Fax: 1/343-5167
The Hungarian Camping and Caravanning Club
Budapest 1085
Mária u. 34. II/4.
Customer Service
Tel.: 1/267-5256
The Hungarian Nature Lovers' Association
Budapest 1065
Bajcsy-Zsilinszky út 31.
Tel.: 1/311-2467, 311-9289, 332-7177
Fax: 1/353-1930
The Hungarian Congress Office Association
Budapest 1118
Szent Adalbert tér 20.
Tel.: 1/319-5667

HUNGARIAN NATIONAL TOURIST OFFICES

www.hungarytourism.hu

www.tourinform.hu

Budapest V., Sütő utca 2. (Deák tér) (8am–8pm)
1/438-8080 (0–24)
Hot-line: (+36) 80/630-800, (+36) 30/30-30-600
Budapest H-1548
Fax: 1/488-8661
E-mail: hungary@tourinform.hu
Internet: www.hungarytourism.hu

An up-to-date list of all the offices making up Tourinform network can be found on the following six pages. Brought to you by Magyar Turizmus Ltd, the addresses on the white sections are arranged according to region and in alphabetical order.

Here, on the yellow sections, Magyar Turizmus Ltd. bring you three pages of foreign representations in Hungary with the addresses written in their relevant languages.

USA
Hungarian National Tourist Office
N.Y. 10155-3398 New York,
150 East 58th Street, 33rd Floor
Tel.: (1)212/355-0240, 355-5055
Fax: (1)212/207-4103
E-mail: hnto@gotohungary.com
www.gotohungary.com

AUSTRIA
Ungarisches Tourismusamt
A-1010 Wien, Opernring 5/2. Stk.
Tel.: (43)1/585-20-1213, 585-20-1214
Fax: (43)1/585-20-1215
E-mail: htvienna@hungarytourism.hu
www.ungarn-tourismus.at

BELGIUM
Office du Tourisme de Hongrie
(Hongaars Verkeersbureau)
B-1050 Bruxelles, Avenue Louise 365
(B-1050 Brussel, 365 Loizalaan)
Tel.: (32)2/346-8630, Fax: (32)2/344-6967
E-mail: htbrussels@skynet.be
www.visithongrie.be; www.visithongarije.be

THE CZECH REPUBLIC
Madarská Turistika
140 21 Praha 4, 5. kvetna 65
Tel.: (420)261/174-166, 174-167
Fax: (420)261/174-169
E-mail: htprague@hungarytourism.hu
www.madarsko.cz

DENMARK
Ungarns Turistkontor, Information Office
DK 2100 Köbenhavn Ö,
Strandvejen 6
Tel.: (45)39/161-350
Fax: (45)39/161-355
E-mail: htcopenhagen@mail.dk
www.ungarn.dk

FRANCE
Office du Tourisme de Hongrie
75116 Paris
140 avenue Victor Hugo
Tel.: (33)1/5370-6717, 5370-6718
Fax: (33)1/4704-8357
E-mail: othon@club-internet.fr
www.hongrietourisme.com

BUDAPEST AND CENTRAL TRANSDANUBIA

Budapest 1052 Sütő utca 2. (Deák tér)
Budapest 1185 Ferihegy Terminals 2A
and 2B
Budapest 1061 Liszt Ferenc tér 11.
Tel.: 1/322-4098
Fax: 1/342-9390
Budapest 1014 Szentháromság tér, (Buda Castle)
Tel.: 1/488-0453, 1/488-0475
Fax: 1/488-0474
Budapest 1062 Nyugati Pályaudvar (Railway Station)
Tel.: 1/302-8580
Fax: 1/302-8580
Budapest* 1054 Steindl I. u. 12.
(Pest megyei iroda),
Tel.: 1/353-2956, 1/428-0377
Fax: 1/428-0375 pest-m@tourinform.hu
Budaörs 2040 M1-M7 AGIP Komplexum
Tel.: 23/417-518
Fax: 23/417-518
Cegléd 2700 Kossuth tér 1.
Tel.: 53/500-285
Fax: 53/500-286
cegled@tourinform.hu
Gödöllő 2100 Királyi Kastély
Tel.: 28/415-403

Tel./fax: 28/415-402
godollo@tourinform.hu
Ócsa 2364 Bajcsy-Zsilinszky utca 2.
Tel.: 29/578-750
Tel./ fax: 29/578-751
ocsa@tourinform.hu
Ráckeve 2300 Kossuth L. u. 51.
Tel.: 24/429-747
Fax: 24/429-747
rackeve@tourinform.hu
Rétság 2651 Kossuth út 1–3.
Tel.: 32/550-155
retsag@tourinform.hu
Szentendre 2000 Dumtsa Jenő u. 22.
Tel./fax: 26/317-965, 26/317-966
szentendre@tourinform.hu
Vác 2600 Március 15. tér 16–18.
Tel.: 27/316-160
Fax: 27/316-464
vac@tourinform.hu
Veresegyház 2112 Fő út 9.
Tel.: 28/558-035
Tel./fax: 28/558-036
veresegyhaz@tourinform.hu
Zsámbék 2072 Etyeki út 2.
Tel./fax: 23/342-318
zsambek@tourinform.hu

FINLAND
**Unkarin Matkailutoimisto,
Information Office**
00100 Helsinki
Kaisaniemenkatu 10
Tel.: (358)9/8240-1040
Fax: (358)9/8240-1041
E-mail: hthelsinki@hungarytourism.inet.fi
www.unkarinmatkailu.fi

NETHERLAND
Hongaars Verkeersbureau
2593 BS Den Haag,
Laan van Nieuw Oost Indie 271
Tel.: (31)70/320-9092,
Fax: (31)70/327-2833
E-mail: hong@euronet.nl
www.hongarsverkeersbureau.nl

IRELAND
Hungarian National Tourist Office
Dublin 2, Hungarian Embassy
2 Fitzwilliam Place

Tel.: (353)1/6612-879,
Fax: (353)1/6612-889
E-mail: info@visithungary.ie
www.visithungary.ie

JAPAN
Hungarian National Tourist Office
106-0031 Tokyo,
Minato-ku, Nishiazabu 4-16-13, 28 Mori Building
11F
Tel.: (81)3/3499-4953
Fax:(81)3/3499-4944
E-mail: info@hungarytabi.jp
www.hungarytabi.jp

POLAND
**Narodowe Przedstawicielstwo Turystyki
Wegierskiej w Polsce**
00-464 Warszawa, ul. Szwolezerów 10.
Tel.: (48)22/841-3024
Fax: (48)22/841-4157
E-mail: huntour@waw.pdi.net
www.wegry.info.pl

TRANSDANUBIA

Bakonyszombathely 2884 Kossuth u. 50.
Tel.: 34/359-155, Fax: 34/359-122
bakonyszombathely@tourinform.hu
Bóly 7754 Erzsébet tér 1., Tel./fax: 69/368-100
boly@tourinform.hu
Bük 9737 Eötvös u. 11.
Tel.: 94/558-419, 94/558-439, Fax: 94/359-322
buk@tourinform.hu
Celldömölk 9500 Dr. Géfin L. tér 1.
Tel./fax: 95/423-940
celldomolk@tourinform.hu
Csurgó 8840 Csokonai u. 24., Tel./fax: 82/571-046
csurgo@tourinform.hu
Dombóvár 7200 Hunyadi tér 27.
Tel./fax: 74/466-053
dombovar@tourinform.hu
Dunaföldvár 7020 Rákóczi u. 2.
Tel./fax: 75/341-176
dunafoldvar@tourinform.hu
Enying 8130 Kossuth u. 29.
Tel./fax: 22/372-952, 22/572-072
enying@tourinform.hu
Fertőd 9431 J. Haydn u. 3.
Tel.: 99/370-182, Tel./fax: 99/370-544
fertod@tourinform.hu

Gárdony 2484 Szabadság út 16.
Tel.: 22/570-078, Tel./fax: 22/570-077
gardony@tourinform.hu
Győr* 9021 Árpád u. 32. (county)
Tel.: 96/522-255 Fax: 96/522-224
gyor-m@tourinform.hu
Győr 9021 Árpád u. 32.
Tel.: 96/336-817 (town) Tel./fax: 96/311-771
gyor@tourinform.hu
Harkány 7815 Kossuth u. 2/a
Tel.: 72/479-624 Fax: 72/479-989
harkany@tourinform.hu
Kaposvár* 7400 Csokonai u. 3. (county)
Tel.: 82/508-150, 82/508-151, Tel./fax: 82/317-133
somogy-m@tourinform.hu
Kaposvár 7400 Fő u. 8. (town)
Tel.: 82/512-921, 82/512-922 Fax: 82/320-404
kaposvar@tourinform.hu
Kárász 7333 Petőfi u. 36.
Tel./fax: 72/420-074
karasz@tourinform.hu
Komárom 2900 Igmándi út 2.
Tel.: 34/540-590 Tel./fax: 34/540-591
komarom@tourimform.hu
Kőszeg 9730 Jurisics tér 7.
Tel.: 94/563-120 Tel./fax: 94/563-121
koszeg@tourinform.hu

THE UNITED KINGDOM
Hungarian National Tourist Office
SW1X 8 AL London,
46. Eaton Place
Tel.: (44)207/823-1032, 823-1055
Fax: (44)207/823-1459
E-mail: htlondon@btinternet.com
www.hungarywelcomesbritain.com

GERMANY
Ungarisches Tourismusamt
D-60313 Frankfurt am Main,
An der Hauptwache 11
Tel.: (49)69/9288-4620
Fax: (49)69/9288-4623
E-mail: sekretariat@ungarn-tourismus.de
www.ungarn-tourismus.de

Ungarisches Tourismusamt
Nord-/Ostdeutschland
D-10178 Berlin, Neue Prominade 5
Tel.: (49)30/243-146-0
Fax: (49)30/243-146-13
E-mail: ungarn.info.berlin@t-online.de
www.ungarn-tourismus.de

Ungarisches Tourismusamt
Süd-Deutschland
D-80637 München,
Dom Pedro Str. 17
Tel.: (49)89/1211-5230, 1211-5253
Fax: (49)89/1211-5251
E-mail: ungarn.info.muc@t-online.de
www.ungarn-tourismus.de

Ungarisches Tourismusamt
Mitte-/West-Deutschland
D-60313 Frankfurt am Main
An der Hauptwache 11
Tel.: (49)69/9288-460
Fax: (49)69/9288-4613
E-mail: ungarn.info.frankfurt@t-online.de
www.ungarn-tourismus.de

ITALY
Ufficio Turistico Ungherese
20145 Milano
Via Alberto Da Giussano 1.
Tel.: (39)02/4819-5434, Fax: (39)02/4801-0268
E-mail: ungotour@tin.it
www.turismoungherese.it

Lenti 8960 Táncsics M. u. 2/A
Tel.: 92/551-188, 92/351-320, Fax: 92/551-189
lenti@tourinform.hu
Magyarhertelend 7394 Kossuth L. u. 46.
Tel.: 72/521-002, Tel./fax: 72/521-001
magyarhertelend@tourinform.hu
Mesztegnyő 8716 Szabadság tér 6.
Tel./fax: 85/329-066
mesztegnyo@tourinform.hu
Mohács 7700 Széchenyi tér 1.
Tel.: 69/505-515, Tel./fax: 69/505-504
mohacs@tourinform.hu
Mosonmagyaróvár 9200 Kápolna tér 16.
Tel./fax: 96/206-304
mosonmagyarovar@tourinform.hu
Nagyatád 7500 Baross G. u. 2.
Tel.: 82/553-012, Fax: 82/553-013
nagyatad@tourinform.hu
Orfű 7677 Széchenyi tér 1.
Tel.: 72/598-115, 72/598-116, Fax: 72/598-119
orfu@tourinform.hu
Paks 7030 Szent István tér 2.
Tel.: 75/421-575 Fax: 75/510-265
paks@tourinform.hu
Pannonhalma 9090 Petőfi u. 25.
Tel./fax: 96/471-733
pannonhalma@tourinform.hu

Pápa 8500 Fő u. 5.
Tel./fax: 89/311-535
papa@tourinform.hu
Pécs 7621 Széchenyi tér 9.
Tel.: 72/213-315, Fax: 72/212-632
baranya-m@tourinform.hu
Pécsvárad 7720 Kossuth L. u. 31.
Tel./fax: 72/466-487
pecsvarad@tourinform.hu
Sárvár 9600 Várkerület 33.
Tel.: 95/520-178, 95/520-181
Fax: 95/520-179
sarvar@tourinform.hu
Siklós 7800 Felszabadulás u. 3.
Tel.: 72/579-090, Fax: 72/579-091
siklos@tourinform.hu
Sopron 9400 Előkapu u. 11.
 Tel.: 99/338-592, Tel./fax: 99/338-892
sopron@tourinform.hu
Sümeg 8330 Kossuth L. utca 15.
Tel.: 87/550-276
Tel./fax: 87/550-275
sumeg@tourinform.hu
Székesfehérvár 8000 Városház tér 1.
Tel.: 22/312-818
Fax: 22/502-772
fejer-m@tourinform.hu

Ufficio Turistico, Punto d' Informazione
00187 Rome, Via Sallustiana 23.
Tel./Fax: (39)06/4744-836
E-mail: romaungotour@virgilio.it
www.turismoungherese.it

THE RUSSIAN FEDERATION
Buro Torgovogo sovetnika po turizmu
Vengerskoj Respubliki
123242 Moscow, Krasznaja Presznya ul. 1-7
Tel.: (70)95/363-3962/3241, Fax: (70)95/363-3963
E-mail: htmoscow@huntourmow.sovintel.ru
www.hungary.ru

ROMANIA
Consulatul General al Republicii Ungare,
Sectia Turism 3400 Cluj-Napoca, C.P. 352
Tel./Fax: (40)264/440-547, E-mail:
htcluj@hungarytourism.ro, www.hungarytourism.ro

SPAIN
Oficina Nacional de Turismo de Hungría
28020 Madrid, Avenida de Brasil 17. piso 10, puerta B
Tel.: (34)91/556-9348, Fax: (34)91/556-9869
E-mail: kepviselet@hungarytourism.ro
www.hungriaturismo.com

SWITZERLAND
Ungarisches Tourismusamt
CH-8035 Zürich, Stampfenbach Str. 78
Tel.: (41)1/361-1414
Fax: (41)1/361-3939
E-mail: info@ungarn-tourism.ch,
www.ungarn-tourism.hu,
www.hongrie-tourisme.ch

SWEDEN
Ungerska Turistbyran I Norden
S-114 34 Stockholm,
Birger Jarlsgatan 22.
Tel.: (46)8/20-40-40
Fax: (46)8/611-7647
E-mail: htstockholm@swipnet.se
www.ungernturism.org; www.ungarnturisme.com

UKRAINE
Komercijnij Viddil Posolstva Ugorskoji Respubliki
Informacijne Bjuro "Ugorshina-Turizm"
01034 Kijev, vul Striletska 16.
Tel.: (380)44/228-0842, 44/228-0811
E-mail: htkiev@hungarytourism.hu
www.ugor.kiev.ua

Szekszárd 7100 Garay tér 18. (town)
Tel.: 74/511-263, Tel./fax: 74/511-264
szekszard@tourinform.hu
Szekszárd 7100 Bajcsy-Zsilinszky u. 7. (county)
Tel.: 74/418-907, Fax: 74/412-082
tolna-m@tourinform.hu
Szombathely 9700 Kossuth Lajos u. 1–3.
Tel.: 94/514-451, Fax: 94/514-450
szombathely@tourinform.hu
Tamási 7090 Garay u. 1–3.
Tel./fax: 74/470-902
tamasi@tourinform.hu
Tata 2890 Ady Endre u. 9. Pf.: 218
Tel.: 34/586-046, Tel./fax: 34/586-045
komarom-m@tourinform.hu
Veszprém* 8200 Megyeház tér 1. (county)
Tel.: 88/545-045, 88/545-047,
88/545-048, 88/545-049, Fax: 88/545-039
veszprem-m@tourinform.hu
Veszprém 8200 Vár u. 4. (town)
Tel./fax: 88/404-548
veszprem@tourinform.hu
Zalaegerszeg* 8900 Kosztolányi u. 10. (county)
Tel.: 92/597-560, Tel./fax: 92/597-561
zala-m@tourinform.hu
Zalaegerszeg 8900 Széchenyi tér 4-6. (town) Pf.: 506
Tel.: 92/316-160, 92/510-696, Fax: 92/510-697
zalaegerszeg@tourinform.hu
Zirc 8420 Rákóczi tér 1.
Tel.: 88/416-816 Fax: 88/416-817
zirc@tourinform.hu

BALATON

Alsóörs 8226 Strand sétány 1.
Tel./fax: 87/575-001 (regional office: 1st June–31st Aug.)
alsoors@tourinform.hu
Badacsony 8261 Park utca 6.
Tel.: 87/531-013, Tel./fax: 87/431-046
badacsonytomaj@tourinform.hu
Balatonalmádi 8220 Városház tér 4.
Tel.: 88/594-081, Tel./fax: 88/594-080
balatonalmadi@tourinform.hu
Balatonboglár 8630 Erzsébet u. 12-14.
Tel./fax: 85/550-168
balatonboglar@tourinform.hu
Balatonföldvár
8623 Széchenyi Imre utca 2.
Tel.: 84/700-036, Tel./fax: 84/540-220
(15th June–15th Sept.)
8623 Kőröshegyi út 1.
Tel.: 84/700-036 Tel./fax: 84/540-220
balatonfoldvar@tourinform.hu

Balatonfüred 8230 Petőfi u. 68.
Tel.: 87/580-480, Fax: 87/580-481
balatonfured@tourinform.hu
Balatonkenese 8174 Táncsics Mihály u. 24.
Tel./fax: 88/491-904
balatonkenese@tourinform.hu
Balatonvilágos 8171 Aligai u. 1.
Tel./fax: 88/446-034
balatonvilagos@tourinform.hu
Buzsák 8695 Fő tér 1/A
Tel./fax: 85/530-070, buzsak@tourinform.hu
Gyenesdiás 8315 Kossuth Lajos u. 97.
Tel./fax: 83/511-790
gyenesdias@tourinform.hu
Fonyód 8640 Ady Endre u. 1.
Tel./fax: 85/363-170
fonyod@tourinform.hu
Keszthely 8360 Kossuth L. u. 28.
Tel./fax: 83/314-144, Tel.: 83/511-660, 83/511-661
keszthely@tourinform.hu
Révfülöp 8253 Villa Filip tér 8/B
Tel.: 87/463-194, Tel./fax: 87/463-092
revfulop@tourinform.hu
Siófok 8600 Víztorony, Pf.: 75.
Tel./fax: 84/315-355, 84/310-117
siofok@tourinform.hu
Tapolca 8300 Fő tér 17.
Tel.: 87/510-777, Fax: 87/510-778
tapolca@tourinform.hu
Tihany 8237 Kossuth u. 20.
Tel.: 87/438-016, Tel./fax: 87/448-804
tihany@tourinform.hu
Zalakaros 8749 Gyógyfürdő tér 10.
Tel./fax: 93/340-421
zalakaros@tourinform.hu
Zamárdi 8621 Kossuth utca 16.
Tel.: 84/345-291, 84/545-052, 84/545-053
Fax: 84/345-290
zamardi@tourinform.hu

THE GREAT PLAIN AND LAKE TISZA

Abádszalók
5241 Füzes Kemping, Strand út 2.
Tel.: 59/535-346, Fax: 59/535-345 (1st May–30th Oct.)
5241 Deák Ferenc u. 1/17. Tel./fax: 59/357-376
abadszalok@tourinform.hu
Baja 6500 Szentháromság tér 5.
Tel.: 79/420-793 Tel./fax: 79/420-792
baja@tourinform.hu
Békéscsaba 5600 Szent István tér 9.
Tel./fax: 66/441-261
bekescsaba@tourinform.hu

Berekfürdő 5309 Berek tér 11.
Tel.: 59/519-007, Fax: 59/319-408
berekfurdo@tourinform.hu
Berettyóújfalu 4100 József A. u. 55.
Tel./fax: 54/400-718
berettyoujfalu@tourinform.hu
Cserkeszőlő 5465 Fürdő u. 1/A
Tel.: 56/568-466, Fax: 56/568-465
cserkeszolo@tourinform.hu
Csongrád 6640 Szentháromság tér 8.
Tel./fax: 63/570-325
csongrad@tourinform.hu
Debrecen 4024 Piac u. 20. (town)
Tel.: 52/412-250, 52/316-419, Fax: 52/535-323
debrecen@tourinform.hu
Debrecen 4026 Kálvin tér 2/a (county)
Tel.: 52/534-544, 52/534-545
hajdu-b@tourinform.hu
Gyomaendrőd 5500 Fő út 173–175.
Tel./fax: 66/386-851
gyomaendrod@tourinform.hu
Gyula 5700 Kossuth L. u. 7.
Tel.: 66/561-681, Tel./fax: 66/561-680
bekes-m@tourinform.hu
Hajdúböszörmény 4220 Kálvin tér 6.
Tel./fax: 52/561-851, 52/561-852
hajduboszormeny@tourinform.hu
Hajdúnánás 4080 Fürdő u. 7.
Tel./fax: 52/702-223 (15th June–31st Aug.)
4080 Köztársaság tér 6.
Tel./fax: 52/382-076
hajdunanas@tourinform.hu
Hajdúszoboszló 4200 Szilfákalja u. 2.
Tel./fax: 52/558-928, 52/558-929
hajduszoboszlo@tourinform.hu
Hódmezővásárhely 6800 Szegfű u. 3.
Tel./fax: 62/249-350
hodmezovasarhely@tourinform.hu
Hortobágy
4071 Pásztormúzeum, Petőfi tér 1.
Tel./fax: 52/589-321 (15th Feb.–15th Dec.)
4071 Czinege János u. 1.
Tel.: 52/589-110, Fax: 52/369-109
hortobagy@tourinform.hu
Jászapáti 5130 Tompa M. u. 2.
Tel./fax: 57/441-008, Fax: 57/441-081
jaszapati@tourinform.hu
Jászberény 5100 Lehel vezér tér 33.
Tel.: 57/411-976/16 m., Tel./fax: 57/406-439
jaszbereny@tourinform.hu
Karcag 5300 Dózsa György u. 5–7.
Tel./fax: 59/503-225
karcag@tourinform.hu

Kecskemét 6000 Kossuth tér 1.
(városi) Tel./fax: 76/481-065
kecskemet@tourinform.hu
Kisköre 3384 Kossuth L. utca 8.
Tel./fax: 36/358-023
kiskore@tourinform.hu
Kiskőrös 6200 Petőfi tér 4/a.
Tel.: 78/514-850, 78/514-851
Fax: 78/414-850
kiskoros@tourinform.hu
Kiskunmajsa 6120 Zárda u. 2.
Tel./fax: 77/481-327
kiskunmajsa@tourinform.hu
Kistelek 6760 Kossuth u. 5-7.
Tel.: 62/597-420, Fax: 62/597-421
kistelek@tourinform.hu
Kisújszállás 5310 Deák Ferenc u. 6.
Tel./fax: 59/520-672
kisujszallas@tourinform
Makó 6900 Széchenyi tér 22.
Tel./fax: 62/210-708
mako@tourinform.hu
Mezőtúr 5400 Szabadság tér 17.
Tel.: 56/550-637, Tel./fax: 56/350-901
mezotur@tourinform.hu
Mórahalom 6782 Röszkei u. 2.
Tel./fax: 62/280-294
morahalom@tourinform.hu
Nagykörű 5065 Május 1 út 1.
Tel./fax: 56/496-305
nagykoru@tourinform.hu
Nyíracsád 4262 Petőfi tér 3.
Tel./fax: 52/207-271
nyiracsad@tourinform.hu
Nyíregyháza 4400 Országzászló tér 6.
Tel./fax: 42/504-647, 42/504-648
szabolcs-m@tourinform.hu
Ópusztaszer 6767 Szoborkert 68.
Tel.: 62/275-133/121 m.,
Fax: 62/275-007
opusztaszer@tourinform.hu
Orosháza 5904 Fasor u. 2/a.
Tel./fax: 68/414-422
oroshaza@tourinform.hu
Pusztamérges 6785 Ifjúság tér 1.
Tel./fax: 62/286-702
pusztamerges@tourinform.hu
Ruzsa 6786 Alkotmány u. 2.
Tel.: 62/585-210
ruzsa@tourinform.hu
Sóstógyógyfürdő
4431 Nyíregyháza Sóstógyógyfürdő, Víztorony,
Tel./fax: 42/411-193 (15th May–15th Sept.)

4400 Nyíregyháza, Damjanich u. 4–6. (off season)
Tel./fax: 42/402-115
sostofurdo@tourinform.hu
Szarvas 5540 Kossuth tér 3.
Tel./fax: 66/311-140, Tel.: 66/210-062
szarvas@tourinform.hu
Szeged* 6722 Tábor u. 7/b. (county)
Tel.: 62/548-092, Fax: 62/548-093
csongrad-m@tourinform.hu
Szeged 6720 Dugonics tér 2. (town)
Tel./fax: 62/488-690, Tel.: 62/488-699
szeged@tourinform.hu
Szeghalom 5520 Szabadság tér 10–12.
Tel./fax: 66/470-380
szeghalom@tourinform.hu
Szolnok 5000 Ságvári krt. 4.
Tel.: 56/420-704, Fax: 56/341-441
szolnok-m@tourinform.hu
Tiszacsege 4066 Fő u. 38.
Tel.: 52/588-036, Fax: 52/588-037
tiszacsege@tourinform.hu
Tiszafüred 5350 Fürdő út 21.
Tel./fax: 59/511-123, 59/511-124
tiszafured@tourinform.hu
Tótkomlós 5940 Marx u. 15
Tel./fax: 68/462-908
maroshatsag@tourinform.hu
Vásárosnamény 4800 Szabadság tér 33.
Tel.: 45/570-206, Tel./fax: 45/570-207
vasarosnameny@tourinform.hu

NORTHERN HUNGARY

Abaújszántó 3881 Szent István tér 1.
Tel.: 47/330-053
abaujszanto@tourinform.hu
Aggtelek 3759 Baradla-oldal 3.
Tel.: 48/503-001, 48/343-073
Fax: 48/503-002
aggtelek@tourinform.hu
Balassagyarmat 2660 Köztársaság tér 6.
Tel.: 35/500-640
Fax: 35/500-641
balassagyarmat@tourinform.hu
Bátonyterenye 3070 Ózdi út 9.
Tel.: 32/553-295
batonyterenye@tourinform.hu
Dédestapolcsány 3643 Petőfi u. 21.
Tel./fax: 48/340-013
dedestapolcsany@tourinform.hu
Edelény 3780 István király út 63.
Tel./fax: 48/342-999
edeleny@tourinform.hu

Eger 3300 Bajcsy-Zsilinszky utca 9. Pf.: 263
Tel.: 36/517-715,
Fax: 36/518-815
eger@tourinform.hu
Encs 3860 Petőfi út 20 –22.
Tel.: 46/587-389
Tel./fax: 46/587-390
encs@tourinform.hu
Gyöngyös 3200 Fő tér 10.
Tel./fax: 37/311-155
gyongyos@tourinform.hu
Hatvan 3000 Grassalkovich Kastély
Tel.: 37/346-415, 37/540-014
Fax: 37/342-383
hatvan@tourinform.hu
Hollókő 3176 Kossuth utca 68.
Tel.: 32/579-011, Tel./fax: 32/579-010
holloko@tourinform.hu
Kazár 3127 Kossuth út 17.
Tel.: 32/341-363
kazar@tourinform.hu
Mezőkövesd 3400 Szent László tér 23.
Tel.: 49/500-285, Fax: 49/500-286
mezokovesd@tourinform.hu
Miskolc 3530 Mindszent tér 1. (county)
Tel./fax: 46/348-921
borsod-m@tourinform.hu
Miskolc 3525 Rákóczi u. 2. (town)
Tel.: 46/350-425
Tel./fax: 46/350-439
miskolc@tourinform.hu
Pásztó 3060 Nagymező út 3.
Tel./fax: 32/563-315
paszto@tourinform.hu
Salgótarján 3100 Fő tér 5.
Tel.: 32/512-315, Tel./fax: 32/512-316
salgotarjan@tourinform.hu
Sárospatak 3950 Eötvös u. 6.
Tel.: 47/315-316, Tel./fax: 47/511-441
sarospatak@tourinform.hu
Sátoraljaújhely 3980 Táncsics tér 3.
Tel./fax: 47/321-458
satoraljaujhely@tourinform.hu
Szécsény 3170 Ady E. út 12.
Tel./fax: 32/370-777
szecseny@tourinform.hu
Tokaj 3910 Serház út 1.
Tel.: 47/552-070 Tel./fax: 47/352-259
tokaj@tourinform.hu

**No over-the-counter services, information
is only available by phone or in writing.*

AT THE HUNGARIAN BORDER

Hungary has been a full member of the European Union since May 2004, and now its citizens can travel within the Union using a valid identification card as well as a passport. Likewise, citizens from EU countries will be able to enter Hungary using their IDs.

Hungarian citizens will now be able to use the EU lanes at border crossings in either direction. However, with the exception of Croatia, Hungarian citizens will continue to have to use their passports for travel outside the EU.

Of those non-EU countries bordering Hungary, citizens of the Ukraine and Serbia-Montenegro may only enter the country with a visa. These may be acquired free of charge at Hungarian foreign representations.

Visa applications can only be applied for at the state border in the most singular of circumstances.

For up-to-date border information phone:
From Hungary: 1/4567-101;
From abroad : 0036/1/4567-101.
Public messages can be heard
free of charge on our green phone line:
Tel.: 80/21-22-23

CUSTOMS REGULATIONS

From 1st May 2004, customs inspections ceased to take place on the interior borders of the European Union.

This means that rather than having the usual customs inspections, the border authorities can make so-called mobile checks within a 30km radius of the border. Likewise the mobile units of the Central Mobile Unit Command can stop and check cars and lorries anywhere in the country.

At all border crossings – and this includes Ferihegy Airport as well – there are separate corridors for EU and non-EU citizens. It is still possible that travellers may be stopped by customs.

For citizens of the EU member states there are no restrictions on what you can buy and what you can take in and out of EU countries, as long as they are for private and not commercial use.

The following quantities are the legal limits for what is deemed to be the personal consumption of tobacco and alcohol, when crossing the border: 800 cigarettes, 400 cigarillos, 200 cigars, 1kg of tobacco; 10 litres of spirits, 20 litres of liqueur, 90 litres of wine (of which 60 litres can be champagne), 110 litres of beer.

Travellers arriving from countries outside the European Union, from a so-called "third country", will have to take the following restrictions into consideration. For tobacco products: 200 cigarettes, or 100 cigarillos, or 50 cigars, or 250 grammes of tobacco; in the case of alcohol: 1 litre of spirits with an alcohol content of over 22%, one litre of pálinka or champagne, 2 litres of wine; 50ml of perfume, 250 Eau de toilette. (Other products brought into the country will remain tax-free up to a value of 175 euros in the case of non-commercial goods.) Those under the age of 17 may not bring in alcohol or tobacco products.

We advise those Hungarians wishing to travel to ask for further information at the foreign representation of the country they intend to visit, as there might be some local variations regarding the movement of goods. When there is a food scare the situation is likely to change almost overnight. It is for this reason that we ask you to make the necessary enquiries just before you leave.

Customs information can be found at: www.vam.hu.

It is there you will find the most up-to-date announcements and most recent regulations.

MONEY MATTERS

As the official currency of Hungary is the Hungarian forint you are advised to change your travellers' cheques or foreign currency prior to purchasing, always changing your money in banks, travel agencies or hotels. Never trust illegal money changers in the street.

Forint coins: 1, 2, 5, 10, 20, 50, and 100.
Forint notes: Ft. 200, 500, 1000, 2000, 5000, 10,000, 20,000
The buying and selling rate of the forint is published weekly by the Hungarian National Bank,

displayed on boards in banks and travel agencies, published in the financial newspapers, the national dailies, and on teletext. Exchange rate information can be found at: www.fornax.hu

In Hungary, most recognised bankcards are accepted in banks, larger department stores, travel agencies, restaurants, hotels and post offices.

There are cash dispensers available on the busier thoroughfares and at petrol stations.

Banks are only open on weekdays, so for those without bank cards it's important that you get your funds ready for the weekend between Monday and Friday.

It's safer to carry a card than a large sum of money. Neither hotels nor cloakrooms undertake responsibility for items left in coats, hotel rooms and suitcases.

TICKETS, PRICES AND TIPPING

From May 2004 there will be times when those visiting the 24 state-run museums, most of which are in Budapest, will be able to visit the permanent collections for free.

Some exhibitions and museums are free on certain days of the week. (In the majority of museums vistors can take photographs for their own personal use if they purchase a special photograph ticket at a price stipulated by the institution concerned. If you require photographs for other uses other than

for your own personal enjoyment you will have to ask for special permission from the museum or picture gallery in question. As regular visitors to exhibitions director of the are already no doubt aware, it is frequently forbidden to take photographs of paintings and other precious exhibits using a flash.)

It is not usually possible to haggle over the prices of goods and services, as the prices include VAT. Tips are usually 10% of bills at restaurants, the hairdresser's, in taxis, for room service, etc., with the amount to be paid rounding up, 922 forints being rounded up to 1000, 86 forints up to 100, or 5400 forints up to 6000. At places where the price of goods or services is not indicated it is better to ask in advance.

If shop assistants or personnel ask you if you require a receipt it is better to ask for one, even if it means the price is a little bit higher, as it will enable you make any necessary claims should the need arise.

When the total amount of a bill is doubtful you are advised to check the price of the items one by one and make the necessary complaint to the manager of the shop. If a dispute arises you are advised to get in contact with the Consumers' Protection Service, which has representatives in all the regional centres.

THE HUNGARY CARD

The Hungary Card entitles you to 10 %–100 % reductions. This is the reason why we highly recommend this card to from both Hungary and abroad.

The Hungary Card is available at petrol stations, larger railway stations, Volán Bus Stations, at the offices of the National Holiday Service and at Tourinform Offices throughout Hungary.

Besides the reductions offered at selected lodgings, restaurants, museums and programmes, the Hungary Card provides free accident insurance courtesy of the Atlasz Insurance Co., as well as a 20% discount on the Budapest Card offering three-days of travel and museum entries.

Other benefits include seven half-price railway tickets and six half-price bus tickets when bought in Debrecen, Miskolc, Pécs and Szeged, as well as a free one-day travel card. The card is also very useful when renting cars, telephoning, travelling by taxi or buying a weekly ticket for motorways M1 and M3.

Visitors to the Capital's Grand Circus, the Ópusztaszer National Historical Memorial Park or the Valley of the Arts should make enquiries about the reductions Hungary Card holders are entitled to. Those with a Hungary Card can also purchase a Budapest Card entitling them to further reductions. Both cards include a list of all the special offers available. Those wanting to know exactly what they can expect from the cards in advance to help them with their planning can find all the information they require on several sites on the Internet.

FURTHER INFORMATION:
www.vendegvaro.hu
www.hotelinfo.hu
www.travelport.hu
www.hungarycard.hu

ACCOMMODATION

Guests generally look for accommodation which will make them forget the rigours of everyday life, so booking the right accommodation is therefore a matter of great importance. What follows is designed to make selecting the right place that little bit easier.

BOOKING

Booking hotel rooms in Budapest and the larger provincial towns like Miskolc, Debrecen, Pécs and Szeged is advisable. The busiest months are May, June, September and October.

On Lake Balaton the season starts in early June and ends around 20th August. The major cultural events, festivals, open-air theatrical performances and sporting events like the Hungarian Grand Prix, held during the second or third week in August at the Hungaroring near Budapest, may

Budapest Kártya

Budapest Card 2004
"the whole city in your pocket"

transportation
FREE

museums
FREE
or discounted

sightseeing
-50%

restaurants
-20%

baths
-10%

The Budapest Card is on sale at main underground ticket offices, tourist information offices, travel agencies and hotels.

for 48 hours 4.350 Ft, for 72 hours 5.450 Ft

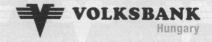

make finding a room very difficult, so it's best to make the necessary enquiries. The hotel rooms can be booked on the premises or at tourist agencies. The major hotel chains and travel agencies are all represented in Hungary, which makes easy pre-booking that much easier. Accommodation searches and bookings can be found on the www.vendegvaro.hu, http://www.vendegvaro.hu website via the AlfaNet-Hotels programme.

On the home pages of Hungarian hotels' database you will find more than 2,600 addresses, together with 7,000 photographs of the accommodation available: www.hotels.hu

Quality

Visitors to Hungary can choose from hotels, guesthouses, camping sites, bungalows, cottages and rooms. All of these have to meet the standards stipulated by the law.

Hotels are graded on a star system. The size of rooms, types of services, fittings and even the aesthetic appearance of the accommodation are stipulated in the legislation. If an institution fails to maintain the standards expected of a particular level of accommodation the institution in question loses a star.

Some of the hotels are controlled or owned by international hotel chains groups. The majority of hotels however are Hungarian-owned and run as family enterprises.

Another option is to stay at one of the beautifully reconstructed palace hotels, country mansions, hunting lodges and lakeside guesthouses, all of which come under the star system. Together with the houses and cottages directly involved in village tourism, they help to provide what is a remarkable cross-section of accommodation possibilities.

Using a system similar to that used for the hotels, the number of sunflowers (1-4) tell you the kind of facilities you can expect to find in a village guesthouse.

Services

Public services meet European standards. Telephones and satellite televisions are accepted stan-dard furnishings. There are no problems with either tidiness, the food or the drinking water. At four- or five-star hotels on Lake Balaton the best-known German, English, French and Italian language newspapers are all available.

The rooms also provide the usual European comforts. The furnishings reflect the grade of the accommodation. In many places you will find local folk architectural designs used.

Family Holidays

At the three- to five-star hotels, in particular, and at the boarding houses in the holiday resorts, you will find accommodation designed especially for families both large and small. Such places are equipped with children's pools and playgrounds and in some places even kindergartens with a resident nursery school teacher.

Accommodation Prices

While prices in the shops and restaurants compared favourably with those in western Europe prior to Hungary joining the EU, the price of accommodation (and fuel) was the same as the European average. Hopefully Hungary's joining the EU will see a stabilisation in the prices, something which experts believe should happen within the next few years, leading eventually to the introduction of the euro in Hungary.

Medicinal Waters

Hungary is richly endowed with thermal waters, Budapest being the only capital in the world which can justifiably claim to be a spa town. Some of the spas have histories stretching back two thousand years, and there are plenty of medicinal hotels offering additional services.

The waters and the mud provide the natural healing powers and there are usually many kinds of balneotheraphy on offer.

Apart from Budapest, there are medicinal hotels at a number of towns, including Hajdúszoboszló, Gyula, Cserkeszőlő, Héviz, Zalakaros, Harkány, Sárvár and Bük.

IN CASE OF TROUBLE

It may just happen that you end up being an eye-witness to an accident or a victim of a crime in which citizens from other countries are involved. In such cases you need to provide the necessary information. The national embassies and consulates in Budapest are only too happy to assist their compatriots in case of an emergency. Listed below are embassies of the German- and English-speaking states and of the countries bordering on Hungary.

USA
BUDAPEST 1054 Szabadság tér 12.
Tel: 1/475-4400 Fax: 1/475-4767 www.usis.hu
Australia
BUDAPEST 1126 Királyhágó tér 8–9.
Tel.: 1/457-9777 Fax: 1/201-9792
www.australia.hu
Croatia
BUDAPEST 1063 Munkácsi M. u. 15.
Tel.: 1/354-1315 Fax: 1/354-1319
PÉCS 7624 Ifjúság útja 11.
Tel.: 72/210-840 Fax: 72/210-575
Ireland
BUDAPEST 1054 Szabadság tér 7–9.
Tel.: 1/302-9600 Fax: 1/302-9599
Levelezési cím:
BUDAPEST 1944 Bank Center, Gránit Torony
Yugoslavia
BUDAPEST 1068 Dózsa György út 92/B
Tel.: 1/322-9838 Fax: 322-1438
Canada
BUDAPEST 1121 Budakeszi út 32.
Tel.: 1/392-3360 Fax: 1/392-3390
www.kanada.hu
Germany
BUDAPEST 1014 Úri u. 64–66.
Tel.: 1/488-3500 Fax: 1/488-3505
The United Kingdom
BUDAPEST 1051 Harmincad u. 6.
Tel.: 1/266-2888 Fax: 1/266-0907
www.britnagykovetseg.hu
Austria
BUDAPEST 1068 Benczúr u. 16.
Tel.: 1/479-7010 Fax: 1/352-8795

Romania
BUDAPEST 1146 Thököly út 72.
Tel.: 1/384-0271 Fax: 1/384-5535
SZEGED 6720 Kelemen u. 5.
Tel.: 62/424-431 Fax: 62/424-429
Slovakia
BUDAPEST 1143 Stefánia út 22–24.
Tel.: 1/460-9010 Fax: 1/460-9020
Slovenia
BUDAPEST 1025 Cseppkő u. 68.
Tel.: 1/438-5600 Fax: 1/325-9187
SZENTGOTTHÁRD 9970 Kossuth Lajos u. 39.
Tel.: 94/383-165 Fax: 94/383-164
Switzerland
BUDAPEST 1143 Stefánia út 107.
Tel.: 1/460-7040 Fax: 1/343-9492
Ukraine
BUDAPEST 1143 Stefánia u. 77.
Tel.: 1/422-4122 Fax: 1/422-4128

LIVING

DATE AND TIME DIFFERENCES
Dates on timetables, tickets etc. are written in the usual Hungarian manner: year/month/day, e.g. 2001. március 1., or if written otherwise 2001. 03. 01., the "03" being the month, not the date. It can also be written III.1., or március 1. To be absolutely sure visitors are advised to double-check the dates on their tickets.
Hungary follows CET, that is Central European Time, GMT +1. Twice a year, at the spring and autumn solstices (March and October), the clock is put one hour ahead, then one hour back at 2am on the Sunday morning.

PUBLIC HOLIDAYS AND OPENING HOURS
1st January (New Year's Day), 15th March (National Holiday), 1st May (Labour Day), Easter Monday, Whit Monday, 20th August (St Stephen's Day), 23rd October (State Holiday), 1st November (All Saints Day), 25th December (Christmas Day), 26th December (Boxing Day) are all holidays.
As shops, restaurants and other public places do not have set Sunday opening hours, holiday opening hours are not uniform. It is a good idea to read

the opening times written in the shops you are likely to need.

Electricity

Throughout Hungary the current is 220 volts, 50-cycle AC. Plugs are the standard continental types, meaning that British and North American appliances need an adaptor.

Frequent Abbreviations

MÁV: Hungarian Railways
Volán: The Bus Company providing local and cross-country bus services.
Malév: Hungarian Airlines

Translation and the Certification of Translations

The translation offices run by the National Translator and Translation Certification Office Co. are available throughout Hungary. They are permitted to make authentic and officially accepted translations.

Insurance

Although it is best to take out an insurance policy at home, there are top-quality insurance companies in Hungary.

ANGLING

In Hungary every angler has to buy an angling ticket. The ticket is valid for a calendar year and for the whole of Hungary. Apart from this ticket local angling associations also issue tickets which are valid at certain fishing waters for a specific length of time.

HUNTING

Hunting in Hungary is subject to state hunting regulations, as well as other terms and conditions stated in the law. Foreign citizens can hunt, though only through hunting organisation offices having trading rights. The county agricultural offices of Ministry of Agriculture and Region Development provide the necessary professional supervision.

GIFTS AND SOUVENIRS

Before buying gifts and souvenirs it is worthwhile consulting the Hungarian Encyclopaedia and the section on Hungarian Specialities in the first chapter of our book.

Apart from that there are sweetshops and bookshops, jewellery and music shops, as well as folk art shops and museum shops, with their reprints and replicas.

Apart from this, plenty of "souvenirs" can be found in the larger supermarkets. You may also find something to your liking at the local markets as well.

It's also worthwhile going out to the various markets and having a look around the stalls . With any luck you might find yourself an antique or a piece of folk art of considerable value.

TELECOMMUNICATIONS

Most of the public telephone boxes can be used for international telephone calls. Telephone cards be bought at petrol stations, tobacconists, supermarkets amongst other places.

International announcer:	190
Sending telegrams:	192
Domestic distance call announcer:	191
Special calls on payment:	
Early morning call:	193
Inland information:	198
Speaking clock:	080
International information:	199

If you want to make a long-distance call within Hungary you have to dial 06 before dialling the local dialling code and the number you want. In the case of international calls, dial 00 first + the country code + the local dialling code + the number you want. Hungary's country code from abroad is 36.

Apart from the Internet cafés and other public institutions offering such services, there are ever more places, including hotels and restaurants, where you can gain Internet access and use the e-mail services available.

TRANSPORT

CAR USE

You should have no particular difficulties when driving to Hungary. The network of petrol stations and their services are excellent and suitable for any type of car.

The locked parking lots at hotels and restaurants are safe, but where such parking is lacking please consult with your host and take their advice. Beware of unguarded parking places and do not leave any packages or valuables visible in the car. Make sure all your doors and windows are locked. The most popular way of stealing cars is when the car thieves stop the innocent, helpful victim pretending they have broken down or that they have just had an accident.

Never get out of your car with the engine still running and be careful when stopping for only a short time as well.

The speed limits for cars are 130 kilometres per hour (81mph) on motorways, 110kph (68mph) on main roads and 90 kph (56mph) on secondary roads.

There are regular speed traps to check whether the compulsory speed limits and temporary limitations announced on signs are being kept.

The police are strict about traffic violations, particularly speeding, where drivers breaking the speed limit may be asked to pay on the spot fines. Use of dipped headlights is compulsory during the daytime on the open road (and for motor bicycles in built-up areas as well) and seat belts have to be worn at all times. Since 1st May 2001 children under the age of 12 can only travel in children's safety-seats. Whilst driving, drivers may not use hand-held mobile phones.

In Hungary, there is zero tolerance on drinking and driving. If police cars (inscribed with the word RENDŐRSÉG) flash the words STOP ELLEN-ŐRZÉS you have to stop.

An inspection can involve the checking of driving and car documents, the state of the car and luggage. In cases of suspected drinking and driving or drug use you may have to take a blood test. Police, ambulance, fire and other special vehicles using blue or yellow flashing lights and a siren have to be given priority.

In the case of a breakdown remember to put out a red warning triangle behind your car. If your car is being towed you have to use your emergency flashing lights. If necessary ask car recovery experts for help.

The Hungarian Automobile Club (Magyar Autóklub) operates a car recovery service on the country's main roads. You can call them on telephone number 188. The emergency services number is 112 where you can call for help in Hungarian and English. In the case of any other languages the operator will switch you through to the appropriate interpreter. Calls are free of charge. You will be put through to the police, ambulance or the fire brigade depending on the nature of the emergency. The individual emergency services can be called on: Ambulance 104, Fire Service 105 and Police 107.

You usually have to pay for parking at busy parking places and at multistorey car parks in the larger towns, although the tariff does not include vehicle supervision.

When parking for a longer period it's best to buy a daily parking ticket. Hotel car-parking is reserved for hotel guests.

There are parking metres in the larger towns, as well as pay and display parking spaces. If you leave your car in a prohibited zone without a parking ticket, or you overstay your parking limit your car is likely to get towed away having been videoed "caught in the act". If you make this mistake you may end up having to pay 50 times the original price of the parking ticket!

Taxis are metered vehicles, distinguishable by their yellow number plates. They are usually available at taxi ranks or can also be hailed in the street. You can of course call a taxi by phone, from a public telephone box if you wish. The drivers are bound to give passengers a receipt on request. Beware of "phoney" taxis without yellow number plates and a taximeter!

TRAVELLING BY AIR

Although there are no timetabled internal flights in Hungary, pleasure flights and air taxi services

Whereever you go in Hungary, you will find OMV petrol stations offering high quality fuel.

Just stop by anytime and try a cup of original "Viennese Coffee" after a long drive. We wish you a pleasant journey.

Move & More. OMV

are available, although the latter are by no means cheap. For further information about airfields and air travel consult the relevant tourist information sections in the regional chapters.

For the time being almost all international flights operate from the two terminals of Budapest's Ferihegy Airport, run by Malév and other foreign airlines.

The booking of tickets and passenger information is not restricted to Budapest, as there are travel agencies and ticket offices selling air tickets in most major towns.

You should shop around when buying air tickets as there are considerable differences in ticket prices, not only between different airlines but between different travel agencies as well.

TRAVELLING BY TRAIN

One quarter of the 160 million passengers who travel on 8,000 kilometres of railway lines run by Hungarian State Railways (MÁV), GYESEV, the State Forestry Narrow-Gauge Railways and the HÉV each year are holidaymakers or tourists. MÁV has more than two dozen ticket offices, in addition to the railway stations where information is also available about fare reductions, timetables and travelling conditions. Also, whether in Hungary or abroad, you can consult the Hungarian Railway homepage:
www.mav.hu

TIMETABLED BUS SERVICES
When the rail tracks stop you can always continue by bus… And this doesn't only mean when it's a question of getting out to the small villages.

Not only do the long-distance bus services cover the whole country, Volán's international bus services take you to numerous major European cities as well.

TAXIS
There are certainly many different kinds of taxis, from the guide conducting a tour in a handful of foreign languages to the van driver transporting some cumbersome item or other. The majority of the taxi drivers, however, transport passengers in the traditional fashion. Taxi drivers are compelled by law to use a calibrated taximeter, so beware of taxi drivers wanting to make deals in advance and those travelling without their taximeter switched on.

Those employed by taxi companies, with telephone numbers that are easy to remember, always give receipts on request.

SHIPPING

Ships and ferries also carry passengers and indeed vehicles on the Danube, the Tisza and on Lake Balaton. The Balaton ferries run to Szántód and Tihany in ice-free conditions.

Departures sometimes depend on the river water levels, so it is wise to ask your hosts about the state of the water.

MOTORWAY

Tolls on Hungarian motorways (M0, M7, M1, M3, M5) apply to the following categories of vehicles:

D1: motorcycles, as well as biaxial vehicles less than 2.1 metres in height and all uniaxial trailers;
D2: biaxial vehicles without trailers exceeding a height of 2.1 metres; buses offering a timetabled service to the public, the D1 category also includes biaxial vehicles pulling trailers;
D3: all those vehicles not in categories D1 and D2.

You can travel on the motorways if you have a display sticker which you have paid for in advance. This should be stuck in a prominent position (e.g. your windscreen). When buying your toll sticker you can choose from those valid for four days, ten days, a month or a year.

Toll stickers are available at the offices of the Állami Autópálya Kezelő Rt. (State Motorways' Management Ltd.) at the relevant border crossing and larger petrol stations.

Their validity is checked electronically with the help of special observation cameras and spot checks.

INFORMATION:
www.autopalya.hu

For over a half a century **Borsod Volán** Transport plc has been at the service of its customers and passengers.

TIMETABLED LONG-DISTANCE SERVICES:

The company provides services to 356 settlements in Borsod County, 266 of which can only be reached by bus. Some 70 million passengers use our services which cover 11 bus stations and about 1800 bus stops.

TIMETABLED LOCAL PASSENGER SERVICES:

The company puts on local bus services in four of the local towns – Ózd, Kazincbarcika, Tiszaújváros and Edelény.

LONG-DISTANCE SERVICES:

Regular bus services run from Miskolc to all the county towns and holiday destinations in eastern Hungary as well as Budapest.

INTERNATIONAL SERVICES:

There are bus services to Rozsnyó (Rozsnava), Rima-szombat (Rimavska Sobota) and Kassa (Kosice) in Slovakia on certain days in the week.

TIMETABLE INFORMATION:

Miskolc	46/340-288
Ózd	48/471-274
Kazincbarcika	48/312-940
Mezőkövesd	49/411-886
Tiszaújváros	49/341-591
Edelény	48/341-420
Sátoraljaújhely	47/321-621
Sárospatak	47/311-027
Encs	46/385-886
Szerencs	47/362-481
Mezőcsát	49/353-334

SPECIAL SERVICES:

Our buses vary from the standard types insofar as the air-conditioned luxury buses are equipped with a refrigerator, a video-recorder and toilets.

Information and bus hire: 46/ 515-060

TECHNICAL SERVICES:

Apart from check-ups, servicing, providing environmental protection measurements, rubber tyre refurbishment, bodywork polishing and other forms of bus and van maintenance, tourists can also use our car and bus washing facilities. Call (46/515-064) for the washing facilities and (48/432-663) for our 24-hour car emergency service.

DUBICSÁNY GUESTHOUSE

Set in gorgeous surroundings the guesthouse offers friendly service and cheap rates.

Information, bookings: 48/432-663

PUT AN ADVERTISEMENT ON OUR BUSES:

Information, orders: 46/515-002

BORSOD VOLÁN – NOT ONLY IN BORSOD

SUMMER DAYS
AT LAKE BALATON...

Lake Balaton day pass

For travelling around Lake Balaton and visiting all the sights of the North and South coast, purchasing a **Lake Balaton day pass** is the best solution. This personal ticket is valid on the railways surrounding the lake. You may take an **unlimited number of trips with unlimited stops** from 12 AM the day featured on the pass until 12 PM the next day.

Price for: 1st **class: HUF 2.718**, 2nd **class: HUF 1.812**

Lake Balaton Mix

If you would like to add a boat trip to your train ride, we recommend the personal discount ticket issued by the Hungarian Railway Co. and Lake Balaton Shipping Co.

Adult price: HUF 3.800

Price for children between 6 and 14: HUF 1.570

You may buy this type of pass for the high season between July 3 and August 22, 2004 and it will be valid for 3 days. The pass entitles you to **an unlimited number of trips and stops** on the railways around Lake Balaton and on the scheduled ship lines of Lake Balaton Shipping Co.

In the case of Inter-city trains, the discounts are only valid together with an IC supplementary and a reserved seat ticket or with an IC supplementary ticket, respectively with a reserved seat ticket.

The Hungarian Railway Network

HUNGARIAN STATE RAILWAYS CO LTD

Symbols:

128	Timetable number
	Main line
	Branch line
	Suburban line
	Narrow-gauge railway
	Covering bus services

© Alappont Kft. 2004.

Major stations and places: Zahony, Zajta, Csenger, Kocsord-alsó, Fehérgyarmat, Vásárosnamény, Kisvárda, Mátészalka, Nyírbátor, Nyírbéltek, Nyírbogát, Nyíregyháza, Nyíradony, Nagykálló, Tiborszállás, Hermánszállás, Görögszállás, Nyékládháza, Hejőkeresztúr, Tokaj, Szerencs, Mezőzombor, Sátoraljaújhely, Sárospatak, Hidasnémeti, Pálháza, Rostalló, Forró-Encs, Abaújszántó, MISKOLC, Sajóecseng, Kazincbarcika, Ózd, Putnok, Bánréve, Rudabánya, Tornanádaska, Jósvafő-Aggtelek, Edelény, DEBRECEN, Hajdúszoboszló, Hajdúnánás, Hajdúdorog, Tiszalök, Tiszavasvári, Polgár, Tiszaújváros, Mezőcsát, Mezőkövesd, Füzesabony, Eger, Mezőkeresztes-Mezőnyárád, Ohat-Pusztakócs, Balmazújváros, Biharkeresztes, Berettyóújfalu, Püspökladány, Báránd, Kisújszállás, Karcag, Sáránd, Derecske, Létavértes, Nagykereki, Kötegyán, Békéscsaba, Gyula, Vésztő, Szeghalom, Füzesgyarmat, Mezőhegyes, Battonya, Hódmezővásárhely, Makó, Orosháza, Szentes, Mezőtúr, Gyoma, Szarvas, Szolnok, SZEGED, Röszke, Kiskunfélegyháza, Kecskemét, Lajosmizse, Kiskunmajsa, Kiskunhalas, Bácsalmás, Baja, Kelebia, Kalocsa, Dunapataj, Szekszárd, Bátaszék, Mohács, Magyarbóly, Villány, Pécs-várad, Szentlőrinc, Sellye, Barcs, PÉCS, Kaposvár, Dombóvár, Tamási, Siófok, Balatonfüred, Tapolca, Keszthely, Nagykanizsa, Zalaegerszeg, Murakeresztúr, Gyékényes, Lenti, Zalalövő, Zalabér-Batyk, SZOMBATHELY, Szentgotthárd, Körmend, Kőszeg, Sopron, Kapuvár, Csorna, Fertőszentmiklós, Hegyeshalom, Mosonmagyaróvár, Rajka, Győr, Pannonhalma, Komárom, Tata, Almásfüzitő, Tatabánya, Oroszlány, Kisbér, Pápa, Celldömölk, Sárvár, Veszprém, Zirc, Székesfehérvár, Várpalota, Börgönd, Pusztaszabolcs, Dunaújváros, Rétszilas, Sárbogárd, BUDAPEST, Esztergom, Szentendre, Vác, Gödöllő, Aszód, Hatvan, Gyöngyös, Vámosgyörk, Salgótarján, Balassagyarmat, Szécsény, Pásztó, Kisterenye, Jászberény, Jászapáti, Újszász, Cegléd, Monor, Dabas, Lajosmizse

MÁV

SUMMER UNLIMITED

HOLIDAY YOUTH
SEASON TICKET
EUR 29.00

Based on the common offer of the Hungarian Railway Company and ÖBB,
between July 3 and August 31, 2004
young people under 20 may
travel freely on the whole territory of Austria
during the validity of the season ticket, even in the case of multiple
entries. Up to the Austrian border, the Hungarian Railway Company
provides a **60%** discount from the international fare for those travelling
with this season ticket.

MÁV

EXCURSION PASS

VISIT THE „NEIGHBOURS"
WITH AN EXCURSION PASS

For those travelling to Austrian cities, we offer excursion passes **valid for 4 days**. Fares on 2nd class for a return trip:

Budapest - Wiener-Neustadt: EUR 22.40

Budapest - Bécs: EUR 34.60

Budapest - Graz: EUR 42.00

With this ticket, you may use the public transportation in **Vienna** and **Graz** free of charge!

MÁV

50%
RETURN TICKET DISCOUNT
FOR EMPLOYEES

Every employee and their dependant family members may benefit from a **50%** discount for a domestic trip once a year. Only the employer's certificate is necessary to receive the discount. **Civil servants may purchase an unlimited number of tickets with 50% discount** based on their valid civil servan Card.

FAMILY
DISCOUNTS

Family discount
You and your family member may benefit from a **33%** discount if you travel with two Children under 18.

Discount for large families
You and your family members may benefit from a **90%** discount if you travel with at least 3 of your children.

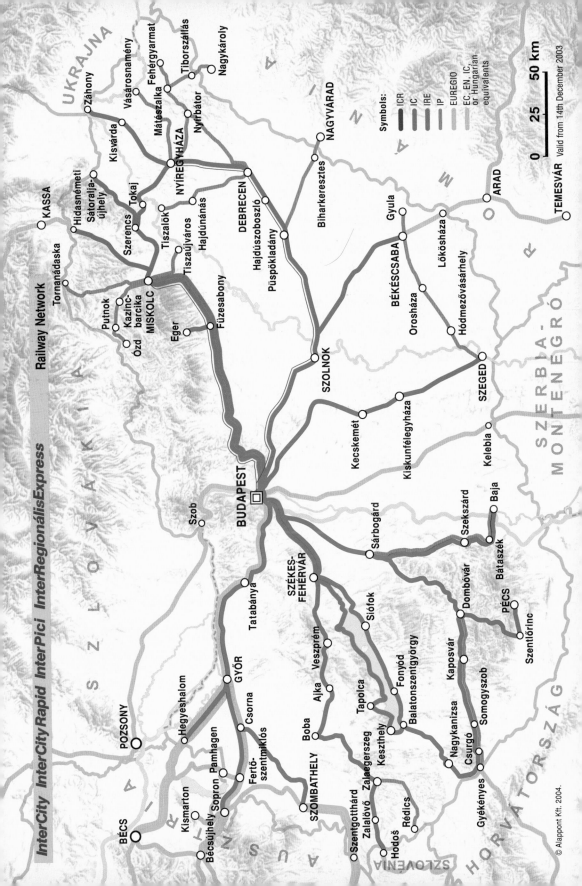

UTILISATION OF HISTORIC MONUMENTS
TREASURY PROPERTY DIRECTORATE

The Treasury Property Directorate (TPD, 1054 Budapest, Zoltán u. 16. Tel.: 1/331-1500) is responsible for exercising the Treasury's rights of ownership on behalf of the Hungarian State. The TPD's central apparatus and its county representations aim to preserve, utilise and develop state properties, and sell those assets (moveable, property, portfolio) which are surplus to requirement.

The properties belonging to the treasury include state-owned ancient monuments and sites of natural and historical (archaeological) importance. Apart from administering and protecting the property rights of such sites, the directorate is also responsible for managing and developing them.

It is not simply a question of utilising the property, there are all the other things which make an ancient monument what it is: the historical setting, the gardens, the outbuildings and the garden architecture, all of which need to be considered during the planning process. The restoration of such elements and their reintroduction into the public domain demands not only that their qualities are acknowledged, but their cultural merits stand at the very forefront of any endeavours to return the property to its former glory. This is something wich requires the necessary art historical rigour.

Within all the groups of ancient monuments enjoying protection, the group made up entirely of state-owned monuments, or groups of monuments (buildings, historical landscapes, historical gardens etc.) of particular cultural importance, amount to an exclusive category. Seen together they are an irreplacable part of our historical, cultural and artistic heritage. It's the task of the TPD, as the "guardian" organisation, to ensure that such a heritage – and such precious assets – be used in a way which will reflect well on the country's great cultural inheritance. Apart from the protection, maintenance, renovation and repair-work which goes on, the directorate, as the trustees, are also involved in research work, the examination of architectural features and details, and the task of finding a use for the property most likely to do it justice. A newly appointed trustee could be any corporate body or individual not working for an organisation financed from state funds. In addition sucessful applicants have to meet the requirements of the tender. The winner of the competition to find the best tender, once selected, would then be entitled to sign a TPD trustee contract.

Administration of the property is impossible without the necessary monument (liability) evaluations carried out by the TPD. In cases where the property is of special historical value less tangible matters also have to be taken into consideration.

At the present time there are 300 ancient monuments under the guardianship of the TPD. For many years now the directorate has devoted a substantial part of its budget to the protection, maintenence, examination and renovation of the sites.

Manorhouses, palaces and castles can only maintain their attraction if they are restored in the correct manner, with the necessary art historical accuracy and with suitable interior furnishings (refurnishing). It is only then that the buildings are in a position to open their doors to the general public and bring the past back to life. This is something which could take place within the context of a cultural event. The country houses you can see in Hungary date from a period when their patrons were prepared to compete with the best. The architectural details (which are for the greater part concealed underneath layers of paint and whitewash) are often the works of internationally recognised artists and craftsmen. The paper and silk wall-coverings, the furniture and other furnishings are the products of eminent factories and workshops. The majority of our ancient monuments have connections with historical personages and families, as well as cultural and historical events of importance not only to Hungary but to Europe as a whole. Such hidden treasures deserve the kind of sensitive art historically correct renovations and future uses which will return them to their rightful place in Hungary's cultural landscape. It is the main job of our directorate, and at the same time its most pressing task, to find the right partners and trustees with whom to realise their plans to provide a context in which the general public can learn about the lives of their ancestors. It would be an environment in which the houses and their outbuildings could be given functions which would not compromise the central principles described above.

Those Hungarian castles which have survived are for the most part ruins. The local climate is unfortunately not conducive to maintaining the fabric of such structures in their current ruined form, hence the need for protective measures.

There are several stages to the renovation process. Following the necessary scientific and archaeological investigations, efforts are turned to a partial or complete reconstruction, which could also result in the building being used. Three years ago the Treasury Property Directorate initiated the Ruin Friend project, which attempts to draw people's attention to buildings which are in a ruinous or otherwise poor condition. Emphasis is placed on the values the building encapsulates, with stress placed on the way people once lived, as well as the structure's cultural and architectural worth. Through the programmes we want to make people realise that history isn't just something you learn from books, and that sensitive renovations and accurate reconstructions and sensibly planned cultural events can provide alternative teaching material.

The garden formed an integral part of the country house complex, its style often depending on when the garden was laid out. Here it was the plants that provided the architectural elements. Managing such gardens consequently also forms an important part of the TPD's work. One task involves returning those parts of the gardens which have been separated off at one time or another back to the houses themselves. Discovering the original extent of the grounds requires careful investigation work (archive work, contemporary documents, plans, maps and aerial photos). Those historical gardens which have managed to stay together in one piece, as an arboretum or something similar, are the fortunate ones. Interestingly, in such cases it is the houses themselves which have tended to get neglected. Nevertheless, Hungary's gardens amount to a considerable resource both in terms of the plants, the layout and the architectural features and the sculptures they contain. Maintaining and renovating the gardens and their contents is therefore a task of considerable impotance.

In the near future the Treasury Board Directorate will be calling for applications from those wishing to take trusteeship of the following properties whilst, abiding by the principles and aims of the directorate

BAJNA (KOMÁROM-ESZTERGOM COUNTY), *Sándor–Metternich Palace*
DABRONC-ÖTVÖSPUSZTA (VESZPRÉM COUNTY), *Szegedy Palace and Manorhouse*
GYULA (BÉKÉS COUNTY), *Harruckern–Almássy–Wenckheim Palace*
HATVAN (HEVES COUNTY), *Grassalkovich Palace*
NAGYKŐRÖS (PEST COUNTY), *Halász–Tanárky Manorhouse*
SOPONYA-NAGYLÁNG (FEJÉR COUNTY), *Zichy Palace*

We will also be calling for tenders for the purchase of the property rights to:
GYÖNK (TOLNA COUNTY), *Magyary–Kossa Manorhouse*
HŐGYÉSZ (TOLNA COUNTY), *Synagogue*

BAJNA (KOMÁROM-ESZTERGOM COUNTY)

The one-time Sándor-Metternich Palace

Bajna Palace (from a postcard in the Hungarian Architectural Museum Collection, franked 1933)

The main building of the palace complex is on the site of the Renaissance palace built by the Bajnai Both family at the end of the 15th century. Between 1690 and 1720, Menyhért Sándor made what remained of the Bot family's palace inhabitable again. In the first half of the 18th century his son Mihály demolished the palace ruins and built a Baroque palace in its place. His son, Antal Sándor, remodelled the building around 1775. It is among the Baroque wall paintings that you can see an equestrian portrait of Sándor Antal holding a depiction of the counties running along the Danube as they appeared at the time, together with architectural features, fountains, human figures, exotic landscapes and a Sala terrena-type arbour.

In 1802, during the time of Vince Sándor, the stable, one of the earliest Neoclassical buildings in Hungary, was built. It was then that the rooms in the palace were given their classical painted schemes. The most recent reconstruction is associated with Móric Sándor, who remodelled the palace in a classical style shortly before his marriage in 1834, to the plans of József Hild. With the construction of the connecting corridor the single-floor outbuildings were joined up with the main building. The rooms were given mid-19th century furnishings, decorations and paintings designed by Scala scenery designer, Alessandro Sanquirico. One room was given Etruscan-style, another Pompeii-style furniture. In another room the wall-paintings are based on the works of Raphael, the ceiling being deco-

rated with stucco by Maria Piazza. The complex also includes a palm house, a green house and an English landscape garden complete with arbours, grottos and hermitages. The park is protected.

Archaeological investigations, research and the location and restoration of the wallpaintings has already been completed, and the renovation of the building is currently in progress – 15–20% of which has already been completed.

HATVAN (HEVES COUNTY)

HG. Grassalkovich- / BR. Hatvany–Deutsch Palace

The Grassalkovich Palace in Hatvan was built by Antal Grassalkivich between 1754 and 1763. The two wings, designed in 1763 by József Jung, Antal, were added to a central portion designed by Ignác Oraschek in 1754. In 1867, the house became the property of the sugar-producing Hatvany–Deutsch family. It was then that a lot of famous guests were known to visit, thus adding to the building's cultural historical importance. The family's stucco programme has a Greek mythological theme. The fire of 1995 damaged one of the wings overlooking the courtyard. A part of the historical garden, containing the Baroque garden, also belongs to the site.

At the present time the Hatvan Municipal Council enjoys the right to use one part of the palace. The TPD is continually renovating the building complex and the historical garden with its own funds and incomes deriving from grant applications.

The façade of the palace following restoration

DABRONC-ÖTVÖSPUSZTA (VESZPRÉM COUNTY)

Szegedy Palace and Manorhouse

The Szegedy family of Mezoszeged owned lands in Vas, Zala and Veszprém counties from the 17th century onwards. The hall at Dabronc-Ötvöspuszta was probably built during the 1740s, hence the presumed association with Ferenc Szegedy. Following the division of the estate, the hall, which was already an L-shaped seven-room building, fell into the hands of Mihály Szegedy. During the first half of the 19th century Ferenc III.'s daughter, Róza Szegedy, lived in the recently renovated house with her husband Sándor Kisfaludy.

During the course of the aforementioned division of the estate, Ignác Szegedy (Mihály's brother) was given the piece of territory on the other side of the road. It was here he built his U-shaped palace. The vaults in the house are decorated with stucco. By using the surviving 1798 inventory it would be possible to reconstruct the interior furnishings. At the end of the 19th century the palace was given some eclectic-style features. The central part of the building dates from the 1927 reconstruction. It was then that the palace acquired its present appearance. The palace once had a substantial landscaped garden.

The façade of the palace from the wildlife park and turtle pond (now the Castle Baths' sunbathing area)

GYULA (BÉKÉS COUNTY)

The one-time Harruckern–Wenckheim–Almásy Palace

János György Harrucker(n) built the palace during the 1720s, on a site lying to the south of Gyula Castle on the edge of what was a farm and then a hussar fortress. His son, Ferenc Harrucker(n), was subsequently to add an additional floor. In the vicinity of the palace lay a fish pond, a crab pond, a turtle pond, a swan lake, a wildlife park, a pheasant range, a formal garden, a kitchen garden and a large vineyard. In those days the moat was still filled with water, and the baroness would organise boat trips around the castle. The male line of the Harrucker(n) ended with the death of Ferenc in 1775, and it was then that the estate was divided up. The Gyula part of the estate ended up in the hands of Teréz Gruber, wife of Count József Wenckheim, and grand-daughter of both Countess Josefa Harrucker(n) and Cecilia Habsburg.

In 1801, Gyula was hit by fire and it was then that the place burnt down. Ferenc Wenckheim invited the architect Antal Czigler to Gyula, and it was to his plans that the palace was completed in 1803. The palace chapel was consecrated by the parish priest Spiegel on 3rd May. It was then that the (water) tower, situated on the eastern wing of the palace, was built, opposite the gatehouse built by the Turks. The spacious stables were built in 1833. It was here that theatrical performances were held during the 1840s. The Erkel family arrived in Gyula in 1806, where József Erkel the Elder was appointed palace steward, becoming the house musician, theatre producer and later tutor of the four Wenckheim boys, József, Károly, Antal and Rudolf (born in 1809, 1811, 1813 and 1814 respectirely). His grandson Ferenc Erkel was born in Gyula on 7th November 1810, son of József Erkel the Younger and Klára Ruttkay. Old József Erkel had been given a room in the palace (situated in the gatehouse built by the Turks). The palace in Gyula was no doubt a formative influence on the future founder of the Hungarian National Opera. József Erkel was first violin in a string quartet that played at the palace. At a very early age Ferenc Erkel was already taking part in concerts as a page turner. By 19th September 1839, he was already conducting at a concert held in the palace's "Coloured Room". The concert featured József Erkel (Ferenc's brother), singing tenor, and Károly Schlesinger on cello, opened with Ferenc Erkel playing Herz's Polonaise on the piano. The Erkel family were active members of the community for more than 40 years. We have documentation of the theatrical performances going on at the palace from 1818 until 1845.

Nine generals and the Russian military commanders came to the house after the surrender at Világos in 1849. The visitors organised a ball which ended abruptly when the Austrian army arrived. Turning in their arms the soldiers threw them in through a window looking onto the courtyard.

The Gyula estate fell into the hands of the Almásy family in 1885. The next phase in the history of the palace is associated with Count Kálmán Almásy, who renovated the building in 1888. It was during this period that lemon and orange trees decorated the areas immediately surrounding the palace during the summer months before being returned to the greenhouse during the winter. In 1902, the first floor was widened by five windows to either side, providing two extra apartments for the Almásy family with their eight children.

The castle and the palace have both enjoyed protected status since 1950. The remodellings of 1956 and 1963 involved the addition of interior walls and a false ceilings. The 24-hectare park was gradually taken over, resulting eventually in the the development of the Castle Baths park. The palace building was first used as a girls' school, before becoming a technical school and finally a nursery in 1959.

Archaeological investigations and the renovation of the façade has already taken place, whilst the restoration of the service buildings is going on at the present time. Documentation concerning the details and the painted areas uncovered at the site arising from the restoration were published in March 2004

The courtyard façade

SOPONYA-NAGYLÁNG (FEJÉR COUNTY)
The one-time Zichy Palace

The Zichy estate in Nagyláng, which belonged to Palota Castle back in the 17th century, was given to István Zichy in recognition for his services to Ferdinand III.

One of the most important dates in the history of the estate was 1768 when, following the death of János Zichy IV. (1764), the Palota estate was divided up leaving János V. with the Sármellék lands, with Nagyláng–Soponya Palace at its centre.

While in 1750, the palace is still referred to as the "Noble Squire's Láng House", in 1757 it is called "the residencial house". It is this building which forms the core of the Baroque palace you can see today, or at least the earliest parts of it. Following the division of the estate in 1768 the owner of the Nagyláng lands moved his permanent residence there from Palota. It was then that the palace became a real aristocratic residence. The old palace was remodelled as well as enlarged in 1772-73. The palace complex also included a garden characteristic of the time.

In 1799, building work on the house started to the designs of Mihály Pollack. It was then that the first floor was built, together with the ceremonial staircase leading down to the courtyard, and the part of the wing making up the vaulted stable block.

Work on the English landscaped garden went on in parallel with developments at the palace. The bridge crossing the lake, created by blocking up the stream, was built in 1822. The surviving plan for the courtyard fountain (1829) was used for the reconstruction of the fountain in 1989-90. Some even greater developments took place in the garden at the beginning of the 20th century. Of particular botanical interest is the variegated leafed maple named after Emperor Leopold. On the lawns you can see several protected roundlobe (white, lilac-blue, pink).

In 1944–45 the palace became a military hospital before becoming a children's home.

HŐGYÉSZ, (TOLNA COUNTY)
Synagogue

The groundplan of the synagogue is typical of the period, the building featuring a long single unified interior and a large women's gallery.

The positioning of the building and the elevations of the late Baroque structure betray the building's date (1815). The details are similar to those at the synagogues in Apostag and Baja. According to old postcards of the building the inscription "This is the gateway to heaven" could be read over the entrance:

Painted decorations on the ceiling and side walls of the women's gallery

The façade of the Manorhouse in Gyönk

GYÖNK (TOLNA COUNTY)
Magyary–Kossa Manorhouse

The classical-style Manorhouse was built by Sámuel Magyary-Kossa between 1837 and 1839. In a letter she wrote from Eszék (Osijek, Croatia) on 2nd January 1838 to Mrs Kornélia Scheartzleiter, Sámuel M-K's niece writes of it "... My Dear Uncle wants the plans to his house to be carried out to his complete satisfaction". The building was built using locally produced bricks marked with an "MS" monogram. It also required large quantities of Sütto "red marble" for the staircases, doorsteps, the interior and exterior window frames, window ledges and corridor floors. The painted decorations for the most part remain, the majority of which can be dated to between 1840 and 1850. Of particular interest are the shutters with their classical detailing, and the two lavatory blocks still in their original positions on the ground floor.

The patron was sub-prefect of the county between 1833 and 1840, and again after 1845. He was a great book-lover with a substantial library and a medal collection. Numbered amongst his guests are Berzsenyi, Csokonai and Petőfi.

Following the death of Sámuel Magyary-Kossa's only son, József, in 1866, the small Manorhouse was inherited by another branch of the family and an heir who was not yet of age. It was during this period that the house was sold to the Grosch family. At the beginning of the 20th century the house fell into the hands of one of the granddaughters and her husband dr. Sándor Kovágó. The Manorhouse has been in state hands since 1947.

HOLLÓHÁZA
Porcelain

1777

HOLLÓHÁZA®
HUNGARY

BAJA, SZABADSÁG ÚT 14. • **BUDAPEST**, RÁKÓCZI ÚT 32. • **BUDAPEST**, LIGET U. 11. • **BUDAPEST**, NAGYTÉTÉNYI ÚT 37-43. CAMPONA ÜZLETKÖZPONT • **DEBRECEN**, BATTHYÁNY ÚT 12. • **DUNAÚJVÁROS**, TÁNCSICS M. U. 8/A. • **ESZTERGOM**, RÁKÓCZI TÉR 2-4. • **GYŐR**, BAJCSY ZS. U. 41. • **GYULA**, VÁROSHÁZ ÚT 2/B. • **HÉVÍZ**, DEÁK TÉR 2. • **HÓDMEZŐVÁSÁRHELY**, SZÁNTÓ KOVÁCS J. U. 1. • **HOLLÓHÁZA**, KÁROLYI ÚT 11. • **JÁSZBERÉNY**, KOSSUTH ÚT 10-12., PIACTÉR • **KECEL**, RÁKÓCZI U. 25. • **KECSKEMÉT**, ARANY JÁNOS ÚT 10. • **MISKOLC**, VÁROSHÁZ TÉR 11. • **NYÍREGYHÁZA**, KOSSUTH TÉR 1. • **PAKS**, DÓZSA GY. ÚT 40. • **PÉCS**, SZÉCHENYI TÉR 6. • **SZEGED**, KÁRÁSZ U. 13. • **SIÓFOK**, SZABADSÁG TÉR 9., VÍZTORONY ÜZLETHÁZ • **SZÉKESFEHÉRVÁR**, FŐ U. 1., KRISTÁLYHÁZ • **SZEKSZÁRD**, KISKORZÓ TÉR 3. • **SZENTENDRE**, BOGDÁNYI U. 8. • **SZENTES**, KOSSUTH U. 11. • **SZOMBATHELY**, KIRÁLY U. 1. • **TATABÁNYA**, FŰZFA ÚT 10. • **ZALAEGERSZEG**, KOSSUTH LAJOS U. 19-23.

CONTENTS

In this final chapter our book turns to a number of themes which we think will be useful to you the visitor. Under each heading you will find the relevant towns and villages arranged alphabetically, followed by a list of the relevant organisations, companies and services registered with Well-PRess Publishing. In some cases information is given in greater detail. By doing this we hope to help those are keen to see some of the annual events or to sample some of the local specialities. Our database is not prepared according to importance, but on the basis of the companies who want to make themselves know. Therefore, if you find just two hotels listed under a town it doesn't mean that they are the only ones.

The information given here is the responsibility of the advertisers. Although the addresses given are not likely to change, the same cannot be said of the telephone and the fax numbers, and the website addresses. It was for this reason that we gave our partners an extra month following the publishing deadline (15th March 2004) to provide all the necessary details. This means that the database reflects the situation as it was in April 2004. The changes currently going on in the telecommunications market may however mean that some of the information will be subject to change, and would like to apologise in advance, if any there prove to be any inconveniences during the course of your visit.

As part of our introduction we would like to tell you what you can do, and where.

The *heritage* section is arranged according to the type of museums or places of cultural importance you may be interested in visiting, whether they be related to local history, a particular branch of the arts or the sciences or the life and work of a particular person. It is here you will find the museums, the history of technology exhibitions, the art galleries, as well as the more specialised collections. (In cases where our partners have made specific requests you might find suggestions which seem more appropriate in the heritage section in one of the other topic areas). The *Folklore* section is made up mainly of peasant cottages fully equipped with furniture and implements, local history exhibitions and outlets where you are likely to be able to buy pieces of folk art, in some cases straight from the craftsman or craftswoman who made them.

Cultural events, however, can either be found in the *Culture* section or in the events listed under the town or village in question. Where settlements have listed all the scheduled events on a month to month basis visitors can be pretty sure that these will take place every year.

The baths' development programme has brought some spectacular changes.

Spas, leisure pools and thermal baths offer ever more attractive surroundings in which to relax and recharge your batteries. For more details see the *Medicinal Tourism* section.

Those consulting the tourist information database will see that we haven't forgotten a host of other leisure activities. You will find that sport, horse riding, angling and walking are all represented in the *Active Relaxation* section, as well as under *Natural Treasures* and *Village Tourism*.

Lodgings, and places where you can enjoy the local cuisine, can be found in the *Accommodation, Gastronomy* and *Wine Tourism* sections.

The size and scope of our database was of course determined by our advertising partners. This doesn't stop you from adding your own particular favourites, or other hotels, restaurants or cellars you have picked up on the grapevine.

If our readers or our advertising partners find that any of the information in our most recent edition is incorrect, or has changed in the meantime, we would be more than happy to hear from you.

The tourist information in *Out and About In Hungary* is brought up to date on a continual basis, and it is this information we drew upon when compiling and publishing our most recent edition.

*For further tourist information
please refer to our website:*
www.vendegvaro.hu

HERITAGE

Interest in the larger state collections and the increasing numbers of private exhibitions has grown significantly in recent times.

It is not rare for ten, or even a hundred, thousand people to visit the provincial collections.

The most popular and well known museums tend to be those concentrating on one or more elements of culture, science or nature.

In some places you are only allowed to take photographs for personal use with the necessary photography ticket. Those wishing to take photographs for other purposes will require the permission of the director of the museum in question. The use of flash photography is forbidden in most exhibitions.

AJKA 8400
The Municipal Library and Museum
Mining Museum
Csinger Parkerdő Tel.: 88/312-033
Open: Tue.–Fri. 11am–4pm,
Wed., Sun.10am–4pm
Local History Museum
Szabadság tér 19. Tel.: 88/312-612
Open: Tue.–Sat. 9am–4pm

BALATONKENESE 8174
Village House
Táncsics u. 24. Tel./fax: 88/594-500
E-mail: faluhaz@mail.uti.hu
Open: 7am–7pm

BÉKÉSCSABA 5600
The Mihály Munkácsy Museum
Széchenyi u. 9. Tel.: 66/323-377
Open: 1st Oct.–31st Mar.
Tue.–Sun. 10am–4pm, 1st Apr.–
30th Sept. Tue. – Sun. 10am–6pm

Permanent exhibitions: The Yurt People – archaeological exhibition; The Munkácsy Memorial Room; Pro Natura – nature exhibition; Identity, Difference, Variety – ethnographical-historical exhibition

BOLDOGASSZONYFA 7937
The János Hoffer Memorial Room
Kossuth u. 24. Tel.: 73/554-036
Open: by appointment,
Key: Mrs Szita
Boldogasszonyfa, Petőfi u. 34.

BUDAPEST
The Béla Bartók Memorial House
1025 Csalán út 29.
Tel.: 1/394-2100
Open: Tue.–Sun. 10am–5pm
The Museum
of Hungarian Trade and Tourism
1014 Fortuna utca 4.

Municipal Library
8230 Balatonfüred, Kossuth L. u. 35.
Tel.: 87/343-070, fax.: 87/341-362
E-mail: balateka@sednet.hu
Open: Sept. 1st–June 30th,
Tue.–Fri. 10am–6pm, Sat. 8am–1pm
July 1st–Aug. 31st Tue.–Fri. 10am–6pm

Local History Collection
8230 Balatonfüred, Arany J. u. 12.
Tel.: 87/340-744
E-mail: helytortenet@freemail.hu
Open: June 16th –Aug. 20th
Mon.–Wed.–Fri. 10am–6pm,
Sat. 9am–1pm Aug. 21st–June 15th
Mon.-Wed.-Fri. 10am–6pm

The Mátyás Jantyik Múzeum
5630 Békés, Széchenyi tér 6.
Tel.: 66/411-437
Open: 1st Oct.–31st Mar.
Tue., Fri.: 9am–1pm,
Wed., Thur., Sat: Noon–4pm
1st Apr.–30th Sept. Tue., Fri.: 10am–2pm,
Wed., Thur., Sat.: 2pm–6pm
Permanent exhibitions: In the Throes of the Millennia (The history and ethnography of Békés), Birds of the Körös Region, The Durkó Room
The Békés Gallery 5630 Békés,
Széchenyi tér 4., Tel./fax: 66/411-943
For the Békés peasant cottage and the schoolmaster's house enquire at the gallery

Galeria Centralis

is the gallery of the Central European University's Open Society Archives. Its unique, theme-based exhibitions are designed to stimulate thought and provoke open discussion on the unresolved and more sensitive issues of our not so distant past.

1051 Budapest, Nádor u. 9.
Tel.: 1/327-3250, fax: 1/327-3260

The Institute of Military History and Museum

1014 Bp., Kapisztrán tér 2–4.
Tel.: 1/356-9522, tel./fax: 1/356-9586
E-mail: info@mail.militaria.hu
www.hm-him.hu

Apr.1st –Sept. 30th: 10am–6pm
Oct. 1st–Mar. 31st : 10am–4pm
Closed Mondays

Permanent exhibitions:
"The Sword is Shinier than the Chain"
"I'm a Mountain Hunter up in the Carpathians..."
Soldiers, Castles, Weapons;
Returning collections;
The Sword and the Wreath –
a thousand years of military iconography
Sergeant, military manager...

Tel.: 1/375-6249
Permanent exhibitions: Hungarian Commerce in the First Half of 20th Century; Budapest as Tourist Resort
Open: Wed.–Fri. 10am–5pm, Sat.–Sun. 10am–6pm
The Hungarian Agricultural Museum
1146 XIV, Városliget, Vajdahunyadvár
Tel.: 1/363-5099,
Tel./fax: 1/363-2711
E-mail: muzeum@mmgm.hu
www.mmgm.hu
www.mezogazdasagimuzeum.hu
Open: Tue.–Fri. 10am–5pm, Sat. 10am–6pm, Sun.10am–5pm (closed Mondays)
The Semmelweis Medical History Múzeum
1013 Apród u. 1–3.
Tel.: 1/2011-577, Fax: 1/3753-936
Open: 1st Mar.–31st Oct.

Tue.–Sun. 10.30am–6pm, 1st Nov.–28th Feb. Tue.–Sun. 10.30am–4pm

DEBRECEN
The Calvinist College Museum
4044 Kálvin tér 16.
Tel.: 52/516-856
E-mail: gszabo@silver-drk.hu
Open: Tue.–Sat. 9am–5pm, Sun. 9am–1pm Permanent exhibitions: Ecclesiastical Art Exhibition (old Hungarian metalwork, textiles and carpentry); The History of the School; The Oratorium: The Scene of the Overthrow of the House of Habsburg; The Great Library

DOMBÓVÁR 7200
The István Fekete Museum
Hóvirág u. 25. Tel./fax: 74/466-087, 20/421-9307
Open: 1st Apr.–31st Oct. Mon.–Fri.

from 3pm, Sat.–Sun. 10am–6pm, 1st Nov.–31st Mar. Mon.–Fri. from 3pm, Sat.–Sun.10am–4pm or by appointment

EGER 3300
The Ecclesiastical Múzeum
Széchenyi u. 5. Tel.: 36/421-332
Open: Tue.–Fri. 9am–4pm

ERCSI 2451
The József Eötvös Memorial Museum
Eötvös u. 33. Tel.: 25/492-075
Open: by appointment

ESZTERGOM 2500
The Dunube Múzeum
Kölcsey u. 2.
Tel.: 33/500-250
Open: Nov–Apr. 10am–4pm, May–Oct. 10am–6pm
closed Tuesdays

Museum of Ethnography

Budapest, V. Kossuth Lajos tér 12.
Open 10am–6pm, closed Mondays

NÉPRAJZI MÚZEUM

MUSEUM OF ETHNOGRAPHY

Telephone: 06 1/473-2400
Fax: 06 1/473-2441
E-mail: infos@neprajz.hu
www.neprajz.hu

Come and visit the Museum of Ethnography!
The Museum of Ethnography not only houses one of the oldest public collections in Hungary, but is also one of the best specialised museums in Europe, with Hungarian and international collections comprising close to 250 thousand ethnographic artefacts. In addition to objects of utility and art, the museum's collection also includes a considerable quantity of manuscripts, photographs, folk music recordings, and film footage, as well as a large, valuable library of books on the field.

In addition to its permanent exhibition of artefacts related to Hungarian folk culture, the museum organises numerous temporary exhibitions and events that introduce the visitor to the broad spectrum of world societies and cultures, from peoples long past to the lifestyles of the present day.

A sample of museum shows and events:
Temporary exhibitions 2004–2005:
• Original–Copy–Forgery. Objects in Conversation.
• "If You Want to Be a Piper…" – Pipes and Pipers in the Carpathian Basin and Beyond
• Boldog / Images • Urban Portraits • Annual Hungarian Press Photo (March-April) and World Press Photo (October–November) Exhibitions
Special Events
• Museum of Ethnography Day (March 5) Easter Exhibition, Show, Bazaar (March–April)
• World Museum Day (May) • Midsummer's Day (closest weekend to June 24)
• Advent Exhibition, Show, Bazaar (November) • Christmas, Nativity Plays, Bazaar (December).

The Museum of the Year 2001; Interactive History of Technology Exhibition (flooding, river-straightening, the water supply – pipes and drains, the history of cartography) www.dunamuzeum.hu

HEREND 8440
The Herend Porcelanium and Porcelain Museum
Kossuth L. u. 140. Tel.: 88/523-197
Open: 1st Nov.–31st Mar. Tue.–Sat. 9am–3.30pm, 1st Apr.–31st Oct.
Mon.–Sun. 9am–4.30pm
Exhibition tours available if organised in advance

HOLLÓHÁZA 3999
The Porcelain Museum
Károlyi út
Tel.: 47/505-400 ext. 155
Open: 1st Apr.–31st Oct.
Mon.–Sun. 9am–5pm

HORTOBÁGY 4071
The Hortobágy Gallery
Petőfi tér 4 . Tel.: 52/369-401
Open: 1st May–31st Oct.
Tue.–Sun. 10am–5pm
Permanent Exhibitions:
The Works of the Hortobágy Art Workshop; The Sculpture of Árpád Somogyi; Temporary exhibitions
The Pastoral Museum
Petőfi tér 1. Tel.: 52/589-321
Open: 15th Mar.- 15. Apr.
10am–2pm; 16 Apr.–30th Apr.
10am–4pm; 1st May–31st Aug.
Mon.–Sun. 9am–6pm;
1st Sept.– 15th Oct.10am–4pm;
16th Oct.–30th Nov. 10am–2pm
Permanent exhibition: Pastoral Life on the Hortobágy
The Local Government Gallery
Czinege J. u. 1. Tel.: 52/369-021
Open: Mon.–Fri. 8am–4pm

Permanent exhibition: The Works of the Hortobágy Art Workshop completed in honour of the Hungarian Conquest and the New Millennium.

IBAFA 7935
The Pipe Museum
Arany J. u. 2. Tel.: 73/354-031
Fax: 73/554-034
E-mail: ibafaonkormanyzat@level.datanet.hu

JÁSZAPÁTI 5130
The Farm Museum
Szentandrási út Tel.: 57/440-827
E-mail: japatimgst@invitel.hu
Open: 1st May–31st Oct.
Sun. 2–5pm, and at other times by appointment
The Pál Vágó Local History Collection
István király u. 23 Tel.:57/441-071
Open: Tue.-Thur. 9am–noon;
Sat. 2–5pm;

Cegléd

Cegléd, situated 70km from Budapest on road no. 4, is the a regional centre of the southern and southeastern parts of Pest County. The name Cegléd is associated with two dates of great significance in Hungarian history. The first is 1514: the year of the Dózsa Peasants' Revolt, and the second 1848: the revolution and the War for Freedom. Indeed, Louis Kossuth's memory has been carefully preserved in the town ever since his rousing Cegléd recruiting speech. The Kossuth statue, the work of János Horvay, has stood in the town since 1902, the one hundredth anniversary of his birth. The only other version of the statue can now be seen in New York. The Kossuth Museum, opened in 1917, is also partly devoted to his memory. There are also numerous other Kossuth-related sites in the town.

The Calvinist Great Church, built to the plans of József Hild, is the biggest Calvinist church in Central Europe. The Lutheran church situated next door and Our Lady of Hungary Chapel in Széchenyi út are also fine examples of traditional Hungarian architecture. Apart from its unique Drum Museum and Sports History Collection, Cegléd can rightly lay claim to having some of the finest thermal waters in Pest County. The Cegléd Thermal and Leisure Baths, which opened their doors to visitors in 2003, are capable of meeting everybody's medicinal, health, wellness and leisure needs, whether they come from locally or indeed abroad.

Cegléd Thermal Baths Ltd.
2700 Cegléd, Fürdő u. 27.
Tel.: 53/505-000
Internet: www.cegleditermal.hu
E-mail: info@cegleditermal.hu

For further information:
TOURINFORM Office
2700 Cegléd, Kossuth tér 1.
Tel.: 53/500-285, 53/500-286
Internet: www.cegled.hu
E-mail: cegled@tourinform.hu

Permanent exhibition:
The Paintings of Pál Vágó;
The Pottery of Béla Mihály;
Farm Museum

KAPUVÁR 9330
The Rábaköz Múzeum
Fő tér 1. Tel.: 96/595-157
Tel./fax: 96/242-557
Open: 1st Apr.–30th Sept.
Tue.–Sun.10am–6pm, 1st Oct.–
31st Mar. Tue.–Sun. 10am–2pm

KECSKEMÉT 6000
The Bozsó Foundation
Klapka u. 34.
Tel.: 76/324-625, 76/417-130
Fax: 76/324-625
E-mail: bozsoal@mail.datanet.hu
Open: Fri.–Sun. 10am–6pm,
and at other times by appointment
Permanent exhibition:
The Paintings of János Bozsó;

Hungarian Folk Art and European
Applied Art of the 15th –19th
Centuries
The József Katona Memorial House
Katona J. u. 5. Tel.: 76/328-420
Open: Tue.–Sat. 10am–2pm
Permanent exhibition: The József
Katona Memorial Exhibition
*The József Katona Museum's
Kecskemét Picture Gallery*
Rákóczi u. 1. Tel.: 76/480-776
Open: 15th Feb.– 15th Dec.
Tue.–Sun. 9am–5pm
Permanent exhibition:
Menyhért Tóth; István Farkas;
The Marcell Nemes Bequest;
The Kecskemét Art Colony
*The Zoltán Kodály Institute
for the Teaching of Music*
Kéttemplomköz 1.
Tel.: 76/481-518
Open: Mon.–Fri.10am–noon and
4–6pm, Sat.–Sun.10am–6pm

*The Museum of Hungarian
Folk Arts*
Serfőző u. 19.
Tel./fax: 76/327-203
Open: Tue.–Sat.10am–5pm
Permanent exhibition:
The Craftsman's Art Today; The
Dezső Zana Kalotaszeg Collection
*The Szórakaténusz Toy Museum
and Workshop*
Gáspár A. u. 11.
Tel.: 76/481-469, 76/506-879,
76/506-889
Open: 2nd Jan.–31st Dec.
Tue.–Sun.10am–noon
and 1–5pm (programmes
for groups by appointment)
Permanent exhibition: Preserving
Our Past Through Toys –
The 20th Anniversary Exhibition of
the *Szórakaténusz Toy Museum and
Workshop*; Handcrafted Toys
through the Ages

Kner Printing Museum

5500 Gyomaendrőd, Kossuth L. u. 16.
Tel.: 66/386-172, fax: 66/386-744
E-mail: knermuzeum@mail.globonet.hu

Open: 1th Apr.–30th Nov.
Tue.–Sun. 9am–3pm;
1st Dec.–31th Mar., Tue.–Fri. 9am–3pm

Permanent Exhibitions:
• Books and Prints from the Kner
  Printing Works in Gyoma
• Lajos Kozma Furniture

At Hungary's one and only printing
museum you can become acquainted
with the work of the Kner family and the
history of the Kner Printing Works in
Gyoma from 1882 to the Present Day.
The fine books, beautiful prints and
working printing equipment make the
exhibition all the more eyecatching.

The Municipal Museum
of Art

Municipal Picture Gallery
– Esterházy Palace 9021 Győr, Király u. 17.
Tel./fax: 96/322-695
E-mail: artmuz@arrabonet.gyor.hu
Open: Tue.–Sun. 10am–6pm
The Péter Váczy Collection – Magyar Ispita
9022 Győr, Nefelejcs köz 3.
Tel./fax: 96/318-141
E-mail: gyormuz@arrabonet.gyor.hu
Open: Tue.–Sun. 10am–5pm
**The Miklós Borsos Permanent Exhibition
and Archive**
9021 Győr, Apor Vilmos püspök tere 2.
Tel.: 96/316-329
E-mail: gyormuz@arrabonet.gyor.hu
Open: Tue.–Sun. 10am–6pm
The Margit Kovács Permanent Exhibition
– Kreszta House 9021 Győr, Apáca u. 1.
Tel: 96/326-739
E-mail: gyormuz@arrabonet.gyor.hu
Open: Tue.–Sun. 10am–6pm

The exhibitions are closed on Mondays

The Kalocsa Archiepiscopal
Treasury

Exhibition: 6300 Kalocsa, Hunyadi u. 2.
Tel.: 78/461-860 (1st Apr.–31st Oct.),
Office: 6300 Kalocsa, Szentháromság tér 1.
Tel.: 78/462-166/210 ext.
Fax: 78/462-166/130 ext.
E-mail: kincstar@archivum.hu
www.asztrik.hu

Open: 1st Apr.–31st Oct.
Tue.–Sun.: 9am–5pm, 1st Nov.–31st Mar.
for group visits arranged in advance.

Permanent exhibition:
1000 Years of the Archdiocese of Kalocsa.
Including: the processional cross and
the burial finds of Archbishop Saul
(12th cent.); chasuble (1450);
the St. Anna reliquary (16th cent.);
Empire-style interior (early 19th cent.);
exhibition of the paintings of Péter Prokop

KESZTHELY 8360
The Balaton Museum
Múzeum u. 2.
Tel.: 83/312-351
Open: 1st May–31st Oct.
Tue.–Sun. 10am–6pm,
1st Nov.– 30th Apr. Tue.–Sat.
9am–5pm
E-mail: balatonimuz@georgikon.hu
The Georgikon Farm Museum
Bercsényi u. 65–67.
Tel.: 88/311-563
Open: 1st May–31st Oct. Tue.–Sat.
10am–5pm, Sun. 10am–6pm

KISKÖRE 3384
Village Museum
Béke út 5.
Tel.: 36/358-311, 36/358-023
Open: 1st May–30th Sept.
Mon.–Sun. 10am–noon,
2pm–5pm

KISKŐRÖS 6200
Petőfi's Birthplace and Memorial Museum
(Sándor Petőfi's birthplace,
Literature and Local History
Museum, Petőfi Picture Gallery,
Translators' Sculpture Park)
Petőfi tér 5.
Tel./fax: 78/312-566
Open: Tue.–Sun. 9am–5pm
E-mail: petofiszulohaz@vitae.hu
www.petofimuzeum.hu
Szlovak Peasant Cottage
(Ethnographic, Dress and
Lifestyle Museum)
Szent István u. 23.
Tel.: 78/414-255
Open: Tue.–Sun. 9am–4pm

KISKUNFÉLEGYHÁZA 6100
The Kiskun Múzeum
Dr. Holló L. u. 9. Tel.: 76/461-468

Open: 1st Apr.–31st Oct.
Wed.–Sun. 9am–5pm
Permanent exhibition: Hungarian
Criminal Law Exhibition;
The Paintings of László Holló;
Kiskunfélegyháza Through
The Centuries

LÉTAVÉRTES 4281
The Nagyléta Water Abbatoir (1905)
4281 Petőfi u. 78.
Tel.: 52/376-101
Open: by appointment
Peasant Cottage – Old Vineyard
Implements (1896) Kossuth zártkert
Tel.: 52/376-101
Open: by appintment
*Greek Catholic Church –
with unique iconostasis*
4281 Károlyi u. 3.
Tel.: 52/376-265
Open: by appointment

The Pintér Museum of Military History and Military Technology Park

Come and see the several thousand military and war exhibits we have
on display. Our park is especially for those interested in military technology.
The exhibits at the Military History Museum and Military Technology Park
are divided into four main parts.
The first part consists of the handguns used by the Hungarian Army as well as
different types of pistols, guns, machine guns and automatic weapons.
It is here you can see János Kádár's hunting rifle.
The second part contains the equipment and uniforms of the Hungarian artillery.
In the model house you can see hundreds of military weapons in miniature.
The fourth part, which is the most spectacular, is an open-air exhibition
and sculpture park set in 3 hectares of land. The refurbished second-hand military
hardware of the Hungarian Army are exhibited here, including the T-34 tank,
armoured war vehicles, reconnaissance planes, rocket-launching stations,
transporting vehicles, (KRAZ, ZIL, URAL, GAZ)
aeroplanes (MIG-15, MIG-17, MIG-21, MIG-23, SZU-22, L-39) and helicopters.

The Museum is open every day 8am–6pm.

Address: 6237 Kecel, II. Rákóczi Ferenc út, ipartelep
Information: 78/420-444 Fax: 78/420-600
E-mail: pinter-muvek@tvnetwork.hu
www.pintermuvek.hu

Lédig Hall – Calvinist Hospice
4283 Irinyi u. 7.
Tel.: 52/376-763
Iriny Leisure Park – Arboretum
4283 Kassai u. 8.
Tel.: 52/585-062

Martonvásár 2462
The Beethoven Memorial Museum
Brunszvik u. 2.
(The Hungarian Academy
Agricultural Research Centre)
Tel.: 22/569-500
Fax: 22/460-213
www.mgki.hu
Open: 1st Nov.–30th Apr.
Tue.–Fri. 10am–noon
and 2–4pm, Sat.–Sun.10am–4pm,
1st May–31st Oct.
Tue.–Fri. 10am–noon and 2–4pm,
Sat.–Sun.10am–6pm
The Cellar Gallery
Budai út 3.
Tel.: 22/460-663, 30/851-8882
Permanent exhibition:
The Graphics of Rozália Sütő Petre;
Plus the works of visiting artists
during the Martonvásár Festival
Open: by appointment

Mezőberény 5650
*The Soma Orlai Petrics
Collection*
Fő u. 1–3. Tel.: 66/352-025
Open: Tue.–Sat. 10am–noon
and 2–4pm

Mezőtúr 5400
The Túr Pottery Museum
Damjanich u 2/a
Tel.: 56/350-174
E-mail:
fazekasmuzeum@netposta.net
www.djm.hu/tagmuzeumok
Permanent exhibition:
The History of Túr Pottery
Info.: Tourinform Office
Tel./fax: 56/350-901

Mosonmagyaróvár 9200
*The History of the Western Hungarian
University of Agricultural and Food*
Vár u. 2. Tel.: 96/566-600
E-mail: nymeovar@mtk.nyme.hu
Open: Mon.–Fri. 9am–noon
The Fire Brigade Museum
Alkotmány u. 16. Tel./fax: 96/215-633
Permanent exhibition: The History
of the Mosonmagyaróvár Brigade
Open: daily 8am–4pm

Nagyhalász 4485
Csuha-Kállay Hall
Arany J. u. 58. Tel.: 42/202-218
Permanent exhibitions:
The Kallay Family Exhibition;
The Artists of Szabolcs-Szatmár-
Bereg County; Everyday Objects
and Implements from Nagyhalász
Open: by appointment

The Highways Collection

The only museum in Hungary –
run by ÁKMI Ltd. –
to give an account of the history
of bridge-building from the Roman
Period to the Present Day.
In the open-air part of
the museum you see an assortment
of road-building machinery.

Open: Daily 9am–4pm
Free entry

6200 Kiskőrös, Dózsa Gy. u. 38.
Tel.: 78/511-935
Fax: 78/511-936
E-mail: kozutigy@mail.externet.hu
www.kozut.hu

Nagyharsány 7822
*Open-air Sculpture Park
and Art Colony*
Tel.: 72/352-257
Fax: 72/326-740
E-mail: artcentr@dravanet.hu
Open: daily

The Diósgyőr Paper Mill

The history of paper production at
the foot of the Bükk Hills goes
back more than 220 years.
The Diósgyőr Paper Mill was founded
in 1782, with the first dated Diósgyőr
watermark we know of coming
from 1802. This is interesting
because the watermark is the oldest
known means of verifying the true
source of paper. Indeed, the Diósgyőr
Paper Mill remains the only place
producing papers of such
a sensitive nature. Today of course we
include several other security elements
so as to prevent forgery of any kind.
The mill is the only one of its kind in
Central Eastern Europe to have its own
exhibition. Visitors can trace both the
history of paper and the history of
the mill itself. The displays include
the various tools of the trade,
historical documents and a fully
fitted 18th century paper-making
workshop, where you can try
cutting the paper to size in the same way
they did it several centuries ago.

Paks 7030
The Municipal Museum
Deák Ferenc u. 2.
Tel./fax: 75/510-448
Open: 1st May–30th Sept. Tue.
10am–4pm, Wed.–Sun.10am–6pm,
1st Oct. –30th Apr. Tue.
10am–4pm, Wed.–Sun. 10am–5pm
Permanent exhibition: The History
of from Prehistoric Times to the

**Paks Atomic Power Station PLC
Information and Visitors' Centre**

Visitor-friendly exhibition on
the civil uses of atomic energy.
Electricity production show,
international comparative studies.
One-hour tour around the production
complex for the over-16s.

7031 Paks, Pf.: 71.
Tel.: 75/508-883, fax: 75/506-662
www.atomeromu.hu

Early 20th Century; Lapidarium;
The István Pákolitz Memorial Room

Páka 8956
The József Öveges Memorial Room
Ifjúság u. 13.
Tel.: 92/579-007

Pálfa 7042
Gyula Illyés's First School
Pálfa-Felsőrácegres, Alkotmány u. 5.
Info.: The Mayor's Office
Tel.: 75/339-011
Permanent exhibition: Objects,
documents, books, school equip-
ment; Illyés Memorial Exhibition
Open: by appointment

Pápa 8500
*The Textile Museum Foundation –
The Blue-Dyers' Museum*
Március 15. tér 12.
Tel.: 89/324-390
Open: 1st Nov.– 31st Mar.
Tue.–Sun. 9am–4pm,
1st Apr.–31st Oct.
Tue.–Sun. 9am–5pm

Rácalmás 2459
The Kovács Gallery
Szentháromság tér 19.
Tel.: 25/441-105
Open: by appointment

Rudabánya 3733
The Mining Museum
Tel./fax: 48/353-151
Open: 15th Apr.–15th Oct.
8am–5pm, 16th Oct–14th Apr.
Tue., Thur. 9am–4pm

Szalkszentmárton 6086
Sándor Petőfi Memorial Museum
Petőfi tér 14.
Tel.: 76/351-968
Open: Tue.–Sun. 9am–4pm
Permanent exhibition: Petőfi
and his Parents in Szalkszentmárton

Szentendre 2000
*The Dobos Cake
and Gastronomy Museum –
The Nostalgia Coffee House*
Bogdányi u. 2.
Tel.: 26/311-660, Fax: 1/486-0336,
30/921-0928
The József C. Dobos Collection –
The History of Chocolate, Sweets,
Gingerbread, Soft Drinks and
Coffee; Grocer's Shop. Cherry
Brandy Chocolate, Sweet and
Cake-making Displays, tasting group
visits, presentations. The cakes at the
coffee shop are made according to
the original recipes.
Open: 10am–6pm Sat.–Sun.,
holidays 10am–1pm

Szentistván 3418
Peasant Cottage, House of Culture
Rákóczi út 16. Tel.: 49/338-662
Open: by appointment

Székesfehérvár 8000
The Aluminium Industry Museum
Zombori út 12.
Tel./fax: 22/333-412
The History of the Hungarian
Aluminium Industry; Hungarian
Bauxite Mines, Geological Museum;
The Paintings of László Drégely
Open: Mon.–Fri. 8am–4pm

Tiszakeszi 3458
*The School and Local History
Collection*
Községháza út 10. Tel.: 49/352-852
Open: by appointment

Tiszavasvári 4400
The Pál Vasvári Museum
Kálvin u. 7. Tel.: 20/951-2193
E-mail: szatmary@tigris.klte.hu
Open: 16th Mar.–14th Oct.
Tue.–Sun. 9am–4pm,
15th Oct.–14th Mar.
Mon.–Fri. 9am–4pm

Permanent exhibitions: The History Pharmacy and Medicine in Szabolcs-Szatmár-Bereg County; The Tiszabüd Room: The History of the Nyír Mezőség from Prehistoric Times until the Middle Ages

TÖRÖKSZENTMIKLÓS 5200
The Straw Gallery
Kossuth L. u. 135. Tel.: 56/590-420
Fax: 56/391-316; Open: Mon.–Fri. 8am–7pm, Sat. 8am–noon

ÚJFEHÉRTÓ 4244
The Municipal Museum
Egészségház u 2. Tel.: 42/290-600
Open: Tue.–Sat. 9am–3pm, by appointment
Permanent exhibitions:
The History of Újfehértó;
Újfehértó peasant cottage interior from the 1920s; Agricultural Tools

VERPELÉT 3351
Blacksmith's Workshop
Kossuth út 62.
(Keeper: Kossuth út 52.)
Tel.: 36/359-014
Info.: The Verpelét Local Council
Open: Tue.–Sun. 9am–3pm

VESZPRÉM 8200
The Queen Gizella Museum
Vár u. 35.
Tel.: 88/426-088
Open: 1st May–23rd Oct.
Tue.–Sun. 9am–5pm
The Csikász Gallery
Vár u. 17. Tel.: 88/425-204
Open: Mon.–Sun. 10am–6pm
The Modern Picture Gallery – The László Vass Collection
Vár u. 3-7.
Tel.: 88/425-204, 88/561-310
Open: Mon.–Sun. 10am–6pm

The Fire Tower
Vár u. 17.
Tel.: 88/425-204
Open: 15th Mar.–31st Oct.
Mon.–Sun. 10am–6pm
The Castle Gallery
Vár u. 29.
Tel.: 88/425-204
Open: 1st May–31st Oct.
Mon.–Sun. 10am–6pm

Hungarian Open-Air Museum – Szentendre

Hungary's biggest open-air museum. Visitors can see the folk architecture of the country's characteristic landscapes, as well as experience the way people lived in both the towns and the villages through the exhibitions and programmes. There are also plenty of additional temporary exhibitions and events.

Open: from the beginning of April to the beginning of November, daily (except Mondays) 9am–5pm. The Museum's Ethnographical Exhibition and Skanzen Gallery are open all year round.

Our main events: Easter, Whitsun, Harvest Celebrations and the St Martin's New Wine Festival

Skanzen – The Pleasure of Tradition

2000 Szentendre, Sztaravodai út
Information: 26/502-519, 26/502-500
www.skanzen.hu

The Ópusztaszer National Historical Memorial Park

Pre-booking of tickets by telephone and tour guide service
62/275-133, 275-257, 275-055, 275-187, 275-167
(extensions 103, 104, 105)
Fax: 62/275-007
Mail: 6767 Ópusztaszer Szoborkert 68.
E-mail: info@opusztaszer.hu
Internet: www.opusztaszer.hu

The History of Hungarian Aviation

5008 Szolnok, Kilián u. 1., Pf.: 5
Tel.: 56/505-100/78-12
Open: 1st April–30th September
Tue.–Fri.: 9am–3pm,
Sat.–Sun.: 10am–4pm

The museum shows the development of military and civil aviation in Hungary up to the present day, including military aircraft manufactured abroad. The collection has grown in recent years with the addition of out-dated aircraft and spare parts.

The Garai Castle, Siklós
– originally Gothic, with Renaissance and Baroque additions

Permanent exhibitions in the castle:
• Wine Museum • Picture Gallery
• The Little Gallery – The István Gádor Pottery Exhibition
• Kálmán Istókovits
• Béla Simon
• Castle History Exhibition
• Dungeon • Waxworks
• Weapons from the Age of Rákóczi
• Glove and Fashion Exhibition
• Hunting Exhibition
• The Castle Chapel, including the tombs of Kázmér Batthyány, minister during the War of Freedom, and Móric Benyovszky, the last owner of the castle

Zamárdi 8621
Peasant Cottage, Ethnographic Collection
Fő u. 82.
Tel.: 84/349-409
E-mail: konyvtar@axelero.hu
Open: 1st Jun.–31st Aug.
Tue.–Sun. 10am–noon and 4–6pm
Groups also at other times by appointment.

Eggs

Red eggs, painted eggs; carved, reticulated eggs, eggs with horseshoes, eggs decorated with leaves, horsehair, seeds, paper; wooden eggs, porcelain- and glass eggs, crystal eggs. Art on eggs, eggs in art. You'll find it all in one place:

The Egg Art Museum

The home of the decorated egg.

Open all year round:
15th Mar.– 31st Oct. 10am–6pm
Otherwise 10am–3pm
Closed: Wednesday

7720 Zengővárkony, Kossuth Lajos u. 6
Tel.: 72/466-605
Fax: 72/566-012
E-mail:tojas@museum.hu
www.tojasmuzeum.ini.hu

FOLKLORE

Etyek 2091
The Swabian House
Magyar u. 7. Tel.: 22/223-325
E-mail: polgarmester@etyek.sednet.hu
Open: by appointment
Stations of the Cross (illuminated at night), Magyar Well, RC Church
Info.: Mayor's Office
Tel.: 22/353-633

Kismaros 2632
The Kismaros Village Museum
Lilliom u. 16.
Tel.: 27/383-121, 20/923-4714
Permanent Local History Exhibition: Faces, Objects from Kismaros's past
Open: Sun. 9am–noon; at other times by appointment

Osli 9354
Local History Collection
Rákóczi u.7.
Tel.: 96/250-144
(out of school hours
Tel.: 96/250-164)
Open: by appointment

Poroszló 3388
Peasant Cottage
Kossuth út 25.
Tel.: 36/553-040
Open: Mon.–Sun. 8am–5pm

Decs: "Capital of the Sárköz"

You will be able to enjoy our peasant cottage all the more for its 100-year-old furnishings. You can also buy some original hand-crafted artefacts. By visiting the Doll Museum, with its more than 100 dolls dressed in local costume, you will become all the more familiar with the Sárköz's rich and varied culture.
7144 Decs, Fő u. 23.
Tel./fax: 74/495-069
Mobile: 20/468-3234, 20/429-4424
E-mail: edit.bomba@freemail.hu

Tard 3416
Peasant Cottage
Tel.: 49/332-367
Open: by appointment

Zánka 8251
Peasant House and Gallery
Fő u. 13.
Open: 1st May–30th July Thur., Sat. 3–6pm, 1st July–20th Aug.
Tue.–Wed. 9am–noon,
Thur.–Sat. 3–6pm
By appointment at any time:
Aranka Andocs
Tel.: 87/568-030, 30/301-1786

Zengővárkony 7722
Peasant Cottage, Country Museum
Kossuth u. 6.
Tel.: 72/466-581
Fax: 72/466-158
Open: Tue.–Sun. 10am–6pm

Heves Folk Art and Handcrafts Co-operative

Heves, Kossuth Lajos út 28.
Tel.: 36/346-811, fax: 36/545-171
E-mail: heveshsz@axelero.hu

Visit our folk art houses and arts & crafts shops for folk art products, hand-woven materials, women's and children's blouses, shirts and felt souvenirs.

Bodony, Kossuth Lajos út 29.
Mátraberecske, Deák Ferenc u. 1.
Recsk, Kossuth Lajos út. 118.
Tarnaméra, Árpád út 15.

Folkart Centrum

1056 Budapest, Váci utca 58.
Tel.: 1/318-5840
Tel./fax: 1/318-4697
www.folkartcentrum.hu
www.nepmuveszethaziipar.hu

The finest Folk-store
full of handicrafts
from the countryside

Open: every day 10–19

There are presently two types of cultural event going on in Hungary: one based on local traditions, religious and folk customs, and the other with a more contemporary and strictly cultural slant.

What the events listed have in common is that they are usually the most popular in the area, and of particular interest to visitors.

The Békés County Jókai Theatre is Fifty Years Old

Founded on 15th September 1954, the theatre celebrates its 50th anniversary this autumn, and not only that, the theatre building itself is celebrating its 125th jubilee. The company puts on nine new productions a year.
The adult season-ticket is valid for five productions (a drama, a musical, an operetta, a comedy and one other) Those with a children's season ticket can see two plays especially for children. The Studio puts on two productions a year.

The Jókai Theatre has one of the most beautiful halls in the Southern Alföld. The so-called Vigadó Hall is well suited for conferences, product launches, balls and concerts. Apart from its aesthetic advantages it also has all the necessary technical equipment (projector, interpreting facilities and quality audio-visual equipment). In addition there is direct access to the town's most elegant hotel, the Hotel Fiumé, so participants attending events don't even have to step onto the pavement when returning to their lodgings.

5600 Békéscsaba, Andrássy út 1.
Telefon: 66/441-730.
E-mail: jokaiszinhaz@axelero.hu

Békés

Local events in around the town that gives the county its name.

THE BÉKÉS-TARHOS MUSIC FESTIVAL
Held every year in June and July.
Three weeks of concerts, courses and masterclasses await classical music lovers.

THE MADZAGFALU FESTIVAL
A day of sport and culture during the second weekend in September and a reunion for residents past and present.
Three days of fun and games for those who happen to be in Békés.

Information: The Municipal Arts Centre
5630 Békés, Jantyik Mátyás u. 21–25.
Tel.: 66/411-142

Algyő Village House and Leisure Centre

Cultural and tourist services:
Community events (balls, markets, conferences, theatrical productions, open-air concerts, information service);
Leisure centre, a youth hostel accommodation for 40 and restaurant for school field trips, outings and families spending their holidays on the banks of the Tisza.

Events calendar:
Village festival (end of April)
Midsummer's Fire Jumping (June)
St Anna's Patronal Festival and International Dance Gala. (End of June)
Equestrian Day (Mid-August)
August 20th Street Market
Algyo Day (October 1st)
Christmas Concert

Village House, 6750 Algyő, Búvár u. 5.
Tel.: 62/517-172, tel./fax: 62/517-173
www.algyo.hu/faluhaz
E-mail: faluhaz@mail.tiszanet.hu

Leisure Centre, 6750 Algyő,
Téglás u. 151., Tel./fax: 62/267-426
The Ferenc Móra Theatre, 6750 Algyő,
Búvár u. 5., Tel.: 62/517-172

APÁTFALVA

May
The Whitsun Brass Convention
July
*The Apátfalva Village Festival
and Equestrian Festival*
August
The Blessing of the Harvest
Info.: Mayor's Office
Tel.: 62/520-040

BUDAKALÁSZ

June
Kalász Festivities – with dance groups
October
*Harvest Parade and Ball
Contemporary Dance Festival*
Info.: Kalász Village House Ltd.
Tel.: 26/ 340-468

BUDAPEST

*The National Philharmonic Orchestra,
Choir and Music Library*
1052 Budapest, Váci u. 16/a
Postal address: 1364 P.O. Box 49
E-mail: info@filharmonikusok.hu
www.filharmonikusok.hu
Tel.: 1/411-6600, Fax: 1/411-6699

CSÓKAKŐ

May
*Spring Farewell Celebrations,
Cooking Competition*
August
Csókakő Patronal Festival
September
*The Csókakő Festival and Castle
Tournament, Market*
December
Classical Concert
Info.: The Mayor's Office
Tel.: 22/422-001

DABAS

September
The Dabas Festival
Info: The Mayor's Office
Tel.: 29/360-166

DEBRECEN

*The Ferenc Kölcsey County
Educational Institute*
4026 Kálvin tér 2/a
Tel.: 52/413-977, Fax: 52/416-040
*The Debrecen Cultural
and Festival Centre Ltd.*
4025 Petőfi tér 10. Tel.: 52/525-270
E-mail: fesztival@debrecen.com
www.fesztivalkozpont.hu

DUNAFÖLDVÁR 7020

The Municipal Cultural Centre
Ilona u. 9.
Tel.: 75/541-000, Fax: 75/541-001
E-mail: foldvarkultura@mail.datanet.hu
www.dunafoldvar-muvhaz.hu

DUNAKILITI 9225

The Mayor's Office and Village House
Kossuth L. u. 86.
Tel./fax: 96/671-033
E-mail: dunakiliti.onkorm@axelero.hu

The Ferencváros Summer Festival
The programme for 2004

Mascagni: **MESSA DI GLORIA** Oratorio
The first public
performance in Hungary
18th June, 7pm and 20th June, 7pm

THE BENKÓ DIXIELAND BAND and
THE BUDAPEST KLEZMER BAND
Open-air concert June 19th, 9pm

DANUBIAN RHAPSODY
Dramatic folk dance production
22rd June, 9pm

A.J. Lerner – F. Loewe: **MY FAIR LADY**
Guest production of the Mór Jókai Theatre
Komárno (Slovakia) 25th June, 9pm

Liszt: **CHRIST** Oratorio-Passion
29th June, 9pm

CAIN and ABEL – BOLERO ballet
3rd July, 9pm

Verdi: **MASKED BALL**
An opera in three acts (own production)
9th July, 11th July, 9pm

Ferencváros Summer Festival Ltd.
1093 Török Pál u. 3., Tel.: 1/218-0193
E-mail: fenyar@hu.inter.net

FONYÓD 8640

The House of Culture
Szabó F. u. 3. Tel.:85/560-058

GYŐR

The Győr Philharmonic Orchestra
9021 Aradi vértanúk u. 16.
Tel.: 96/312-452, 96/524-900
Fax: 96-319-232
E-mail: filhgyor@axelero.hu
www.filharmonikusok.gyor.hu
The Győr National Theatre
9022 Czuczor G. u. 7.
Tel.: 96/312-044, Fax: 96/313-276
E-mail: szervezes@gyoriszinhaz.hu
www.gyoriszinhaz.hu

GYULA

July
*The International Fire Brigade Brass
Band and Majorette Festival*
Info.: The Fire Brigade
Tel.: 66/463-533

Enjoy the Harmony
WITH
ZOLTÁN KOCSIS
AND THE
HUNGARIAN NATIONAL PHILHARMONIC

 Hungarian National
Philharmonic Orchestra

Tel.: 1/411-6600
E-mail: info@filharmonikusok.hu
www.hunphilharmonic.org

Jásszentandrás 5136
Traditional Harvest Parade
Info.: The Mayor's Office
Tel.: 52/446-006

Kaba 4183
The Pál Mácsai Cultural Centre
Szabadság tér 8. Tel.: 54/522-000

Kalocsa 6300
The Archdiocesan Library
Szentháromság tér 1. Tel.: 78/465-280
Open: 1st Apr.–31st Oct.
Tue.–Sun. 9am–5pm

Kartal 2173
The House of Culture
Felszabadulás út 107. Tel.: 28/437-241
E-mail: muvhazkartal@freemail.hu
May
Kartal May Day Celebrations
June
Arts and Crafts Workshop

September
Folk Music Convention,
Pest County Choral Competition
October
"By the People for the People"
December
Village Christmas
Info.: The House of Culture
Tel.: 28/437-241

Kecskemét
July–August
The Kodály Festival (annual)
The Kodály Seminar (in years ending
in odd numbers)
Info.: The Kodály Institute
Tel.: 76/481-518

Kiskunfélegyháza
May
Founders' Day (Symphonic concert,
cultural programmes,
entertainment, prize-giving)

July
Ferenc Móra Celebrations
(statue ceremony,
cultural programme),
Petőfi Celebrations
August
The Kiskunfélegyháza Festival
(The rock opera Stephen the King,
cultural programmes, entertainment)
September
Gastronomic Festival
(goose festival, harvest ball,
wine competition,
gastronomic exhibition,
presentations)
October
World Music Day – Exhibition and
Concert
December
Anniversary of Sándor Petőfi's Birth
and Farewell to the Year Past
Info.: The Mayor's Office
Tel.: 76/461-255

Celldömölk

In May: the Alsóság Spring Festival
In September:
St Mary's Patronal Festival
and the Ság Hill Harvest Festival
The Vulkán Cup International
Youth Football Tournament,
9th–11th July 2004

Info.: Tourinform Office
Celldömölk, Dr. Géfin tér 1.
Tel.: 95/420-037, 95/423-940
E-mail: phcell@cellkabel.hu

Cibakháza

Popular annual events:
arts and crafts workshop,
harvest ball and grape-picking ball.
Things to see: the Turul statue,
the Arad memorial and wooden
grave post in Szabadság tér.

Information:
Mayor's Office
5462 Cibakháza, Szabadság tér 5.
Tel.: 56/477-001
Fax: 56/577-032
E-mail: cibakh@mail.externet.hu

Csesznek

Travelling through the Bakony on road
82 linking Győr with Veszprém (110 km
from Budapest and 50 from Lake
Balaton), you come upon the unique
spectacle of the Gothic ruins of 13th
century Csesznek Castle perched up on
the ridge of Castle Hill. The CSESZNEK
SUMMER festival, which takes place at
the castle and the Quarry Open-air
Stage, amounts to a major cultural event
including: THE CASTLE TOURNMENT,
the historical archery competition,
the castle musical evenings,
the tarogato festival, rock concerts
(including EDDA), THE BLUES FESTIVAL,
theatrical productions:
Stephen the King (rock opera)
and THE STARS OF EGER (musical).
Info.: The Csesznek Programme Office
8419 Csesznek, Vár út 51.
Tel./fax: 88/436-110
e-mail: info@cseszprog-hu
www.cseszprog.hu

Philharmonia Eastern Hungary Ltd.

For organising concerts,
ticket sales and information
about cultural events

4024 Debrecen, Vár u. 10/c., I. em. 3.
(The Kálvin tér Shopping Centre,
above Papp Optika)
Tel./fax: 52/314-139
E-mail: filharmonia@cablenet.hu

Kisgyőr
Come to Kisgyőr!

The wood carvers' village
at the southern foot of the Bükk Hills
Traditional events:
– Woodcarvers' workshop
– Equestrian festival
– Grape harvest
– Folk art exhibition

Accommodation
Tel./fax: 46/477-897
E-mail: kisgyor@freemail.hu
http://kisgyor.uw.hu

KÖRMEND 9900
The Centre of Culture and Youth,
Theatre
Dr. Batthyány-Strattman László u.
Tel.: 94/410-107
E-mail: cultcent@axelero.hu
www.kormend.hu

KŐSZEG 9730
Jurisics Castle – Cultural Centre
and Castle Theatre
Rajnis u. 9.
Tel.: 94/360-113
Fax: 94/563-244
E-mail: jurisics@koszeg.hu
www.koszeg.hu

MISKOLC 3525
The Miskolc National Theatre
(Main Theatre, Workshop Theatre,
Stage)
Déryné u. 1.
Tel.: 46/516-700

NYÍREGYHÁZA 4400
Philharmonia Eastern Hungary Ltd.
Szabadság tér 9. Tel.: 30/399-7934
Fax: 30/800-1671
E-mail: filharm@westel900.hu

OROSHÁZA
April
Civic and Saint George's Day
Celebrations
April–May
The Spring Arts Festival
May
The VI. Poultry Festival
June
MotOros Convention
OPEN 2004 National Ballroom
Dancing Competition
August
XXXVI. National Equestrian
Championship
Info.: (about all the events)
The Mayor's Office Tel.: 68/413-022

PALOZNAK 8229
Organ Recitals in
the Catholic Church
Info.: The Mayor's Office
Tel./fax: 87/446-623
Concers and arts and crafts events
in the yard of the peasant cottage at
weekends
Info.: Peasant Cottage,
Fő utca 10.
www.paloznak.hu

PÉCS
The Croatian Theatre, Pécs –
The Pécs Open-Air Festival
7621 Anna u. 17.
Tel.: 72/210-197,
72/510-093,
Fax: 72/514-300
E-mail: phsz@freemail.hu,
phszbalatinacz@vnet.hu
www.horvatszinhaz.hu
www.pecsiszabadteri.hu

The Apáczai Cultural Centre,
House of Culture
7632 Apáczai Csere János krt. 1.
Tel.: 72/550-600, 550-601
Fax: 72/550-621

PÉCSVÁRAD 7720
The Lajos Fülep Cultural Centre
Kossuth L. u. 31.
Tel.: 72/465-123, 72/565-096
E-mail: muvhaz@pecsvarad.hu
www.pecsvarad.hu

PELLÉRD 7831
The Cultural Centre
Iskola u.2.
Tel.:72/373-224
E-mail.:pellisk@matavnet.hu

PILISCSABA 2087
May
The Piliscsaba Church Music Festival
– In the churches of Piliscsaba
and at the Péter
Pázmány Roman Catholic University
Info.: The Foundation for
the Klotildliget Parish
Piliscsaba 3. Klotildliget Pf. 28.
Tel.: 26/375-095

PILISSZENTKERESZT
September
*The Festival of the Raising
of the True Cross*
Info.: The Roman Catholic parish
Tel.: 26/347-619

RÁTKA
July
Ethnic Minorities' Festival
Info.: The Mayor's Office
Tel.: 47/374-019

SELLYE 7960
Cultural Sports Centre and Library
Batthyány u. 14. Tel.: 73/480-245
Fax: 73/580-025
www.ormansag.hu

SOPRON 9400
Pro Cultura Sopron Ltd.
*The Ferenc Liszt Conference and
Cultural Centre*
Liszt F. u. 1. Tel.: 99/517-500
Fax: 99/517-516
E-mail: info@prokultura.hu

SZARVAS 5540
*The Péter Vajda Cultural Centre
and Tourinform Office*
Kossuth tér 3.
Tel.: 66/311-464, 66/311-140
The organisation of the summer tour-
ist events and an information service.

SZATYMAZ
March
The Peach Blossom Celebrations
July
Village Days, Peach Festival
Info.: The Mayor's Office
Tel.: 62/583-560

The Diósgyőr Castle Festival
The Main Events

May: "The Market's Open",
The Diósgyőr Castle Tournament
May–June: The Borsod Spinners
National Folklore Festival
July: The International Dixieland Festival
The Kaláka International Folk Festival
July–August: "The Golden Arrow"
Historical Archery Competition
August: Diósgyőr Castle Theatre Evenings
The Medieval Castle Festival in Diósgyőr
The Feast of Saint Stephen the King
October: The Diósgyőr Wine Festival

Information: Diósgyőr Castle
3534 Miskolc-Diósgyőr, Vár u. 24.
Tel.: 46/533-355
E-mail: adymuvhaz@chello.hu
www.diosgyorivar.com

SZENTGOTTHÁRD 9970
House of Culture and Theatre
Kossuth L. út. 7.
Tel./fax: 94/554-106

SZOLNOK 5000
*Municipal Cultural and Musical
Centre Ltd.*
Hild J. tér 1. Tel.: 56/514-569
E-mail: vmzk@szolnok-vmzk.hu
The House of Science and Technology
Kossuth u. 4.
Tel./fax: 56/425-524, 56/510-410
E-mail: pelikan@mtesz.hu
www.szolnok.mtesz.hu
Education, organising events,
video-conferences, European
information service.

TISZANÁNA 3385
Cultural Centre
Hunyadi u. 1.
Tel.: 36/566-018

Miskolc's House of Youth and Leisure present:
The Diósgyőr Tournament
The last weekend in May
The International Dixieland Festival
The first Saturday in July
The Festival of Music and Light –
Miskolctapolca
The last Saturday in July
The International Formation
Dancing Festival
In October
3531 Miskolc, Győri kapu 27.
Tel.: 46/411-747, 46/412-508
Fax: 46/320-716
E-mail: ifihaz@chello.hu

Sárisáp

Sárisáp's cultural centre takes the form of the Miners' Cultural House, It's a venue which often sees the Miners' Brass Band, the Ethnic Slovak Women's Choir and the mixed choir take to the stage. The highlights of the calendar are: Ethnic Minorities' Day and Old People's Day in April, the Village Festival on 20th August, including St Stephen's Day and the Breaking of the New Bread, and the Patronal Festival in November, celebrating St Emerich's Day.
Tel.: 33/508-390, Fax: 33/450-001

VÁRPALOTA 8100
May
The Flowers of the Bakony Folk Art Day
Info.: Municipal Sports Hall
Tel.: 88/372-103
June
VÁREXPO Exhibition and Trade Fair, Várpalota
Info.: The Municipal Sports Hall
Tel.: 88/372-103
August
International Wind Band Festival, International Folk Dance Festival, Várpalota
Info.: The Municipal Sports Hall
Tel.: 88/372-103
Oktober
The Várpalota Festival
Info.: The Mayor's Office
Tel.: 88/592-694
The Cultural and Human Resources Institute
Honvéd u. 1.
Tel.: 88/472-305

VILLÁNY 7773
April
Emmaus with Wine and Dance (Easter)
Info.: Bortrezor Cellar
Homann u. 1.
Tel.:72/492-053

ZÁKÁNYSZÉK
April
Calling in the Spring
Info.: Youth Office Tel.: 62/590-010
June
Patronal Festival
Info.: The Mayor's Office
Tel.: 62/590-490
July
Harvest Festival
Info.: László Papp Tel.: 62/290-417
August
The Zákányszék Paprika Festival
Info.: The Cultural Centre
Tel.: 62/590-080
September
Health Week
Info.: Lajos Mester Tel.: 62/590-050
Village Day
Info.: The Mayor's Office
Tel.: 62/590-490

Orosháza

2004 Events Calendar:
15th–16th May: The VI. "Szárnyas" Festival
18th–20th June: The IV. MotOros Convention
19th June: OPEN 2004. National Ballroom-Dancing Competition
25th June–4th July: Orosháza-Gyopáros Summer Cultural and Leisure Festival
10th July: "We've got something to grill!" I. Gyopáros National Bacon-Grilling Competition
31st July–1st Aug.: I. European Folk Dance and Gastronomic Festival
19st–22nd Aug.: I. European Bread Festival
22nd Aug.: The XXXVI. International Equestrian Championship
25th–30th Oct.: International Hawkers' Convention

Information: 68/413-022

October
World Music Day – Concert
Info.: The Cultural Centre
Tel.: 62/590-080
December
Village Christmas
Info.: The Cultural Centre
Tel.: 62/590-080

ZALALÖVŐ 8999
The Municipal Cultural Centre and Library
Szabadság tér. 1.
Tel.: 92/371-004

ZEBEGÉNY
June–July
The Danube Bend Arts Festival
Info.: The Danube Bend Cultural Foundation
Tel.: 27/572-545

Ludi Savarienses
Savaria Historical Carnival

In Szombathely in August every year The Savaria Historical

Carnival Foundation
Carnival office
9700 Szombathely, Széchenyi u. 1.
Tel: 94/510-160, 94/510-161
E-mail: savariakarneval@axelero.hu
www.savariakarneval.hu

ZEMPLÉN *festival*

13th–19th August 2004

30 picturesque cities with 60 cultural
and gastronomical events
symphonic and chamber concerts
Ancient Music, World Music, New Music, Opera, Dance

Information: **Interkultur Hungaria Kht.**
H-1074 Budapest, Rottenbiller u. 16-22. Tel.: (+36) 1/462-0330 • Fax: (+36) 1/342-9362
E-mail: info@zemplenfestival.hu • Tickets: ticket@zemplenfestival.hu
www.zemplenfestival.hu • www.vendegvaro.hu
Hotel booking: **Zemplén Tourist**
E-mail: zemplen.tourist@axelero.hu • Phone: (+36) 47/361-151 • Fax: (+36) 47/362-952

MEDICINAL TOURISM

The country's extraordinarily rich stock of thermal and medicinal waters mean that almost 70% of the country has thermal waters lurking under the surface. The thermal waters along the Danube, in Southern and Western Transdanubia and along the eastern border have had a beneficial effect on development of the local communities. Numerous towns and villages have a lot to thank hot waters for. During the Turkish period the prevalent bathing culture produced some significant results. Following a temporary lapse, spa culture re-emerged triumphant in Hungary during the 19th century. It was then that medicinal waters dominated balneological research. The Hungarian Balneological Association came into being in 1891. From the end of the 19th century numerous spa buildings of considerable architectural interest were constructed – some of which are currently undergoing restoration today. Medicinal waters are recommended for numerous illnesses, treatments etc. – whether bathing cures, drinking cures, or mud treatment.

Alongside the medicinal services and the thermal baths there are also opportunities to do sport, aerobics or some of your other favourite hobbies. In most places you will find accommodation and some excellent restaurants in the vicinity of the baths.

In the following section you will not only find baths with medicinal and thermal waters, but waters of all types. The choice is wide and the list here far from complete. Wherever you happen to be in Hungary it is worthwhile enquiring whether there is an outdoor swimming complex nearby as the answer is usually in the affirmative, with "near" usually meaning no longer than half an hour's drive away.

BATTONYA 5830
Thermal Baths and Outdoor Bathing Complex
With medicinal waters and boarding house from 2004
Bajcsy-Zs. E. u. 72.
Tel./fax: 68/456-048
www.myland.hu

BÜK 9740
The Bük Medicinal Baths
Termál Krt. 2. Office: 94/358-022
BÜKIT.: 94/359-539
Medicinal bath services: 94/358-660

CSONGRÁD 6640
Medicinal Baths and Swimming Pool
Dob u. 3. Tel.: 63/481-918
Tel./fax: 63/483-631
Open: Mon. 7am–5pm,
Tue.–Thur. 7am–8pm, Fri.–Sat. 8am–10pm, Sun. 8am–8pm

DÉVAVÁNYA 5510
Outdoor Swimming Complex and Medicinal Services
Sport u. 5. Tel./fax: 66/483-127
E-mail: dvfurdo@bekesnet.hu
Open: Mon.–Fri. 10am–7pm,
Sat.–Sun. 9am–8pm

DOMBÓVÁR 7200
The Gunaras Medicinal and Thermal Baths
Alkotás tér 1. Pf. 2. Tel.:74/465-335
Open:Mon.–Fri. 7am–6pm,
Sat.–Sun. 8am–6pm,
Outdoor Swimming Pool
1st May–30th Sept. Mon.–Fri.
7am–6pm, Sat.–Sun. 8am–6pm

EGER 3300
The Eger Thermal Baths
Petőfi tér 2
Tel.: 36/511-810
Open: 1st May–31st Sept.
Mon.–Sun. 6am–8am, 9am–7pm,
1st Nov.–1st May 9am–7pm

Balatonlelle

Sunny, friendly, flowery Balatonlelle is one of the most popular holiday resorts on the southern shore of Lake Balaton. Its colourful image is due not only to its wonderful setting and picturesque surroundings, but to its attractive and atmospheric buildings, its ancient monuments, its history culture as well as its visitor-friendly wine cellars. Balatonlelle's most recent attraction is the new leisure pool at the Sunshine Lido, which is popular with young and old alike. There is a swimming pool, a children's and adults' leisure pool, including a jacuzzi, water massage, water tunnel and slides. As the waters are heated you can even bathe when the weather gets cooler.

Medicinal and Outdoor Baths
5465 Cserkeszőlő, Fürdő u. 1.
Tel./fax: 56/568-465
E-mail: cserkeszolofurdo@externet.hu
Open all year round, with covered winter pool; medicinal swimming, leisure and wave pools; slides; physiotherapy; galvanizing tub; massage; tangentor; traction bath; carbon dioxide bath; mudpack; pedicure
Thermál Camping***Touring Hotel **
Tel.: 56/568-450, fax: 56/568-464
Open all year round
Direct access to the Baths

Travelling with Béres

Visiting Hungary's unique natural, cultural and historical treasures can only be a completely relaxing experience if all the family are feeling one hundred per cent. Under the motto "Béres for the healthy individual" Béres Pharmaceuticals has been helping to protect people's health with a range of products designed to meet the needs of the modern world; and that includes making sure the whole family gets the most out of their holiday.

Béres Drops and Vitamin C

Béres drops are made of trace elements and minerals designed to strengthen the immune system. In doing so they improve performance by putting people's natural resistence mechanisms back on track. Health care is not simply a question of curing illnesses and aiding recovery, but taking the necessary preventative measures. If our bodies are strong, we are not only better placed to prevent problems, we can also embark on a recovery from illness from a position of strength rather than weakness. Apart from Béres Drops we would also recommend taking Béres C vitamin. Just one small drop of vitamin C a day is all you need to give your body the vitamin C it requires.

Béres Drops are a roborant which can be purchased without a prescription.
For the risks and any possible side effects read the directions, or ask your GP or chemist.

Actival Multivitamins

The Actival multivitamins, a new product from Béres Pharmaceuticals, has been developed following all the necessary scientific research. By contributing to the body's vitamin, mineral and trace element requirements, the multivitamins maintain your body's powers of resistance whilst helping you to hit top form. Actival gives the whole family a complex vitamin, mineral and trace element supplement: Actival Kid for the children, Actival Max for adults and Actival 50+, specially designed for the over-50s.
Of all the multivitimins available in Hungary, Actival Max is the first to contain ingredients such as lutein, likopin and ß-carotin. The lutein helps to protect your eyes and maintains the arterial system, likopin helps prevent the oxidation processes which lead to aging, and the ß-carotin keeps your nails, hair and skin healthy.

Antifront Drops and Capsules

Traditional herbal remedies are currently enjoying something of a renaissance. Not only do they help us get better, they bring us a little closer to nature. The Antifront Drop and Capsule developed by the Béres Pharmaceutical Company is one such herbal product, designed to overcome any discomfort resulting from weather change, new weather fronts and travel sickness. The herbal ingredients (ginger, liquorice, lemon-balm and turmeric) have a positive effect, reducing such unpleasant symptoms as dizziness, sleeplessness and headaches. Containing as it does natural ingredients, Antifront is a great alternative to the strong sedatives, painkillers and other drugs which are usually prescribed.

♫ BÉRES

Orosháza-Gyopárosfürdő, "Pearl of the Great Plain"

The Gyopárosfürdő Medicinal Baths and Lido, lying in a protected area on the shores of Lake Gyopáros, are just 3 kilometres from the centre of Orosháza. Its natural alkaline hydrogen carbonate waters are good for various locomotor and rheumatic problems, as well as inflammations and aching joints. They are also recommended for gynaeocological complaints and post-accident and post-operation rehabilitation.

The Medicinal Baths and Lido offer a complete range of treatments, including physiotherapy, electrotherapy and balneotherapy, together with services specially designed to make our guests feel refreshed and relaxed.

The state-of-the-art Leisure Complex was opened during spring 2004. 6200m^2 of leisure facilities, consisting of seven pools, giant slides, water features, a gym, a conference hall, a bar and a restaurant now await. In addition the "Szaunapark" supplies our guests with various types of sauna, as well as a steam cabin, a danarium and aroma and light therapies.

Orosháza-Gyopáros Medicinal Baths Ltd.
5904 Orosháza, Fasor u. 3.
Tel./fax: 68/411-962, 68/512-260
E-mail: furdort@oroshaza.hu
www.gyoparosfurdo.hu

The Gyula Castle Baths – The Bastion of Health

The Castle Baths in Gyula is one of the most famous destinations on Hungary's health tourism map. It is here that the thermal waters bursting up to the surface promise visitors refreshment, regeneration and recovery. This all happens at the outdoor swimming complex and medicinal baths in what is a 220-year-old 8.5-hectare park. The recently renovated Castle Baths offer up-to-date medical services, medicinal and leisure pools, a children's water paradise, 25m and 50m pools which are open all year round, as well as the southern Alföld's one-and-only Wellness Centre, where the 480m^2 leisure pool, saunas, steam cabins, billiard room, fitness gym and card tables provide some great ways to relax.

Suggested accommodation: **Hotel Park*****
5700 Gyula, Part u. 15., e-mail: parkgyula@civishotels.hu

Gyula Castle Baths Ltd
5700 Gyula, Várkert u. 2.
Tel.: 66/561-350, 561-360, Fax: 66/561-060
E-mail: varfurdo@bekes.hungary.net, www.gyulavarfurdo.hu

VÁRFÜRDŐ
GYULA

Join us at Europe's largest spa complex!

13 pools, an indoor swimming pool, 9 water slides, a Mediterranean atmosphere, sandy beaches, palm trees, a pirate ship and a lighthouse – you can find these all in one place! The older ones can wash away their weekday stress in the attractive pools filled with internationally renowned medicinal water. In addition, there are 40 different types of treatment based on the unique water, making complete relaxation possible. A crystal-clear lake with a sandy shore offers further opportunities for an active holiday for the young. Water lovers will spend many a pleasant hour at the Aquapark.

HUNGUEST HOTEL
AQUA-SOL
HAJDÚSZOBOSZLÓ
★★★★

4200 Hajdúszoboszló, Gábor Áron u. 7–9.
Telephone: 52/273-310, fax: 52/273-340
E-mail: reserve@hotelaquasol.hunguesthotels.hu

Spa therapy section: Our guests can reach the medicinal spa through a covered, air-conditioned bridge. In the baths you can find medicinal water with excellent qualities.
Medical services: rheumatological examinations, massage (medical, refreshing, foot, lympho), medical gymnastics (individual, group, in a gym, underwater), balneotherapy (traction bath, mudpack, fango, underwater jet massage, effervescent bath), physiotherapy (cryotherapy, ultra sound), laser shower, salt therapy, physiatry, cure packages (pause, after-care treatment, Bechterew, constriction of the vessels). Hotel guests can have the above-mentioned treatments in the newly-built medical centre, in a medical section which is available to those staying at the hotel.
Wellness, sport and fitness: in the hotel's Wellness Island: jacuzzi, pool (9 m), sauna, steam bath. In the spa-centre: solarium, on gym, Dermalife spa & wellness therapy, from May till September (see opening times) open-air swimming pools, jacuzzi, wave-bath, fun-bath, children's pools and a unique artificial Mediterranean beach.

4200 Hajdúszoboszló, Mátyás király sétány 10.
Telephone: 52/361-411, fax: 52/361-759
E-mail: reserve@hotelbeke.hunguesthotels.hu

HUNGUEST HOTEL
BÉKE
HAJDÚSZOBOSZLÓ
★★★

Spa therapy section: The hotel has its own medical section – connected to the hotel wing. Two indoor and one outdoor thermal pools (with leisure bath) are available.
Treatment available: physician's examinations (general, rheumatological, dental) massage (medical, refreshing, reflex), medical gymnastics (individual, group, in a gym and underwater), balneotherapy, (mud-pack, weight bath, underwater jet massage, effervescent bath), physiotherapy (Tens-treatment, cryotherapy, galvanic treatment, ultra sound, etc.), salt chamber, light therapy.
Sport and fitness: 1 indoor and 2 outdoor (seasonal opening) swimming pools, sauna, solarium. Nearby: tennis courts, bowling, bike rental

1000 m² water surface

Outdoor fun bath
Swimming pool with Sauna-Island
Luxury Roman Thermal bath
Traditional Spa Therapies and Vital-Wellness Programmes
Detoxicational and fasting cures...
are waiting for you!

To your health...

**NaturMed
Hotel
Carbona** ****

www.carbona.hu
Tel.: +36 83/543-582
Fax: +36 83/340-468
hotel@carbona.hu
H-8380 Hévíz, Attila u. 1.

HAJDÚNÁNÁS 4080
*Outdoor Swimming Complex and
Medicinal Baths*
Fürdő u. 7. Tel.: 52/381-858
Fax: 52/381-272
The 67°C-waters are recommended
for curing locomotor diseases.
Services: rheumatological treatment,
medicinal massage, tangentor, medi-
cinal gymnastics, sauna, 2 tennis
courts; Open: Covered medicinal
bath: Tue.–Thur. 9am–6pm;
Fri.–Sat. 9am–8pm; Sun. 9am–7pm
Outdoor swimming pool: 1st Jun.–
15th Sept. Mon.–Sun. 9am–7pm

JÁSZBERÉNY 5100
LEHEL Sports and Leisure Ltd.
Kiserdei sétány 5. Tel.: 57/415-267
Open: Swimming pool: 2nd Jan.–
31st Dec. Mon. 8am–6pm; Tue.–Fri.
6am–6pm; Sat.–Sun.10am–6pm;
19th May–31st Aug. Mon.8am–6pm;
Tue.–Fri. 6am–6pm; Sat.–Sun.
10am–6pm; Outdoor swimming
pool: 5th May–31st Aug.
Mon.–Sun. 8am–7pm
Water type: simple thermal water,
good for rheumatic illnesses

JÁSSZENTANDRÁS 5136
Outdoor Swimming Complex
Mártírok u. 14. Tel.: 57/446-025
Open: 1st May–31st Oct. 8am–7pm
The ferruginous thermal waters are
good for those suffering from
rheumatic and gynaecological illnesses.

MEZŐTÚR 5400
*The Municipal Outdoor Swimming
Complex*
Erzsébet-liget Tel.: 56/350-684
Fax: 56/350-215
E-mail: vizmumt@mail.externet.hu
Open: Outdoor complex 1st May–
15th Sept. Mon.–Sun. 9am–7pm;
Swimming pool: 15th Sept.–31st
May Mon.–Sun. 6am–8pm

NAGYBÁNHEGYES 5668
Thermal Bath
Erzsébet királyné útja 36.
Tel.: 68/426-768
Open:
off season: Fri., Sat., Sun.:
noon–9pm,
high season:
Tue., Wed., Thur.: noon–8pm,
Fri., Sat., Sun.: noon–9pm

Heves Thermal Bath & Camp Site

Holiday and relax in the thermal baths
of southern Heves County in what are
tranquil atmospheric surroundings.
3360 Heves, Arany J. u. 41.
Tel.: 36/346-869
Open: May 1st–Sept. 31st 8am–7pm.

Tarnaméra Thermal Bath and Camping Site

The varied programme of summer
entertainment will make your stay
all the more pleasant.
Camping Site:
3284 Tarnaméra Dobó u. 2/a.
Manager: The Tarnaméra Local
Government
Tel.: 36/479-116, 36/479-101
Thermal Baths:
3284 Tarnaméra, Dobó u. 2/a
Tel.: 36/479-317
Open: May 15th–Jun. 15th 10am–6pm,
Jun. 16th–Aug. 30th 9am–7pm
The bath can be found in beautiful
woodland in the middle of the village.

The Cave and Spa Miskolc-Tapolca

Experience and Recovery

• situated on the edge of Miskolc,
centre of the northeastern
Hungarian region
• therapeutic effects known as far
back as the 16th century
• Europe's one and only natural
cave bath, complete with 30°C thermal
spa waters   • leisure features in
the cave, with a children's pool
outside in the garden
• the services of the medicinal
compound: hydrotherapy, tangentor,
medicinal and tonal massage,
electrotherapy, in-house
rheumatological consultant, sauna
• restaurant   • valuables safe
• wheelchair-friendly
• open: daily 9am–6pm,
summer opening 9am–7pm
• annual maintenance break:
in January

The Cave and Spa
3519 Miskolc-Tapolca, Pazár sétány
Tel.: 46/560-030, fax: 46/560-035
E-mail: barlangfurdo@miviz.hu
www.barlangfurdo.hu

NAGYKÁTA 2760
Medicinal and Outdoor Swimming Complex
Hosszútó u. Tel.: 29/442-971
Open: 1st May–30th Sept.
9am–5pm

PÉCS 7623
Wave Bath
Szendrey J. u. 7. Tel.: 72/512-935
Open: all year round 6am–10pm
Wave complex: spring-autumn
9am–7pm
Services: sauna, jacuzzi,solarium, massage and foot massage, rheumatological examinations, electrotherapy, medicinal swimming

SÁROSPATAK 3950
The Végardó Swimming Complex
Határ u. 2/b Tel.: 47/311-639
Open: Mon.–Sun. 8am–6pm

SZENDRŐ 3752
Outdoor Swimming Complex
Kovács u. 6.
Tel.: 48/560-511
Open: seasonal

SZULOK 7539
Outdoor Swimming Complex
Dózsa Gy. u. 8.
Tel.: 82/487-297
Open: 1st May–30th Sept.
Tue.–Sun. 9am–6pm

TATABÁNYA 2800
Sports Facility Operations Ltd.
Ságvári E. út 9.
Tel./fax: 34/339-999, 34/316-642
www.sportkht.hu
E-mail: sportkht@mail.datanet.hu
Open: Swimming pool:
Mon.–Fri. 6am–7pm,
Sat.–Sun. 8am–4pm

Outdoor swimming complex:
Mon.–Fri. noon–7pm,
Sat.–Sun. 9am–7pm
Sports hall: according
to requirement

ZÁHONY 4625
Municipal Swimming Pool
József Attila u. 54
Tel.: 45/425-111
Fax: 45/425-979
E-mail: zahony@tvrt.hu
Open: 8am–8pm,
closed Mon.

ZALAKAROS 8749
AquaTherm Hotel***
Üdülő sor 6.
Tel.: 93/541-910
Fax: 93/541-911
E-mail: info@hotel-aquatherm.com
www.hotel-aquatherm.com

Szeged Baths

Those of all ages looking for relaxation, fun or respite from their aches and pains will find something suitable amongst Szeged's wide selection of pools all the year round. Since its renovation, the Anna Baths now offers its guests a wide range of medicinal and wellness services, as well as a leisure pool, all in the surroundings of a grand building. We can also offer a camping site in what are pleasant surroundings, 2–3 bed accommodation and access to the outdoor swimming complex.

Szeged Bathing Water Ltd.
6720 Szeged, Tisza Lajos krt. 24.
Tel.: 62/425-721, fax: 62/426-659
E-mail: szegedfurdo@tiszanet.hu
www.furdovizek.hu

The Tisza Thermal Bath Camp Site and Restaurant

6060 Tiszakécske, Tisza-part
Tel.: 76/441-363, fax.: 76/540-363
E-mail: thermal@thermaltiszapart.hu,
www.thermaltiszapart.hu

All-year-round services:
medicinal waters, medicinal, honey, refreshing massage, pedicure- manicure, Finnish sauna, jacuzzi, covered bath, seven pools, giant slide bath, night bathing, leisure pool : massage cabin, water massage bed, underwater jet currents, geyser, neck and torso water massage

Thermal Complex, Tiszaújváros

We can offer a modern medicinal and leisure bathing complex, sauna, solarium, massage, rheumatological consultation and treatment, as well as a camping site.

Tiszaújváros-Termálfürdő
3580 Tiszaújváros, Szederkényi u. 12.
Tel.: 49/544-170, 49/540-460
E-mail: termal@tujvaros.hu
www.termal.tujvaros.hu

AquaTherm Hotel***

This family hotel, situated 400 metres from the medicinal baths, contains 22 tastefully furnished rooms. Each room has a shower/WC, a TV (satellite), a telephone and a fridge, as well as a terrace or balcony. On the ground floor there is a small restaurant with a small coffee shop. The hotel also has a lift, a massage parlour, a safe, dressing gowns, hair dryers and secure parking.

8749 Zalakaros, Üdülő sor 6.
Tel.: 93/541-910, fax: 93/541-911
E-mail: info@hotel-aquatherm.com
www.hotel-aquatherm.com

Granite Medicinal Baths Ltd.

Hungary's 6th biggest medicinal, leisure and outdoor swimming pool

Those who come will get the most out of our excellent spa waters and the up-to-date treatment we can offer. Our leisure pool offers a great opportunity to switch off and relax. We also have a seasonal thermal outdoor complex with a medicinal pool, a swimming pool, a children's pool, a paddling pool and a wave pool – excellent for the whole family.

OPEN ALL YEAR ROUND!

8749 Zalakaros, Thermál u. 4.
Tel.: 93/340-420, fax:93/340-318
E-mail: thermalfurdo-zkaros@axelero.hu
www.furdo-zalakaros.hu
www.bad-zalakaros.hu

ACTIVE TOURISM

Why not relax – actively! The large towns have facilities covering more or less all sports, whilst the opportunities available in the smaller towns and villages are increasing. So why not adopt the motto, "a bit of physical activity didn't do anyone any harm" and look for a suitable venue to test your powers of endurance.

It's great when active relaxation happens to correspond with a particular hobby of yours. Combining health and happiness may come in the form of horse riding, angling or hunting, not to mention some of the more extreme two or four-wheeled pursuits you can find in the following pages. In the regional sections you should be able to find something which takes your fancy.

Bakodpuszta Tourist Centre

Built on the site of a former medieval village not far from Kalocsa, Bakodpuszta has put its name on Hungary's tourist map. It is here that you can share in the relationship between men and horses which has existed for many thousands of years. The stud's gallop and the buildings, which manage to preserve the most beautiful traditions of folk architecture, form the backdrop for the horseherds' breathtaking display of equestrian skill.
Attractions:
The equestrian show, pony-trekking, carriage-driving, the equestrian school, carriage driving courses.
6328 Dunapataj, Külterület 061.
Tel.: 78/461-819, fax: 78/461-676
30/9459-771, 20/466-3487
E-mail: szallar@mail.externet.hu
www.koronatours.hu

Let Bugac Tours be your hosts in Bugac!

Horseherd show for small groups and individual visitors.
From April to October we can guarantee the following daily horseherd programme:
12.00 Arrival
at the Karikás Csárda in Bugac
12.15 The teams of horses leave for the Herdsman Museum
13.00 Horseherd Show
at the Bugac Stud Farm
13.45 The horses start their return for the Karikás Csárda
14.00 Lunch at the Karikás Csárda.
In June, July and August the very same programme is repeated at 2pm
Info.: Bugac Tours
Tel.: 76/575-117
Tel./fax: 76/362-220, 76/372-827
E-mail: bugactours.kft@axelero.hu

Danube Panorama

Dunaújváros – National Sports Town

Dunaújváros is a surprisingly dynamic new town, and one whose undulating site reads like an A-Z of post-war Hungarian architecture. Taken together the Intercisa Museum and the Contemporary Arts Institute take you many thousands of years back before bringing you right up to Present Day. It is an experience which can be combined with the superb views which can be had from the upper shores rising 50 metres above the River Danube, just 200 metres from the town centre.

The sports facilities (Danube Bay, the airport, ice rink, covered swimming pool, sports hall, stadium etc.) have provided the venue for some important events, including a number of world championships. Dunaújváros will be hosting the Formula-2000 and Formula-3000 Speedboat World Championships, the Modern Dance World Championships, the Junior Swimming World Championships (the Golden Bowl) around Easter and the Indoor Carpathian Basin Hungarian Student Games.

The Dunaújváros Municipal Council
2401 Dunaújváros, Városháza tér 1.
Tel.: 25/410-525, 25/409-214, fax: 25/410-404
E-mail: polgduna@dunanet.hu

Speedboat Competition

BUDAPEST 1092
The Association for Hungarian Equestrian Tourism
Rádai u. 8 1/4.
Tel.: 1/456-0444
Fax: 1/456-0445
www.equi.hu

GYŐR
*The Achilles Park
Lake Leisure Park
and Holiday Village*
At the junction of the M1
and road 83
Tel.: 96/556-011
Fax: 96/556-012
E-mail: info@achilles.hu

KECSKEMÉT 6000
*The Hung. Hunting Assoc.
Bács-Kiskun Branch*
Árpád krt. 2.
Tel.: 76/418-800

Karcag

Cycling and bridle paths
in and around Karcag
For those visiting Karcag you can take advantage of four different routes
(taking you to Zádor Bridge,
the Kecskeri Reservoir,
the Kun Memorial and Ágota Hill),
all of which will prove an unforgettable experience for cyclists and those
on horses. As these tours take you towards, and indeed into, the Hortobágy National Park you will need to make the necessary arrangements with the local Tourinform Office.

Tourinform Office 5300
Karcag, Dózsa Gy. u. 5–7.
Tel.: 59/503-225
E-mail: karcag@tourinform.hu

The North Hungarian Angling Association

Come to our office for information about angling tickets, permits and fishing areas

The North Hungarian Angling Association
3525 Miskolc, Széchenyi u. 73.
Tel./fax: 46/354-500
E-mail: e.horgasz@chello.hu

Opening hours:
Mon., Tue., Wed., Fri. 7.30am–noon,
1pm–3pm Thur. 7.30am–noon, 1pm–5pm

CROSS-BALATON SWIM

Révfülöp – Balatonboglár
2004. július. 31
www.balaton-atuszas.hu

KISSOMLYÓ 9555
The Albert- Major
Riding School
Kossuth u. 37.
Tel./fax.: 95/458-188
www.reittour.de
Sport and equestrian tourism
all year round.

PAKS 7031
Charon Boating Ltd.
Deák Ferenc u. 15.
Tel.: 20/9415-476
Fax: 75/421-801
E-mail: kiszl@axelero.hu
www.paksnet.hu/charon

PÁKOZD 8095
The Kapaszkodó Foundation
Riding School
Therapeutic Riding Lessons
Pákozd-major
Tel.: 22/505-000

PÁPA 8500
The Municipal Sports Hall,
Stadium
Várkert u. 4.
Tel.: 89/510-301

SÁTORALJAÚJHELY 3980
The Lénárd Jagd Hunting Travel
Office
Benczúr út 8.
Tel.: 47/321-683
E-mail: lenar@enternet.hu

SZEKSZÁRD 7100
The Angling Association Tolna
County Branch
Rákóczi F. u.46.
Tel./fax: 74/312-593

SZILVÁSVÁRAD 3348
The State Stud
Egri út 16.
Tel.: 36/355-155

SZOLNOK 5000
The Szolnok Sports Centre
Rita u.
Tel.: 56/414-590
The Dead-Channel Water Centre.
Accommodation and water camps

TOKAJ 3910
Kékcápák Canoe Rental
Malom u. 11.
Tel.: 30/214-3942
Fax: 47/353-227
E-mail: info@turak.hu
www.turak.hu

NATURAL TREASURES

SZARVAS 5540
The Szarvasi Arboretum
István király krt. 9.
Tel.: 66/312-344
E-mail: kert@szarvas.arbor.hu

Nyíregyháza Wildlife Park Sóstó Zoo

4431 Nyíregyháza-Sóstógyógyfürdő
Tel.: 42/479-702, tel./fax: 42/402-031

Hungary's premier wildlife park awaits.
Situated in 24 hectares of oak forest,
visitors will see over 2,500 animals
representing 250 species
in their natural habitats.
Seal display, African panorama,
sea aquarium, tropical house,
peasant farmyard
and much much more.
Special rates for groups.
Open all year round 9am–7pm

AquaCity

Water Slide and Leisure Park
Zalaegerszeg • www.aquacity.hu

13 giant slides • 12 pools
5,6 million litres of water • covering
6000 m² • 7,5 hectares of parkland
• changing rooms • valuables safe
• concerts • star guests
Entertainment programmes

The Erdőspuszta Exhibition House

At our house and at the neighbouring
arboretum, lying 15km from Debrecen,
you can enjoy the sights, sounds and
the tranquil atmosphere of the wooded
plains. It's worthwhile acquainting
yourself with what is a tract of unspoilt
Alföld countryside. You can visit
the Peasant Cottage as well.
4079 Debrecen, Fancsika u. 93/a
Tel.: 52/441-118, www.nyirerdo.hu
Operator: Nyírerdő Nyírség Forestry Ltd.
4400 Nyíregyháza, Kótai u. 29.
Tel.: 42/598-450, fax: 42/501-170
E-mail: info@nyirerdo.hu

From here you are within easy reach of
the Hortobágy and the sights of Szatmár
and Bereg, whether you are driving,
cycling and perhaps even hiking.

CONFERENCE TOURISM

TATABÁNYA
August
The Vértes Expo –
Regional Trade Fair
Tatabánya, Sports Hall
Info.: Alfadat-Press Ltd.
Tel.: 34/310-717

The Northern Hungarian Regional Labour Development and Retraining Centre

The centre is
situated at the foot of the Bükk Hills,
halfway between Miskolc and Lillafüred.

The brand new EU-conference room,
equipped with modern technical,
catering for 100 people,
constitutes part of
the NRRC's top-quality professional
education service in Borsod,
Heves and Nógrád counties.
Besides distance-learning,
postgraduate courses and information
technology the conference room
is an ideal venue
for professional events, symposiums
and video-conferences.

Miskolc, Erenyő út 1.
Tel.: 46/530-150, fax: 46/530-153
E-mail: erakinfo@mail.erak.hu
www.erak.hu
Green number: 06-80/204-077

VILLAGE TOURISM

Those who are keen preserving everything we have inherited from our ancestors will need to have the necessary modern conveniences if they are planning to branch out into the field of village tourism. The term village tourism has indeed come to mean many things. It could involve staying in a 10-20-year-old house, an original peasant cottage or a recently built boarding house.

Perhaps the ideal lodgings are those where visitors can experience the realities of life on the farm from the distance of separate lodgings, and where you can milk the cows and shepherd the sheep whenever you feel the urge. Such holiday houses are few and far between, the most romantic solutions tending to be the nicely renovated old rural residences.

Balástya

Accommodation available at the **Orchidea Hotel**, the **Camion Guesthouse** and the **Zöldmező Leisure Centre**. Events: **Patronal Festival – St Anthony's Day** (June, the Sunday following St Anthony's day); the 3-day **Flower and Vegetable Festival**, as well as the **Village Festival** (first weekend in October); and **Pig-sticking Day** (November)
Mayor's Office:
6764 Balástya, Rákóczi u. 5.
Tel.: 62/278-222
E-mail: hivatal@balastya.hu

Sándorfalva

Traditional pig-sticking is held
in Sándorfalva on the last Saturday
in November.

VESZPRÉM 8200
The Veszprém County Village Tourism Association
Rózsa u. 21/a
Tel.: 88/328-994
www.balaton.hu/falusiturizmus

The Boronaház Inn

Come and discover the Őrség with us!
Pleasant and comfortable lodgings,
a full range of children's facilities,
a huge garden, grill, oven,
playground, animals, cycling,
angling, bathing at the lido.
Handicrafts

9941 Szalafő, Alsószer 15.
Tel.: 94/428-635
Information, booking: Emilia Rikker
Tel.: 1/257-7764
Mobile: 06-20/956-6120
Tel./fax: 1/258-7125

ACCOMODATION

AGÁRD 2484
The Simon Boarding House and Cellars
Bikavölgyi út 2.
Tel.: 22/570-085, 20/975-6319, 30/956-7652, Fax: 22/570-086
E-mail: sl@simonessimon.hu, www.simonessimon.hu

BAKONYBÉL 8427
The Gerence Inn
Fürdő út 59. Tel./fax: 88/461-042
www.hotels.hu/gerence

BUDAPEST 1184
The Irini Boarding House
Ferenc u. 51.
Tel./fax: 1/294-3695
E-mail: irinipanzio@freestart.hu
www.vendegvaro.hu

CEGLÉD 2700
Kossuth Hotel
Rákóczi u.1.
Tel.: 53/310-990, 53/311-812
Fax. 53/311-940

CSONGRÁD 6640
Private Accommodation, the Erzsébet Hotel, the Árnyas Camping Sites
Bookings: Idegenforgalmi Kft.
Fő u. 3. Tel./fax: 63/483-631
E-mail:
idegenforgalom@csongrad.hu

Aggtelek National Park

Aggtelek National Park Directorate
Accommodation Service:
E-mail: info.anp@axelero.hu
www.anp.hu

Tengerszem Hotel and Education Centre
3758 Jósvafő, Tengerszem oldal 2.
Tel/fax: 48/350-006

Baradla Camp Site and Hotel
3759 Aggtelek, Baradla oldal 1.
Tel./fax: 48/503-000, 48/503-002

The Bánkút White Eagle Guesthouse

Go on, take a break in **Bánkút**!
We offer our guests a pleasant and peaceful environment at reasonable prices, including a restaurant, accommodation, organised leisure activies and music and dance events.

Contact Marika Ligeti.
Tel.: 46/390-371, tel./fax: 46/390-603
E-mail: fehersas@pannonv.hu
www.hotels.hu/fehersas

Zöldvár Villa

Everything from a tent to a luxurious apartment!
Come and be our guest at the thermal water holiday village of Bogács in the Bükk National Park. We have 75 beds and cellar programmes.

3412 Bogács, Zöldváralja u. 7., 11.
Tel./fax: 49/534-077, 30/349-4334
E-mail: info@zoldvarvilla.hu
www.zoldvarvilla.hu

Hotel Europa ***

Apartments and Holiday Houses
The hotel, the apartments and the holiday houses are all situated around the thermal bath at the Domdóvár–Gunaras holiday complex. Services: breakfast, half-board and full-board.
TIEGEL Travel Office
7200 Dombóvár–Gunaras, Hableány u. 5.
Tel./fax: 74/463-337
E-mail: info@gunaras.hu
www.gunaras.hu

*** Helios Club Hotel

Hajdúszoboszló, Mátyás király sétány 1.
Fax: 52/362-246
Tel: 52/362-642
E-mail: helios52@axelero.hu
www.heliosclubhotel.hu

*** Helios Club Hotel, completely renovated in 2001, awaits guests looking for relaxation and refreshment. Our hotel is situated in beautiful parkland in the town's holiday quarter, just 1,100 meters from the baths. We have 62 twin-bed rooms, including rooms specially fitted for the disabled, containing a bathroom, TV and mini-bar, and there are extra beds if necessary. The restaurant seats 120, and there are also conference rooms, an atmospheric coffee house, a lift, sauna, jacuzzi, a fitness gym, and a beer garden serving hot meals during the summer. Secure parking is available for our guests.

The hotel can put on: conferences, in-service training, buffet receptions, weddings, product presentations and other events. We also organise health cure programmes, excursions and the other leisure activities. Guests can enquire about National Insurance-supported health cures at the medicinal baths.

DEBRECEN
Civis Hotels Aranybika
4025 Piac u. 11–15.
Tel.: 52/508-600
Fax: 52/421-834
E-mail:
aranybika@civishotels.hu
www.civishotels.hu
Civis Hotels Kálvin
4025 Kálvin tér 4.
Tel./fax: 52/418-522
E-mail:
kalvin@civishotels.hu
www.civishotels.hu

Park- Hotel
and Restaurant
4032 Kartács u. 27.
Tel./fax: 52/413-627
E-mail:
enigmadb@axelero.hu
www.hotelpark.tsx.org
www.hotelpark.de.tf

DUNABOGDÁNY 2023
Irene Haus
Erzsébet királyné u. 36.
Tel./fax: 26/390170
E-mail: schill.@axelero.hu
www.vendegvaro.hu

DUNAKESZI 2120
The Kikelet Boarding House
Kikelet u.1.
Tel.: 27/342-554
www.hotels/kikelet_panzió

ESZTERGOM 2500
The Mátra Boarding House
Bocskoroskúti u.1.
Tel.: 33/311-983

GALYATETŐ 3234
The BM Andezit Hotel
Mező Imre u. 6–21.
Tel./fax: 37/376-026, 576-009
E-mail: andezit@axelero.hu

GYŐR 9024
Hotel Kálvária
Kálvária u. 22/d
Tel.: 96/510-800, Fax: 96/510-801
E-mail: info@hotel-kalvaria.hu
www.hotel-kalvaria.hu
The Pető Boarding House
Kossuth u. 20. Tel.: 96/313-412
Fax: 96/312-195

HAJDÚSZOBOSZLÓ 4200
Civis Hotels Délibáb
József A. u. 4
Tel.: 52/360-366
Fax: 52/362-059
E-mail: delibab@civishotels.hu
www.civishotels.hu

JÁSZBERÉNY 5100
Hotel Lehel Neszür
(on road 31 heading towards
Budapest)
Tel.: 57/415-122

A genuine Pearl far away from the noise of the world…

The Count Apponyi Palace Hotel

The medicinal waters of the Count Apponyi Palace Hotel's Klára Well awaits those guests who are particularly interested in looking after their health and taking the first steps to recovery.
The 36–38° C waters, which contain sodium chloride and hydrogen carbonate, are there to heal, relax and refresh. The waters are also one of the most important elements of our wellness centre.

Go on spoil yourself, enjoy the tranquility and the freedom you are guaranteed here.

The facultative programmes can all be part of the regeneration process. They might involve looking at the deer in the Gyulaj woods, or discovering the region by bike or on horseback. You can even survey the Tolna Hills from a hot-air balloon, not to mention taste the excellent wines of the historical Szekszárd Wine Region.

7191 Hőgyész, Ady Endre u. 2.
Tel.: 74/588-800, fax: 74/588-801
E-mail: info@apponyi.hu;
www.apponyi.hu

…where you can put your worries aside.

The Dubicsány Boarding House

The Vay Residence is situated
in Dubicsány on road 26
about 30km from Miskolc,
not far from the Aggtelek National Park
and the Slovakian border.

The imposing 18th century residence
was rebuilt by Arnold Barta
at the beginning of the last century.

It now functions as
a boarding house owned
by the Borsod Volán Bus Company.

Address:
3635 Dubicsány, Kossuth u. 55.

Excellent for family holidays,
friendly get-togethers,
business meetings, camps,
school reunions and weddings.
Group catering is available on demand.

Bookings, information:
Tel/Fax: 48/432-663
E-mail: gyorto@borsodvolan.hu
www.borsodvolan.hu

Favourable prices.

KESZTHELY 8360
The Muschel Guest House
Nádasköz 5. Tel./fax: 83/314-380
E-mail: muschel@axelero.hu
web.axelero.hu/muschelo

MEZŐKÖVESD 3400
Mercurius Private Tours
Mátyás király u. 59.
Tel.: 49/411-522

MEZŐZOMBOR 3931
The Bortó Boarding House
Conference-Restaurant
Lido-Camping
In a beautiful valley
in the Tokaj-Hegyalja
Lake Dorogi, near road 37
Tel./fax: 47/369-475, 47/569-015

Aranyhomok Hotel ***

Our hotel in Kecskemét's main square,
with its 111 rooms,
is open all year round.
From August 2004 we will be able
to offer our guests additional
swimming and wellness facilities.

6000 Kecskemét, Kossuth tér 3.
Tel.: 76/503-730, fax: 76/503-731
E-mail: aranyhomok@axelero.hu
www.hotels.hu/aranyhomok

The Hort Dunube Inn

Our boarding house offers ten
comfortably furnished rooms all
of which have bathrooms.
The alkaline hydrogen carbonate waters
in the small covered swimming
pool are excellent for
the treatment of locomotor
and rheumatic problems.

9233 Lipót, Fő út 65.
Tel./fax: 96/674-029
Tel: 96/674-028

MISKOLC 3519
*The Zenit Boarding House
and Car Hire*
Miskolctapolca, Tapolcai u. 25.
Tel.: 46/561-561
Fax: 46/368-313
E-mail: zenitpanzio@axelero.hu

NAGYBERÉNY 8656
The Fűzfa Boarding House
Szabadság u. 44/a
Tel.: 84/582-922, 30/226-6437
Fax: 84/582-923
E-mail: fuzfa@hotmail.com
www.fuzfapanzio.hu
We can offer you relaxation
in wonderful surroundings
near Lake Balaton
and the Thermal Baths

The Gerébi Hall Hotel

The Gerébi Hall Hotel, situated in
picturesque surroundings, offers
guests 47 double rooms.
Those who come can make the most of
the swimming pool, the sauna, the
tennis courts and other sporting
facilities, as well as the stables and
the restaurant. There are also special
rooms available, a garden, a gift shop,
a playground and secure parking.
We host conferences, in-service
training, wedding receptions and family
events, and can offer Alföld equestrian
displays, goulash supper parties
and folk dance programmes.

6050 Lajosmizse, Alsólajos 224.
Tel.: 76/356-555, fax: 76/555-080
Mobile: 30/955-9056, www.gerebi.hu
E-mail: gerebi@gerebi.hu

The Palace Hotel***☆

3517 Miskolc–Lillafüred
Erzsébet sétány 1.
Tel.: 46/331-411, fax: 46/533-203
E-mail:
reserve@hotelpalota.hunguesthotels.hu
www.hunguesthotels.hu

• 129 top-quality rooms –
accommodation for 240
(tv, minibar, telephone)
• Two restaurants
*New: the cuisine of historical Hungary,
and Renaissance delicacies at the
Matthias Restaurant*
• Swimming pool, sauna, jacuzzi, steam
bath, fitness gym, bowling, billiards
• 8 conference rooms (15–250 people)
and conference programmes
• International cuisine

HUNGUEST HOTEL
PALOTA
LILLAFÜRED
★★★☆

SÍKFŐKÚT-NOSZVAJ
The Korona Holiday Complex_3325
Várhegyi út Tel./fax: 36/463-073
Mobile: 30/262-3063
Open all year round

SIROK
The Sirok Motel
3332 Sirok Lenin u. 22.
Tel.: 36/561-000 Fax: 36/361-633

City Hotel Miskolc***

• Five-floor, three-star hotel containing
17 two-bed, 3 three-bed rooms and
3 apartments all with air-conditioning
• Each room has a telephone,
Internet access, TV, minibar
• Breakfast room, bar, lounge, terrace
• Conference room for 50 people,
• Special room for 14 people
• Sauna, Jacuzzi, steam chamber

3529 Miskolc, Csabai kapu 6.
Tel.: 46/555-100, fax: 46/555-105
E-mail: hotelmiskolc@chello.hu

"Kőkapu… where the peace begins."
Kőkapu
Hunting Lodge and Hotel

Come and visit our hotel situated
on a rock overlooking a picturesque
lake. The former hunting residence
of the Károlyi family it can be found in
Kőkapu in the Zemplén Hills,
7km from Pálháza. Nowadays it's not
only popular with hunters but with
those seeking the tranquility of
the countryside.

3994 Pálháza–Kőkapu
Tel.: 47/370-032 Fax: 47/570-042

SOPRON 9400
*The Woodland Hide
Boarding House**
Nemeskúti u. 1.
Tel.: 20/429-00-95
Fax/recorded messages:
99/323-566
E-mail:
rejtekado@hotmail.com
www.hotels.hu/rejtekado

Szarvaskő 3323
Villa Bikavér
Rózsa u.33.
Tel.: 36/352-052

Szilvásvárad 3348
The Bükk Boarding House
Dózsa u. 16. Tel.: 36/355-444
Fax: 36/355-537
Open: all year round 9am–10pm

The Szidónia Palace Wellness Hotel

9451 Röjtökmuzsaj, Röjtöki u. 37.
Tel.: 99/544-810, fax: 99/380-013
E-mail: szidonia@axelero.hu
www. szidonia.hu

A bridge between past and present,
"the palace of regeneration"
– palace hotel
– manor house
– villa
You can enjoy 7 hectares of woodland
and a wonderful bathing house,
giving you the opportunity to relax,
recharge your batteries and
become acquainted with the harmony
of the wellness lifestyle

Royal Hotel

Szeged's Royal Hotel has special
weekend offers for those wishing
to stay for 2, 3 or 4 nights.
Between 15th November
and 15th March you can make the
most of our services for 19.99* euros.
For more information see our website.
www.royalhotel.hu

6720 Szeged, Kölcsey u. 1–3.
Tel.: 62/475-275, fax: 62/420-225

**For further details about our 19.99-euro rooms
see our website.*

Szolnok 500
Hotel Kőrösi**
Kőrösi út 43.
Tel.: 56/420-514
Fax: 56/210-121
Mobile: 30/958-4718,
30/626-7643
Open all year round.

Telkibánya 3896
Children's and Youth Camp
Hegyi u. 19.
Tel.: 46/ 443-521
Fax: 46/388-502

Tihany 8237
*Club Tihany Holiday, Conference,
Wellness, and Medicinal Centre*
Rév u. 3.
Tel.: 87/538 564
Fax: 87/448 083
E-mail: reserv@clubtihany.hu

Tisza Hotel***

At the heart of the "palatial town",
in Szeged's main square,
the Tisza Hotel in its 120-year-old
premises is the region's most
well-established hotel. We offer
exclusive services and rooms complete
with bathroom suites beautifully
furnished in a colonial style,
all designed to ensure you have
a perfect stay.

Stately comfort in grand surroundings.
Feel at the centre of things!

6720 Szeged, Wesselényi u. 6.
Tel./fax: 62/478-278
E-mail: info@tiszahotel.hu
www.tiszahotel.hu

Tiszacsege 4066
The Holdfény Camping Site
Bocskai u. 7.
Tel./fax: 52/373-071
Open: 1st May–end of Sept.

Tiszaújváros 3580
Civis Hotels Phőnix
Bethlen G. u. 4. Tel.: 49/341-511
Fax: 49/341-952
E-mail: phoenix@civishotels.hu
www.civishotels.hu

Velem 9726
The Kern Boarding House
Rákóczi u. 56.
Tel./fax.: 94/363-612, 20/341-0861
E-mail: kernhaz@freemail.hu,
www.kern.info.hu
11 rooms for 38 people in 2 houses
Open: all year round by
appointment

Betekints Hotel**** and Restaurant

Our hotel, set in wooded surroundings,
is now offering its guests more
services than ever.

38 rooms or apartments – 85 places
TV, telephone, mini bar, air-conditioning,
secure parking with security
camara system, sauna, fitness gym,
solarium, massage, pool

Hungarian cuisine, a restaurant
with a garden
Conference rooms (for up to 250 people)

Special family offers!
Conferences, in-service training,
presentations and other events

8200 Veszprém, Veszprémvölgyi u. 4.
Tel: 88/579-280, fax: 88/579-289
E-mail: betekints@betekints.hu
www.betekints.hu

GASTRONOMY

The country's geographical and ethnic diversity is reflected in the cuisine. Here it is the local traditions and the characteristic ingredients which determine the flavours you are likely to encounter.

From the famous coffee houses and patisseries to the restaurants of great repute, you are likely to find numerous "good places". As the great culinary expert and writer Gyula Krúgy once said: there are some people who travel merely for the pleasure of eating well, as a good lunch or dinner is well worth the effort.

Restaurant owners are making ever greater efforts to ensure that local dishes make their way onto the menu. The fact is, visitors are curious to sample the local flavours.

Traditional seasoning is making a real come-back, and tarragon, pepper-grass, allspice and marjoram are becoming popular once again.

As a break from fast food a visit to a hunting lodge or a fish restaurant can come as really pleasant change. The same goes for an evening meal at an inn oozing 19th century atmosphere. Whilst there are restaurants offering internationally popular dishes, there are also ever greater opportunities to sample specialities from other countries. So, the choice is yours à la carte!

CSERSZEGTOMAJ 8372
The Napraforgó Inn
Sümegi u. 9. Tel.: 83/330-173,
30/22-63-473, 30/226-3473
Fax: 83/510-242
E-mail: elekati@axelero.hu
www.elekpension.ini.hu

EGER
The Nótafa Inn
Szépasszonyvölgy
Tel.: 36/313-484
(Hungarian dishes,
stews, ham knuckle
specialities)

KECSKEMÉT 6000
The Liberté Coffee House
Szabadság tér 2.
Tel.: 76/506-343
Fax: 76/328-863
E-mail: pirtours@axelero.hu

OROSHÁZA 5900
Aranypatkó Csárda
Szentesi u. 62/a
Tel.: 68/411-621
Home-made dishes
with live music on Saturdays
and Sundays

SopronkÖvesd 9483
Fehér Csárda
Kossuth út. 58.
Tel./fax.: 99/536-041
Open: 8am-10pm
Seating: for 100 inside,
for 200 in the garden
Our chef promises some gastronomic
delights and Hungarian flavours.

Szigetvár 7900
The Flórián Inn
József A. u.58.Tel./fax.: 73/311-939
We offer our guests a wide choice
of fish, venison, poultry, pork
and beef dishes.

Tolcsva 3934
The Ős Kaján Restaurant
Kossuth u. 16. Tel./fax: 47/384-195
E-mail:
oskajan.restaurant@matavnet.hu

Régiposta Motel

Miskolc-Lillafüred, Erzsébet sétány 21.
Bookings:
Tel./fax: 46/401-670

The RÉGIPOSTA MOTEL is open
all year round. We are situated in one
of Hungary's most beautiful hill resorts
just opposite Saint Stephen's Cave.
We have eight 2-3-bed rooms, all with
showers, and serve breakfast and supper
as required. Our 80-person restaurant is
suitable for conferences, receptions
and family programmes. Apart from
our closed courtyard, landscaped garden
and parking facilities we can also
offer leisure programmes.

WINE TOURISM

The sunshine, the soil and the hard endeavour of the vinedressers, not to mention the necessary expertise, combine to create the characteristically fragrant and fruity wines of the Hungarian wine regions. It is a wine culture with a history stretching back two thousand years, to a time when the Romans of ancient Pannonia were happy to lay the noble wines they had produced at the altar of Bacchus. The processing of grapes was also not unknown to the settling Hungarians, who had made wine for medicinal as well as recreational purposes for many centuries. Although wine production has had its difficulties over the years, it is now enjoying something of a renaissance.

The wines of the Mór wine region, the Etyek–Buda and Ászár–Neszmély wine regions, Somló's legendary *juhfark,* the Balaton Highlands and the wines of the southern shores of Lake Balaton in the Villány, Siklós and Szekszárd wine regions are the highlights in Pannonia, west of the Danube. On the southern part of the Great Plain you can find the Kunság, Hajós and Csongrád wines, whilst in Northern Hungary there are the famous Tokaj varieties, as well as the Bükk, Mátraalja and Eger wines, which also feature well at international wine festivals. A visit to one or two of the local wine cellars would not be time wasted, for it is there you can see how wines are handled and to sample a few for yourself. So as an introduction: *Storage:* Store bottled wines horizontally so as to allow the wine and the cork to touch each other. It should be an airy, not particularly bright place, being neither too wet nor too dry, of a temperature of 10–14 °C. Avoid shaking and moving during storage.

Serving Temperature of Wines: Red Wines: Kékoportó 14–15 °C, Barrique Cabernet 18–20 °C and other types of red wines 16–18 °C
Sauvignon Rosé 8–10 °C
White Wines with Meals: 10–12 °C
White Wines as Aperitifs: 6–8 °C
Aszú Wines: 9–11 °C
Keep bottles in ice-filled bucket or in a flask because even when cooled bottles warm up quickly at room temperature. Cut the edge of plastic foil on the top of the bottle before unscrewing, but keep the lower part on because it is considered to be part of the wine's clothing. Prior to wine-tasting smell the cork after drawing it out of the bottle to ascertain whether the wine has any basic imperfections. Unscrew red wines of special quality one hour before consumption to allow the wine to breathe. Pour a small amount of wine for yourself partly to take out the small cork pieces from the wine resulting from the unscrewing, and partly to taste whether the wine is satisfactory. For cultured wine-drinking the glass should be clean, dry, and should have a stem and a goblet which narrows to the rim. Glasses can of course come in different sizes. It is usual to pour white wines into a smaller glass and red wines into a larger one, filling it no more than two-thirds high so as to allow the wine in the glass to move freely, thus bringing out the bouquet.

Wine-Tasting: First of all, take the glass by its stem to warm the wine up without at the same time dirtying the glass. Take a good look at the colour of wine before smelling it, holding the glass up to the light whilst swilling the wine gently.

By doing this you can catch the aroma given off from the glass. Finally taking one gulp of wine in the mouth "move it around" the palate and tongue to taste all the components.

The Balla Cellar

(Number 18) in Eger's Valley
of the Beautiful Woman
(Szépasszonyvölgy)
is open all year round.
You can try our 12 types of wine,
either bottled or straight
from the barrel.
Open: 9am–8pm

István Balla
3300 Eger, Koszorú u. 58.
Tel.: 06-36/413-902

BALATONBOGLÁR 8630
*The Southern Balaton Wine Road
Association*
Erzsébet u. 11. Tel.: 85/ 550-333
Fax: 85/ 350-469
E-mail: balatonboglar@somogy.hu
www.dbb.hu

EGER 3300
The Sándor Csabai Wine Cellar
Szépasszonyvölgy Cellar no. 36
Tel.: 36/320-758
Istenes Cellar (run by Hotel Eger)
Szépasszonyvölgy
Tel.: 36/522-222
E-mail: hotelegerpark@axelero.hu
www.danubuisgroup.com/eger-park

SOPRON 9400
Taschnervin Ltd.
Zsilip u.18. Tel.: 20/931-5225
www.taschnervin.hu
Cellar visits if organised in advance.

Villány Winery Inc.

Cellar visits and wine-tasting
for groups
7773 Villány, Ady fasor 2.
Tel.: 72/492-14, fax: 72/492-009

Apart from seeing the WINE MUSEUM's
rich collection of exhibits, visitors also
have the opportunity to become
acquainted with the company's wines
during what is a pleasant programme.

7773 Villány, Bem u. 8.
Tel.: 72/492-130, fax: 72/492-009

Béres Vineyard

The Béres Vineyard
was founded in 2002
with the aim of producing
the very best Tokaj wines.
The wine processing plant
and guesthouse can be found
in the historic Lőcse-dűlő
near Erdőbénye.

3932 Erdőbénye
Tel.: 47/536-000

8630 Balatonboglár, Epres u. 10.
Tel.: 20/945-0842
E-mail: katonab@mail.tvnet.hu
www.katonaborhaz.hu

Katona-Borház Ltd. was founded in
the autumn of 1996, with the intention
of developing the family's wine-making
traditions. We presently grow grapes
on 52 hectares of land south of Lake
Balaton in the Boglár Wine Region.
Our preferred grape types are Muscat,
Sauvignon, Cabernet, Merlot
and Chardonnay. Although our bottled
wines are stored in our Budafok cellars
we also sell our wines from here.
For further information about visits,
events and orders please
consult our website.
We look forward to hearing from you!

The Takács Family Vineyard and Cellarage

(Mád, in Batthyány út
next to the Catholic church.)
Excellent Tokaj–Hegyalja wines,
wine specialities • Cellar tour, private
wine-tasting for groups of up to 40
• Explanation of the wine-making process.

Address: Miklós Takács ,
3909 Mád Vöröshadsereg út 17.
Tel.: 47/348-064 from 4pm
Mobile: 06-20/364-4758

The Páll Cellar

The Páll family farms a 12-hectare vineyard growing Yellow Muscat, Furmint,
and Hárslevelű grapes, all of which are
ideal for wine-making. This quality
makes it possible to produce
the special "Szamorodni"
and 3–6 puttony "aszú" wines.
These much-prized wines mature
in oak-barrels stored in cellars covered
in mould. Our principle is to produce
quality wines using traditional
techniques from the choicest types
of grapes grown on the most fertile
lands. The Páll Cellar is situated
amongst the cellars in Tarcal.
We can cater for up to 45 guests
if the visit is organised in advance.

János Páll
3915 Tarcal, Szondi ltp. 3/2.
Tel.: 47/380-016, fax: 47/380-639
Mobile: 30/955-2167, 30/983-2253
E-mail: palpince@mail.matav.hu

The Rákóczi Cellar

3950 Sárospatak, Szent Erzsébet út 26.
Tel.: 47/311-902

This nearly one-kilometre-long cellar, housing 900 barrels situated under the Sárospatak Castle Park, is one of the most attractive cellars in the Hegyalja. It bears witness to how wines were made back in the Middle Ages. Open on weekdays from 10am to 5pm for visits and wine-tasting, and for larger groups at any time if the relevant arrangements have been made.

Pajzos Co. & Megyer Co.
3950 Sárospatak, Nagy Lajos u. 12.
Tel.: 47/411-902, Fax: 47/312-320
E-mail: pajzosmegyer@axelero.hu

Tokaj-Hegyalja Wine Road association

3915 Tarcal, Fő út 57.
Tel.: 47/580-444, 47/580-440, 47/580-450, Fax: 47/580-441
E-mail: tarcal@tarcal.hu, patakysam@hotmail.com
www.tokaji-borut.hu
Office: 3910 Tokaj, Bethlen G. út. 11.
Telephone: 47/352-000

The organisation, responsible for co-ordinating wine tourism in the Tokaj-hegyalja, is made up of 55 recognised members offering guests reliable and high-quality services.

The Furmint Vinotéka

Wine shop in Tokaj's main square

Our products:
the widest choice of local wines available, bottled wines from more than thirty different cellars

Our services:
local programmes: wine-tasting, wine road information

For more information:
www.furmintvinoteka.hu

3910 Tokaj, Bethlen G. u. 12/a
Open: daily 9am–5pm
Tel./fax: 47/353-340, 47/352-919
E-mail: tokajwac@enternet.hu

Hilltop Neszmély
Wine Hotel and Restaurant

A place where you can find:
- top quality winemaking,
- Ákos Kamocsay's wines (the winemaker of the year 1999),
- the excellent cuisine of our very own master chef,
- breathtaking views over the River Danube and our sundrenched vineyards,
- pleasant leisure activities (winery visits, wine-tasting, tennis, pony-trekking, cycling)
- lodgings with a bright, warm atmosphere.

Once we have tempted you here it will be the memories that draw you back!

Hilltop Neszmély
Wine Hotel and Restaurant
2544 Neszmély Melegeshegy, Pf. 4.
Tel.: 34/550-440
Mobile: 30/525-8490
Fax: 34/550-441
E-mail: hillhot@hu.inter.net
www.hilltop.hu

HILLTOP
NESZMÉLY

TOURIST ORGANISATIONS

ABÁDSZALÓK 5241
Tourinform Office
Deák F. u. 1/17. Tel.: 59/357-376,
59/535-357, Fax: 59/357-376
E-mail: abadszalok@tourinform.hu
www.abadszalok.hu
Open: high season Mon.–Sun.
8am–9pm, low season Mon.–Fri.
8am–4.30pm

BÉKÉSCSABA 5600
Tourinform Office
Szent István tér 9. Tel./fax: 66/441-261
E-mail: bekescsaba@tourinform.hu,
www.turizmus.bekescsaba.hu

BUDAPEST 1086
Friendship Club
Magdolna u. 5–7.
Tel./fax: 1/210-0115
www.baratsagklub.uw.hu

DUNAFÖLDVÁR 7200
Tourinform Office
Rákóczi u. 2. Tel./fax: 75/341-176
E-mail: dunafoldvar@tourinform.hu
Information about programmes,
accommodation, entertainment and
places to eat

FONYÓD 8640
PP Tours Ltd.
Szent István u. 5.
Tel./fax: 85/362-125
E-mail: pptours@axelero.hu

MEZŐTÚR 5400
Tourinform Mezőtúr (Regional infor-
mation and marketing office)
Szabadság tér 17.
Tel.: 56/530-637, Fax: 56/350-901
E-mail: mezotur@tourinform.hu
Information service: accommoda-
tion, places to eat, events,
sights, famous places, baths

MOSONMAGYARÓVÁR 9200
Tourinform Office
Kápolna tér 16.
Tel./fax: 96/206-304
E-mail:
tourinform@mosonmagyarovar.hu
www.mosonmagyarovar.hu

SZERENCS 3900
*Zemplén Tourist Travel
Office Ltd.*
Rákóczi út 67.
Tel./fax: 47/560-059, 30/925-8555
E-mail:
zemplen.tourist@axelero.hu
– accommodation bookings for
the whole of Zemplén County
– cellar visits, wine-tasting meals
with musical accompaniment,
currency exchange,
group programmes
– Hungarian holiday coupons
accepted

Kalocsa-Korona Tours Ltd

Recommended programmes: The folk
art exhibition and folklore programme
at Aunt Juca's Inn, the equestrian
show at Bákodpuszta, sightseeing in
Kalocsa, the peasant cottage, the Paprika
Museum, the paprika harvest, cellar
visits, wine-tasting at the Hajós Cellar
Village, the organisation of events.
The office runs the international quay
on the River Danube at Kalocsa-Meszes
making it possible for our guests to
get to "the town of thousand colours",
Kalocsa, on one of our floating hotels.

6300 Kalocsa, Szent István út 6.
Tel./fax: 78/461-819, 78/462-186
E-mail: szallar@mail.externet.hu,
www.koronatours.hu

Kisköre, The Family Paradise

Kisköre is situated in the southern part
of Heves County on the banks
of Lake Tisza. Its main attraction is
its outdoor swimming complex,
whose clean waters and various
attractions guarantee a great day out
for children and adults alike.
There's also great fishing to be
had both in the Tisza and
in the local reservoir.
Whilst cycling round the reservoir you
can get a real taste of the local landscape.
Visitors have plenty of programmes
to choose from between May and
September, and there is a wide variety
of accommodation on offer,
from local homes and quality
guesthouses to hotels and apartments.
There are also atmospheric restaurants,
inns and cafés.

Tourinform Kisköre
Kisköre, Kossuth L. u. 8.
Tel./fax: (06-36) 358-023
E-mail: kiskore@tourinform.hu
www.kiskore.hu

The Ararát Tours Travel Agency

4600 Kisvárda, Szent László u. 2.
Tel./fax: 45/500-046, 45/500-047
E-mail: ararat@enternet.hu
www.ararattours.hu
Branch office:
4400 Nyíregyháza, Kosbor u. 1.
Tel.: 42/595-594, fax: 42/595-593
A full range of travel services,
domestic and foreign travel, visas,
air-tickets, international bus-tickets,
passenger insurance,
and the organisation of business trips.

Savaria Tourist Travel Agency

Services:
Currency exchange
Accommodation
Travel organisation
Air ticket sales

9600 Sárvár, Várkerület 33.
Tel./fax: 95/320-578, 95/325-848
E-mail: savariatourist.sarvar@enternet.hu
www.savariatourist-sarvar.hu

Szombathely 9700
Tourinform Office
Kossuth Lajos u. 1–3.
Tel.: 94/514-451, Fax: 94/514-450
E-mail: szombathely@tourinform.hu
www.szombathely.hu
Open: high season: 15th Jun.–15th
Sept. Mon.–Fri. 9am–8pm,
Sat.–Sun., holidays: 9am–6pm, low
season: 15th Sept.–15th Jun.
Mon.–Fri. 9am–5pm, Sat. 9am–3pm

SZENTENDRE

Regional Information and Marketing Office

For eleven years we have been offering information and providing leaflets about Hungary, the Danube Bend, as well as accommodation, museums, events, trips and holidays in and around Szentendre.

OUR TOWN IS WAITING FOR YOU!

www.szentendre.hu

2000 Szentendre
Dumtsa Jenő u. 22.
Tel./fax: 26/317-965,
26/317-966
E-mail: szentendre@tourinform.hu

LOCAL RECOMMENDATIONS

Municipal and Local Councils help their residents in many different ways, bringing happiness being one of their prescribed roles. It is a consideration which can also help make a town or a village all the more attractive to the passing visitor. In the list that follows you will see what can be done to make a settlement or a region all the more popular.

Csömöri Hívogató

Situated in the immediate neighbourhood of the capital this 900 year-old town, with its Slovak, Swabian and Hungarian population, can justly look back on its multicultural traditions with pride. Visitors can make the most of the 6-hectare fishing lake and the riding stables in the area. Those requiring sustenance should head for the Zöldfa, which offers some fine home-made dishes.
Regular events:
January-February: The Ball Season, Puff Pastry Competition
March: Women–Beauty–Health event
April: Choir Festival
June: Whitsun Festival
Csömör Village Festival, Corpus Christi Procession
August: St Stephen's Day Celebrations
September: The Csömör Autumn Festival Grape Harvest Celebrations
October: Health Day
December: Advent and Christmas Events Series

Petőfi S. House of Culture
Tel./fax: 28/543-790

Balatonszemes

Balatonszemes, a peaceful holiday resort on the southern shores of the lake, has three camping sites, several small hotels and hundreds of holiday homes all guaranteeing our visitors a comfortable stay. The town has a Roman Catholic church (where weekend organ recitals are held during the summer) as well as Baptist and Lutheran Chapels. The landing stage is the starting point for local boat trips, and you can also go in search of Bagolyvár and the museums featuring the life and work of graphic artist Károly Reich and the actor Zoltán Latinovics.

Mayor's Office
8636 Balatonszemes, Bajcsy-Zs. u. 23.
Tel.: 84/560-900

Bükkszentkereszt
Clean air and a subalpine climate at 600 metres

Here the climate and air are ideal for those suffering from asthma and other respiratory illnesses and those who just need a rest. As for accommodation, there are inns, guesthouses, hotels, a youth camp and a camping site.
Things to see: • The Bükk Glassworks Museum • The Open-air Ethnographic Exhibition • Woodcarving Exhibition • Lime-burning
Things to do: • Sports facilities • Nature trail • Ski lift • Winter taboggan run • Stables
Come to Bükkszentkereszt
for active relaxation.
Events: 29th May: The Slovak National Day
3rd-4th July: The Bükkszentkereszt Festival
30th December: Sleigh Competition
We look forward to seeing you!

Cserépfalu Tourism

Set in the wonderful natural, architectural and cultural environment of the Bükkalja you can make the most of the village's 30 guesthouses, the Túrbucka Outdoor School, the Youth Hostel, the Ördögtorony Nature Trail and the excellent local wine cellars and wine programmes.

Information: The Notary's Office
Cserépfalu, Kossuth út 125.
Tel./fax: 49/423-935, 30/207-9977
E-mail: hivatal@axelero.hu
www.cserepfalu.hu

Kóspallag

Our village is well placed for journeys into the Börzsöny Hills and visits to all the local sights:

The Kisinóc Hostel: food and accommodation all year round
• The Nagyhideghegy Hostel, the Nagyírtáspuszta St Urban Inn: food and accommodation
• Robbers' Den Holiday House: accommodation, leisure activities, walking possibilities
• There's plenty of sport to be had next to the fishing lake
• Three hunting associations operate in the village

The Mayor's Office, Kóspallag
Tel.: 27/585-660

Tarcal

Land of Honey-Sweet Springs
Part of the World Heritage Site since July 2002 Tarcal is a settlement situated on the southern edge of the Zemplén Hills dating back to period of the Hungarian Conquest. It's one of the Tokaj-hegyalja Wine Region's finest wine-producing areas. The village, which has the air of a small agricultural town, is famous for its ancient monuments, the beauty of the surrounding countryside, the excellent sporting opportunities as well as its superb wines.
Information Office: Cellar Gallery, Local History Museum Fő út 61.
Tel.: 47/580-444, fax: 47/580-441
E-mail: tarcal@tarcal.hu

The Crypt Villa, The House of Eternal Love

Fonyód's most recent ancient monument

8640 Fonyód, József u. 16.
Open: 1st May–30th Sept.
Daily 3pm–7pm,
1st Oct.–30th Apr. by appointment
Contact:
The Károly Eötvös Municipal Library
Tel.: 85/362-802
E-mail: fonyodkt@axelero.hu

Ödön Abrudbányay-Rédiger had the house built in 1939.
It is a monument to lost love, recorded in the photographs he took and the life-size marble statues he made.
Love's mystery lives on.

Monor

While the area around the spring enjoys environmental protection, Monor's great tourist attraction is Strázsa Hill with its one thousand wine cellars and press houses. The Monor May Festival is a lively event. St Urban's Day offers a good opportunity to visit the cellar village and perhaps climb the recently built lookout-tower, which offers some fine views of the surrounding settlements if the skies are clear. In the autumn the most spectacular event is the Harvest Parade organised by the local agricultural association. Those coming from some distances can make the most of the town's boarding houses.
The Mayor's Office
2200 Monor, Kossuth u. 78–80.
Tel.: 29/412-215

Zalakaros

The waters at this spa town situated just a few kilometres from Kis-Balaton are excellent for the cure of gynaecological ailments, locomotor and vegetative nervous complaints, as well as the treatment of those recovering from accidents. At the baths you will find a spa centre, a leisure pool, as well as swimming, wave and children's pools. In 2002, Zalakaros won the title of the most flowery town in Hungary. Those who visit will be able to enjoy the picturesque countryside, the extraordinary natural habitats around Kis-Balaton, as well as the excellent local wines and cuisine.

Tourinform Zalakaros
8749 Zalakaros, Gyógyfürdő tér 10.
Tel.: 93/340-421
E-mail: zalakaros@tourinform.hu
www.zalakaros.hu

Paks

. A great deal has survived from this once small agricultural town. But now, while there is still much that is old, there is just as much which is new. The Roman fortress of Lussonium can be seen on top of Sánc Hill, a loess mound which has no equal in Europe. Those arriving from Budapest will be greeted by the Baroque and classical buildings lining Deák Ferenc utca. From there it's only a short walk to the chestnut avenue lining the banks of the River Danube, where there always seems to be something going on at the weekends from May through to September. It is here that Paks fish soup chefs cook against one another, where both big and small can relax at the family events, where the active take part in the Daróczy cross-river swim and the odd angling competition takes place. The Paks Picture Gallery, in the old casino building, is a must for lovers of modern art. The first weekend in July will once again belong to the Gastroblues Festival, at which music, cuisine and fine wines combine to make one happy event. The organisers couldn't have chosen a better venue, as the town is one of the stopping off places on the Tolna Wine Road. The event provides tourists with an opportunity to try Paks's famous siller rosé at the wine cellers in Sörgödör tér. The Church of the Holy Spirit, designed by Imre Makovecz, has become one of the most immediately recognisable symbols of the town. Visitors will get all the help they need from the local Tourinform Office, which offers much in the way of local equestrian programmes and accommodation.

Telephone: 75/421-575

 ## Solymár

Situated in the basin between the Buda and the Pilis Hills, Solymár's setting, the locals' friendliness and the fact that people here tend to be multilingual, mean that visitors will feel at home irrespective of where they come from. The Jegenye Valley, the only waterfall in the region, the Rózsika Spring, Zsiros Hill, the ruins of the medieval castle and the Ördöglyukbarlang offer peace and quiet to those in search of it. The rich and varied events going on in the village and the great atmosphere mean that those who come are guaranteed more than their fair share of fun and enjoyment. At the concerts and dance events you have the chance to become familiar with the local Swabian traditions and the local costume, while the village museum and the Baroque Roman Catholic church give you an insight into Solymár's historical past. Visitors can make the most of our quality boarding houses and restaurants. For all the possibilities available you can log on to our www.solymár.hu website, or call us on 26/560-600.

The main cultural events and forms of entertainment:
April: • Traditional Easter Sprinkling Ball • The National English-Language Drama Festival for Middle Schools • Putting Up the Village Maypole
May: • The Jegenye Valley May Day Festivities
• Keffee, Kuchen und Kultur • Heroes' Day
June: • Whitsun Beer Afternoon • Jazz Weekend
July and August: • Open-air music and beer afternoons every second Sunday
August: • Ecumenical Gospel Concert
September: • The Solymár Patronal Festival (Cultural Festival)
October: • Harvest Parade and Ball
November: • The Catherine Ball
December: • Advent Village Day

OTHER SERVICES

Many thousands of minor incidents contribute towards the complete travelling experience. Much could depend on taking the right turning, being able to rent a car or buy a replacement for the medicine you left at home. These are all things that could well make or break a trip. What you can find here, therefore, is a collection of the types of services which could prove important in such eventualities. To start with here are a few useful telephone numbers:

Police (National)
Central green number: 81/201-303
Police (Budapest)
Drug help-line: 80/202-502
Stolen vehicles: 80/201-334
Lost property: 80/201-343
Matáv information plus   197

The Ferihegy Aircraft Park

Hungary's one
and only civil aircraft park,
situated near terminals 2A and 2B,
awaits flying enthusiasts
from 1st March and 30th November.

Open daily:
1st March–30th September
9am–6pm
1st October–30th November
9am–4pm

*Get to know the mysterious
world of aviation, its history
and how airports function.
Bus trips into the airport are put on
for groups during the week.*

Bookings and enquiries:
296-7489
(answerphone, fax)

Budapest Airport Rt.
1675 Budapest Pf. 53

www.bud.hu

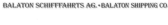

Animal Health Centre

4080 Hajúnánás, Bocskai u. 94

Veterinary services:

Medication
Mobile: 20/481-5130
Tel./fax:52/383-664

Pet care, operations
Mobile: 30/262-3893

Dog-cat cosmetics
Mobile: 30/570-3330

24 hours a day

Mezőkövesd Ker Coop plc

Mezőkövesd, Mátyás király u. 74.
Tel.: 49/505-450, fax: 49/505-490

Our "Matyóföld", "Matyótáj" and "ABC"
food, fittings and clothing shops
and supermarkets can be found in
Mezőkövesd and 26 of the surrounding
settlements, offering reliable quality,
a wide selection of products
at favourable prices.

If you are either visiting Mezőkövesd,
spending your holiday here or just
passing through, why not drop
into one of our shops. It's worth it!

BUDAKALÁSZ 2011
The Hercules Pharmacy
Cora Shopping Centre
Omszk park 1.
Tel.: 26/342-393

BUDAPEST 1121
BKV Libego Ltd.
Zugligeti 97.
Tel./fax: 1/394-3764; 1/200-9993
Open: May–Sept. 9am–5pm
Sept.–May 9.30am–4pm

CSÖMÖDÉR 8957
Woodland Narrow-Gauge Railway
Vasút u. 6.
Tel.: 92/579-033
Lenti–Csömödér–Kistolmács
E-mail: zalaerdo@zalaerdo.hu

SZEGED 6726
ISA Rent a Car
Kállay Albert u. 13.
Tel.: 62/431-577, Fax: 62/430-194,
Non-stop: 20/9557-887,
20/955-7887
E-mail: ISA@tiszanet.hu,
www.tiszanet.hu/ISARentaCar
Open: Mon.–Thur. 9am–4pm,
Fri. 9am–3pm, Sat.–Sun.,
holidays 9am–1pm

SZÉKESFEHÉRVÁR 8000
The Viktória Pharmacy
József u. 2. Tel.: 22/502-700
Fax: 22/502-699

Mahart PassNave

Tokaj Boat Trips

Sail with us on the Bodrog and
the Tisza from the world-famous
wine town of Tokaj.
Boats can be hired either
by phone or fax.
Tel.: 47/352-937
Fax: 47/352-108

Domestic Sewerage Appliances

for homes, guesthouses,
holiday complexes,
schools, factories
together with application planning

Enquiries: KRODA Ltd.
3527 Miskolc, Bajcsy-Zsilinszky u. 17.
Tel.: 46/413-202
Tel./fax: 46/506-032

Zánkai Gyermek és Ifjúsági Centrum Kht.

Europe's largest children's and youth centre is waiting
for both groups and individuals all the year round
on the northern shore of Lake Balaton.
Besides children and young people we also welcome families,
groups, organisations and companies,
as well as participants at courses and events.
The Zánka Children and Youth Centre is situated on a site covering
209 hectares on the shores of Hungary's largest lake, surrounded by the
picturesque landscape, the natural beauties and the cultural monuments
of the Balaton Highlands and close to many popular tourist destinations.
The extensive site means Zánka has a long shoreline along
Lake Balaton with its own beach and jetty which are ideal for sport
and relaxation. It is big enough for 2–3000 people and popular among
those who are fond of sailing and windsurfing
The Holiday Centre has its own bus stop and railway station with
direct connections to Budapest and Tapolca. You can drive to the centre
by car directly from road no. 71.
Our jetty waits for those who arrive by ship or yacht.
A wide range of accommodation and catering possibilities are
available at the Youth Centre. We can offer lodging in a two-star hotel,
in stone buildings and wooden bungalows with 2, 3, 4, 6, 8 and
10 beds and at our camping site.
Breakfast, lunch and dinner are all available at our restaurants.
A pizzeria and a waterside restaurant can also be found
in the Centre which are ideal for dinners with your family and friends.
Nature lovers can find well-marked hiking paths
and other open-air sports facilities in the forest.
Buses and boats are available to those wishing to go on a day out.
There is also a stadium, a sports hall, a fitness centre, a sauna,
and other sports facilities in the Youth Centre,
as well as a computer room, theatre hall, conference rooms,
a cinema, a supermarket, a hairdresser's,
a souvenir shop, a buffet, an Ice Cream Stand and a disco helping
to make our visitors' stay even more memorable and relaxing.
There is a lifeguard service on the shore of the lake and a doctor on duty.

Information and bookings:
Zánkai GyIC Kht.
8250 ZÁNKA
Tel.: 87/568-581, 568-582
Fax: 87/568-588
E-mail: centrum@zanka.hu
www.zanka.hu

Zánkaház
1119 BUDAPEST
Náday Ferenc u. 3
Tel./fax: 1/204-0123

List of Settlements

The settlements listed below include those places which appear in the main text of the regional chapters, their first mention being acknowledged by being printed in CAPITAL LETTERS.

Bőszénfa	400	Csongrád	480	Égerszög	590
Brennbergbánya	303	Csopak	366	Egervár	322
Bucsuszentlászló	335	Csorna	288	Egyek	566
Budajenő	211	Csömödér	338	Egyházasdengeleg	633
Budakeszi	215	Csömör	196	Egyházasgerge	628
Budaörs	210	Csurgó	393	Elek	469
Budapest	164	Csurgónagymarton	393	Encs	601
Bugac	486			Eplény	269
Buják	632	Dabas	205	Ercsi	256
Buzsák	377	Debrecen	519	Érd	209
Bük	313	Decs	428	Erdőtelek	559
Bükkösd	419	Dédestapolcsány	603	Esztergom	220
Bükkszenterzsébet	612	Dég	257	Etyek	254
Bükkszentkereszt	600	Délegyháza	207		
		Déványa	479	Fadd	430
Cák	311	Devecser	271	Farkasgyepü	273
Cece	257	Diósgyőr	598	Fehérgyarmat	530
Cégénydányád	530	Diósjenő	191	Fehérvárcsurgó	261
Cegléd	201	Diszel	357	Feldebrő	614
Ceglédbercel	201	Dobogókő	218	Felpéc	291
Celldömölk	319	Dombóvár	433	Felsőörs	367
Cibakháza	507	Dombrád	539	Felsőrajk	338
		Döbrönte	273	Felsőtárkány	613
Csákberény	246	Dömös	224	Felsővadász	601
Csákvár	247	Dömsöd	208	Fenékpuszta	351
Csány	625	Dör	288	Fenyőfő	269
Csaroda	536	Dörgicse	360	Fertőd	296
Csatár	335	Drávaiványi	405	Fertőrákos	303
Csehimindszent	320	Drávatamási	395	Fertőszentmiklós	296
Csempeszkopács	320	Drégelypalánk	192	Fertőszéplak	298
Csenger	532	Dunaalmás	240	Fonyód	376
Csengersima	532	Dunaegyháza	448	Forró	601
Csepreg	312	Dunaföldvár	435	Fót	195
Cserépfalu	605	Dunafüred	209	Füle	264
Cserépváralja	605	Dunaharaszti	206	Füzér	587
Cserhátsurány	635	Dunakeszi	196	Füzérradvány	587
Cserkeszőlő	508	Dunakömlőd	436	Füzesabony	558
Cserkút	418	Dunapataj	447	Füzesgyarmat	477
Cserszegtomaj	354	Dunaszekcső	412		
Csertő	403	Dunaszentmiklós	240	Gacsály	531
Csesznek	270	Dunaújváros	255	Galambok	353
Csesztreg	332	Dunavecse	448	Galgamácsa	197
Csesztve	635			Galyatető	618
Csisztapuszta	378	Écs	291	Ganna	273
Csobánka	217	Edelény	593	Gánt	247
Csókakő	246	Eger	606	Gárdony	252
Csokonyavisonta	394	Egerszalók	613	Geszt	477

Komló	420	Máriabesnyő	194	Murakeresztúr	339
Kórós	405	Máriagyüd	407	**N**adap	249
Kóspallag	189	Márianosztra	190		
Kovácshida	405	Máriapócs	527	Nádasdladány	265
Kölcse	533	Márokpapi	536	Nádudvar	518
Kömlő	559	Mártély	466	Nagyar	534
Körmend	324	Martfű	507	Nagyatád	391
Kőröshegy	372	Martonvásár	253	Nagybajom	391
Köröstetétlen	202	Martonyi	593	Nagybörzsöny	190
Kőszeg	307	Máta	514	Nagycenk	305
Kőtelek	560	Mátészalka	529	Nagydorog	437
Kővágóőrs	359	Mátraballa	622	Nagyecsed	529
Kővágószőlős	418	Mátraderecske	622	Nagygeresd	317
Kunfehértó	453	Mátrafüred	618	Nagyhalász	540
Kunhegyes	563	Mátraháza	618	Nagyharsány	408
Kunmadaras	563	Mátraszentimre	618	Nagyiván	566
Kunszentmárton	508	Mátraverebély	621	Nagykálló	544
Kunszentmiklós	486	Mecseknádasd	423	Nagykanizsa	336
Kustánszeg	332	Mecsekrákos	418	Nagykapornak	334
		Megyefa	419	Nagykarácsony	257
Lajosmizse	486	Mesztegnyő	391	Nagykáta	199
Lakitelek	489	Mezőberény	477	Nagykereki	518
Leányfalu	218	Mezőcsát	557	Nagykopáncs	474
Lébény	294	Mezőhegyes	470	Nagykovácsi	215
Lendvadedes	334	Mezőkövesd	603	Nagykőrös	202
Lengyeltóti	377	Mezőtúr	509	Nagykörű	560
Lenti	333	Mikepércs	523	Nagylózs	306
Letenye	339	Miklósfa	339	Nagymaros	188
Levelek	545	Milota	533	Nagynyárád	412
Lillafüred	598	Mindszent	466	Nagyszakácsi	392
Lispeszentadorján	338	Miske	448	Nagyszekeres	531
Litér	268	Miskolc	595	Nagytótfalu	408
Lónya	537	Miskolctapolca	598	Nagyvázsony	360
Lovasberény	249	Mogyoród	195	Nemeskér	307
		Moha	262	Nemesnádudvar	449
Mád	579	Mohács	410	Nemesnép	332
Madocsa	436	Mohora	635	Nemesvámos	365
Magyarcsanád	463	Molnári	339	Németkér	435
Magyaregregy	421	Monok	580	Neszmély	240
Magyarhertelend	420	Monor	204	Nikla	379
Magyarlukafa	403	Monostorapáti	360	Nógrád	191
Magyarpolány	270	Mór	245	Noszvaj	613
Majk	244	Mórágy	428	Nova	332
Makó	463	Mórahalom	459		
Mályi	601	Mosonmagyaróvár	291	**N**yékládháza	601
Mánfa	420	Mozsgó	403	Nyíracsád	523
Marcali	379	Muhi	601	Nyírbátor	526

Picture Credits

Baczúr, János 149a, b, 150a, 151b
Bartók, István 19c, 556a, b
Blaumann, Ödön 262a
Bodnár, Mihály 564b, 565b
Bócsi, Krisztián 596b
Boldogh Jr, Sándor 143b, 590c
Borzsák, Péter 50, 51b, 53, 90a, 143a, 144a, 145a, 146a, 147, 184b, 572, 591a,
Burián, György 23c, 54, 55a, b, 56a, b, c, 57, 84c, 284b, 285, 286, 287a, b, c, 288a, b, 289a, 290a, b, 291a, b, 292a, b, 293a, 294a, b, 296a, b, c, 298b, c, 299a, b, 300a, b, c, 301a, b, c, 303b, 306, 307a, b
The Lace House (Kiskunhalas) Archive 451
Csizmazia, György 29d, 445, 489c
Dávid, János 345, 370b, 371a, b, 372a, b, 373a, b, 374a, c, 375b, 376, 378, 379a, b, 380a, b, 382, 388, 391, 392c, 393a, b, 394, 399b, c, 400b, c, 401a, 429b
The Disznókő Rt. Archive 71b, 72b, c
Dozvald, János 42a, b, 43b, 44a, b, 45a, b, 158b, 161a, 168b, 271c, d, 172a, 174, 175a, 176a, 177, 179a, 180, 181a, c, 185a, 369b, 435c, 614b
The Danube–Ipoly National Park Archive 159, 216a
E. Nagy Lajos 243c
Endrődi, Zoltán 578a, 579a
Enyedi, Zoltán 17a, 465a, 482b
Felső, Barnabás 119a, b
The Fertő-Hanság National Park Archive 99a, b, 100a, b, 101a, 102, 279, 295, 298a, 304a
Fésüs, Ádám 183
Fésüs, László 52a, 605b, 648
Futó, Tamás 16a, 17b, d, 19a, 20c, 21b, 22c, 23b, e, 24a, 25c, d, 26b, 27a, 28a, 29c, e, 32c, 33c, 34a, b, c, 36b, 37a, d, 75b, as well as the water-colours used at the beginning of the regional chapters
Füri, András 94b, 163, 188a

Most of the pictures you will find in the guide were taken specially for the purpose, and the names of the photographers can be found below arranged in alphabetical order. We also acknowledge all those organisations and institutions which provided us with opportunity to use their picture archives.

The FVM Agrármarketing Centrum Archive 27c, 31, 33d, 35a, b, 36a, c, 37b, 234, 346, 390, 574
Gelencsér, Ferenc 264b
The Gödöllő Royal Palace Museum Archive 193b
The Győr-Moson-Sopron County Tourist Centre Archive 293b, 302, 303a
Halmai, László 72a, 73, 568, 573, 575a, b, 577a, b, 579b, c, 580a, b, 581a, b, c, 583a, b, 584a, 585a, 586c, 587a, b, c, 589a, 590b, 591b, 592a, 593a, b, 594a, b, 595a, b, 596a, c, 597a, b, 598b, c, 599a, 600a, b, 601a, b, 602, 603a, b, 604a, b, c, 605a, 713
Haraszti, Norbert 221a, 223a, b, 225a, 228, 232a, 235a, 236a, b, 237, 238a, b, c, 239, 240a, b, 241a, b, 242a, b, 243a, b, 244a, 245a
The Herend Porcelain Factory Archive 33a, b, 270b
The Hollóház Porcelain Archive 588b
Horváth, Benő 557a
Horváth, Róbert 592b
The Hungaroring Archive 195a
The Ibrány Town Council Library 540
Istvánovics, Eszter 534b,
Kantár, Gyula 84a
Kapfinger, András 20a, 425a, b, 426a, b, 427a, 428a, b, c, 429a, 430a, b, 431, 432a, b, 433a, b, c, 434a, b, 435a, b, d, 436a, b, 437b
Kardos, Tamás 19d, 499b, 506c, 564a
Károly Pump (Nürnberg) 51a
Kiss, Sándor 233, 265c, 266, 267a, 268a, b, 269b, c, 270a, c, 271b, 272a, b, c, 356b, 357a, b, 358, 359a, 360a, b, 362a, b, 363, 364a, 365b, 366a, b, 367a, b
Korniss, Péter 2
Kovács, Béla 111a, b, 112a, 113a, 114, 359b
Kovács, Gábor 5, 58, 59a, 60b, c, 61, 90c, 137a, b, 138b, 139a, b, 140, 515a, 566b